D1609206

THE Casas Grandes World

TO THE MEMORY OF

J. Charles Kelley

AND

Daniel Wolfman

Manufactured in the United States of America

∞ The paper on which this book is printed meets the minimum requirements of American National Standard for Information Science–Permanence of Paper for Printed Library Materials, ANSI Z39.48-1984.

Index prepared by Andrew L. Christenson

LIBRARY OF CONGRESS CATALOGING-IN-PUBLICATION DATA

The Casas Grandes world / edited by Curtis F. Schaafsma, Carroll L. Riley

p. cm.

Includes bibliographical references.

ISBN 0-87480-595-3 (alk. paper)

1. Casas Grandes Site (Mexico). 2. Indians of Mexico—Commerce. 3. Indians of Mexico—Antiquities. 4. Pueblo Indians—Commerce. 5. Pueblo Indians—Antiquities. 6. Mexico—Antiquities. 7. Southwest, New—Antiquities. I. Schaafsma, Curtis F., 1938- . II. Riley, Carroll L.

F1219.3.C6C37 1999

972'.16—dc21 99-18367

BRITISH LIBRARY CATALOGUING-IN-PUBLICATION DATA AVAILABLE

THE Casas Grandes World

EDITED BY

Curtis F. Schaafsma

Carroll L. Riley

The University of Utah Press
Salt Lake City

CONTENTS

List of Illustrations ix
List of Tables xiii
Acknowledgments xv

I Introduction
Plates following page 11

II The Core Area
1 Reflections on the Casas Grandes Regional System from the Northwestern Periphery 27
Paul R. Fish and Suzanne K. Fish
2 The Villa Ahumada Site: Archaeological Investigations East of Paquimé 43
Rafael Cruz Antillón and Timothy D. Maxwell
3 Investigating the Paquimé Regional System 54
Michael E. Whalen and Paul E. Minnis
4 A West Central Chihuahuan Perspective on Chihuahuan Culture 63
Jane H. Kelley, Joe D. Stewart, A. C. MacWilliams, and Loy C. Neff
5 The Robles Phase of the Casas Grandes Culture 78
David A. Phillips Jr. and John P. Carpenter
6 Was Casas a Pueblo? 84
Stephen H. Lekson
7 A Preliminary Graph-Theoretic Analysis of Access Relationships at Casas Grandes 93
David R. Wilcox

III The Outer Sphere
8 The Black Mountain Phase in the Mimbres Area 107
Darrell G. Creel
9 The Mimbres Classic and Postclassic: A Case for Discontinuity 121
Harry J. Shafer
10 Cerro de Trincheras and the Casas Grandes World 134
Randall H. McGuire, Maria Elisa Villalpando C., Victoria D. Vargas, and Emiliano Gallaga M.

IV The Larger View
11 The Aztatlán Tradition of West and Northwest Mexico and Casas Grandes: Speculations on the Medio Period Florescence 149
Michael S. Foster
12 Tlalocs, Kachinas, Sacred Bundles, and Related Symbolism in the Southwest and Mesoamerica 164
Polly Schaafsma
13 The Sonoran Statelets and Casas Grandes 193
Carroll L. Riley
14 The Postclassic along the Northern Frontiers of Mesoamerica 201
Alice B. Kehoe
15 The Mexican West Coast and the Hohokam Region 206
Clement W. Meighan
16 Shell Exchange within the Southwest: The Casas Grandes Interaction Sphere 213
Ronna J. Bradley
17 The Dentition of Casas Grandes with Suggestions on Epigenetic Relationships among Mexican and Southwestern U.S. Populations 229
Christy G. Turner II

V Toward a New Synthesis
18 The Casas Grandes World: Analysis and Conclusion 237
Curtis F. Schaafsma and Carroll L. Riley

References 251
Contributors 281
Index 283

ILLUSTRATIONS

Figures

1 Map of Casas Grandes interaction sphere ca. 1200–1425 8
2 Map of the Casas Grandes world and related areas to the north and south. Adapted from McGuire et al. 1994:Figure 11.1 9
1.1 Late prehistoric sites in the Malpais study area 28
1.2 Selected site plans with compound architecture 31
1.3 Comparison of residential units in idealized compound and room-block architecture 32
1.4 Selected site plans with room-block architecture: (a) Pendleton Ruin; (b) Box Canyon; (c) Joyce Well 32
1.5 Late prehistoric settlement and ball-court distribution in the Malpais study area 37
1.6 Distribution of Chihuahuan polychrome styles as outlined by J. Carpenter (1992) 39
1.7 Distributions of public architecture in the regions north and west of Casas Grandes 41
2.1 Northwestern Chihuahua 44
2.2 The Villa Ahumada site 45
2.3 Pottery recovered at the Villa Ahumada site 48
2.4 Faunal assemblages 49
3.1 The four 1989 reconnaissance areas 55
3.2 Three styles of Chihuahuan ball courts 59
3.3 Three postulated interaction zones around the primate center of Paquimé in northwestern Chihuahua 61
4.1 Map of the PAC (Proyecto Arqueológico Chihuahua) study region showing locations of sites with radiocarbon dates 64
4.2 Pithouse at CH-125 (1993) 65
4.3 Medio period rooms at CH-156 (1996) 67
4.4 Thirty-nine PAC radiocarbon determinations 72
7.1 Basic graph theory concepts (after Hillier and Hanson 1984:148–149) 97
7.2 The Casas Grandes site in the Medio period 97
7.3 General access graph, Unit 11, Casas Grandes, Chihuahua 100
7.4 Justified gamma graph, Unit 11, Casas Grandes, early Buena Fé phase 100
7.5 Justified gamma graph, Unit 11, Casas Grandes, late Buena Fé phase 100
7.6 General access graph, Units 14, 12, 13, 16, 8, and 6, Casas Grandes, Chihuahua 103
7.7 Subgraph of Units 14, 12, 13, 16, 8, and 6, Casas Grandes, showing plazas, hallways, trails, and large doorways 103
8.1 Map of southwest New Mexico and adjacent area showing locations of sites mentioned in the text 106
8.2 Map of the Old Town site (LA 1113) showing the principal portions of the site investigated 1989–1996 111
8.3 Map of Old Town Area C showing known rooms, surface wall segments, and general area of Black Mountain phase surface architecture 112
8.4 Plan of Rooms C1 and C2 with locations of intramural features 113
9.1 Map of the Mimbres System ca. A.D. 1050–1100 122
9.2 Mimbres population model taken from Blake et al. (1986) 122
9.3 South room block at the NAN Ruin 124
9.4 Building episodes at the NAN Ruin 125
9.5 Map showing the geographic distribution of large Classic Mimbres towns 126
9.6 Room 12 at the NAN Ruin 127
9.7 Graph showing mean numbers of burials per hearth type at the NAN Ruin 127
9.8 Drawing of Mimbres bowl depicting a ceremony in progress (taken from Moulard 1981:Plate 1) 129
9.9 Photo of bowl from the NAN Ruin showing the same ceremonial scene as depicted in Figure 9.8 129

9.10 Mimbres Style III Black-on-white showing warped form and chipped paint 130
10.1 Map of Northwest Mexico 135
10.2 Map of Northwest Sonora 137
10.3 Cerro de Trincheras, Trincheras, Sonora 137
10.4 Map of Cerro de Trincheras 138
10.5 Habitation terraces at Cerro de Trincheras 140
10.6 Round stone room at Cerro de Trincheras 140
10.7 Some incised shell ornaments from Cerro de Trincheras 144
11.1 The distribution of the Aztatlán tradition in western and northwestern Mexico 157
11.2 The Guasave jar decorated in codex style from the Schroeder site, Durango 159
11.3 The hypothesized route and linkage of the Late Aztatlán mercantile exchange network in west and northwest Mexico 159
12.1 Masked impersonator of Tlaloc, *Codex Magliabechiano,* Aztec (redrawn from Townsend 1992:Figure 3) 169
12.2 Aztec Tlaloc effigy vase from the Templo Mayor, Tenochtitlán 169
12.3 Tlaloc holding a lightning serpent surrounded by sparks and flames in one hand and a Tlaloc effigy vessel or bundle wearing a Tlaloc mask in the other 169
12.4 Tepantitla mural fragment 169
12.5 Bas-relief Panel 6, South Ball Court, El Tajin 170
12.6 Map of the Southwest with various cultural and Pueblo linguistic provinces indicated 172
12.7 Seven Tlaloc figures painted in a single rock shelter, Hueco Tanks State Park, Texas (redrawn from Davis and Toness 1974:Figure 28-A) 172
12.8 Design from a Mimbres bowl depicting a female figure carrying a burden basket in the form of a Southwest Tlaloc (redrawn from Davis 1995, p. 171) 173
12.9 Jornada-style petroglyph Tlaloc at Vado, New Mexico 176
12.10 Jornada-style Tlaloc, Three Rivers, New Mexico 176
12.11 Petroglyph Tlaloc with stepped cloud motif, Three Rivers, New Mexico 177
12.12 Goggle eyes attached to a free-form design of scrolls and stepped elements symbolizing clouds 177
12.13 Tlaloc painting in red on cave ceiling, Hueco Tanks, Texas 178
12.14 Petroglyph mask with goggle eyes and jagged teeth, Three Rivers, New Mexico 178
12.15 Tlaloc boulder, Samalayuca, Chihuahua 179
12.16 Wooden effigies from U-Bar and Stanton Caves in southern New Mexico 180
12.17 Cloud terrace painted in solid black at the bottom of limestone sinkhole near Gran Quivira, New Mexico 180
12.18 Fifteenth-century kiva mural painting of a stepped cloud terrace with a bird on top 181
12.19 Pueblo IV (A.D. 1325–1680) rock paintings of kachina masks in the form of water jars, Tompiro Pueblo province, New Mexico 182
12.20 Early Pueblo IV petroglyph masks in the form of bowls with cloud symbolism, Piro province, New Mexico 182
12.21 Pueblo IV kiva mural from Kuaua Pueblo on the Rio Grande 183
12.22 Funerary bundle wearing Tlaloc mask and cave 186
12.23 Masked Tlaloc bundle seated on a cave maw 186
12.24 Head resting on a trapezoidal/triangular support 187
12.25 From Teotihuacan tomb, a clay bust with detachable mask thought to represent a funerary bundle 190
12.26 Hopi shalako manas 190
13.1 Map of Sonoran statelets and related areas in the sixteenth century 196
16.1 Paquimé, or Casas Grandes, and other sites in the Southwest 214
16.2 Plan map of the site of Paquimé 215
16.3 Diversity plot of type richness 218
16.4 Diversity plot of type evenness 219
16.5 Cluster analysis of all shell artifacts 220
16.6 Cluster analysis of the marine shell artifacts 221
16.7 Results of the cluster analysis of marine shell, illustrating the Hohokam and Casas Grandes networks 222
16.8 Special artifact shapes 223
17.1 Dendrogram of multivariate phenetic relationships based on Mean Measures of Divergence clustered with the Unweighted Pair Group, Arithmetic Averages method 233

18.1 Wall cross section near Olla Cave west of Casas Grandes 243

Plates following page 11

1 Early Mesilla phase pithouse at LA 3135 near Hatch, New Mexico.
2 Doña Ana phase pithouse at LA 3135 near Hatch, New Mexico.
3 Doña Ana phase coursed-adobe structure at LA 3135 near Hatch, New Mexico.
4 Desert landscape east of Casas Grandes.
5 Plateau nature of the Sierra Madre Occidental southwest of Casas Grandes looking west.
6 Typical situation of a cliff dwelling in a shallow cave in the Sierra Madre Occidental southwest of Casas Grandes.
7 View of the Alamo Hueco Mountains in Hidalgo County, New Mexico.
8 Ball court defined by parallel rows of rocks with a central cleared area in the Arroyo el Alamillo area.
9 Michael Whalen on row of rocks defining the west side of the ball court at the Joyce Well site in southern Hidalgo County, New Mexico.
10 Casas Grandes, or Paquimé, with a new coat of mud plaster.
11 Flat-topped pyramid at Casas Grandes.
12 Coursed-adobe walls with plaster remaining in cliff dwelling southwest of Casas Grandes.
13 Coursed-adobe rooms in the rear of Olla Cave in Cave Valley.
14 Adobe and grass granary in Olla Cave west of Casas Grandes.
15 T-shaped doorway in Casas Grandes.
16 Cuarenta Casas cliff dwelling in the Sierra Madres Occidental south of Casas Grandes.
17 Situation of Cuarenta Casas cliff dwelling.
18 Detail of burned hearth in the Joyce Well site.
19 Arnold Withers viewing a row of turkey pens at Casas Grandes.
20 Turkey pen with turkey burial at Casas Grandes.
21 Horned and plumed serpent painting on the roof of a cave near Fort Hancock, Texas.

TABLES

1 Chronology of Areas Related to Casas Grandes Culture 7
1.1 Comparison of Relevant Chronological Sequences for the Northwest Periphery 30
1.2 Absolute Dates for Sites in the Northwest Periphery 30
1.3 Comparison of Groundstone Frequencies among Sites in the Northwest Periphery, Hohokam, and Salado Regions 33
1.4 Interregional Comparison of Estimates for Demographic Parameters and Resource Requirements 35
1.5 Distribution of Casas Grandes Architectural Traits among Excavated Late Prehistoric Sites in Southeastern Arizona and Southwestern New Mexico 38
2.1 Ceramic Types at Villa Ahumada Site 47
3.1 Frequency of Room-Block Size Classes in Inner and Middle Zones 58
4.1 West Central Chihuahua Radiocarbon Dates Discussed in This Chapter 69
5.1 Di Peso's Robles Phase Dates 79
5.2 Reevaluation of Di Peso's Dates 83
10.1 Shell Artifact Forms from Cerro de Trincheras and Paquimé 145
11.1 Concordance of West Coast Archaeological Sequences 154
12.1 Chronology of Selected Cultures and Areas 166
15.1 Parallels between Hohokam Archaeology and that of the West Coast of Mexico 212
16.1 Ornament Types by Site 216
16.2 Site Code for Richness and Evenness 218
16.3 Diversity Plot of Type Richness 218
16.4 Diversity Plot of Type Evenness 219
16.5 Cluster Analysis of all Shell Artifacts 220
16.6 Cluster Analysis of the Marine Shell Artifacts 221
17.1 Casas Grandes Morphological Crown Trait Frequencies (Individual Count, Sexes Pooled, Standard ASUDAS Breakpoints) 230
17.2 Mean Measures of Divergence (MMD) Matrix Based on 20 Crown Traits 231
17.3 Ranking of MMD Values of Casas Grandes and Other Dental Samples 232

ACKNOWLEDGMENTS

A BOOK SUCH AS THIS owes a great deal to the generosity of colleagues. We wish to thank members of the Museum of Indian Arts and Culture/Laboratory of Anthropology, especially the past and current directors, Bruce Bernstein and Patricia House, who wholeheartedly supported the *Casas Grandes World* project. Laura J. Holt, librarian of the MIAC/LAB, also gave invaluable assistance, as did Phoebe Hackett, assistant director; Edmund J. Ladd, curator of ethnology; Laura Morley, division secretary; and Louise Stiver, curator of collections.

Directly involved with the *Casas Grandes* manuscript and bibliographies were Susan Yewell and Eugene C. Sheeley, and their continued assistance is greatly appreciated. Polly Schaafsma helped with illustrations and is also a contributor to the volume. Another contributor, David A. Phillips Jr., was in a sense the progenitor of this book, for he helped organize the 1995 conference from which the work came. We are grateful for the good advice of conference members R. Ben Brown of the Chihuahua office of INAH and Jeffrey S. Dean of the University of Arizona. Let us also note with sadness the death of our friend and fellow volume author, Clement W. Meighan.

I

Introduction

Introduction

A NUMBER OF SCHOLARS have suggested that the current conceptual framework of southwestern archaeology is deficient. In our opinion this deficiency stems partially from adherence to two broad themes that are now mutually reinforcing. These are (1) devotion to a view defined by A. V. Kidder as the "San Juan hypothesis" and (2) belief in a mandate that all "significant" cultural changes can be explained as the result of ecological adaptations. For nonadherents such explanations seem as likely as the notion that Tibetan Buddhist religion and society are the autochthonous result of ecological adaptation on the Tibetan Plateau.

The San Juan hypothesis was articulated by A. V. Kidder in 1933 as he prepared for excavations in the far southwestern corner of New Mexico:

> The southern part of the Southwest has been neglected because the spectacular ruins of the northern pueblos and cliff houses drew early and long held the almost undivided attention of archaeologists. Perhaps because of the greater knowledge of the north thus acquired, there was gradually formulated what may be called the "San Juan hypothesis," according to which a nomadic people resident in the general region of the San Juan drainage acquired from the south, at about the opening of the Christian Era, the knowledge of maize agriculture; and they built up, in almost complete isolation and with little further borrowing from the south, a culture which grew and ramified to give rise to that of all subsequent sedentary groups from Chihuahua to Utah and from eastern New Mexico to California.... The culture thus established spread and matured, giving rise to many local specializations and passing through the several chronological phases recognized in the Pecos classification, as the Pueblo periods numbered I–V. All Southwestern developments, under the hypothesis, were believed to be derived from the San Juan nucleus and all variations from the Basket Maker–Pueblo pattern were supposed to be environmental specializations or peripheral thinnings-out, rather than the effects of impingement by extraneous cultures. (Kidder et al. 1949:115–116)

The details of the San Juan hypothesis, as well as a clear presentation of most of its elements, were published in 1939 by one of its most tenacious apostles, Earl H. Morris:

> The Pueblo area may be considered to comprise all of Arizona northward of the Gila Valley, most of Utah, the southwestern corner of Colorado, and all of New Mexico west of the open plains. Beyond these limits there are marginal extensions westward into Nevada, eastward into

> Kansas and Texas, and, as has been previously mentioned, strong and contributory contacts with the cultures of southern Arizona and northern Mexico. However, these peripheral occurrences may be regarded as no more than radiations and spill-overs from the great parent center. (Morris 1939:5)

The last sentence, of course, tells all and exemplifies the basic perspective described by Kidder. Morris's 1939 overview of southwestern archaeology is important because his belief in the San Juan nucleus as the "great parent center" is still the background against which many southwestern archaeologists operate. In this regard McGuire et al. observed, "Most authors seem to agree that the culture traits they use to define the area sprang from a climax, or hub, and then spread out over the region; some stress the study of this hub, and others emphasize the borders of the area" (McGuire et al. 1994:240–241).

Central to this view is the belief that southwestern cultural developments continued in isolation with little outside interference from early agricultural times to the historic period. Morris argued strongly that even pottery making was "a purely local invention" (Morris 1939:21; see also chapter 13 of this volume). Accordingly, even if the notion of firing had "crept up from the south . . . nothing else came with it" (Morris 1939:23). As Ferguson and Rohn put it, "The Anasazi are one of the very few cultures of the world that show a continuity and homogeneity of culture from 700 B.C. (Basketmaker II) to modern times and a remarkably consistent culture from Pueblo III (1100 to 1300) to the present day" (Ferguson and Rohn 1987:275).

The complementary theme that all cultural developments can be explained as the result of ecological adaptation is perhaps most fully illustrated by Martin and Plog's 1973 book, *The Archaeology of Arizona.* Wills has summarized Julian Steward's influence on southwestern archaeology, noting that in this approach "cultural progress (evolution) could only be understood by reference to economic strategies, which were in turn conditioned by ecological factors. . . . Steward's belief that ecology determined economy (and hence social organization) was adopted by Southwestern archaeologists as an explanation for the geographical variability apparent in the archaeology of the Southwest" (Wills 1994:291). This strongly recalls Kidder's summary that "all southwestern developments . . . were supposed to be environmental specializations or peripheral thinnings-out" (Kidder et al. 1949:116). Wills adds, "For the most part, Southwestern researchers continue to seek causes of change in the archaeological record by reference to environmental factors." Occasionally other causal factors are cited, such as trade and migration, "but environment is without question the most compelling 'motivation' found in the literature for temporal and spatial patterns of variation in prehistoric material remains" (Wills 1994:291). McGuire et al. cogently summarized this development: "Since the 1960s most archaeologists have turned . . . to ecological studies of resources and technology" (McGuire et al. 1994:241).

Three associated volumes develop these two broad themes into a current interpretive framework for southwestern archaeology. These are *Dynamics of Southwest Prehistory* (Cordell and Gumerman, eds. 1989), *Themes in Southwest Prehistory* (Gumerman, ed. 1994), and *Understanding Complexity in the Prehistoric Southwest* (Gumerman and Gell-Mann, eds. 1994). The first volume grew out of a 1983 advanced seminar at the School of American Research in Santa Fe. Subsequently, two conferences led to the other volumes that ostensibly consider the Southwest as a whole. In spite of the extraordinary sophistication and expertise represented in these volumes, the two themes discussed above stand unquestioned: The Southwest is a closed system with changes primarily explained by ecological adaptation.

Gumerman and Gell-Mann recognized that numerous agents of change have been proposed for explaining southwestern prehistory and that although all of them had some role, "Traditionally, environmental conditions have been the most common explanation for stability and change in the prehistoric Southwest" (Gumerman and Gell-Mann 1994:30). This explanatory framework offers precious little room or tolerance for "impingement by extraneous cultures." The isolation advocated by Morris sits well with those seeing "significant" culture change as a result of local environmental adaptation.

The persistence of the San Juan hypothesis is illustrated by Gumerman's effort to seek explanations for southwestern cultural developments primarily from the "initial conditions" that came into being with the arrival of domesticated plants from Mexico. Gumerman maintains that from this beginning subsequent developments were inevitable. Although he does not want to "suggest that Southwestern society was a closed system," and he acknowledges that a "changing relationship with more complex societies to the south and less complex entities in other directions also played a role in the evolution of Southwestern society" (Gumerman 1994:5), his fundamental effort (and that of most of the other volume contributors) is toward explanation of southwestern cultural change as the result of local ecological adaptation, uninterrupted by impinging cultures.

Casas Grandes

In the three volumes mentioned above, the Casas Grandes regional culture or interaction sphere is largely ignored. The bias is clear in the regional map of Cordell and Gumerman (1989:Figure 1), in which discussion of general regions and groups stops at the international border. Only in LeBlanc's summary of the southern Mogollon area is a strong position taken on the nature and importance of the "Casas Grandes interaction sphere," and he is somewhat hampered by improper dating (LeBlanc 1989:192–204). Otherwise, these volumes make only occasional references to Casas Grandes, with the exception of the chapter by McGuire et al. (1994).

A primary focus of these volumes is on Chaco and the Hohokam: "Chaco was one of two major 'regional systems' in the tenth, eleventh, and twelfth century Southwest, the other being the very impressive Hohokam developments of the southern Arizona desert" (Lekson et al. 1994:21). This statement seems inconsistent with the summation of Kelley and Villalpando: "The Casas Grandes system, then, is generally acknowledged to be the third major regional system within the larger culture area, and the one with the least diluted Mesoamerican characteristics. As such, it needs to be studied along with the Chacoan and Classic Hohokam regional systems, and the similarities and difference between these need to be charted more fully" (Kelley and Villalpando 1996:74). Ignoring it is even more troublesome if these authors are correct in contending that "the Casas Grandes system is, arguably, the most complex regional system found north of Mesoamerica in this culture area" (Kelley and Villalpando 1996:72). Whalen and Minnis also recognized this oversight, maintaining that in the Casas Grandes area there is still another major regional system of the Greater Southwest (Whalen and Minnis 1996b).

We contend that there are deep-seated, largely implicit reasons for this oversight that need to be made explicit. They relate to the dissatisfactions expressed in the "Open Letter to Southwestern Archaeologists" that was the basis for the Durango Conference, from which this volume also originates.

People developing computer-simulation models utilizing initial conditions, demographic change, and environmental variables are generally very intolerant toward arguments that individual people "negotiate" events within a society (see the relevant chapters in Preucel 1991). As the "Open Letter" observed, "Interaction within a society is not viewed as a meaningful source of historical change. Instead, change is explained by appeal to the interaction between the entire 'system' and external factors such as environmental change or independent demographic growth" (Anonymous 1995:14). The organizers of the Durango Conference expressed in their open letter their "dissatisfaction with tracing all historical change to environmental or demographic roots." Although they focused on the internal dynamics of societies that they asserted are "far from being a passive aspect of systemic change," their main dissatisfaction was with computer-simulation models that essentially cannot accommodate the unpredictable effects of individuals negotiating their lives. Such models must treat individuals within social systems as entirely passive actors.

The nature of these models is evident in the workshop prospectus entitled "Growing Artificial Prehistoric Worlds: A Workshop and Demonstration of Agent-based Modeling in Archaeology," which was also held at the Durango Conference:

> A computer program designed to simulate existing or prehistoric societies, as well as to create artificial social worlds, is used to model actual and systematically altered Anasazi economic and settlement behavior in Long House Valley, northeastern Arizona. The agent based model is used to predict individual household responses to changes in agricultural productivity in annual increments from A.D. 400 to 1500 based on reconstructions of yearly climatic conditions, as well as long term [*sic*] hydrologic trends and cycles of erosion and deposition. Population parameters and site distribution characteristics of the valley at A.D. 400 are used as the initial state for the

operation of a few simple rules about how households interact with each other and with their changing environment over the 1100-year test period. The performance of the model will be evaluated against actual population, settlement, and organizational parameters. By manipulating numbers and attributes of households, climate patterns and other environmental variables, it should be possible to evaluate the roles of these factors in Anasazi culture change. (Dean et al. 1995:9)

If the designers of such computer-simulation models have difficulties including "negotiating" individuals in their programs, rest assured they have no tolerance for outside cultural "influences" or "impingement by extraneous cultures." Such random, undirected input from outside the closed system would be most undesirable indeed. It is extremely difficult (perhaps impossible) to allow for such influences and much easier to dismiss possible input into the southwestern "system" over the 1100-year test period. Further, it seems acceptable to acknowledge that some kind of reflected involvement with other cultures occurred at a higher scale (Lekson et al. 1994:21), although that involvement may not be "meaningful" (i.e., important enough to alter the outcome of the computer simulation). This brings us back to the old San Juan hypothesis, now armed with computers and in agreement with Julian Steward's view that once agriculture is accepted, environmental and ecological variables, plus intrinsic population flux, condition all meaningful culture change. It is a monolithic block indeed, and there is little surprise that the Casas Grandes regional culture was essentially ignored in the three volumes cited above.

In this book we seek to acknowledge the Casas Grandes regional culture. It was there. It was important. It requires understanding in its own right (Kelley and Villalpando 1996:77) and as a conduit or nexus between the Anasazi and all that was to the south. Moreover, our point in this book is that *after* A.D. 1250–1300 one cannot disregard the outside input from the south, which by and large arrived by way of the "Casas Grandes interaction sphere" during the period roughly A.D. 1250–1425. Those who adhere to a modern version of the San Juan hypothesis and Julian Steward's cultural ecology must come to grips with a dynamic regional culture that was not simply a "peripheral thinning out" from the Anasazi heartland.

About This Book

This volume originates from a symposium on the regional culture related to the site of Casas Grandes in northern Chihuahua. Entitled "The Casas Grandes Interaction Sphere: Origins, Nature, Contacts and Legacy," the symposium was organized by Curtis F. Schaafsma and was held in September 1995 as part of the Durango Conference on Southwest Archaeology, Durango, Colorado. A number of scholars gave papers on various aspects of Casas Grandes and the many other sites in the region. It was apparent to all participants that the Casas Grandes interaction sphere becomes very different if we focus on the regional culture and not primarily on the single, large site of "Paquimé" or Casas Grandes itself (Figure 1). Symposium members quickly saw the need for new models that explain the site of Casas Grandes in its regional setting.

Carroll Riley opened the symposium with a historical overview of research on the Casas Grandes culture, focusing on the long-standing issue of connections between Mesoamerica and the Southwest and the role of Casas Grandes. Riley maintained that the Casas Grandes culture is essential to understanding the contacts between Mesoamerica and the Southwest (Figure 2).

Curtis Schaafsma offered a regional map outlining his interpretation of the Casas Grandes interaction sphere. The map was accompanied by a history of research that has led to the recognition that this large region is indeed related to Casas Grandes. Schaafsma also offered a time chart that ordered the different regional manifestations according to current data (Table 1) and suggested the "Cacique Model" for the origin of the culture (see chapter 18 of this volume).

Michael Whalen summarized current survey work with Paul Minnis, especially near Casas Grandes and to the north near Janos, Chihuahua. Whalen was impressed with the general lack of large sites near Janos and suggested that the earlier stages of the Casas Grandes culture may have seen a dispersed series of relatively small sites and that only later did people concentrate in the large site of Paquimé. He also suggested that this settlement pattern may have been like that of Teotihuacan. This, of course, is a complete reversal of Di Peso's (1974) assumption that Paquimé was settled first and that the

Table 1. Chronology of Areas Related to Casas Grandes Culture.

TIME	CASAS GRANDES AREA		MIMBRES AREA	JORNADA AREA
1598	Sumas, Conchos Tarahumaras,		Janos, Jocomes,	Sumas, Mansos, Chinarras
1540	Janos, and Jocomes		and Mansos	
1500				
1450				
1425		MEDIO PERIOD		
1400				
1350	MEDIO PERIOD		Cliff Phase	El Paso Phase
1325	See note below			
1300				
1250			Black Mountain Phase	
1200				
1150				Doña Ana Phase
1100	Perros Bravos Phase	VIEJO PERIOD		
1050	Small Pueblos		Mimbres Phase	
1000				
950	Pilon Phase Pithouses			Late Mesilla Phase
900			Late Pithouse Period	(Pithouse Period)
800	Convento Phase Pithouses			
750				
700				
600	Plainware Period Pithouses			
500			Early Pithouse Period	
400				Early Mesilla Phase
300				(Pithouse Period)
200				
100	Late Archaic Preceramic		Late Archaic Preceramic	Late Archaic Preceramic
100+				

NOTE: We agree that there is no longer justification for dividing the Medio period into phases. The A.D. 1300 line dividing early and late periods at Paquimé is retained for guidance only. Gray highlighted sections indicate periods characterized by significant scholarly disagreement.

satellite communities developed subsequently to support the central place.

Jane Kelley summarized the research she and Joe Stewart have been conducting in the southern areas near Babícora and the upper Santa María and Carmén river drainages. She discussed a wide array of new dates, which are presented in this volume.

R. Ben Brown was the INAH archaeologist in charge of Paquimé for many years and gave a much-needed overview of the subject as seen from the Mexican perspective. He saw in Casas Grandes a strong religious component related to Quetzalcoatl. It is clear that Mesoamerican elements in Casas Grandes culture are readily apparent to Mexican archaeologists.

Paul Fish discussed a parallel-sided structure at the Ringo site in southeastern Arizona, rejected as a ball court by earlier Arizona archaeologists because of its dissimilarity to Hohokam courts. Fish pointed out that this Ringo structure was similar to the ball court at the Joyce Well site in the southwestern corner of New Mexico. Both resemble the many small ball courts near Casas Grandes that Minnis and Whalen have found and recorded (1996a).

Alice Kehoe provided a macroregional perspective on connections between Mesoamerica and regions to the northeast and northwest. She compelled us to reconsider the notion of "Nuclear America," maintaining that there were two main routes of contact, one along the Gulf Coast toward the southeastern United States and the other along the Sierra Madre Occidental into the southwestern United States.

David Wilcox discussed trade routes and travel

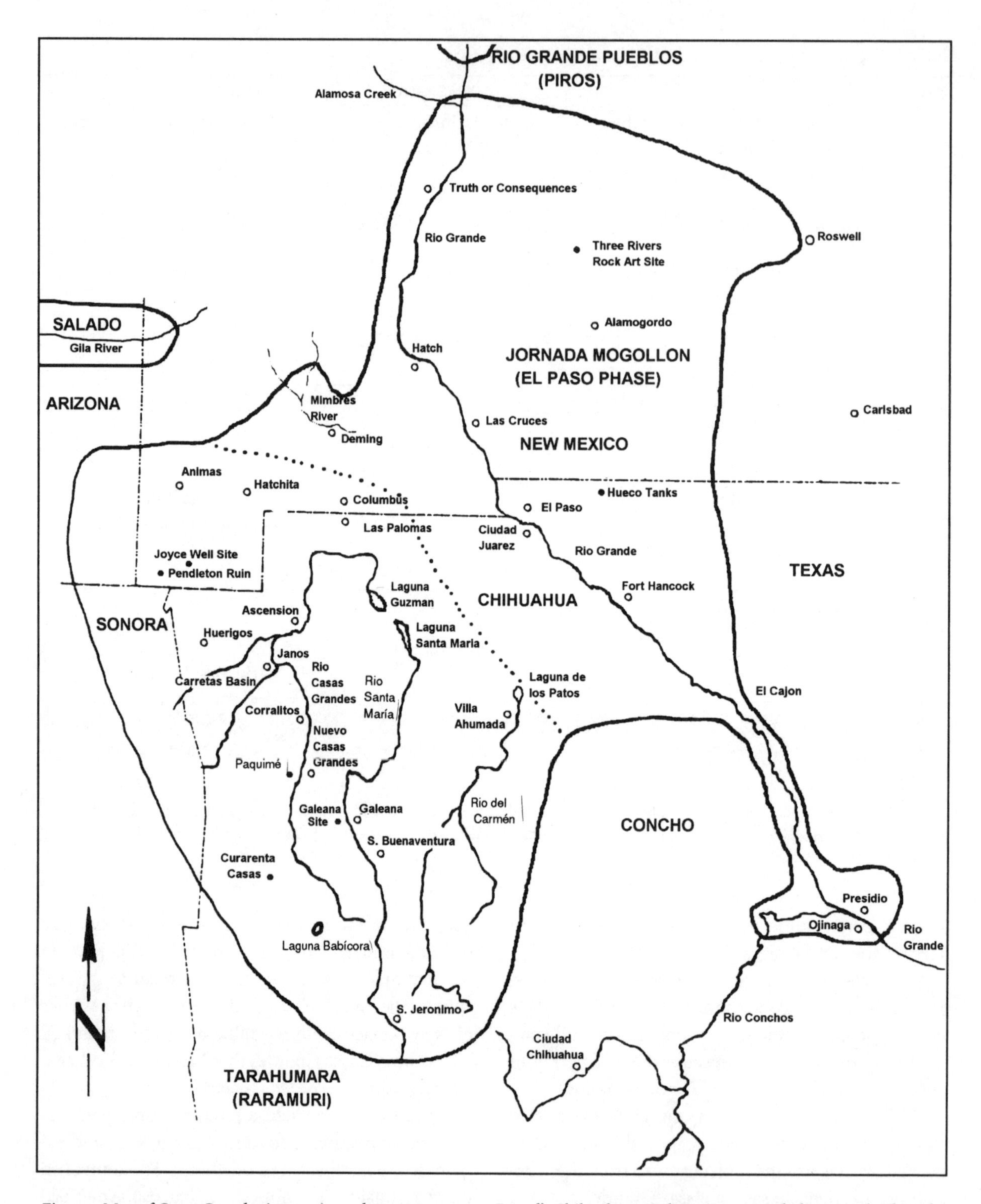

Figure 1. Map of Casas Grandes interaction sphere ca. 1200–1425. Brand's Chihuahuan Culture area extended to near the dotted line in Northeastern Chihuahua.

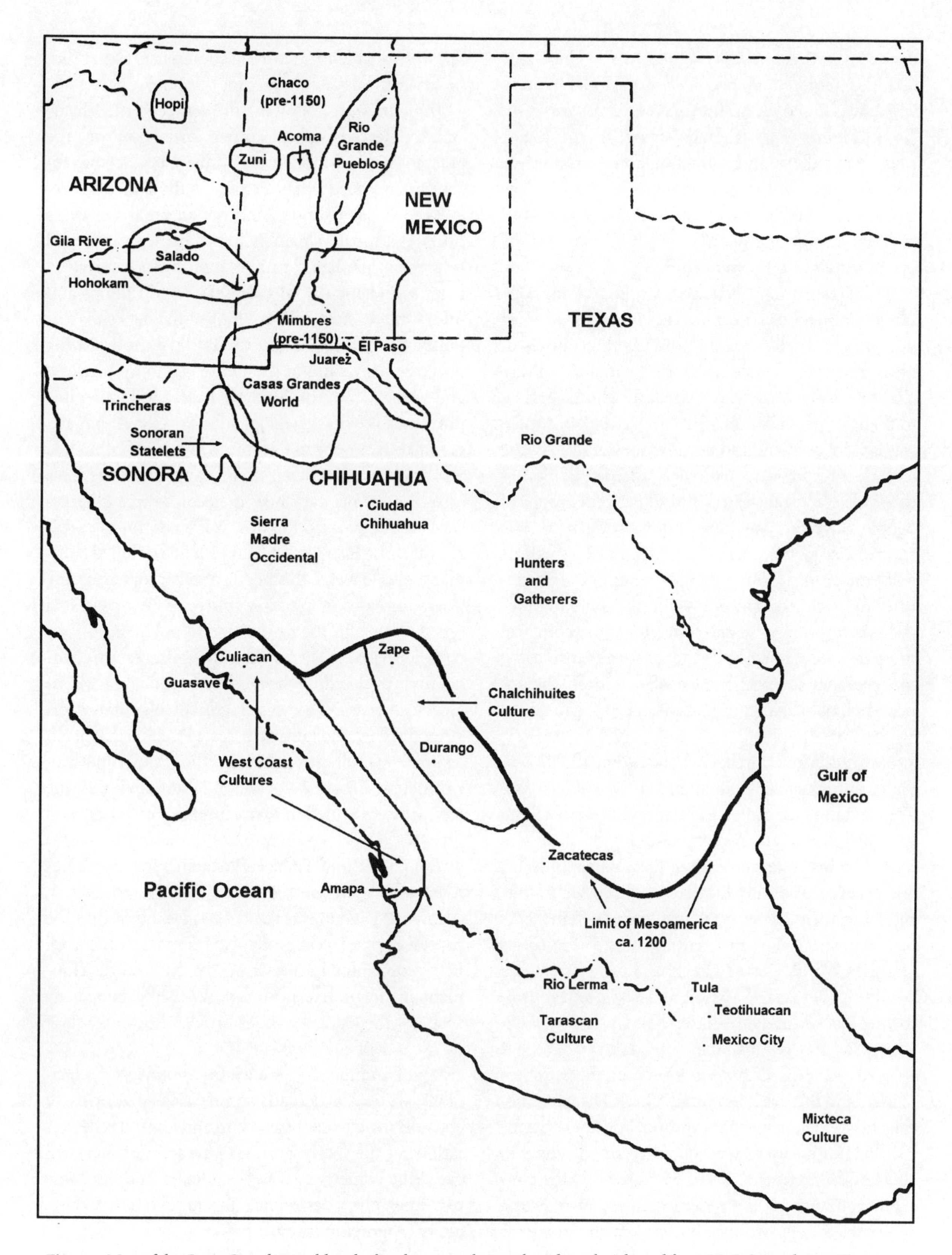

Figure 2. Map of the Casas Grandes world and related areas to the north and south. Adapted from McGuire et al. 1994:Figure 11.1.

distances between diverse settlements in the Casas Grandes region and provided a regional map—which was based on Brand (1943) and Di Peso et al. (1974:5:Figure 284)—showing many of the major sites, river valleys, and habitation zones in the river bottomlands. He recognized the diversity of ideas that are currently being considered and urged us all to "keep our options open"—which in a sense sums up the results of the symposium.

The symposium participants reflected the Durango Conference objectives in several ways. Most notable was a willingness to discuss the transfer of ideas and even people as causal factors in culture change. Participants did not advocate a simple return to theories of "diffusion" and "migration," but there was clearly no dictum to perceive all changes as due to in situ response to ecological adaptation. Sometimes ideas are transferred, and sometimes groups of people move carrying ideas around with them. The sudden rise of the Casas Grandes culture—with its ball courts, platform pyramids, complex architecture, and rich iconography—did not come into being as a response of local populations to ecological pressures. It is a significant topic for reconsidering interregional contacts, the transfer of ideas, the appearance of religious organizations, and the actual movement of people.

Two additional archaeologists, Randall H. McGuire and Darrell Creel, attended the symposium. They did not give conference papers but were willing to contribute to the present volume. McGuire was joined by his colleagues María Elisa Villalpando C., Victoria D. Vargas, and Emiliano Gallago M. in summarizing their recent work at Cerro de Trincheras and explaining how that work relates to the Casas Grandes World. Darrell Creel has long advocated a continuity between the Mimbres Classic and the following Black Mountain phase. His chapter details evidence for that. On the other hand, Harry Shafer has long advocated a *discontinuity* between the Mimbres Classic and the Black Mountain phase. His paper details his evidence for that position. Together they illustrate our desire to present a diversity of views in this book. Steven H. Lekson, who attended the conference though not the symposium, was also willing to contribute, providing a view from the north, as well as an insight into the attitude of Chaco archaeologists toward Casas Grandes. Michael S. Foster, John C. Ravesloot, and Thomas O'Laughlin were invited but were unable to attend the conference. Foster did, however, produce a chapter for this book.

In the months following the symposium, Schaafsma contacted various other specialists on the greater Casas Grandes area. Ronna J. Bradley has recently completed a major study on the shell trade related to Casas Grandes, and her summary of these findings is most welcome. Christy Turner was invited to present his data on population histories derived from epigenetic dental analyses. David Phillips and John Carpenter take a hard look at the data substantiating the Robles phase of the Tardio period, finding no basis for retaining the phase. Timothy Maxwell and Rafael Cruz Antillón have been conducting important new work at a major site near Villa Ahumada, Chihuahua, under the auspices of INAH Chihuahua and contributed a paper on this important site. This is the kind of primary, new archaeology that is necessary. We are pleased to know it is a continuing project. Suzanne Fish joined Paul Fish in a detailed summary overview of the northwestern corner of the Casas Grandes interaction sphere. Polly Schaafsma sets the stage for the next round of publications and conferences on Mesoamerican-southwestern connections by detailing the manner in which the Mesoamerican cosmology was essentially like that of the ethnographic and late prehistoric Pueblos inasmuch as they are all grounded in the "Mesoamerican worldview" (Preucel 1996:125). Jane Kelley and Joe Stewart were joined in their summary of survey and excavation work and new dates in the southern area by Loy C. Neff and A. C. MacWilliams. To balance Kehoe's report on the region east of the Southwest, Clement Meighan was invited to give a paper on the coastal regions west of Casas Grandes, and Carroll Riley contributed a paper on the cultural development in northeastern Sonora. With the increasing scope of the Casas Grandes project, Riley also took on the task of coeditor.

The Durango Conference on Southwest Archaeology was a particularly appropriate platform for considering current research in and revised interpretations of the Casas Grandes interaction sphere because the conference was designed to address some of the perceived deficiencies in southwestern archaeology (Anonymous 1995:14–15).

Both the symposium and the resulting volume were organized to give a variety of views on Casas Grandes. Because of basic differences among specialists, the editors feel that at this stage of Casas Grandes research no reasonable consensus can be reached. What can be done is to establish the parameters of the problem as it appears at the end of the twentieth century. One obvious step is to determine which differences are real and which are simply a matter of terminology. From this point a consensus may eventually be forged.

It seems clear there is a basic need for more information from the many sites in the region, as well as a return to Di Peso's extraordinarily detailed data from Casas Grandes, viewing them from different perspectives. Overall, the Casas Grandes interaction sphere was on a par with other better-known regional cultures, such as Chaco and the Hohokam. We sincerely hope that this volume will bring the topic to the attention of a wider audience.

C. F. S.
C. L. R.

PLATE 1 (*Above left*). Early Mesilla phase pithouse at LA 3135 near Hatch, New Mexico. This is typical of hundreds of pithouses throughout the desert country in the years before about A.D. 1000.

PLATE 2 (*Above right*). Doña Ana phase pithouse at LA 3135 near Hatch, New Mexico. Ceramics indicate that the pithouse (ca. A.D. 1150–1200) was contemporaneous with nearby coursed-adobe surface rooms (see Plate 3).

PLATE 3 (*Left*). Doña Ana phase coursed-adobe structure at LA 3135 near Hatch, New Mexico, occupied at the same time (ca. 1150–1200) as nearby pithouses. This structure and others of this transitional phase mark the change from pithouses to coursed-adobe pueblos.

Plate 4. Desert landscape to the east of Casas Grandes looking toward the Santa Maria River valley from high on Sierra Escondida.

Plate 5. Plateau nature of the Sierra Madre Occidental southwest of Casas Grandes looking west. The hills in the distance are on the border with the modern state of Sonora. There are many cliff dwellings as well as open puebloan sites in this high country.

PLATE 6. Typical situation of a cliff dwelling in a shallow cave in the Sierra Madre Occidental southwest of Casas Grandes.

PLATE 7. View of the Alamo Hueco Mountains in Hidalgo Country, New Mexico from the Casas Grandes River valley near Ascencion, Chihuahua. The distance is about twenty-five miles.

Plate 8. Group in 1993 viewing a ballcourt defined by parallel rows of rocks with a central cleared area in the Arroyo el Alamillo area southwest of Casas Grandes. The eastern escarpment of the Sierra Madre Occidental is in the background.

Plate 9. Michael Whalen on row of rocks defining the west side of the ballcourt at the Joyce Well site in southern Hidalgo Country, New Mexico. The Animas Mountain Range is in the distance.

Plate 10. Casas Grandes, or Paquimé, with a new coat of mud plaster. The trees along the nearby Casas Grandes river are beyond the site to the east.

Plate 11. Flat-topped pyramid at Casas Grandes.

PLATE 12. Coursed-adobe walls with plaster remaining in cliff dwelling southwest of Casas Grandes.

PLATE 13. Coursed-adobe rooms in the rear of Olla Cave in Cave Valley along the upper Piedras Verdes River west of Casas Grandes.

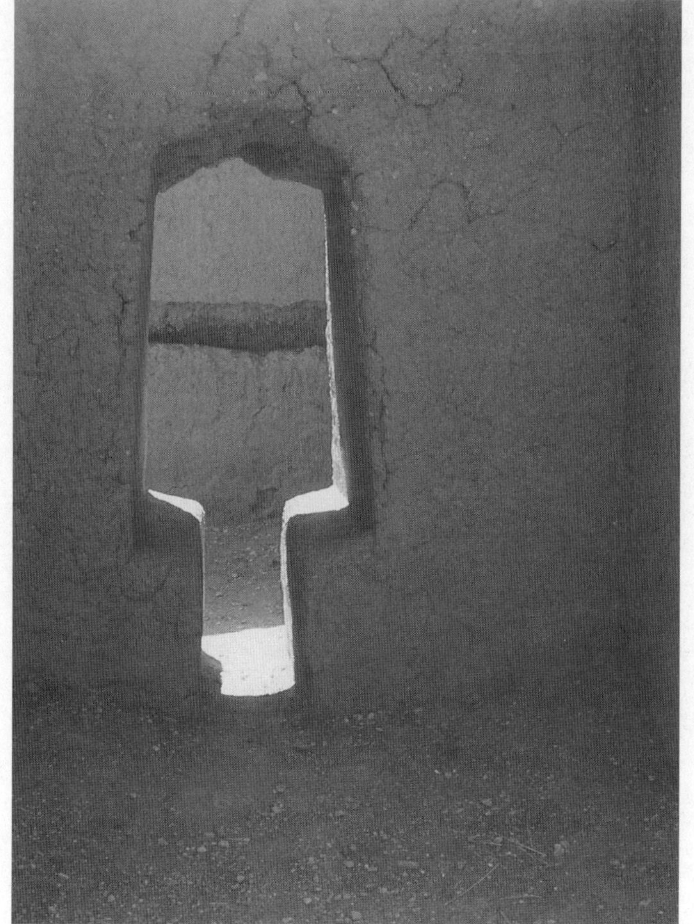

PLATE 14 (*Above*). Adobe and grass granary in Olla Cave west of Casas Grandes.

PLATE 15 (*Left*). T-shaped doorway in Casas Grandes.

Plate 16. Cuarenta Casas cliff dwelling in the Sierra Madres Occidental south of Casas Grandes. Photo by John Ware.

Plate 17. Situation of Cuarenta Casas cliff dwelling. Photo by John Ware.

Plate 18. Detail of burned hearth in the Joyce Well site in southern Hidalgo County, New Mexico. This is typical of hearths in nearly all known sites in the Casas Grandes interaction sphere. Daniel Wolfman is preparing an archaeomagnetic sample that yielded a date of approximately A.D. 1370.

Plate 19. Arnold Withers viewing a row of turkey pens at Casas Grandes.

Plate 20. Turkey pen with turkey burial at Casas Grandes at the time of excavation. Photograph by Arnold Withers.

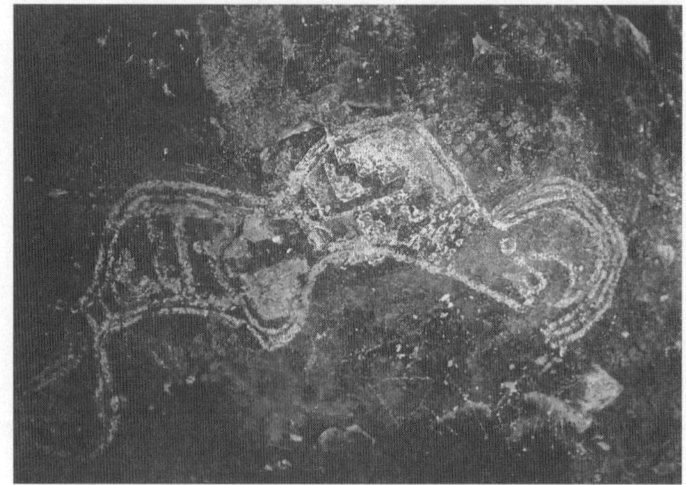

Plate 21. Horned and plumed serpent painting on the roof of a cave near Fort Hancock, Texas. Note the pronounced muzzle mouth, the side-view single eye and the checkerboard necklace. The plumes arc in front of the forward-projecting horn.

II

The Core Area

1

Reflections on the Casas Grandes Regional System from the Northwestern Periphery

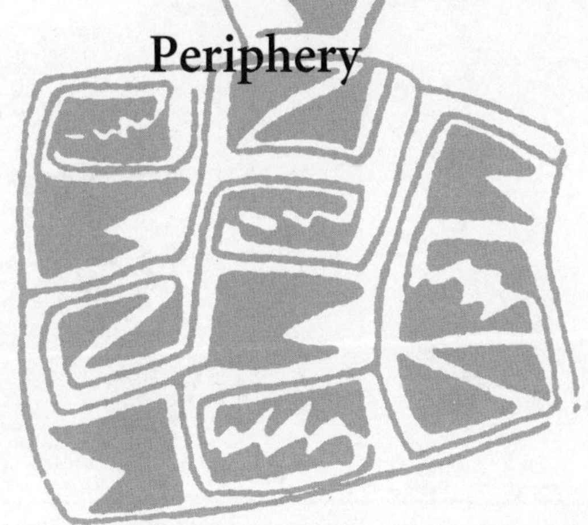

Paul R. Fish

Suzanne K. Fish

THE ADOBE PUEBLOS and compounds of southwestern New Mexico and southeastern Arizona that recall Chihuahuan styles have attracted sporadic archaeological attention since the 1920s (e.g., Brand 1943; Sauer and Brand 1930; Sayles 1936; Gladwin 1934; Kidder et al. 1949). This stylistic complex has been termed the Animas phase in the archaeological literature. It is characterized by large, coursed-adobe pueblos and compounds, room blocks built around plazas, an absence of kivas, and a high proportion of Ramos Polychrome and other Chihuahuan ceramics. Interpretation of these manifestations is almost always in terms of interaction with the preeminent site of Casas Grandes, although the nature and strength of such relationships have been hotly debated.

We recently had occasion to review the archaeological patterns and relationships of a portion of the Animas sphere in the course of preparing an overview of the Malpais Borderlands Ecosystem study area for the U.S. Forest Service (P. Fish and Fish, in press). As defined for this purpose, the 2600–sq km Malpais Borderlands encompasses large segments of the San Bernardino Valley in Arizona and the San Luis, Animas, and Playas valleys in the boot-heel region of New Mexico. Boundaries for this study area almost precisely correspond to the northern distribution of ceramic assemblages with high proportions of Chihuahuan polychromes and sites within the United States assigned to a Chihuahuan tradition (Sauer and Brand 1930).

The Malpais Borderlands and adjacent territories represent both a boundary and a crossroads between cultural expressions bearing the prominent imprint of Casas Grandes and contemporary modes designated as Classic Hohokam and Salado. It also lies within an intervening zone between Casas Grandes and the late prehistoric Trincheras sphere, centered to the west in Sonora. The Malpais Borderlands represent a key segment of the perimeter in which the Casas Grandes regional system reaches its limits and is thus defined. In part, the scale and shape of the Casas Grandes systems on the north must be understood in terms of dynamics and interactions within this area. Archaeological information in southeastern Arizona and southwestern New Mexico is insufficient to examine this issue in detail or achieve any final resolution. Rather, we attempt to summarize and synthesize currently available patterns from some new perspectives and to place the Borderlands within a wider context during late prehistory.

Some geographic correlations appear pertinent in assessing cultural configurations at the broadest level

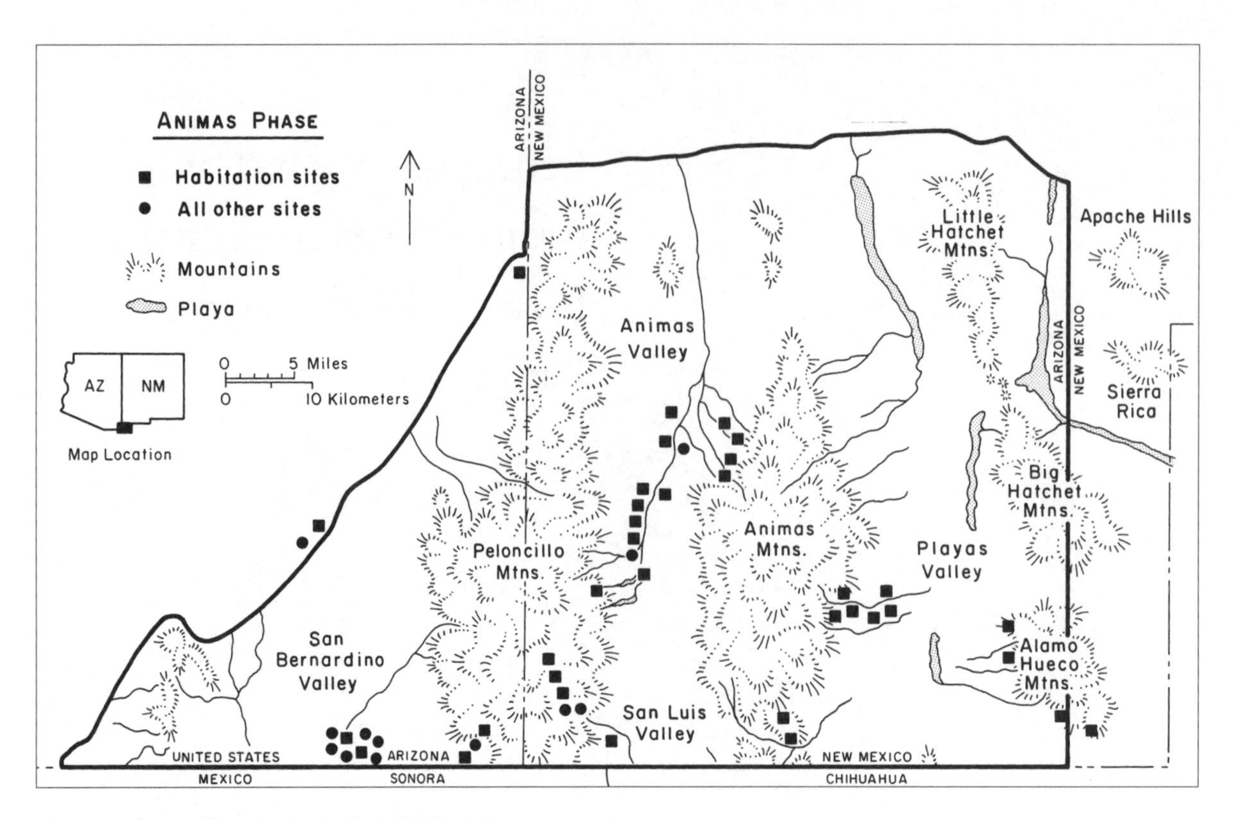

Figure 1.1. Late prehistoric sites in the Malpais study area.

of shared elements of economic orientation and ease of interaction. The northwest boundary between Chihuahuan-influenced styles of material culture that includes the Borderlands and those conforming to the Hohokam and mound-building Salado roughly follows the environmental contact between the shrub- and grass-dominated Chihuahuan desert and the Sonoran Desert, with large cacti and small trees. On an east-west axis, however, a natural flow of items, ideas, and people can be envisioned along the northern front of the Sierra Madre Occidental, across both Chihuahuan and Sonoran deserts from Casas Grandes to the Gulf of California coast (P. Fish and Fish 1994:7).

Although the Casas Grandes sphere encompasses a huge block of territory in the International Four Corners, events in the Malpais Borderlands or any other segment reflect still broader regional trends. The late prehistoric era throughout the Southwest witnessed abandonments, aggregation, and congregation in irrigable and other hydrologically favored locales (S. Fish and Fish 1994; P. Fish et al. 1994; Adler 1996). In the Greater Southwest below the Mogollon Rim, settlement nodes with public architecture and associated modes of territorial organization appear widely in regional sectors where such features were formerly absent (P. Fish and Fish 1994:19–24).

Background of Malpais Borderlands Studies

In the Malpais Borderlands, locations of the largest pueblos (100+ rooms) are well known and are reiterated in regional archaeological reconnaissances (e.g., Brand 1943; Kidder et al. 1949; Sayles 1936; De Atley 1980). The next tier of even moderate-sized sites is so spottily documented that most scholars have focused on these larger settlements for organizational interpretations. Figure 1.1 shows the locations of large, late prehistoric sites in the study area. Systematic survey data are very limited. Archaeological surveys in the boot-heel segment of New Mexico and in the San Bernardino Valley of Arizona are environmentally stratified samples at 2 percent levels. Nothing comparable to full-coverage data exists for any significant subsection; consequently, relationships between large pueblos and the smaller units of settlement pattern are problematic. Sample survey in the boot-heel region of New Mexico suggests to Suzanne De Atley

(1980:30) a hierarchical settlement pattern with large central sites (100 to 500 rooms) separated by distances of approximately 15 km. On the other hand, John Douglas (1995) infers largely autonomous villages from settlement distributions in the eastern part of the study area. Needless to say, models of interaction between territorial units are currently speculative.

Casas Grandes, only 100 km to the south, is undoubtedly the single most important factor in interpretations of Malpais Borderlands prehistory. The presence of Chihuahuan polychrome ceramics and architectural styles encouraged early Borderlands investigators to look to Casas Grandes for their comparisons and expectations. Extensive reconnaissance surveys south of the San Luis and Playas valleys (Brand 1943; Sayles 1936) and the San Bernardino Valley (Sauer and Brand 1930; Di Peso n.d.; Braniff 1992) demonstrated spatial continuity in ceramic and architectural styles. Large-scale excavations by Charles Di Peso (1974) at Casas Grandes during the 1960s reinforced this point of comparison. The level of information for the intervening area did not approach that available for the Borderlands and Casas Grandes for many years. Only recently have systematic survey efforts begun to provide measures of Casas Grandes influence in Mexico at varying distances to the north from that site (Minnis and Whalen 1990, 1995; Braniff 1992).

Chronology is a pivotal issue for correctly placing late prehistoric developments in the Malpais Borderlands study area. On the basis of ceramic cross-dating, most archaeologists working in southwest New Mexico and southeast Arizona placed the large, late pueblos in the range of A.D. 1250 to 1450 (Brand 1935; Kidder et al. 1949; McCluney (1965b). In fact, the constellation of decorated ceramic types occurring at these sites (St. Johns Polychrome, Gila Polychrome, Tonto Polychrome, Pinedale Polychrome, El Paso Polychrome, Chupadero Black-on-white, and an assortment of Chihuahuan types) came to be regarded as the hallmark of fourteenth- and fifteenth-century occupations in the southern Southwest (Thompson 1963; Doyel 1976; Wilcox and Shenk 1977:64–68). Recent reevaluation of the tree-ring evidence for Casas Grandes clearly demonstrates that the major occupation at the site occurs between A.D. 1200–1250 and 1450, and perhaps as late as A.D. 1500 (Dean and Ravesloot 1993:96–98). Table 1.1, comparing current regional chronologies for southwestern New Mexico, southeastern Arizona, and northern Chihuahua, conforms to this dating.

In a complication for regional chronology, Di Peso (1974:46) accepted and reported three radiocarbon dates suggesting a sixteenth-century occupation at the Joyce Well site in the Borderlands. He interpreted these dates as evidence that scattered Tardio period populations from Casas Grandes occupied the boot-heel section of New Mexico and nearby areas after the collapse of that site. Both De Atley (1980) and Carpenter (1994) point out that these dates were all derived from carbonized corn and never corrected for differential absorption of C13 and C14 fractions. If an estimated average correction of 200 years were made, all three samples would date to the latter half of the 1300s.

Table 1.2 presents chronological data from excavated sites with radiocarbon and tree-ring dates in and immediately adjacent to the Malpais Borderlands. Obsidian hydration dates from two analyses (De Atley 1980:77–80; Stevenson et al. 1983) tend to broadly confirm associated radiocarbon dates and estimates from ceramic assemblages. Table 1.2 underscores the limited number of absolute determinations. Poorly understood proveniences and lack of current correction factors for radiocarbon dates further obscure the chronological picture. However, available dates from most large sites parallel ceramic estimates and postdate A.D. 1200. The very late dates from Ojo de Agua are intriguing because they are in clear association with ceramic assemblages (the range of polychrome types and Cloverdale Corrugated utility ceramics) and architecture that characterize late Animas phase occupations.

Geographic Variability

The presence of two stylistically discrete late prehistoric occupations in the Malpais Borderlands study area has been long distinguished on the basis of distinct plainware utility types (Brand 1943; Sauer and Brand 1930). One subdivision is located in the Animas/San Luis and San Bernardino valleys and corresponds to utility ceramic assemblages dominated by Cloverdale Corrugated; the other is located in the Playas Valley, where utility ceramics are principally Playas Red. Differences in frequencies of Chihuahuan and Salado polychrome types (Nelson and Anyon 1996:284) also figure in this distinction;

Table 1.1. Comparison of Relevant Chronological Sequences for the Northwest Periphery.

	PHASE SEQUENCE SOUTHWEST NEW MEXICO (Stuart and Gautier 1981; Nelson and Anyon 1996)	PERIOD SEQUENCE SOUTHWEST NEW MEXICO (Stuart and Gautier 1981; Nelson and Anyon 1996)	REVISED CASAS GRANDES PHASE SEQUENCE (Dean and Ravesloot 1993)	REVISED CASAS GRANDES PERIOD SEQUENCE (Dean and Ravesloot 1993)	PHASE SEQUENCE MALPAIS BORDERLANDS (De Atley 1980)
A.D. 1500					
1400	Cliff (Salado)		Diablo		Salado
1300		LATE PUEBLO	Paquimé	MEDIO	
1200	Black Mountain (Animas)		Buena Fe		Animas
1100			Perros Bravos		
1000	Classic Mimbres	EARLY PUEBLO			
900	Three Circle			VIEJO	San Luis
800	San Francisco				
700		LATE PITHOUSE			
600	Georgetown				
500					
400		EARLY PITHOUSE			
300	Cumbre				
200					
100					?
A.D. 1	Late Archaic	LATE ARCHAIC			

Table 1.2. Absolute Dates for Sites in the Northwest Periphery.

	CERAMIC CROSSDATING	RADIOCARBON	TREE RING	ARCHAEOMAGNETIC
Clanton Draw	1350–1375 (1)			
Box Canyon	1350–1380 (1)			
Joyce Well	1250–1400 (2)	1620±110; 1590±100; 1565±110 (9)	1249p–1308vv (9)	late 1300s (12)
Pendleton	1300–1375 (3)			
Culberson	1200–1450 (4)	1360±60 (8)	1183–1282vv; 1185–1284vv (9)	
Boss Ranch	1150–1450 (5)	1400±80; 1430±50 (5)		
Kuykendall	1300–1450 (6)			1385±23; 1375±18 (11)
Slaughter Ranch	1300–1500 (6)			
Ojo de Agua	1250–1450 (7)	1580±180; 1522±41; 1420±70; 1666±40 (7)		
Double Adobe Cave	?	545±90 (8)		
Maddox Ruin	1000–1400 (4)	1230±60 (8)		
Hidalgo Survey 1	?	1420±60; 1060±60; 1200±60 (8)		
Hidalgo Survey 65	?	1185±60 (8)		
Hidalgo Survey 15	?	1060±60; 875±60 (8)		

NOTE: References: (1) McCluney 1965a; (2) McCluney 1965b; (3) Kidder et al. 1949; (4) O'Laughlin et al. ca. 1984; (5) Douglas 1996; (6) estimate by P. Fish; (7) Braniff 1992:547; (8) De Atley 1980:69; (9) Di Peso 1974:46; (10) Robinson and Cameron (1991); (11) Mills and Mills 1969a; (12) Curtis Schaafsma, personal communication.

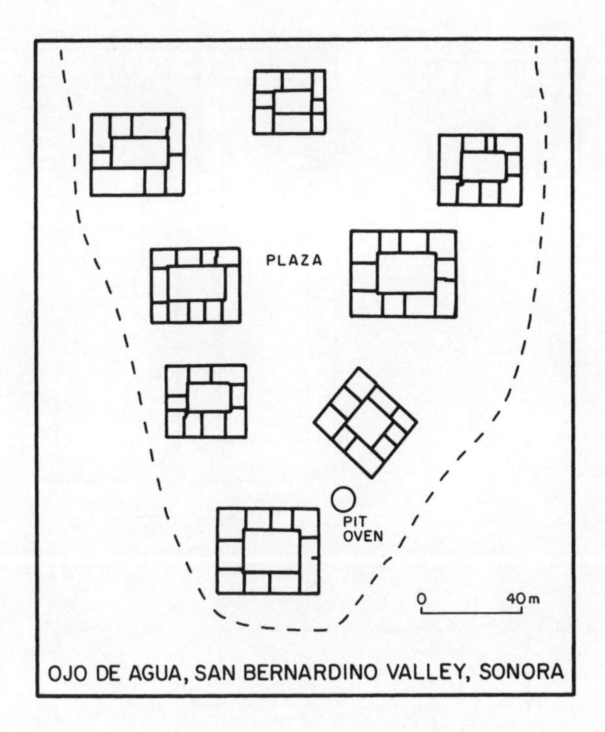

Figure 1.2. Selected site plans with compound architecture.

Salado polychromes are more common with Cloverdale Corrugated, and Chihuahuan polychromes are more frequent with Playas Red.

Architectural tendencies crosscut these ceramic spheres. Compounds and cimientos-type wall footings (cobble or slab alignments without discernible accompaniment of melted adobe) are more frequent in the west, particularly in the San Bernardino Valley with Cloverdale Corrugated. At the largest sites, such as Kuykendall (Mills and Mills 1969a, 1969b), a short distance northwest of the study area, and Ojo de Agua (Braniff 1992), spatially separate compounds are formed by a single row of rooms on all four sides of an open interior. At Ojo de Agua and other Sonoran sites recorded by Di Peso, large open areas among the compounds may represent a central plaza (Figure 1.2). Contiguous room blocks and plaza arrangements that have been designated as "puebloan" are recorded in the Animas and Playas valleys. Massive, coursed-adobe construction of the room blocks, resulting in architectural remains of mounded adobe, is more commonplace in the Playas Valley. Smaller sites in the San Bernardino, Animas, and Playas valleys exhibit great variability and range from isolated structures, or field houses, to sets of contiguous rooms, to compounds with a few rooms dispersed in the courtyard or attached to the outer wall.

Geographic and stylistic contrasts have been noted between spatially discrete compounds and room blocks of contiguous units (e.g., Douglas 1995:243–244; Brand 1943:117). The designation of "puebloan" for the room-block layouts suggests underlying cultural and organizational differences as well. However, room-block sites are more "puebloan" than compound sites only in the sense of larger masses of contiguous rooms; neither of the architectural types exhibits northern elements such as kivas.

Among sites with compound and room-block arrangements, questions concerning organizational carryovers or similarities also can be raised, if not resolved, by our current understanding of site layouts. Di Peso's sketch of Ojo de Agua compounds (Figure 1.2) shows eight units, each outlined by a single row of rooms. If those compounds were conjoined along their outer edges, they would form a series of plaza and room-block arrangements, with a row of two (or sometimes more) back-to-back rooms between adjacent plazas (Figure 1.3). Such a structure generally parallels the layout of the Joyce Well site (Figure 1.4c), which has five identified internal plazas and several

Figure 1.3 (Right). Comparison of residential units in idealized compound and room-block architecture.

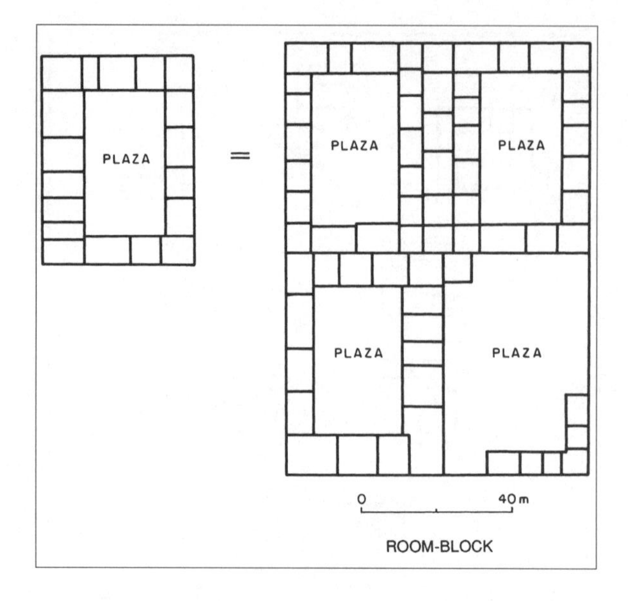

Figure 1.4 (Below). Selected site plans with room-block architecture: (a) Pendleton Ruin; (b) Box Canyon; (c) Joyce Well.

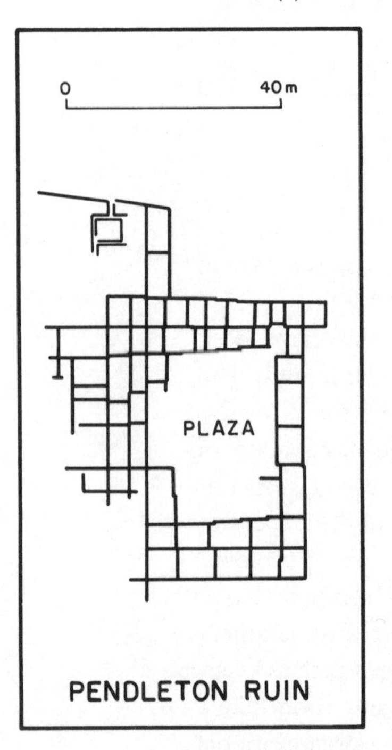

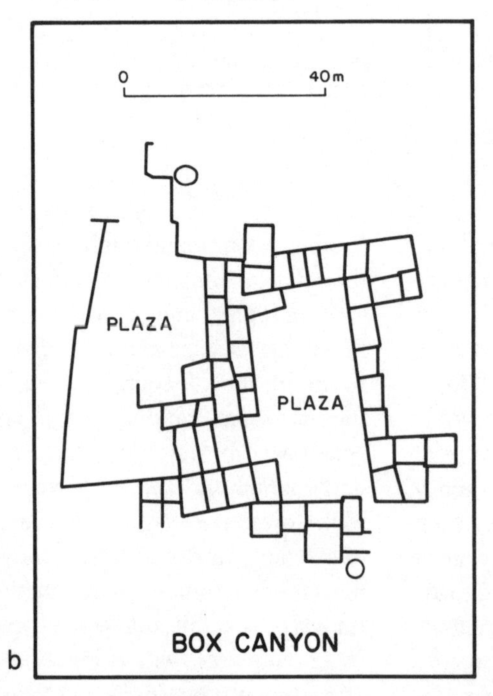

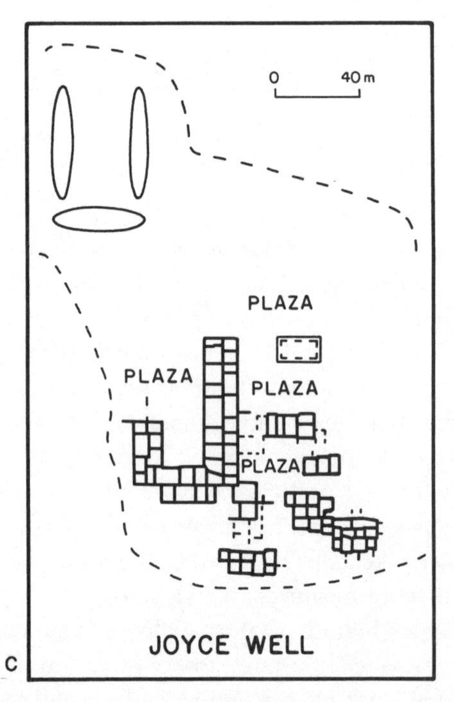

more probable ones. The open area in the center of Ojo de Agua compounds could conceivably correspond to the large plaza at Joyce Well. Pendleton and Box Canyon could be smaller multiples of similar arrangements (Figure 1.4a, 1.4b). Precise comparison is not possible with sketch maps of most large sites, but the dimensions of plaza units at the three sites in Figure 1.4 appear similar to dimensions of Sonoran compounds provided by Di Peso (see Figure 1.2). Thus, sites with separate compounds and sites with room blocks and plazas may share aspects of demographic and organizational structure.

Architectural and ceramic styles of the late prehistoric Malpais Borderlands are more closely allied to expressions to the south than to the north. Sites with high frequencies of Cloverdale Corrugated extend to the south in the northern portion of the Carretas Basin and along the southward flowing streams immediately across the border from the San Bernardino Valley in Sonora. Whereas many of the larger sites in the Carretas Basin have even more massive, coursed-adobe walls than in the study area, Ojo de Agua and other large Sonoran sites west of the Carretas Basin consist of compound and cimientos-style architec-

Table 1.3. Comparison of Groundstone Frequencies among Sites in the Northwest Periphery, Hohokam, and Salado Regions.

SITE OR SITE GROUP	LOCATION	# OF SHERDS	# OF MANOS AND METATES	GROUNDSTONE RATIO	REFERENCE
Pendleton	Cloverdale Creek	2765	261	9.45	Kidder et al. 1949
Joyce Well	Deer Creek	9985	78	0.78	McCluney 1965b
Box Canyon	Animas Valley	1017	17	1.67	McCluney 1965a
Clanton Draw	Animas Valley	1167	14	1.19	McCluney 1965a
Boss Ranch	San Bernardino Valley	28959	42	0.15	Douglas 1985
Los Morteros	Tucson Basin	39002	258	0.66	Wallace 1995
La Lomita	Phoenix Basin	9943	66	0.66	Mitchell 1990
U:9:95 (ASM)	Phoenix Basin	5216	33	0.63	Doyel et al. 1995
U:9:97 (ASM)	Phoenix Basin	907	23	2.54	Doyel et al. 1995
Livingston Site Group	Tonto Basin	75628	331	0.31	Jacobs 1995
Roosevelt Community Development Sites	Tonto Basin	90316	192	0.21	Elson et al. 1995

NOTE: The groundstone index is calculated by dividing number of manos and metates by total number of sherds and multiplying by 100.

ture. Brand and others record many mounded Chihuahuan sites with evidence for massive coursed adobe south of their Borderlands counterparts at Joyce Well and the Culberson Ruin in the Playas Valley.

Subsistence

Qualitative evidence indicates a strong commitment to agriculture. Ratios of formal groundstone grinding implements to sherds appear well within the range of excavated assemblages from Hohokam and Salado contexts to the north and west (Table 1.3). In fact, high frequencies of well-worn grinding implements have often been used by study area researchers to characterize Animas phase remains (Kidder et al. 1949:142; Brand 1943:119–122).

Corn remains are consistently described as abundant in dry caves and excavated sites (e.g., Kidder et al. 1949:142; McCluney 1965a:21, 36; 1965b:83–84; Lambert and Ambler 1965). At Joyce Well corn was present in many rooms and described as stacked like cordwood in several (Cutler 1965a:104–105). In the single systematic flotation study, 92 percent of 25 samples contained corn at the Boss Ranch site (Douglas 1996; Adams 1988)—a high rate of recovery when compared with analyses for other prehistoric southwestern farmers. Four varieties of corn, which Cutler classified as Pueblo, Onaveno, Pima-Papago, and Reventado/Chapalote, were usually present in assemblages at the dry caves, Box Canyon, Clanton Draw, and Joyce Well (Cutler 1965a, 1965b; Cutler and Eickmeier 1965; York 1961). Other cultivated crops include cotton, several varieties of beans, cucurbits, and bottle gourd. The frequency of cotton in excavated samples is of note, particularly in light of the fact that systematic methods such as flotation or even screening were seldom attempted. Cotton is reported from the Alamo Hueco Caves (Lambert and Ambler 1965), Boss Ranch (Adams 1988), and Joyce Well (Cutler 1965a).

Tabular knives, usually associated with the harvest and processing of agave, are conspicuous components of lithic artifact assemblages, and large roasting pits are frequently found in both residential sites and as isolated features. Amerind Foundation site file information indicates that large ovens may be formal elements of plaza arrangements surrounded by compounds in the San Bernardino Valley and in the valleys of northwesternmost Sonora. Although this archaeological evidence suggests that agave or perhaps yucca or sotol were important sources of food and fiber, no direct evidence currently supports cultivation of agave as now recognized in the Hohokam region (see Fish et al. 1985).

The record of wild plants from excavated study area sites, including dry caves, is modest compared to cultivated resources. Potential food resources include grass, yucca, sotol, mesquite legumes, acorns, walnuts, dock, and prickly pear, but identification of these is often limited to a single instance; the ubiquity of any wild resource is always much lower than that of corn. Likewise, animal bones do not appear to have been particularly common in excavated contexts. Kidder et al. (1949:142) specifically comment on their rarity at the Pendleton Ruin. With systematic recovery through screening and flotation at Boss Ranch, only 178 faunal specimens could be classified into the broad categories of canine (coyote and dog), artiodactyl (deer and antelope), or lagomorph (cottontail and jackrabbit). This assemblage was dominated by lagomorphs. Aside from the addition of a few small mammals (fox, rock squirrel, skunk, bobcat, wood rat) and unidentified birds, a composite faunal assemblage from all reported late prehistoric sites is almost identical to that of Boss Ranch.

Little direct information on agricultural technology and field locations is available. Location near surface flows and alluvial fans suggests an emphasis on small-scale irrigation and floodwater strategies. In a catchment analysis for residential sites, Frank Findlow (1979) suggests that there is a primary emphasis on first- and second-order streams suitable for ditch irrigation and a secondary emphasis on alluvial fans. On the basis of farming observed in Mexico, Sauer and Brand (Brand 1933, 1943:117–122; Sauer and Brand 1930:426, 443–444) drew similar conclusions about the importance of irrigation during early reconnaissance surveys in the region. By comparing catchments around these sites and randomly placed plots on landsat photographs of the study area, Findlow and Confeld (1980) identified at stream margins distinctions in soil composition that could have resulted from past farming activity. Al Dart's (1986) subsequent correlation of Soil Conservation Service water-laid soil types with paths of Hohokam irrigation canals in the Phoenix Basin lend support to their earlier interpretation.

Stone features associated with prehistoric agriculture are not well documented in the Borderlands. Without locations or descriptions, Brand (1943:117) mentioned considerable use of stone for terracing in the San Bernardino Valley and along the Rio Bavispe but noted its absence in the Animas drainage. In a large-scale map of Casas Grandes settlement pattern, Di Peso et al. (1974b:Figure 284-5) indicated several instances of extensive check dam systems in the Playas Valley. However, the few instances in site files of features that might be agricultural in function are of very restricted extent and usually consist of only one or two alignments.

Issues in Demography and Settlement

Relative Population

Estimates by Findlow and De Atley (1976) and by Lekson (1992a) suggest that Borderland population was relatively low in both total numbers and densities. Findlow and De Atley proposed a population of approximately 1300 persons with a density of .96 individuals per square mile. Using Longacre's (1970) formula, Lekson (1992a:113) projected back from this estimate to derive a figure of approximately 640 contemporary rooms within the study area outlined by Findlow and De Atley in their Hidalgo Project. Possibly a few hundred additional occupants could be added from southeast Arizona portions of the Malpais Borderlands not included in the Hidalgo Project design. Brand (1943; Sauer and Brand 1930) believed that population sizes and densities were significantly greater among related peoples near Janos and in the Carretas Basin, the Bavispe drainage, and portions of the San Bernardino Valley to the south.

To put modest Borderlands population into perspective, contrasts can be made with more densely settled populations in surrounding areas. For example, residents of Casas Grandes alone have been estimated to range between 2500 and 5000 persons (Lekson 1996a; Di Peso 1974); unfortunately, there is no sound basis at present for estimating outlying population in any area approximating the size of the Borderlands. A rough comparison of magnitude vis-à-vis Hohokam large-scale irrigators along the Gila River also is revealing (Table 1.4). An average population of 2300 has been calculated for a single community consisting of one mound center and its outlying settlements. Six such communities share an extensive canal network on the Gila River, for a possible total of 13,800 in an area a fraction of the size of the Borderlands.

Short-term Sedentism

Restricted refuse, limited architectural remodeling and superpositioning of features, and low numbers of burials at late prehistoric sites in the study area and in adjacent regional sectors have led researchers to believe occupation spans were short (Kidder et al.

Table 1.4. Interregional Comparison of Estimates for Demographic Parameters and Resource Requirements.

	ESTIMATED POPULATION (a)	HECTARES OF FARMLAND (b)	CORDES OF FIREWOOD (c)
Late Prehistoric Animas Pueblos	1300	520	2600
Average Hohokam Platform Mound Community in the Casa Grande Irrigation Community	2300	1041	3450
Casa Grande Irrigation Community	13800	6245	9370

NOTE: (a) The estimate for late prehistoric Animas population is by Findlow and De Atley (1976:40) as amplified by Lekson (1992a:113). Population estimates for an individual Hohokam platform mound community and the entire Casa Grande system are based on available irrigated land estimated by Crown (1987) and the ratio of population to hectares for Pima irrigated land in Castetter and Bell (1942:54).
(b) Hectares of irrigated land for the Hohokam examples are estimated by Crown (1987) and derived for the Animas region by the ratio of population to hectare of Pima irrigated land.
(c) Following Ravesloot and Spoerl (1994), fuel-wood consumption is based on a modification of Plog's (1992) per capita estimates. Requirements are arbitrarily reduced by 25% for Animas estimates and by another 25% for the Hohokam because of increasingly milder climates.

1949:146; Douglas 1990; Carmichael 1990; Nelson and LeBlanc 1986; Upham 1992). Nelson and LeBlanc (1986) coined the descriptor "short term sedentism" to describe agriculturally committed and aggregated populations that occupy sedentary communities in sequential locations. More recently, Nelson and Anyon (1996) have presented a model of "fallow" valleys in which sedentary populations shift from valley to valley in order to allow regeneration of critical resources. They posit a sequence of shifts in sedentary villages from the Mimbres valley south to the Animas and Playas valleys and then north to the Cliff and Mule Creek regions.

Depletion of faunal (e.g., Nelson and LeBlanc 1986; Douglas 1996) and fuelwood (Minnis 1985) resources are mentioned as examples of factors that might precipitate cycles of population movement. Soil exhaustion (Sandor and Gersper 1988; Sandor et al. 1986) is also sometimes cited as a factor influencing regional settlement. Sequential movement might be the simple and convenient solution to resource depletion under conditions of low and discontinuous regional population.

It is also clear, however, that long-term sedentism was maintained in other sectors of the Southwest under environmental constraints as stringent as those cited for southwest New Mexico by Nelson and Anyon (1996). To develop a general comparison, fuelwood and agricultural land requirements are examined for late prehistoric inhabitants of the Malpais Borderlands and a single irrigation community of settlements sharing a canal network on the Gila River that was continuously inhabited for at least 800 years (Table 1.4). Estimates for emory oak in low-yield zones near the study area (Touchon 1988) suggest that sustained fuelwood needs could be supplied for the entire Borderlands population from approximately 155 sq km. Sustainable fuel for the Classic period Hohokam in the Casa Grande irrigation community is a problem of substantially greater spatial scale, however. Between approximately 350 and 1000 sq km of Sonoran Desert would be required to sustain the estimated level of fuelwood consumption by the Casa Grande community. This population was concentrated in an area of 75 sq km. Problems of resource sustainability for even the largest Borderlands settlement clusters were minor compared to similar challenges for these densely packed Gila River irrigators.

Ceramic variability from one valley to the next is critical to Nelson and Anyon's (1996:279) argument of sequential movements among fallow valleys. They reason that regional phases are difficult to establish because the ceramic assemblages in each valley differ somewhat, probably because of a lack of contemporaneity. Their model does not take into account the fact that the ceramic divisions among Borderlands valleys continue to the south into Chihuahua and Sonora, as do distributions of settlement during this period (Brand 1943; Sauer and Brand 1930; Minnis and Whalen 1992). Crossing the border at Antelope Wells, Brand (1943) continued to record Animas-like sites into the Carretas Basin. Site files at the Amerind Foundation document six large sites (100 to 400 rooms) along the San Bernardino River between Fronteras and the International Border in Sonora, suggesting that Slaughter Ranch and perhaps the Boss Ranch/San Bernardino complex are northernmost expressions of a settlement distribution that stretches a considerable distance into Mexico.

The quality and extent of archaeological work in the Malpais Borderlands study area make it difficult to evaluate the "Short-term Sedentism/Fallow Valley" hypothesis. Site survey records do indicate that some continuity exists in settlement location between Mimbres horizon and later prehistoric villages. Large assemblages of heavily worn and worn-out grinding implements are present at many sites (for example, see Kidder et al. 1949:Figures 22 and 23 and Brand 1943:118–120, particularly the description of Double Adobe Creek on 119), suggesting some span of stable occupation. The same degree of ceramic variability noted by Nelson and Anyon (1996) for Borderlands sites also occurs to the south among the contemporary sites of northern Sonora and Chihuahua and must reflect cultural factors in addition to time. Finally, as will be discussed in the following section, even the most generous population estimates suggest that the Borderlands region always had relatively low populations, which should have put less pressure on resources than did populations of various other southwestern regions.

Settlement Hierarchies and Territorial Communities

Several discussions of late prehistoric settlement hierarchies in the study area have focused on site size rankings. Stephen LeBlanc (1989:193) uses differences in site size as evidence that large pueblos were lower-order centers in the Casas Grandes polity. Findlow and De Atley (De Atley 1980; Findlow and De Atley 1976) also suggest an Animas phase settlement hierarchy, although they do not imply a dependency relationship with Casas Grandes. Their hierarchy is based primarily on site size, supported by artifact densities and diversity. The hierarchy consists of primary and secondary villages and at least some field houses.

Douglas (1995:247–248) takes issue with attempts to define any sort of settlement hierarchy or integrative settlement structure above the village level. He observes a strong correlation between settlement size and agriculturally favored locales and favors a strong likelihood that tendencies toward larger site size may occur later during the Animas phase. He notes that archaeologists in the region frequently divide occupational loci dispersed over several kilometers but functioning as a single village into multiple sites; separate designations for the Boss Ranch and San Bernardino sites are a good example (Douglas 1996; Myers 1985). Finally, Douglas (1995:246–247) and De Atley (1980) both note the apparent absence of ritually integrative features that mark integrative or communal nodes in a settlement hierarchy.

Review of earlier records, new comparative information, and recent site visits reveal that multiple nodes of this sort marked by ball courts are indeed present in late prehistoric Borderlands settlement. These features may have been frequently overlooked because of their unobtrusive character and their failure to match expectations for Hohokam-like ball-court morphology. Current survey investigations in the Casas Grandes region demonstrate numerous instances of ball-court structures and provide new criteria for their recognition (Whalen and Minnis 1996a; Naylor 1995). Orientation is consistently north-south. Although some Chihuahuan ball courts are clearly I- or T-shaped, others are marked on the surface by simple parallel arrangements of rocks (Whalen and Minnis 1996a). In locales with appreciable settlement near Casas Grandes, courts do not invariably occur at the largest site.

The clearest examples of ball-court structures in the Malpais Borderlands are at Joyce Well (Carpenter 1992) and in the vicinity of Timberlake Ruin (O'Laughlin et al. 1984). Both consist of north-south parallel embankments delimiting field areas of 650 and 850 sq m, respectively. A third possible instance is a heavily disturbed depression and set of embankments at the Maddox Ruin in the Animas valley (Thomas O'Laughlin, personal communication). This feature is also oriented north-south and has an area of approximately 700 sq m. A fourth probable ball court, at New Mexico EE:5:1 (ASM), is located to the south in the Animas valley and was recorded by Roger Kelley (1963; Arizona State Museum site files). The structure is oriented north-south, with a field area of 480 sq m and is associated with a pueblo of approximately 100 rooms. On the site card Kelley suggests the court is associated with School of American Research Site 62Hi5 (the Cowboy site). Recent

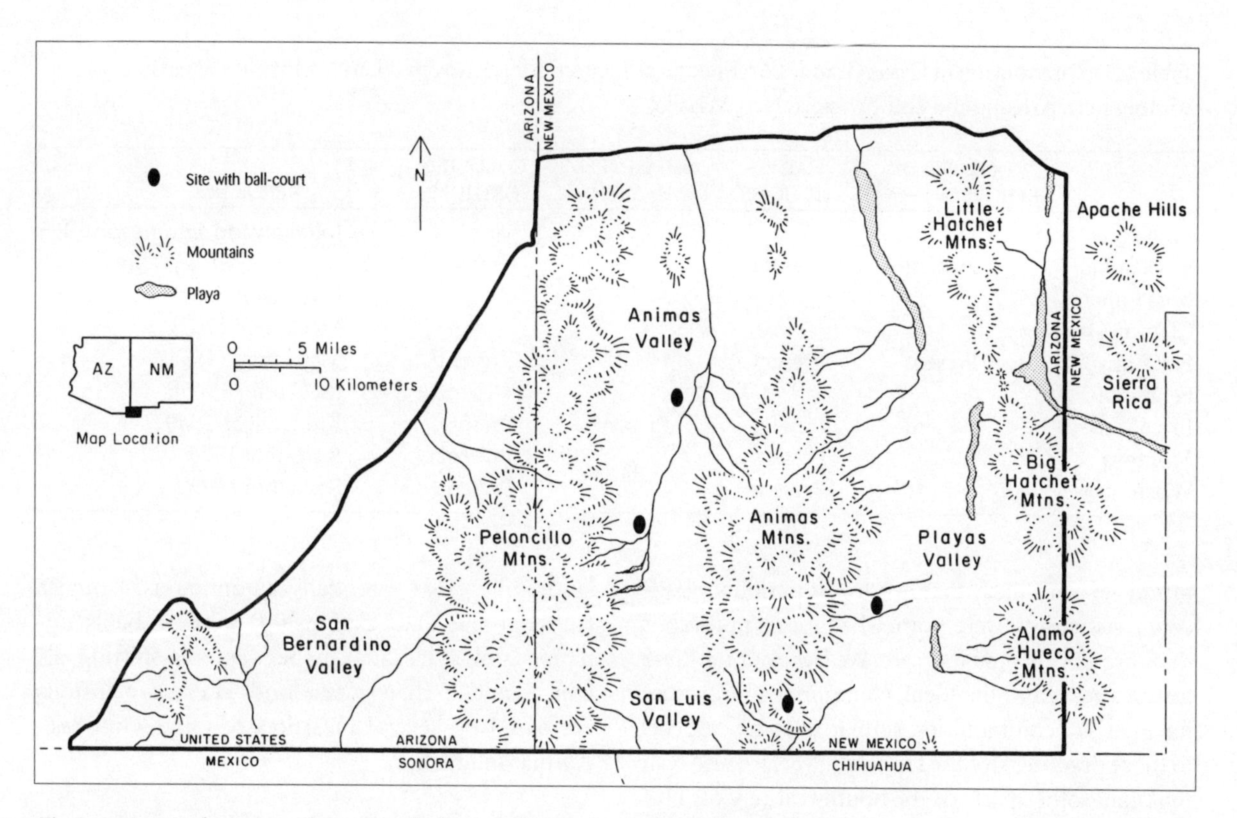

Figure 1.5. Late prehistoric settlement and ball-court distribution in the Malpais study area.

conversations between Roger Kelley and Curtis Schaafsma (personal communication) indicate that the actual site location might be near Clanton Draw. However, a brief reconnaissance by the authors in the vicinity of Clanton Draw and the Cowboy site failed to locate this feature. Figure 1.5 illustrates late prehistoric settlement, in conjunction with probable ball-court distributions, by plotting locations of known ball courts and approximate locations for others.

Several ball courts and possible ball courts are reported just beyond the boundaries of the Malpais Borderlands study area. A court was recorded immediately west of Janos by Minnis and Whalen (1995), and Naylor (1995) describes a ball court at Las Palmas just off the Janos–Carretas Pass Road in Chihuahua. William Doolittle (1984) identifies two probable ball-court structures in the Rio Sonora farther west. Braniff describes two rectangular enclosed structures (*corrales*) that Whalen and Minnis (1996a) believe may be ball courts elsewhere in northern Sonora. A north-south Casas Grandes–type court is also recorded at the Santa Cruz site east of Nogales, Sonora (Kelley 1963; Wilcox and Sternberg 1983:127). North-south parallel stone alignments at two sites north of Nogales along the Santa Cruz reported by Frick (1952, also Whittlesey 1996) fit the criteria for additional instances.

The "great kiva," a likely ball court at the Ringo site northwest of the Borderlands, may have implications for ball-court recognition. The feature was marked on the surface by a shallow depression. Excavation revealed court delimitation by low adobe walls and patches of an adobe surface on a flat floor. Walls are oriented north-south and enclose approximately 900 sq m. The excavators, Albert Johnson and Raymond Thompson (Thompson 1963; Johnson and Thompson 1963:469), considered the possibility that the structure was a ball court but rejected the idea because it was clearly rectangular, unlike the oval courts of southern Arizona. Based on current knowledge of the Chihuahuan instances, Raymond Thompson (personal communication) now believes that this feature probably is a Casas Grandes style ball court. Without surface markers, other adobe courts might be dismissed as in the Ringo site instance.

Given conceptual and physical problems of recog-

Table 1.5. Distribution of Casas Grandes Architectural Traits among Excavated Late Prehistoric Sites in Southeastern Arizona and Southwestern New Mexico.

	T-SHAPED OR KEYHOLE DOORWAYS	RAISED HEARTHS	SCALLOPED HEARTHS	COLLARED POSTHOLES	REFERENCE
Ringo Site					Johnson and Thompson 1963
Kuykendall	Present	Present		Present	Mills and Mills 1969b
Boss Ranch					Douglas 1985, 1996
Clanton Draw					McCluney 1965a
Box Canyon	Present	Present		Present	McCluney 1965a
Pendleton					McCluney 1965b
Joyce Well	Present	Present	Present	Present	Kidder et al. 1949
Montoya		Present		Present	Ravesloot 1975
Walsh		Present		Present	Ravesloot 1975

nition, it seems likely that northwest periphery ball-court structures were somewhat more numerous than present records indicate. We believe that these features served as the focal, communal architecture for multisite communities, similar in some respects to those described for the Hohokam (S. Fish and Fish 1994) and other parts of the Southwest (e.g., P. Fish and Fish 1994; Adler 1996; Lekson 1991). In the apparent absence of kivas, platform mounds, or other integrative structures, ball courts probably represent institutions and activities that crosscut social constituencies and promoted community identity.

Regional Integration and Interaction

The degree to which settlements were integrated by the Casas Grandes polity has been the crux of a central debate in Borderlands prehistory. Charles Di Peso (1974:778) initially viewed Animas phase sites as satellites providing Casas Grandes with turquoise and obsidian and later as population refuges after the collapse of that city in the early fourteenth century. Similarly, Steve LeBlanc (1989) portrays Animas settlements as outposts of Casas Grandes that developed following the collapse of the Chaco Canyon and Mimbres cultural systems and the demise of their role in trade with central Mexico.

Other models involve considerably less economic and political dependency on Casas Grandes. De Atley (1980) and De Atley and Findlow (1982) describe Animas phase settlements as a frontier phenomenon, with loose participation in a Casas Grandes exchange system. Paul Minnis (1984, 1990) finds little linkage between the two areas and describes Borderlands villages as essentially autonomous. Douglas (1995) argues that relationships were probably dynamic and situational, dependent on shifting alliances and exchange relations. These conclusions are based on several measures of Casas Grandes–Animas interaction.

Architectural Traits

Archaeologists have evoked Chihuahuan styles of architecture to both support (Brand 1943; Di Peso 1974; LeBlanc 1989; Ravesloot 1975; Carpenter 1992) and negate (Kidder et al. 1949:146; Douglas 1995:243) Animas phase affinity with Casas Grandes. The absence of T-shaped or keyhole-shaped doorways, raised and scalloped hearths, collared postholes, and subfloor inhumations at the Pendleton Ruin caused Kidder to reject a Chihuahuan affiliation and to adopt the term "Animas." As indicated in Table 1.5, subsequent excavations have demonstrated the widespread existence of these traits in southwestern New Mexico and southeastern Arizona. These traits indicate relationships at the level of horizon style and reflect some degree of acceptance of "norms" that serve to distinguish broad cultural patterns. It is significant that these traits often linked to Casas Grandes crosscut the east-west divisions in the Borderlands between room-block and compound architecture and utility wares.

Ceramic Styles and Production

John Carpenter (1992) shows that Ramos Polychrome distributions in the Borderlands are separated from a similar zone encompassing Casas Grandes by an intervening area of Carretas and

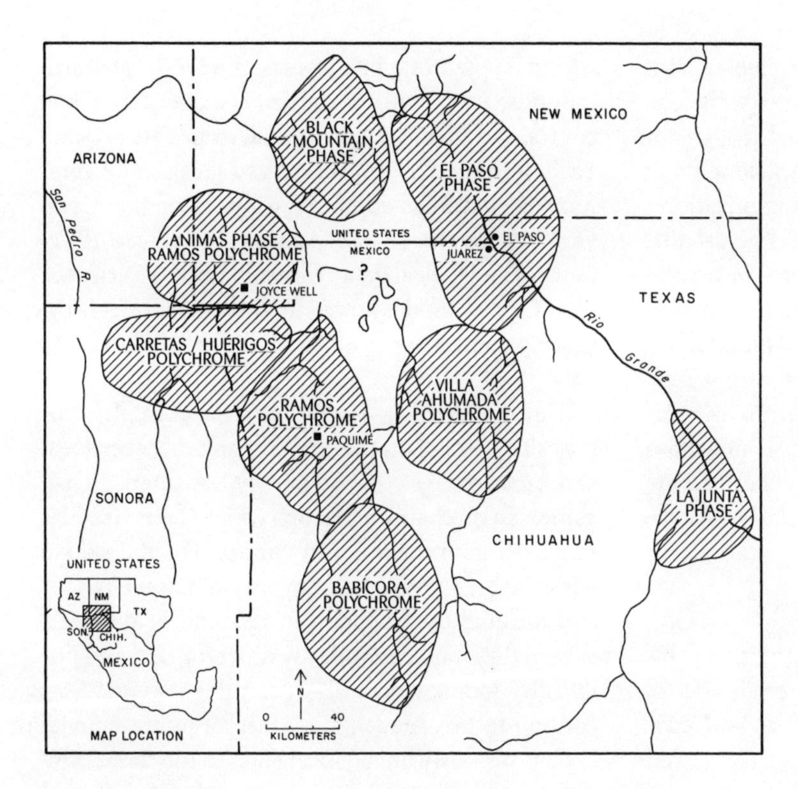

Figure 1.6. Distribution of Chihuahuan polychrome styles as outlined by J. Carpenter (1992).

Huérigos polychromes (Figure 1.6). Suzanne De Atley (1980; Findlow and De Atley 1982) attempted to measure the integration of the Borderlands region by Casas Grandes through attributes of style, but her results have been seriously challenged on grounds of sample size and an untested assumption of local ceramic production within Borderland valleys (Douglas 1995:247; Minnis 1984, 1989). Recently, some compositional evidence has indicated that Ramos Polychrome was produced in the Sulphur Springs valley in southeastern Arizona (Woosley and Olinger 1993) and at the Culberson Ruin (Woosley and Olinger 1993) and Joyce Well (Carpenter 1992) in southwestern New Mexico.

Access to Prestige Goods

Paul Minnis (1984, 1988, 1989) argues that certain types of prestige goods characteristic of Casas Grandes are rare (shell, turquoise) or absent (copper, macaws) in Animas phase sites. On the other hand, John Douglas (1995:246) points out that frequencies of prestige items may not equate with level of interaction or strength of integration. He also notes that, with few burials and no exposed ritual contexts, excavated data may not be adequate to make such comparisons. In addition to Douglas's observation, Animas site comparisons would be more appropriate with similarly sized settlements in the Casas Grandes vicinity rather than directly with this unique center. Comparative data from such sites are not currently available.

In spite of these caveats, a body of qualitative data from the Borderlands and adjacent locations shows a degree of access to prestige goods. Abundant shell and numerous artifacts of turquoise, slate, and hematite were recovered from funerary contexts at Joyce Well (McCluney 1965b), the one site where significant numbers of burials have been excavated. Two small copper pendants were recovered from the San Bernardino site (Myers 1985). Farther south in the San Bernardino Valley, Braniff (1992:496) reports three copper bells from Ojo de Agua and two from Rancho Baviso. U-Bar and Pinnacle caves produced large quantities of scarlet macaw feathers (Lambert 1965:101; Curtis Schaafsma, personal communication), and a possible macaw pen was identified at Slaughter Ranch (Mills and Mills 1971).

Di Peso (1974) proposed Antelope Wells obsidian

as a Borderlands resource of economic value to Casas Grandes. X-ray florescence studies of obsidian samples from Casas Grandes confirmed that a substantial proportion is derived from Antelope Wells sources (Steve Shackley, personal communication). Furthermore, regional obsidian studies reveal that Antelope Wells material seldom occurs in assemblages to the north and west outside the distribution of Chihuahuan polychrome ceramics. Although this pattern of overlapping distributions does not confirm any kind of dependency between the Borderlands and Casas Grandes, it is a significant indication of the dual directionality and spatial concentration of some kinds of economic relationships.

Conclusions

Most discussion of Casas Grandes–Borderlands interaction has focused on the presence or absence of dependency relationships in a political and economic sense. We can agree with Douglas (1995) and Minnis (1984, 1989) that current evidence for such asymmetric interaction is limited. On the other hand, it seems likely that late prehistoric Borderlands inhabitants participated at some level in an ideology that was shared with and most elaborately encoded at Casas Grandes. This ideology involved the construction of ball courts, and related tenets were probably symbolized in certain ceramic and architectural "horizon styles" (see Wilcox 1995:289). This ideology was clearly differentiated from a Hohokam and western Salado ceremonial focus on platform mounds to the northwest and an Anasazi kiva and plaza orientation to the north. Massive hillside structures of the major trincheras villages may delineate a similarly distinctive realm of ideological orientation to the west in Sonora (Downum et al. 1994:292–293; P. Fish and Fish 1994:22).

Casas Grandes was clearly a central exponent of this ideology. As defined archaeologically, this ideology likely represents a phenomenon broader than religion per se, perhaps in the realm of "worldview." Archaeologically recognized variants of architecture and ceramics are subsumed by the most conservative distribution of ball courts (Whalen and Minnis 1996a). This stylistic diversity is increased if most of the instances proposed herein prove viable. The number and variety of ritual features at Casas Grandes set this site apart from all other sites in the region containing ball courts. Eighteen platform mounds, each with a different shape, three ball courts, and a wide range of ritual rooms are present. Each of these probably served as a location for ceremonies that affected some segment of the Casas Grandes population (see Minnis 1989:277–280). Current archaeological data are insufficient to clarify the roles Casas Grandes served in this regional ideology; sharply contrasting models can be fitted to existing data.

David Wilcox (1995:289–292), for example, proposes a system of ceremonial exchange between local elites, fostered by a version of the Mesoamerican ball game, as a mechanism through which Casas Grandes exercised its influence and control. For the sphere within a three-and-a-half-day walk of Casas Grandes that includes the Malpais Borderlands, he defines a system that was economically differentiated and politically dominated by the preeminent center. According to this model, the Casas Grandes regional system variously linked local elites to the center, and differentially facilitated exchange and tribute flowed among village or community nodes. As a result of recent and ongoing surveys designed to illuminate the role of Casas Grandes in regional settlement, Minnis and Whalen (1990, 1995) find little support for Casas Grandes hegemony or integration of outlying settlements beyond a range as short as 30 km. Thus, based on the distribution of elements such as site size, ball courts, production of crafts and other exotics such as macaws and ceramics, they would exclude the Borderlands and adjacent areas in Mexico from any direct political and economic influence of Casas Grandes. Furthermore, they argue that the notable sparsity of courts at a distance from Casas Grandes denotes substantially weaker local integration and that their presence need not imply any type of integration into the Casas Grandes regional systems (Whalen and Minnis 1996a:741–744).

Plausible models for ideological centrality and directional emphasis in material exchange can be offered that do not emphasize political or economic domination. For instance, Casas Grandes could have been the destination for regional pilgrimages, serving to ideologically reinforce and unite outlying populations without tribute or political control. Models featuring pilgrimage have been considered for Chaco Canyon (Judge 1983, 1989). Examples of such pilgrimages appear in the ethnographic literature. For

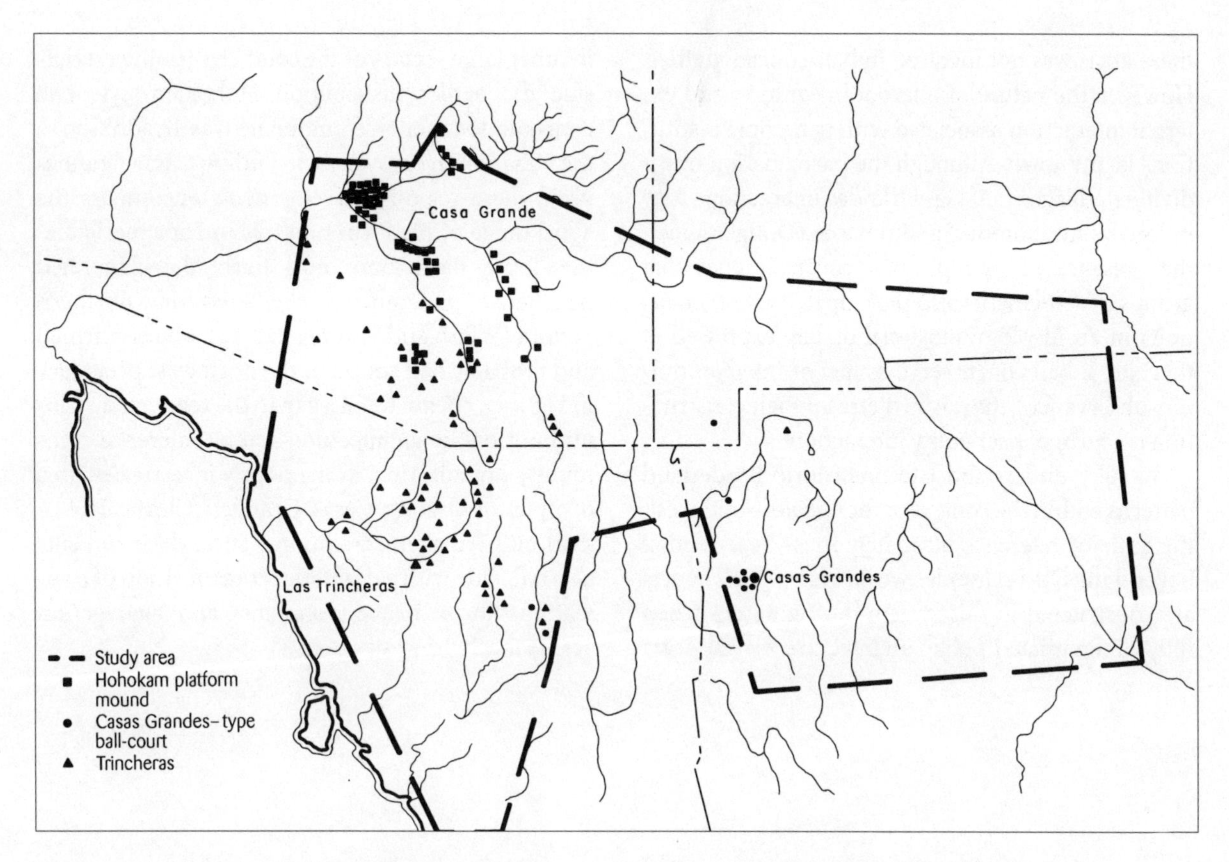

Figure 1.7. Distributions of public architecture in the regions north and west of Casas Grandes.

example, the annual Festival of San Francisco in Magdalena, Sonora, involves multiethnic participants from all parts of Sonora and southern Arizona and is thought to have precontact origins (Griffith 1992; Dobyns 1960). Pilgrimages represent an individualized mechanism through which widely separated communities might participate at different levels in Casas Grandes ideology. Trade, local alliances, and a variety of other political and economic negotiations are likely by-products of such occasions.

Just as it is difficult with existing data to detail the kind of regional integration embodied by Casas Grandes–style ball courts, it is difficult to specify their significance at the local Borderlands level. Although all northern and western examples would fit into Whalen and Minnis's (1996a:737) simple, open–ball court category, these too are morphologically variable. This variability includes size, construction material, and labor investment, which may have functional, ideological, and hierarchical implications. Unfortunately, none of the northwestern periphery sites with consensual or suspected ball courts can be viewed in a context of comprehensive local settlement.

Despite these problems, the nature of the ball courts themselves offers some insights into probable roles in local territorial organization. The communal nature of ball-court construction is generally accepted. Furthermore, events held at these structures are also considered to be communal and to frequently involve the competitive interaction of separate territorial entities. This interaction could involve individual villages, but in the case of Hohokam ball courts, interaction is generally conceived as taking place between "communities" or groups of settlements (Wilcox and Sternberg 1983). This kind of interpretation of ball-court function seems no less applicable for Casas Grandes–style structures. It follows, then, that Borderlands sites with ball courts served as integrative nodes for some community-like set of additional settlements.

Whalen and Minnis (1996a) observe that the small number of courts at a distance from Casas Grandes indicates the majority of population in these areas was not involved in ball-court activities. However, the nature of internal integration and external interaction associated with ball-court institutions is unknown. Although the participation of individual villages in Casas Grandes interactions may indeed be autonomous in some cases (Douglas 1995), the presence of multiple ball courts implies that groups of settlements also participated as territorial units in an ideology most elaborately expressed at that site. If ball courts serve as loci of intercommunity observances, the raison d'etre for their construction is a form of peer polity interaction.

To fully understand late prehistoric Borderland patterns within the context of the Greater Southwest, the scale of reference ultimately must be extended beyond the Casas Grandes world system. Ball courts are constructed in this system during an era when fully differentiated public architecture first appears in other large sectors of the southern Southwest outside the earlier distribution Hohokam-style ball courts and Mogollon communal kivas. In addition to the Casas Grandes system, including Casas Grandes itself, these regional developments encompass the appearance of platform mounds in Papagueria and the Tonto Basin and most likely the elaborated trincheras phenomenon centered in northern Sonora (P. Fish and Fish 1994:21–24). The confirmed and probable ball courts of the northwest periphery in Figure 1.7 begin to fill a gap in the regional distribution of public architecture, and by inference community organization, in the poorly investigated area of juncture among Casas Grandes, Classic Hohokam, and Trincheras traditions. These developments also coincide with a dramatic reorganization of populations through abandonments and aggregation across the Southwest.

2

The Villa Ahumada Site

Archaeological Investigations East of Paquimé

Rafael Cruz Antillón

Timothy D. Maxwell

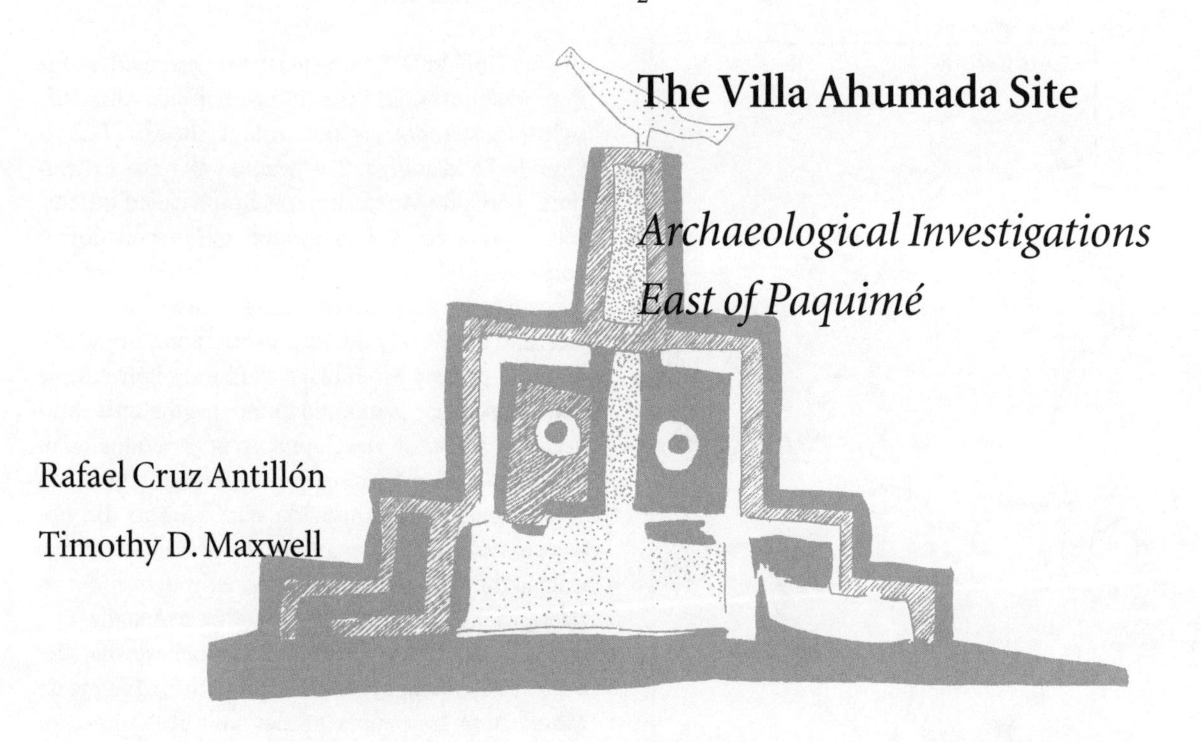

SEVERAL ARCHAEOLOGICAL STUDIES have suggested that the site of Paquimé served as the central authority in a complex cultural network formed by hundreds of archaeological sites in northwestern Chihuahua sometime after A.D. 1050. However, several different models have been proposed regarding the complexity and the extent of the network (Di Peso 1974; Di Peso et al. 1974; Bradley 1993; Minnis 1989; Wilcox 1995; Whalen and Minnis 1996a, 1996b), and other studies have reevaluated the proposed dates for the development of this network (Dean and Ravesloot 1988; Ravesloot et al. 1995a). Although researchers have addressed the possible integrative structure of the network and its geographical extent, the extant database has limited the development of a widely accepted explanatory model. Recognizing that current views on the regional nature of Paquimé's influence are based on modest information from a scattering of sites, limited and perhaps misinterpreted chronological data, and the regional distribution of pottery whose production centers are sometimes disputed, researchers such as Paul Minnis and Michael Whalen have begun surveying the region northwest of Paquimé (Minnis and Whalen 1990; Whalen and Minnis 1996a, 1996b), and Jane Kelly and Joe Stewart (1991) have been looking at the Namiquipa-Babícora-Cuauhtémoc region to the south. These researchers are conducting surface analyses and testing of sites to establish a more comprehensive view of regional interactions.

In 1992 the Instituto Nacional de Antropología e Historia–Centro Chihuahua (INAH) decided to approach the problem of an inadequate database through an excavation program. After surveying and recording 41 sites along the Río Santa María and Río el Carmén drainages, INAH selected two sites for long-term study: the Villa Ahumada site, along the Río el Carmén, and the Galeana site, bordering the Río Santa María (Figure 2.1). In 1993 excavations began at Villa Ahumada, and the following discussion focuses on the results of the first year of excavation. Since 1994 the University of New Mexico has participated in these studies under the direction of Robert D. Leonard, and in 1994 and 1995 archaeologists from the Museum of New Mexico assisted in the regional studies.

Physiographically, the region encompassing the two sites consists of the two river basins and surrounding mountains. The Río Santa María drains into a lake of the same name, whereas the Río el

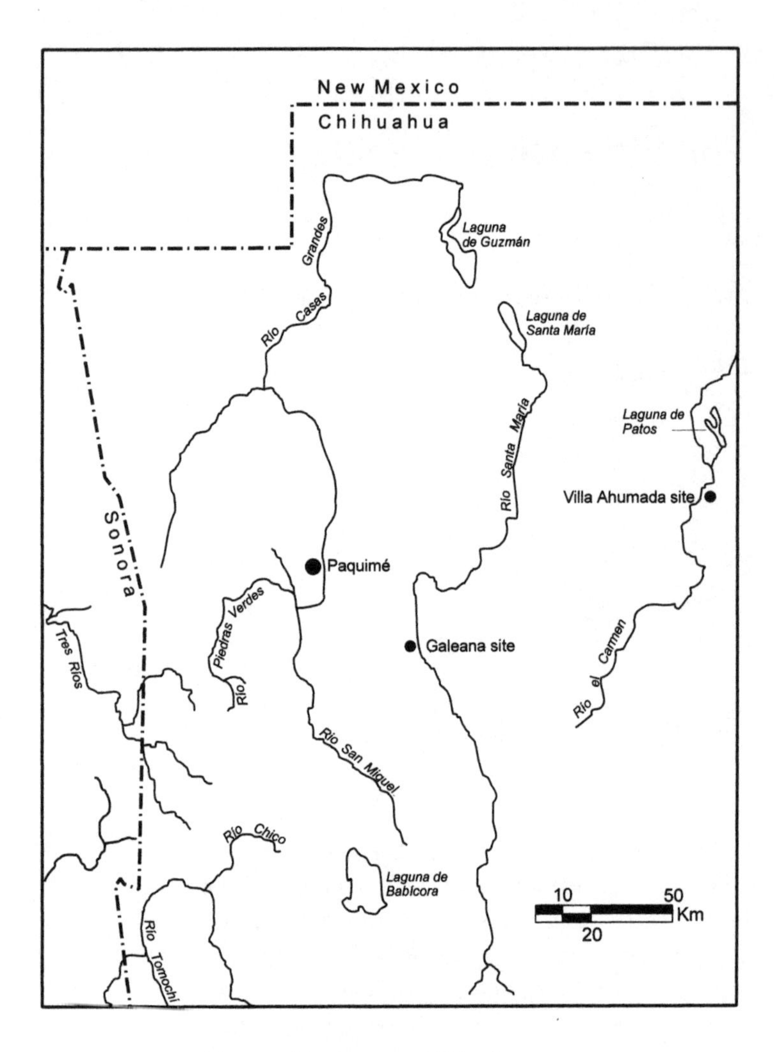

Figure 2.1. Northwestern Chihuahua.

Carmén empties into the Laguna de Patos. Several intermittent water bodies exist throughout both river basins. Topographically, the land is uneven, with mountain ranges of volcanic origin, some isolated mounts of limestone, and deeply dissected arroyos.

As a warm-temperate desertland, the Chihuahuan desert scrub around the sites is typical of xeric regions, and the plant cover includes agave, ocotillo, ash, sage, vauquelinia, and yucca. Mammals observed historically are mountain lions, rabbits, hares, mice, and mule deer, but domesticated cattle dominate today. Reptiles and amphibians such as chameleon, snakes, toads, and tortoises are present, and large avifauna includes duck, heron, hawk, eagle, vulture, and various migratory species.

The Villa Ahumada Site

In 1943 Donald D. Brand (1943:154) described a large mound about two miles southwest of Villa Ahumada as "the most important archaeologic site east of Casas Grandes" and as a site that "would well repay excavation." Loma de Montezuma, as Brand called the site, was characterized as a mound of "melted down" adobe walls about 2 m high at the central point and covering an area of about 13,400 sq m. On the site surface, and in several pothunting intrusions, Brand observed a pottery assemblage of El Paso Polychrome and Chihuahuan wares and found that the site exhibited the "greatest development of a Chihuahuan black-on-red-on-white slip polychrome which has been termed Villa Ahumada ware." Brand did not wish to discuss the reasons for the prevalence of this ware at the site because nothing was known about its stratigraphic relationships with other regionally produced wares. However, Brand did believe that the pottery assemblage reflected occupation of Loma de Montezuma by people of two cultures—those of "Chihuahuan affinities" and those of the "El Paso culture" (Brand 1935:303, 1943:153–154). Although his findings did not necessarily contradict Brand's observations, Lehmer (1948:11) would later contend that the Villa Ahumada site should be placed within the region occupied by Jornada Mogollon populations.

As related by Brand (1943:153–154), the Loma de Montezuma was an unreported distance east of, but close to, the Río el Carmén, the drainage that Brand believed marked "the eastern-most advance of Chihuahua culture," a characterization with which Di Peso (1974:9) later agreed. Brand further recounted that the site was in a *mesquital* surrounded by arable land and that a spring, probably used by prehistoric farmers as a source of irrigation water, is near the site. The site had experienced some looting by the time of Brand's report, and he remarked that pothunters had turned up great quantities of pottery, human bones, and turquoise beads and pendants. Brand collected samples of potsherds from the site—which today are in the collections of the Museum of New Mexico, Laboratory of Anthropology (ARC Catalog Number 13897)—and the site was assigned the number LA 507.

INAH began excavations at the site believed to be that described by Brand, now commonly called the "Villa Ahumada site," in 1993. Located about 3 km

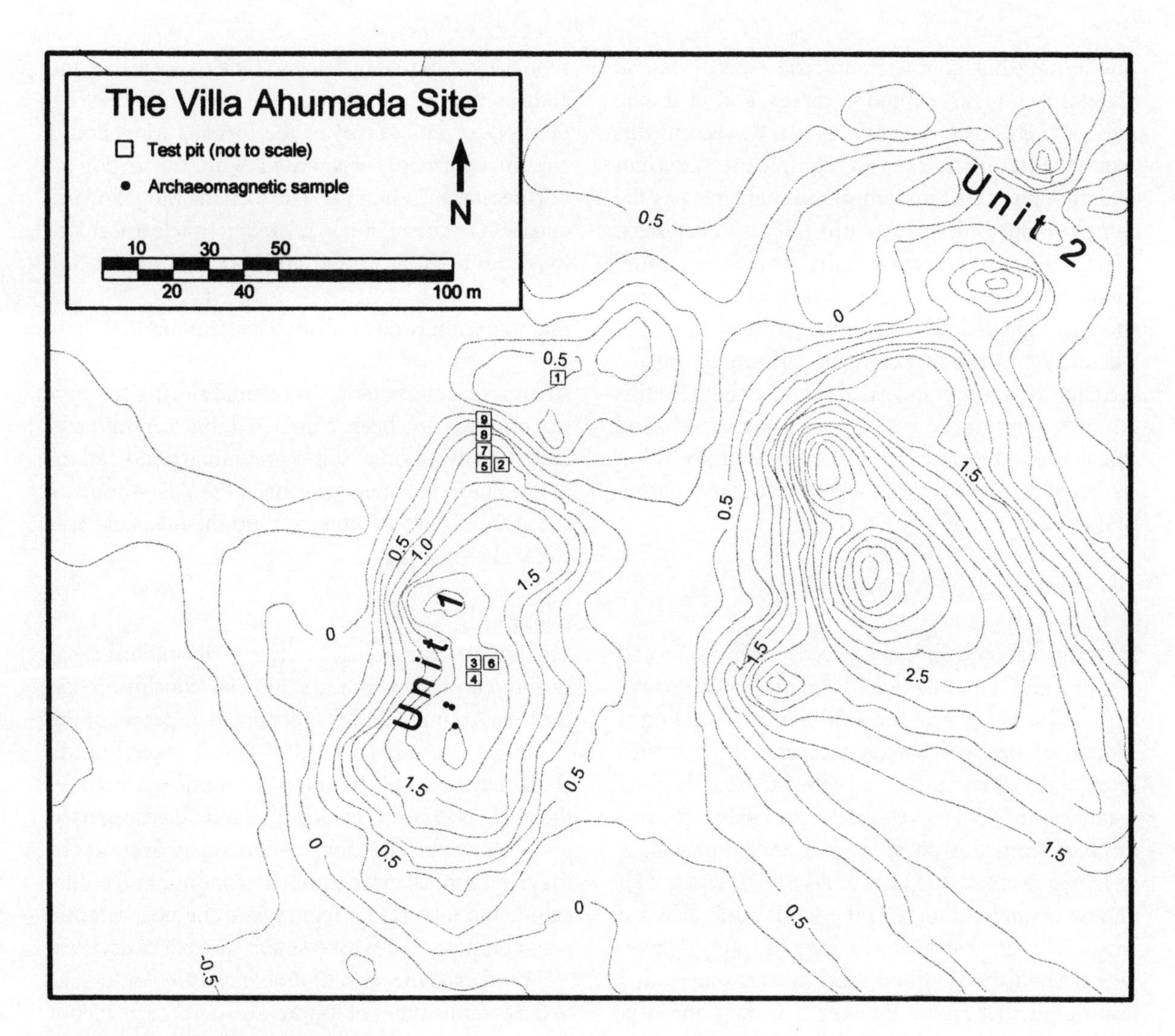

Figure 2.2. The Villa Ahumada site.

southwest of the town of Villa Ahumada, the Villa Ahumada site fits Brand's general description of the location, surrounding environment, and site characteristics. Following INAH's investigations, Brand's earlier characterization of the site can be amplified and his tentative conclusions evaluated. The room blocks are in a small plain about 500 m east of the Río el Carmén. Rather than the one mound observed by Brand, the site has two room blocks, one larger than the other (Figure 2.2). The larger room block, Unit 1, is the mound described by Brand. The second room block, Unit 2, lies to the northeast, about 200 m from the center of Unit 1. Unit 2 is also a mound of melted adobe, measuring 20 m by 10 m and about .5 m high. The second unit sits among large dunes and was likely unseen by Brand, who may have not visited that locale because of a break in artifact distribution between the two areas. Although the two mounds have similar assemblages of pottery, the lack of study in Unit 2 prevents a more accurate evaluation of their contemporaneity.

During the first excavation season, nine exploratory trenches were dug to determine stratigraphic sequences at the site (Fig. 2.2). Three were excavated in the central part of Unit 1 and six at its northern edge. Four natural strata were detected, and arbitrary levels between 15 and 20 cm in thickness were excavated within each stratum. Stratum I is loose, medium-grained sand and averages 15 cm in thickness. It has been severely disturbed by continuous looting but contains numerous sherds, faunal skeletal fragments, turquoise pieces, and charcoal. Several prehistoric use surfaces can be seen in this stratum. Stratum II has an average thickness of 50 cm and, though of a more compacted character, has the same soil attributes as Stratum I. It also contains a high frequency of artifacts. In Stratum III more medium-grained sand is a dark brown and even more compacted. The stratum averages 25 cm in thickness and has inclusions of calcium carbonate. Artifact frequency increases dramatically in this stratum. Stratum IV is also medium-grained sand that is about the same compaction as Stratum III but darker in color. No artifacts were found at the bottom of this level.

Dating

Six radiocarbon samples were recovered from several test pits and a looting hole during the 1993 excavations. All samples were of a bulk nature, consisting of individual pieces of charcoal recovered throughout a level. With two exceptions, all dates are from the thirteenth century. All reported dates are calibrated. Two samples from test pit 5, levels 1 and 2, provide a weighted average date of A.D. 1259 (A.D. 1212–1278), and two samples from test pit 9, levels 2 and 4, have a weighted average date of A.D. 1267 (A.D. 1259–1279). Two dates from disturbed areas include one from a looting pit that ranges between A.D. 1413 and A.D. 1436 and one from an exterior firepit that ranges between A.D. 1522 and A.D. 1648.

Archaeomagnetic samples taken from other locations and processed by the Museum of New Mexico, Archaeomagnetic Dating Laboratory, correspond with the radiocarbon dates. Excavators expected to find an early occupation level in the southern part of the site, and an archaeomagnetic date of A.D. 960–1030 supports that impression. One thermal feature in the approximate site center dated between A.D. 1255 and A.D. 1290, and one to the north dated between A.D. 1255 and A.D. 1285.

Excepting the disturbed areas, these results fall within the revised Medio period dates ascribed to Casas Grandes (Dean and Ravesloot 1988; Ravesloot et al. 1995a). Di Peso's original dates of A.D. 1060–1340 for the Medio period were reevaluated by Dean and Ravesloot (1988), who believe that the beginning of the period may date closer to A.D. 1200 than the A.D. 1060 date proposed by Di Peso. The radiocarbon and archaeomagnetic dates also fall within the El Paso phase (A.D. 1200–1450) of the Jornada Mogollon, a culture commonly associated with the region of northeastern Chihuahua. The Jornada Mogollon occupation of the region is related, in unclear fashion, to Medio period Casas Grandes (Phillips 1989:384).

Material Culture and Subsistence Remains

Analyses of all materials recovered during the 1993 season have not been completed, but ceramic and faunal analyses offer some preliminary indications on the character of occupation at the Villa Ahumada site. Analysis of assemblages from the 1994 field season is also ongoing.

Ceramics

The pottery assemblage recovered during test excavations contradicts Brand's informal conclusion that the Villa Ahumada site was occupied by people of the "Chihuahuan complex" and "El Paso" people. Brand's characterization of the surface ceramic assemblage, the only observations made until now, has been used by subsequent researchers to develop an overview of the geographical extent of socioeconomic and political interactions in the region, and the new ceramic data compel some reassessment of such overviews.

Brand used the term *Chihuahuan complex* to refer to the ceramic types of Ramos Polychrome, Babícora Polychrome, Carretas Polychrome, Huérigos Polychrome, Madera Red-on-black, Médanos Red-on-brown, Playas Red, Ramos Black, and Villa Ahumada Polychrome. He reported that these types were found in the same approximate frequency at this site as wares such as El Paso wares. He also noted that trade wares were well represented at the site (Brand 1943: 154) but did not mention their approximate frequency. Records at the Museum of New Mexico, Laboratory of Anthropology, and a footnote by Brand (1943:157) show that he included Mimbres Black-on-white, Mimbres smoothed/corrugated wares, St. Johns Polychrome, Chupadero Black-on-white, and Three Rivers Terracotta as trade wares.

The 1993 excavations recovered 4,782 sherds (Table 2.1), of which 39 types were identified and classified into six groups: brown wares, corrugated wares, incised wares, El Paso series, miscellaneous wares, and types associated with the Casas Grandes

Table 2.1. Ceramic Types at Villa Ahumada Site.

STRATUM	I		II				III				IV			
LEVEL	Surface		1		2		3		4		5		6	
CERAMIC GROUP	#	%	#	%	#	%	#	%	#	%	#	%	#	%
Plain brown wares	288	21.8	485	27.6	244	33.7	181	35.8	73	31.9	71	33.6	12	38.7
El Paso wares	643	48.6	706	40.2	213	29.4	102	20.2	52	22.7	43	20.4	1	3.2
Casas Grandes wares	32	2.4	57	3.2	22	3.0	6	1.2	5	2.2	1	0.5	0	0.0
Incised wares	42	3.2	67	3.8	34	4.7	43	8.5	10	4.4	9	4.3	0	0.0
Corrugated wares	139	10.5	126	7.2	110	15.2	77	15.2	59	25.8	49	23.2	5	16.1
Miscellaneous	179	13.5	317	18.0	102	14.1	96	19.0	30	13.1	38	18.0	13	41.9
Total	1323		1758		725		505		229		211		31	

culture, such as Babícora, Ramos, and Villa Ahumada polychromes. As Table 2.1 shows, sherds of the Casas Grandes ceramic complex occur in low frequency, showing their highest frequency in the upper levels of the site. In contrast, El Paso series sherds dominate the surface assemblage and continue to predominate in the first subsurface level. At that point, brown wares constitute the majority of the assemblage, a pattern that continues through the lowest levels (Figure 2.3).

Therefore, in contrast to Brand's original observation, the Casas Grandes and El Paso wares do not occur on the site in similar proportions. The El Paso wares are far more abundant than those associated with Casas Grandes, and the brown ware occurs in a frequency approaching that of the El Paso wares. The high percentage of brown ware suggests that there may have been local production of the ware, but further research is necessary to verify this.

Of the 771,274 sherds found at Paquimé (Di Peso et al. 1974:6:77), those of nonlocal origin accounted for 7.3 percent of the ceramic assemblage, including Gila Polychrome, which Di Peso et al. (1974:8:141) suggest may not have actually been a trade ware. Among the nonlocal sherds specifically identified in the nonlocal assemblage (Di Peso et al. 1974:8:141), 50 percent were Gila Polychrome, 39.7 percent El Paso Polychrome, and 8.1 percent Tonto Polychrome (Di Peso et al. 1974:6:77). For Di Peso et al. (1974:8:149–150), the Gila Polychrome was probably of local manufacture, although others question this interpretation (Whalen, personal communication; Wilcox 1995:291). If the Gila Polychrome was manufactured outside the Paquimé region, it came from the Salado region; if it was locally manufactured, it appears that Paquimé people were appropriating the Gila Polychrome style. In either case this would suggest strong interaction with populations residing northwest of Paquimé and perhaps different functional or ideological treatment of the two major pottery types. Whereas the Gila Polychrome appears primarily in bowl forms, 94.8 percent of the El Paso Polychrome consists of jar forms (Di Peso et al. 1974:8:141; Douglas 1992:9). Di Peso (1974:8:141) believed that El Paso Polychrome vessels were important to Paquimeños as a container, perhaps to hold spume salt from the lower Rio Grande region. This implies that El Paso Polychrome was more important for storage and that stylistic elements may have had less importance in maintaining economic or political relationships. The large amount of El Paso wares at the Villa Ahumada site may indicate that Villa Ahumada served as a central trade location with other Jornada Mogollon people and that Villa Ahumadans in turn traded pottery into Paquimé, but more research is needed.

Fauna

Faunal remains were analyzed by Oscar Polaco and Ana Fabiola Guzmán of the Laboratorio de Paleozoología del INAH. Identified specimens numbered

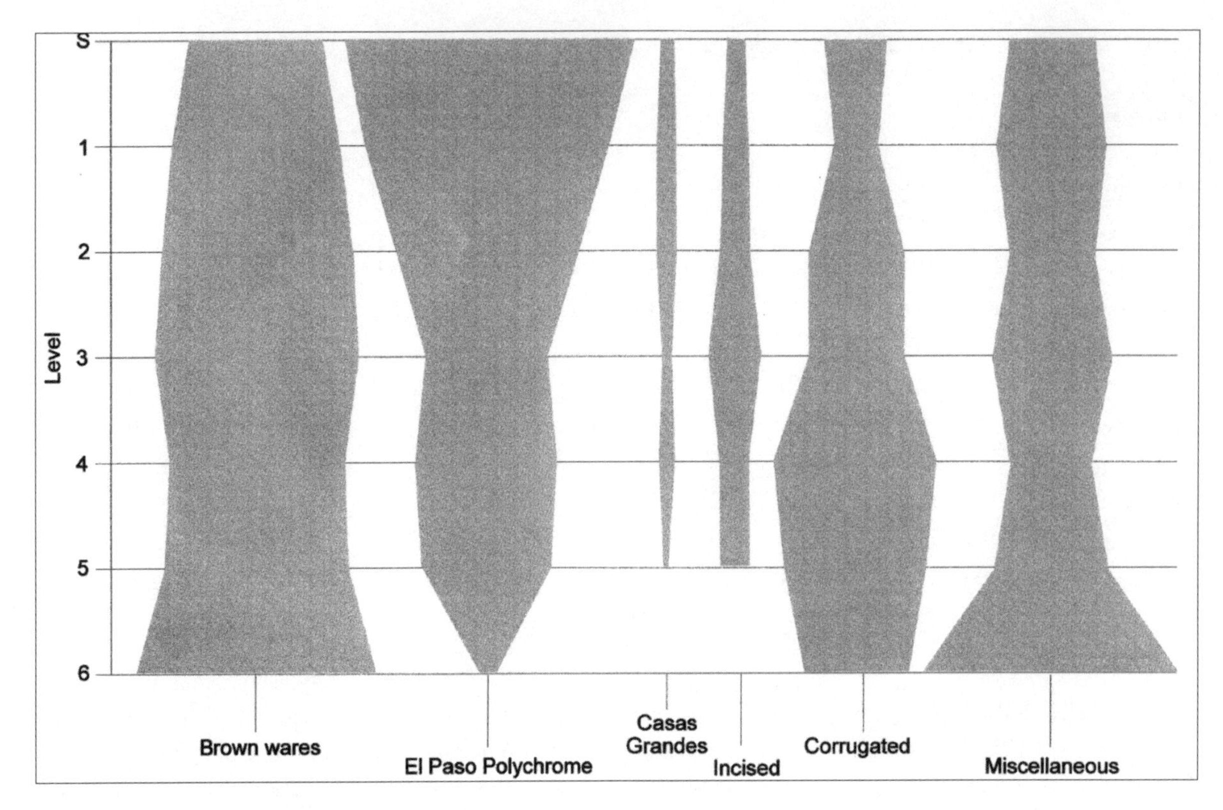

Figure 2.3. Pottery recovered at the Villa Ahumada site.

11,196, but another 10,976 small fragments could not be identified. In total, 28 taxa were recognized, including fish, amphibians, reptiles, birds, and mammals. At least 26 percent of all the recovered elements show signs of burning, which may indicate their use as a food source.

Identified fish include the remains of *Gila nigrescens,* known locally as the Chihuahua carp. For amphibians, 26 elements were determined to be *Bufo cognatus,* whereas reptiles included two tortoise individuals, a rattlesnake (*Crotalus* sp.), and an unidentified snake. An interesting characteristic for the tortoise species *Trachemys seripta* is that it requires a permanent water source of large size.

In the category of birds, 61 elements were found from six taxa. The most abundant elements were from roadrunner (*Geococcyx californianus*), a common species in the region, followed by owl (genera *Strix*), quail (*Callipepla squamata*), and duck (genera *Anas*). Only two elements of turkey (*Meleagris gallopavo*) were recovered.

Mammals constitute the bulk of the faunal remains, and 14 taxa were recognized. However, 11 of the taxa have less than ten skeletal elements. Of interest is *Microtus pennsylvanicum,* now extinct in the region but a species requiring a humid, marshy habitat. The other abundantly represented taxa include weasel (*Mustela frenata*), kangaroo rat (*Dipodomys merriami*), and mule deer (*Odocoileus hemionus*).

The most abundant skeletal elements ($N = 10{,}871$) were from four species of lagomorphs—two of *Sylvilagus* sp. and two of *Lepus* sp. These remains formed 97.1 percent of the identified remains, and elements of *Lepus* sp. outnumbered *Sylvilagus* sp. 2:1. Polaco and Guzmán maintain that the Villa Ahumada site has a greater percentage of lagomorphs than any other known site in Mexico, but far fewer sites have been excavated in northern Mexico, and even fewer samples are available for comparison. Research by Szuter and Gillespie (1994:68) shows that in faunal samples from Hohokam sites, lagomorphs account for more than 50 percent of all recovered faunal remains and as much as 95 percent of the identified specimens in samples from lowland sites. They also point out that in these lowland sites, jackrabbits predominate in the assemblages (Szuter and Gillespie

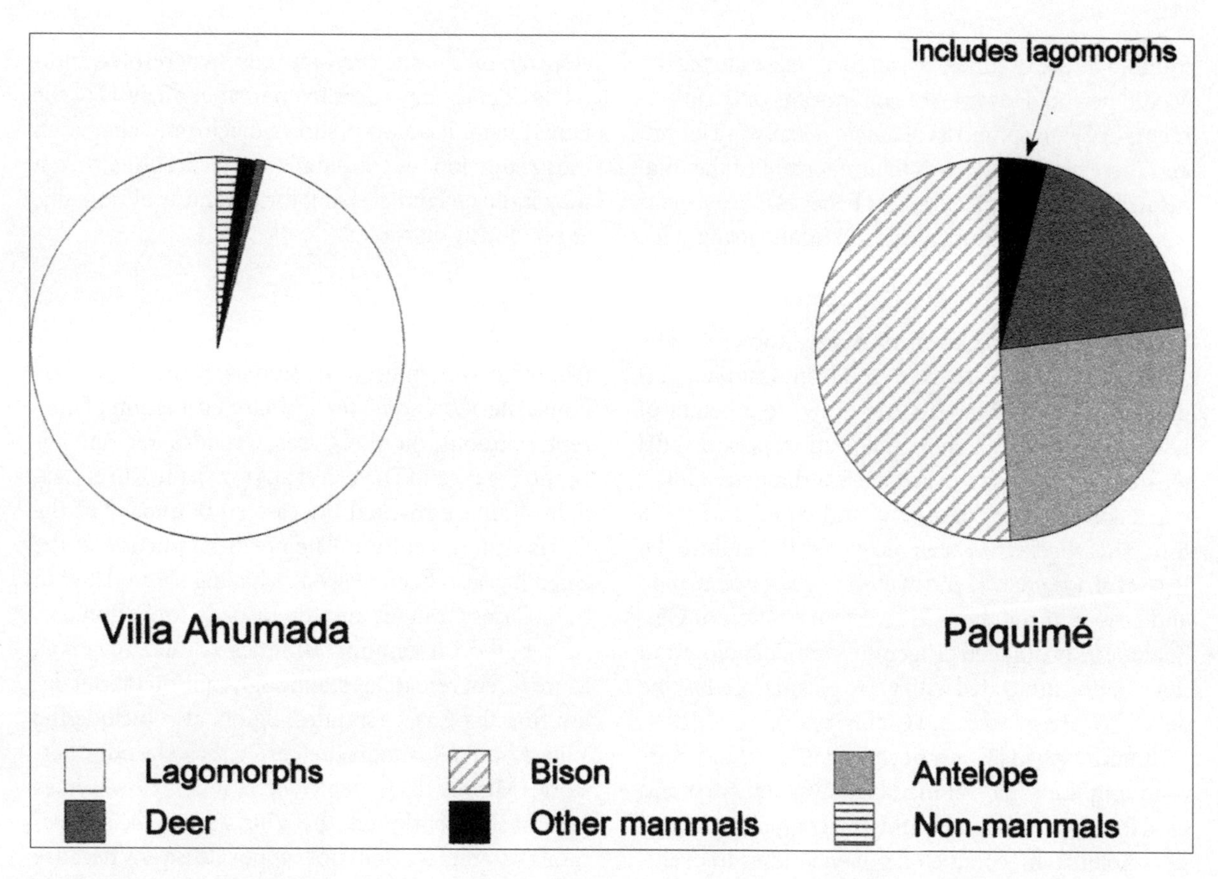

Figure 2.4. Faunal assemblages.

1994:71). Similar patterns have been found in Jornada Mogollon sites (Foster et al. 1981).

The dominance of *Lepus* sp. in assemblages may be related to the density of vegetative cover. Jackrabbits inhabit less-dense vegetative settings, whereas cottontails live where greater brush cover occurs (Anyon and LeBlanc 1984; Szuter and Gillespie 1994). Jackrabbit populations are therefore larger in desert settings and may also increase as land is cleared for farming or building construction (Anyon and LeBlanc 1984; Gillespie 1989). Relative population size between species may also fluctuate as precipitation patterns change. A period of increased rainfall fosters expanded vegetation cover, permitting cottontail populations to grow concomitantly, whereas decreased precipitation would cause population decline. Other researchers also point out that dissimilar social organization between communities is somehow associated with some differential patterning in the relative proportions of jackrabbits and cottontails (Akins 1987; Bertram and Draper 1982).

Clearly, at the Villa Ahumada site, more investigation is needed to see if the proportions of the two species reflect diachronic changes related to land clearing or climatic change or if, perhaps, the representation of lagomorphs is isomorphic with their proportion in the environment. However, lagomorphs apparently played an important role in the subsistence of site occupants. The animals would supply not only meat but also raw materials, such as fur for garments or bags and bone for specialized tools such as needles or awls. The 300 individuals represented in the assemblage would have supplied between 150 and 300 kg of meat, assuming that each individual contributed between 500 and 1000 g of meat.

Comparison of the Villa Ahumada site faunal assemblage to that from Casas Grandes provides clear differences (Figure 2.4). Di Peso et al. (1974:8: 242) report that during the Medio period, bison was the primary meat source and antelope the second, although a small quantity of white tail deer and coyote was also found. The use of turkey began to increase during the Medio period. However, of lagomorphs only 119 elements of *Lepus* sp. and 43 of *Silvilagus* sp. were found, and these contributed less than 1 percent of the total meat. Di Peso (1974:8:244–245) believes these species were communally hunted by sub-adults using nets.

Plant remains

Several charred specimens of maize, known locally as "maize gordo," were recovered from test pit 4 and one looting hole. Maize gordo grows to a height of 1.8–2.0 m and has a short maturation period. This ten-rowed maize has an average ear diameter of 8.37 cm, a cob diameter of 4.5 cm, and cupules of 3 × 6 mm. This species has been recovered at Paquimé (Di Peso et al. 1974:8:242) and at elevations between 2000 and 2500 m throughout the western portion of Chihuahua. Its postulated progenitors are Chapolote and Reventador, infiltrated with germ plasm from Harina del Ocho (Hernández and Glafiro 1970).

Brand (1943:154) proposed that the land surrounding the Villa Ahumada site was irrigated and used for crop production, and INAH palynologist, Susana Xelhuatzin, conducted pollen studies to evaluate Brand's suggestion. It was recognized, however, that the local sediments are sandy and have a high silica content with a low probability for finding preserved pollen grains. Therefore, Xelhuatzin took samples from the adobe walls and floors of the site, assuming that the adobe came from clayey sand deposits near the Río el Carmén, a relatively moist area where crops may have been cultivated.

The samples from the architectural features contained no maize pollen, but pollen from *Pinus* sp. and *Quercus* sp. was found. These species do not occur locally but are known to grow in the Sierra Madre, over 100 km away. The reasons for the presence of this pollen are unclear. It is possible that wind-borne *Pinus* sp. pollen was transported such a distance. However, should wood samples be found in the future, analysis may indicate that some wood was transported from that region. Alternatively, tree elements such as pine boughs may have had ceremonial uses as they do in other parts of the Southwest.

The lack of pollen evidence does not suggest an absence of agricultural activity at the Villa Ahumada site, but there is little direct evidence other than perhaps the maize specimens. However, maize could have been traded into the site, a possibility that future research on the site surroundings may resolve. Indirect evidence may come from further analysis of the faunal data. If analysis shows diachronic change in the proportions of cottontails and jackrabbits, then it may indicate land clearing for agricultural pursuits, as previously discussed.

Discussion

Although still embryonic, studies at the Villa Ahumada site allow some preliminary evaluation of current opinions on the Casas Grandes region. For Brand (1943) and Di Peso et al. (1974), the Río el Carmén drainage marked the eastern boundary of the Casas Grandes culture. The northern portion of the basin has also been viewed as having sites related to both Casas Grandes and the Jornada Mogollon culture, based on ceramic affinities (Brand 1943:153). More recent researchers, although cautious about delimiting the Casas Grandes region, also include the Villa Ahumada site in the core Casas Grandes network (Minnis 1984, 1989; Wilcox 1995). However, as previously mentioned, the Villa Ahumada site ceramic assemblage does not support this view because El Paso ware, pottery associated with the Jornada Mogollon, predominates in the assemblage. In this regard Lehmer (1948:11) also maintained that the southern limit of the Jornada Mogollon was to the south and west of the Villa Ahumada site. The presence of other material culture generally associated with Paquimé, such as turquoise, does, however, indicate some interaction with Paquimé during the Medio period. Although such interaction existed, it does not appear that the economic ties that Villa Ahumada had with Paquimé were as strong as those between Paquimé and northwestern populations.

Di Peso (1974:2:329–332) used the phrase "Casas Grandes culture" to refer to the central community of Paquimé and the outlying area, which contained several hundred satellite villages that were culturally or politically associated. Di Peso described this relationship based on common architectural elements and material culture and believed that a hierarchical organization existed, with lesser villages producing finished products that entered a central market at Paquimé.

Minnis (1984) and Bradley (1993) point out that the problem with Di Peso's interpretation is its basis in the minimal data on the sites surrounding

Paquimé. The Joint Casas Grandes Project (Di Peso 1974; Di Peso et al. 1974:5:Figure 284-5) produced a distributional map of regional sites, and although the map provides important data, its indication of distribution is based on very cursory and unverifiable site information (Minnis 1989:290). To evaluate Di Peso's viewpoint, Minnis (1989) argues that if Paquimé was the center of a political and economic system that incorporated the hundreds of surrounding communities, then there were probably secondary centers that should be recognizable. He proposes that some criteria through which such sites might be recognized are size, presence of elite goods, communication systems, and the presence of public or ritual architecture. On the last criterion, for example, if secondary centers existed within a regional political system controlled by Paquimé, they should have ball courts or mounds (Minnis 1989:293), features that presumably indicate a more powerful hierarchical level.

Minnis (1989:294), Naylor (1995), and Whalen and Minnis (1996a:743) report that the occurrence of the I-shaped ball-court form associated with Paquimé is rare. Such forms are limited to the region west and northwest of Paquimé on the eastern flank of the northern Sierra Madre. Based on the distribution of large sites, public and ritual architecture, and fire communication features, Minnis (1989:298) originally proposed that the influence of Paquimé extended outward in a 130-km radius. He also cites De Atley and Findlow's (1982:277) studies on the distribution of Ramos Polychrome and Animas phase settlement distributions and Bradley and Hoffer's (1985) study of Playas Red sherds as corroborating evidence. After 130 km the fire-signaling system seems to fade, and site density drops, which Minnis saw as evidence for declining incorporation in the Casas Grandes network of control.

In a more recent analysis of ball courts, Whalen and Minnis (1996a) use the regional distribution of their forms to reassess the extent and the nature of Paquimé's dominance. Noting that the highest density of formal I-shaped ball courts is within a one-day walk of Paquimé, they maintain that this pattern reflects a zone of intense interaction among regional communities (Whalen and Minnis 1996a:743). A wider, second zone is defined by sparse, scattered ball courts to the west and northwest. No I-shaped ball courts are known within this zone. A third area contains no ball courts, but ceramic data still suggest ties with Paquimé. Included in the third zone are areas to the northeast, east, and southeast of Paquimé, including the Villa Ahumada locale (Whalen and Minnis 1996a:743). Whalen and Minnis (1996a:744) offer further support for their hypothesis by referring to the regional distribution of "macaw stones," or the doors of macaw pens, which shows isomorphic patterning with the ball-court distribution.

Earlier, Minnis (1989:295) proposed that the absence of ball courts in the Santa María and Carmén river drainages may be because (1) the communities were not integrated into the Casas Grandes system; or (2) the communities were under the control of Paquimé but not controlled by regional elites; or (3) the ball courts exist but have not been recorded; or (4) the ball courts or mounds are not symbols of a regional hierarchy; or (5) there are no elites within the Casas Grandes system.

In the more recent model, Whalen and Minnis (1996a:744) argue that the increasing scarcity of ball courts outside the Paquimé core area implies lower levels of integration, but not necessarily interaction, between Paquimé and the more distant communities. Therefore, the outlying communities still maintained economic and social alliances with Paquimé, but they were not formally integrated into a centralized regional political organization. Whalen and Minnis (1996a:745) suggest that alliances between Paquimé and outlying communities occurred at several different levels, which were not necessarily closely related to simple distance. Previous analyses of the distribution of possible second-order centers led Minnis (1989), as well as Braniff (1986) and Wilcox and Sternberg (1983), to assert that Paquimé probably interacted more closely with communities to the north and west, a finding supported by Whalen and Minnis's (1996a) recent study.

In contrast, Wilcox (1995) outlines a model of a functionally differentiated economy based on the inclusion of diverse "local systems" within a larger system that had Paquimé at its center (Wilcox 1995:Figure 15.4). These local systems are nested within a system politically dominated by Paquimé (Wilcox 1995:289), which he suggests encompassed a region about 125 km in diameter, based on the distance a person on foot can travel in three and a half days. Wilcox (1995:291) views this integrated network as a macroeconomy (Baugh 1984), an economic system that sustains a division of multiethnic labor but not political integration. Relying on Brand's (1943) observation of the large amounts of Villa Ahumada Polychrome, Wilcox (1995:291) proposes that the Villa Ahumada site was the center of such a local system and was dominated by Paquimé. Wilcox (1995:291) further posits that the Villa Ahumada site, as a Paquimé outlier, served as a center for trade with Jornada Mogollon populations to the east, which may account for the large quantities of Villa Ahumada and El Paso Polychrome found at Paquimé. Also depending on Brand's accounts of numerous turquoise beads at the site of Ojos Calientes de Santo Domingo, east of Laguna de Patos, Wilcox (1995:291) believes that the site also served as a Casas Grandes trading center for Jornada Mogollon goods.

Conclusions

The recent work at the Villa Ahumada site suggests it is doubtful that Villa Ahumada Polychrome was produced at the site or that it exists in large quantity, which is sometimes used as evidence for political ties with Paquimé. In fact, Sayles (1936:13–17) originally proposed that this pottery type centered around Galeana, on the Río Santa María, and noted that the name "Villa Ahumada Polychrome" was a synonym for Gladwin's "Galeana Polychrome." In contrast with Brand's commentary on the frequency of pottery types and the implication for the cultural affiliations of Villa Ahumada site residents, the pottery assemblage suggests that the site was occupied by Jornada Mogollon people.

The implication from the pottery assemblage would be that Villa Ahumada site residents were politically independent of Paquimé and that the boundary of the Casas Grandes political system lies somewhere to the west of the site. The absence of ball courts throughout the Río el Carmén drainage also suggests there was no formal social or political affiliation with Paquimé. Ties, however, were probably maintained with the Casas Grandes economic system, a point made by Whalen and Minnis (1996a). As previously discussed, however, Paquimé seems to have had its strongest ties with sites to its north and west. Therefore, any model that makes use of flat, homogeneous circles of hierarchical political integration may not extend to the Villa Ahumada site. The model developed by Wilcox (1995) for economically independent "local systems" that interact with Paquimé might appropriately be applied to the Villa Ahumada locale, but including the Villa Ahumada site as one under Paquimé's political dominance may be inapplicable.

Villa Ahumada site residents likely controlled their own forms of production and distribution networks, but the size of their local trade network is unclear. Furthermore, although we believe that Villa Ahumadans were politically independent of Paquimé, that does not mean that the political organization of Paquimé did not affect their lives. The society, political structure, and economy of a nearby large system undoubtedly affected Villa Ahumada site residents, but determination of those effects must await further research.

The important issue of economics is also raised by the faunal assemblage at the Villa Ahumada site. Obviously, site residents were doing something much different from Paquimé residents, and that difference may have resulted from environmental differences across the region. Few of the models for the Casas Grandes system developed to date have examined the role that topography, hydrology, climate, or resource distribution may have had in the organization of northern Chihuahuan local and macroeconomic systems. The intensity of relations with the Casas Grandes system may have been conditioned by these largely unexplored factors, and models that utilize these variables have yet to be developed.

The current data from Villa Ahumada suggest that the boundary of any formal Casas Grandes political system, at least if measured through the distribution of ball courts and pottery, lies somewhere to the west of the site. The boundaries of the Casas Grandes political region as proposed by Wilcox (1995) should also be slightly smaller because Ojos Calientes de Santo Domingo, which he used to define an eastern boundary, lies about 20 km west of Laguna de Patos, instead of the east as reported. If, as Whalen and Minnis (1996a) suggest, Paquimé was organized as a "midlevel" complex society where there was local competition for power among emergent elites, this would have prevented singular political dominance, preventing widespread regional political control but not interaction with outlying communities. These conditions likely oscillated through time, and boundaries of political control probably also fluctuated. Likewise, the area bounding Jornada Mogollon interactions probably also changed over time; however, at this point the data from the Villa Ahumada site suggest that during the Medio period the site was politically independent of Paquimé and, although perhaps having economic ties with Paquimé, was probably more involved in economic interaction with Jornada Mogollon populations.

ACKNOWLEDGMENTS. We wish to thank Mike Whalen, Paul Minnis, John Roney, Bob Leonard, Jeff Cox, Curt Schaafsma, Linda Mick-O'Hara, and Regge Wiseman for their counsel, help, review, and comments. Also thanks go to Todd Van Pool, Dwight Fieselman, and Kierson Crune, who produced the map of the Villa Ahumada site.

3

Investigating the Paquimé Regional System

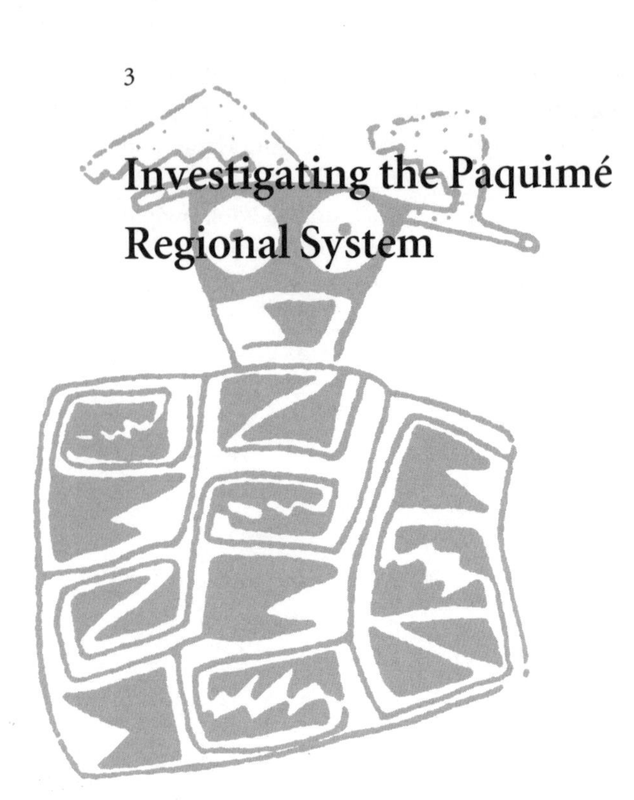

Michael E. Whalen

Paul E. Minnis

Perspectives on Paquimé

ARCHAEOLOGISTS HAVE LONG been aware that northwestern Chihuahua, Mexico, was the scene of important cultural development in late prehistoric times, and the ruins of the great adobe pueblo at Casas Grandes, or Paquimé, have impressed all of the region's visitors, from the earliest Spanish explorers to modern archaeologists. The high point of regional research was the well-known Joint Casas Grandes Project, which involved fieldwork conducted from 1958 to 1961 (Di Peso 1974; Di Peso et al. 1974). Most of this work focused on the site of Paquimé, which reached its peak during the Medio period, originally placed at A.D. 1060–1340 (Di Peso 1974:2:283) and now convincingly repositioned about 150 years later than Di Peso's beginning and ending dates (e.g., Dean and Ravesloot 1993). Chronological questions aside, there is wide agreement that Paquimé was the center of a complex polity in northwestern Chihuahua. There is less agreement, however, on the society's size, kind, and level of complexity.

In the original and highly influential interpretation, Di Peso (1974:2) described Medio period Paquimé as the center of a complex society of Postclassic Mesoamerican size and structure. He argued that the community was established on the edge of the Southwest through Mesoamerican commercial interests in order to control trade between the two regions. In this interpretation shell, exotic birds and their feathers, turquoise, and copper and other minerals were all funneled through Paquimé. Di Peso further envisioned extensive use of slaves and corvée labor for production of trade goods and for construction of public works under the direction of the lords of Paquimé. The community was seen as the "prime mover" and principal consumer of much of the region's productive effort, and it was asserted to have exercised sovereignty over a vast area of nearly 88,000 sq km (Di Peso 1974:2:667). Beyond this, however, Di Peso's work provided little other information on the region's interacting with Paquimé. He clearly saw the rise of the center in exogenic, diffusionist terms, as a direct result of Mesoamerican commercial interests. From this perspective the question of the regional context of Paquimé was of minor importance; the region simply served its primate community.

Today, archaeologists are increasingly aware that regional systems can be understood only through careful study of all of their components, not simply those at the top. This approach permits us to define, rather than assume, patterns of regional development and interaction. Unfortunately, extant northwestern Chihuahuan data have for many years been inadequate to the task. In 1988, for instance, we found some 200 sites on record for an area about one-sixth the size of the state of New Mexico. Moreover, most of these sites had been recorded half a century ago or earlier (e.g., Robles 1929; Noguera 1926; Brand 1943; Sayles 1936; Lister 1946), and they had only brief descriptions and approximate locations. Neither are there any existing descriptions or locations for the majority of the hundreds of sites shown on the small-scale regional map published in the Casas Grandes report (Di Peso et al. 1974:5:Figure 284-5). By the late 1980s, then, there were only a handful of precisely recorded sites in the entire northwest Chihuahua region. The goal of our work has been to remedy this situation and to turn these data to consideration of the origin, extent, and nature of the system of regional interaction that focused on Paquimé. This chapter seeks to summarize the results of the research that we carried out between 1989 and 1995 under the title of the Paquimé Regional Survey Project.

Initial Investigations

In 1989 we received a small grant from the National Science Foundation to carry out a pilot survey in four areas around Paquimé (Figure 3.1). All four survey areas lie at the eastern foot of the Sierra Madres, in a basin-and-range physiographic setting (Schmidt 1973). The climate and rainfall are typical of the arid Southwest and northern Mexico, where the availability of water is a critical variable in determining the distribution of human populations, especially those dependent on agriculture. Not surprisingly, all previous work in the area shows that major foci of human habitation are the drainages descending from the Sierra Madres. Major streams like the Rios Santa María, Casas Grandes, and San Pedro offer a combination of water and arable land unmatched anywhere else in the region.

There are also many seasonal drainages, some of which are very large, close to the mountains. These arroyos cross wide alluvial slopes that offer broad expanses of arable land and many opportunities for water management. Finally, a few small, permanent streams descend through narrow, deeply cut valleys in the foothills of the Sierra Madres. Although these

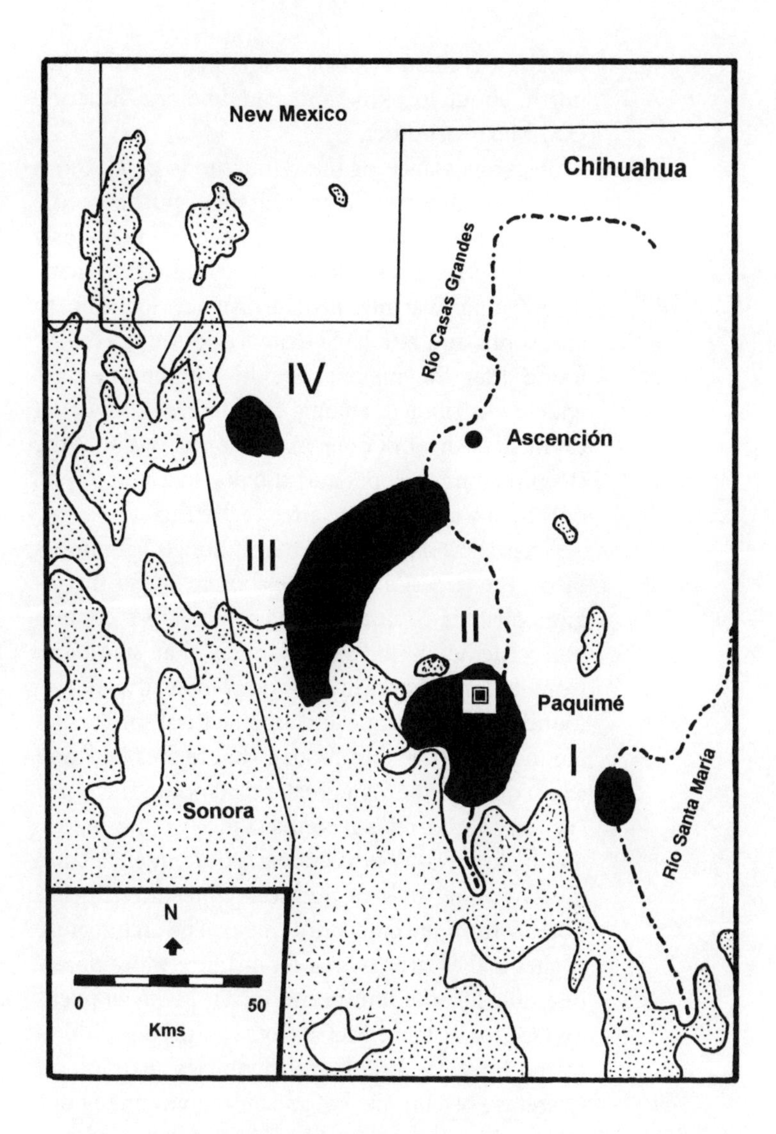

Figure 3.1. The four 1989 reconnaissance areas. Areas I–III are named after the river valleys they surround, respectively Santa Maria, Casas Grandes, and San Pedro. Area IV is named after the Carretas Basin, in which it lies.

valleys are well watered, arable land is circumscribed by the steep topography. We expected to find sites in all of these zones, which we subdivided as described below. Note that each of the first three units are named for the major river valleys that they contain. The Casas Grandes unit lies within a radius of about 30 km around the primate center, including much of the region's best agricultural land. The Santa Maria and San Pedro units lie, respectively, to the south and north of the Paquimé unit, at distances of about 60 to 90 km. The Carretas survey unit, the only one that does not contain a major river valley, is in the far north, about 100 km from Paquimé and near the U.S.-Mexican border.

Reconnaissance in these four units produced a sample of about 80 large and small pueblos, only eight of which could be identified as previously recorded ones. These sites lay in the immediate vicinity of Paquimé, at intermediate distances to the north and south and at a large distance to the north. We found that the region's pueblo communities are widely distributed among the different kinds of drainages. All work done in the area shows that the steep piedmont slopes and the dry mesa tops were only lightly used for specialized activities.

These new data showed that although Paquimé is by far the largest and most elaborate site in the region, all four of our reconnaissance areas contain other Medio period communities that stand out from their neighbors in size and complexity. We also found notable ceramic and architectural similarities among pueblos within about 60 km to the north and south of Paquimé. At a greater distance to the north (i.e., in the Carretas reconnaissance unit, lying ca. 90–100 km away), both ceramic type frequencies and the prevailing style of pueblo architecture differed notably from the other study areas. The architecture of sites in the Carretas area, for instance, more closely resembled that of southwestern New Mexican pueblos (see, for instance, McCluney's [1965b] description of the Joyce Well site), and frequency of the local Carretas Polychrome was greater than in any of our other reconnaissance areas.

We confined our distant reconnaissance to the north, both for reasons of economy and because ceramic data argue that this was the principal direction of Paquimé's interaction. It is noteworthy that other work in southern Chihuahua (Kelley and Stewart 1992), about 140 km from Paquimé, shows a situation similar to what we found in the north: notable ceramic and architectural variation from the patterns common around the primate center. Such observations supported earlier suppositions (e.g., Minnis 1989) that whatever regional system existed around Paquimé might not have been as large as originally thought.

We were also led to suspect that the organizational structure of the region may have been simpler and less comprehensive than argued originally. Our 1989 survey showed that the most ritual architecture, most imported items, and the clearest evidences of widespread production of exotica (i.e., macaw cages) were all present in greatest quantity in the Casas Grandes reconnaissance unit, or within about 30 km of the primate center. Most discussions of preindustrial centralization (e.g., Renfrew 1975) note that this is about a day's walk, and it is commonly the most tightly integrated part of polities that rely on foot transport. It is noteworthy that the ritual architecture and exotic goods, which we think were important in integration of the communities of the Casas Grandes interaction sphere, appeared to be rare only a little farther away. In the San Pedro unit, for instance, we found no ball courts and no macaw cage doors, and we judged that local site hierarchies were smaller and simpler than those near Paquimé. Extant data were not strong enough to form a clear picture, but we suspected that an area only 60–90 km (or two- to three-days' walk) from the primate center showed a considerably simpler settlement pattern and organizational structure than did the core area (i.e., the Casas Grandes unit).

The 1989 reconnaissance also hinted at interesting demographic patterns in the core area itself, where there appeared to have been local Medio period polities lying within approximately 15–30 km of Paquimé. The Arroyo la Tinaja subunit (a component of the larger Casas Grandes unit) is one of the populous valleys that form major corridors for movement from the flatlands around Paquimé up into the Sierra Madre mountains. Here we recorded a variety of pueblos, large to small. Only the largest site had an associated ball court, but we recorded examples of isolated ball courts lying between several smaller sites. It is also notable that stone entryways for macaw cages (see Di Peso 1974:2:598) were found on the large site, on the medium site, and on one of the small sites (Minnis et al. 1993). The Arroyo la Tinaja thus emerges as a localized area with its own site hierarchy, attached and isolated ritual structures, and production facilities for at least some exotica (i.e., macaws). Also within the Casas Grandes unit is the nearby El Alamito subunit (see Figure 3.1). El Alamito shows a similar pattern of a site hierarchy, ritual facilities, and macaw production.

Another independent study supports this picture of local productive units. Schmidt and Gerald (1988) analyze water control systems of the eastern Sierra Madre, and they argue convincingly that these systems were not built under the direction of Paquimé and for its benefit as originally argued (Di Peso et al. 1974:5:823). Instead, the systems seem to have been constructed by local units to improve the productivity of their own environs.

These simple observations took us as far as we could go with the small amount of data collected in 1989. We still needed to know a great deal about settlement pattern characteristics, community interaction, and internal community structure to more clearly define the mode of operation of the Paquimé regional system in northwestern Chihuahua. This was obviously a large job and would require a great deal of work spread over years. Moreover, no single investigative approach is capable of providing all of the necessary data. Accordingly, the first stage of subsequent fieldwork sought to build on our regional reconnaissance with intensive survey designed to shed light on organization, integration, differentiation, function, and chronology in the communities that composed the Paquimé regional system.

Intensive Survey Work in 1994 and 1995

Succeeding survey work was based on the understandings generated by the 1989 reconnaissance. With funding from the National Science Foundation and authorization from the Mexican National Institute of Anthropology and History, we carried out twenty weeks of intensive survey in the summers of 1994 and 1995. In total these projects covered some 270 sq km of land in the 1989 Casas Grandes and San Pedro reconnaissance units, which we renamed, respectively, the inner and middle zones, based on their evident degree of interaction with Paquimé. Work in these two areas gave us an intensive look at the structure of settlement in large, contiguous areas at a range of distances around Paquimé, including the center's immediate environs, its near vicinity (15–30 km away), and a neighboring region at an intermediate distance (60–90 km) from the primate center. Moreover, these survey areas were chosen to pursue some of the issues raised by our earlier reconnaissance. Our goals were to collect data on chronological and spatial variability in the size, type, and distribution of sites, in the frequency of productive and ritual facilities from agricultural terraces to macaw cages to ball courts, and in the distribution of artifacts, from local ceramics to exotic and imported items such as seashell and pottery from the southwestern United States. We recorded more than 400 prehistoric sites, making this by far the largest survey data set ever accumulated in northwestern Chihuahua. The data are still being analyzed at this writing, but we can offer a few basic observations.

Survey Results

Our site sample includes examples from the late Archaic through the Ceramic era (or the Viejo and Medio periods in the chronology of Casas Grandes). The present discussion focuses on the communities that were contemporary with Paquimé, which amounts to about 80 percent of our total sample, or about 300 sites. These yielded Medio period ceramics together with mounds that are the remains of adobe-walled blocks of contiguous rooms. We use mound area as a simple measure of size because we do not yet have the data necessary to convert mound volumes into room counts. We use room blocks rather than sites as the primary analytical units described and compared here. Most room blocks do not lie in close proximity to another block, although some do. These neighboring room blocks could be lumped together to form sites, although the decision on how close blocks must be before they are considered a single "site" is largely arbitrary. To compound the problem, we are unable to determine room-block contemporaneity beyond the period level, as we have noted elsewhere (Whalen and Minnis 1996a, 1996b).

In the inner-zone survey area of 124 sq km, we recorded 222 room blocks, which total 244,496 sq m of area. In the middle-zone survey area of 145 sq km, 171 room blocks amount to 168,439 sq m of area. As these data suggest, the room blocks of the inner zone are slightly larger than their middle-zone counterparts, averaging, respectively, 1101 sq m and 985 sq m. Inner-zone room blocks also occur at higher density, averaging 1.79 blocks per sq km. In the middle zone, in contrast, the comparable figure is only 1.18. Still another way to reflect settlement system scale is to note that the inner zone averages 1972 sq m of room-block area per sq km of surveyed land, whereas the middle zone's figure is only 985. By every measure it is apparent that the middle-zone settlement system was smaller than its inner-zone contemporary.

Another point of comparison is the extent to which the two zones show differences in the frequencies of room blocks of different sizes. A histogram of

Table 3.1. Frequency of Room-Block Size Classes in Inner and Middle Zones.

ZONE	SMALL	MEDIUM	LARGE	V. LARGE	TOTAL
Inner	163	46	9	1	219
Middle	133	32	6	1	172
Total	216	78	15	2	391

mound sizes suggested four modal categories: small (<1000 sq m), medium (1000–4999 sq m), large (5000–9999 sq m), very large (>10000 sq m). Table 3.1 shows these size-class data, omitting those room blocks that were too badly damaged to permit accurate estimates of original sizes. We also omit Paquimé itself, which has about 70,000 sq m of mound area, making it the largest community in the region by a factor of ten.

The chi-squared statistic can be used to test the hypothesis that the frequencies of different room-block size classes are the same in both survey zones. Table 3.1 forms a contingency table in which we combine the "large" and "very large" columns in order to achieve adequate cell values. We calculate $X^2 = 3.46$ with three degrees of freedom. The associated probability is approximately 0.17, which does not permit rejection of the null hypothesis of no significant frequency difference. These data lead to the conclusion that the two survey zones contain about the same relative frequencies of the five mound size classes.

It is also evident that settlement systems in the inner and middle zones consisted of many small pueblos and few larger ones. Nevertheless, over 80 percent of the residential-site area of both zones was contained in the medium, large, and very large pueblos. We can therefore conclude that the majority of the area's Medio period population lived in larger communities.

Finally, we note the absence of significant architectural variation between inner- and middle-zone pueblos. Many wall sections were exposed by looting in both zones, and construction techniques appeared to be very similar. It is difficult to say much about room sizes because we were able to measure only the few walls where both corners had been exposed by looters' excavations. Until we have better data, we can only note that room sizes seemed to be about the same in both zones. We were unable to observe other architectural details in the unexcavated sites. In sum, inner- and middle-zone pueblos appear to have been built in the same style, and the two zones have about the same relative frequencies of the different room-block size classes. Nevertheless, it is apparent that the middle-zone pueblos were somewhat smaller than their contemporaries of the inner zone.

Features and Facilities

Many different categories of feature were encountered by the survey, but here we focus on two: ball courts and macaw cages. In Mesoamerica the ritual ball game was important in social, political, and economic contexts, and the presence and distribution of playing fields has been taken to reflect systems of social integration (e.g., Scarborough and Wilcox 1991). The same argument has been made for the ball courts of the Hohokam region of the U.S. Southwest (e.g., Wilcox 1991b).

Three ball courts at the site of Paquimé were described by Di Peso et al. (1974:4, 1974:5), and our survey work recorded twelve additional ones, bringing the total Chihuahuan sample to 15. Briefly, they ranged in playing-field area from 244 to 1194 sq m, and their shapes included the familiar Mesoamerican I, several T-shaped specimens, and a number that were simply formed by two parallel rows of upright stones. These have been illustrated and described in detail elsewhere (Whalen and Minnis 1996a), and a sample is illustrated in Figure 3.2. The region's largest and most elaborate court was at Paquimé, and the primate center is the only known Chihuahuan community with more than one of these facilities.

Most Chihuahuan ball courts were found to occur with Medio period pueblos; that is, they lay within an average of about 70 m from a pueblo room block. It is noteworthy that courts were not common with these sites. Of the 46 medium-sized pueblos recorded in the inner zone, for instance, only 5 (about 11 percent) have associated ball courts. Including Paquimé itself, only 3 of the 11 large inner-zone pueblos (ca. 27 percent) have courts. It is clear, therefore, that these facilities are not as common in northwest Chihuahua as their earlier counterparts have been shown to be in the Hohokam area of the U.S. Southwest (e.g., Wilcox 1991b).

Notably, our study area also contains ball courts that are not proximate to any Medio period residential site. Elsewhere (Whalen and Minnis 1996a) we have termed these "isolated" courts, and they are al-

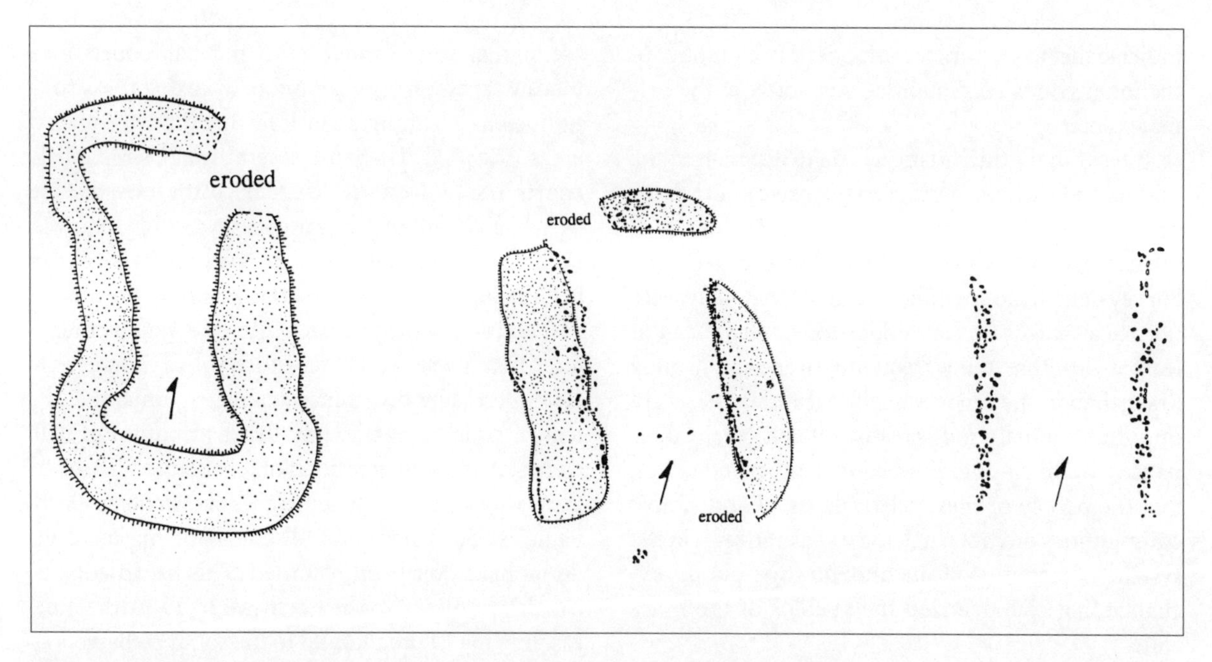

Figure 3.2. Three styles of Chihuahuan ball courts: (a) Mesoamerican-style I-shape; (b) T-shaped court; (c) simple, open-style court. The last style is the most common in the region. Arrows indicate north. Stippled areas are earth embankments, and black dots are stones.

ways among the smallest ones in our sample. Three isolated courts lay an average of 400 m (std. dev. = 60) from the nearest community, which was always a small or medium-sized pueblo without an attached ball court. Each isolated court was found to have four to six of these pueblo communities within a radius of a kilometer.

There is a dramatic contrast between ball-court distributions and frequencies in the inner and middle survey zones. One of the 15 known Chihuahuan ball courts lies in the Sierra Madre mountains, outside of our survey areas. Of the remaining 14, all but one are in the inner zone, or within about a day's walk of Paquimé. Our survey of some 145 sq km of the middle zone, which lies between 60 and 80 km from Paquimé, yielded only one small, simple, isolated court. It is evident, therefore, that the inner and middle zones have dramatically different frequencies of ball courts, despite their high levels of architectural and ceramic similarity.

This discovery is consistent with the middle zone's relatively simple demographic pattern, as described in preceding pages. Together with the majority of our colleagues in Mesoamerica and in the Hohokam region (e.g., Krickeberg 1966; Castro-Leal 1986; Wilcox 1991b), we assume ball courts to have been ceremonial-civic facilities, which is to say that they functioned in social, political, and economic integration of surrounding populations, as well as in ritual. If Chihuahuan ball courts served even broadly similar functions, then we can suggest a relatively high level of integration in the inner zone. In the middle zone, in contrast, the ball court data argue for a relatively low level of integration, both among themselves and with their neighbors closer to Paquimé.

Another category of feature or facility to which we ascribe considerable importance is the macaw cage. At Paquimé, investigators found many cages for keeping macaws, the plumes of which were one class of prestige item. The doors of these cages were formed by stone disks about 30 cm in diameter. These disks had central holes about 15 cm in diameter, which were closed by a cylindrical stone plug. Complete cages from Paquimé are illustrated by Di Peso (1974:2:598), by Contreras (1986:32), and by Braniff (1994b:30). Our inner-zone survey found whole or partial perforated stone disks that are nearly identical to those from Paquimé on the surfaces of twelve Medio period sites. In one case we found not only the perforated disk but also the stone plug used to close it. These data are described in more detail in an earlier publication (Minnis et al. 1993). They indicate that aviculture was practiced in a number of the inner zone's communities, not solely at the primate center.

Interestingly, the situation is quite different in the middle zone, where, despite an intensive effort to locate them, we found no macaw cage doors on any of the nearly 200 Medio period pueblos recorded here. Survey data do not permit us to argue that there were no macaw cages in the middle zone, but we can at least assert that their frequency was significantly lower than in the inner zone. If macaw feathers were important ritual and prestige items, then their paucity in the middle zone is yet another indication that the people of these relatively small and simple communities did not participate at a high level in the system of ceremonialism and prestige goods exchange that characterized the pueblos of the inner zone.

Concluding Thoughts

We have made some simple observations about the settlement systems, the presence of ritual architecture, and the existence of facilities for production of at least one category of exotic or prestige goods in two areas of northwest Chihuahua. The inner zone lies within about a day's walk (ca. 30 km) of the primate center of Paquimé, whereas the middle zone is two to three days' walk away (ca. 60–90 km). Given the scale of interaction that has been suggested for the region (e.g., Di Peso 1974:2), these two zones are not very far apart. Nevertheless, we found some interesting differences between them. These observations may be used to suggest several tentative conclusions about the magnitude and structure of interaction in the Paquimé region:

1. Based on investigation of ceramic type distributions, styles of domestic architecture, patterns of occurrence of ritual architecture, and distributions of exotic and imported goods, we argue that there were several different levels of contact between Paquimé and its neighbors. There was a zone of maximum interaction extending about 30 km around the primate center. Here the ritual activities and production and exchange of exotica appear to have been at their highest levels. A second level of interaction characterized our survey areas to the northwest of Paquimé, roughly 60–90 km away. Architecture and ceramics are similar to the inner zone, but ball courts and macaw cages were not common. Note that this situation seems to continue a little farther than our survey areas extended. There are several small, simple ball courts in southwestern New Mexico, the most distant of which is about 120 km northwest of Paquimé (Whalen and Minnis 1996a). No ball courts have ever been reported from the desert lowlands to the northeast and east of the primate center. We suggest, therefore, that there was a second level of interaction asymmetrically distributed about Paquimé, the extent of which is marked by the distribution of ball courts. A third interaction zone is defined by those areas whose ceramic assemblages show contact with Paquimé but where no ball courts or macaw cage doors have ever been recorded. This broad zone is roughly bounded to the northeast by El Paso, to the east by Villa Ahumada, and to the south by Babícora, as shown in Figure 3.3.

These three interaction zones thus appear to have been characterized by at least three levels of interaction with the primate center. Communities within a day's walk of the center appear to have participated relatively heavily in a system of ball court ritual and prestige goods exchange. Communities in the postulated second zone, up to about four days' walk to the northwest, seem to have participated in the ritual and exchange system at a considerably lower level. There are ball courts known here, for instance, but they are few, simple, and sparsely distributed. If there was aviculture, it was practiced at too low a level to be detected by our survey. Shell seems to be present on site surfaces in about the same frequency in the inner and middle zones. By the "production step measure" (Feinman et al. 1981), the simple *Olivella* beads, which make up most of what we see on site surfaces, were a relatively cheap prestige item. The middle zone, then, may be characterized as a marginal participant in the ritual and exchange activities of the inner zone. The postulated outer zone to the east shows no indication of this participation.

2. These arguments lead to the conclusion that the Paquimé regional system existed at a geographic scale comparable to those described for Chaco or the Hohokam in the southwestern United States (Crown and Judge 1991). This idea stands in marked contrast to the Mesoamerican-scale regional polity originally postulated by Di Peso. Such a suggestion also has implications for the level of organization that would be

necessary to integrate such a system. Prestige goods distributions, perhaps made in ritual contexts, may have been all that was required. Paquimé might thus be seen as the most prominent participant in a regional prestige-goods system rather than as a mercantile center. This supposition has been considered in more detail elsewhere (e.g., Minnis 1988; Bradley 1993; Whalen and Minnis 1996a). In short, it seems to us that the Paquimé regional system may have been smaller and simpler than its original investigator proposed.

3. Our work in the inner survey zone hints at the existence of several local polities within 15–20 km of Paquimé. As noted earlier, these complexes with their hierarchies of sites, ball courts, and facilities for producing at least one category of exotica (macaws) may be seen as peer polities that may have rivaled Paquimé at an early point in its history.

4. The developmental history of the Paquimé polity is still obscure because we cannot seriate sites within the Medio period, as indicated earlier in this chapter. Accordingly, there are several plausible growth models for the Paquimé regional system, and we cannot presently decide among them. We present two very different alternatives here.

In the first scenario, Paquimé, most of the recorded inner- and middle-zone pueblos, and the inner zone's ball courts and macaw cages are all roughly contemporary, growing together and reaching their apogees sometime after the early part of the Medio period. Paquimé monopolizes ball-court ritual and whatever political and economic functions were associated with it only in its near vicinity, about 15 km. Contemporary outliers beyond 15 km (but still within the inner zone) maintain their own ball courts, some of which are nearly as large as Paquimé's, and they presumably carry out whatever political, ritual, and economic activities may have been associated with the courts. They also produce exotica, as demonstrated by the macaw cage stones.

The existence of a number of contemporary ball courts in proximity to Paquimé could imply a relatively low level of regional centralization. Late Postclassic Mesoamerican ball courts were recently asserted (Santley et al. 1991) to have been most common in regional systems that lacked strong, centralized political control and that were fragmented into competing units. In cases where decision making was competitive and decentralized, and where there was a

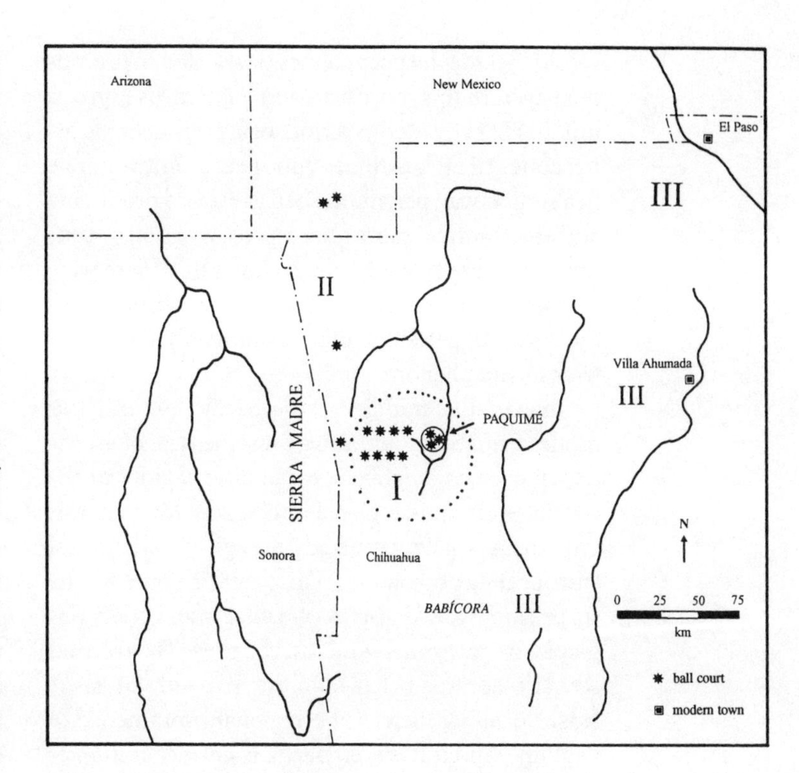

Figure 3.3. Three postulated interaction zones around the primate center of Paquimé in northwestern Chihuahua. Note that a few small ball courts are also known from neighboring parts of northeastern Sonora.

good deal of factional competition for power, prestige, and resources among elites of near-equal status, ball courts were argued to have been stages where rivalries were played out in a ritualized context. The effect of increased political centralization is suppression of factional competition and concomitant reduction in numbers of ball courts. Brumfiel (1994) has also noted the inverse relation between extent of political centralization and intensity of factional competition in human societies.

If the Chihuahuan ball courts functioned even partially as stages for personal or factional competitions, then their relative abundance among communities within about a day's walk of Paquimé may indicate a high level of factional rivalry among the elites of the core zone, which in turn hints at a relatively low level of political centralization within that area. This interpretation sees the regional power of Paquimé in a very different light from that originally proposed.

In an alternative scenario, a number of the inner zone's pueblos, macaw cages, and ball courts are not contemporary with the florescence of Paquimé. This would include the peer polities postulated in preceding pages. In this reconstruction Paquimé is one of a number of early Medio period local polities in the inner zone. All of these inner-zone peer polities operate in a similar way, playing the ball game and producing and distributing exotica in a prestige-goods economy. Our survey work, which shows that there were no comparable units in the slightly more distant middle zone, suggests that this was probably not a very widespread phenomenon.

Toward the middle of the Medio period, this model requires Paquimé to gain some type of ascendancy over its neighbors, expanding rapidly to the central position in regional interaction. Much of this growth may have occurred through absorption of surrounding populations. This would account for the surprisingly low densities of artifacts and trash observed on our inner-zone survey sites. This second scenario accords better than the first with Di Peso's (1974) original view of the regional prominence of Paquimé, and if it is even partially correct, it implies significant changes in regional demography, organization, and power structure after early Medio times.

Finally, it is interesting to note that we do not have evidence of this postulated population concentration in our middle-zone survey area, where we envision a somewhat lower level of development and centralization, although there was clearly significant interaction with Paquimé.

THE INTERPRETATIONS PRESENTED here should all be taken as working models rather than as definitive pronouncements because we still have far to go toward understanding the origin, development, and structure of the Paquimé regional system. Our greatest need is for chronometric information to convincingly seriate our survey sites. We have begun to accumulate this information, and at this writing we are processing the first sets of chronometric dates obtained since Di Peso's excavations in the late 1950s and early 1960s. We hope that these dates, and our ongoing analyses of the settlement data, will assist us in our investigation of the Paquimé regional system.

ACKNOWLEDGMENTS. The Paquimé Regional Survey was funded by two grants from the National Science Foundation (BNS 88-20597 and SBR-9320007). A Faculty Research grant from the University of Oklahoma also assisted in this work. Authorization for the work was provided by Mexico's National Institute of Anthropology and History. Last, but not least, we recognize the efforts of our field and lab crews over the past few years. All of this support, assistance, and hard work is most gratefully acknowledged.

4

A West Central Chihuahuan Perspective on Chihuahuan Culture

Jane H. Kelley

Joe D. Stewart

A. C. MacWilliams

Loy C. Neff

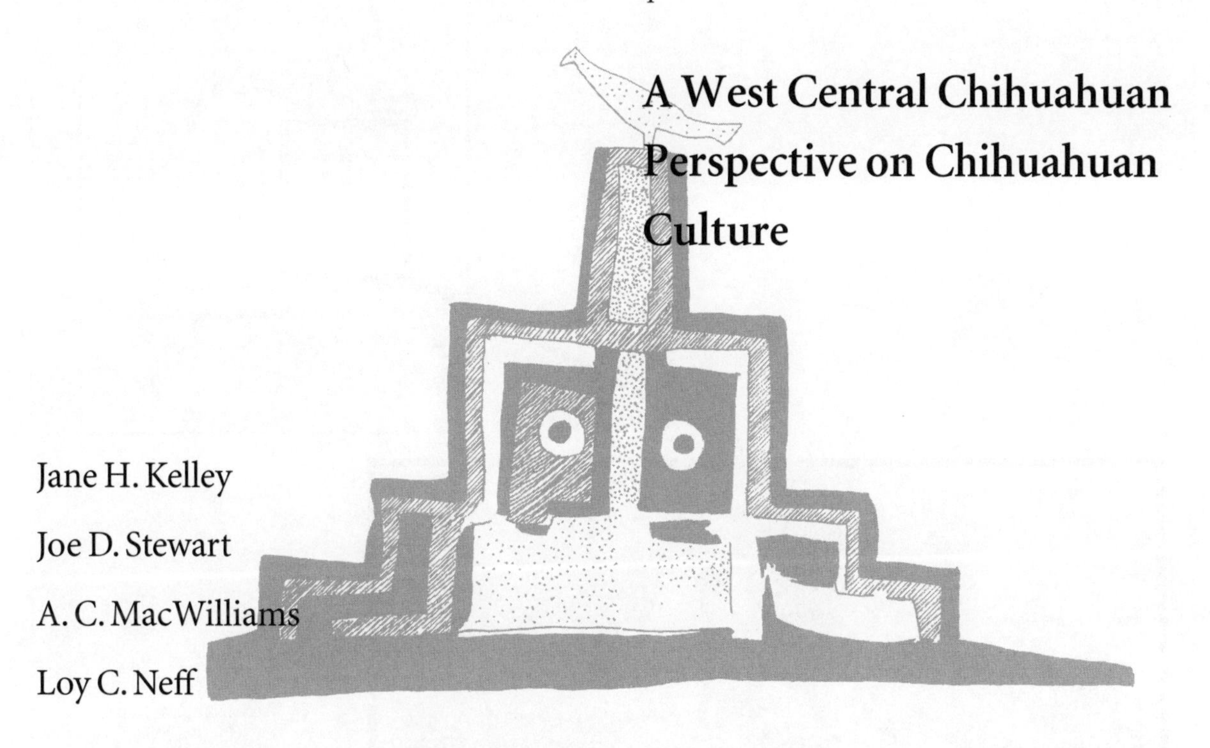

West central Chihuahua, as defined here, includes the Babícora Basin, the Middle and Upper Río Santa María drainage, and the Río Santa Clara drainage (Figure 4.1). This corresponds to the southern portion of the area Brand (1933; 1935; 1943) ascribed to the prehistoric "Chihuahuan culture." The northern portion of Brand's Chihuahuan culture encompasses the Río Casas Grandes but includes a wide area extending into Sonora and the United States. Di Peso et al. (1974:1:4) estimate the entire area as being 87,750 sq km, whereas LeBlanc (1989) estimates an interaction area totaling 100,000 sq km. The site of Paquimé (or Casas Grandes) and its environs is often considered the core area of this culture (Di Peso 1974; De Atley 1980). The inner core is more specifically delineated by Minnis and Whalen (1993:36) as the territory within a 30-km radius of Paquimé. Habitual reference by archaeologists to the whole of Brand's Chihuahuan culture area as the Casas Grandes culture, the Casas Grandes phenomenon, the Casas Grandes interaction sphere, and so forth reflects a Casas Grandes–centered perspective of the entire region. This is due largely to the preeminence of the Joint Casas Grandes Expedition excavations in the Casas Grandes valley (Di Peso 1974; Di Peso et al. 1974) and to Di Peso's "pochteca" (Di Peso 1968) and "world systems" (Di Peso 1983) explanations of regional events as centered at Paquimé. Here, we reactivate Brand's term "Chihuahuan culture," not particularly to endorse the culture-area concept but to use an existing term that more accurately reflects regional structure.

During the 1920s and 1930s the southern half of Chihuahuan culture was often incorporated into Chihuahuan archaeological research. In part this reflects the prevalent research concerns and strategies of that era; rambling surveys resolved limits of known groups and often provided a needed first sense of what existed over vast areas. Archaeologists such as Amsden (1928), Carey (1931), Sayles (1936), Kidder (1939), and Brand (1933; 1935; 1943), who were concerned with Chihuahuan and related sites, seemed as interested in central Chihuahua sites as those closer to Paquimé. They recorded many sites in west central Chihuahua and collectively excavated in more than a dozen of them, primarily in the Babícora Basin.

For six decades relatively little research followed this valuable early work in this southern zone, and it remained sufficiently unknown to be usable for any

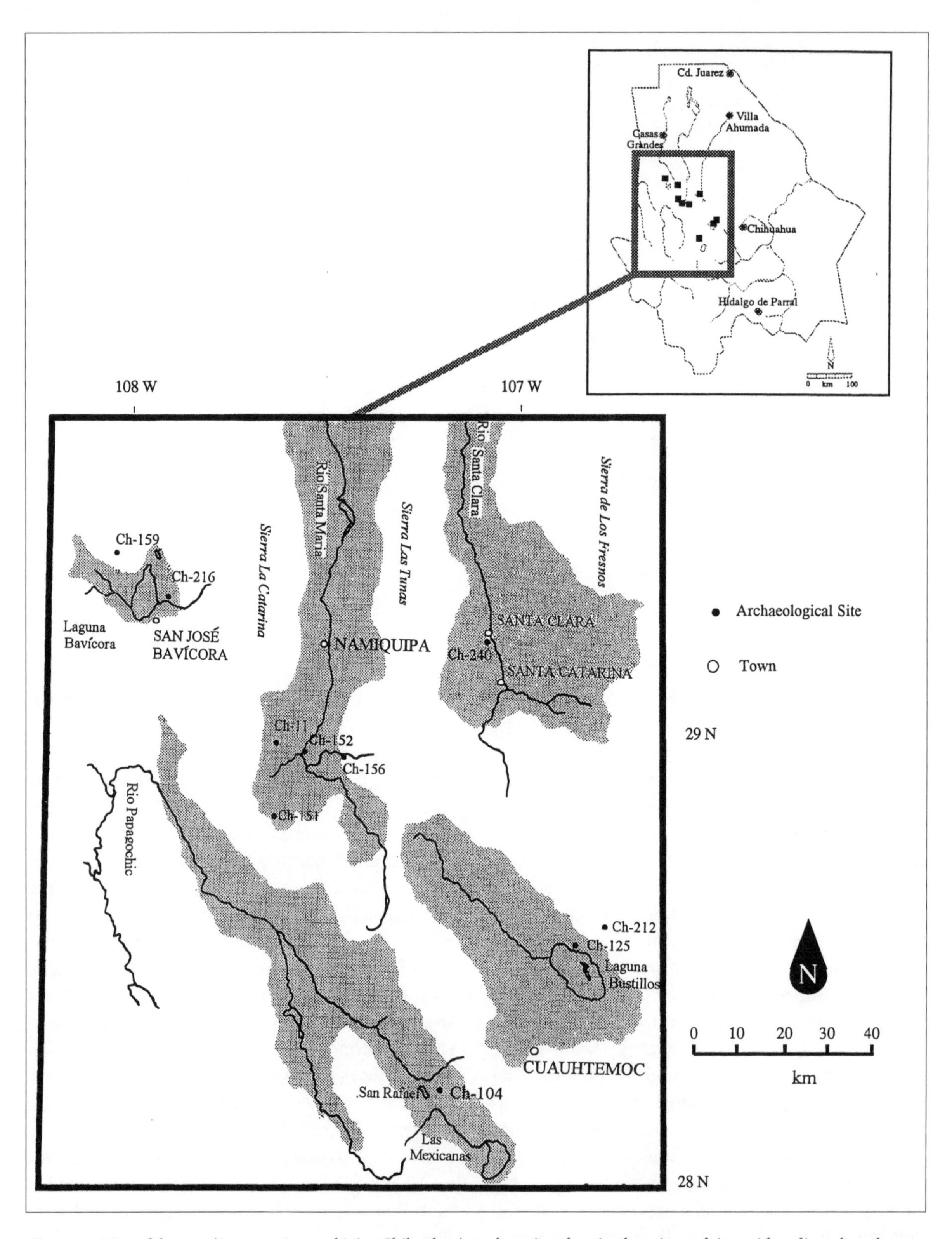

Figure 4.1. Map of the PAC (Proyecto Arqueológico Chihuahua) study region showing locations of sites with radiocarbon dates. CH-151 marks the known southerly extent of Chihuahuan culture sites and the division between the northern and southern PAC study areas. The shaded areas indicate major internal and external drainages.

Figure 4.2. Pithouse at CH-125 (1993).

assigned role in various interpretations of Chihuahuan archaeology. For example, central Chihuahua was a corridor to Brand (1933, 1943) and Brooks (1971) but a separate culture to Amsden (1928) and Carey (1931). Brand (1935) also saw it as peripheral to the Paquimé area, as did later advocates of the pochteca hypothesis and world systems theory.

However, recent work by the Proyecto Arqueológico Chihuahua (PAC) provides a foundation for a fresh perspective on west central Chihuahua. Following reconnaissance in 1989, a major program of survey and excavation proceeded from 1990 to 1993, with additional fieldwork during 1995 and 1996. The research was conducted in basin and range country immediately east of the Sierra Madre Occidental, stretching from the Babícora Basin in the northwest to Laguna Bustillos, Laguna Las Mexicanas, and Laguna San Rafael basins in the south (Figure 4.1). This large region is divisible across the upper Santa María and Santa Clara valleys into southern and northern PAC research areas. Only the northern PAC area exhibits the Chihuahuan culture pattern and may be thought of as the southern zone of the Chihuahuan culture.

Non-Chihuahuan Culture Sites in the Southern PAC Research Area

South of the Santa María Valley in west central Chihuahua there are a series of basins, many internally drained with intermittent lakes, that contain archaeological remains distinct from Chihuahuan culture. This pattern includes hamlets of pithouses and jacals, agriculture, and predominantly undecorated pottery. Known sites are concentrated in the Laguna Bustillos Basin but extend as far west as the Guerrero area. At Ch-125, on the north shore of Laguna Bustillos, one pithouse (Figure 4.2) and two jacal structures were excavated. Subsistence evidence includes corn, two kinds of beans, and a faunal assemblage dominated by lagomorphs and artiodactyls. The most acceptable of several radiocarbon dates from Ch-125, along with one from a corresponding feature at Ch-104, range from ca. A.D. 800 to 1225, taking in the early and late ends of the 2-sigma ranges, calibrated (see CHRONOLOGY, below, for details). One southern date reported here (TO-4118) is from Ch-212, a cave site not easily relatable in material culture to the open habitation sites, probably because of its greater antiquity.

The dated southern habitation sites are contemporaneous with the Viejo period and perhaps early Medio period at Casas Grandes, using the chronology of Dean and Ravesloot (1993), but there are clear differences, particularly in site locations and pottery. For example, the Viejo Red-on-brown pottery types defined by Di Peso et al. (1974) do not occur this far south, although red-on-brown pottery is present. Other than a few Babícora Polychrome sherds from only three locations, there is no indication that Medio period influences extended south of the Santa María drainage, at least east of the Sierra Madre. Most significantly there are no adobe room blocks this far south. As well, the hamlets concentrated around Laguna Bustillos Basin lack known counterparts in the northern PAC research area. Whether this geographical contrast in material culture reflects some sort of ethnic or linguistic boundary is beyond the scope of this chapter, although this possibility is congruent with Schaafsma's (1997) suggestion that the southern area was ancestral Concho territory.

Chihuahuan Culture Sites in the Northern PAC Research Area

Sites with Chihuahuan culture attributes are known in the upper Santa María and Santa Clara drainages and in the Babícora Basin area, where approximately 100 ceramic period sites have been recorded. Interestingly, there is only modest evidence for Archaic use of this region in contrast to the Bustillos Basin. PAC research includes some excavation at seven of the ceramic period sites.

Obvious physiographic contrasts exist among the three sections of the northern PAC research area. One is a closed basin, whereas the other two are externally drained valleys. Perhaps not coincidentally, room blocks in the Babícora Basin tend to occur in clusters, whereas those along the Ríos Santa María and Santa Clara are more dispersed. These distinct settlement patterns are most economically explained by drainage patterns and availability of arable land. Drainages from mountains flanking the Río Santa María cross wide, low-gradient bajada, providing suitable locations for farming across the breadth of the valley. The broad extent of marshland and intermittent lake in the Babícora Basin limits site locations to the basin margin and drainages entering the basin. Although there is less information for the Santa Clara drainage, it is clear that larger sites are close to the river and not clustered.

The Upper Santa María Drainage

The upper Santa María Valley contains the southernmost sites that can be ascribed to Chihuahuan culture (Brand 1933; Kelley and Stewart 1991). At least two Viejo period sites and seven Medio period mound sites are among the 29 sites recorded within and adjacent to this valley. Both Viejo period sites are located on river terraces in similar physiographic settings to the Convento site. Ceramics are largely plainwares with some Leal/Fernando/Pilon and Mata textured Red-on-brown sherds.

Medio period sites are dispersed beside tributary streams across the width of the basin, along the main drainage, and, in one case, at the mouth of a side valley. Sites range in size from one to at least sixteen residential mounds, with site Ch-11 on the west side of the valley being the largest. Room blocks in these sites are massive adobe and where excavation data are available sometimes contain such Chihuahuan hallmarks as raised floor features and T-shaped doorways. Ch-151, the southernmost Medio period site known, is located approximately 170 km south of Paquimé. This site has one relatively small room block and only a sparse associated artifact scatter. Both rectangular and T-shaped doorways and Chihuahuan polychrome pottery occur. Site Ch-152, located approximately 13 km north of Ch-151, is interesting for having some remaining plaster walls that are almost 2 m high and covered with up to six layers of plaster. Guevara Sánchez (1991) offers some similar observations about Medio period architecture in this region.

Site Ch-156 is located at the mouth of El Picacho Valley, which enters the Río Santa María from the east. This site consists of perhaps four low room blocks (Figure 4.3). Site Ch-156 is notable for having two excavated collared posts and a broken spindle whorl comparable to those found at Paquimé, which

Figure 4.3. Medio period rooms at CH-156 (1996).

Di Peso (1974:2:540) attributes to Chalchihuites sources in Durango (see also Lazalde 1987:115). The larger of the collared postholes, built to accommodate a post approximately 35 cm in diameter, differs from Paquimé counterparts only in lacking a seating stone as usually occurs there.

Site Ch-11 is located beside a small wash on the middle bajada west of the Río Santa María. Sayles (1936) originally recorded and tested this site as GP CHIH I:15:1. Several room blocks at this site were clearly more than one story high. This is the largest site in the area but does not contain any visible evidence of public architecture. The assemblage from Ch-11 includes Babícora Polychrome as the dominant painted ware, with lesser amounts of Madera Black-on-red, Ramos, Carretas and Corralitos polychromes. There is conspicuously little textured pottery at this site. Two molded spindle whorls were also found here, adding to one reported by Sayles (1936:59). Plant remains from the site include cheno-ams and corn (Adams 1992).

Medio period sites in the upper Santa María Valley typically have shaped metates, with plainwares, textured wares, Playas Red, Playas Black, and Madera Red-on-black pottery. Babícora Polychrome is the dominant polychrome ware, although Ramos Polychrome is consistently present wherever the former occurs. Artifacts originating outside western Chihuahua are rare. Public space is present in the form of plazas. Although these are the southernmost Medio period sites, they are much like sites nearer Paquimé, other than lacking exotic artifacts for the most part and having no clear evidence for public architecture such as platform mounds or ball courts (Whalen and Minnis 1996a).

The Babícora Basin

There are surprisingly few indications of preceramic use of this closed basin. Isolated points and points with lithic scatters are comparable to defined Archaic types from northeast Chihuahua and adjacent Texas (see Mallouf 1992). One site (Ch-159) that includes a Viejo period component is discussed below.

Mound sites in the Babícora Basin were excavated by Kidder in 1924 (1939), Carey in 1928 and 1929 (1931), and Sayles during 1933 (1936). Kidder's report of one partially excavated small mound in the Las Varas area gives a good summary description of architecture and artifacts. Carey's (1931:336) map of the Babícora Basin shows three site clusters designated as the Las Varas, Babícora (near San José Babícora), and San Juan groups. He completely excavated three mounds and partially excavated four other Las Varas sites close to Kidder's 1924 excavation (1931:335). Sayles (1936) recorded nine sites in the Las Varas drainage (GP CHIH I:9:1–9) and another two sites elsewhere in the basin.

Like Carey's and Sayles's, PAC efforts were concentrated in the Las Varas mound group, although we located and surface-collected sites in the other groups, and elsewhere in the basin. Primary investigations were carried out at Ch-159, or the El Zurdo site, during 1991 and 1992. Site Ch-159 (equivalent to Sayles's site GP CHIH I:9:6) is located beside Arroyo El Zurdo, which drains into the Babícora Basin. This 15,000 sq m site is 5 km from the basin edge and is at about 2200 m elevation. It comprises a central mound area, small outlying room blocks, and midden deposits up to 2 m deep (Hill 1992). A large stone-outlined patio exists along the northeast of the central mound. In unpublished notes from May of 1933, Sayles mentions that sites in this area, including the El Zurdo site, have distinct sizable outside hearths, which unfortunately are no longer visible due to surface disturbances.

Remains from Ch-159 include diverse Chihuahuan pottery, abundant carbonized corn and beans, and one fragment of two-ply, s-twist cotton. Hill (1992) established that the proportional frequency of textured sherds decreases moving from bottom to top in Ch-159 midden deposits. Proportions of painted wares, particularly Babícora Polychrome, increase in upper levels of the midden. Lower midden deposits, containing some Red-on-brown sherds, produced six radiocarbon dates that reflect a pre-Medio component at this site (Table 4.1), although the major occupation is within the Medio period. In a faunal study of Ch-159 collections, Hodgetts (1996) recognized 36 bird taxa, including water fowl, 33 mammalian taxa, plus incidental fish and reptile bones. This includes remains from five turkey burials and scattered turkey bones. In spite of the diversity of taxa, Hodgetts suggests that animal foods played a relatively small role in the Medio period diet, with most hunting having occurred as "garden hunting" near the site.

Extensive survey of the El Zurdo valley allows us to place this site into a local context. In total, 22 sites were recorded in a 9-km stretch of this valley. This total includes several smaller room blocks within 1 km of Ch-159. Isolated field houses are not dated but may be contemporary with Ch-159. Obsidian and vitrophyre, curated from a large acquisition site and workshop at the head of the valley, occur in sites throughout the drainage, including Ch-159. The only prehistoric water control features known for west central Chihuahua occur in this valley and consist simply of several small check dams. In sum, this information suggests considerable reliance on local resources.

The Santa Clara Valley

The Río Santa Clara, which becomes the Río Carmen farther downstream, is the next drainage east of the Río Santa María. Both Sayles (1933) and Brand (1943) recorded mound sites along the main valley. Several of these sites were relocated during 1993 along with previously unrecorded sites near the towns of Santa Catarina and Santa Clara. Site densities are relatively low along the Río Santa Clara as compared to much of the research area. One site on a terrace near Santa Clara (Ch-240) shares some characteristics of Viejo sites, including Red-on-brown pottery and an absence of contiguous adobe rooms. Polychrome types associated with Medio period room blocks in this area include Ramos, Babícora, Villa Ahumada, and El Paso. Unfortunately, none of the Santa Clara Medio period sites is dated other than by ceramic cross-typing.

Comparative Observations Regarding West Central Chihuahua Medio Period Sites

Local variability in Medio period sites in the northern portion of the PAC study area is recognizable on a site-by-site basis and between regions. Variability exists within a general Chihuahuan pattern of subsistence, architecture, material culture, and probably belief systems, in the Santa María Valley, Santa Clara Valley, and Babícora Basin. Architecture in Medio period room blocks, so far as it is studied, is consistent from site to site. Room blocks are built with adobe and often have cimientos (single courses of cobbles set into the adobe) and attached plazas. Rooms are usually rectangular, with plaster floors and walls. Floor features are sometimes raised, although small plaster or adobe floor hearths and ash pits set into the floor are more common.

Subsistence information is less extensive for the Santa María Valley sites than for the Babícora Basin, reflecting the scale of PAC excavations in each region. The evidence suggests that people generally were opportunists, mixing subsistence strategies involving corn (*Zea mays*), beans (*Phaseolus* cf. *acutifolius* and *Phaseolus vulgaris*), and squash (*Cucurbita pepo*) agriculture (Adams 1992) with collecting and hunting. Isotopic studies of human bone from Ch-159, and Ch-216 in the San Juan mound group, confirm the importance of corn in the diet (Abonyi and Katzenberg 1992).

Table 4.1. West Central Chihuahua Radiocarbon Dates Discussed in This Chapter.

LAB. NO.	SAMPLE TYPE	RADIOCARBON AGE BP ± 1-SIGMA	CAL AGE(S) A.D., UNLESS B.C. IS SPECIFIED	1-SIGMA CAL AGE RANGE(S) WITH PROBABILITIES	2-SIGMA CAL AGE RANGES(S)WITH PROBABILITIES	SITE NO.
AA-10516	*Zea mays*	985 ± 45	1027	1010–1054 (.49) 1083–1122 (.34) 1138–1156 (.17)	985–1167 (1.00)	Ch-125
AA-10517	unidentifiable seed	1135 ± 50	894, 918, 952	881–984 (1.00)	791–1003 (1.00)	Ch-125
AA-11953	unidentifiable twig	1649 ± 45	416	344–370 (.15) 370–451 (.74) 484–500 (.09) 525–530 (.02)	263–283 (.04) 327–539 (.96)	Ch-125
AA-11954	*Zea mays*	1007 ± 45	1020	986–1047 (.76) 1094–1116 (.16) 1143–1154 (.07)	968–1163 (1.00)	Ch-125
AA-13015	unidentifiable grass stems	618 ± 58	1317, 1345, 1391	1306–1364 (.73) 1375–1398 (.27)	1289–1419 (1.00)	Ch-240
AA-16832	*Fulica americana* bone collagen	780 ± 65	1275	1205–1294 (1.00)	1049–1088 (.04) 1119–1141 (.02) 1155–1312 (.90) 1351–1387 (.04)	Ch-152
AA-18017	unidentifiable grass stems	1045 ± 45	1008	900–901 (.01) 965–1029 (.99)	890–1047 (.96) 1094–1117 (.03) 1143–1154 (.01)	Ch-125
Beta-44458	*Zea mays*	1340 ± 80	671	637–781 (1.00)	565–581 (.01) 592–885 (.99)	Ch-159
Beta-52997	human bone collagen	600 ± 50	1328, 1333, 1395	1308–1359 (.69) 1380–1404 (.31)	1298–1421 (1.00)	Ch-159
Beta-52998	human bone collagen	670 ± 50	1300	1288–1315 (.39) 1347–1390 (.61)	1278–1402 (1.00)	Ch-159
Beta-52999	human bone collagen	660 ± 50	1302	1292–1317 (.35) 1345–1391 (.65)	1282–1402 (1.00)	Ch-216
Beta-65674	*Phaseolus* spp.	940 ± 60	1046, 1097, 1115, 1144, 1153	1034–1161 (1.00)	1003–1226 (1.00)	Ch-125
Beta-65675	*Zea mays*	570 ± 50	1403	1312–1350 (.49) 1388–1423 (.51)	1304–1369 (.49) 1371–1434 (.51)	Ch-159
TO-2557	*Zea mays*	1100 ± 50	973	893–933 (.41) 942–996 (.59)	820–841 (.02) 959–1026 (.98)	Ch-159
TO-2708	*Zea mays*	990 ± 60	1025	999–1060 (.50) 1078–1125 (.34) 1135–1158 (.16)	899–903 (.00) 963–1212 (1.00)	Ch-104
TO-2875	*Zea mays*	640 ± 50	1307, 1360, 1379	1300–1321 (.28) 1340–1393 (.72)	1288–1405 (1.00)	Ch-159
TO-2877	*Zea mays*	940 ± 40	1046, 1097, 1115, 1144, 1153	1037–1064 (.26) 1075–1126 (.50) 1134–1159 (.24)	1020–1195 (1.00)	Ch-159
TO-2878	*Zea mays*	670 ± 40	1300	1289–1312 (.40) 1350–1388 (.60)	1283–1328 (.41) 1332–1396 (.59)	Ch-159

continued on next page

Table 4.1 continued

LAB. NO.	SAMPLE TYPE	RADIOCARBON AGE BP ± 1-SIGMA	CAL AGE(S) A.D., UNLESS B.C. IS SPECIFIED	1-SIGMA CAL AGE RANGE(S) WITH PROBABILITIES	2-SIGMA CAL AGE RANGES(S)WITH PROBABILITIES	SITE NO.
TO-2879	*Zea mays*	1060 ± 50	997	987–911 (.12) 977–1024 (.88)	883–1047 (.97) 1095–1116 (.02) 1143–1153 (.01)	Ch-159
TO-2880	*Zea mays*	1050 ± 50	1005	897–909 (.09) 959–1029 (.91)	886–1050 (.94) 1088–1120 (.04) 1140–1155 (.02)	Ch-159
TO-4118	*Juglans* type nutshell	1230 ± 50	786	721–737 (.10) 769–883 (.90)	678–894 (.96) 920–948 (.04)	Ch-212
TO-4119	*Phragmites* spp. stems	640 ± 50	1307, 1360, 1379		1288–1405 (1.00)	Ch-152
TO-4120	*Zea mays*	560 ± 60	1405	1312–1350 (.43) 1388–1432 (.57)	1301–1443 (1.00)	Ch-156
TO-4121	*Zea mays*	640 ± 60	1307, 1360, 1379	1299–1324 (.30) 1337–1394 (.70)	1282–1414 (1.00)	Ch-156
TO-4122	*Zea mays*	700 ± 60	1293	1274–1316 (.54) 1345–1391 (.46)	1233–1399 (1.00)	Ch-156
TO-4123	*Zea mays*	820 ± 60	1229	1179–1279 (1.00)	1046–1098 (.10) 1115–1145 (.06) 1153–1293 (.85)	Ch-159
TO-4124	*Zea mays*	560 ± 60	1405	1312–1350 (.43) 1388–1432 (.57)	1301–1443 (1.00)	Ch-159
TO-4125	*Zea mays*	620 ± 60	1315, 1347, 1390	1306–1365 (.73) 1375–1397 (.27)	1288–1420 (1.00)	Ch-159
TO-4126	*Zea mays*	520 ± 50	1421	1396–1445 (1.00)	1308–1358 (.17) 1381–1471 (.83)	Ch-159
TO-4138	*Zea mays*	4810 ± 120	B.C. 3634	B.C. 3704–3499 (.93) 3452–3435 (.06) 3535–3429 (.02)	B.C. 3940–3852 (.03) 3821–3334 (.96) 3152–3145 (.00)	Ch-212
TO-4140	*Zea mays*	3410 ± 120	B.C. 1731, 1728, 1686	B.C. 1874–1837 (.11) 1816–1803 (.04) 1783–1592 (.69) 1582–1528 (.16)	B.C. 2015–2006 (.00) 1979–1427 (1.00)	Ch-152
TO-4141	*Zea mays* (TO-5042)	4540 ± 220	B.C. 3336	B.C. 3505–3411 (.15) 3384–2924 (.85)	B.C. 3757–3740 (.00) 3721–2846 (.93) 2828–2621 (.07)	Ch-156
TO-5033	carbonized residue on sherd	500 ± 60	1431	1397–1469 (1.00)	1306–1365 (.14) 1374–1514 (.84) 1595–1619 (.03)	Ch-011
TO-5034	carbonized residue on sherd	500 ± 40	1431	1410–1441 (1.00)	1328–1333 (.01) 1395–1473 (.99)	Ch-011
TO-5035	*Zea mays*	880 ± 50	1176	1050–1087 (.24) 1120–1140 (.14) 1155–1226 (.62)	1036–1257 (1.00)	Ch-011
TO-5036	*Zea mays*	540 ± 40	1410	1329–1331 (.02) 1396–1435 (.98)	1309–1355 (.22) 1384–1444 (.78)	Ch-011
TO-5037	*Zea mays*	700 ± 40	1293	1279–1308 (.69) 1358–1381 (.31)	1254–1324 (.63) 1337–1394 (.37)	Ch-151

continued on next page

Table 4.1 continued

LAB. NO.	SAMPLE TYPE	RADIOCARBON AGE BP ± 1-SIGMA	CAL AGE(S) A.D., UNLESS B.C. IS SPECIFIED	1-SIGMA CAL AGE RANGE(S) WITH PROBABILITIES	2-SIGMA CAL AGE RANGES(S)WITH PROBABILITIES	SITE NO.
TO-5038	*Zea mays*	630 ± 40	1310, 1353, 1385	1305–1322 (.26) 1339–1368 (.42) 1372–1393 (.32)	1296–1402 (1.00)	Ch-151
TO-5039	*Juglans* type nutshell	570 ± 60	1403	1310–1353 (.50) 1386–1425 (.50)	1300–1439 (1.00)	Ch-151
TO-5040	*Zea mays*	1070 ± 60	989	894–923 (.23) 945–1022 (.77)	818–844 (.02) 857–1054 (.93) 1084–1122 (.03) 1138–1156 (.02)	Ch-152
TO-5041	*Zea mays*	670 ± 50	1300	1288–1315 (.39) 1347–1390 (.61)	1278–1402 (1.00)	Ch-156
TO-5042	Reed grass (*Phragmites* spp.)	1110 ± 70	967	882–1012 (1.00)	724–735 (.01) 771–1044 (.99) 1105–1112 (.00) 1148–1151 (.00)	Ch-156
TO-5043	*Zea mays*	610 ± 50	1322, 1340, 1393	1307–1360 (.71) 1379–1400 (.29)	1295–1416 (1.00)	Ch-156

NOTE: Cal (calibrated) ages and age ranges are A.D. except where specified B.C. Calibrations by program CALIB 3.0.3c (Stuiver and Reimer 1993a, 1993b).

The same major ceramic categories are present in the Santa María as in the Babícora Basin, but textured wares, and especially short-necked textured ollas, are more abundant in the Babícora Basin assemblages. The Medio period sites at Santa Catarina and Santa Clara have similar ceramic types and frequencies, with the dominant polychrome being Babícora. In contrast to assemblages at other PAC regions, Santa Clara Valley assemblages contain El Paso and Villa Ahumada polychrome sherds. This contrast is not surprising given the abundance of both types at Villa Ahumada to the northeast (Cruz 1997).

Chronology

An integral part of this project is obtaining chronometric dates, thus far limited to the radiocarbon determinations summarized here. Of the more than 150 sites recorded in the areas described above, ten sites now have at least one radiocarbon date (Table 4.1). Of the 43 dates on archaeological samples, TO-4138, TO-4140, and TO-4141 are rejected as inexplicably early by millennia, considering both sample type (corn) and, at least for the latter two dates, archaeological contexts. These three dates are omitted from the graph of calibrated dates (Figure 4.4). Of the remaining 40 dates, AA-11953, from a pithouse at Ch-125, is clearly an early outlier and is omitted from Figure 4.4 simply to increase the scale for plotting the other 39 dates. In this case the omission does not necessarily mean rejection, but the date does stand alone at this stage. Certain other problematic results are mentioned below under the discussions of "early group" and "late group" dates.

All determinations are corrected for isotopic fractionation by sample measurements, except one corrected using an estimated δ13C value for corn (as per Stuiver and Polach 1977). All are on relatively short-lived materials, including cultigens (mostly corn, some beans), other charred plant parts considered cultural remains, and human and animal bone collagen. Wood (e.g., house posts, hearth charcoal) was avoided because of the potential "old wood" problem (Schiffer 1986).

Using program CALIB 3.0.3c (Stuiver and Reimer 1993a, 1993b), the dates were calibrated by the international standard bidecadal atmospheric data set, although the decadal data set could be used for short-lived sample types (Stewart et al. 1991; Taylor, Haynes, and Stuiver 1996; Taylor, Stuiver, and Reimer

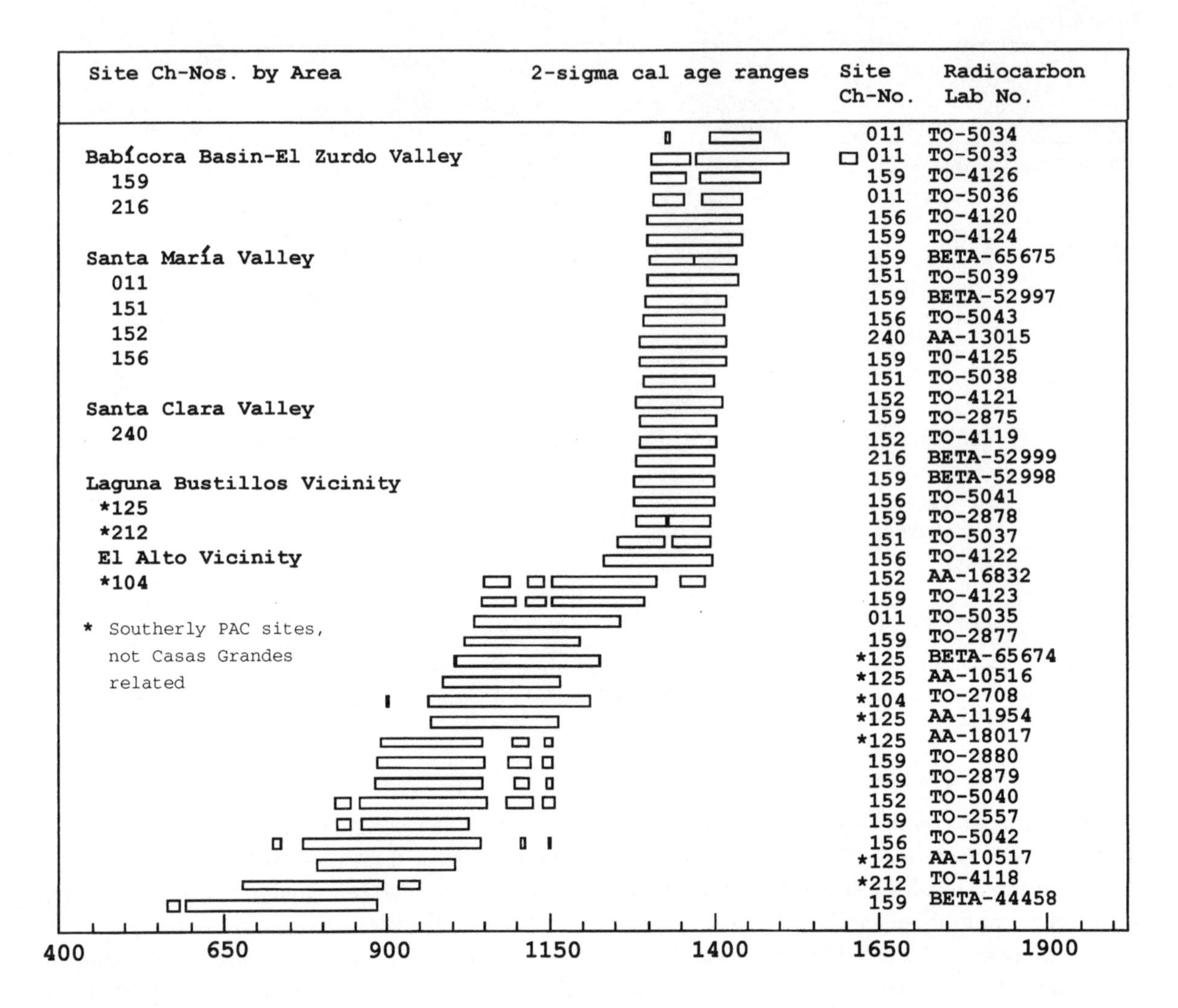

Figure 4.4. Thirty-nine PAC radiocarbon determinations, 2-sigma cal age ranges as calibrated using CALIB 3.0.3c, Method B. (For probabilities associated with intercepts, see Table 4.1.) Cited in Table 4.1 but not graphed are (a) three dates rejected as inexplicably early (TO-4138, TO-4140, and TO-4141) and (b) an early outlier (AA-11953) not necessarily rejected but excluded to increase the scale of the graph.

1996:3). All references here to "cal age ranges" are to calibrated radiocarbon ages with 2-sigma (rather than 1-sigma) errors. Probabilities associated with cal age ranges, as computed by CALIB's Method B, are given in parentheses. The calibrations take into account error in the calibration curve, as well as laboratory-reported error, but no other sources of variance. As no added variance or laboratory error multipliers (Reimer 1994; Stuiver and Reimer 1993a) have been applied, the present results are first approximations with precision exaggerated to some degree.

The 39 cal age 2-sigma ranges in Figure 4.4 are ordered by radiocarbon age, and all adjacent pairs overlap each other. However, testing via CALIB by the statistic T' (Ward and Wilson 1978) shows that this whole set of dates does not constitute a statistical grouping ($T' = 708.95 < 43.80 = X^2$; df, 38; $p < .05$). Hence, it is not valid to calculate the pooled average and standard deviation and then calibrate the result to obtain a summary for the set. However, in CALIB one can still sum the probability distributions for the 39 2-sigma cal age ranges, which gives a summary 2-sigma cal age range of cal A.D. 790–1458 ($p = 1.00$). This can be taken as a well-demonstrated time frame for all presently dated ceramic period sites in west central Chihuahua, leaving open the possibility of a somewhat earlier lower limit, considering the lone outlier, AA-11953.

Informal inspection of Figure 4.4 suggests a cline from early to late but with a noticeable bend at ca. cal A.D. 1250–1300, between AA-16832 and TO-4122, resulting in the impression of an "early group" versus a "late group" of dates. Although the two distributions do overlap slightly, the overall distribution is bimodal and presents the following three intriguing features.

EARLY GROUP DATES. First, the 17 lower dates (AA-16832 downward in Figure 4.4) constitute a loosely packed "early group" with the earliest and latest cal age ranges spanning cal A.D. 565–1294. The samples were excavated from various contexts in both northern and southern PAC sites. Of the northern sites, the five samples from Ch-159 all come from nonarchitectural, "lower midden zone" contexts with ceramics more comparable to Casas Grandes Viejo than Medio period ceramics. Other northern samples come either from less stratigraphically or ceramically indicative contexts or from contexts considered equivalent to the Medio period. In particular, samples TO-5040 from Ch-152 and TO-5042 from Ch-156 come from apparent Medio contexts. If these early dates are not, in Dean's (1978) sense, "erroneous" (something wrong with the dates themselves), they may be "anomalous" (e.g., the dates are correct but are older materials secondarily deposited in more recent contexts). In any case the "early group" does represent at least some site contexts in both our southern and northern research areas. Assuming that none of the 17 dates is erroneous (in Dean's terms), as a set they exhibit considerable dispersion and do not constitute a classical statistical grouping ($T' = 80.75 > 226.30 = X^2$; $df = 1,16$; $p < .05$). Therefore, these dates cannot be pooled. However, summing the probability distributions provides a valid summary for the 17 cal age ranges: cal A.D. 711–747 ($p = .02$) and 755–1289 ($p = .98$). These results suggest a time span of approximately 550 years, ca. cal A.D. 750–1300, for the early group dates. Although the beginning of the Viejo period in the Casas Grandes valley remains unclear, this time span incorporates (and exceeds) a Viejo period time frame. Thus, sites throughout the PAC study area have deposits contemporaneous with the Viejo period although not associated with Viejo ceramic wares in sites south of the upper Río Santa María.

LATE GROUP DATES. Second, the 22 dates from TO-4122 upward in Figure 4.4 form a "late group" of tightly packed 2-sigma cal age ranges spanning cal A.D. 1233–1514 (ignoring the intercept of 1595–1619, which has a probability of only .02 and is clearly out of line with the upper termini of the other 21 age ranges). The late group dates are marginally statistically the same ($T' = 32.46 < 32.70 = X^2$; df, 21; $p < .05$), and the pooled average radiocarbon age is 610 ± 10 B.P. This calibrates to cal A.D. 1308–1358 ($p = .78$) and 1381–1400 ($p = .22$). Using the essentially Bayesian summed probability distribution approach (cf. Taylor, Haynes, and Stuiver 1996; Taylor, Stuiver, and Reimer 1996) for the 22 calibrated dates gives a summary of cal A.D. 1279–1446 ($p = 1.00$). Considered together, these results show that the late group samples come from essentially fourteenth- and early-fifteenth-century contexts, with a strong likelihood of ranging from the middle thirteenth to the middle or late fifteenth centuries. This dating corresponds closely to the revised Medio period dating of Paquimé proposed by Dean and Ravesloot (1993).

All but two of the 22 late group dates are on samples from contexts provisionally considered Medio, based on ceramics or architecture. One of the exceptions is TO-2878 from a "lower midden zone" context at Ch-159 expected to date earlier, like other samples from that stratigraphic zone, as discussed above. The other problematic late group date is AA-13015 from Ch-240, which seems Viejo-like in material culture.

LACK OF LATE GROUP DATES IN THE SOUTH. Third, all the late group dates are from Medio period–related sites in the northern PAC research area. This raises certain questions, one of the more interesting being why we have no late group dates from the south. Although this lack is probably due to sampling limitations, withdrawal from the southernmost area, paralleling withdrawal from some areas of the American Southwest in the late A.D. 1200s, is conceivable.

Evaluation of Radiocarbon Dating

With the exception of problems noted above, the radiocarbon dates correspond well with both the redefined chronology for Paquimé (Dean and Ravesloot 1993) and earlier assessments of the age of Babícora area polychrome sites based on ceramic cross-typing (e.g., Brand 1933; Sayles 1936) and one dendrochronologic date from a site west of El Zurdo given as 1374 + x by Haury (1938:3). At this point, even with the largest suite of radiocarbon dates from Chihuahua, it is impossible to precisely define an interval for the transition from the Viejo period to the Medio period, although the latter clearly was well established by A.D. 1300. There is little basis for arguing whether the Viejo-to-Medio change is coeval or diachronic in western Chihuahua, as the one perhaps anomalous late date from Ch-240, associated with red-on-brown pottery, may mean. Uncertainties such as this ca. A.D. 1300 date with Viejo period artifacts require careful verification.

Given such uncertainties about Viejo period chronology, and the transition from Viejo to Medio, arguments for the temporal priority of any part of Chihuahua over other parts cannot be sustained. The important points are that the seedbed of Chihuahuan culture was very large and that the southern zone was an active participant in these broadly based cultural developments.

Regional Dynamics: A Southern Perspective

The southern zone of Chihuahuan culture (corresponding to the northern PAC research area) is clearly tied to northwest Chihuahua during both the Viejo and Medio periods. There are close similarities in settlement and material culture between Viejo period sites over the same areas through which later Medio period sites are distributed in west central Chihuahua. Correspondingly close similarities in Viejo period subsistence seem likely, although this remains to be proven.

Paquimé has butterfly-shaped rooms, extensive public architecture, macaw pens, and enormous shell caches—things with few or no parallels in the southern Chihuahuan culture zone. No archaeologist could seriously dispute the uniqueness of Paquimé as compared to any other site in the region. Not surprisingly, the immediate region around Paquimé mirrors its characteristics more than sites farther away (Whalen and Minnis 1996b:285). With a few known exceptions to the north, ball courts are largely confined to the Paquimé area (Naylor 1995; Whalen and Minnis 1996a). So far, ball courts have not been identified in the PAC study area. The presence of ball courts to the north, but not south of the Casas Grandes valley area, may give some indication of how autonomous the southern region was from any semblance of formal centralized control. The stone-circle roasting pits reported by Minnis and Whalen (1993) are not known farther south than the Galeana area about 50 km south of Paquimé (Sayles 1933).

The most important differences between northwest and west central Chihuahua may be rooted in demography and environment. Clearly, site density is greatest along the Río Casas Grandes, which has a relatively wide floodplain (e.g., Sayles 1933; Brand 1943), and perhaps more locally in the Carretas Basin (Carr 1935; Brand 1943). Similarly, there is no question that land use was generally most intensive around Paquimé and discontinuously westward into the adjacent Sierra Madre Occidental (e.g., Leubben et al. 1986; Herold and Miller 1995). This is reflected in the concentration of major water management systems across these areas. By contrast, overall site density is lower in west central Chihuahua, but there is no remaining evidence for water management features, other than small check dams in the El Zurdo drainage. Nor are there accounts of major water management features in the Río Carmen and Villa Ahumada areas. Some features have probably been lost to mechanical agriculture, but the basic contrast with the Casas Grandes valley and adjacent sierra surely holds.

Little is known about Holocene climate changes in this area, although Metcalfe et al. (1997) do suggest that Laguna Babícora existed into the early Holocene, was interrupted by a dry interval of Younger Dryas age, and then possibly expanded during the mid-Holocene. Unfortunately, data for the later Holocene are not available. The modern pattern is for considerably greater rainfall moving south through the Chihuahuan desert along the east flank of the Sierra Madre Occidental (see Schmidt 1992). The net difference is largely provided during the summer monsoons critical to modern bean and corn farming. Some earlier workers implied relative backwardness in outlying areas of Chihuahuan culture, in part, because of what was absent in comparison to Paquimé and environs (e.g., Amsden 1928; Kidder et al. 1949). However, these outlying areas did not necessarily deal with needs or challenges identical to those of their neighbors around Paquimé.

By stressing what is shared across this region, we see an overall pattern of loosely assembled social organization, with subscription to common beliefs and practices that were defined in local terms. Although referring specifically to montane Medio sites, Di Peso defines Medio period Casas Grandes hallmarks as "multi-storied structures that contain T-shaped entries, raised fire hearths, subfloor burials, similar ceramic types, and a multitude of other material culture ties" (Di Peso 1974:2:335). These similarities apply equally to the southern Chihuahuan culture area and discussions of putative cores and hinterlands or peripheries must accommodate them.

Architecture illustrates this point. Known late prehistoric sites in both areas are typically adobe pueblos with plastered floors and walls. Rooms are normally rectangular with occasional variations such as L-shaped or T-shaped rooms. Walls are generally aligned within a few degrees of the cardinal directions in both regions, and rectangular and T-shaped doorways co-occur. Sites nearer sources of cobbles typically have cimientos, whereas those in rock-poor floodplains do not. Internal and adjacent plazas are common, with the latter sometimes being marked by cimientos. Several floor features are distinctive, albeit inconsistent, markers, including raised hearths and collared postholes. The collared posts from Ch-156, for instance, were constructed much like those reported at Paquimé by Di Peso et al. (1974:5:214), providing an example of very specific construction knowledge shared between two sites over 100 km apart.

Lithic technology is an aspect of Chihuahuan culture virtually ignored. It is worth mentioning that the Medio period point types noted by Di Peso are indistinguishable from those recovered from PAC room blocks. Elliptical, oval, and rectangular manos are characteristics of mound sites throughout western Chihuahua, as are shaped legless metates. Rock types suitable for flaking, such as chert, silicified rhyolite, and obsidian, are almost ubiquitous in gravels within the study area.

Other interesting similarities between the Casas Grandes area and the southern zone may illustrate a shared symbolic system. Turkey burials in midden deposits occur in both areas, and macaw raising may have occurred in the southern zone as well (Minnis et al. 1993). Human burials were usually placed below room floors throughout the southern room blocks, as first reported by Carey (1931) and Sayles (1936). Approximately 60 percent of the burials excavated at Paquimé are from under room floors (Di Peso et al. 1974:8).

The Southern Chihuahuan Culture Zone in Centralization Models

In Di Peso's interpretation of events at Paquimé, following the introduction of a hierarchical mercantile system, "it is assumed that the lesser villages produced both surplus goods and population which were funneled into the Paquimé market center" (Di Peso 1974:2:332). Di Peso's interpretation of the "Casas Grandes Sovereignty" in the Medio period, depicted in graphic form (Di Peso 1974:2:Figure 20), clearly includes the northern PAC study area. We see no basis for this area having been under political or economic control from Paquimé at any time. However, the question of how Di Peso's centralization model can be assessed from a southern perspective deserves consideration. Much discussion, although not specifically in the context of west central Chihuahua, has revolved around ceramic distributions. There is no evidence of a manufacturing monopoly for any Chihuahuan pottery type, although it is intuitively satisfying to think of specialists producing the finest light-colored Ramos Polychrome vessels. Multiple production sources of Playas Red are suggested by Bradley and Hoffer (1985) and for Ramos Polychrome by Woosley and Olinger (1993). At the same time regional polychrome styles, such as Huérigos and Carretas, seem remarkably persistent within Chihuahuan culture. This regionalization of Chihuahuan pottery assemblages, including the southern Chihuahuan culture area, does not suggest strong economic centralization.

For the south, and using pottery frequencies as the basis for discussion, visible ties to other parts of the Casas system vary according to geographical positioning. The Santa Clara region shows the closest ties to the Villa Ahumada sites downstream. The Santa María Valley and Babícora Basin sites possibly had their closest external relations to the Casas Grandes valley, perhaps via the intervening Galeana area, because most of the potentially imported pottery is Ramos Polychrome, with occasional sherds of Villa Ahumada, and rare sherds of Carretas and Corralitos polychromes. Trade wares from beyond the Chihuahuan sphere, including the American Southwest, are virtually nonexistent in the Santa María and Babícora areas. Planned ceramic provenancing work should help clarify ceramic production patterns in PAC Medio period sites.

Evidence for exchange in exotic artifacts and materials originating outside the Chihuahuan area is undeniable at Paquimé. The southern zone apparently received little of the materials for which Paquimé is famous. Even large sites in west central Chihuahua have few or none of the nonlocal goods seen at Paquimé. One copper bell collected by Sayles from a Las Varas site is reported by Withers (1946). No other copper artifacts are known from this far south in Chihuahua. Indeed, Withers (1946) and Vargas (1995) argue that West Mexico was the manufacturing source for copper bells found at Paquimé and in the American Southwest (see also Brand [1933:111–113]). Shell is not common in PAC sites and most of what has been collected are freshwater bivalves. Marine taxa from southern Chihuahuan culture sites include *Glycymeris, Conus, Laevicardium elatum, Haliotis,* and *Vermetid* (Bradley 1996:197). These shells are available in the Gulf of California. Interestingly, Harrington (1939) describes an impressive trove of shell from an unspecified cave somewhere along the Río Santa María. There are no identified Gila Polychrome or El Paso Polychrome vessels or sherds, and only one Chupadero Black-on-white sherd from the Babícora Basin or middle Santa María Valley. Sayles's sherd collections at the Arizona State Museum look much like PAC collections in types. Two Mimbres Black-on-white sherds are reported from pre-Medio Santa María contexts.

The low frequency of items for which Paquimé is so famous, coupled with the scarcity of trade pottery from outside the Chihuahuan sphere, suggests that little entered the southern zone from outside of the Chihuahuan culture. Moreover, some of the northern Chihuahuan polychrome types—such as Carretas, Corralitos, Huérigos, and Escondida—are scarce or unknown in west central Chihuahua. Nor is there substantial evidence for trade with neighbors from Durango or farther south. Only the molded spindle whorls, copper bell, minor amounts of shell, and one possible Sinaloan sherd in Sayles's collections offer any hints of southern or West Coast connections. It is much easier to see relationships to the north than the south. Although there is still vast unsurveyed terrain in west central Chihuahua, from what we do know there is no indication of a sustained trade route from the Durango area, such as J. C. Kelley (1986, 1993) posits.

Conclusions

Related cultural developments occur along much of the eastern flank of the Sierra Madre Occidental over at least the past five centuries of prehistory. An archaeological contrast between the upper Santa María Valley and basins farther south extends at least back into the Viejo period time interval. This contrast was not recognized previously because ties to the Viejo period, although suggested (e.g., Foster 1995b), were never actually identified in west central Chihuahua. It is intriguing that the overall distribution of Viejo period sites is evidently much the same as for Medio period sites. The Medio period in the Santa María Valley, Santa Clara Valley, and Babícora Basin closely parallels developments in northwest Chihuahua. The variability observed in PAC Medio period sites reflects participation defined and controlled at a local level, within a loosely, flexibly organized region. Region-wide participation has deep historical roots but not a demonstrable coercive element, which may explain the absence of such features as ball courts in the south. Shared Medio period iconography, such as serpents and parrots, along with turkey burials, implies that an ideological connection also existed. It is not only the southern zone that is seen as politically independent of, but obliquely involved with, Paquimé. De Atley and Findlow (1982) and Douglas (1995) have developed a similar position for Animas sites, although the supporting arguments differ.

The essentially descriptive information offered here does little to explain why Paquimé became such a remarkable site but underscores the fact that Paquimé's characteristics are tied in many ways to developments that unfolded during several centuries over much of western Chihuahua.

ACKNOWLEDGMENTS. The PAC was principally funded, 1990–1992 and extended to 1994, by a research grant to Kelley (principal investigator) and Stewart (coinvestigator) from the Social Sciences and Humanities Research Council of Canada (SSHRC file no. 410-90-1070) and by smaller grants to Kelley from the University of Calgary (1989, 1996–1997), Stewart from Lakehead University (1989), MacWilliams from the University of Arizona (1992, 1993) and the Arizona Archaeological and Historical Society (1993), and Neff from the University of Calgary

(1995). The research was conducted with permission from the Consejo de Arqueología of the Instituto Nacional de Antropología e Historia (INAH, Consejo reference no. 401-36-039-90). We thank the INAH Chihuahuan Regional Center for much assistance and collaboration with our project. Local officials and friends in Chihuahua greatly facilitated the field operations. Karen R. Adams and David H. Kelley critically read various drafts of this paper, and Paula J. Reimer specifically commented on the chronology section. Reviews by the editors of this volume led to improvements in the final draft. Hugh Gibbins, Bryan Wells, and Mitchel Hendrickson drafted the map (Figure 4.1).

5

The Robles Phase of the Casas Grandes Culture

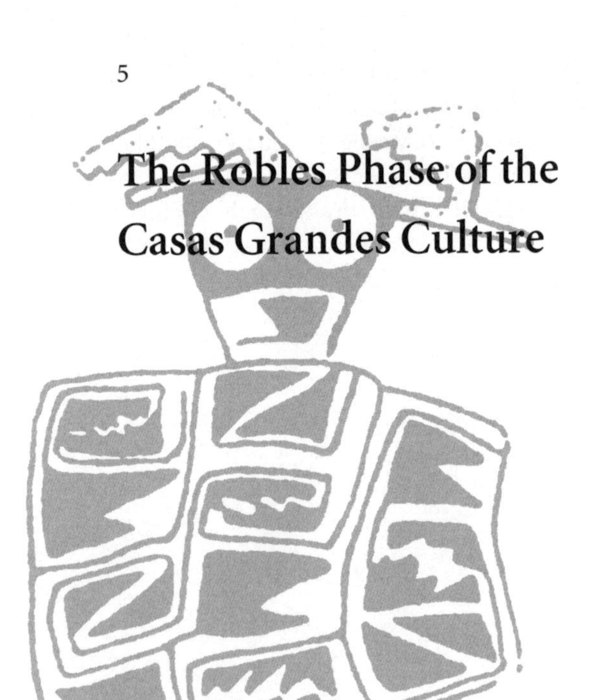

David A. Phillips Jr.

John P. Carpenter

In 1974 Charles C. Di Peso published his massive and lasting contribution to northwest Mexican archaeology, the eight-volume *Casas Grandes: A Fallen Trading Center of the Gran Chichimeca* (Di Peso 1974; Di Peso et al. 1974). Among many of Di Peso's novel ideas was an argument that the Casas Grandes culture survived the destruction of its principal town, Paquimé, and lingered until the arrival of the Spanish. Di Peso believed that in 1565 a Spanish expedition clashed with members of the culture in the northern Sierra Madre Occidental. He therefore defined the Robles phase as the period between the fall of Paquimé and the arrival of the Spanish.

We wish to reexamine here the arguments made for the existence of the Robles phase. Most archaeological reexaminations of earlier studies focus on the presentation of new data or apply newly developed methods to existing data. We wish to do neither. Our question is not "Does the Robles phase exist?" Instead we ask, "Was Di Peso justified in defining a new phase, based on the data and methods available *at the time*?" By taking this approach we hope to provide a study in archaeological reconstruction. New information available on the Robles phase has been relegated to the end of the chapter. In the main text we will evaluate the Robles phase in terms of the data and methods that were available to Di Peso. If the point is to evaluate the decision-making process behind the definition of the Robles phase, relying on methods or information not available to Di Peso would be unfair.

What Is the Robles Phase?

In Di Peso's 1974 synthesis the Casas Grandes culture epitomized Mesoamerican domination of the Greater Southwest. In A.D. 1060 Toltec merchants, or *puchteca,* established Paquimé as their base for economic and cultural control of the region. When the Toltec Empire collapsed, Paquimé became a beleaguered outpost. In A.D. 1340 nomads burned the town, leaving their victims where they fell (Di Peso 1974:2:320–325).

Inspired by late radiocarbon dates and by accounts of the Ibarra expedition of 1565, Di Peso was convinced that the Casas Grandes culture lingered into the historic period (Di Peso et al. 1974:4:8; Di Peso 1974:3:833–834, 836). He concluded that survivors of the attack on Paquimé abandoned the town and moved north (where they established new villages) and west (where they joined existing settlements in the Sierra Madre Occidental). The survivors

Table 5.1. Di Peso's Robles Phase Dates.

SAMPLE USED	DATE USED IN SYNTHESIS	CORRECTED DATE/COMMENT/SOURCE
Beam, Chih. H:11:1	1374+x	Undated (Breternitz 1966)
Maize cobs, CHIH D:9:1, Hearth 5 in Room 24-11; CG(p)/233, A-612	470± 90 B.P., A.D. 1480	660 ± 90 B.P., A.D. 1290 (Correction as reported by Di Peso)
Maize cobs, Joyce Well Site, ASR #776, I-1789	385 ± 100 B.P., A.D. 1565	620 ±120B.P., A.D. 1330 (Correction based on Damon et al. 1974)
Maize cobs, Joyce Well Site, ASR #2574, I-1790	355 ± 100 B.P., A.D. 1595	590 ± 160 B.P., A.D. 1355 (Correction based on Damon et al. 1974)
Maize cobs, Joyce Well Site, ASR #2657, I-1791	330 ± 110 B.P., A.D. 1620	565 ± 165 B.P., A.D. 1375 (Correction based on Damon et al. 1974)
Roof support post, CHIH G:2:3, CG(d)/319, A-610	300 ± 90 B.P., A.D. 1650	390 ± 90 B.P., A.D. 1560 (Correction as reported by Di Peso)

maintained their culture and continued to produce the distinctive Casas Grandes pottery types (Di Peso 1974:3:778, 830–839; Di Peso et al. 1974:4:868–875).

The most critical bit of evidence in Di Peso's thinking was obtained by Di Peso himself. In a site in the Sierra Madre, along the upper Bavispe, Di Peso recovered a radiocarbon sample that yielded a date of A.D. 1650—obvious evidence of a Casas Grandes occupation after the abandonment of Paquimé in A.D. 1340. Di Peso found further evidence for a remnant population in independently reported dates from two other Casas Grandes sites (Di Peso 1974:3:836–837; Di Peso et al. 1974:4, 1974:5). A tree-ring date from a cliff dwelling in the Sierra Madre yielded a date of A.D. 1374+x (Haury 1938; Scott 1966). Three radiocarbon samples from the Animas phase Joyce Well site (McCluney 1965b), on Deer Creek in New Mexico, yielded dates of A.D. 1565, 1595, and 1620 (reported by McCluney to Di Peso in 1965; Di Peso 1974:3:778, 838:Figure 38-3, 970; Di Peso et al. 1974:5:870). Di Peso reported one additional Robles phase radiocarbon date from a hearth at Paquimé itself, attributing this date to postabandonment use of the site (Di Peso et al. 1974:4:8–33) (Table 5.1).

The tree-ring date, presumably the most accurate of the six, was from at least 34 years after Di Peso's A.D. 1340 abandonment date for Paquimé. The five radiocarbon dates ranged from A.D. 1480 to A.D. 1560, with no sigma values of greater than 110 years. The dates therefore neatly filled the gap between the end of Paquimé and the permanent arrival of the Spanish in the region in 1660. There seemed to be no reason to doubt the existence of the phase.

Unlike Di Peso, however, we will assume that defining the Robles phase as a new cultural taxon is justified only if there is a strong reason to reject the "null hypothesis"—namely, that the supposed Robles phase remains were contemporary with Medio period Paquimé. To do so, however, we must begin by understanding the basis for Di Peso's A.D. 1340 date for the abandonment of Paquimé.

The End of the Medio Period

Di Peso's major effort at chronology building took place between 1965 and 1967, when the results of tree-ring and radiocarbon studies (including the Joyce Well dates) became available to him (Di Peso et al. 1974:4:8). The Joint Casas Grandes Expedition had made every effort to secure accurate dates, including the collection of 386 tree-ring samples from Paquimé itself, but only 54 tree-ring samples from the site yielded dates, and none was a cutting date. Despite a sustained effort, Di Peso was unable to correlate his noncutting dates with the Gregorian calendar. In the end Di Peso correlated noncutting dates with selected radiocarbon dates and concluded that he could treat the noncutting dates as reasonably accurate (Di Peso et al. 1974:4:9–14).

Noncutting dates for the major construction episodes at Paquimé fell no later than A.D. 1261vv, but one highly fragmentary specimen yielded a noncutting date of A.D. 1338vv. Di Peso concluded that this last sample was from a replacement timber brought in toward the end of the occupation. He related the late tree-ring date to a radiocarbon date of A.D. 1310 ± 30 from Pit Oven 4-1. The pit contained carbonized agave hearts, and Di Peso inferred that an agave roast was under way when nomads destroyed the town. Di Peso noted that the "upper limit" of the stated range for the radiocarbon sample was A.D. 1340, which jibed with the tree-ring date of A.D. 1338vv. Di Peso therefore used A.D. 1340 for the end of the Medio period (Di Peso et al. 1974:4:14).

Di Peso's arguments relied heavily on the contents of Pit Oven 4-1's dating to the end (literally the last day) of the occupation of the site. Di Peso actually obtained a later radiocarbon date from Paquimé of A.D. 1480 ± 90 from Fire Hearth 5 in Room 24-11 (Di Peso et al. 1974:4:25), but he argued that the late date reflected casual postabandonment use of the site. The evidence suggests otherwise. The hearth in question was an adobe-lined feature set into the earlier of two formal floors in the room (the schematic drawing in volume 4 is incorrect), was of a form that occurred 54 times in assumed Medio period contexts, and was sealed by a remodeling episode (Di Peso et al. 1974:5:519). These attributes are more consistent with hearth use during the main life of the site than with casual use after abandonment. Thus, the Fire Hearth 5 date was a "red flag" that could have warned Di Peso of problems with his chronology.

A second red flag was provided by the 63 obsidian hydration dates from the final occupation of Paquimé. When combined, these yielded an average date of A.D. 1404 ± 52, or a 2-sigma error range of A.D. 1300 to 1508 (Di Peso et al. 1974:4:26–29). Although the obsidian hydration data were problematic and did not rule out an end date of A.D. 1340, they indicated at least the possibility of a site occupation after that date.

A third red flag was ceramic cross-dating based on the accepted date ranges for trade pottery in the U.S. Southwest. By looking at contemporary sources (such as McGregor 1965, especially pp. 107–108, and Breternitz 1966), we can appreciate the lack of fit between Di Peso's Medio period chronology and those date ranges. Based on his interpretation of noncutting dates at Paquimé, Di Peso placed that start of the Medio period at A.D. 1060; based on accepted date ranges for trade pottery, the start of the period was more likely to fall between A.D. 1175 and 1200. This is a discrepancy of at least 115 years. Based on the same noncutting tree-ring dates, Di Peso dated the transition between the Buena Fé and Paquimé phases of the Medio period to A.D. 1205, but the trade wares indicated a date about A.D. 1300 (Di Peso et al. 1974: 4:4). This is a discrepancy of 95 years. In other words application of readily available pottery dates should have indicated that the tree-ring results, far from being near-cutting dates as Di Peso supposed, were early by many decades.

Di Peso did not heed these three "red flags." We now wish to explore what he might have determined about Casas Grandes chronology, had he chosen to do so.

Given the methods and knowledge available to Di Peso, we can propose two basic methods for resolving the problems with the Casas Grandes chronology. First, Di Peso could have assumed that outer-ring loss was fairly uniform in the Paquimé samples and added 100 years (as a rough correction) to the final date in the tree-ring sequence, which was A.D. 1338. This approach yields a revised final construction date at Paquimé of roughly A.D. 1438, which is also within the then-accepted date ranges for the trade pottery found in late Medio period contexts. The second and more conservative approach would have been to dismiss the problematic tree-ring and radiocarbon dates altogether and to fall back on ceramic cross-dating as the primary source of chronological information. Based on the Medio period sample of over 20,000 trade sherds, and using accepted date ranges for those sherds, the end of the Medio period could be placed as late as A.D. 1450. Thus, extrapolation from tree-ring dates and ceramic cross-dating both suggest that the Medio period could have lasted until about A.D. 1450. This conclusion also eliminates the red flags raised by the Hearth 5 radiocarbon sample and the obsidian hydration data, resulting in a tentative but internally consistent picture of Casas Grandes chronology.

Sites "After" the Medio Period

If the Medio period actually lasted until about A.D. 1450, what becomes of the chronological evidence for the Robles phase?

What appears to be the most precise date cited by Di Peso, the tree-ring date of A.D. 1374+x, now falls within the Medio period. According to Breternitz (1966:25), however, "Recent reexamination of the dated tree-ring specimen has not verified the published date; consequently this specimen should be ignored for interpretive purposes." Because Breternitz's publication is contemporary with Di Peso's analytical efforts, we feel justified in stating that this date should not have been used either in support of or against the validity of the Robles phase.

As for the five Robles phase radiocarbon dates: In 1965 through 1967, as Di Peso established his master sequence for Casas Grandes, he used only uncorrected radiocarbon dates and single sigmas. It was only about 1971, well after he had committed to his master sequence, that Di Peso became aware of the need to correct and calibrate his radiocarbon dates. Di Peso reported the revised radiocarbon dates for two samples (one from his upper Bavispe site, the other from Hearth 5) using information provided to him by Paul V. Damon in 1971 (Di Peso et al. 1974:4:25). Di Peso did not revise the three dates reported to him by Eugene McCluney for the Joyce Well site. More critically, Di Peso did not revise his interpretations based on the changed Robles phase radiocarbon dates but instead relegated the inconsistency to comments in the report's descriptive sections (see Di Peso et al. 1974:4:8, 24–25; end papers:Figure 327-4). The main narrative of the report continued to use the old dates.

In Table 5.1 we have provided the two corrected dates as reported (but not applied) by Di Peso. We have also corrected the three dates from the Joyce Well site, and as all three are from maize cobs, we have first applied the Lowdon (1969) correction used by Di Peso in his own report (Di Peso et al. 1974:4:24). The calibration used is from Damon et al. (1974), which we assume is consistent with the calibrations that Damon applied for Di Peso in 1971. The result is a series of calendar dates of A.D. 1290, 1330, 1355, 1375, and 1560, with sigmas of 65 to 165 years. Five of the six dates therefore indicate that Di Peso's "Robles phase" survivors were, in fact, contemporary with Medio period Paquimé.

The one exception, from a Bavispe River site, is the date of A.D. 1560. If forced to take this date at face value, we can point out that the 2-sigma range for this latest date is A.D. 1380 to 1740, providing a 70-year overlap with an A.D. 1450 end date for the Medio period. We prefer, however, to argue that in any series of radiocarbon dates it is possible to have a "wild card" date that is unexplainable except by factors such as contamination and processing errors. As a consequence, it is important to examine the overall patterns of dates rather than only individual results. The pattern, in this case, is that three of the four "Robles phase" radiocarbon dates from sites other than Paquimé are contemporary with the principal occupation of Paquimé—that is, with the Medio period.

It appears, therefore, that if Di Peso had applied the information available to him in a more critical fashion, he would have been reduced to a single radiocarbon date to support the concept of a Casas Grandes occupation after the abandonment of Paquimé. Although his evidence did not negate the possibility of a post-Paquimé phase, the similarities between his supposed Robles phase sites and Medio period remains, combined with the absence of firm evidence for a later occupation, indicate that there was little reason to establish the Robles phase as a new cultural taxon.

Discussion

Was there a Robles phase, in the sense of a Casas Grandes occupation after the abandonment of Paquimé? We suspect not (see endnote), but that is beside the point. Instead, we have tried to illustrate how the data and methods *available to Di Peso* do not support his conclusions. It is therefore important to understand how such a respected scholar could have reached such conclusions. It appears that Di Peso was an enthusiastic advocate for his own hypotheses, instead of using a "null hypothesis" approach, in which one does not accept a hypothesis until the alternative (or alternatives) are eliminated. As a consequence, Di Peso appears to have ignored at least three "red flags" that might have told him of flaws in the Casas Grandes chronology.

Based on work by Irving Langmuir, Dennis

Rousseau (1992) has identified three characteristics of error in scientific synthesis: (1) ambiguity in the standards of research success, (2) a readiness to disregard prevailing ideas and theories, and (3) an unwillingness to pursue additional studies that may confirm the new synthesis but that are also likely to discredit it. All three apply to the definition of the Robles phase.

First, the measure of "success" in establishing the distinction between the Medio period and the Robles phase was ambiguous. Di Peso did not require the two to be substantially different. For example, although he defined a series of "Robles Variant" forms of Medio period pottery types (Di Peso et al. 1974:4:6), there were no formal differences between Robles and earlier variants of those types. If the two were mixed on a table, it would be impossible to distinguish them. Only one measure, the apparent later age of certain sites, served as the basis for establishing the new ceramic taxa.

Second, Di Peso was well known for his willingness to discard prevailing ideas and theories. Such an approach was sometimes justified, but in this case Di Peso's chronology, as he readily acknowledged (Di Peso et al. 1974:4:9, 39), flew in the face of the regional ceramic sequence. Although the regional sequence was based on decades of research and hundreds of tree-ring dates (including cutting dates), Di Peso rejected the possibility that something was wrong with his chronology. Instead, he demanded "serious rethinking of accepted time relationships as they have hitherto been ascribed to by archaeologists" (Di Peso et al. 1974:4:9).

Third, it appears that Di Peso was intellectually unprepared or unwilling to see the full implications of new information and to make the corresponding drastic changes in his own findings as that new information became available to him. Di Peso apparently created the heart of his chronology between 1965 and 1967, as raw data from tree-ring and radiocarbon studies became available to him. About 1969, apparently, the results of the obsidian hydration study became available, and in 1971 Di Peso became aware of the need to correct his radiocarbon dates (Di Peso et al. 1974:4:8). To his credit, Di Peso reported the new information that threatened to unravel his chronology, but he did not go back and change his conclusions.

It seems that in developing a chronology that now finds no support among scholars, Di Peso was following fairly standard steps toward scientific error as described by Rousseau. As for the Robles phase, we cannot prove that it did not exist, but given the evidence and methods available to Di Peso, we see no reason to conclude that it did exist. Neither of these statements is intended to be a dismissal of a scholar who, as we are painfully aware, is no longer able to defend himself. If anything, we admire his many accomplishments and his habit of presenting data and methods in such detail that we can use his research in a case study. What we do assert is that error is common in archaeology, that it follows patterns, and that by analyzing and learning from those patterns we can hope to develop a more rigorous and effective discipline.

ACKNOWLEDGMENTS. This essay is based on a paper presented at the 55th Annual Meeting of the Society for American Archaeology, with the assistance of the Committee for Excellence of the Museum of New Mexico. Our thanks to Joe Stewart and the late Dan Wolfman for comments on radiocarbon dating, to Curt Schaafsma for information on the new archaeomagnetic dates from the Joyce Well site, and to Curt Schaafsma, Cal Riley, and the University of Utah Press faculty review board for their input on later drafts.

Note

Since publication of Di Peso's report, a number of authors have criticized the Casas Grandes chronology as a whole (Wilcox and Shenk 1977; LeBlanc 1980; Lekson 1984b; Braniff 1986; Phillips 1989; Dean and Ravesloot 1993). The most important critique is that of Dean and Ravesloot, who devised a computer protocol to estimate the number of rings missing from the Paquimé samples. Their results suggest that the Medio period began no earlier than about A.D. 1200 and lasted at least until A.D. 1400, possibly as late as A.D. 1500. Ahlstrom et al. (1991) have also noted the problems inherent in the Casas Grandes chronology, based on tree-ring studies at Walpi in northeast Arizona.

Table 5.2 illustrates results obtained by using newer methods to reevaluate the dates discussed in the main part of this chapter. These revisions are in line with De Atley's (1980:Table 3) revised radiocarbon dates for the Joyce Well site. Applying Suess's (1970) calibration curve and Stuiver and Polach's

(1977) corrections for isotopic fractionation, De Atley obtained calibrated dates of A.D. 1330 ± 121, 1340 ± 112, and 1365 ± 121, or a combined date of A.D. 1340 ± 68. As Curtis Schaafsma remarked to us in a 1998 letter, "An average in this case is sensible since all dates were from a pile of burned corn in Room 24 and were probably all contemporaneous."

The revised Joyce Well dates find further support in the work of Wolfman and Schaafsma (1989), who in April 1988 returned to the site and obtained archaeomagnetic samples from four hearths. Three of the hearths yielded usable dates:

Room 21, Hearth	A.D. 1220–1295 or 1335–1390
Room 18, Subfloor Hearth	A.D. 1245–1285 or 1330–1360
Room 12, Hearth	A.D. 1335–1390

Wolfman and Schaafsma (1989) also used the combined data from these hearths to yield a tighter date of A.D. 1345–1370. Similarly, Stevenson et al. (1989) obtained a median obsidian hydration date estimate of A.D. 1296 ± 108 from Joyce Well site artifacts.

In summary, although we cannot disprove the existence of a post–A.D. 1450 Casas Grandes phase, except for a single date from CHIH G:2:3 the data do not suggest a continuation of the Casas Grandes culture after the abandonment of Paquimé. Our postulated collapse of the Casas Grandes culture during the early 1400s does not mean that the Casas Grandes area was abandoned, only that subsequent inhabitants of the area had an archaeologically distinct way of life.

Table 5.2. Reevaluation of Di Peso's Dates.

SAMPLE	METHOD A	METHOD B
Maize cobs, Hearth 5, Room 24-11	1150(1273)1400	1143–1409
Maize cobs, Joyce Well ASR #776	1190(1336)1470	1160–1490
Maize cobs, Joyce Well ASR #2574	1230(1369)1480	1210–1500
Maize cobs, Joyce Well ASR #2657	1230(1382)1560	1230–1570
Post, CHIH G:2:3	1420(1616)1955	1426–1830 @ .93
		1905–1955 @ .07

NOTE: The A.D. dates are estimated by using Lowdon (1969), the Radiocarbon Calibration Program of the University of Washington's Quaternary Isotope Lab (Rev. 2.0, 1987), and 2 sigmas.

6

Was Casas a Pueblo?

Stephen H. Lekson

What's a Pueblo?

SOUTHWESTERN CULTURAL NOMENCLATURE is notoriously slippery. Native terms have been taken from one group and rudely applied to another, geographic names have been stretched beyond tectonic plasticity, and descriptive terms have been elevated to ethnic identities. "Pueblo" was originally the conquistador's first-cut classification of any *Indios* living in settled towns—more a tactical category than a cultural tag. The Treaty of Guadalupe Hidalgo separated the *Indios Pueblos* of New Mexico from the pueblos of old Mexico, and in the United States *pueblo* was elevated to a cultural label: The Pueblo Indians. That usage predominates, but *pueblo* has other, different archaeological uses. Specifically, *pueblo* is used descriptively to refer to any above-ground, contiguous-room structure. Masonry or mud, five rooms or five hundred—if a site sticks up, it's a small-*p* pueblo. A capital-*p* Pueblo means a site historically linked to the Hopi, Zuni, Acoma, Laguna, or the several Rio Grande tribes.

In these days of conflicting tribal claims, many Pueblo sites are being demoted to pueblo sites—"Pueblos" become "pueblos" to avoid the tangle of tribal rivalries. Yet even the lowercase term remains archaeologically charged. Was Casas a pueblo? Was Casas a Pueblo? Both questions raise hackles: Casas Grandes was the "Fallen Trading Center of the Gran Chichimeca" (Di Peso 1974).

When Bandelier called Casas Grandes a pueblo (Bandelier 1884, in Lange and Riley 1970:292 ff), did he mean a ruined town or Pueblo ruin? Probably both. "He wanted to find out how far Pueblo architecture had penetrated into Chihuahua" (Lange and Riley 1996:74), and there seemed to be little doubt in his mind that Casas was a pueblo/Pueblo. Edgar Hewett, about 25 years later, had no hesitation in labeling Casas a pueblo (Hewett 1908, in Schroeder 1993). Not everyone was comfortable with a Puebloan Casas, and in his 1924 *Introduction to Southwestern Archaeology,* A. V. Kidder sounded a warning and raised a call for "analytical studies of the remains to enable us to ascertain which elements are Southwestern and which are Mexican" (reprinted 1962:321).

The office sought the man, and that man was Charles Di Peso. Di Peso's excavation, analysis, and publication of the Casas Grandes spanned 16 years, from 1958 to 1974; but early in that monumental program Di Peso realized that he'd hooked a live one. First in conference papers, then in journal articles, and finally in a classic multivolume publication, Di

Peso stated with admirable assurance and clarity that Casas was *not* a Pueblo: It was "a trading center," a "city," a "capital" planned and built by Mesoamerican "merchant-priests, in their managerial capacity as overlords"—"the union of sophisticated donor plans with recipient Chichimecan labor" (Di Peso 1974:2: 293). The word *pueblo* was conspicuous by its plateau specificity and, consequently, its near absence in Di Peso's magisterial summary (e.g., Di Peso 1974:2). Casas ceased being a Pueblo and became the bête noire of traditional, territorial southwesternists.

The subsequent battles that raged between "indigenists" and "Mexicanists" (Judge 1991:29) need not be recounted here. No one could deny the Mesoamerican qualities of Casas Grandes—those ball courts! those pyramids! those parrots!—but entrenched Puebloan archaeologists drew the line at the border or, in strategic retreat, raised barricades along the Mogollon Rim, defending what J. Charles Kelley scornfully called the "Chaco Alamo" (Kelley 1986). The Pueblo defense was more successful than the mythopoetic Texas defeat. When it came to southwestern regional nomenclature, the conclusion was clear: Don't mess with taxa. Pueblo sites were Pueblos, and Casas wasn't.

Puebloan archaeologists learned to live with a Mesoamerican Casas Grandes—the site was, after all, actually *in* Mexico—and for almost two decades Di Peso's Chichimec capital spun in a distant orbit around the Real Southwest. At rare intervals pourparlers were advanced, inviting Casas back into the southwestern fold, but those bids came not from the Pueblo Plateau but from the Hohokam desert (more on this later). With a few brave exceptions—Steven LeBlanc and several authors in this volume, among others—most Puebloan archaeologists left Casas to Mexicanists. Certainly, I wanted no part of Casas as a southwestern site, as a Pueblo (Lekson 1983, 1984b).

But times change, and in this case, the times literally changed. The dramatic redating of Casas Grandes (summarized in Dean and Ravesloot 1993) turned all the old arguments on their heads: Instead of Casas being a Pueblo II *cause,* it now is possible to consider that great center as a Pueblo IV *effect.* Elsewhere, I make an irrefutable, undisputable, lead-pipe-cinch case for Casas being the last of a series of three historically linked, geographically aligned southwestern political centers: Chaco (900–1125), Aztec (1110–1275) and Casas (1250–1450). I will not repeat that argument here (Lekson 1996c, 1997, 1999a). Here I address only one of the stumbling blocks that impedes its advancement: Many Puebloan archaeologists have grown so accustomed to ignoring Casas as a bizarre Mesoamerican satellite—a highly localized anomaly—that we have grave difficulties in linking the words *Casas* and *Pueblo.* But Casas Grandes was, in some very important ways, a Pueblo.

I am not dismissing those spectacularly Mesoamerican features (ball courts! pyramids! parrots!). My position, paralleling that of many colleagues, is that Casas represents an intersection of southernmost Pueblo and northernmost Mesoamerica. Casas was the key link between the two areas throughout the fourteenth and fifteenth centuries, and that geographic position gave it much of its political power. This interpretation parallels Di Peso's in many ways, but the realignment of Casas with Puebloan prehistory, rather than events and processes of the Mesa Central, corrects what I perceive as the major flaw in Di Peso's argument. Casas was not a Mesoamerican center; it was, instead, the last of the great Pueblo regional centers.

Why would I say that Casas was a Pueblo? Well, it looks like a Pueblo, it had Puebloan antecedents, and Pueblo people say it was. In the following sections I will (1) compare architectural and other dimensions of Casas and Puebloan archaeology, (2) explore the historic implications of Casas's regional sequence, and (3) summarize some Pueblo traditional histories that appear to link Casas and the larger Pueblo world.

Pueblo Paquimé?

In form Casas Grandes was remarkably, almost stereotypically, Puebloan. As mapped by Di Peso, Casas was a massive, terraced, U-shaped pueblo-style building surrounding a central plaza (Di Peso's "east plaza," Di Peso 1974:Figure 125-4). The view from the south entrance to the site would have been much like Taos Pueblo today: terraced adobe room blocks surrounding a large, well-defined plaza. Like Taos, Casas has ceremonial architecture and mounds located around the outside of the building.

I do not mean by this comparison to imply a historic linkage between Casas and Taos but simply to rectify widespread misconceptions about Casas's form. Di Peso excavated the ritual and ceremonial precincts outside the pueblo itself and only nibbled at the edges of the massed adobe room blocks, all but ignoring the real central plaza of the site. His presentation of the site's layout was biased by his excavation strategy (e.g., Di Peso et al. 1974:4:Figure 124-4, comparing "domestic and public/ceremonial settlement patterns" at Pueblo Bonito, Casas Grandes, and Tula). Subsequent redrawings derived from Di Peso's map deemphasize and even delete the central plaza and the east wing, showing only a single room block facing the river valley, with ball courts, mounds, and detached compounds on the reverse, away from the river (cf. Ravesloot 1988:Figure 1.2 and Bradley 1993: Figure 2). Compared to Di Peso's original map, we've lost half the pueblo!

Might these editorially truncated presentations be, in fact, correct? David Wilcox suggested at a professional forum that the east arm of Casas Grandes is not real, that is, that the east arm is, in fact, a natural ridge on the Rio Casas floodplain (David Wilcox, remarks at the Southwest Symposium, Tempe, Feb. 10, 1996). Wilcox proposed his hypothesis based on his surface examination of the site and on a manuscript map by Adolph Bandelier.

Bandelier's unpublished and published maps of Casas Grandes (Bandelier 1892:Plate 7; reprinted, along with an "unpublished" Bandelier map, in Di Peso 1974:Figure 14-4; the latter published by Burrus 1969:Plate 26) indeed do not include the east arm and eastern outbuildings shown by Di Peso on his maps of Casas Grandes (e.g., Di Peso et al. 1974:4:Figure 121-4). However, in his field journals Bandelier noted that modern Mexican settlement encroached on the ancient ruins of Casas Grandes: "[T]he dozen [Mexican] houses, east of the ruins, still partly stand on ruins, and some of them are built on ancient walls. On the whole, the [ancient] settlement has been very extensive, and expanded into the river bottom proper" ("Field-Notes of Casas Grandes" in Lange and Riley 1970:294–295). In Bandelier's phrase "east of the ruins," the term *ruins* almost certainly refers to the west arm (as represented on Bandelier's maps). Bandelier recognized but did *not* map "ruins" and "ancient walls" east of the west arm; I assume that these "ruins" and "ancient walls" were at least in part the architectural units Di Peso later called the east arm. Thus, Bandelier's maps did *not* present the entire site as it was known to him but only the better-preserved western half. Wilcox's doubts about Di Peso's east arm are not, in fact, supported by Bandelier's notes, maps, and published conclusions.

My admittedly brief examinations of the "east arm" indicate that it is, in fact, a very large adobe room block. This opinion is shared by others familiar with the site (e.g., Paul Minnis, personal communication, Feb. 10, 1996; John Carpenter, personal communication, Feb. 10, 1996), although other archaeologists share Wilcox's view (e.g., David Phillips, personal communication, Aug. 10, 1996). Di Peso, of course, expressed no doubt that the east arm was real. He described and mapped Casas Grandes as "a south oriented, multistoried apartment building having three arms or wings (east, north, and west) built around a large public plaza which was walled on its south side (the 'East' Plaza)" (Di Peso et al. 1974:4: 201). Di Peso stated that "the outline of the east half of the city was obtained from data gathered from ground survey and aerial photos" (Di Peso et al. 1974:4:Figure 129-4). Why did Di Peso not excavate the east arm? "Due to the fact that the eastern sector of the city was occupied by some 53 families, which the government of Mexico wisely decided not to move, the target area was confined to the west, where eleven families lived. To these, the Republic gave not only land and riparian rights, but also new homes" (Di Peso et al. 1974:4:128).

The reality of the east arm is a resolvable issue; the east arm can be confirmed or disconfirmed through excavation. However, the possibilities for excavation in the east wing are currently remote and will probably remain so in our lifetimes. Absent new excavation data, I prefer to believe Di Peso. In addition to the mutually supporting archival and published evidence, my reasons for trusting Di Peso are frankly ad hominem. Whatever the interpretive or theoretical quibbles one might have with Di Peso's work at Casas Grandes, few doubt his remarkable abilities as a field archaeologist. Di Peso knew the site better than anyone before or since his extended fieldwork.

Because (1) Bandelier's field notes negate the ambiguities of his maps and (2) Di Peso's knowledge of the site was and is unrivaled, I accept the east wing as real. But what if Wilcox is right (and he very often is right), and Di Peso was wrong? Casas was still Puebloan: not the unmistakably Pueblo IV form of Di Peso's original map perhaps, but even without the east wing, the massing remains northern and Puebloan—but more like Walpi than Taos.

The question is not so much finding a plateau parallel (and they are legion) as drawing a distinction between Puebloan and north Mexican architectural traditions. Puebloan massing, during Casas's time, joined multiples of contiguous rooms in stepped, terraced room blocks. Northern and western Mexican domestic architecture (insofar as it is known) was founded on separate cells—typically, three or four separate one-room structures around a sunken central patio (Lekson 1983). In the Southwest that pattern is mirrored in Hohokam courtyard clusters (and perhaps in early Mogollon pithouse groupings) but not in the unit pueblos of Pueblo II or the larger pueblos of Pueblo III and IV. The massing of Casas Grandes—four or five stories tall, hundreds of contiguous rooms—with or without the east wing was Puebloan. Indeed, it was emphatically Puebloan, in that Casas was notably *not* west or north Mexican in form, and if not Mexican, then Puebloan.

A wide range of architectural details connect Casas and more northerly Pueblos. Comparisons to Chaco (a century and a half earlier) have been summarized in detail by Di Peso (Di Peso et al. 1974:4: 208–211; see also Lekson 1983, 1996c, 1997). Colonnades, "sleeping platforms," massive post-support disks, T-shaped doors, and a variety of other Casas features can be confidently linked to Puebloan prototypes at Chaco and Aztec. Even the massive poured- or puddled-adobe walls of Casas Grandes were presaged by massive-walled adobe Great Houses at Chaco (Breternitz et al. 1982) and Aztec (Stein and McKenna 1988). (See also chapter 18 of this volume.)

Of course, there are as many differences as similarities. I am not trying to imply that Casas was a copy of Chaco or a clone of Kuaua, but Casas falls (just barely) within the range of variation of sites we call pueblos. Tsiping was a very different place than Awatovi, but both of them are archaeological "pueblos." There was enormous variation within Pueblos above the Mogollon Rim and proportionately more, perhaps, between desert pueblos and plateau pueblos. Casas in particular was its own place, unique in its time as Chaco was unique in its era. There is nothing like Casas Grandes's room shapes in the northern Pueblos (or anywhere else, for that matter). Colonnades are ubiquitous at Casas but absent in the northern Rio Grande, and Zuni, and Hopi. I do not claim that Casas mirrors northern Pueblo forms; rather, both northern and southern pueblos are part of a larger, inclusive array with multiple dimensions of variability.

Chaco, Aztec, and Casas each represented the distinct architectural canons of their time. Casas differed as much from Aztec as did Aztec from Chaco, or—for that matter—as Chaco differed from Blue Mesa or Shabikechee. Within the context of changing Puebloan architectural vocabularies, changing notions of space and landscape, the continuities of both detail and form over a span of centuries was remarkable.

Casas was a Pueblo IV site, later than Aztec and much later than Chaco, and it is to Pueblo IV sites, perhaps, that it should be compared. Two key aspects of Pueblo IV architecture were enclosed plazas and conspicuous kivas (Adams 1991). The problematic status of Casas's plaza has been discussed, at length, above. Pay your money and take your choice. But if Casas was a Pueblo, where are the kivas? This question may be plateau-centric, but the audience I seek to reach is a plateau group.

Puebloan (and particularly Anasazi) archaeologists are obsessed with "kivas"—an archaeological term for a class of subterranean rooms that may or may not have parallels in modern Puebloan ceremonial architecture. There is no need to rehash arguments about archaeological kivas here (see Lipe and Hegmon 1989 for a sample); rightly or wrongly, the kiva remains the ill-defined but diagnostic signature of Anasazi and, by extension, all Puebloan archaeology.

Where are the kivas at Casas? Although Di Peso noted a number of "ceremonial rooms," his best candidate for a kiva is Room 38 in Unit 11 (the House of the Serpent). Di Peso argued that Unit 11, a compound of four plazas and about 25 rooms, was "the best and least contaminated evidence of the Buena Fe phase" (Di Peso et al. 1974:5:475); however, neither tree-ring dates nor pottery support an early placement of this unit.

Room 38 was a large (ca. 8 × 9.3 m) subterranean chamber with a long ramp entry in the middle of its south wall. It appears to have been built as a unit with Room 33, to its east, which was also subterranean. Flanking the entry ramp of Room 38, on its east side, was an associated small surface room, Room 36. The room had been "secularized" (to use Di Peso's term) with two raised fire hearths along its west wall. The original floor features included two very elaborate post supports in the center of the room. These flanked an area about 1 m in diameter that had been excavated and disturbed prehistorically. Di Peso suggested that this area was a looted central ceremonial cache (Di Peso et al. 1974:5:509); the possibility that it was originally a central hearth should also be entertained. Fire Hearth 4, a rather generic small, adobe-lined hemispherical pit, is well positioned for a sipapu, if we need one (Di Peso et al. 1974:5:509)—they are rare indeed in Mogollon-area kivas.

Room 38 and associated Room 33 had the only examples of kiva-related mural art found at Casas Grandes: a figure Di Peso interpreted as a plumed serpent in Room 38 and a one-horned katsina-like figure on the walls of Room 33 (Di Peso et al. 1974:5:Figures 24-5 and 30-5; cf. Di Peso et al. 1974:4: Figure 150-4). Di Peso dismisses this mural art as "doodlings" (Di Peso et al. 1974:5:Figure 29-5, caption 4), and they are indeed scruffy; but their subject matter and architectural association suggest that the mural art of Rooms 33 and 38 may be more significant than Di Peso and other Casas scholars have heretofore understood.

The size, depth, and ramp entry of Room 38 are quite comparable to known twelfth-century through fourteenth-century Mogollon great kivas (Anyon and LeBlanc 1984). Great kiva–like forms were part of the Chihuahuan architectural tradition long before Casas Grandes: Earlier great kivas were present at the nearby Convento site (Di Peso et al. 1974:4:142). Thus we should not be surprised to find Room 38 at Casas Grandes.

There was only one candidate kiva at Casas Grandes, but there were generally only one or two great kivas at most big Pueblo IV Pueblos (and recall that Di Peso excavated only 40 percent of Casas Grandes). I am arguing that Casas was a pueblo/Pueblo, and we all know that the essence of Pueblo was Anasazi: Is a square Mogollon great kiva a reasonable proxy for a real rootin'-tootin', perfect-circle, slab-lined Anasazi kiva? It is, I think, because Anasazi kivas (real and/or archaeological) do not all look like Casa Rinconada. The Colorado Plateau is rife with square kivas, early and late, from Kayenta to the Rio Grande, Mesa Verde to Tularosa. Again: Of course there are differences, but I submit we have not yet understood the range of variation within architectural archetypes, like "kivas," over the appropriately broad scales. What, for instance, was the real difference between a ramp entry into Room 38 (typical of Mogollon great kivas) and the stairway into Casa Rinconada? If you know, tell us.

Casas was not Anasazi, in archaeological terms; Casas was Mogollon. But Mogollon *was* profoundly Puebloan. An explanation of this statement requires a somewhat extended treatment of Casas Grandes's Mogollon antecedents and the relationship of Mogollon culture post-A.D. 1000 to the Pueblo-Anasazi north.

What Was Mimbres, Really?

On maps of the ancient Southwest, Casas Grandes is conventionally shown as Mogollon (e.g., Cordell 1994:13). On more detailed maps, where that vast Mogollon region was divided into a surprising number of subregions and "branches," Casas usually falls within the still-considerable area called Mimbres Mogollon (e.g., Lekson 1986; Brody 1977a:Map 3; but see Brody and Swentzell 1996:25). Was Casas a Mimbres Mogollon Pueblo? Dear me, no; layers of cross-bedded resistance would meet that claim. Not the least of that resistance devolves from the inherent confusion of temporal and spatial semantics: "Mimbres Mogollon" is a geographic entity that conventionally includes Casas, but the "Mimbres phase" is a century earlier (ca. A.D. 1100–1130) and many miles distant from Casas. Casas Grandes and the Classic Mimbres phase were separated by 250 km and 100 years (see chapters eight and nine of this volume).

We know a great deal about Mimbres and quite a bit about Casas; we know much less about what lay between, both in time and in space. Working from known to known ("tussocks of empirical certainty to guide our speculation across the fens of time," as Earl Morris once said), we can at least extrapolate from Mimbres to Casas—with obvious risks. Whatever the twists and turns in that currently dark century that separates Mimbres from Casas, a Puebloan Mimbres region would provide a promising substrate for a Puebloan Casas. That is, if the Mimbres region was demonstrably Puebloan, the foundation is well laid for a Puebloan Casas Grandes a century later (see chapters 8 and 18 of this volume).

The first proponents of Mogollon maintained that Mogollon ceased to mean much, culturally, after A.D. 1000 (Haury 1936; Wheat 1955). Their original model had Mogollon hillbillies succumbing to a vague Anasazi "swamping": Shortly after the millennium a powerful surge out of the Four Corners spilled over the highlands and created Mimbres (and other Mogollon pueblos) in its own Anasazi image.

The swamping model was roundly rejected by the New Archaeologists of the 1970s, who maintained that "the post-A.D. 1000 occupation in the Mimbres area (the Classic Mimbres) was fully Mogollon" (LeBlanc 1986:299). At the time, the distinction between Anasazi and Mogollon seemed important. Today, that insistence on a separate-but-equal evolution seems strained. We now have more details, much better dating, and far more complete distributional data (thanks to research by Darrell Creel, Steven LeBlanc, Harry Shafer, and many others), but the material patterns that led Haury and Wheat to look north after A.D. 1000 have not changed: black-on-white and corrugated-indented pottery, stone-masonry contiguous room blocks, and small square "kivas" (much like the quintessential Anasazi unit pueblo: Lekson 1990, 1999b, Ice 1966, Moyer 1980). Those elements remain the stock-in-trade of Classic Mimbres. Despite well-attested local sequences, architectural evolutions, and synoptic ceramic progressions, we are left with a similarity of basic material culture that encompasses both Mimbres and Pueblo/ Anasazi within the same general taxon. To insist on separate-but-equal segregation of Mimbres and Anasazi requires an act of equifinality that simply defies belief. Of course Mimbres was "local," but it was also part of a larger cultural formation that exceeds both our research scales and (perhaps) the ancients' own geographies.

Part of the difficulty in making Mimbres (and by extension Casas) part of the Pueblo world rises from the historical inferiority of Mogollon vis-à-vis Anasazi. In its infancy Mogollon was denied by many Anasazi archaeologists; in its maturity Mogollon has turned on its cruel stepparent and denied Anasazi. A simple speculative exercise—"plausible worlds" or alternative history—might restore parity and alleviate the historical burdens of parvenu Mimbres, *ancien* Anasazi. Consider: the Four Corners' reputation is architectural, whereas Mimbres's fame is artistic. If the pioneer archaeologists had excavated Mimbres first and Mesa Verde last, the ruins of the Four Corners might be seen as secondary and subordinate, "swamped" by the artistic and ideological center to the south. One can imagine the perplexity aroused in a hypothetical turn-of-the-century Mimbres-centric archaeologist by Chaco: "They built surprisingly well—for ideologically impoverished heathens who couldn't paint their way out of a yucca sack. . . ."

Instead of looking to the Four Corners, rightly or wrongly, as source and center, we should view Mimbres and Anasazi as samples of a much larger geographic and historical Pueblo continuum. "Pueblo," in the eleventh and twelfth centuries, encompasses a range of material remains from Fremont (reaching north to Pocatello, Idaho) to Virgin (as far west as Las Vegas, Nevada) and various ill-defined Great Plains interfaces (in southeast Colorado and northeast New Mexico). And how far south? That issue lies at the heart of this chapter.

Within that vast broad Puebloan spectrum, Mimbres and Mesa Verde become two cases among many, each remarkable and distinctive in some dimensions but mundane and undistinguished in others. The whole vast heterogeneous conglomeration—united by broad themes in pottery, architecture, economy, and symbolism—was "Puebloan." Those same themes evolved and survive in the remarkably diverse living peoples we group today under that same term. There may be no direct genetic representation of northernmost Fremont or southernmost Chihuahua in today's Pueblos (see chapter 17 of this volume), but both of those far-flung developments contributed, by providing social context, to the evolution of modern Pueblo peoples. Fremont was Puebloan (Talbot 1996); Mimbres was Puebloan (Lekson 1992c; Lekson and Cameron 1995; see also Lekson 1993 for a a *really* confusing take on all this).

If Mimbres was part of that larger Pueblo world—tangentially or integrally—then it becomes much less of a leap to say the same for Casas Grandes, the center that dominated the Mimbres region a century after Mimbres's end. The standard view of the Mimbres sequence posited a dramatic depopulation about 1130 followed by a greatly diminished Black Mountain phase, which was originally seen as a new population (LeBlanc 1980; Anyon et al. 1981). Reanalyses of survey data (Lekson 1992a) suggest that population decrease was not nearly so drastic as originally proposed and indicate strong continuities of detail between the black-on-white, stone-masonry Mimbres pueblos and the polychrome, adobe Black Mountain sites (Darrell Creel, personal communications 1995, 1996). I have argued that the Black Mountain phase (in the Mimbres) and taxonomically identical El Paso phase (to the south and east) may represent a temporal link between large pueblos in the Mimbres and the huge political center—Di Peso's "city," my pueblo—that arose a century later on the Rio Casas Grandes (see chapter 18 of this volume). But our knowledge of these intermediate phases is northern: from southern New Mexico and the western tip of trans-Pecos Texas, but conspicuously not from Chihuahua. What came before Casas?

Immediately pre-Casas archaeology in northwest Chihuahua remains foggy and opaque—a treacherous fen indeed. There are now large gaps in Di Peso's (1974) originally continuous sequence. (The archaeology of northern Chihuahua in the twelfth and thirteenth centuries is only now being defined by Paul Minnis and Michael Whalen [see chapters three and four of this volume]). But whatever immediately preceded Casas in northwestern Chihuahua followed a long architectural tradition that paralleled both Mimbres and Anasazi paths. At the early Convento site, Di Peso documented a transition from a small pithouse village with a central "community house" (equated to a "kiva" by Rinaldo [Di Peso et al. 1974:4:143]) to a small "unit pueblo" (my term, not Di Peso's or Rinaldo's) of 10 rooms and "community house" or kiva (Di Peso et al. 1974:4:Figure 36-4). The prehistoric sequence at the Convento site ended about 1150 or 1200 (contra Di Peso's 1060; Di Peso et al. 1974:4:Figure 36-4), but the "unit pueblo" pattern apparently continued at the later Reyes 2 site: three pueblo-style rooms and a round "community house" (Di Peso et al. 1974:5:846), with Ramos Polychrome but no Salado polychromes. Prior to Casas the architectural record of northern Chihuahua falls within the broad Pueblo tradition of small pueblos with kivas or kiva-like structures—a pattern familiar in Anasazi and demonstrable in Mimbres.

Di Peso also recorded large, unmistakably pueblo-style sites that he believed immediately postdated Casas Grandes. The "stone pueblos" (Di Peso's own term: Di Peso et al. 1974:5:872) of the Tres Rios area, west of Casas Grandes, fall comfortably within any late Mogollon pueblo pattern. CHIH G:2:2, for example, was a rectangular, 90-room, multistoried, stone-masonry pueblo built around a small square interior plaza (Di Peso et al. 1974:5:Figure 240-5). Di Peso dated the Tres Rios sites to the Spanish Contact period, but it seems likely that some of these unexcavated sites were fifteenth century or even earlier (see chapter five of this volume).

Thus, northern Chihuahua pre- and post-Casas looked pretty solidly Puebloan. I argue that Casas itself looks Puebloan—but that, of course, is the point at issue.

Casas Grandes also looks Hohokam. In making this statement I use the term *Hohokam* (as I use *pueblo*) as a description, not a derivation. Southwestern cultural nomenclature is not only slippery, it is semantically dangerous: Names have proprietary power far beyond their original delineative intentions. But instead of saying "Casas Grandes looks Hohokam" I may as well have said "Casa Grande looks Chihuahuan" (and I have; Lekson 1996c).

Beyond a strong sense of similarity, there are no clearly articulated models for Hohokam and Casas. Di Peso, Crown, McGuire, Wilcox, and many others have considered the Sonoran-Chihuahuan desert axis, linking Phoenix and Paquimé, a fruitful field for study and reflection. Cult-status pottery, the old ball game, the old shell game, adobe big houses (castles made of sand?), and big-time canal irrigation (known for Hohokam, safely inferred for Casas)—a series of suggestive ties link the riverine oases that punctuate the desert from Bill Williams River to the Bolson de Malpimi.

The east-west axis across the low deserts may prove as important for understanding Casas Grandes as the north-south alignment of Anasazi/Pueblo and Mimbres Mogollon. Rushing in where wiser, better angels decline to tread, I explore that east-west axis elsewhere (Lekson 1996b, 1996c); to summarize, Casas Grandes may have been far more important to the configuration of Classic period Hohokam than the reverse. But our understanding of social histories spanning the upper Sonoran and Chihuahuan deserts is even less developed than considerations of Casas Grandes and the northern Pueblo world.

What Do the People Say?

Pueblo origin stories, particularly from Acoma and Zuni, probably refer to Casas Grandes (Lekson 1996c). The Acoma version is most elaborated and detailed. In the Acoma tales, the people left White House (probably Chaco or Aztec, taken as inclusive regional systems; Lekson and Cameron 1995). The movement from White House to Acoma was always south. The people carried two birds' eggs, one a parrot's and the other a crow's; they were to choose and open one egg when they reached their presumed destination. "They decided to go to the south, where lay a place called Ako. They wished to go there and raise parrots" (White 1932:145). When they reached Acoma (Ako), they chose eggs and opened the blue, presumed parrot, egg, but it contained crows. The people who had chosen the other egg continued far to the south. "'The rest must journey on to Kuyapukauwak and take the other egg with them.' . . . This was a very sad time for both groups. The parrot group left toward the south and it is not known how far they went" (Sterling 1942:83).

The Zuni tell a similar story, with the tribe choosing between two eggs and a sizable portion of the tribe following a parrot (which had hatched, again, from the plainer egg) far south to the Land of Everlasting Sunshine, never to return (Ferguson and Hart 1985:22). Ed Ladd (personal communication, 1996) adds some important points to this story. The division of the people occasioned by the choice of eggs happened before either Zuni or Acoma was established. Thus, the people who went south were neither Zuni nor Acoma, and through time those southern people developed their own language, which was not Zuni or Acoma; but they looked very much like Zuni and Acoma people. After the southern people had established their homes in "the land of eternal summer," a few returned as traders, bringing macaw feathers, live macaws and parrots, and sea shells.

Those stories very likely refer to Casas Grandes, with its remarkable evidence for commercial macaw breeding (Di Peso 1974; Minnis 1988). In the Greater Southwest, only Casas (and its immediate dependencies) engaged in macaw production on these large scales. That only Acoma and Zuni (and perhaps Laguna) recount this story is, perhaps, significant: If Chaco is White House (Lekson and Cameron 1995), the line south from White House to Casas Grandes runs right between Acoma and Zuni. The alignment and juxtaposition of Chaco, Acoma, Zuni, and Casas form the basis of a much larger, longer argument of historical continuity between Anasazi regional centers and Casas Grandes (Lekson 1996c, 1999a). Whatever the merits of that larger argument, Pueblo memories of groups who went due south a great distance to raise macaws seem a close fit to the archaeological facts of Casas Grandes—if not an intrusion, at least a late, major transformation of local populations into a magnificent, cosmopolitan pueblo conspicuously adorned with macaws, parrots, and other trappings of the great civilizations to the south.

What Was the Question, Again?

Claiming Casas as a Pueblo upsets two decades of Puebloan archaeological thought that largely dismissed Casas as *Mexica manqué:* a peddler of parrots, a penetration without issue. Casas-as-Pueblo also runs counter to current research directions at the site itself, which frame its history in profoundly local contexts (Whalen and Minnis 1996c). Archaeologists on the Plateau and in Chihuahua seem content to ignore each other; why force a confrontation?

One clear lesson of the past decade's research is that small scales are pernicious (Lekson 1996b). On a terrain of thin resources, southwestern adaptations, Paleoindian to Hopi, were always geographically large. Logistical arrangements varied and changed, but even maize and turkeys, wheat and sheep could not transform this marginal land into a garden of earthly delights. Only commercial economies and convenience stores reduced the width of native niches to politically containable scales.

The whole history of human-land relations in the Southwest counters the Jeffersonian ideal of small, single-family farms. A great deal of human misery and tragedy—from Bosque Redondo to the Bursum Bill—resulted from that conflict in scales. Archaeological errors of scale have less-serious consequences, but they do impede the growth of knowledge and they are avoidable. We might erase map lines that segment the Southwest into divisions as much professional as substantive and look again at the Greater Southwest.

I'm Sorry, But Your Response Must Be Phrased as a Question

I've lost patience with those (happily, few) who summarily dismiss Puebloan arguments in Mogollon and Chihuahuan regions as warmed-over versions of the "San Juan hypothesis"—the historically accidental notion that all good things in the Southwest emanated from the Four Corners. Most of us have gotten past antiquated sectional rivalries, and we now try to reconstruct a prehistory of the Greater Southwest that reflects its remarkable facts, freed from turf and territory. The stunningly obvious central matter of that prehistory was Chaco, Aztec, and, from 1300 to perhaps 1500, Casas Grandes.

But for those in the South who wince at a Casas-Pueblo linkage, be satisfied with this: At Casas Grandes's peak, in the fourteenth and fifteenth centuries, there was nothing on the Colorado Plateau or the Rio Grande that challenged it as a political center. During that critical span of southwestern development, many Pueblos were larger, but no pueblos were more important than Casas Grandes. The South rose again.

7

A Preliminary Graph-Theoretic Analysis of Access Relationships at Casas Grandes

David R. Wilcox

THE OBJECTIVE OF THIS chapter is to present a preliminary analysis of access relationships at the site of Casas Grandes (Paquimé), Chihuahua. An application of graph theory is the method used. A large sample of the architecture of Casas Grandes was excavated by the late Charles C. Di Peso from 1958 to 1961, and he published an impressive eight-volume report in 1974 (Di Peso 1974; Di Peso et al. 1974). The sheer size of this corpus of information has been rather intimidating, and it is only gradually that southwestern archaeologists have begun to digest it and to contribute fresh analyses based on it. Di Peso set a very high standard for reporting the data resulting from his work, as well as his own interpretations of them. Consequently it has been possible to revisit his data from methodological or theoretical perspectives very different from his own and to rethink their behavioral or historical implications (e.g., Wilcox 1987, 1995). Such analyses, I believe, renew the value of Di Peso's contributions to archaeology, demonstrating the relevance of his findings to the scientific debates of a later generation. In this way we may hope to stand on his shoulders and, perhaps, to see a bit farther than he could (see Merton 1993).

Before taking up the specifics of this analysis of Casas Grandes architecture, and the implications of the access relationships embedded in it, I want to make more explicit the methodological perspective I bring to this analysis. After first discussing the background of my own approach to southwestern architecture, I contrast that with insights drawn from a new theory on the social logic of space (Hillier and Hanson 1984) and the mathematics of graph theory, which supports it (Hage and Harary 1983; Harary 1969). In that light I apply a combination of these ideas to the data from Casas Grandes. Although only preliminary, the results of this analysis will, I hope, introduce more archaeologists to the potential of this kind of analysis and stimulate some among them to pursue these studies more fully.

Background

When I first came to work in the Southwest at the Grasshopper Field School, nearly thirty years ago, there was a standard way used to excavate collapsed pueblo buildings. First, the tops of the standing walls were found, either by noting wall-stone alignments or by trenching to find them, and then a map of the "rooms" so defined was made. Next, a trench was dug along one wall and a profile drawing was made of the "fill" deposits. Then the fill was removed, roughly following as best one could the fill deposits of wall-fall, roof-fall, or trash-fill, eventually exposing "the floor," being careful to leave all floor-contact artifacts in place so that a photograph and map could be made of their context. After recording and collecting those artifacts, "subflooring" proceeded, the main object being to find and excavate human burials. This method had been devised at the earlier Point of Pines Field School (Haury 1955) and was still being rather mechanically applied in 1969.

In my first year at Grasshopper I dutifully followed this method, but I quickly found that it was cumbersome and constraining to someone who thought that the recording of depositional units and their relationships was a key to formulating and testing behaviorally meaningful models of the archaeological record and how it came to be as it was. Before coming to the Southwest, I had had intensive training in stratigraphic or depositional analysis. After a field class with the late William S. Godfrey at Beloit College, I worked as Alice Kehoe's field assistant in Saskatchewan, spending an entire summer drawing profiles and learning how to interpret them. Following another winter-to-summer stint of work in Saskatchewan, working first for Thomas Kehoe in the laboratory and then with Anthony Ranere in the field, I returned to Beloit to take Robert Salzer's first class in North American archaeology. That semester I was to learn an enduring lesson.

My most vivid memory of Salzer's excellent class is his discussion of Stuart Streuver's field methods somewhere in Illinois. The usual method of digging trash pits at that time was to section them and then to draw a profile of their deposits and the pit shape. Streuver did this, but he also tried digging some pits horizontally, deposit by deposit. In one of them, dug in the latter way, he found the claws and paw bones of a small animal arrayed in such a way that it was clear the whole animal pelt had been placed in the pit. Streuver went on to infer from this and other evidence that what he had found was a medicine bag. Clearly, if the pit had been sectioned, the relationships that documented this inference would very likely have been missed. The way exposures are created by the archaeologist's interaction with the archaeological record can have a profound effect on the evidence of past behavior that can be recorded.

After graduating from Beloit, I worked for two and a half years for William A. Ritchie and Robert Funk at the New York State Museum. In 1967 I went with Ritchie's crew to dig shell heaps on Martha's Vineyard (Ritchie 1969) and alluvial sites in the Binghamton area of New York. The following summer I again worked with Ritchie's crew, on Maine shell heaps. It was on Martha's Vineyard, however, that I first understood the key importance of surfaces as both a provenience category and a point of departure for understanding the depositional history of the archaeological record in general.

Ritchie had for years followed Sir Mortimer Wheeler's (1956) stratigraphic methods, using five-foot squares, leaving balks that were profiled, and then collecting artifacts in terms of cultural strata defined on the basis of both stratigraphic discontinuities and changes in artifact form. After learning how to recognize distinct shell deposits, by noting the relationships of all the shells to one another, the species composition, and the shells' relationships to thin soil deposits, I also began to notice that most of the artifacts being found were *on* the contact surfaces of the shell lenses, not *in* them. Using appropriate exposure techniques, I was also able to document relationships between postholes and larger pits with particular surfaces.

Reflecting on these findings, I soon saw that we could conceive of a site in terms of a surface on which people in the past had carried on various activities—building a house here, processing shell there, depositing shell lenses over here—the physical loci of such activities shifting about over time. Our excavations were punching a "window" into this palimpsest of physical, depositional outcomes, providing a sample of the sequence of different living surfaces.

Within what we had classified as "cultural strata," there were often multiple surfaces. That fact raised many questions about the bearing the artifacts from those strata had as a measure of past behavior. In some cases they were from the sandy floor of a structure, in others from a work surface outside a structure, in others from a deposit farther afield. Yet we were lumping them together in "cultural strata." Closer attention to microstratigraphic deposits seemed warranted.

Coming from this background, I soon showed at Grasshopper Pueblo that the deposits lumped together as "fill" were often quite complex, with far more potential for shedding valuable light on behaviorally meaningful depositional and predepositional processes than was being exploited. Similarly, I found that the floors of the "rooms" were not simple, unitary phenomena. Rather, they frequently had been replastered or patched, and floor features like hearths or mealing bins were added or eliminated during the use history of these spaces. New exposure techniques, and, indeed, a whole new philosophy of archaeological fieldwork, were necessary if we were to take full advantage of these potential data.

So with the amused acquiescence of William Longacre, the director of the Grasshopper Field School, I began to experiment with new exposure techniques. Short papers on "how to draw profiles" and "how to take useful field notes" sketched the general philosophy (see Wilcox and Shenk 1977:213–221). First we tried digging trenches down the center of "rooms," but this approach turned out to afford little advantage. In 1973, at the Vernon Field School during Paul S. Martin's last summer, we tried digging half-rooms, but we found that this approach took as long as digging whole "rooms." Yet it did afford better exposure of wall-fall arrays.

The site in question was a 25-room, single-story surface-masonry pueblo in West Hay Hollow Valley, which we called the Swannie site after Swannie Willis, the local rancher's wife, who was fascinated by archaeology. Besides being manageably small, the site offered another advantage: The walls were built using tabular sandstone laid up with clay mortar. The collapse of such walls, we had found, resulted in coherent arrays of these stones, but because a wall can fall over in two or more directions from a given room space, interpreting the rock arrays in individual room spaces still did not provide a wide enough exposure to test alternative hypotheses. Accordingly, in 1974 we changed strategy and began by stripping the blow-sand off the whole pueblo and then chopped out the top of the mortar linking the wall stones. We thus were able rapidly to reveal *all* the fallen walls. By noting the strike and dip of coherent wall-stone sets in relation to the top of wall remnants, we were able to show the order of wall collapse and its direction. Furthermore, it was also possible to very accurately document original wall heights for each room space, to define doorway heights, and even to identify whole doorways that were part of a fallen wall. Once recorded, all the wall-fall was quickly and efficiently removed, leaving the cells of the room spaces as depositional units that could be dug in quadrants, leaving exposures to draw cross-sectional profiles. Once the uppermost floor was reached, slit trenches were dug so that the sequence of micro-floor-strata could be defined and stripped, one by one.

Based on this experience, and building on the opportunity to analyze the data recovered by others from another site in the Hay Hollow Valley, the Joint site (Wilcox 1975), I have proposed a formal concept of a "living surface" and a terminology for discussing architecture that is consistent with David Clarke's (1973) general notions of archaeological theory (Wilcox 1982, 1995; Wilcox and Shenk 1977; Wilcox et al. 1981:147–156). The central importance of surfaces as provenience categories has also been recognized by Edward Harris (1975, 1979), and his "Harris matrix" provides an excellent graphic method of operationalizing the broader concept of a living surface.

Once we recognize that the physical spaces we can observe in a collapsed building are no longer "rooms," it becomes apparent that new terminology is required. We thus can call the excavation units we design "recovery spaces." Given that the wall remnants that bound a space that was once a room with a roof may have more than one floor surface associated with them, and hence there were, in fact, a sequence of "rooms" in much the same physical space, I have suggested the term "room space" for the set of all such rooms. In this way we can reserve the term "room" for those behaviorally meaningful space-times where human behavior occurred during a certain interval (the interval during which a particular floor surface was in use). Sometimes recovery spaces defined by a set of wall remnants contain deposits from the collapse of multiple stories. As they therefore contain deposits from more than one room space, I suggest that we call them "room tiers" (see Wilcox and Shenk 1977).

The Social Logic of Space

Space is a universal of human experience. All of us have some notions about it and how our actions structure or configure it to suit our purposes. Spatial concepts have long been central to the way southwestern archaeologists have chosen to describe the archaeological record. T. Mitchell Prudden's (1903) definition of a "unit-type" pueblo as an ordered set composed of a small, surface-masonry room block, a circular ("kiva") depression, and a midden arranged north to south is a classic example (Lipe and Hegmon 1989). So, too, are Rohn's (1965) and Dean's (1969) delineations of household domains in cliff dwellings based on doorway-access patterns, and the definition of a Hohokam "courtyard group" (Wilcox et al. 1981; Wilcox 1991a). The site structure of southwestern settlements and the internal structure of buildings have been the focus of intensive study since at least the 1950s (Chang 1958; see also Steward 1938). And we have learned a lot in these ways. Fortunately, new, more formal and mathematical methods of spatial analysis are now available that should significantly increase the ability of archaeologists everywhere to learn more about the social meanings of the way humans deploy themselves in space and how they structure it to suit the modes of their behavior.

Two such methods are discussed here. The first is called graph theory (Harary 1969). "A graph is a structure consisting of points [or nodes] joined by lines" (Hage and Harary 1983:3). An excellent introduction to anthropological and archaeological uses of the mathematics of graph theory is provided by Per Hage and Frank Harary (1983) in their *Structural Models in Anthropology.* Graphs are an abstract way of displaying relationships between objects. "Graph theory is a branch of finite mathematics that is both topological and combinatorial in nature. Because it is essentially the study of relations, graph theory is eminently suited to the description and analysis of a wide range of structures that constitute a significant part of the subject matter of anthropology, as well as of the social sciences generally" (Hage and Harary 1983:2). As in other branches of mathematics, a description of graph theory begins with a series of definitions and builds more and more elaborate concepts, and hence a more and more involved terminology, as the discussion proceeds. As I assume most of this argot is unfamiliar to most southwestern archaeologists, and still is only partially understood by me, I refrain from trying here to introduce more than the most basic of its methods or terminology. Graphs of Casas Grandes architecture are presented below and the potentialities for their rigorous analysis using graph theory are discussed.

Quite a different language is developed by Hillier and Hanson (1984) to express a theory of "space syntax" or what they call "the social logic of space." At issue is the relation between space and social life, and they develop approaches to both the outdoor space of settlement layouts and the interior space of buildings. The first they call alpha analysis and the latter gamma analysis. Both use aspects of graph theory as a descriptive calculus. In contrast to the way many archaeological studies of site structure proceed, which is by looking for patterning in the internal structure of settlements, Hillier and Hanson (1984) start from the perspective of the interaction between its inhabitants and strangers outside the settlement. It is the nature of this interaction, they argue, that accounts for significant patterns of settlement layout and differences of layout from one society to another. Similarly, in gamma analysis they argue that the internal layout of buildings results in many respects from the nature of the interaction between residents and visitors. The morphology of settlements and buildings, at different systemic levels, structures the encounter probabilities between inhabitants and strangers or visitors. These arguments are stimulating and merit careful consideration by archaeologists, who can bring a wealth of empirical data to the table for further testing.

What archaeologists have more often called "access relations," Hillier and Hanson (1984) call "permeability" (see also Hage and Harary 1983:31–33; Hammond 1972). In gamma analysis, which is applied in a limited way below to analyze buildings at Casas Grandes, two spaces "a" and "b" are

> symmetric if a is to b as b is to a with respect to c, meaning that neither a nor b control permeability to each other; asymmetric if a is not to b as b is to a, in the sense that *one controls permeability to the other* from some third space c; distributed if there is more than one independent route from a to b including one passing through a third space c (i. e., if a space has more than one locus of control with respect to another); and nondistributed if there is some space c, through which any route from a to b must pass. (Hillier and Hanson 1984:148; emphasis added; see Figure 7.1).

The "carrier," in gamma analysis, is the space outside the building under consideration; it is represented as a circle with a cross (Hillier and Hanson 1984:148). With these concepts in mind let us move on without further delay to their application to a preliminary analysis of access relations (permeability) at the site of Casas Grandes, Chihuahua.

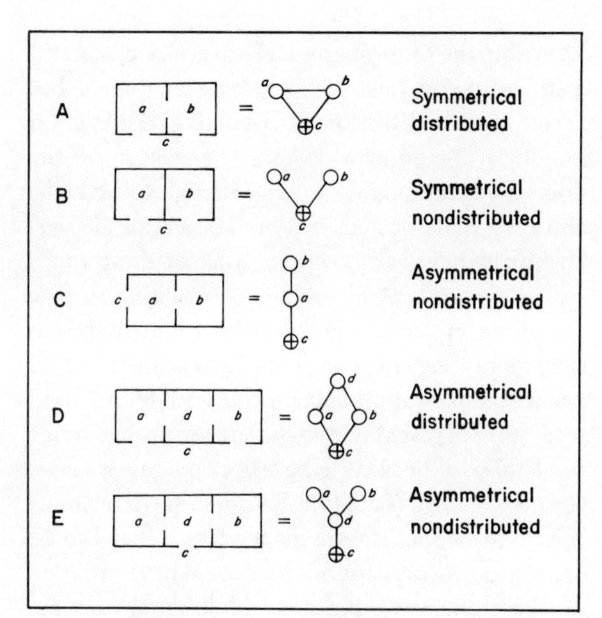

Figure 7.1 (Left). Basic graph theory concepts (after Hillier and Hanson 1984:148–149).

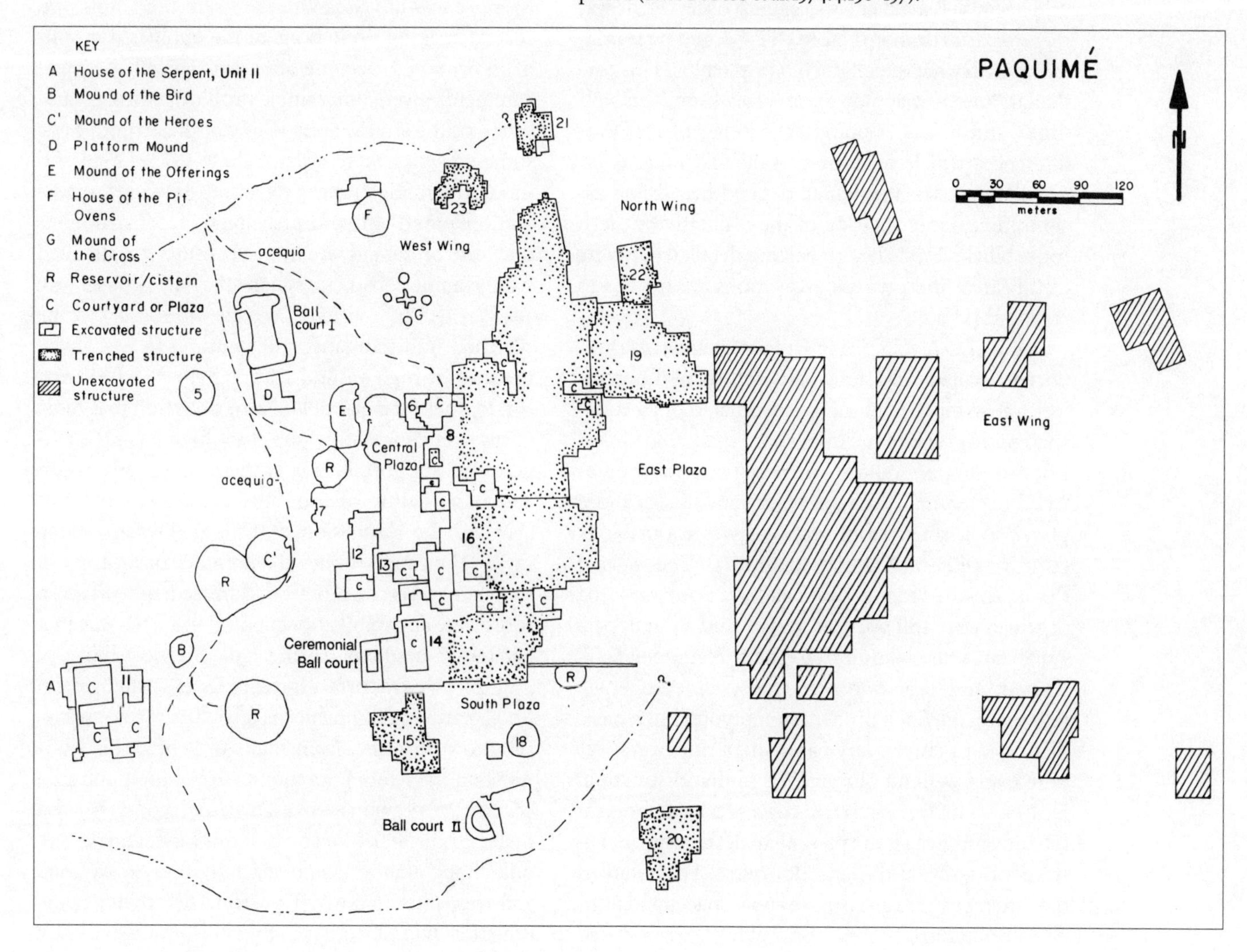

Figure 7.2 (Below). The Casas Grandes site in the Medio period (after Di Peso et al. 1974:4:196–197).

Casas Grandes Architecture

Casas Grandes (Paquimé) is one of the largest nucleated pueblo-like sites in the North American Southwest. Like contemporaneous Pueblo IV pueblos in the Rio Grande and the southern Colorado Plateau, it consists of multistory room blocks and large open plazas. Di Peso's excavations were concentrated on the western side of the site, where the majority of ceremonial mounds and ball courts are located. In his general map of the site (Figure 7.2) he postulates a series of room blocks east of the main ruin whose overall layout, he implies, defined a large plaza. If true, this would make the site seem even more like a Pueblo IV pueblo. However, as I have discussed elsewhere (Wilcox 1996), Bandelier's (1892; Burrus 1969) map of Casas Grandes does not show such a plaza. This is odd because Bandelier was a superb observer, he was there 75 years or more before Di Peso, and he was familiar with what we call Pueblo IV pueblos. This particular "plaza" may not exist (cf. Lekson, this volume), and if it does not, certain other of Di Peso's inferences will have to be reevaluated, such as his population estimates, which depend heavily on assumptions about the size of these putative eastern room blocks. Fresh field research, a detailed mapping of this area, and perhaps excavations are needed to resolve this issue.

Most of two volumes of Di Peso et al.'s (1974) report is devoted to a detailed description of the architectural sample. Out of an estimated 942 room spaces, only 157 ground-floor room spaces, 86 upper-story room spaces, and 16 enclosed plazas were excavated in the main ruin, and 39 room spaces and 4 plazas in a single-story "ranch-style" room block (Unit 11; Di Peso et al. 1974:4:201, 203). The walls of these excavated room spaces had 472 doorways, 402 of which were still open, 36 sealed, and 34 in upper-story contexts. Within the basic rectangular, T-shaped, and oval doorway types, Di Peso et al. (1974:4:233) defined numerous subtypes, but a basic distinction between large and small doorways was noted, and we limit our analysis to that distinction. Di Peso et al. (1974:4:232) recognized an important relationship (which the present analysis confirms) in the distribution of the large doorways: They marked the difference between private room spaces and public or ceremonial spaces "and were often associated with worn trails in hallways, colonnades, and plazas."

Within the room spaces Di Peso et al. (1974:4:238) distinguished a class of 201 subspaces that he believed were bed platforms. Averaging 2.01–2.87 m long by 1.58–1.90 m wide, and 0.77–1.07 m off the floor, they certainly were large enough to be beds, and they were located in room corners or alcoves. Strikingly, however, nowhere in all of these room spaces does Di Peso identify specialized storage spaces, except to designate a few room spaces as storerooms (e.g., for shell). At Chaco Canyon, where a few examples of these platforms were found, Judd (1964:29) suggested that they were for storage, and I think this is quite likely to have been the case at Casas Grandes as well. If artifact distributions in relationship to these spaces were mapped, or if they can be reconstructed, perhaps this idea could be tested.

The moment we begin to think about how the room spaces at Casas Grandes were used, however, several striking limitations in the published corpus of information become apparent. For all the measurements given, not a single profile drawing is published of the stratigraphy in any of these room tiers, some of which were at least three stories high. Although helpful, the few elevation drawings, cross-sections, and three-dimensional reconstructions that are presented are no substitute for detailed stratigraphic profiles. When Bartlett (1965:2:348, 364–365 [1854]) visited the site in the 1850s, he sketched wall remnants still standing 30 feet above the 20-foot-high mound. Although there is little reason to doubt the claim, Di Peso's assertion that most of his sample was only one story high has little evidence to support it, nor is there much discussion about the nature of roof surfaces as activity areas (but see the discussion of Unit 11, Di Peso et al. 1974:5). Questions about the presence or location of roof hatchways can rarely be addressed; the collapsed roofs were apparently not exposed in such a way that hatchways could be delineated. The possibility of multiple floor surfaces, replastering, changes in floor-feature relationships is also difficult or impossible to determine. Even maps of artifact distributions on the "floors" are not a part of the published corpus. In previous work Di Peso (1953, 1956) did make exquisite field records of this kind, and we can only hope that they do exist in the excavation's archives, thus making it possible to pursue many other behavioral studies of this still-impressive body of data. For now, what is possible is to examine the relationship of room spaces to one another but not of rooms to one another.

The occupation of Casas Grandes encompasses what Di Peso called the Medio period. The excavated room blocks were not all built at once, however, and Di Peso et al. (1974:4, 1974:5) divide them into a series of units that they thought were socially or ceremonially discrete. The walls of these room blocks they classified into a sequence of temporal phases and subphases. Although their attempt to calibrate this phase sequence with the Christian calendar has not withstood critical testing, the *architectural* sequence has yet to be critically evaluated.

The basic issue with Di Peso's calibration of the phase sequence was whether only few rings were missing from the tree-ring-dated specimens or many (Wilcox and Shenk 1977:65). Fortunately, many of those specimens are wood, which means that the relationship of heartwood and sapwood can be reexamined. When this was done, it was found that most sapwood rings were missing (Dean and Ravesloot 1993). By retrodiction from modern trees of appropriate size in the area, it has also been possible to estimate a correction factor for the tree-ring dates, giving a better approximation of construction dates at Casas Grandes (Dean and Ravesloot 1993). Accordingly, the Medio period can now be bracketed between A.D. 1200 and 1500, with the height of the occupation falling in the late 1300s and early 1400s (Dean and Ravesloot 1993; Wilcox 1994). These findings fit the ceramic cross-dating evidence far better than Di Peso's failed chronology (Wilcox and Shenk 1977:67–68; Carlson 1982b; Wilcox 1986a).

Access Graphs of Selected Casas Grandes Housing Units

A reassessment of the architectural sequence at Casas Grandes is beyond the scope of this chapter. In what follows I exclude the walls Di Peso et al. (1974:4, 1974:5) classified into the Diablo phase, when the original structure of these buildings was considerably modified. For Unit 11, a Buena Fé phase "ranch-style" room block that was totally excavated, it is possible to consider both an early and a late graph of this building. Units 14, 12, 13, 16, 8, and 6 form a contiguous series for which a single graph is generated from the walls classified as Buena Fé or Paquimé phase. My assumption is that these room spaces were absolutely contemporaneous for at least some interval of their use lives.

Only the first story of the contiguous room blocks is considered in the graphs, although the stairwells to the second story are indicated. The two second-story room spaces in Unit 11 are included in the graphs. A relatively small number of the doorways were blocked, or originally solid walls were pierced to form a doorway. As I have no way in most cases to decide how these events are temporally related to one another, I show all open doorways in the graphs as open circles. The blocked doors, as well as walls that were later pierced, are shown as solid circles. The rooms are shown as small squares and the plazas as larger squares. Access relations are shown as lines connecting the squares and circles. As some of the room spaces were markedly long and narrow, and some of these Di Peso et al. (1974:4, 1974:5) regarded as hallways, I show such room spaces as narrow rectangles in the graphs. Some unroofed areas that are long and narrow and appear also to have acted as hallways or alleys are also shown as narrow rectangles.

Unit 11

The initial access graph of Unit 11 (Figure 7.3) is drawn to scale as an overlay of Di Peso et al.'s (1974:5: 476) Figure 1-5. What Di Peso et al. (1974:4:238–240) regarded as "bed platforms," and I suggest were storage alcoves, are shown as "Bs" in the graph. The X, Y, and Z spaces are unroofed, hallway-like spaces that stand between one plaza and another. They also could be called alcoves that are the arm of an L off a plaza. Room space 18-19, when it was a single colonnaded space, is a roofed example of this type of alcove.

Starting with Figure 7.3, a "justified gamma map" (Hillier and Hanson 1984:149) can be constructed for both the early and late Buena Fé phases (Figures 7.4 and 7.5). The basic idea in a justified graph is that the doorways can be arranged in successive "steps" away from the carrier, which defines their "depth" from the carrier. Thus, in Figure 7.4 the depth of room space 38B is seven, whereas Plaza 4-11's depth is only two. Transforming the graph of Figure 7.3 into these two justified graphs clarifies the question of contemporaneous doorway access and simplifies the analysis of significant properties of the graphs.

The "degree" of a node is the number of lines

Figure 7.3 (Right). General access graph, Unit 11, Casas Grandes, Chihuahua.

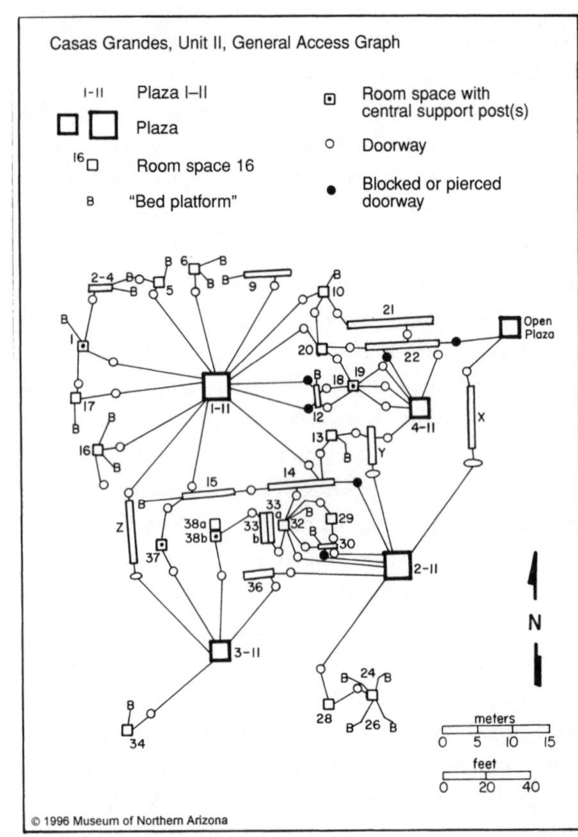

Figure 7.4 (Bottom left). Justified gamma graph, Unit 11, Casas Grandes, early Buena Fé phase.

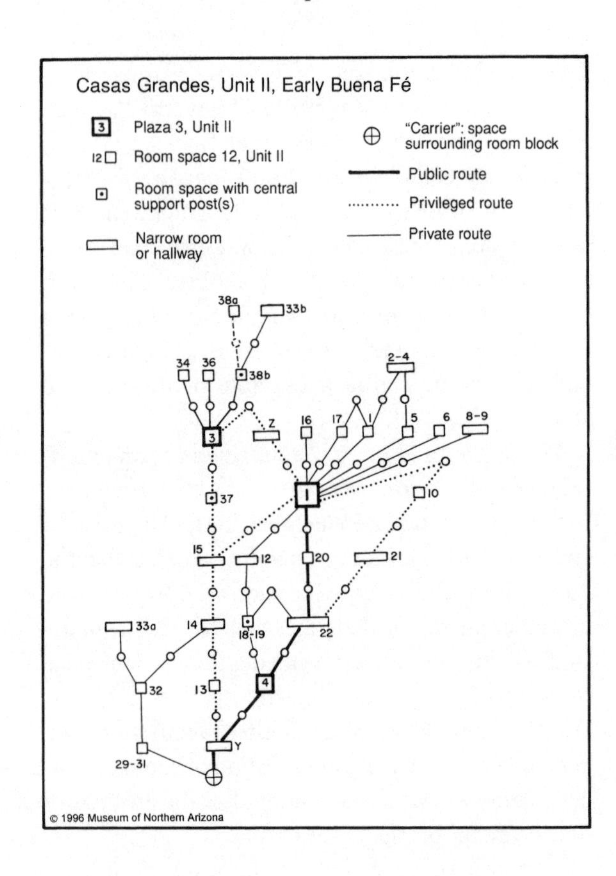

Figure 7.5 (Bottom right). Justified gamma graph, Unit 11, Casas Grandes, late Buena Fé phase.

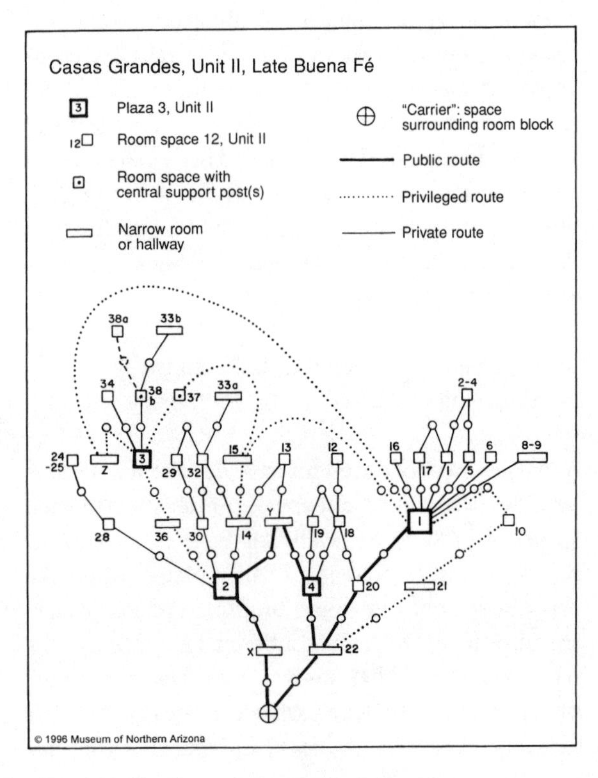

incident to it. In Figure 7.4 the space with the largest degree is Plaza 1, whose degree is eleven. The degree of room space 34 is one. A "trail" in a graph is any sequence of alternating lines and nodes, beginning and ending with nodes. A trail with all the nodes distinct is called a "path." A walk with distinct lines and nodes, whose first and last nodes are the same, is called a "cycle" (Hage and Harary 1983:17) or a "ring" (Hillier and Hanson 1984). Thus, in Figure 7.4 the sequence from room spaces X-13-14-15-Plaza 1-12-(18-19)-Plaza 4 to X is a cycle, and many similar walks are apparent in this graph. The spaces on cycles are distributed. In contrast, room space 34 is not on any cycle, and in Hillier and Hanson's (1984) terms it is nondistributed. It sticks off the rest of the graph like the branch of a tree. "In most, but by no means all cases, . . . the distributed system is the set of spaces through which the visitor, subject to more or less control, may pass; while the nondistributed system, (that is, the set of trees connected to each other only through the distributed system) is the domain of the inhabitants, with stronger sanctions against penetration by the visitor" (Hillier and Hanson 1984:167).

The most unique spaces in Figure 7.4 are 38B and 33B, which were built in a large pit dug into the ground, with a second story above them. Room space 38B, with a floor area of 75 sq m, had a pair of central roof supports and a wide-ramp entryway: It is reminiscent of a Mogollon great kiva, and, indeed, although they do not draw this analogy, Di Peso et al. (1974:5:475) do interpret it as the principal ceremonial room of Unit 11. These two room spaces are nondistributed, and access is apparently controlled by Plaza 3, which is on two cycles, one connected directly to Plaza 1 via space Z and one connected both to Plaza 1 and to the Carrier via room space 37. The latter had a central roof support and two postholes that suggested to Di Peso et al. (1974:5:499) a ladder to the roof.

No connections to 38A are indicated in the data, but in Figure 7.4 a roof hatch from 38B is suggested here. Of greater interest is the question whether there was a roof hatch in 33B connecting it to 33A, and hence to the Carrier via room spaces 32 and 29-31. If there was such a hatch, the structure of the graph would be very different than shown in Figure 7.4. Regrettably, there is no way from current data to evaluate this possibility.

A second space of great interest is room space 18-19, with a floor area of 62 sq m, which was colonnaded and opened off of Plaza 4, being connected to Plaza 1 by an "antechamber," room space 12. From the Carrier one could access Plaza 4 directly via space X, or via a roundabout route through Plaza 1 and then through either room spaces 12 and 18-19 or 20 and 22. It thus appears that room space 18-19 can be interpreted as a ceremonial space that mediated between visitors, who could be ushered into Plaza 4, and the occupants of Unit 11, who could meet the visitors by moving from Plaza 1 via the room space 12 antechamber or via the hallways, room spaces 20 and 22.

Which space in Unit 11 is the most central, the one most readily accessed from any other space? Graph theory provides a mathematical way to answer this question. In the first place the degree of a node is a measure of its communication activity (Hage and Harary 1983:31). The "eccentricity" of a node is the maximum distance between it and any other. The center of a graph is thus the set of nodes with minimum eccentricity. In Figure 7.4, as we have seen, Plaza 1, with degree eleven, has the greatest claim to the largest communication activity. Its eccentricity is four relative to all other spaces in Unit 11 and five if the Carrier is included. This is the smallest eccentricity of any node in Figure 7.4. Its "communication efficiency" vis-à-vis all other spaces in Unit 11 thus appears to be the highest.

A third graph-theoretic measure of centrality is called "betweenness." Starting with the idea of the shortest path ("geodesic") between any two nodes, betweenness is defined as the frequency of occurrence of each node on the geodesics between all pairs of other nodes (Hage and Harary 1983:33). It is a measure of the potential for control of communication. In Figure 7.4 Plaza 1, again, apparently has the highest betweenness value.

The three plazas of Unit 11 during the early Buena Fé phase are thus found to have distinct functions. Plaza 4 appears to be a reception area that mediates between visitors and occupants, being the staging area for ceremonies conducted in room space 18-19. Plaza 1 is the center of domestic life within the unit. Plaza 3 is a staging area for occupants of the unit to attend private ceremonies held in room space 38B. Connecting Plaza 1 to Plaza 4 are two room spaces, 20 and 22, which have a worn pathway in the floor, testifying to the frequency with which this route was used. Accordingly, in Figure 7.4 a heavy line marks what we may infer was a "public route" from the Carrier to plazas 4 and 1.

Associated with Plaza 3 is room space 37, which has its own access route to the Carrier independent of Plaza 1. Only two doorways away from room space 38B, room space 37 appears to have been the locus of a special group or set of activities. Its possible ladder to the roof might also indicate a secret access to 38B, if there was a hatchway in the roofs of both 38A and 38B. Because of its unique role and position in the graph, in Figure 7.4 a "privileged route" is shown connecting the Carrier to Plaza 3 via room space 37. Similarly "privileged routes" bypass the public route to Plaza 1, one via hallway 15 and another via hallway 21 and room space 10. There is also a "privileged route" connecting Plazas 1 and 3 via space Z.

Two other room-space sets stand out in Figure 7.4 as having special properties. The first is 33A, 32, and 29-31. They are the most isolated from the rest of the unit and are among the farthest spaces from Plaza 1. Their role, however, remains unclear. The second set consists of room spaces 1 and 17, 5 and 2-4. The latter is a small hallway that connects 1 and 5, whereas a doorway directly links 1 and 17. Of all the room spaces around Plaza 1, therefore, room space 1 comes into focus as the most central and the least controlled by the Plaza. Perhaps we can hazard to suggest that room space 1 was the domain of the unit's leading family. Alternatively, room space 37 might have had that role.

Later during the Buena Fé phase, doorways were punched through a series of walls, and the structure of Unit 11's access relationships was changed significantly (Figure 7.5). Correlated with these changes is the secularization of the ceremonial spaces, 38B and 18-19 (Di Peso et al. 1974:5:483, 510–514). Colonnades in the latter were walled up, a "bed platform" (space 11) was added to the antechamber (room space 12), and the doorways to Plaza 1 were blocked. Adjacent to the Carrier, Plaza 2 was added, with eccentricity five, the same as Plaza 1. Its degree (six) is, however, less than that for Plaza 1 (ten). Public, privileged, and private routes are still shown, and it is interesting to note that Plaza 4 is as close to Plaza 2 as is Plaza 3 and is closer to it than is Plaza 1. Each of the plazas has what appear to be sets of domestic space associated with them, and in plazas 1 and 3 a set of macaw nesting boxes were built along one wall.[1] In general it appears that the social solidarity of groups occupying Unit 11, which had formerly been quite strong, became marked by a sharp contrast between internal and external social relations and was weakened significantly, having no internal ceremonial focus.[2] Each of the four plaza groups has a more or less equal relation to the Carrier and hence to the rest of the Casas Grandes community. Perhaps it was during the late Buena Fé phase that the outside, public ceremonial facilities became critically important as the locus of *community* solidarity. One wonders, for example, if the nearby serpent mound was built in the *late* Buena Fé phase (cf. Di Peso et al. 1974:5:478).

Units 14, 12, 13, 16, 8, and 6

Figure 7.6 presents an initial graph of the set of contiguous units on the west side of the great mound at Paquimé. Di Peso et al. (1974:4, 1974:5) say that most room tiers in these units are single story, but two or more stories are present along their east side, where a series of formal stairways mark points of access to them. Figure 7.6 is a complex graph whose full interpretation is beyond the scope of this discussion. Any attempt at interpretation should take into account the warning provided by Hillier and Hanson (1984: 163): "The larger buildings become, and the more removed from intuitive experience, the more hazardous becomes the use of the abstract model to try to construct a sociological picture of a particular type of building." Nevertheless, graph theory and Hillier and Hanson's (1984) abstract model of the social logic of space are tools that can produce a mathematical and replicable basis for interpretation that can move us far beyond what intuition alone affords us. Only a few suggestions for such research can be made here.

Several of the basic structural features of the Figure 7.6 graph can be seen more clearly by considering a subgraph, Figure 7.7. This subset of the elements from Figure 7.6 includes all the plazas; the linkages between the plazas, which are marked by footpaths or hallways; stairways; all the large doors (Di Peso et al.'s [1974:4:232–233] types 1C and 2B); and the two shell storerooms. No room spaces (except several of the hallways) with "bed platforms" are included.

Several conclusions can be drawn from this graph. First, the connection of what Di Peso et al. (1974:4) called the Central Plaza to plazas in units 13, 14, and 16 (in two nested cycles) is apparent. The unenclosed "South Plaza" (carrier) is connected to the

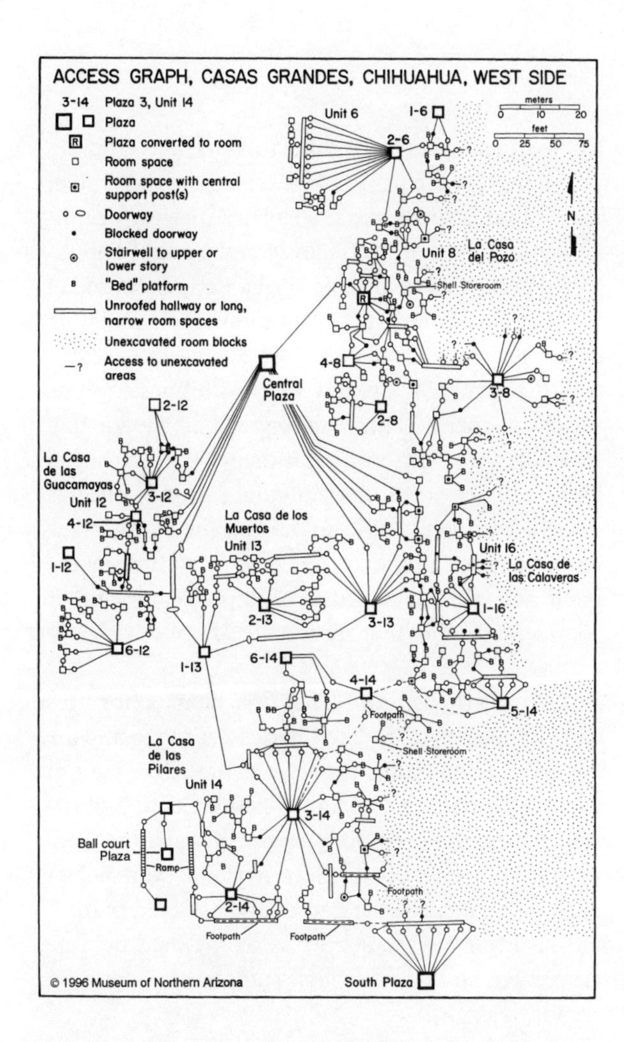

Figure 7.6. General access graph, Units 14, 12, 13, 16, 8, and 6, Casas Grandes, Chihuahua.

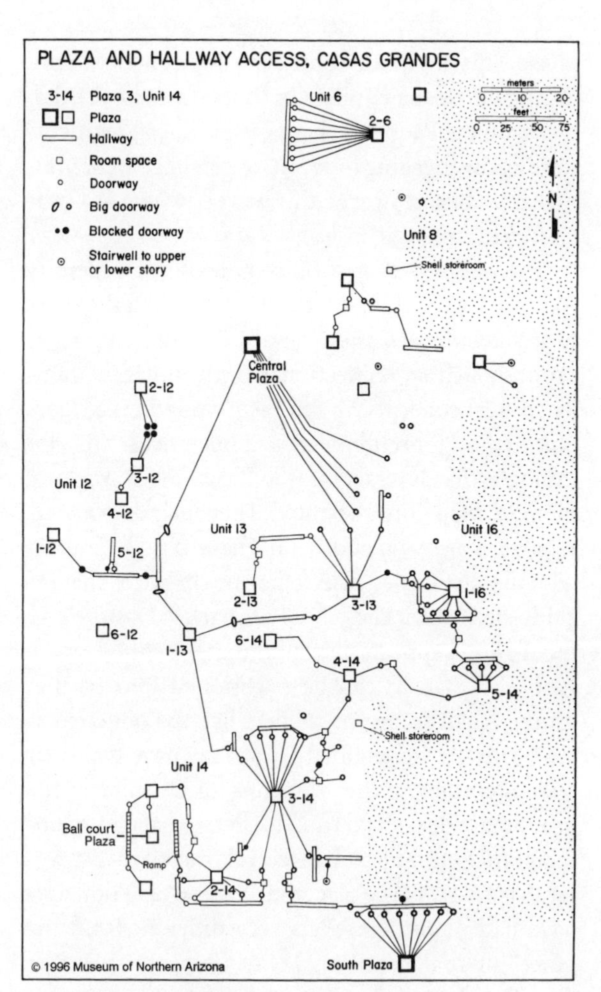

Figure 7.7. Subgraph of Units 14, 12, 13, 16, 8, and 6, Casas Grandes, showing plazas, hallways, trails, and large doorways.

Central Plaza by a series of hallways and plazas through a series of large doorways. Second, the disjunction of Units 6 and 8 from the rest of the graph is readily apparent, as is the disjunction of both shell storerooms from the main access paths and cycles among the plazas for all of these units. Third, two strikingly different paths provide access to the ceremonial ball court in Unit 14, but both of them begin from enclosed Plaza 3-14. One appears to be a semipublic or "privileged" route via Plaza 2-14 or a hallway that bypasses this plaza, leading out to the ramp on the east side of the ball court. The second also goes through Plaza 2-14 but then proceeds along a "private" route, exiting through a large doorway to a small plaza or courtyard at the north end of the ball court and continuing to the west ramp and to a small plaza or courtyard at the south end of the ball court.

In sharp contrast to the I-shaped courts at the north and south ends of Casas Grandes, where access appears to be directly from the carrier, the ceremonial ball court is deeply embedded on the interior of the main Paquimé building, and both privileged and private access to it is evident. A close association between the domestic space in the southwestern quadrant of Unit 14 (southwest of Plaza 3-14) and the ceremonial ball court is indicated. As the access of the players to the playing field was presumably attained via the small plaza or courtyard just north of it, it may be that the players actually lived in the southwest part of Unit 14. Alternatively, groups responsible for the care and maintenance of the ball court may have lived there.

Di Peso et al. (1974:5:613) indicate that the ceremonial ball court was not built until late in the Paquimé phase. This implies, in contrast to the sequence found during the Buena Fé phase in Unit 11 (see above), that by late in the Paquimé phase certain social segments were again engaging in secret, or privileged, ceremonial activities. How true this was elsewhere at Casas Grandes remains to be learned.

This raises the question of how one can identify the domains of discrete social segments in the mass of architecture at Casas Grandes. Di Peso et al. (1974) propose such a classification in their "unit" and "family cluster" concepts. Graph theory provides a rigorous method for rethinking such inferences. Note, for example, that several plazas in the connected part of Figure 7.7 are nondistributed. They include plazas 1-12, 5-12, 2-13, 2-14, and 6-14. These plazas contrast with the distributed plazas that are on cycles that include the Central Plaza. Looking back at Figure 7.6 in this light, it appears that the "units" defined by Di Peso et al. (1974) can be partitioned into smaller groupings of room spaces that, like the one associated with the Ceremonial Plaza, may have had their own identities as the domains of distinct social groupings. Plazas "external" to such social-group domains include the South Plaza, Central Plaza, Plaza 3-14, Plaza 1-13, Plaza 3-13, and Plaza 4-14. They may have had public functions very different from the other "internal" (domestic) plazas. Linkages between these "public" plazas and the "domestic" ones are often mediated by a hallway or only one or two doorways (see Figure 7.6). Further analysis of these relationships is needed.

Conclusion

The excavations of the architecture of Casas Grandes (Paquimé) have been published in more detail than most other large sites in the North American Southwest. It is likely that an equally large corpus of unpublished archival data on this site can also be found at the Amerind Foundation, Dragoon, AZ. The nature of the exposure strategies used during the excavations has probably limited the possibilities of some forms of analysis, but this paper has shown that methods derived from graph theory and the social logic of space create the potential for fresh insights into the sociology of this important site. More intensive analyses along the same lines may further expand scientific knowledge of this site and other southwestern sites that are equally complex.

ACKNOWLEDGMENTS. The first thanks for this chapter must go to the late Charles C. Di Peso and the Amerind Foundation for their remarkable work at Casas Grandes. I also want to thank Curtis Schaafsma for inviting me to prepare this chapter. Jodi Griffith, Museum of Northern Arizona Exhibits Department, prepared the figures and endured numerous revisions as the subtleties of the data became clearer. For any errors or faulty judgment, I alone am responsible.

Notes

1. Di Peso et al. (1974:5:475) claim that the macaw pens in Plaza 3 replaced those in Plaza 1; however, no evidence to support this inference is given, and I here adopt a different position.

2. Di Peso et al. (1974:5:475) suggest that room space 38B continued to be a ceremonial room into the late Buena Fé phase, being secularized at a later period toward the end of the phase. On the basis of the temporal data available, this is possible, but so, too, is the position adopted here.

III

The Outer Sphere

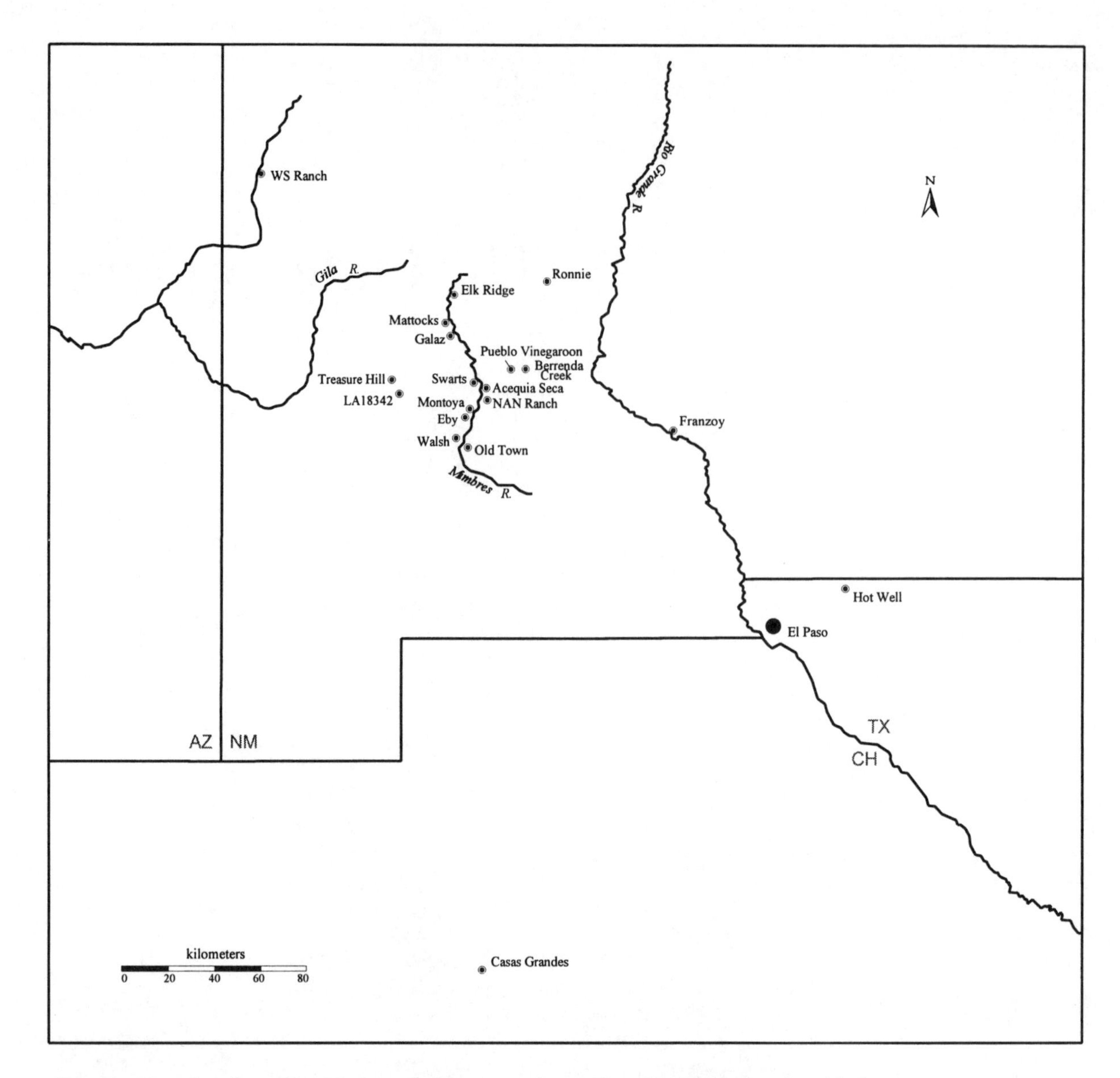

Figure 8.1. Map of southwest New Mexico and adjacent area showing locations of sites mentioned in the text.

8

The Black Mountain Phase in the Mimbres Area

Darrell G. Creel

In the archaeology of southwest New Mexico, there is perhaps no issue with such divergent views as the transition from Classic Mimbres to Black Mountain phase around A.D. 1130 to 1150 and the role played in that transition by Casas Grandes. In very general terms, some archaeologists believe that the Mimbres Mogollon occupation of the area ceased sometime after A.D. 1130 with fairly abrupt abandonment and was followed by reoccupation some years later by a population that may or may not have included some Mimbreños. Indeed, some archaeologists believe that the rise of Casas Grandes was an important factor in the so-called collapse of the Mimbres system. Other archaeologists are more inclined to interpret the evidence as indicating continuous Mimbres occupation of the region as a whole but with notable changes in material culture and settlement pattern. Regardless of the specific interpretation for transition advocated, all have perceived elements of material culture, especially ceramics and coursed-adobe architecture, in the Black Mountain phase potentially attributable to influence from developments in the Casas Grandes area.

Recent excavations at the Old Town site on the lower Mimbres River (Figure 8.1) have yielded a modest amount of new data on the late Classic and Black Mountain phases, including evidence relevant to the transition between them. As discussed below, on the basis of these data and evidence from other sites, I submit that some of the material culture changes long considered to have occurred in the earlier portion of the Black Mountain phase actually occurred late in the Mimbres Classic and can be attributed in part to increased interaction with populations to the east, north, and northwest, as well as with people to the south in Chihuahua.

Given the disparate views on the Classic–Black Mountain transition, we must first determine what happened and when before we can explain the cultural changes that occurred late in the Mogollon occupation of southwest New Mexico. More specifically, the changes occurring in the first few decades of the twelfth century are directly relevant to understanding the Black Mountain phase and the possible early influence of Casas Grandes, and yet they are the subject of much disagreement. Thus, I begin with a brief review of the Mimbres Classic and Black Mountain phases, with particular attention to criteria used by archaeologists to assign remains to one or the other.

The Mimbres Classic and Black Mountain Phases

Early in the history of archaeological investigations in southwest New Mexico, it was recognized that some sites possessed characteristics labeled as Mimbres, that others had attributes like those of Casas Grandes, and that still others had a combination of the two. For many decades the nature of these differences was of comparatively little interest to researchers because the driving concern was acquisition of the much-sought-after Mimbres Black-on-white and polychrome pottery. Indeed, it was not until the investigations of the Mimbres Foundation in the 1970s that substantial attention was devoted to developments after what was generally thought to be the end of the Mimbres occupation of southwest New Mexico.

Based on extensive review of previous investigations in the region and on their own survey and excavation, Mimbres Foundation researchers proposed a phase sequence that, for the first time, dealt at some length with occupation after about A.D. 1130 (e.g., Anyon and LeBlanc 1984; LeBlanc 1977, 1983; Ravesloot 1979). These remains, distinguished most notably by adobe pueblos and a new suite of ceramic types, were assigned to the Black Mountain phase (ca. A.D. 1130 or 1150–1300), newly designated to distinguish it from the partially contemporaneous and somewhat different Animas phase in extreme southwest New Mexico and adjacent Arizona and Chihuahua. Acknowledging traits suggesting population continuity (i.e., burial practices), LeBlanc (1989:192) nonetheless has argued that the Black Mountain phase represents a cultural break from the preceding Mimbres sequence following the collapse of the Classic social system (see also Shafer 1996). Moreover, LeBlanc suggested that the marked changes in material culture from the Mimbres Classic to the Black Mountain phase reflect the rise of a Casas Grandes interaction sphere and its incorporation of the Mimbres area.

To some extent differences of opinion on the Classic–Black Mountain transition issue hinge on the criteria used to distinguish one phase from the other. Moreover, this distinction has significant implications for assessing the timing and nature of interaction between Mimbres area populations and Casas Grandes. First and foremost is the occurrence of El Paso Brown Ware (bichrome and early polychrome), Chupadero Black-on-white, Playas Red series, White Mountain Red Ware, and some late Reserve-area ceramic types that are traditionally viewed as indicators of a Black Mountain phase component in the Mimbres area. In the Mimbres drainage itself, coursed-adobe architecture and round hearths, as opposed to Classic phase rectangular hearths and masonry construction, are also considered among the most important new material culture traits of the Black Mountain phase when they occur with the supposedly non-Mimbres ceramics noted above. The presence of these pottery types on Classic Mimbres sites has for the most part been interpreted as indicating a reoccupation at the beginning of the Black Mountain phase (the immediate Postclassic of Anyon and LeBlanc 1984).

In fact, some of the key traits used to distinguish the Black Mountain phase from the preceding Classic occur in what are arguably late Classic contexts at numerous sites. It is the recent finding of such occurrences by the Mimbres Foundation investigations, the Texas A & M University NAN Ranch Project, and the investigations on the east side of the Black Range by Margaret Nelson and Michelle Hegmon, with their solid contextual information, that permit us to understand the significance of similar occurrences found many decades ago and mostly inadequately reported.

As is commonly the case in the Southwest, ceramic assemblages in the Mimbres area have been quite important in phase definition and assignment and are particularly pertinent in regard to the Black Mountain phase and other nearby contemporaneous complexes. Therefore, it is critical that we acknowledge that there are numerous instances in which the Black Mountain phase pottery types listed previously occur with Classic phase Mimbres Style III Black-on-white, most of them in what would generally be understood as contemporaneous Classic context. A few of the more significant of these are summarized here.

Among the most important is the suite of large storage vessels on the floor of Room 74 at the NAN Ranch Ruin. The careful excavation reported by Shafer (1986:14–18) revealed numerous Mimbres Classic Corrugated jars, at least four Mimbres Style III B/W vessels, one El Paso bichrome jar, and other vessels, all evidently broken when the room burned and its roof collapsed. Like several of the other late

Classic rooms at the site, Room 74 had a round, clay-lined hearth. There are no direct dates on Room 74 itself, but it was added on to Room 84, which was remodeled on more than one occasion, the latest likely being in about A.D. 1128. Exactly when Room 74 was built is unknown, but Shafer (1986:18) estimates it to have been ca. A.D. 1125. Thus, we have contemporaneous use in late Classic context of ceramic types characteristic of both the Classic and Black Mountain phases, with reasonable evidence for dating.

Similar occurrences of Classic and Black Mountain pottery types together have been documented at Ronnie Pueblo on the east side of the Black Range and at the Franzoy site along the Rio Grande valley near Hatch. At the former, 2 Mimbres B/W Style III bowls and a Chupadero B/W jar were found on the floor of Room 2. (This site is not necessarily considered Classic Mimbres by its excavators, nor do they see it as Black Mountain phase, preferring instead to refer to it as Postclassic [Nelson 1993a:29].) At the Franzoy site, 2 Mimbres B/W Style III bowls, 2 Mimbres Corrugated jars, 1 or 2 El Paso bichrome jars, and 2–3 early El Paso Polychrome jars occurred on the floor of a room that had been partially destroyed by bulldozing (O'Laughlin 1985:49).

Black Mountain phase pottery types also have been found in burials in contexts that are in all other regards Classic. One of the more important sites with such contexts is Galaz, although the critical burials were all excavated in the 1920s and have documentation of variable quality. Nonetheless, among the most significant cases is Room 108, a Classic masonry room with two floors, the later (108) being ca. 40 cm above the earlier 108A floor (Anyon and LeBlanc 1984:Appendix 1). Room 108 had burned, and its roof lay on the upper 108 floor (Anyon and LeBlanc 1984:105). One burial without offerings may have been interred beneath this upper floor. Two Mimbres B/W Style III bowls lay on the lower floor, and beneath the floor were 9 or 10 inhumations and one secondary cremation deposit in a Playas Red Incised jar covered by a smudged indented half-corrugated jar. The inhumations were typical Classic interments, the individuals being placed in the flexed position in small pits with Mimbres Style III vessels, at least some of them over the face and with kill holes. One inhumation had a Style II vessel. With the burned roof material lying on the Room 108 floor, itself some 40 cm above that of the earlier 108A floor, it seems reasonable to infer that the cremation deposit was interred from the same floor (108A) as were the inhumations with Style III pottery; indeed, there is no evidence to the contrary. Thus, it seems further reasonable to infer that Playas Red Incised was in use at Galaz at the same time as Mimbres Style III.

Similarly, at Galaz an El Paso Polychrome bowl was interred with Burial 15-235 beneath, and apparently originating from, the lower of two floors in Room 97A, as were three other inhumations, one of them with a killed Mimbres Style III bowl (Anyon and LeBlanc 1984:Appendices 1, 2, and 3). A Chupadero B/W bowl was over the skull of Burial 15-316 beneath the lower of two floors in Room 117A that, like Rooms 97A and 108, was a typical Classic masonry room. Occurring elsewhere at Galaz in other Classic rooms with only one floor were burials with St. Johns Polychrome (Room SWM-3, Burial 8), St. Johns Black-on-red (Room 99, Burial 15-189), Three Rivers Red-on-terracotta (Room 18A, Burial 2-146), and Playas Red Obliterated Indented Corrugated (Room 83, Burial 15-211), in some cases there also being burials with Mimbres Style III vessels beneath the same floors. These are distinct from the burials associated with an entirely separate, later adobe pueblo overlying part of the Classic architecture.

Similar occurrences were found by the Cosgroves (1932) at the Swarts Ruin but are difficult to evaluate with the information presented in the original report. Only recently has their context been reevaluated by Mara Hill in her thesis research. The latest rooms added to the south room block at Swarts had several contexts relevant to the present discussion. For example, masonry Room 24 had 2 floors, the earlier designated as Room B and ca. 30 cm below the upper (Hill 1997). The hearth on the lower floor was a rectangular slab-lined hearth characteristic of Classic Mimbres habitation rooms, whereas the upper floor had a round, clay-lined hearth. Burial 308 was interred from and beneath the lower floor and had an associated unkilled Chupadero B/W bowl; there were also similar burials accompanied by Mimbres Style III vessels. A St. Johns Polychrome bowl with Burial 171 was associated with the upper floor. Moreover, Rooms 112–121 were added to the room block after Room 24; and several of these late rooms had round, clay-lined hearths and burials with Mimbres Classic phase ceramics.

In addition, several burials were interred beneath,

and originating from, the floor of Room 16 at Swarts; its hearth was round and clay-lined (Hill 1997:Table 37). Most of these were inhumations accompanied by Mimbres Style III vessels, but one was a secondary cremation deposit (Burial 112) in an El Paso Polychrome jar covered by two Tularosa Fillet Rim bowls (Cosgrove and Cosgrove 1932:Plate 18).

The most parsimonious explanation of these cases, taken together, is that many of the so-called Black Mountain phase pottery types occurred in very late (probably post–A.D. 1100) Classic contexts at NAN Ranch, Galaz, and Swarts; but unfortunately, these specific contexts are not tightly dated. It seems likely that the occurrence of such ceramics at other Classic sites was in similar contexts. Indeed, the literature is replete with examples of relatively small numbers of Black Mountain phase type vessels and sherds from virtually all of the major, well-known Classic sites in the Mimbres drainage. In addition, the NAN Ranch Project has recorded at least two small, one- or two-room sites in the Mimbres valley with both Classic and so-called Black Mountain types; and such assemblages are common at sites on the east side of the Black Range, where there is good evidence for contemporaneous usage (see Nelson 1993a, 1993b); in cases such as Ronnie Pueblo, the co-occurrence is in what the excavators consider to be a Postclassic site.

As noted previously, it is not uncommon for late Classic rooms, or the later floors in remodeled rooms, to have round, clay-lined hearths unlike the rectangular, slab-lined hearths characteristic of most of the Classic phase. This is well-documented at NAN Ranch (Shafer 1986, 1987), Swarts (Hill 1997), and Mattocks (Patricia Gilman, personal communication) and has been found as well at Old Town (Creel 1991). Thus, as is the case with El Paso Polychrome, Chupadero B/W, Playas Red, and the other types discussed above, round hearths occur in both late Classic and Black Mountain phase rooms.

Finally, it is worth noting that most researchers have recognized that the marked similarity of mortuary practices in the Classic and Black Mountain phases strongly suggests continuity. Subfloor interment with killed pottery vessels over the face of the deceased is a comparatively rare practice elsewhere in the Southwest but is typical of both Classic and Black Mountain phases. In excavations at the Walsh and Montoya sites, however, cremations constituted a slightly larger proportion of interments than is believed to be the case in the Classic (Ravesloot 1979:50–53), although a reassessment of Creel's (1989) phase assignments for other purported Black Mountain phase cremations might reduce the apparent difference in proportions. It should also be noted that the sample of Black Mountain phase burials from sites without Classic components is fewer than 20 and perhaps should not be taken as representative. Moreover, recent excavations at the NAN Ranch Ruin reveal that our understanding of Classic mortuary variability may well be incomplete and that cremation may have been more common than previously thought (Shafer and Judkins 1997). It may well be, thus, that there was little if any difference in the frequency of cremation between the Classic and Black Mountain phases.

Overall, there is good evidence that some of the well-known material culture traits ascribed to the Black Mountain phase actually occurred first in the later portion of the Mimbres Classic phase and that, with other changes discussed below, they reflect not only the disintegration of the old Mimbres social order but also new patterns of regional interaction (see also Anyon and LeBlanc 1984:143, 316; Nelson and LeBlanc 1986:246 for earlier versions of this interpretation). Within a brief time and with a population shift to lower elevations documented by the Mimbres Foundation survey (Blake et al. 1986; see also Lekson 1992b), the Classic room blocks were completely abandoned, and entirely new, mostly coursed-adobe pueblos were built. It is these adobe pueblos with round hearths and a decorated ceramic assemblage dominated by Playas wares, El Paso Polychrome, and Chupadero B/W that are most usefully designated as Black Mountain phase.

In my opinion there is meaningful evidence for actual population continuity between the Classic and Black Mountain phases (see chapter 17 of this volume), although Hegmon et al. (in press) present data suggesting that there may have been immigration on a limited scale on the east side of the Black Range. Hegmon et al. (in press) have dealt with the situation by noting that we should not equate the term *Postclassic*, a commonly used alternative for Black Mountain phase, with the term *post-Mimbres;* indeed, they do not consider it appropriate to assign their "post-Classic" sites to the Black Mountain phase. Anyon and LeBlanc (1984:143) referred to an "immediate postclassic" occupation at Galaz but were careful to note that it may very well represent continued occupation by at least some of the same inhabitants after the collapse of the Classic Mimbres system (Anyon and LeBlanc 1984:316). Their use of the term "immediate postclassic" is equivalent to "terminal Classic" as used occasionally herein. As will be discussed below, the nature of changes in Mimbres culture during the twelfth century is not fully understood, although recent research in the eastern Mimbres area is yielding significant new data on this issue.

Excavations at the Old Town Site

With the perspective outlined above, the occurrence of Late Classic and Black Mountain phase remains at Old Town (LA 1113) is more readily understandable. Long known as a major Classic site and, unfortunately, the scene of extensive looting for more than a century, Old Town has been the subject of excavations by Texas A & M University (1989, as part of the NAN Ranch Project) and the University of Texas at Austin since 1989. Sponsored in part by the Bureau of Land Management, Las Cruces District, these excavations have revealed architectural and artifactual remains dating from perhaps A.D. 500 to ca. A.D. 1300. Of interest here are the investigations in the Classic pueblo and in an entirely separate Black Mountain phase pueblo (Figure 8.2). Not only has there been excavation of the latter, but we have devoted special effort to dating and to addressing the ceramic differences and continuities between the two phases. In addition, we have conducted a program of chemical sourcing of ceramics in an effort to test the common assumption that the pottery types typical of the Black Mountain phase were imported (a cooperative project with researchers at Texas A & M University, University of Missouri Research Reactor, Arizona State University, University of Oklahoma, Texas Historical Commission, and Fort Bliss).

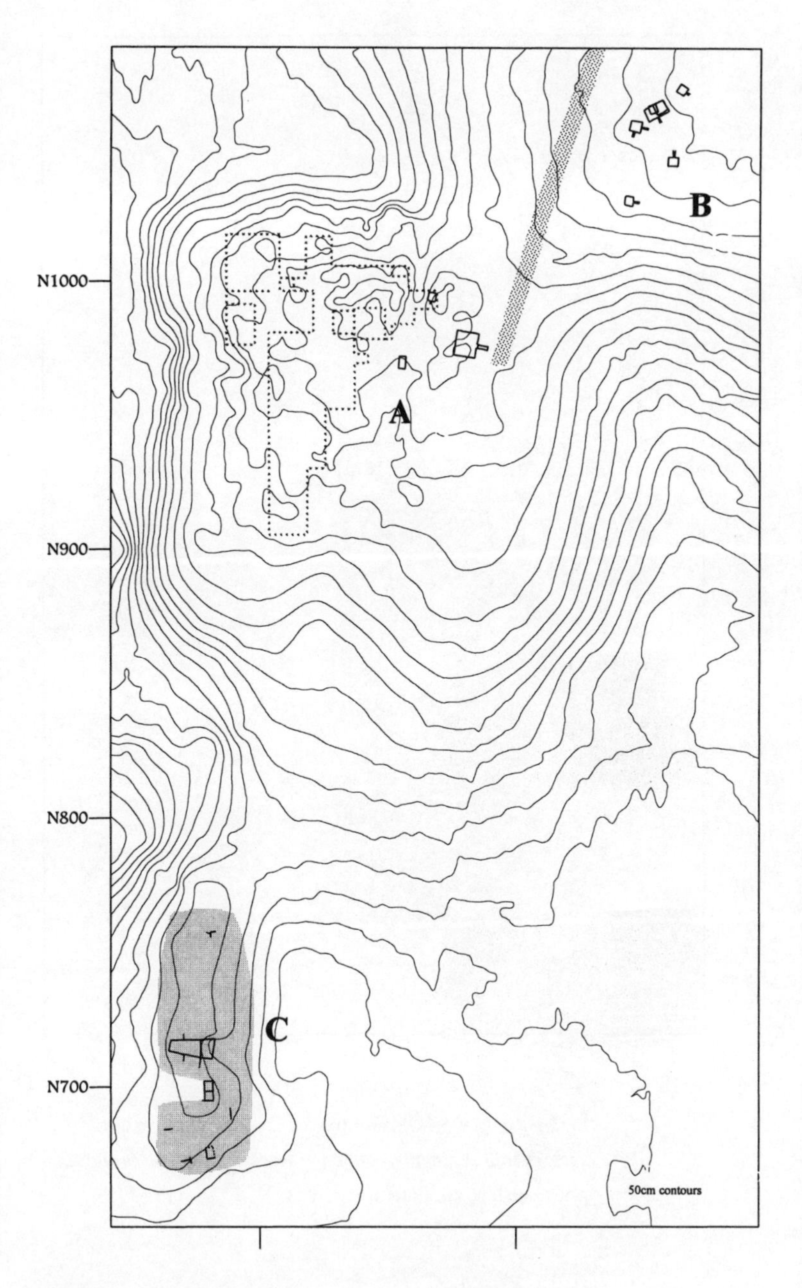

Figure 8.2. Map of the Old Town site (LA 1113) showing the principal portions of the site investigated 1989–1996. In Area A the dotted line marks the approximate location of the Classic Mimbres surface pueblo as mapped by Nels Nelson in 1920. The locations of excavated Three Circle phase pit structures are shown for Areas A and B but not Area C.

Relevant Classic Mimbres Architecture and Dating

Although the exact extent of the Classic Mimbres pueblo is not fully known, in part because of the extensive disturbance, a few rooms have been partially or wholly excavated. The masonry walls are for the most part still intact, but the floors were largely destroyed by pothunters digging for burials. Where portions of floors were preserved, important data on

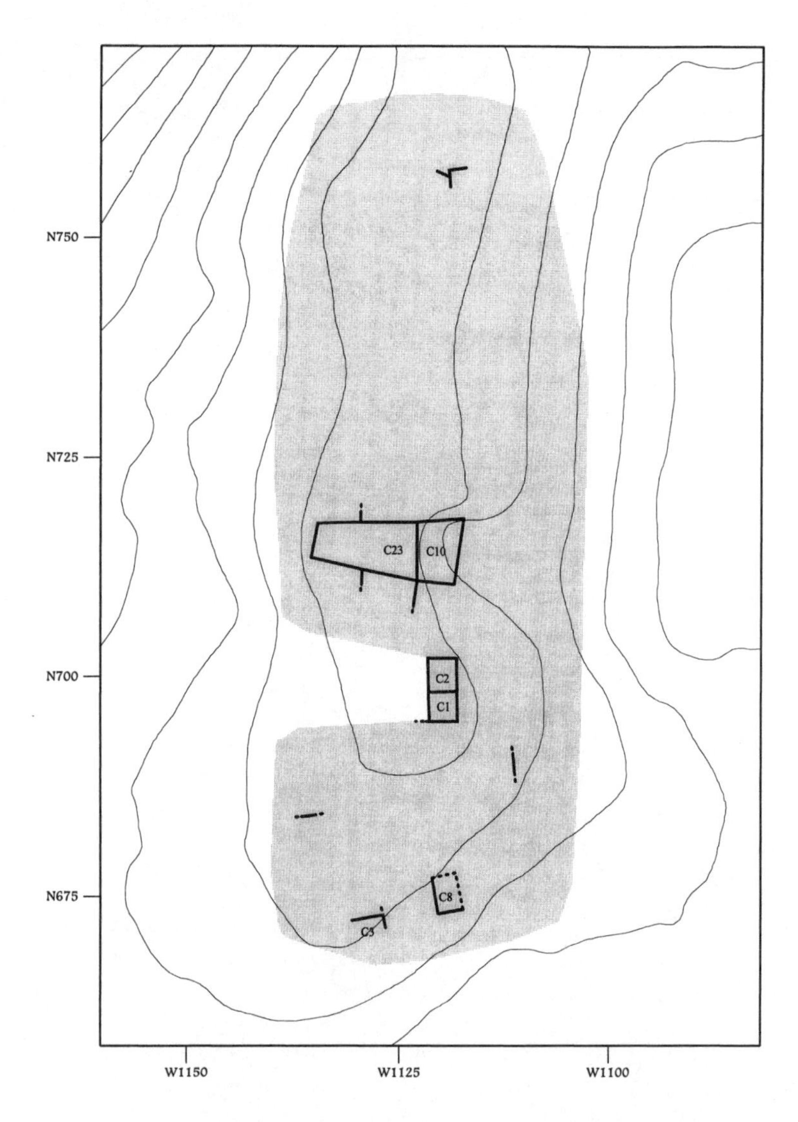

Figure 8.3. Map of Old Town Area C showing known rooms, surface wall segments, and general area of Black Mountain phase surface architecture.

ceramic assemblages, floor features, and dating were acquired.

The hearths in two rooms were round and clay-lined, and in one of these rooms (A2) there were round hearths on most of the five clearly defined adobe floors (none of the hearths yielded an archaeomagnetic date). Playas Red and Mimbres Classic sherds occurred within the adobe of two of these floors, evidently representing vessels used and broken prior to being incorporated into construction adobe. Room A2 and perhaps the nearly completely destroyed room to its east were remodeled after construction of Room A2's uppermost floor. This remodeling involved dismantling the east wall to the lowest course, removing the upper four floors in the northeast corner of Room A2, the walling-in of this smaller area, and at some point, the interment of a breeding age scarlet macaw in the base of the doorway into the newly created space, all occurring in the late Classic after the introduction of Playas Red. Overlying the southwest corner of Room A2 are the remains of at least one and perhaps two later, sequential masonry rooms. There are as yet no direct dates on these later remains, nor at this point can the removal of the south and west walls of Room A2 be specifically linked to the remodeling of the east side of this room.

Adjacent to Room A2 on the north is Room A7, but destruction of the common corners by pothunters precludes determining whether they were bonded or abutted. Room A7 also had a circular hearth, and there were Classic pottery types, as well as several Playas Red and El Paso Brown Ware sherds, in undisturbed fill below the lower floor remnant. Room A7 had burned, but most of the timbers had been displaced or extensively broken by pothunters. Two Douglas fir beam fragments, however, did yield tree-ring dates of A.D. 1074+vv (MIM-760) and 1107+v (MIM-758) (Creel 1992:2). The date of construction is unknown but apparently postdates A.D. 1107 by some number of years.

It is thus reasonably clear that at least some of the rooms on the north side of the Classic pueblo were built and/or remodeled late in the Classic phase. There is also modest evidence that Playas Red and some El Paso brownware were present prior to and during use of these rooms. Disturbed fill from these rooms contained substantially larger numbers of sherds of these two types as well as El Paso Polychrome, Chupadero B/W, Three Rivers Red-on-terracotta, and Tularosa Smudged-Corrugated, some of them modified after breakage. Ceramic types occurring with burials in these rooms are unknown because no looted vessels can be attributed to this area of the site. It is believed that some evidence of superimposed Black Mountain phase adobe pueblo architecture, if ever present, would have escaped pothunter destruction and would have been recognized. Because none was, and given the Classic context of some Playas Red and El Paso brownware sherds, these ceramics are provisionally interpreted as representing vessels in use late in the Classic phase. This would be consistent with the previously cited occurrences at other sites in the area. For what it is worth, such late ceramics occur over most of the Classic Mimbres pueblo at Old Town.

The Black Mountain Phase Pueblo at Old Town

Located on the crest of a narrow ridge nearly 200 m south of the Classic ruin at Old Town, there is a Black Mountain phase pueblo of undetermined size (Figures 8.2 and 8.3). It too has suffered significant damage from pothunting, and some rooms have eroded down to and slightly below floor level. As a result it is difficult to determine the layout and number of rooms; but the occurrence of wall segments, architectural rock, and distinct vegetation patterns and the distribution of melted adobe (especially clear on some aerial photography) suggest that structural remains occur over much of an area ca. 100 m N-S and 30 m E-W. Wall segments, definite rooms, different vegetation, and the results of test excavations indicate the presence of a small plaza open to the west, with rooms on at least some of the other three sides (Figure 8.3). As is the case with the Classic pueblo, these Black Mountain phase rooms overlie an extensive pithouse component.

To date, two rooms have been fully excavated, two others partially excavated, and several additional rooms minimally tested or walls partially traced. Construction is basically coursed adobe, although much rock was also incorporated into walls. In some cases there was nearly as much rock as adobe, with courses in some walls composed of horizontally laid slabs and rocks; in other walls materials were vertically placed. Most walls were set in footing trenches dug either into the underlying tuff bedrock or into the fill of pithouses (in regard to the latter, no different from the construction requirements of Classic rooms).

At present, little information on construction sequence is available, but it is clear that rooms were, to some extent, added incrementally rather than all built at once. Room C2 was clearly added on to Room C1 (Figure 8.4) and was remodeled at least once. The hearth on its upper floor yielded an initial archaeomagnetic date of A.D. 1000–1325. This date has since been reevaluated and reported at A.D. 1000–1350, but a closer inspection of the data reveals that the best estimate of the age is A.D. 1200–1225, a much shorter range that is consistent with the context (Creel 1995: 20). If the latter is an accurate date range, and given the fact that the hearth relates only to the upper floor of C2, it implies that adjacent Room C1 was built by perhaps A.D. 1200. The only other chronometric date for the Black Mountain phase component is also an archaeomagnetic date on the hearth in Room C3. Two ranges are possible, A.D. 1025–1150 and A.D. 1250–1275 (Creel 1993:16). Nothing precludes the former, but the latter seems more probable. Thus, there is limited evidence for construction and use of rooms east and south of the small plaza over a period of perhaps 50 years or more.

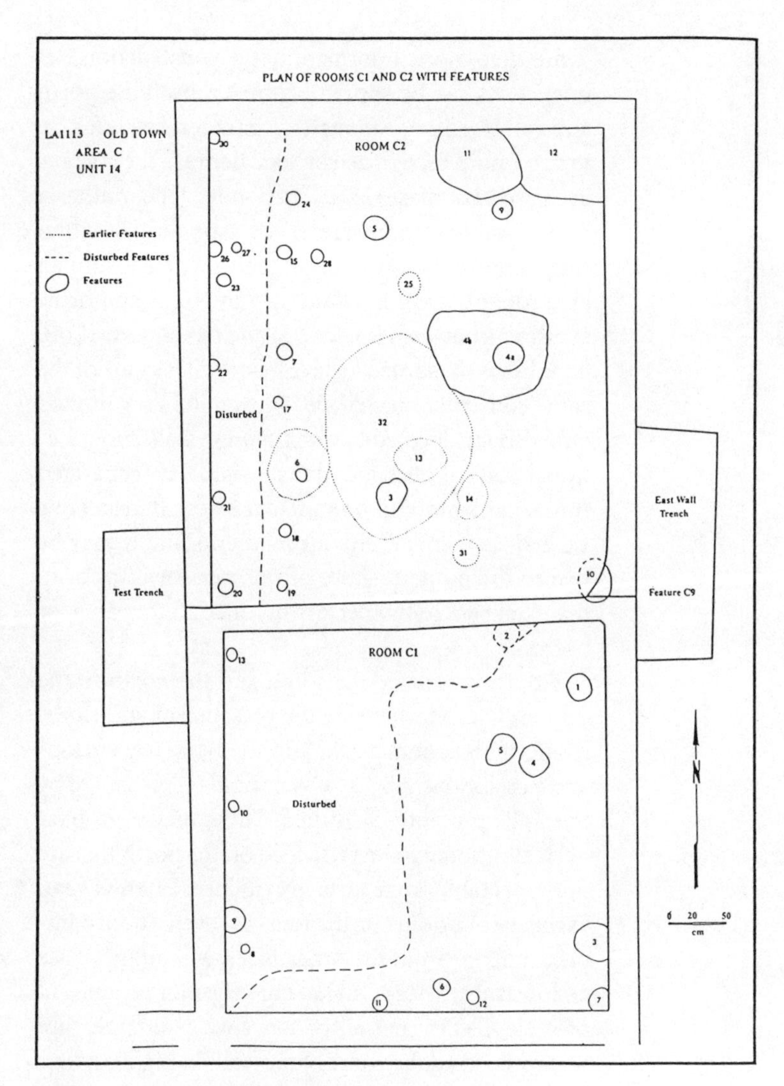

Figure 8.4. Plan of Rooms C1 and C2 with locations of intramural features; the earlier features date to an underlying pithouse component.

In contrast, there are no chronometric dates for the room block north of the plaza, although there is somewhat more information on construction sequence. As can be seen in Figure 8.3, both the north and south walls of Rooms C10/C23 extend west for ca. 17 m without recognized breaks. Because the corners at each end of these walls were bonded (the southeast corner was too poorly preserved to be sure), we infer that they were built at the same time, enclosing an area roughly 17 m E-W and 4–7 m N-S. The north-south wall between Rooms C10 and C23 abuts on both ends but is presumed to have been built as part of the same construction episode. During the very limited effort so far devoted to tracing these walls, no additional wall has been found that would have separated Room C23 from a third room to the west. If in fact one existed, as seems likely, our failure to find it may be due to the limited nature of our investigation or to the extensive pothunter disturbance in this area, or both.

Abutting walls to the south and the north of the C10/C23 complex indicate the presence of additional rooms in this room block. Minimally, there were four and possibly as many as seven rooms represented by the walls presently identified. There may even have been additional rooms attached on the north that are not detectable from surface evidence. In any event, exclusive of Room C10, the four- to seven-room complex differed from the other Black Mountain phase architecture in Area C in having a substantial amount of rock. Clearly, not all of this surface architecture was coursed adobe, some of the walls being masonry, at least in their lower portions.

The two completely excavated rooms (C1 and C2) are contiguous and have about 10 and 13.5 sq m of floor area, respectively (Creel 1993:12–13). Nearby Room C10 was substantially larger at ca. 35 sq m, and adjacent but unexcavated Room C23 also appears to be fairly large. Other rooms for which there is some information appear to be nearer the size of C1 and C2.

Because of erosion and pothunting, comparatively little information is available on interior features. The only preserved hearths were in Rooms C2 and C3 (a nearly totally destroyed room probably about the same size as C2), both of them round and clay-lined. Disturbed Room C1 had postholes and small pits, as well as what was probably an infant burial covered by a killed plain smudged bowl (Figure 8.4). This burial was clearly interred from the floor, the pit having been sealed by a distinctive plug of hard adobe. Only a few infant bones were inside the bowl, the remainder apparently having been displaced by rodent burrowing.

In adjacent Room C2, there was a small round hearth, two roof-support postholes, and numerous small postholes on the west side that presumably represent interior furniture of some sort (Figure 8.4). There were also two pits containing burned rocks and a disturbed pit in the northeast corner that contained cranial fragments of a child probably interred from the upper of the two floors. No features could be unambiguously assigned to large Room C10, although a north-south line of postholes down the center may mark the location of roof-support posts.

Extramural features believed to be associated with the Black Mountain phase occupation include shallow pits filled with burned rock and presumed to be roasting pits. In addition, a shallow, circular, basin-shaped pit lined with small, thin rhyolite slabs was found in the center of the apparent plaza. This feature was ca. 1 m in diameter and ca. 8 cm deep; it had no evidence of burning, and its function is unknown. Simply because of its location in the probable plaza and because its upper edges were barely below ground surface, this feature is also believed to be associated with the Black Mountain phase.

Lithic and Ceramic Assemblages

Relatively little is known about Black Mountain phase lithic assemblages anywhere in the Mimbres area, including Old Town. Nonetheless, the investigations at Old Town have revealed a style of arrowpoint that appears to date to the late Classic and Black Mountain phases. Like many of the arrowpoints from Classic contexts at Old Town and other sites, these have side notches, but they also have distinct basal notches. Such arrowpoints occur in both the Classic and Black Mountain phase pueblos at Old Town, but the more typical side-notched points occur only in the former part of the site. These side-notched and basally notched arrowpoints have been recovered from numerous other sites in the Mimbres area, including NAN Ranch (Dockall 1991), Swarts (Cosgrove and Cosgrove 1932), and Saige-McFarland (Lekson 1990); but no one has yet had the data to determine their temporal occurrence. The Old Town data are not conclusive but do suggest that this style most likely dates to the late Classic and Black Mountain phases.

Not surprisingly, much more is known about

Black Mountain phase ceramics than about lithics. The ceramic assemblage from the Black Mountain phase pueblo at Old Town comprises plain wares, both slipped and unslipped variants of Playas Red (with variations of incising, tooling, corrugation, and cord-marking), early El Paso Polychrome, Chupadero B/W, variants of Reserve/Tularosa smudged corrugated, and plain smudged, with small amounts of Tularosa B/W, White Mountain Red Ware (including St. Johns Polychrome and Wingate Black-on-red), Three Rivers Red-on-terracotta, Tucson Polychrome, and Villa Ahumada Polychrome (tentative identification). Together these types indicate a date range of ca. A.D. 1130 or 1150 to somewhat beyond A.D. 1300.

Although it is widely asserted that there was a wholesale replacement of ceramic types during the Classic-Black Mountain transition, there was actually considerable continuity in corrugated pottery. That is, one of the most common kinds of pottery on Black Mountain (and at least some Classic) sites is a rubbed or obliterated corrugated variety virtually indistinguishable from Mimbres Classic Corrugated except for its more common reddish color and more micaceous paste. In some cases, though, this corrugated pottery is also red-slipped and in general fits comfortably in the range of variation of Playas. In addition, chemical characterization studies indicate clearly that this corrugated pottery typically clusters with incised, tooled, and cordmarked varieties of Playas. As discussed more fully below, chemical characterization also indicates that much of the Playas was made in the Mimbres drainage.

Neutron activation analysis (NAA) of Classic Mimbres sherds, especially Style III, from numerous sites in the Mimbres and nearby Jornada Mogollon areas has consistently indicated manufacture at multiple localities in the former area, with extensive movement of vessels to sites in the latter area, from Hatch, New Mexico, to the El Paso, Texas, vicinity (Brewington 1997; Gilman et al. 1994; James et al. 1995). Mimbres area sites sampled range from Treasure Hill and Cameron Creek to Mattocks to Old Town. In contrast, NAA data on the so-called Black Mountain phase types derived from many of the same sites, as well as others, and from what are here considered late Classic and Black Mountain phase contexts reveal a rather different picture. Williams (1996) and Creel et al. (1998) have shown that there is good evidence that virtually all of the El Paso Polychrome occurring in Mimbres sites was manufactured in the El Paso area, although a small amount does seem to have been made in the Mimbres valley. Similarly, the Chupadero B/W was also apparently made elsewhere and traded into the Mimbres area; evidence from other analyses indicates that Chupadero was made in the area east and north of the Tularosa Basin (e.g., Warren 1981; Stewart et al. 1990). Little attention has been given to most of the other types; but the typological data, more frequent occurrence in distant areas, and certain physical differences such as sherd temper in some types suggest that these, too, were made outside the Mimbres area.

Determining the place of manufacture of Playas wares has proven a bit more complex. Interestingly, much of the Playas tends to group with Mimbres Classic Corrugated and smudged wares. There are several related compositional groups with this range of types, as well as including Mimbres B/W Style III (Creel et al. 1998; Williams 1996), and there is reasonable evidence for multiple manufacturing locales in the Mimbres valley and perhaps upper Gila areas. In addition, one group contains numerous Playas members and also several Mimbres valley clay samples. Thus, there is good evidence for manufacture of Playas in the Mimbres valley, but the NAA data alone do not permit us to identify more specific manufacturing locales.

A few of the compositional groups containing only Playas are strongly site specific, but for the most part these groups are quite small. Two such groups contain only two specimens each, with both members from the same site (WS Ranch and Hot Well). Finally, the largest exclusively Playas group ($N = 21$) is dominated by Old Town members, the only two other members being from Acequia Seca (a Black Mountain phase pueblo adjacent to NAN Ranch) and LA 18342 (a Classic and possibly Black Mountain phase site in the Rio Arenas drainage near Treasure Hill). This group contains approximately 80 percent of the Playas sherds analyzed from Old Town and at the present time cannot be confidently linked via clay samples to a specific locale.

Virtually every site with more than one Playas NAA sample has multiple compositional groups represented. To a large extent, the number of compositional groups represented per site is a function of the number of sherds analyzed, but it seems likely that this multigroup representation reflects fairly widespread manufacture and movement of Playas vessels. With the present sample, the only known exception is Old Town, where, as noted previously, most of the Playas is in a single compositional group.

It is interesting in this regard to consider the small group of six Playas sherds analyzed from Casas Grandes. Five of these are presently unassigned, whereas one is a member of a group that contains most of the Playas sherds in the sample. It also contains Mimbres valley Classic pottery type members (from numerous sites) and is closely related to other groups also containing predominantly Mimbres valley members, including clay samples.

Overall, then, there is NAA evidence that Playas was made and moved over a large area in the southern Southwest; this is consistent with the findings of a previous X-ray fluorescence study by Bradley and Hoffer (1985). To an extent, the same appears to be true of El Paso Polychrome and Chupadero B/W, although our NAA data do not reveal manufacture over nearly so large an area as Playas. Too few samples of the other pottery types characteristic of the Black Mountain phase have been analyzed in our joint NAA efforts to be meaningful, but other kinds of evidence indicate that they were also being widely traded. From a Mimbres valley perspective, perhaps the most important observation is how the manufacture and exchange of pottery began to change late in the Mimbres Classic. It was then that non-Mimbres painted ceramics began to be imported, whereas utility ware continued for the most part to be locally produced. The painted pottery apparently derived from a number of neighboring regions, presumably reflecting increased interaction with a number of different populations. How much longer Mimbres B/W Style III continued to be made is unknown.

Implications of the Findings at Old Town: Overview

Despite modest sampling, the excavations at Old Town and associated research have yielded significant information on the late Classic and Black Mountain phases. As noted previously, this has resulted in a suggested revision of the definition of the Black Mountain phase; but unfortunately it has not contributed to any substantive improvement in dating of the phase. Indeed, because there has still been far too little investigation of the Black Mountain phase, perhaps the most important contribution of the Old Town project may be identification of critical questions to be addressed in future research. Nonetheless, it is useful to summarize what is known about the Black Mountain phase in terms of architecture, community plan, dating, and settlement pattern.

Architecture and Community Plan

As noted previously, there is good evidence that many of the material culture traits long considered characteristic of the Black Mountain phase actually began late in the Mimbres Classic. That is, people began to make round hearths in addition to the square or rectangular slab-lined hearths typical of most of the Classic while still using and probably still building masonry pueblo rooms. As best as can be ascertained, importation of painted pottery from most surrounding regions began while the well-known Mimbres Black-on-white and polychrome were still being used locally. The data support the contention that these were Classic occurrences (see also Anyon and LeBlanc 1984:143).

Moreover, the occasional use of coursed-adobe construction was known to the Mimbreños as early as A.D. 900 (Cosgrove and Cosgrove 1932:8; Lucas 1996:64), but it seems not to have been widely used until the Black Mountain phase. The most recently excavated example is Three Circle phase pit structure B11 at Old Town, with two noncutting tree-ring dates on roof timbers of A.D. 831+vv and A.D. 881vv and an archaeomagnetic date on burned wall plaster of A.D. 900–950 (Creel 1995:14; Lucas 1996:67–68). Room B11 had unambiguous coursed-adobe wall construction and a floor assemblage including ceramic vessels of Three Circle phase types Mimbres B/W Style II and Three Circle Neck Corrugated. An earlier but larger pit structure in the same location, Room B9, apparently was also constructed of coursed adobe (Creel 1995:10–11; Lucas 1996:56–61). Similarly, pit structure Room E at Swarts was built of coursed adobe (described as puddled adobe in the report); it underlay and thus clearly predated Classic Mimbres surface pueblo rooms (Cosgrove and Cosgrove 1932:8).

Construction of a number of entirely separate adobe pueblos, particularly along the lower reaches of drainages in the Mimbres area, has generally been believed to postdate, and to have resulted from, the complete abandonment of Classic villages and the so-called collapse of the Mimbres system. Relatively little excavation has been done at any of these Black Mountain phase sites, however, and we know far less about them than about Classic sites. On the east side of the Black Range, early Postclassic (or Black Mountain) architecture was masonry (Nelson 1993a), although later Black Mountain phase construction was coursed adobe (see also Laumbach and Kirkpatrick 1985).

The Mimbres Foundation excavated four rooms at the Walsh site, estimated to contain as many as 100 rooms arranged in a U shape around a plaza (LeBlanc 1977:13; Ravesloot 1979:25). Hearths were round and clay-lined, and some rooms had been remodeled. Size of excavated rooms ranged from ca. 12 to 21 sq m. Ceramics include those previously mentioned non–Mimbres series types occurring in terminal Classic contexts but also include small numbers of Chihuahuan polychromes and Tucson Polychrome.

A few miles up the Mimbres River, the Mimbres Foundation also excavated two rooms at the Montoya site, a smaller village than Walsh, with perhaps 20 to 40 rooms (LeBlanc 1977:13; Ravesloot 1979:24). The site evidently had something of a U shape, with small room blocks around a plaza. Material culture was similar to that at Walsh. Much the same is true of the Black Mountain phase pueblo at Old Town except that it may have been larger than Montoya and perhaps more nearly comparable in size to Walsh. It too appears to have had at least one small plaza.

The only other site in the Mimbres valley for which there is possible Black Mountain phase data is Galaz. The University of Minnesota excavated 20 rooms that have been tentatively dated by Anyon and LeBlanc (1984:148) at ca. A.D. 1300. Room size ranged from about 12 to 53 sq m, with two large rooms; most rooms, however, ranged from ca. 16 to 26 sq m (Anyon and LeBlanc 1984:147). The hearths in this component were more like those of the following Cliff phase than like those at Walsh, Montoya, or Old Town.

Most rooms in these four sites were 12 to 26 sq m in size; but as noted previously, at Montoya, Old Town, and Galaz, there was at least one room with a floor area greater than 35 sq m. Rooms excavated at sites in the eastern Mimbres area (east of the Black Range) have a comparable size range (see Nelson 1993a; Nelson and Hegmon 1996). This difference in room size is similar to that in Classic sites and may well reflect the presence of, and differentiation in use between, smaller domestic and larger communal/ceremonial rooms. No semisubterranean communal rooms (kivas) are known for the Black Mountain phase, nor have any small, presumably storage, rooms been confidently identified as such except in the eastern portion of the Mimbres area (Anyon and LeBlanc 1984:146; Nelson 1993a:58).

Dating

As noted previously, neither the material culture changes that evidently began late in the Classic nor the beginning of the Black Mountain phase as defined here are adequately dated. However, we know more about the former, especially the shift in ceramic production and exchange that began in the late Classic, because of the extensive excavations in Classic sites. In particular, the previously cited evidence from NAN Ranch suggests that painted El Paso Brown Ware might have reached the Mimbres valley by perhaps A.D. 1125. Interestingly, none of the Black Mountain phase types was found during the excavations of Pueblo Vinegaroon, a late Classic site investigated by the NAN Ranch Project (Armstrong 1990). This 15- to 20-room pueblo has several tree-ring dates in the early A.D. 1100s (latest is A.D. 1110+v for Room 5 and A.D. 1116vv for Room 8; Shafer 1986:40). The excavations at the Elk Ridge Ruin in the upper Mimbres valley have yielded similar tree-ring dates but no Black Mountain phase pottery types (Karl Laumbach, personal communication). On the basis of these meager data, the best we can say is that these later ceramics probably did not reach the Mimbres valley earlier than perhaps the A.D. 1120s. Moreover, the extent of remodeling of Classic rooms after the introduction of these pottery types suggests that at least some Classic pueblos continued to be occupied for some period of years.

How much longer they were occupied is unknown, but the limited evidence from Old Town suggests that some Black Mountain phase rooms there were built by about A.D. 1200. This is perhaps supported by the dating information from the nine-room Berrenda Creek site, which the excavators believe was built in a fairly short time. There was no recognized evidence of extensive remodeling at Berrenda Creek, and the single tree-ring date of A.D. 1105vv (MIM-637) and three archaeomagnetic dates of A.D. 1215 ± 27, 1180, and 1190 for hearths (Gomolak and Ford 1976:127–129) are difficult to interpret. On the one hand, the archaeomagnetic dates seem too late for Classic rooms, but there are some El Paso bichrome sherds among the far more numerous Classic sherds at the site. They do not, however, seem to be numerous enough, nor are there any other late types, to indicate extensive occupation of the site in the late A.D. 1100s. On the other hand, there is no evidence of which I am aware that necessarily precludes these being accurate dates for this site (but accepting them would seem to imply that there was either little or no new construction at the excavated Classic sites in the Mimbres valley or that extensive reuse of construction timbers has given us an incorrect notion of Classic dating).

Small sites with insubstantial field houses on the east side of the Black Range, built during the Classic, appear to have been remodeled into more substantial masonry structures early in what Nelson and Hegmon (1996) designate the Postclassic. The excavators believe that this remodeling was done by small Mimbres family groups moving permanently out of the large Classic villages nearby. Whether there was literal continuity in these cases or, in the Mimbres valley, from the occupation of the Classic pueblos to the building and habitation of the Black Mountain pueblos is not presently determinable. The extant settlement pattern data do, however, indicate that Classic Mimbres communities in higher elevations like the upper Mimbres valley were abandoned, with no nearby Black Mountain phase pueblos. In contrast, most Classic sites from about the Mattocks site on down the Mimbres valley have Black Mountain phase pueblos immediately adjacent or within a short distance (see below and Ravesloot 1979:Figure 2).

Conventional wisdom places this abandonment at ca. A.D. 1130 (LeBlanc 1983:162), about the time of a multiyear drought. The lack of Classic dates after the A.D. 1120s (other than Berrenda Creek) is consistent with this scenario, as is the relatively modest quantity of the late pottery types at many Classic sites. The Berrenda Creek dates suggest that the Classic lasted considerably longer, but they are difficult to reconcile with what other dating evidence exists. If the archaeomagnetic dates from Old Town are accurate, at least one of the Black Mountain phase pueblos was established by about A.D. 1200, perhaps earlier. These dates and the occurrence of such pottery types as Villa Ahumada Polychrome (tentative identification) and Tucson Polychrome at these sites is consistent with occupation throughout the thirteenth century and even into the fourteenth. The absence of later types such as Gila and Tonto polychromes were argued by Anyon and LeBlanc (1984:146, 148) and Nelson and LeBlanc (1986:246) to indicate an end date of ca. A.D. 1300 for the Black Mountain phase. Archaeomagnetic dates and tree-ring dates from nearby sites with these pottery types are in the A.D. 1300s and thus support a date of around A.D. 1300 for the end of the Black Mountain phase (Nelson and LeBlanc 1986: 106; Robinson and Cameron 1991:23; Nelson and Anyon 1996:283). The occurrence of Tucson Polychrome and perhaps Villa Ahumada Polychrome at Old Town and Walsh suggest that the end of the Black Mountain phase and the beginning of the Cliff phase may date slightly later than A.D. 1300 and perhaps was not as distinct as once thought (see Nelson and LeBlanc 1986:246).

Settlement Pattern

There is evidence for terminal Classic occupation at essentially all of the larger Classic communities below about 6000 feet in elevation (see Anyon and LeBlanc 1984:316; Laumbach and Kirkpatrick 1985:35; LaVerne Herrington, personal communication). For the most part, this evidence is in the form of late Mimbres Style III B/W and the new pottery types such as El Paso Polychrome, Chupadero B/W, and Playas. There is similar evidence at some smaller sites as well. The apparent lack of these ceramics at Classic sites in the upper Mimbres valley suggests that these villages were abandoned prior to the influx of the imported ceramics and thus earlier than Classic sites at lower elevations. From this we can infer that major changes in settlement pattern began during the Classic phase and continued to occur in the following Black Mountain phase.

As noted previously, there is a Black Mountain phase pueblo adjacent to or near virtually all of the Classic sites below about 6000 feet, but we know little about their size, layout, dating, etc. In at least some cases these are substantial pueblos, and our experience at Old Town leads me to suspect that the size of other sites may have been underestimated. This and an overly narrow conception of community as influenced by modern arbitrary site designations may affect our notions of village abandonment. Indeed, it is possible that none of these Classic communities was abandoned at the end of the Classic phase; instead, it may simply be that some room blocks in those villages were abandoned and new adobe ones built nearby. The lack of Black Mountain phase adobe room blocks at or near upper Mimbres valley Classic sites is consistent with earlier abandonment of villages in this portion of the drainage.

In any event, survey has revealed rather clearly that there was far more Black Mountain than Classic phase floor area (and inferentially more people) in the lower Mimbres valley and that there were no Black Mountain phase sites at all in the upper portion of the Mimbres drainage (e.g., Blake et al. 1986:Table 13). This is considered by the Mimbres Foundation researchers to indicate a substantial population increase in the lower portion of the Mimbres valley at about the same time that, or perhaps somewhat later than, the upper valley was abandoned (Blake et al. 1986:Table 13).

It has been suggested that the purported abandonment of Classic sites may have resulted from drought-induced stress in the A.D. 1130s. Although it is not clear why the upper valley would have been abandoned under drought conditions, it is possible that hydrologic conditions in the lower valley were to some extent better during drought than conditions in the upper valley (Creel 1996). Although it is likely that the drought had substantial negative impact that may well have pushed the limits of the Classic population's local resources (see Herrington 1979:199–202; Minnis 1985:146–155), it is not clear what options the population had in their efforts to adjust to stress. On the one hand, this drought prevailed over a much larger region than just the Mimbres area (Creel 1996); indeed, it occurred over virtually all of the southern Southwest, including northern Chihuahua. The population as a whole, or even substantial portions of it, may not have had significant options for better places to live.

On the other hand, if Nelson and Anyon (1996) are correct, some of the population could have moved to what may have been vacant areas and survived even during a severe drought. Presumably, this would have enabled the remnant population at the old villages to have survived as well. That is, one would expect those families with access to the most productive land (and presumably the ability to provide food for themselves during the drought) to remain in their villages while those without adequate resources had to move elsewhere temporarily (see Levy 1992 for an ethnographic example). This may be what happened in the Mimbres area and is an explanation at least partially consistent with the occurrence of some Classic rooms with late ceramics at sites such as Galaz and Swarts.

On a more local basis, no one has yet identified where those forced to abandon their villages may have gone within the Mimbres drainage except potentially the Black Mountain phase pueblos. Until more of these sites are excavated and dated, however, this matter will remain unresolved. It may even be, as Nelson and Anyon (1996:287) suggest, that the Mimbreños first moved to the Animas valley in Hidalgo County, New Mexico, and then moved back to and reoccupied the Mimbres valley during the Black Mountain phase. This suggestion is not without merit in arguing that there were unoccupied areas in southwest New Mexico temporarily inhabited by some of the Mimbreños forced to leave the Mimbres valley.

In any event, no one has yet offered a good explanation for the apparent settlement shift to the lower Mimbres valley and the lack of resettlement of the upper valley. LeBlanc (1983:165) and Creel (1996), however, have suggested that emphasis on the growing of cotton may explain, at least in part, the shift to the lower valley, which is more suitable for cotton cultivation. This possibility is supported by the occurrence of cotton seeds in Black Mountain phase sites, but cotton seeds have also been found at the Classic phase Eby site (personal communication, Gloria Greis, Peabody Museum, Harvard University, Catalog number 95752) and another Classic site near Deming (Minnis 1985:62, 182, Table 8). If true, this suggests that the Classic Mimbreños began producing a nonfood commodity that could be exchanged and widely distributed. However, the extent to which they or the Black Mountain phase population engaged in cotton cultivation is presently unknown.

Summary

It seems clear that in the mid and late twelfth century populations over most of the southern Southwest began interacting with one another to a much greater extent than they had previously. This is perhaps reflected most obviously in the sudden widespread distribution of significant quantities of pottery types such as Chupadero B/W and El Paso Polychrome. The nature of this seemingly sudden change in ceramic production and exchange is poorly understood, and no one has systematically addressed questions about vessel type, form, size, and their relevance to whether it was pottery vessels or their contents that were the important commodities being exchanged (see, however, Di Peso et al. 1974:4:141 regarding the use of El Paso Polychrome to transport spume salt; and Smiley 1979).

LeBlanc (1983:160–166; 1989:192–194) has suggested, though, that the establishment of Casas Grandes in Chihuahua and its influence throughout the southern Southwest accounts for the changes in settlement pattern and material culture seen in the Classic–Black Mountain transition in the Mimbres area. More specifically, LeBlanc suggests that the Black Mountain phase population may have shifted to the lower elevations to produce cotton for Casas Grandes. Dean and Ravesloot's (1993:102) revision of the Casas Grandes chronology is consistent with this possibility.

On the other hand, Dean and Ravesloot (1993) note that much of the construction at Casas Grandes occurred too late to be related to the Mimbres Classic–Black Mountain transition. The growing of cotton during the Classic, thus, may well have preceded Medio period Casas Grandes and would not be consistent with LeBlanc's hypothesis. However, the early Buena Fé phase construction at Casas Grandes is not adequately dated, and there is no evidence to preclude this phase's actually beginning before A.D. 1200. It may be, then, that LeBlanc was correct in his suggested linkage of the Mimbres and Casas Grandes areas.

In any event, at what point and to what extent Casas Grandes became a major participant in the newly expanded interaction network in the southern Southwest is unknown. The role of Casas Grandes in the notable shift in ceramic production and exchange seen in the early-to-mid twelfth century is difficult to evaluate, particularly with regard to production of Playas wares. Although the production of Playas pottery has long been considered to have been Chihuahuan, recent studies have shown that it was also produced in the Mimbres area and perhaps in the El Paso/Jornada area as well (Bradley and Hoffer 1985:175; Creel et al. 1998; Williams 1996). Based on the lack of Playas Red types in Viejo period sites in the Casas Grandes area (Di Peso 1974; Di Peso et al. 1974), its apparently earlier occurrence in terminal Mimbres Classic contexts, and current notions on dating of the Perros Bravos and Buena Fé phases, it is difficult to perceive much Casas Grandes influence, at least ceramically, in the Mimbres area until the thirteenth century. As noted above, though, it is possible that the Perros Bravos–Buena Fé transition occurred earlier than thought; but until this dating issue is resolved we cannot adequately consider interaction in a very meaningful way. Indeed, judged on the basis of ceramic type frequency, the Jornada area would appear to have had more influence than any other area during the middle half of the twelfth century; but the nature of interaction between the Jornada and adjacent regions is difficult to define.

In sum, it is perhaps most prudent to emphasize critical issues to be addressed in research on the Black Mountain phase and its relationship to Casas Grandes. First and foremost, we need more basic research on Black Mountain phase sites; clearly, our present sample is far too small. Second, we need adequate dating of the Black Mountain phase, as well as such other complexes as the Perros Bravos and early Buena Fé phases. Finally, I think we need to consider more carefully the nature of changes reflected by the sudden and widespread distribution of pottery types made in so many different parts of the southern Southwest after about A.D. 1130.

9

The Mimbres Classic and Postclassic

A Case for Discontinuity

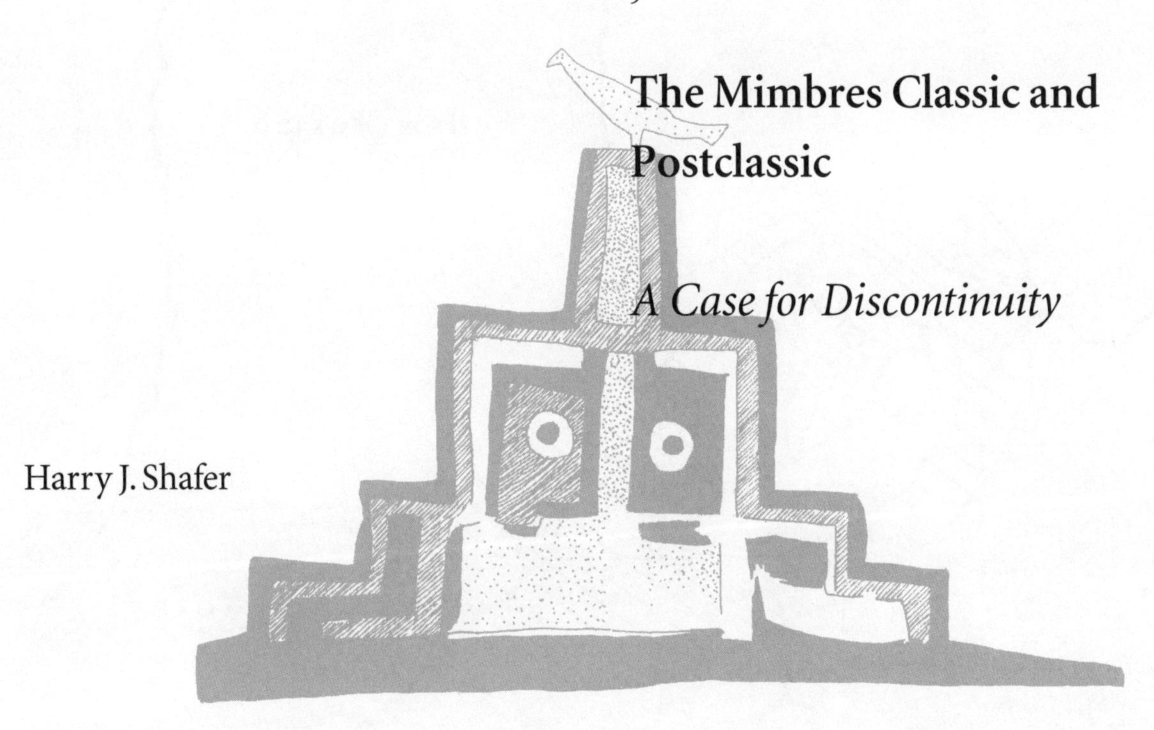

Harry J. Shafer

THIS CHAPTER PRESENTS the view that the Mimbres Postclassic Black Mountain phase was the result of a reoccupation of the lower half of the Mimbres River valley following an occupational hiatus of about 50 to 75 years. The core of this argument lies in the strong regional patterns established in the Mimbres heartland building up to and including the Classic Mimbres phase and the abrupt end of these patterns at the end of that phase. I contend that the abandonment of large Mimbres towns and sudden decrease in population were the result of an out-migration. Construction of new pueblos in the Black Mountain phase using different architectural methods, marked changes in ceramic styles and loci of ceramic production, and changes in mortuary behavior from the Classic Mimbres phase to the Black Mountain phase indicate a later in-migration and substantive differences between the two cultural systems. These differences are hard to explain if the occupation was uninterrupted.

The Mimbres Phenomenon

In the period from A.D. 900 to 1140, the Mimbres valley was an oasis for agriculturally dependent groups (Figure 9.1) and supported one of the densest populations in the American Southwest at that time. The Mimbres regional system became one of the most influential in the Southwest, on par in many ways with the Chaco and Hohokam regional systems.

Survey work carried out by the Mimbres Foundation provided the first population model for the Mimbres valley (Blake et al. 1986). This model was based on the numbers, size, and density of a stratified sample of sites through time and reflects trends showing population growth and population peaks (Figure 9.2). The Mimbres Foundation data suggest a high rate of population growth in the late Pithouse period. The architectural and mortuary evidence from NAN and Swarts ruins and the NAN Ranch survey data also indicate a rapid population growth in the late Three Circle phase; in fact, this phase has the most rapid population growth of any phase in Mimbres history.

The population peak occurred in the Classic Mimbres period. The original definition of the Classic Mimbres was based on work in the Mimbres River system, and indeed, it is within the Mimbres drainage where the greatest concentration of large Mimbres pueblos are found, numbering at least 15. A few large Mimbres pueblos are also found along the upper Gila and its tributaries, including the Sapillo (Lekson

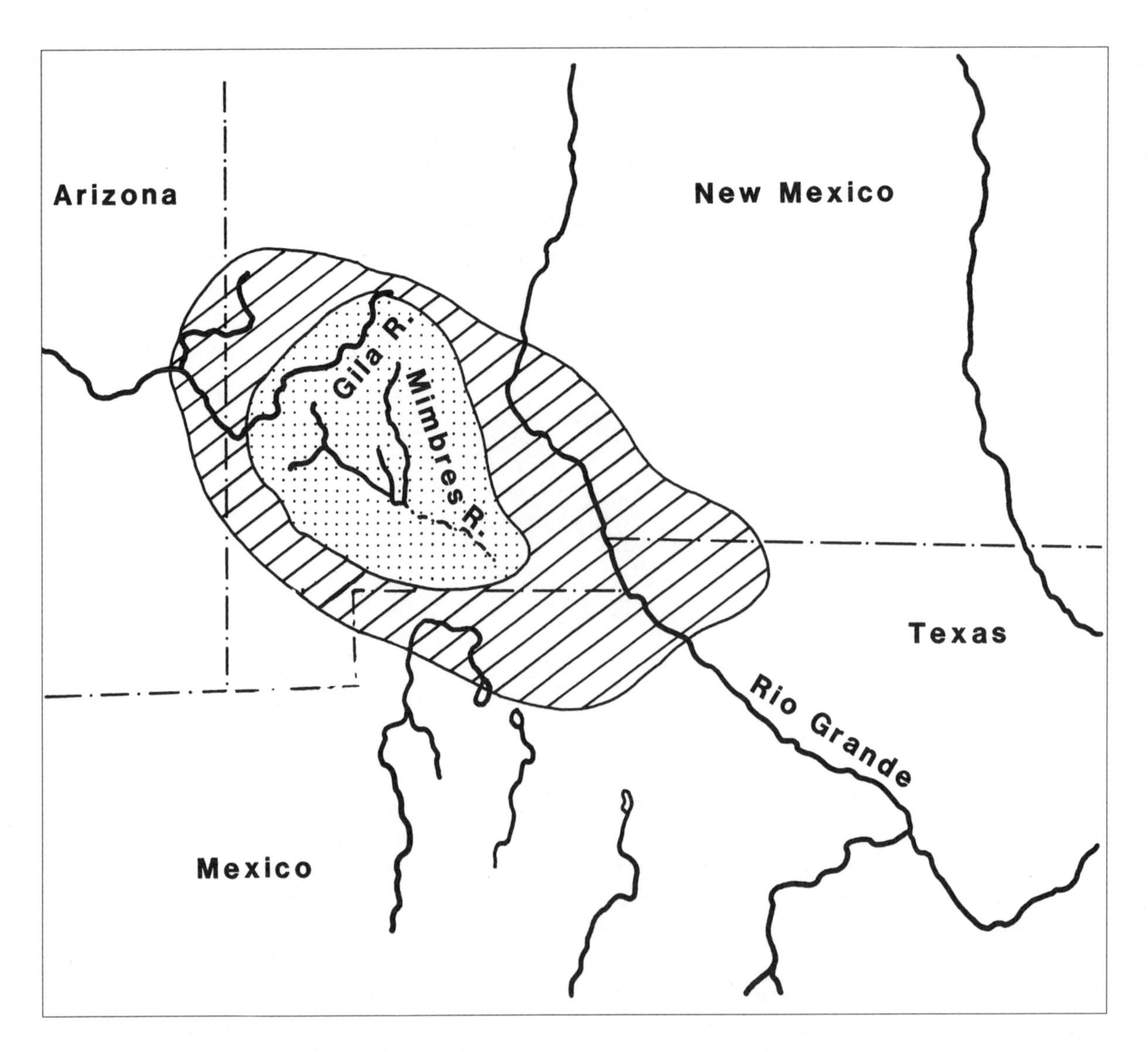

Figure 9.1 (Above). Map of the Mimbres System ca. A.D. 1050–1100. The Mimbres heartland is defined on the distribution of large towns; the extent of the Mimbres system is based on the significant occurrence of Mimbres Style III pottery.

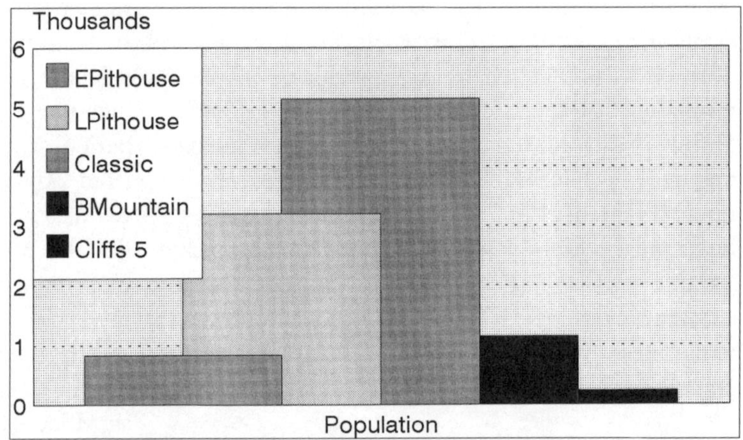

Figure 9.2 (Right). Mimbres population model (estimated 0.3% annual growth rate) taken from Blake et al. (1986).

1984a; Stokes 1996). The distribution of the large Classic Mimbres pueblos, as discussed below, defines the Mimbres heartland (Figure 9.1). Archaeologists have detected some variation between the Gila and Mimbres valleys, such as subtle differences in ceramic designs (Brewington 1992), decreasing frequency of intramural burial on the Gila (Gilman 1980), and fewer but larger towns on the Gila (Lekson 1984a).

There may also be some differences between the Mimbres valley and the Mimbres period material documented from east of the Black Range (Nelson 1984; 1993b), although data gaps, namely an absence of mortuary data and information on large pueblos, do not allow for comfortable comparisons at this time. I do feel these broad regional differences are worth pointing out because they imply differences or variability between the respective populations.

The evolution of the Mimbres system, which began at least by the San Francisco phase, if not earlier, took shape in the Three Circle phase and culminated in what we call the Classic Mimbres phase (Shafer 1995). During the A.D. 900s, pithouses were being abandoned and the first pueblo structures were being built in the Mimbres valley. This time was marked by a great deal of experimentation in ceramic design and vessel form and the greatest variability in mortuary behavior. Burial practices included intramural burials with killed or smashed vessels, extramural burials with unkilled vessels or none at all, primary and secondary cremations. As mentioned previously, population growth in the Mimbres valley was rapidly increasing in the late Pithouse and Classic Mimbres periods, probably much faster than can be explained by biological processes alone (Blake et al. 1986). The behavioral variability seen in the ceramic styles and mortuary behavior may signify an in-migration—that is, outside groups joining the indigenous settlements and thus inflating the population (see chapter 17 of this volume).

Storage practices also were changing in the A.D. 900s, with the appearance of formal granaries constructed above ground. At first these were isolated structures, but they soon became incorporated into or were built as part of residential complexes in Classic Mimbres times (Shafer 1995).

Change also occurred in civic-ceremonial architecture and space use. The use of great kivas and kiva-like structures had reached a peak in late Pithouse–early Classic times and began to decline (Anyon et al. 1981), perhaps correlating in a shift away from secret ceremonies to public plaza ceremonies by ca. A.D. 1050 (LeBlanc 1983). I favor Rapapport's (1971) and Wilshusen's (1989) idea that such public rituals served as a means of organizing people in the absence of formal or powerful authority. Great kivas ceased to be a major element in the architectural plan although large communal rooms with multiple functions were built into Classic Mimbres room suites after A.D. 1050 (Figure 9.3). The demise of the kiva seemed to parallel the rise of rooms that served as family or lineage shrines marked by a dual hearth arrangement, a feature whose significance will be discussed later.

The Mimbres phenomenon should not be viewed as a static entity isolated in time and space. Rather, it was extremely dynamic, sensitive to what the climate was doing and what neighboring people were doing. The stability of the towns may have centered on the core (or founding) families. If modern pueblo behavior can be used as a model, these core households farmed the best lands based on the rule of first occupancy (McAnany 1996; McGuire and Saitta 1996). Our analysis of architectural patterning at the NAN Ruin (Shafer and Taylor 1986; Shafer 1995) and Mara D. Hill's (1997) architectural reconstructions at Swarts Ruin suggest that these large valley towns also were not static communities. Their stability rested on core households that endured for up to five or six generations. These core households, composed of one large room with a hearth and a smaller storeroom (Shafer 1982), eventually attracted, or begat, later joined households that eventually formed room clusters. Community fluidity was marked by attached or unaffiliated households whose rooms were used only for a generation or so and abandoned, with the space reclaimed for later construction or other uses. These short-lived households probably failed to become established for a variety of reasons, one possibly being that the inhabitants were only taking refuge in the larger towns temporarily. This translates to a Mimbres town being composed of both permanent families and attached-temporary or transient families. Such a dual strategy of stability and intermittent mobility could have provided an important adaptive advantage for the Mimbres during cycles of drought or above-average precipitation.

Recent data reported by Darrell Creel (1996)

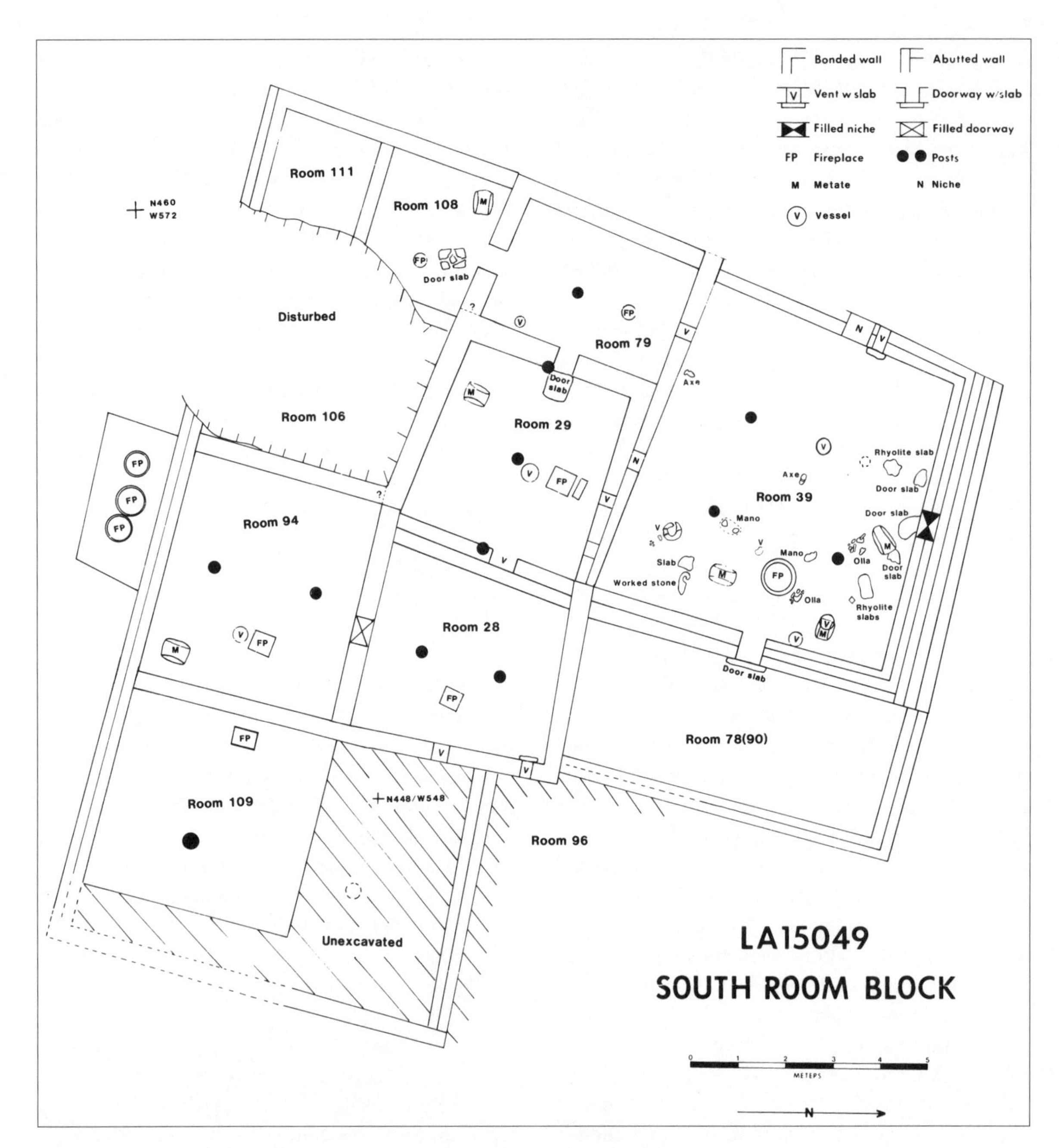

Figure 9.3. South room block at the NAN Ruin showing habitation (H), storerooms (S), civic-ceremonial room (CC), and granary (G).

indicate that when the population in the Mimbres valley approached its apogee in ca. A.D. 1050–1100, annual rainfall rates were fluctuating between episodes of good and bad years. Based on a 13-inch annual rainfall average, measurements for the years between A.D. 1043 and 1066 were good, with one exceptional spike in 1048. The period from A.D. 1080 to 1093 fluctuated between good and bad years, but most were good. From A.D. 1090 to 1100 rainfall was generally below average, and there may have even been a pretty serious drought. The record shows some rather serious dribbles back and forth from A.D. 1100 to 1130 and a severe drought beginning at A.D. 1130.

When these climatic intervals are correlated with building spurts at the NAN Ruin, the results—although preliminary—are intriguing (Figure 9.4). Each dot on Figure 9.4 represents a cutting date from

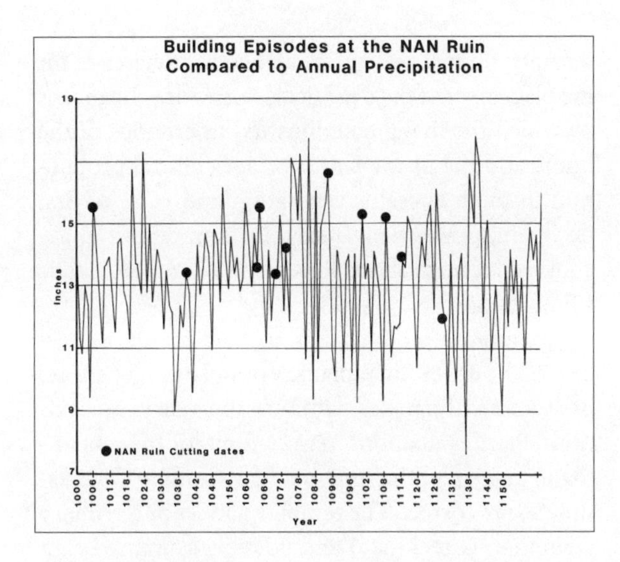

Figure 9.4. Building episodes at the NAN Ruin (dots) based on tree-ring cutting dates superimposed over rainfall pattern also reconstructed from tree-ring data (after Creel 1996).

one of the NAN Ruin rooms. Although at first glance it looks as though building episodes took place only during wet cycles and good years, the evidence may be deceiving because all dates fall above the 13" average rainfall line. Many of these building episodes follow immediately or a year or two after serious dry years or periods. The evidence seems to suggest that transient families are attracted to the large towns following one or two above-average-rainfall years. If the Mimbres practiced irrigation farming, this building pattern may be correlated with years of anticipated good river discharge for irrigation.

Despite disturbances caused by 100 years of ranching and modern development in the Mimbres valley and throughout the Mimbres drainage, recent archaeological evidence confirms historic references to ancient irrigation ditches (Webster 1912). LaVerne Herrington (1979, 1982) documented extensive Classic Mimbres irrigation networks along the Rio de Arenas. Lain Ellis (1995) has documented a major diversion ditch system in the Mimbres valley that fed into an artificial reservoir at the NAN Ruin, and the NAN Ranch Project documented a well-preserved prehistoric rainfall irrigation system in the Gavilan Canyon that is probably Mimbres in age (Creel and Adams 1985). These findings illustrate that the Mimbres practiced riverine irrigation, allowing them to overcome intermittently poor years of rainfall. As Creel (1996) has shown, river discharge can vary more dramatically than rainfall, and a poor discharge year may not correlate directly with a low-rainfall year. The geomorphology of the river, which creates numerous underground reservoirs and affects the water table, could offset short periods of drought (Creel 1996).

What might this be telling us? Judging from architectural evidence at the NAN Ruin, during the wet cycle—beginning about A.D. 1043 and ending ca. A.D. 1080—there was an influx of new families into the large towns in the valley. Families in peripheral areas were attracted to the large towns, where food stores and the best productive lands occur. Even in bad years there was probably enough discharge in the river for some irrigation (Creel 1996). During dry cycles between moderately good years after ca. 1080, some of these attached families would again disperse to other locales because they did not hold claim to prime valley lands. This scenario fits the architectural patterns of building and abandonment at the NAN and Swarts ruins. It may also help to explain ruins that were built late in the Mimbres sequence, like NAN 15, and abandoned after a generation or so. NAN 15 is a 25- to 30-room pueblo ruin near a spring along a middle Mimbres River tributary. Ceramic style and tree-ring dates obtained from Texas A & M University investigations in 1984 (unpublished) suggest construction after A.D. 1080.

In short, climatological, tree-ring, and architectural data are providing circumstantial evidence of a combined strategy of long-term sedentism established by the core families who held claim to the most productive lands through the rule of first occupancy and short-term sedentism (Nelson and LeBlanc 1986; Nelson and Anyon 1996) for families who held no ancestral claim to the well-watered valley lands. The ebb and flow of transient families likely depended on the standard of living they could maintain on second- and third-choice agricultural lands around springs and subirrigated plots of drainages and marshes. Some of these itinerant families may have spent time hunting and gathering in traditional lands in the Chihuahuan desert to the south and east. In other words, sites similar to the Florida Mountain site (Minnis and Wormser 1984) may be out there that are Classic Mimbres in age. The late Pithouse period Florida Mountain site was possibly a plant processing locality based on the amount of burned rock and burned rock features present.

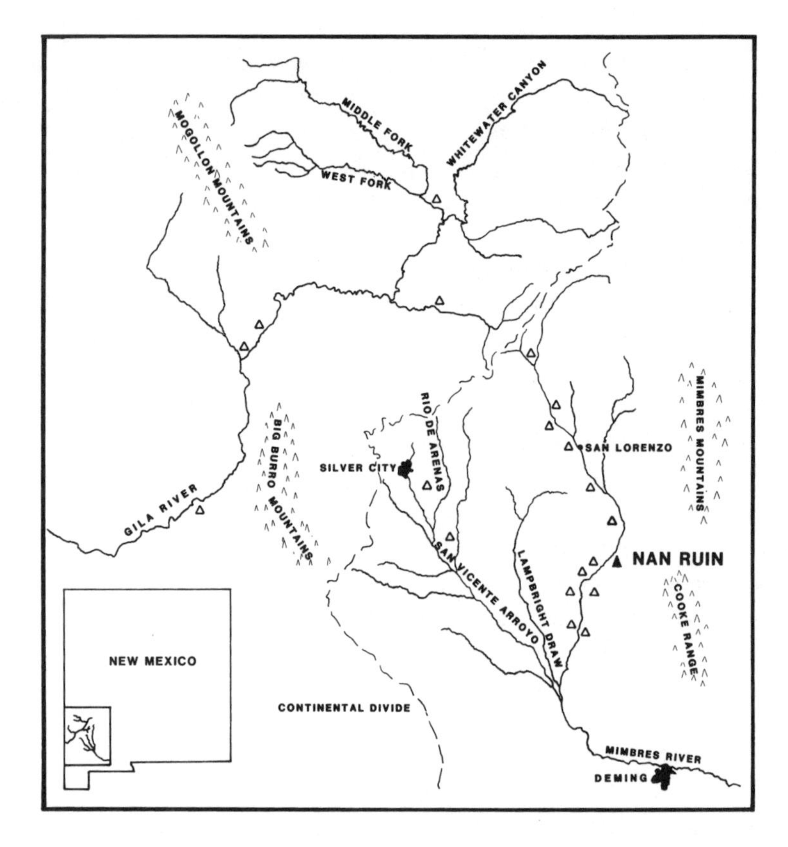

Figure 9.5. Map showing the geographic distribution of large Classic Mimbres towns.

Classic Mimbres mortuary practices and Mimbres Style III pottery are among the definable traits of the Mimbres phenomenon and together with the large pueblo communities (Figure 9.5) serve to define the Mimbres heartland. The importance of the Mimbres phenomenon to contemporary populations in the greater region can be seen in the geographic distribution of Mimbres Style III pottery (Figure 9.1). For example, it occurs with significant frequency throughout the Jornada area. I will argue that there is a correlation between Mimbres mortuary behavior, large towns, Mimbres Style III pottery, and the presence of Mimbres pottery in the Jornada area.

Mortuary Practices

The shift to intramural family cemeteries did not occur until the A.D. 900s based on archaeological data from the NAN Ruin (Shafer 1995); prior to that time the few intramural burials were limited to infants and occasionally an adult female. The intramural cemetery not only represents a change in preference for the placement of the dead; it also provided the means by which the living could justify inheritance of the home and the prime lands for agricultural production through ancestor veneration and rules of first occupancy (McAnany 1996). Intramural burial accounted for up to about 80 percent of the NAN Classic Mimbres sample.

Extramural inhumations account for ca. 10 percent of the NAN Ruin mortuary population. These are predominantly males without mortuary associations. Plaza cremations may account for the remaining 10 percent of the NAN mortuary sample if our estimates are correct. The sample includes one primary cremation (Creel 1989) and possibly as many as ten secondary cremations, subadults and adults. The number of plaza cremations at the NAN Ruin—estimated to number at least 100—suggests this was not reserved just for exceptional circumstances but was a treatment applied to a significant percentage of the mortuary population. The rules that distinguished the more public extramural inhumations and cremations from the more private intramural inhumations are of course unknown and beyond speculation at this time. Presumably, the patterns reflect social and perhaps residential differentiation within and between Mimbres communities.

Based on data from both the NAN and Swarts ruins (Hill 1997) and, as noted earlier, specific rooms possibly were household shrines; as such, most of the dead were interred there (Figure 9.6). These household shrines, often marked by a dual hearth complex (Figure 9.6) composed of a slab-lined hearth and an adjacent slab-lined bin, were maintained through as many as five generations. Comparing rooms with a dual-hearth complex to those with no hearths, circular hearths, and slab-lined hearths shows that most of the intramural burials were placed in the dual-hearth complex rooms (Figure 9.7). The mortuary pattern supports the contention that these rooms may have been dedicated to the ancestors; the slab-lined bin also may have been a *sipapu,* or a small floor drum (Wilshusen 1989). Further supporting the idea that these were somehow special are the dual shelves, which very likely were a shrine, placed in the west wall of Room 12 (Figure 9.6). Rooms with dual-hearth complexes may be analogous in an organizational sense to the circular kivas of Pueblo II and Pueblo III room blocks in the San Juan district

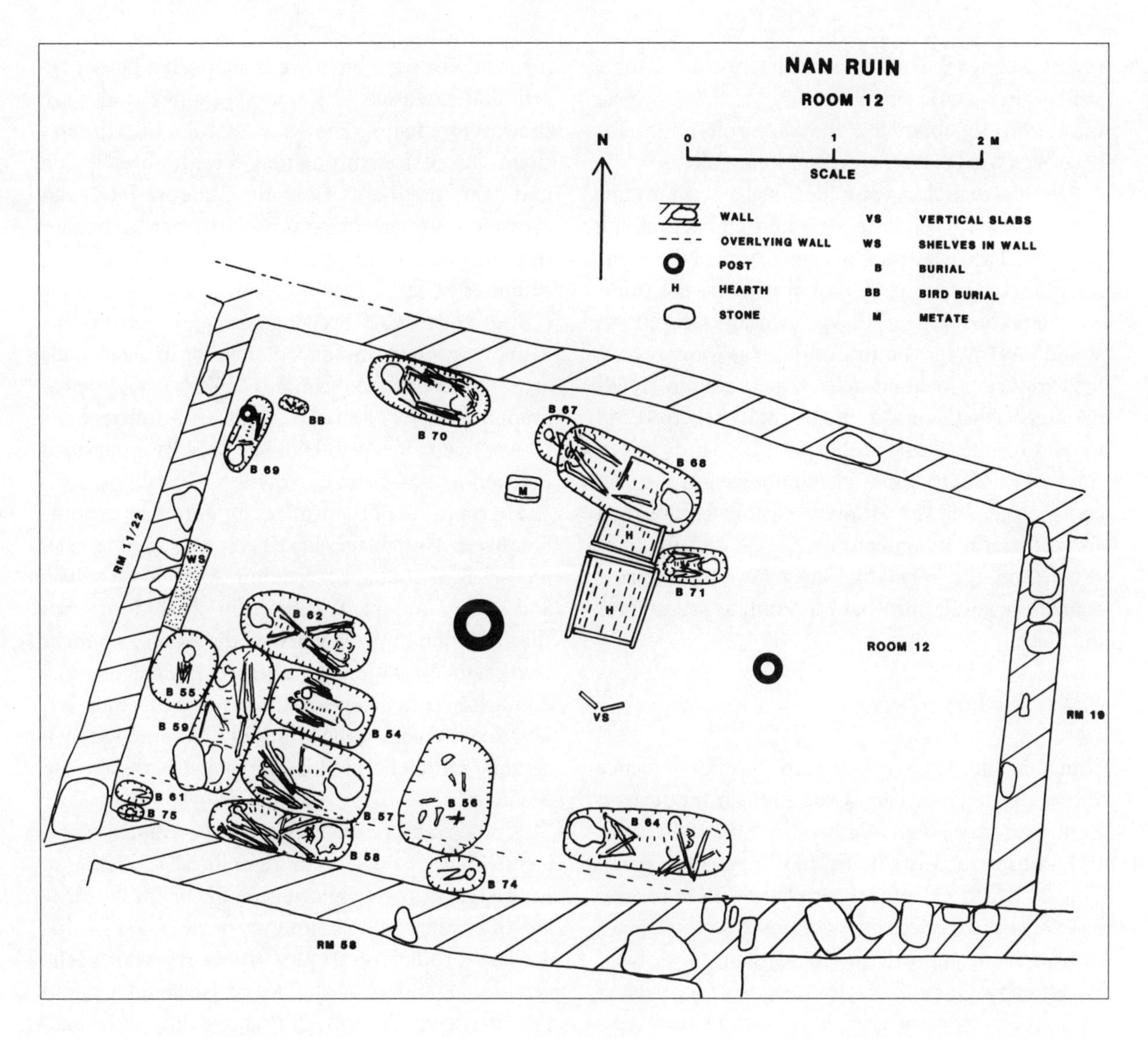

Figure 9.6 (Above). Room 12 at the NAN Ruin showing the placement of burials relative to hearth location.

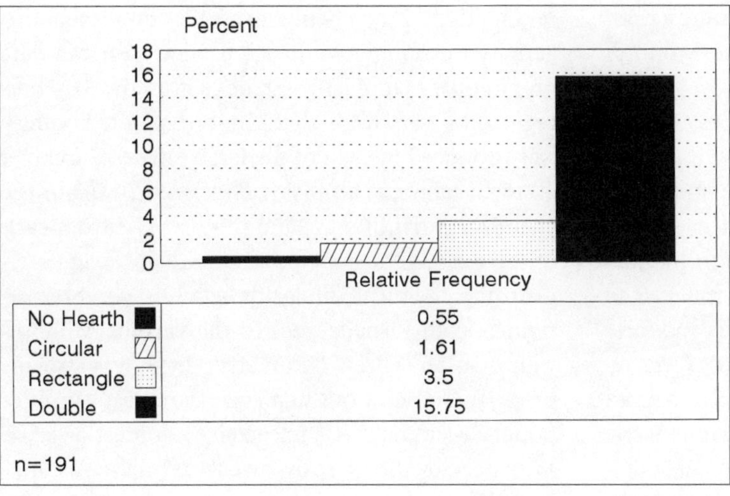

Figure 9.7 (Left). Graph showing mean numbers of burials per hearth type at the NAN Ruin.

(Wilshusen 1989). Furthermore, attached storerooms are another characteristic feature for these rooms, raising the possibility that the room suites may also have been used to store ritual paraphernalia.

Despite their longevity, the dual-hearth rooms went through periodic destruction and rebuilding episodes. These destruction episodes involved burning the rooms and rebuilding directly on the ruins. Although burning of Classic Mimbres rooms at abandonment was common, this behavior may have held important symbolism. Patricia McAnany (1996) has argued that a similar practice of destruction and rebuilding after burial in the Maya Lowlands was to show or exemplify a new generation's control of the core household. The Mimbres customarily burned structures at abandonment, perhaps as a termination ritual, and the rebuilding may have symbolized something similar to what McAnany is arguing for the Maya.

Classic Mimbres Pottery

Using the deeply stratified architectural sequence and associated mortuary associations from the NAN Ruin, we have seriated Mimbres Style II and III into a series of microstyles (Shafer and Brewington 1995). This stylistic development correlates with the evolving network of social interactions that took place from ca. A.D. 900 to 1110 (Brewington et al. 1994; Wobst 1977). This microstylistic sequence, correlated with tree-ring dates and dated architectural episodes, can be used as a means of ceramic cross-dating for Mimbres Style III outside the Mimbres valley.

When the material expression that best defines the Classic Mimbres period was in full swing, from A.D. 1050 to 1110, production of Classic Mimbres or Mimbres middle Style III pottery was at its height. Mimbres Style III pottery is widespread in the Jornada region, where it may account for as much as 10 percent of the ceramics in some late Mesilla and early Dona Ana phase sites (Shafer et al. 1998). Over 90 percent of the Mimbres pottery we have analyzed from the Tularosa Basin and sorted by microstyle falls in the middle to late Style III (Shafer et al. 1998). In other words, the time from A.D. 1050 to 1110 was when the Mimbres-Jornada interaction was at its peak.

The assumption that the Mimbres ceramics in the Jornada area were intrusive is supported by our recent and extensive NAA analysis (James et al. 1995; Brewington 1996). The NAA analysis of Mimbres sherds from sites throughout the Mimbres region and Mimbres sherds from the Tularosa basin has shown two important patterns: First, there were multiple manufacturing sites in the Mimbres area for Mimbres Style III Black-on-white and Polychrome (James et al. 1994; Brewington 1996). Second, the Mimbres pottery was indeed intrusive in the Jornada area (Shafer et al. 1998). Myles Miller's (1992) petrographic analysis of a large sample of Mimbres Style III B/W from the North Hills site in El Paso provided independent confirmation of the NAA findings.

High production estimates for ceramics in some Southwest assemblages have been attributed to various levels of craft specialization (Mills 1995; Wilson and Blinman 1995). The question of Mimbres craft specialization came up when we discovered a potter's grave at the NAN Ruin some years ago (Shafer 1985). I doubt, however, that ceramic craft specialization was ever a component in the Mimbres economic system if ceramic production in historic pueblos is taken into account.

A much better explanation may be found in nineteenth-century pueblo ethnographies. According to Fewkes (1891:16), women at Zuni pueblo in the nineteenth century held community-wide pottery firing events to produce pottery for various roles during the ceremonies and associated feasts. He counted about 150 such open kiln fires going at one time and makes no mention of men being involved. I doubt that this activity was unique to the Zuni. Given the NAA data on multiple manufacturing loci within the Mimbres region, it is very likely that Mimbres painted pottery was produced in each of the large towns (Gilman et al. 1994; James et al. 1995). This would explain the chemical variability in Mimbres Style III from each of the major sites sampled; it would also help to explain the chemical similarity between Mimbres ceramics from Jornada sites to the various Mimbres valley clusters (Brewington et al. 1995). It is also appropriate to point out that even the finest Mimbres pottery eventually was relegated to domestic use, as evidenced by the extensive use wear on the vast majority of the vessels (Lyle 1996). It was from the domestic context that vessels were drawn for use in the mortuary context.

Major calendar ceremonies at Zuni in the nineteenth century were attended by locals as well as by visitors from distant pueblos and even Apaches and Navajos (Cushing 1920). Visitors witnessed the ceremonies, participated in the feasts, received gifts, and apparently bartered items of exchange (Fewkes 1891). Visitors also left with knowledge of some of the ceremonies and practiced variations of them at their own pueblos. These events served to unify or standardize ritual behavior among the pueblo populations through shared experiences and also served as mechanisms to move great quantities of material goods such as pottery over considerable distances. I think it is precisely this mechanism of ceremonial activity and feasting that resulted in the spread of iconographic-rich pottery across the American Southwest (Crown 1994).

Depictions of Mimbres pottery showing dances or processions (Figures 9.8 and 9.9) and Mimbres ceremonial paraphernalia recovered from cave sites in the Mimbres region (Cosgrove 1947) indicate that the Mimbres also held public ceremonies, and it is assumed that feasting was an important element in these events, given traditional pueblo practices. The Mimbres ceremonies and feasts likely drew visitors from within the valley and beyond. Whether visitors contributed to the food and material preparation is not known. There is surprisingly little identifiable intrusive material culture other than obsidian and shell. Intrusive ceramics—such as Cibola White Ware, for example—uniformly constitute a minor percent of ceramics in the late Pithouse period at the NAN Ruin and are rare in the Mimbres valley (but less so in the upper Gila) during the Classic Mimbres period. Plain El Paso Brown Ware, however, is the most common intrusive ware in Mimbres sites throughout the late Pithouse and Classic Mimbres periods. If equal exchange was a factor, we would expect an equal amount of intrusive wares to balance the amount of exported Mimbres wares. This is certainly not the case.

When intrusive ceramics do occur, however, they may not meet our expectations. Consider the ceramic assemblage from Room 74 at the NAN Ruin, a large storeroom dating to ca. A.D. 1130 that contained a large El Paso Red-on-brown jar, a large Chihuahua indented corrugated jar, and several large Mimbres corrugated and Style III Black-on-white jars (Shafer 1991). I propose these large jars were used for brewing some kind of ceremonial drink like tesvino—similar to the Tarahumara practice (Lumholtz 1902:253)—but we have no evidence to support this theory. My point is that the widespread distribution of Mimbres Style III vessels throughout the Jornada region can be attributed, in part, to the Jornada people's attending Mimbres feasts and leaving with gifts and items of exchange, including Mimbres Style III bowls.

Figure 9.8. Drawing of Mimbres bowl depicting a ceremony in progress (taken from Moulard 1981:Plate 1).

Figure 9.9. Photo of bowl from the NAN Ruin showing the same ceremonial scene as depicted in Figure 9.8.

Figure 9.10. Mimbres Style III Black-on-white showing warped form and chipped paint.

This scenario of ceremonial events and feasts evidently has a long history in the pueblo Southwest. Also, judging from historic Pueblo behavior (McGuire and Saitta 1996), status among lineages was defined on the basis of ceremonial knowledge and keepers of ceremonial paraphernalia. Ranked kin groups gained their prestige through ownership of the secrets and knowledge of the most important ceremonies because they had inherited this knowledge and access to the best agricultural lands. I think the mortuary evidence from the South Room Block at the NAN Ruin (Shafer 1991), which was occupied for some five to six generations, is an archaeological example of this pattern. When these Mimbres lineages hosted important ceremonies, the entire community participated in the preparation of feasts (if nineteenth-century pueblo behavior can be used as a model).

Middle and late Mimbres Style III ceramics often display poor technological preparation and are technologically inferior to Style II (Shafer and Brewington 1995). Although warpage occurred throughout the Mimbres black-on-white series, warped vessels and vessels with peeled and chipped slip and paint are noticeably more frequent in Style III (Figure 9.10). These imperfections could be due to rapid production under less-than-ideal conditions in preparation for ceremonial events much like what Fewkes observed at Zuni. I am arguing that much of Mimbres Style III pottery was produced in the context of ceremonial and feasting activity rather than being the product of economic craft specialization.

The symbolism on Mimbres painted pottery has drawn more than its share of attention. We will never get into the minds of the Mimbres women who dreamed up the designs to know their meanings, but there are enough symbolic rules that are observable and that have contextual parallels to known ideologies. I think the graphic themes on Style III vessels do indeed reflect the worldview of the Mimbres as persuasively argued by Barbara Moulard (1981; see also Thompson 1994; Shafer 1995), and many of the images likely represent mythical elements, symbols, or metaphors, as argued by Mark Thompson (1990, 1994). Nowhere else in the ancient Southwest was such symbolism more graphic than among the Mimbres. Certainly Moulard's layered universe model—elements of which survive into historic pueblo beliefs (Hieb 1994)—was symbolized not only in the ceramics but in the architecture and mortuary behavior (Shafer 1995). Although these themes may parallel those of the Maya as presented in the Popul Vuh, as Thompson (1990, 1994) suggests, I believe that the similarity is more historical in nature. I think Thompson (1994) is correct in suggesting the Maya and Mimbres shared a common ideology, but not from diffusion; they may have shared a common, albeit distant, ancestry. Certainly, many of the themes that appear in both Maya and Mimbres iconography have been documented in the Chihuahuan Desert Archaic by Carolyn Boyd (1996), dating to about 4000 years ago. I am currently of the opinion that Mesoamerican influence on Mimbres material culture and symbolism was virtually nonexistent (see chapter 12 of this volume).

Collapse of the Mimbres System

Rather suddenly, probably over a period of about 20 years—from A.D. 1120 to 1140—or one generation, the big Mimbres towns were abandoned and the whole cultural system ended. Why this occurred is anything but certain. Minnis (1981) has argued for an ecological failure created by too many people and a restricted resource base correlated with diminishing rainfall. Creel's (1996) data substantiate a significant drought period that could have been the catalyst. Certainly, sustained failure in agricultural production for whatever reason could have set a demographic shift in motion. But I strongly believe the problem developed in a failure at the point of the prime lands. Perhaps the river flow dropped to the point that irrigation was no longer possible. If you cannot get water to the fields, nothing will grow. The reasoning that this is the locus of the failure is that the strength in the social network lay in the ancestral ties and reinforcing ceremonies. Once the bond between the land and the ancestors/families was broken, the ceremonies and the associated religious and symbolic media—including Mimbres Style III pottery—were no longer relevant.

The people abandoned the large Classic Mimbres towns and relocated elsewhere. I believe that most probably went back to the desert to the south and joined the desert populations that were there all along. Christy Turner's (1993) analysis of dental traits of the NAN Ruin population places them in the greater northern Mexico group (see chapter 17 of this volume). This evidence may either reflect a northern Mexican ancestry, as stated previously, a descendant Mimbres population, or more likely both. The Gila Mimbres may have done likewise or may have become absorbed in the mountain Mogollon groups.

Argument for Discontinuity

I adhere to the interpretation that the Mimbres heartland was abandoned for a period of time, possibly until about A.D. 1200. This is in contrast to some who argue for a continuity in valley occupation (Creel 1996 and chapter eight of this volume). The occurrence of Black Mountain phase ceramics and urn burial at Swarts Ruin (Cosgrove and Cosgrove 1932) and Postclassic presence at Galaz (Anyon and LeBlanc 1984b) is well documented. Also, there is a very small amount of El Paso Polychrome and Chupadero Black-on-white at the NAN Ruin, either mixed in with the architectural rubble or in deposits capping the rubble. I attribute much of this Black Mountain material at the NAN Ruin to a scatter that came from the large Black Mountain pueblo located only ca. 150 m north of the NAN Ruin. Creel (this volume), in making his case for continuity, reviews the Classic Mimbres–Black Mountain phase association data, so I need not repeat it here. The fact that the Black Mountain people used previous sites in addition to numerous new locations does not in itself demonstrate continuity. It also is possible that pilgrimages were periodically made to certain ancient ruins for some time after abandonment. But my main argument against continuity lies more in the behavioral realm, that is, in the complete break with the system of behaviors that left us with the large towns, a highly developed mortuary pattern, and Mimbres Style III pottery.

A theory as to why Mimbres Style III pottery production ceased was presented earlier. To briefly reiterate: I believe that it was made to display or communicate and reinforce a belief system and cosmology that tied the ancestors to the prime agricultural lands and to the households of the descendants. The public ceremonies that reinforced the cosmology and acted out the myths also involved public feasting. The Mimbres painted pottery that displayed the abstract and figurative symbols of this cosmology was produced to be used in the ceremonial/feasting events. These mythical bonds were severed when those residential links were abandoned and the material culture that was produced to project or communicate the reinforcing symbolism ceased to be produced.

Mortuary behavior played an important role in defining the households with ancestral connections to the land and as a powerful reinforcing mechanism for the cosmology and mythical relations. Specific rooms with dual-hearth complexes served as core household shrines to the ancestors. Again, once the ancestral ties to the land were broken at abandonment, these practices also ceased. Perhaps Cushing (1920:24) explained the relationship between pottery style, ancestors, and land tenure when he quoted a Zuni informant who said, "Is not the bowl the emblem of the earth, our mother?"

After the Classic Mimbres abandonment, the valley was occupied by short-term sedentary groups (Nelson and LeBlanc 1986; Nelson and Anyon 1996). The desert Jornada people of the Black Mountain phase soon moved into the lower and middle sections of the valley, reoccupying a few of the ruins at Old Town, Swarts, and Galaz for a brief time until they constructed their own adobe pueblos, often nearby. The Black Mountain people were very likely descendants of the Mimbres, but enough time had elapsed between the Classic Mimbres abandonment and the Postclassic reoccupation that certain themes had dropped out of the cultural repertoire. Virtually all of the painted ware in the Black Mountain phase was intrusive El Paso Polychrome, Chupadero Black-on-white, St. Johns Polychrome, early Chihuahua polychromes, and Three Rivers Red-on-terracotta; about the only locally produced pottery was the culinary ware Playas Red in its various textured varieties (Williams 1996).

Although the mortuary behavior of the Black Mountain phase has some continuities in the form of intramural burial with killed vessels placed over the heads, cremation burials were more frequent than before. Cremation was practiced among the Classic Mimbres probably in a frequency higher than has been documented archaeologically, as noted earlier. To me the compelling body of evidence for an occupational discontinuity includes differences in the mortuary behavior, the absence of especially marked shrine rooms with high numbers of burials, and the absence of a locally produced painted ware with motifs and iconography that provided a reinforcing mechanism to the cosmology of the new system.

The Black Mountain phase was apparently short-lived; the people took advantage of a short wet-cycle and maintained distant relationships with Casas Grandes but soon moved out again, probably back to the desert. Sometime later, they returned once again for a brief time in the 1300s as Cliff phase groups with strong Salado ceremonial connections, only to abandon the valley forever after about two generations. It is important to note that neither of the Postclassic occupations created their own brand of decorated pottery to reinforce new ancestral ties to the land. It seems that their affiliation was with distant power centers—Casas Grandes, Cibola, Salado—where such ties became established.

Summary

The Mimbres phenomenon consisted of a region in the Mimbres and upper Gila river drainages in which large pueblo towns and associated dispersed outliers were clustered. The populations in these communities participated in shared ceremonial and feasting events whose basic function was to reinforce the value system and worldview with an emphasis on maintaining harmony and bringing rain. Part of this value system included the use of indoor cemeteries. Indoor cemeteries in specific rooms—the dominant mortuary pattern after A.D. 1000—encoded the cosmology, historical events, and inheritance of agricultural plots through the household architecture. Descendants laid claim to the architecture, fields, and important ceremonies. The social spheres created by the ceremonial occasions stimulated vivid symbolic expressions of the sacred themes in the material culture; one such medium was Mimbres Style III pottery. Material exchange through gift giving and mutualism during these occasions helped to level out the material expression among the large towns and to distribute ceramics and other paraphernalia throughout the Jornada region. The Mimbres legacy among the Jornada desert population can be seen in the rock art and *katsina* ceremonialism (P. Schaafsma 1994).

Because of regional geography, there is some variability within the Mimbres region. Differences in such things as mortuary behavior and subtle differences in frequencies of ceramic motifs between the towns in the Mimbres and upper Gila drainage, for example, may be attributed to stylistic drift; that is, the Gila settlements were simply more familiar with each other than they were with settlements in the Mimbres valley proper.

The system failed when the ranking families who owned the ceremonies and prime lands abandoned their fields and, by extension, their households possibly because of worsening drought conditions or other environmental hardships. The value system previously sustained by the ceremonies, along with the beliefs and intramural mortuary practices, began to fade. Abandonment severed ancestral ties to house, land, and inheritance rights of first occupancy and put an end to intramural burial as a dominant mortuary pattern. Without the ranking families' ceremonial knowledge the major ceremonies and associated feasts were no longer held, and the material expression of these occasions—as represented by the symbolism on the Classic Mimbres pottery—was no longer sanctioned. Mimbres Style III pottery was one material element of the ceremonial-feasting process. The termination of this process led to the termination of Mimbres Style III pottery production and its characteristic symbolism and iconography and thus ended the material expressions that define the Mimbres phenomenon, which is perhaps more appropriately labeled "the Mimbres ceremonial and feasting complex."

I have argued for depopulation of the Mimbres heartland and an occupation hiatus of some 50 to 75 years before a substantial short-term sedentary population returned to the middle and lower parts of the Mimbres valley. Interestingly, the hiatus on the upper Gila in the Cliff valley was much longer. Material evidence for occupational discontinuity is documented in the areas of architecture, mortuary behavior, and ceramics. The most compelling evidence, however, lies in the symbolic and ceremonial behaviors, which reflect fundamental changes in the way the societies were organized and how they related to their natural and ancestral worlds. These are the kinds of cultural behaviors that establish group identity and are bonded by both historical and lineal relationships.

ACKNOWLEDGMENTS. Without my long-term experiences in the Mimbres valley and at the NAN Ruin this paper would not have been possible. I wish to acknowledge certain individuals for their support and encouragement over the years: Margaret and C. A. Hinton, LaVerne Herrington, Darrell and Ann Creel, and the students and staff at Texas A & M University who contributed so much effort toward expanding our knowledge of the Mimbres people. I particularly want to thank Robbie L. Brewington, Connie Judkins, and Carolyn Boyd for the insightful discussions on various topics that were brought together in this chapter. Funding sources that have aided our research over the years include the National Geographic Society, Earthwatch, College of Liberal Arts, Program to Enhance Scholarly and Creative Activities at Texas A & M University, Advanced Research Program Grant from the Texas Higher Education Coordinating Board, and private contributions. Comments on a previous draft of this paper were provided by Robbie L. Brewington, Darrell Creel, and Steve Lekson; however, I assume full responsibility for any error of fact or interpretation.

10

Cerro de Trincheras and the Casas Grandes World

Randall H. McGuire

Maria Elisa Villalpando C.

Victoria D. Vargas

Emiliano Gallaga M.

PREHISPANIC NORTHWEST MEXICO, that area from the international frontier south to the southern borders of the Mexican states of Sonora and Chihuahua, is an immense gray zone. Whether it was peripheral to the prehistory of the Southwest United States/Northwest Mexico Culture Area or not, it has been peripheral in the minds and theories of archaeologists (Phillips 1989). Traditionally they have explained cultural developments in the region using one of two models. Either these developments were simply the southern fringes of the Hohokam or Mogollon traditions of the Southwest (Haury 1976), or they resulted from the intrusion of Mesoamerican merchants from the south, who set up major centers as trade outposts (Di Peso 1974, 1983). More recently these debates have been recast in models of world systems that reach south to Mesoamerica (Di Peso 1983; Whitecotton and Pailes 1986; Weigand 1982) or peer polities developing in situ based primarily on local ecological relationships (Minnis 1989). At the core of all of these debates is the nature of economic relations at and between major Northwest centers such as Casas Grandes in Chihuahua and Cerro de Trincheras in Sonora (Figure 10.1).

Charles Di Peso (1979a:158–159) identified Casas Grandes and Cerro de Trincheras as Mesoamerican commercial centers. Two groups of Mesoamerican donors entered the Northwest by A.D. 1100 to establish the two centers, and they both withdrew south in the mid-fourteenth century. The two groups of merchants operated independently of each other, gathering goods from the southwestern cultures to the north and then shipping them south to their home polities in Mesoamerica. Di Peso argued that Cerro de Trincheras was "a spectacular hillside trenched defense system" built by Mesoamerican merchants to protect the marine shell industry at the nearby site of La Playa (Di Peso 1979a:158). From the site of La Playa these merchants shipped bulk raw materials to the Hohokam shell artisans.

Di Peso's theory about Cerro de Trincheras is only one of several that attempt to account for the site in terms of specialized functions or in terms of processes centered outside of northern Sonora. Among the oldest of these ideas are the notions that the site was a refuge fort (McGee 1898) or that it was a massive terraced agricultural field (Huntington 1912). Numerous scholars have suggested that Cerro de Trincheras was a rude station, specializing in the production of shell jewelry, at the southern periphery of

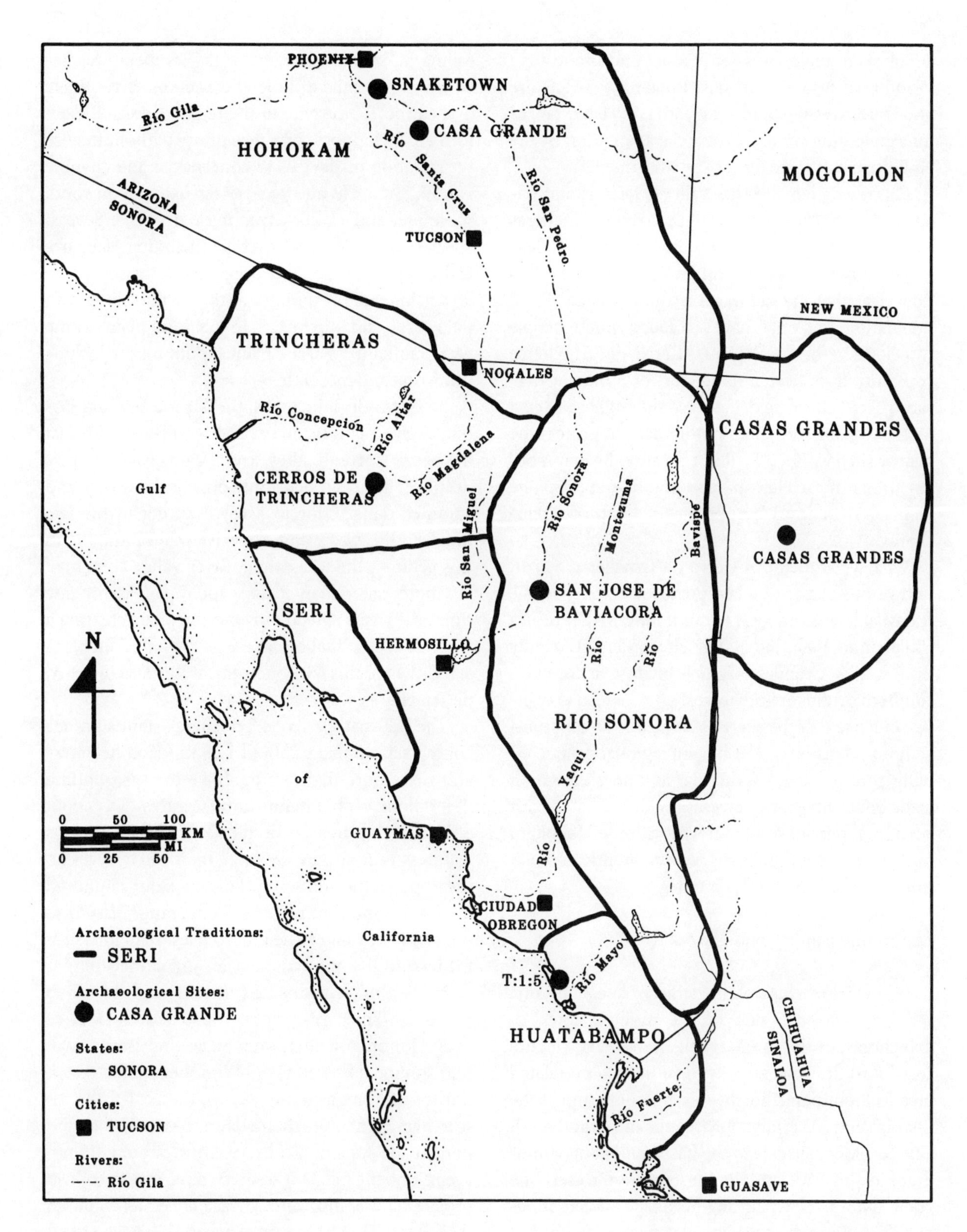

Figure 10.1. Map of Northwest Mexico.

a Hohokam regional system (Sauer and Brand 1931; Woodward 1936; Tower 1945; Robles 1973; McGuire and Howard 1987). Johnson (1960) and Haury (1976) interpreted the site as a provincial adaptation by the Hohokam culture to the local environment.

Our research in the Altar Valley (McGuire and Villalpando 1993) and at the site of Cerro de Trincheras (McGuire et al. 1993; O'Donovan 1997) has challenged most of these hypotheses (Figure 10.2). It is now clear that the site was a terraced village with a population that may have exceeded 2,000 people (McGuire et al. 1993). Thus, Cerro de Trincheras could not have been a refuge fort or a massive terraced agricultural field. It also could not have been a massive defensive system put in place to protect the nearby shell works at La Playa because the major occupations of La Playa predate the late Prehispanic (A.D. 1300 to 1450) occupation of Cerro de Trincheras.

We have argued that Cerro de Trincheras was an indigenous center of a late prehistoric polity in the Río Magdalena drainage (Braniff 1985; McGuire and Villalpando 1989, 1993). The site differs strikingly from Casas Grandes, arguing against a common southern origin for both towns. There is also very little evidence that the site was culturally or economically an extension of a Hohokam regional system. Finally, contrary to most theories and lines drawn on trade-route maps, we have no evidence to suggest economic relations to the north with the Hohokam but some evidence that suggests economic connections to the east, to Casas Grandes.

Environment and Previous Work

Cerro de Trincheras covers a large, isolated, volcanic hill on the south side of the modern town of Trincheras, in the Río Magdalena drainage (Figure 10.3). This drainage was the most heavily populated area in Prehispanic northwestern Sonora and at the Spanish entrada (Spicer 1962; Sauer and Brand 1931). The Río Magdalena is in the basin-and-range topographic province and in the Sonoran Desert life zone. Before arroyo cutting began in the late nineteenth century, the river was permanent, wide, and shallow, with marshes common along its course. Precipitation comes to the region primarily in the form of summer cloudbursts, with lesser amounts of rain falling in extensive winter fronts. Temperatures between the months of June and September routinely exceed 100°F. Nowhere in the region does sufficient rain fall to support corn agriculture without the use of irrigation or devices to concentrate and channel runoff. Creosote and to a lesser extent ironwood, mesquite, and cholla cover the flat plains. Several species of columnar cactus, including saguaro, cadron, garambillo, and organ pipe, thrive on the lower slopes of the mountain (the bajada) along with palo verde and other cacti. In the flood plains of the river remnant riparian plant communities include ironwood and mesquite.

At Cerro de Trincheras, the Magdalena and Boquillas rivers empty out of narrow valleys onto a vast flat basin. Currently these rivers carry water in their deeply entrenched beds only during the winter and summer rains. Prior to arroyo cutting in the late nineteenth century and extensive water pumping in this century, the Magdalena River valley contained far more water than it does today. In Prehispanic times the rivers spread out over the plain, creating a vast cienaga, or shallow lake. The town of Trincheras stands where this lake once did, at the base of Cerro de Trincheras.

The hill that Cerro de Trincheras stands on encompasses an area of about 1 sq km (100 hectares) and rises more than 150 m above the surrounding desert floor. Visible architectural features cover about a third of this area (31 hectares). The most obvious features at the site are the more than 900 terraces on the slopes of the hill. Some of these run for a hundred meters or more, but most are in the range of 15 to 30 m long. They range in height from less than 100 cm at the base of the hill to more than 3 m at the summit.

Numerous scholars had visited and described Cerro de Trincheras prior to our research (McGee 1898; Huntington 1912, 1914; Sauer and Brand 1931; Johnson 1960; Bowen 1976). With the notable exception of Huntington (1912, 1914), none of these researchers spent more than a day or two at the site, and none made systematic observations. Several did not even climb the hill. Our research has consisted of two projects: a mapping and surface collection done in the fall of 1991 (McGuire et al. 1993; O'Donovan 1997) and two seasons of excavation in the springs of 1995 and 1996.

In the fall of 1991 Elisa Villalpando and Randall

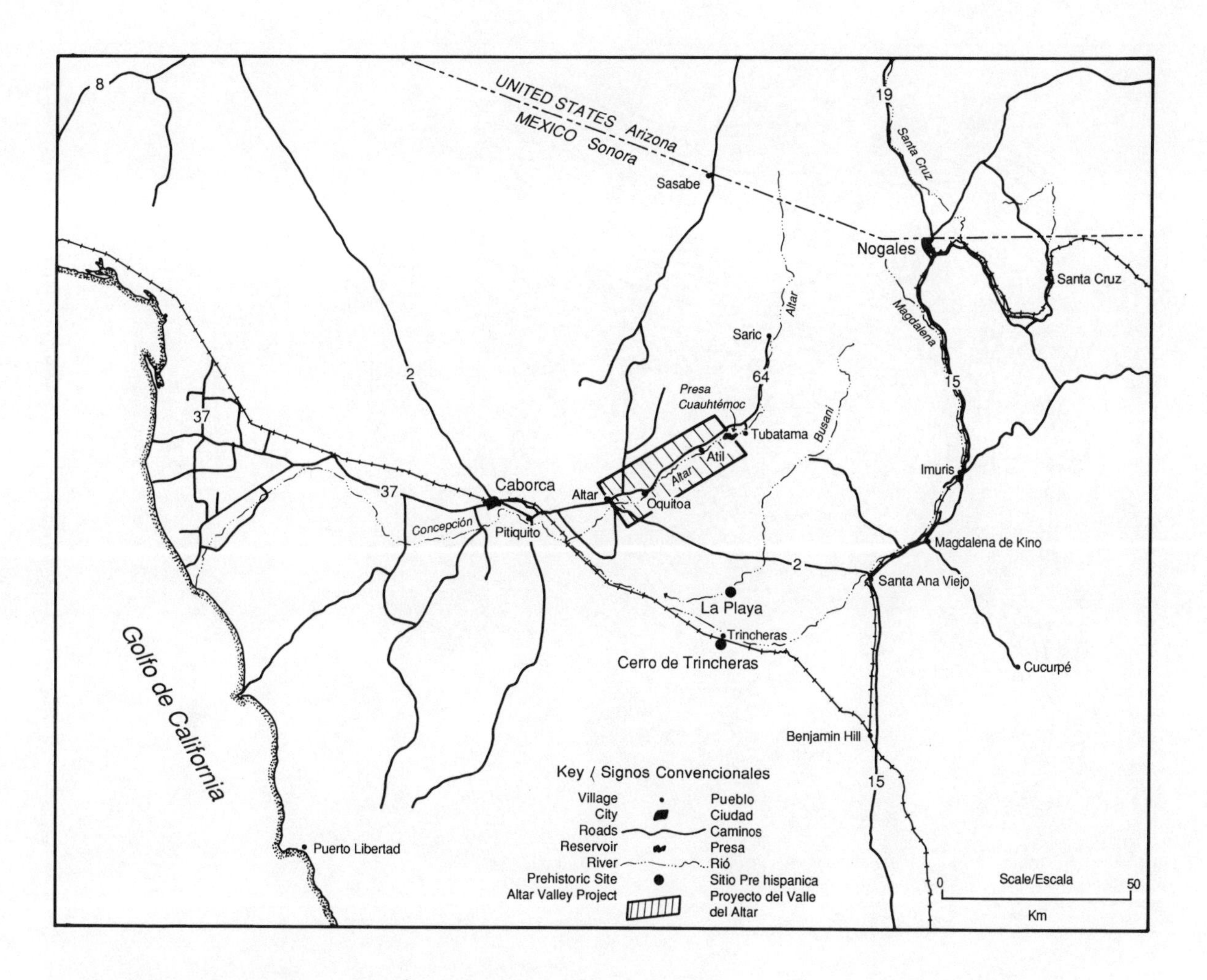

Figure 10.2 (Above). Map of Northwest Sonora.

Figure 10.3 (Left). Cerro de Trincheras, Trincheras, Sonora.

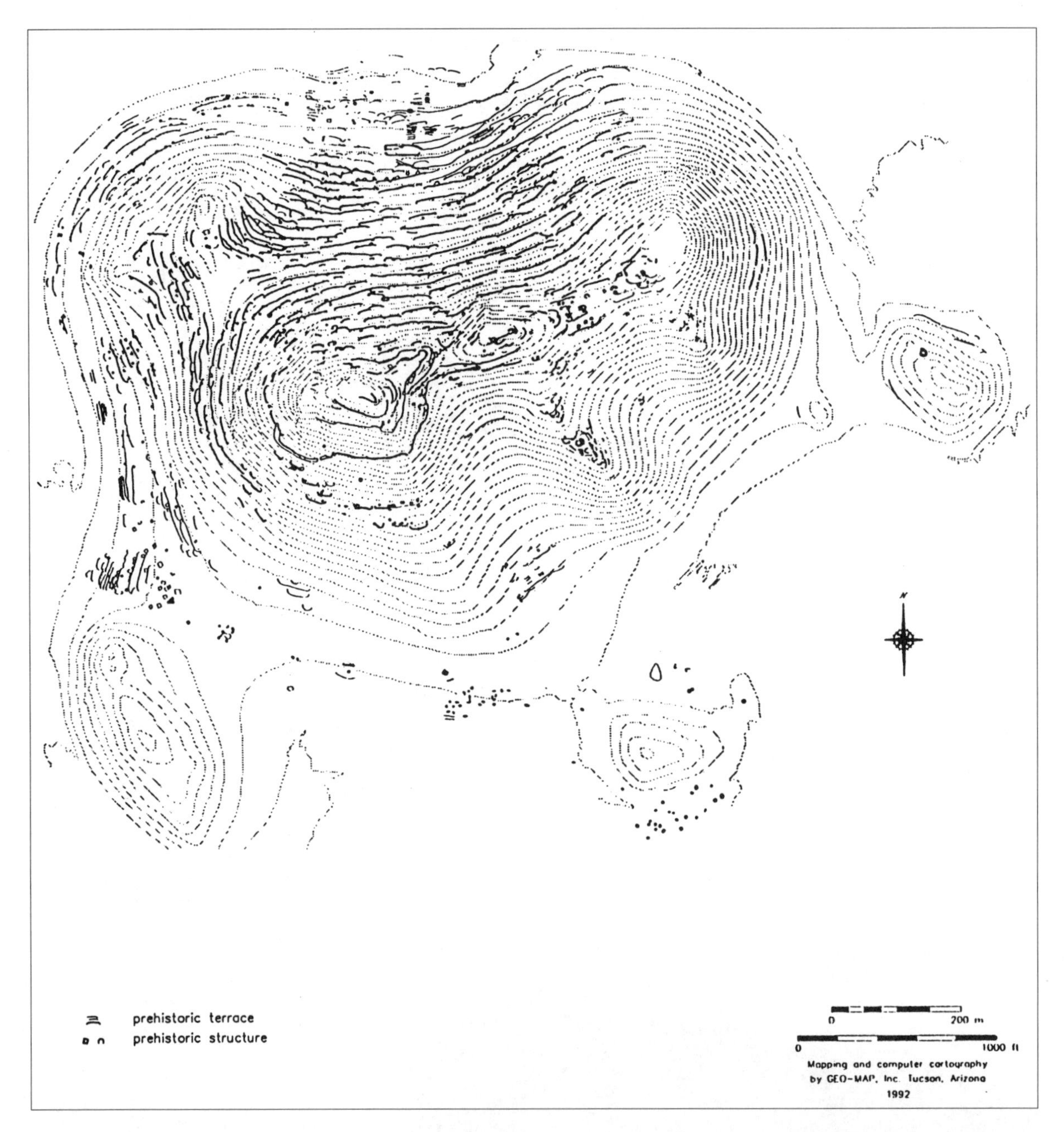

Figure 10.4. Map of Cerro de Trincheras.

McGuire conducted a surface survey and mapping project at the site of Cerro de Trincheras (McGuire et al. 1993). The National Geographic Society sponsored this work with grant number 4454-91. The project contracted with Geo-Map of Tucson, Arizona, to produce a photometric contour map of the site. Survey crews then systematically walked over the entire site to locate all features visible on the surface of the site, even amorphous rock piles and isolated rock alignments. Each feature was measured, and then the crews plotted the features on aerial photographs. In Tucson Geo-Map transferred the features from the aerial photos to the contour map (Figure 10.4). The survey crews made systematic, controlled surface collections from each terrace and feature. We recovered more than 23,000 artifacts in these collections. These materials included ground stone, chipped lithics, ceramics, large quantities of marine shell, and a handful of stone beads, including two of turquoise. Artifact density ranged from one or two artifacts per square meter to over 200 artifacts per square meter on different parts of the site, with an overall average artifact density of 10 artifacts per square meter. Our analyses of the artifacts indicate a variety of activities—including food preparation, burial of the dead, shell working, pottery making, and stone-tool production—that archaeologists normally associate with a habitation site that is a village or a town.

We returned to the site in the springs of 1995 and 1996 with support from the National Science Foundation (SBR9320224) to conduct extensive excavations. The project excavated about half of a hectare, or 1.5 percent of the total site area. Local laborers and project archaeologists did all excavations by hand. The archaeologists drew stratigraphic profiles whenever appropriate and collected artifacts by natural and cultural levels. With the exception of exploratory trenching, all fill was passed through ¼-inch screens to increase artifact recovery. When buried features were encountered, they were excavated, collected, mapped, and photographed in their entirety. We plotted all excavations and features on the site map generated by the mapping project. We intentionally did not excavate in the known cremation cemeteries, but we did encounter burials in some of the terraces. Field crews collected both C-14 and archaeomagnetic samples, but because of the magnetic characteristics of the hill the archaeomagnetic samples did not work out. The project collected three types of biological samples in the excavation: pollen, animal bone, and flotation samples.

Archaeological deposits at Cerro de Trincheras tended to be very shallow, usually 10 to 20 cm. This meant that the preservation of materials was generally quite poor. Organic materials were present only if charred, and the preservation of bone, both animal and human, was generally poor. Features were also not well preserved. Houses, stone rooms, surface jacales, and pithouses usually showed evidence of much disturbance and poor preservation. Artifacts also have suffered damage as a consequence of the shallowness of the site. For example, potsherds tended to be quite small. A second consequence of the shallowness of deposits is that an unknown but clearly large amount of material has been removed from the surface of the site. Residents of Trincheras frequently spoke to us of items such as metates, pots, and skulls that they knew had been picked up from the surface of the ruin. Older residents said that in the past much more material was visible on the surface of the ground but that it had been collected over the years. Little of this material seems to remain in the community because it has been sold to U.S. collectors, who apparently visit Trincheras fairly regularly.

These excavations exposed a considerable number of features and recovered many artifacts. In two seasons of fieldwork we have excavated, recorded, and mapped over 20 terraces, more than 40 houses, 2 public architectural features, and over 75 other features. Artifact recovery included nearly one million pottery sherds, over 100,000 lithics, and over 3,000 pieces of marine shell.

The Site of Cerro de Trincheras

Analysis of the materials from Cerro de Trincheras is ongoing, and our conclusions here are based largely on the first year's materials. We can, however, draw some preliminary conclusions with the information that we have on hand. These conclusions tend to confirm our inference that the site was a late Prehispanic agriculturally based town.

Ceramics and radiocarbon dating suggest that the occupation of Cerro de Trincheras was limited to a single phase. Bowen (1976) has suggested a chronology of four numbered phases for the Trincheras tradition. Phase 3 (A.D. 800–1300) sites yield Trincheras Purple-on-red and Nogales Polychrome and include large pithouse villages like La Playa. We found only a handful of Purple-on-red sherds at Cerro de Trincheras, and the rest of the painted ceramic types we found were late Prehispanic polychromes, including various Chihuahua types, Gila Polychrome, and Santa Cruz Polychrome. This assemblage suggests that Cerro de Trincheras dates to Bowen's Phase 4 (A.D. 1300–1450). Eleven C-14 dates collected in the first season's excavations confirm this phase assignment. These dates were very consistent and suggest an occupation of the site from around A.D. 1300 to around A.D. 1450. We currently believe that people lived at the site over most or all of this 150-year period. We base this inference both on the distribution of the dates and the fact that our excavations revealed complex sequences of building and rebuilding of terraces.

Both botanical specimens and artifacts demonstrate that Cerro de Trincheras was an agricultural settlement. Over 50 percent of the first year's flotation

Figure 10.5. Habitation terraces at Cerro de Trincheras.

Figure 10.6. Round stone room at Cerro de Trincheras.

samples had corn in them, and we also found evidence of squash and possibly cotton. One interesting outcome of the flotation was the common occurrence of agave in the samples. Agave would have been an important plant for food, fiber, and basketry. The natural range for agave starts approximately 300 m higher than the elevation of Cerro de Trincheras. In southern Arizona, Hohokam peoples used specially constructed agricultural features to grow agave at elevations comparable to Cerro de Trincheras. The artifact assemblage from the site also supports the inference of an agricultural town. The ground-stone assemblage includes manos and metates of types generally interpreted as being for grinding corn. We have a diverse range of other artifact types and good evidence for shell jewelry production. Ceramic vessels included a wide range of forms, among them large ollas, which were probably used for water storage, and sooted cooking pots.

The most obvious features at Cerro de Trincheras were terraces (900+ examples). Approximately 50 of these terraces were narrow and defined by a single row of rock. Based on comparison to similar features in Arizona, and the appearance of agave spines in flotation samples, we think that these terraces may have been used for raising agave. The vast majority of the terraces (420 to 600) were probably platforms for habitations (Figure 10.5). We have consistently found domestic artifact assemblages including ceramic jars, bowls, and plates; manos and metates; shell jewelry; chipped stone tools and debitage; and ash and charcoal on these terraces. The occupants constructed two types of structures on these platforms. Stone rooms had foundations of dry laid stone and were either round or rectangular (Figure 10.6). These features are usually visible from the surface of the ground, and we have recorded over 300 at the site. Our excavations uncovered jacales on many of these terraces. These structures had pole and ocotillo-branch superstructures that the builders had packed with daub. In addition to these two types of houses on terraces, we excavated a cluster of a dozen shallow pithouses below the hill and to the south.

The two most prominent features at the site are La Cancha and the Plaza del Caracol. La Cancha (feature 8) lies near the base of the hill on the north side. It is a large 15-m-×-57-m elongated oval. Unlike the other terraces, which the town's occupants filled primarily with rocks and cobbles, La Cancha has a 20 to 30 cm layer of fine, hard-packed silt over a deeper layer of rocks and cobbles. The builders used this silt layer to create a very flat, smooth, and uniform surface over the entire feature. In the center of the feature on its north wall the builders constructed a round stone room. Other than this room we found no other evidence of subfeatures within La Cancha, nor did we find posts that would suggest that La Cancha was roofed. The Plaza del Caracol lies on the crest of the hill toward the east end. El Caracol (feature 9) itself is built of dry laid cobbles with walls still standing to a height of 1.6 m. In plan view these walls form a

13-m-×-8-m spiral that looks like a snail shell cut in half. There is a small round rock room attached to the south side of the feature. The whole complex of features that forms the Plaza del Caracol covers an area 50 m × 55 m and included a plaza, about a dozen terraces, more than 20 stone rooms, and a series of walls that controlled access and limited sight lines into the complex.

The builders of Cerro de Trincheras combined these features, terraces, jacales, pithouses, and stone rooms in different ways, suggesting a complex activity structure to the town. Most of the occupation of the hill was on the north and west sides, with a single cluster of pithouses to the south of the hill. One cremation cemetery lies between this cluster of pithouses and the base of the hill, and a second lies to the north of the hill, in what is now the town of Trincheras. At the base of the hill the builders laid in the narrow terraces that we believe they used for agave cultivation. They constructed La Cancha just above these narrow terraces and filled the north face of the hill from this point to just below the crest with habitation terraces. Whatever went on in La Cancha would have been very public, visible from all of the households on the north side of the hill. The highest and the most prominent of these habitation terraces, a cluster of three terraces, we have called El Mirador because the occupants of this terrace were the only ones with an unobstructed view of every household on the north side of the hill. Above El Mirador there are fewer terraces. These terraces have few artifacts, reddish desert soils (unlike the gray midden-like fill of lower terraces), and appear to be platforms for presentations to the households below. A combination of walls and terraces controls access to the crest of the hill, where a series of architectural complexes including the Plaza del Caracol lie. Whatever went on in the Plaza del Caracol must have been private, visible only to those people in the plaza. The highest point of the site, El Pico de Zopilotes, lacks architectural features other than a series of walls that may create observation points for the winter and summer solstice.

Cerro de Trincheras in the Context of the Southwest/Northwest Culture Area

We argue that Cerro de Trincheras was a central place for the Trincheras Tradition. We are skeptical that it can be understood as an extension of events and processes happening in either Mesoamerica or southern Arizona. If the site were the twin pochteca outpost to Casas Grandes, as Di Peso theorizes, then we would expect the two towns to be similar in significant ways. If the site were a provincial outpost of the Hohokam tradition, then we would expect it to have a Hohokam artifact assemblage.

Cerro de Trincheras is the largest known town in the Trincheras Tradition. Given the paucity of archaeological research in northern Sonora, however, it is difficult to know exactly how it fit in a regional settlement pattern. Archaeologists have long recognized that Cerro de Trincheras is the largest *cerros de trincheras* in Arizona, or Sonora. With over 900 terraces, the site is easily four times larger than the next largest *cerros de trincheras.* Tio Benino (SON:F:6:6), a site with over 40 terraces in the Altar Valley, is the next-largest *cerros de trincheras* in Sonora (McGuire and Villalpando 1993). The largest *cerros de trincheras* in southern Arizona are the Cerro Prieto, with around 30 terraces and 250 round and square stone rooms, and Linda Vista, with over 200 terraces (Downum 1993). Given the size and visibility of Cerro de Trincheras it seems reasonable at this time to conclude that it was a central place in the Trincheras Tradition.

In a very broad sense Cerro de Trincheras and Casas Grandes are comparable sites. Both are among the largest of southwestern/northwestern settlements that archaeologists commonly classify as towns. Casas Grandes was slightly larger, covering 36 hectares to Cerro de Trincheras's 31 hectares. Population estimates are also comparable, with Di Peso et al. (1974:4:199) reckoning a maximum population at Paquimé of 2,995 people and with McGuire et al. (1993:74) calculating a maximum population for Cerro de Trincheras of 2,100 persons. Both stand out as the largest and most impressive towns in their respective regions. As towns, both were internally differentiated with areas of specialized production, cemeteries, sacred precincts, and socially differentiated residences. Beyond these very broad similarities of scale, however, the two sites are strikingly different.

The most obvious difference between the two sites lies in their architecture. The people of Casas Grandes built a substantial town out of adobe and surrounded it with earthen mounds and ball courts. By southwestern/northwestern standards this architecture is monumental in scope. In many ways the site of Cerro de Trincheras presents us with a paradox. The site is massive and visually monumental because of the hundreds of terraces that cover this prominent hill. These terraces represent an investment of labor that is quite high for the Northwest. The structures that the inhabitants built on these terraces, however, appear to have been quite insubstantial, resulting from a minimum of labor investment. The people of Paquimé lived in large, contiguous apartment structures built around plazas and compounds. In this context a variety of activities must have occurred within architectural spaces. The people of Cerro de Trincheras lived in small ephemeral stone and jacal rooms that would have been suitable only for sleeping and storage. These differences are not in any simple way the result of environmental differences. The Hohokam, who also lived in the Sonoran Desert, built massive adobe towns, such as Los Muertos, that were contemporary with Cerro de Trincheras. The plan, logic, and organization of both towns are clearly quite different.

Key to Di Peso's (1983) arguments was the idea that the Mesoamerican donors took up residence with local populations at Casas Grandes and Cerro de Trincheras. If this were the case we would expect evidence at both sites for the residences of this foreign population. This is not the case at Cerro de Trincheras, where no area of the site stands out as a foreign precinct.

Braniff (1985) and McGuire and Villalpando (1993) have argued that the Trincheras Tradition was a distinct development from the Hohokam Tradition of southern Arizona. Our excavations at Cerro de Trincheras have tended to confirm this evaluation. The only feature that the two traditions shared was the *cerro de trincheras* site type. Terraced hills in Sonora and in southern Arizona look quite similar, but the Hohokam of southern Arizona built different structures and deposited different artifacts on their hills than our Sonoran subjects did. We have also found no evidence to support the idea that Cerro de Trincheras was an outpost producing shell for the Hohokam (Craig 1982; McGuire and Schiffer 1982). Most of the objects produced at the site seem to have been used there, and we found no evidence for long-distance trade north into the Hohokam region.

Evidence For Long-Distance Exchange

Only a very small percentage of the artifacts that we recovered at Cerro de Trincheras obviously originated from outside of the region. We found no objects that came from Mesoamerica and only a handful of sherds that may derive from southern Sonora. The two categories of artifacts that gave the clearest evidence for long-range exchange were polychrome pottery and marine shell.

Ceramics

The most common artifacts that we recovered from Cerro de Trincheras were plainware pottery sherds. Trincheras Lisa 3 made up over 70 percent of the total pottery sherds recovered in the first year's excavations. This type is a coil-and-scrape-produced brownware that is the last type in the Trincheras Tradition plainware sequence. The next-most-common type, making up almost 30 percent of the total ceramics found in the first year, was Lisa Tardia (McGuire and Villalpando 1993). This is a paddle-and-anvil-produced, polished brownware that differs little in appearance from the Sells Plain of the Papagueria. We do not know if Cerro de Trincheras potters made Lisa Tardia or if it came from the Altar Valley 55 km to the north, where it is the most common plainware in the late Prehispanic period.

The painted ware from the site can be divided into two groups. The first group includes Phase 3 painted ceramics of the Trincheras Tradition (Trincheras Purple-on-red, Trincheras Purple-on-brown, Trincheras Polychrome, and Nogales Polychrome), and we have identified fewer than 20 sherds of these types from the first year's sample. The second group consists of non-Trincheras Tradition types, including Gila Polychrome, Santa Cruz Polychrome, and several types of Chihuahuan polychromes. Both groups make up only .15 percent of the total ceramic collection from both years of excavation.

Santa Cruz Polychrome and Gila Polychrome can appear very similar when recovered as small sherds. Both types are black and white painted over a red slip and are best distinguished by characteristics of the paste and paint (Santa Cruz Polychrome is consistently coarser on both counts). Gila Polychrome is one of the most widespread types found in the late Prehispanic Southwest/Northwest, with a range from southern Arizona to southern New Mexico and into northern Chihuahua. Less than 20 of the black-and-white-on-red sherds that we found in both years were Gila Polychrome. The vast majority were instead either Santa Cruz Polychrome, with slightly less than 300 sherds from both seasons, or Babocomari Polychrome, with slightly more than 30 sherds. These poorly known late Prehispanic types occur in the upper Santa Cruz River valley on both sides of the international border (Di Peso 1956).

The most common painted ceramics were the Chihuahuan polychromes. Sherds of these types made up almost half of the decorated ceramics but less than .1 percent of the total number of sherds recovered in both seasons. We identified Ramos Polychrome, with more than 500 sherds, and Babícora Polychrome, with almost 150 sherds.

The ceramic evidence from Cerro de Trincheras does not support any of the theories that interpret the site in terms of processes centered outside of northern Sonora. Ceramics of probable foreign manufacture make up a very small proportion of the total assemblage, far less than might be expected at a major trade outpost. The vast majority of ceramics at the site are the end product of a long-term ceramic sequence in the region and do not reflect ceramic types found to the north or south. Furthermore, the preponderance of Chihuahuan polychromes in the sample suggests economic relations to the east rather than to the north as is usually speculated. Along these lines it is noteworthy that we have found no Tucson Basin or Phoenix Basin types at Cerro de Trincheras or in our survey of the Altar Valley. The absence from northwestern Sonora of the Tucson Basin type Tanque Verde Red-on-brown, which is found throughout southern Arizona, is especially noteworthy in this respect.

Shell

The impression given by the shell we recovered at Cerro de Trincheras is very similar to that of the ceramics. The assemblages of shell artifacts from Medio period Paquimé (Casas Grandes) and Cerro de Trincheras bear several interesting similarities and differences. The similarities included several traits, distinct from groups in the Southwest. Similarities between the two assemblages include the shared presence of a "saucer-shaped" bead form and shared iconography between Chihuahuan polychromes (particularly Ramos Polychrome) and incised shell designs at Cerro de Trincheras.

Archaeologists rarely find saucer-shaped beads in the U.S. Southwest, and they have traditionally interpreted these beads as indicating interaction with California coast groups who produced and widely traded this form of bead (Jernigan 1978:37; Nelson 1981:58). California saucer-shaped beads and those examples found at sites in the U.S. Southwest that could be identified to genera are usually made from *Olivella* gastropods (Nelson 1981:58). Nelson (1981:58) lists only three sites in Arizona with these beads, including only six or seven examples total from Escalante Ruin, Los Muertos, and Babocomari Village. Cerro de Trincheras, however, yielded 180 of these beads, and Paquimé yielded 844 specimens (Di Peso et al. 1974:430).

Of the 180 saucer-shaped beads recovered from Cerro de Trincheras, we identified 25 to the *Conus* genera, whereas Paquimé's analysis identified only four specimens to genus, also *Conus*. Neither analysis assigned any of these beads to the genera *Olivella*. Given the large quantities of the beads at Paquimé, it is impossible to know how representative these four are of the whole assemblage. Our analysis identified numerous examples of in-process saucer-shaped beads at Cerro de Trincheras, but Di Peso et al. (1974) do not record any in-process examples at Casas Grandes. The lack of production evidence for these beads at Paquimé suggests that shell workers there did not make this form. Therefore, it is possible that these *Conus* saucer-shaped beads originated in the Trincheras area because Cerro de Trincheras is the only locale in the Southwest/Northwest to yield evidence for production of this form. Although the overall quantities of these beads are relatively small for both sites, they serve as one identifiable indicator of interaction between the two areas.

In addition to the saucer-shaped bead data, incised shell designs from Cerro de Trincheras provide another line of evidence supporting interaction with Paquimé. Incised shell enjoyed a greater popularity at Cerro de Trincheras than at Paquimé, but incised shell goods occur infrequently at both sites. At Cerro de Trincheras we recorded a variety of incised designs on *Glycymeris* bracelets and *Conus* rings. The majority of these designs appear similar to designs used by Hohokam artisans, including geometric motifs interpreted by Haury (1976) and Jernigan (1978)

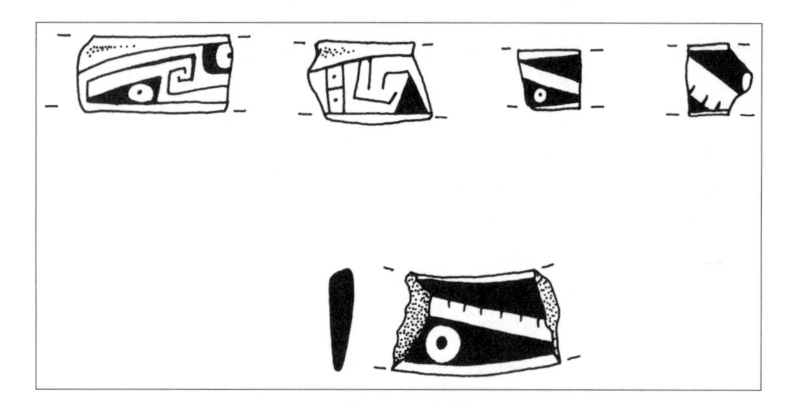

Figure 10.7. Some incised shell ornaments from Cerro de Trincheras. Top row: *Conus* ring fragments. Bottom row: *Glycymeris* bracelet fragment.

as representing an idealized serpent motif. Additionally, Cerro de Trincheras has several incised shell designs that researchers have not reported from sites in the Southwest. This style includes geometric interlocking scrolls and angled lines, often with hatching, and with the design portion in relief to the background. Integrated into the design is a circle or square with a small dot depression in the center. The design is bracketed with a raised-edge border (Figure 10.7). This incised shell style, especially the interlocking angled scrolls, is strikingly similar to several Chihuahua polychromes, especially Ramos Polychrome (Arlin Simon, personal communication). Shell workers at Cerro de Trincheras would have encountered Chihuahuan designs on the Chihuahuan polychrome trade ware found at the site. Apparently Casas Grandes shell workers did not use these designs, because none of the incised shell work at Paquimé includes these motifs.

However striking these similarities are, it must be emphasized that there exist significant differences in the shell assemblages: differences in the quantity of shell, differences in genera present, differences in the sources, and differences in the types of items produced.

The most glaring difference is in the sheer quantity of shell at Casas Grandes: 3,907,402 individual pieces of marine shell (Di Peso et al. 1974), compared to 6,793 pieces from Cerro de Trincheras. The vast majority of the Paquimé shell (3,307,024 pieces) were *Nassarius* sp. beads that the excavators found in three rooms in unit 8.[1] If we omit these beads, then the count of shell for Casas Grandes is 600,378. Di Peso also excavated a far greater portion of Casas Grandes (about 40 percent) than the roughly 1.5 percent of Cerro de Trincheras that we excavated. If we extrapolate from these samples, then the total population of shell at Casas Grandes would be 1,500,000 pieces and the total population for Cerro de Trincheras would be 453,000 pieces.[2] The raw counts overstate the differences in the quantity of shell at each site, but even if they are adjusted, the difference remains on the order of three times more shell at Paquimé than at Cerro de Trincheras.

The assemblage at Paquimé includes several California coast marine shell species: *Haliotis cracherodii, Haliotis fulgens* Philippi, 1845, and *Dentallium* cf. *D.* (*D.*) *neohexagonum* Sharp and Pilsbry, 1827 (Di Peso et al. 1974:4:401). Our analysis found no California coast species for Cerro de Trincheras, indicating that Paquimé most likely had a source for these shells not exploited by the people at Cerro de Trincheras.

It is also clear that Paquimé imported shell from farther south on the gulf coast of West Mexico than did the shell workers at Cerro de Trincheras. The excavations at Paquimé recovered 1,122 examples of a rare shell type, *Persicula bandera* (Di Peso et al. 1974: 6:Figure 660-6). The only known natural habitat for this shell is at Banderas Bay, Jalisco (Keen 1971:635). In the Casas Grandes sample one shell in 535 was *Persicula bandera.* Applying this ratio to the Cerro de Trincheras sample we would expect to have found 12 specimens of this species instead of none. Its absence from Cerro de Trincheras supports the probability that Paquimian shell workers obtained marine shell from yet another source not used by the people of Trincheras.

The marine shell analysts on the Paquimé project concluded that the majority of shell found at Paquimé was obtained from the coastal region around Guaymas and/or the nearby deltas of the Yaqui and Matape rivers (Di Peso et al. 1974:4:401). The site of Cerro de Trincheras is at the confluence of two possible shell trade routes (Villalpando 1988). The most obvious would have followed the Magdalena River to the coast at Desemboque near Puerto Lobos. The second would have come up the Bacoachi Arroyo, which enters the Gulf of California north of Kino Bay and heads immediately to the south of Cerro de Trincheras (Robles 1973). Both of these potential sources are much farther north than the Guaymas area. The shell species available in this northern re-

Table 10.1. Shell Artifact Forms from Cerro de Trincheras and Paquimé.

ARTIFACT FORM	TRINCHERAS QTY	TRINCHERAS %	PAQUIMÉ QTY	PAQUIMÉ %
Beads	1058	34.24	80292	74.64
Bracelet/Armlet	836	27.06	434	0.4
Rings	969	31.36	387	0.36
Tinklers	68	2.2	21849	20.31
Pendants	144	4.66	4231	3.94
Spangles	11	0.36	141	0.13
Strand Dividers	0	0	9	0.01
Containers	0	0	2	0
Disks	0	0	8	0.01
Trumpet/Altar Pc	0	0	176	0.16
Cuff	1	0.03	0	0
Tool	1	0.03	0	0
Tessarae	2	0.06	44	0.04

gion of the coast match the genera at Cerro de Trincheras. It appears that the primary sources for both sites are quite geographically distant. The differences in the makeup of the shell species assemblages from both sites reflect the disparities in the source areas. Paquimé has 73 marine shell species represented by 40 species that do not occur at Cerro de Trincheras. Cerro de Trincheras, on the other hand, has 78 recorded marine shell species, 44 of which do not occur at Paquimé.

Consideration of the shell artifact forms also shows marked differences between the two sites (Table 10.1). Several revisions of the data sets were necessary to provide comparable assemblages. For example, Di Peso et al. (1974) recorded what are traditionally called "*Conus* rings" as truncated beads. These items were moved into a ring category for the Paquimé assemblage. Additionally, all unidentified fragments and objects, as well as manufacturing debris, were not included. This has little effect on the Casas Grandes data because the researchers there found negligible quantities of manufacturing debris. *Nassarius* sp. beads constituted the overwhelming majority of the recovered Paquimé shell (*N* = 3,711,930; 97.18 percent of the total assemblage) (Di Peso et al. 1974:6:Figure 660-6). Three rooms in Unit 8, interpreted as storerooms, yielded 3,307,024 of these shells. In order to provide some basis of comparability for the other shell artifacts, this obvious outlier of all *Nassarius* sp. shell has been omitted from the Paquimé inventory for Table 10.1.

The differences in artifact forms between the two sites are striking. The occupants of Cerro de Trincheras emphasized bracelets/armlets (27.06 percent) much more than the folks at Paquimé (0.04 percent). *Conus* rings have a significantly higher frequency at Cerro de Trincheras (31.36 percent) than at Paquimé (0.36 percent). The inhabitants of Paquimé obviously focused much more on beads (74.64 percent) and tinklers (20.31 percent) than did the people of Cerro de Trincheras (34.34 percent and 2.2 percent, respectively). If we add the *Nassarius* sp. beads back into the Paquimé assemblage, the bead frequency rises to 99.29 percent of the site's total. These differences between the sites are important because they express the cultural differences in shell artifact form preferences (possibly tied to use and meaning) that indicate a considerable cultural distance between the two shell-working traditions.

Overall, there is negligible manufacturing debris recorded for Paquimé, suggesting that many artifacts must have been imported as finished products. Bradley (1995) indicates that the lack of manufacturing debris most likely results from the emphasis on only slightly modified gastropod beads at the site and the resulting minimal manufacturing debris that the methods of production would produce. However, there are significant quantities of shell jewelry items at Paquimé, such as bracelets, tinklers, and Conus shell rings that, if produced at the site, should have left distinctive manufacturing waste. Production of these pieces at Paquimé should also be evidenced by in-process pieces broken or discarded prior to completion, such as those recovered in great quantities at

Cerro de Trincheras. The Paquimé reports indicate that only 20 partially worked pieces were identified during analysis (Di Peso et al. 1974:6:523–525). Therefore, Paquimé likely imported the great majority of these goods in finished form, some of which may have originated in the Trincheras area. A review of the unidentified fragments from Paquimé for evidence of production waste is needed to completely resolve the question of production at the site.

Overall, the differences between the marine shell assemblages of Paquimé and Cerro de Trincheras far outweigh any similarities. That Paquimians were acquiring shell from at least two or more sources seems certain; it is possible that one of these sources was Cerro de Trincheras. Specifically, evidence suggests that Cerro de Trincheras traded saucer-shaped beads to Paquimé. The lack of saucer-shaped bead production evidence from Paquimé indicates that these items were likely traded into the site in finished form. Cerro de Trincheras is thus far the only known site with evidence of the production of this bead form in the Greater Southwest, thereby making it the logical source for Paquimé. Additional evidence for interaction lies in the shared iconography on Cerro de Trincheras incised shell bracelets and rings and Chihuahuan polychrome ceramics.

The nature and level of interaction between the two sites is still unclear. This initial investigation shows that interaction did occur at some level. We still do not know how much Paquimé shell in raw or finished form originated in the Trincheras region. Our preliminary study does clearly indicate that the overall quantities of shell traded were not great and that Cerro de Trincheras was not the primary marine shell source for Paquimé.

Given that most previous researchers have interpreted Cerro de Trincheras as an outpost of another region or as an extension of processes occurring elsewhere, it is striking how distinctive the site is and how little evidence there is for long-distance exchange. A comparison of Cerro de Trincheras and Casas Grandes shows not how similar the two sites are but rather how markedly different they are. If both were in fact trade outposts of Mesoamerican polities we would reasonably expect them to be more alike. Not surprisingly, Cerro de Trincheras resembles most closely other sites in the Sonoran Desert, specifically the Hohokam Tradition of southern Arizona. However, we have found no artifacts from southern Arizona at Cerro de Trincheras or in our survey of the Altar Valley. The trade goods we have found suggest contacts to the east, to Casas Grandes. Our work in northern Sonora has dismissed much speculation about the Trincheras Tradition. It is clearly not an extension of the Hohokam to the north, nor is it an outpost of Mesoamerican civilizations. Defining what it is remains the goal of our future research and analyses.

Notes

1. *Nassarius* shell appears at Cerro de Trincheras, but it does not make up as large a proportion of the shell assemblage. There were 109 pieces, all of which were perforated whole-shell beads. They made up only about 1.6 percent of the total shell assemblage.

2. There are numerous problems in our calculations of the total populations of shell from the Casas Grandes and Cerro de Trincheras samples. Both excavations used judgmental samples that tended to emphasize contexts that would be rich in shell, and therefore both samples may overestimate the population of shell at each site. Excavation methods differed significantly between the sites both in terms of earth removal (primarily by trowel at Cerro de Trincheras, primarily by shovel at Casas Grandes), and screening (¼ inch at Cerro de Trincheras and ½-inch to 1-inch mesh at Casas Grandes). Given these differences we would expect that the Cerro de Trincheras excavations recovered a higher proportion of the shell present than did the excavations at Casas Grandes. Thus, our calculations probably underestimate the magnitude of the difference in quantity of shell at the two sites. Our approximations serve only to make gross relative comparisons between the two sites and not to make accurate or precise estimates of the total populations of shell at either site.

IV

The Larger View

11

The Aztatlán Tradition of West and Northwest Mexico and Casas Grandes

Speculations on the Medio Period Florescence

Michael S. Foster

There can be little argument that the Medio period florescence of Casas Grandes represented the most complex socioeconomic and political development in the Greater Southwest (the vast Mesoamerican hinterlands northwest of the Mesoamerican frontier). There can be even less argument regarding the significance of Charles Di Peso's monumental Casas Grandes project to Mesoamerican and southwestern archaeology. This volume, published 25 years after the publication of the Casas Grandes report, is a testament to Di Peso's enduring contribution in that every paper herein uses and builds on his ideas and data.

Two major points of controversy arose immediately with the publication of the Casas Grandes report. Undoubtedly, the greatest argument centered on the dating of the Medio period. Using noncutting tree-ring dates, "vv" dates (Scott 1966), Di Peso dated the Medio period between A.D. 1060 and 1340, believing that only a few of the outer rings were missing. Many individuals working in the American Southwest believed that the Medio period dates clearly contradicted accepted archaeological and chronometric data from adjacent areas in the Southwest (see chapter five of this volume).

The second major point of contention focused on Di Peso's interpretation of the origin of the Medio period:

> It is believed that sometime around the year A.D. 1060 a group of sophisticated Mesoamerican merchants came into the valley of the Casas Grandes and inspired the indigenous Chichimecans to build the city of Paquimé over portions of an older Viejo Period village. . . . These organizers, who may have come from somewhere along the Pacific coast of Mexico, brought with them an aggregate of technological knowledge such as one might associate with an advanced hydraulic society. (Di Peso 1974:2:290)

Di Peso (1974:2:292) further emphasized the Mesoamerican connection by stating, "The general Gran Chichimecan continuum of events proposed herein was somehow associated with the missionary activities of certain Mesoamerican cults of the gods Tezcatlipoca, Quetzacóatl, and Huizilopochtli, in that order." Although Di Peso notes a probable connection to the cultures of Mexico's west coast, in a subsequent discussion he (Di Peso 1974:2:299) clearly attributes the rise of the Medio period to the economic expansion of the Toltec Empire at Tula in the northern Valley of Mexico. This argument is repeated and emphasized in several subsequent discussions (Di Peso 1976:12, 1979:160).

Di Peso's argument regarding the "Toltec connection" derives clearly from his dating of the Medio period and thus contemporary Mesoamerican history. Despite arguments to the contrary, Di Peso held steadfast to his dating of the Medio period.

However, with the recent reassessment of the Casas Grandes tree-ring dates (Dean and Ravesloot 1993; Foster 1992; Ravesloot et al. 1995a, 1995b) and a substantial amount of supporting dating from surrounding areas, it is now clear the Medio period is best placed between ca. A.D. 1200 and the late A.D. 1400s. Thus, it is important to reassess Di Peso's proposition regarding the origins of the Medio period florescence and the role Mesoamerican culture(s) played in that florescence. Explanations for the Medio period florescence fall into two groups. There are those who see it as a local phenomenon stemming from an indigenous Mogollon base (e.g., McGuire 1980; McGuire and Villalpando 1989). The second category of explanations focuses on Mesoamerican interaction, by either direct colonization or economic integration, as a catalyst for the Medio period development.

One of the more intriguing and well-articulated arguments regarding the role of Mesoamerican influence in west and northwest Mexico, including Medio period developments at Casas Grandes, is that of J. Charles Kelley (1986, 1992, 1993). In this series of evolving discussions Kelley has detailed his arguments regarding the development of the Aztatlán tradition of the highlands and coastal lowlands of west and northwest Mexico and its link to the Mixteca-Puebla tradition based in central Mexico. With regard to Casas Grandes, Kelley argues that the expansion of a mercantile system with links to central Mexico operating within the Aztatlán tradition during the Postclassic period established a trading outpost at Casas Grandes incorporating it into the Aztatlán sphere of influence. The result of this was the introduction of a series of new traits that led to the development of the Casas Grandes Medio period. This discussion reviews the Kelley model and offers some elaboration and variation of key points in his discussion.

The Aztatlán Tradition: Background

In order to understand Kelley's model of Aztatlán–Casas Grandes interaction, it is necessary to have a basic understanding of the Aztatlán phenomenon itself. Furthermore, because I will argue that the Aztatlán phenomenon contributed to the florescence and character of the Medio period in a variety of ways, a basic knowledge of the archaeology of the northern west coast and northwest Mexican highlands is necessary. Sauer and Brand (1932) introduced the term *Aztatlán* into the archaeology of coastal west Mexico. The Aztatlán area, as originally defined, extended from southern Sinaloa (the Mazatlán area) into northern Nayarit. In their summary of the Aztatlán area Sauer and Brand (1932:31–41) noted that a variety of remains were associated with their Aztatlán "culture."

The most striking trait observed by Sauer and Brand was the well-made polished pottery. Considerable variation in vessel form and decoration, including dotted circles, motifs thought to represent feather headdresses, and engraving, was noted. A common utility ware was decorated with a broad red rim and in bands of various widths across the vessel body. Monochrome and polychrome vessels were often engraved with geometric or stylized patterns cut into color bands or the background color or around the edges of colored designs.

Other ceramic items included figurines, pipes, incised spindle whorls, and cylindrical clay stamps. Urn burials also appear to be a characteristic trait of Sauer and Brand's Aztatlán culture. Obsidian blades and debitage were common and believed to be mostly imported.

Sauer and Brand (1932:37–41) also described the local variation observed elsewhere along the coast. At Culiacán the red-rimmed and red-decorated types were generally missing or occurred in very low frequencies. The most striking ceramic type noted was Culiacán Polychrome. A fluted ware and a well-polished black-brown type occurred along with Culiacán Polychrome and appeared to be restricted to the Culiacán area. Also of note was a "walnut or mahogany colored" type that exhibited incising on the upper half of bowl exteriors. Bowls with incised interiors were common, as were tripod vessels, often molcajetes, with ball feet.

At Chametla the only type Sauer and Brand (1932:38–39) observed that seemed to tie Chametla to Culiacán was Mazatlán Polychrome. Aztatlán ware (the red-rimmed red-on-buff incised type sometimes decorated with white paint) was fairly common but took on some local variation with the addition of black painting. Chametla Polychrome was also defined.

Sauer and Brand (1932:40–41) defined another subregion of their Aztatlán culture, the Tacuichamona subregion, in the foothills north of Culiacán. They indicate this cultural expression was less sophisticated or complex than those to the south. None of the finely made wares of the Chametla and Culiacán areas were found. Some relatively crude polychromes, incised, and punched types were noted, along with pipes decorated by incision and punctation.

The work by Sauer and Brand (1932) was pioneering for several reasons. Not only were they the first to conduct archaeological research on the northern west coast of Mexico, but they recognized the area's importance as a zone of Precolumbian cultural development. Their recognition of the Aztatlán phenomenon laid the foundation for addressing the nature of regional and panregional interaction and cultural development among the cultures of northwest Mexico and adjacent areas. Sauer and Brand were among the first to recognize the west coast as a likely and major land and cultural route between Mesoamerica and the American Southwest.

Subsequently, Isabel Kelly excavated in the Chametla area, dividing the occupation into four complexes (Kelly 1938:34–44): Early Chametla, Middle Chametla, Late Chametla II (Aztatlán complex), and Late Chametla I (El Taste–Mazatlán). The first two, the Early and Middle Chametla, predate Aztatlán related materials in the Chametla zone.

Basic Chametla ceramic types consist of red-rimmed utility and black-banded wares. Although they were found throughout the ceramic sequences identified in the sites investigated, frequencies varied from site to site, as did their distribution through time. A similar pattern was also noted in the red and black wares. A series of polychromes, many of which were engraved, was also identified.

Kelly's (1938:36) Aztatlán and El Taste–Mazatlán complexes are Aztatlán associated. The Aztatlán complex ceramics are characterized by red-rim decorated, black-on-buff, Aztatlán Polychrome, and Cocoyolitos Polychrome. She notes that red-rim decorated was a basic element of the Aztatlán complex ceramic assemblage. The El Taste–Mazatlán ceramic assemblage was dominated by El Taste Red-bordered, El Taste Polychrome, Mazatlán Polychrome, El Taste Satin, and El Taste Rough. Other items associated with these two late complexes include smoking pipes, large incised spindle whorls, and late El Taste slab figurines.

Ekholm (1942), excavating a burial mound at Guasave, recovered a variety of ceramic, shell, and metal artifacts, as well as ground, chipped, and carved stone artifacts. Ekholm believed the Guasave material was clearly Aztatlán related but postdated the Aztatlán and El Taste–Mazatlán complexes at Chametla. He also believed the Aztatlán phenomenon was more widespread in Sinaloa than anything that predated it (Ekholm 1942:123–124) and that the Guasave remains reflected a single temporal component.

The Guasave ceramic assemblage comprised elaborate polychromes, incised and engraved types, polished red-on-buff, red and plain wares, and grooved wares in a variety of bowl, tripod, and jar forms. Types identified include Guasave Red-on-buff, Aztatlán Polychrome, Cerro Isabel Engraved, Sinaloa Polychrome, Aguaruto Incised, Guasave Polychrome, and Navalato Polychrome. Other ceramic objects included spindle whorls, smoking pipes, and masks. Small numbers of clay plaques, animal and human figurines, whistles, beads, earplugs, and a cylinder stamp were also found. Paint cloisonné decorated gourd fragments, stone bowls, a pipe, manos, metates, pestles, and axes were recovered, along with shell beads, pendants, and bracelets. Copper artifacts included bells, an ear spool(?), a finger ring, a flat plate, and a necklace. Turquoise was also recovered.

It is important to remember that the Guasave assemblage was recovered from a large burial mound. The richness and elaborate nature of the collection clearly reflect that fact. Despite this, the Guasave materials demonstrated that the Aztatlán phenomenon was more complex and elaborate than initially envisioned by Sauer and Brand and reported for the Chametla area.

Also of significance was Ekholm's (1942:125–132)

recognition of links between the Guasave materials and central Mexican cultures. He listed 44 traits identified at Guasave that emulate or were derived from central Mexican culture(s), several of which were derived from the Mixteca-Puebla tradition. Ekholm even went as far as to suggest Mixteca-Puebla peoples migrated into the area.

Isabel Kelly also excavated at Culiacán, dividing the sequence into four complexes (Kelly 1945:120): Early Culiacán II (Aztatlán complex), Early Culiacán I, Middle Culiacán, and Late Culiacán. Aztatlán-related ceramics at Culiacán included Early Culiacán, Navolato and Aguaruto Polychromes, Aguaruto Incised, and Cerro Izábal and Alamitos Engraved wares. The Red-rimmed and Aztatlán wares found elsewhere along the Sinaloa coast are present but limited. Other artifact types recovered were similar to the Guasave materials and included ceramic cylindrical stamps, human figurines, rattles, smoking pipes, incised spindle whorls, and copper bells, pendants, and wire.

Aztatlán materials were not abundant in the Culiacán area (Kelly 1945:118–121) although evidence for a "pure" Aztatlán component was found. Some Aztatlán materials occurred in association with Early Culiacán I materials indicating that an Aztatlán manifestation preceded and was partly contemporaneous with Early Culiacán I. The work at Culiacán also led Kelly (1945:119) to suggest that the Aztatlán phenomenon itself may have been quite dynamic.

Thus, the work done in the 1930s along Mexico's northwestern coast resulted in the definition of three major cultural provinces: Guasave, Culiacán, and Chametla. The occupational sequences developed for these three areas partially overlap and fall within the Classic and Postclassic periods.

Following the work of Kelly and Ekholm, archaeological investigations of the west coast languished for more than 15 years. In the 1950s a series of projects conducted by the University of California at Los Angeles was initiated (Nicholson and Meighan 1974 [see chapter 15 of this volume]). These projects included work on the coastal lowland of Nayarit and excavations and survey in the highlands of Jalisco. However, it was not until 1960 that the issues and questions raised by the work of Kelly and Ekholm along the Sinaloa coast received renewed interest. This was the result of research conducted in the highlands of Durango by J. Charles Kelley and his associates.

Working at the Schroeder site, a Guadiana Chalchihuites site (see Kelley 1971, 1990), near the city of Durango, Kelley recovered many intrusive west coast artifacts. Kelley and Winters (1960) used chronometric and other data from the Schroeder excavations to reevaluate the west coast sequences established by Kelly and Ekholm. Three groups—A, B, and C—of intrusive ceramics were identified at the Schroeder site. Group A types were consistently found in Ayala phase contexts, A.D. 550–700 (Foster 1995a; Kelley 1971). Group A intrusives included Middle Chametla Polychrome, Middle Chametla Polychrome Engraved, Chametla Red-rimmed utility ware (including marbleized surface and mano colorado variants), Chametla white-filleted figurines, and small incised spindle whorls. A few Middle Chametla Black-banded Engraved and Scalloped-rim decorated sherds also occurred. No Aztatlán-related materials were recovered from Ayala phase contexts, thus placing the Ayala phase and Middle Chametla complex clearly before Aztatlán times (confirming Kelly's relative temporal placement of the Middle Chametla complex).

Groups B and C intrusive ceramics recovered were clearly Aztatlán associated. Group B types included red-rimmed ware, locally called Lolandis Red-rimmed (Kelley and Kelley 1971), Aztatlán ware, Cocoyolitos hollow figurines, and large round incised spindle whorls. Sherds of Cerro Izábal Engraved and Aguaruto Exterior Incised were tentatively identified. Group B intrusive ceramics were recovered primarily in Las Joyas phase contexts, A.D. 700–950, and rarely in Río Tunal phase contexts, A.D. 950–1150 (Kelley 1971).

The Group C intrusive assemblage included Guasave and Sinaloa Polychromes and a group of sherds that resembled Cocoyolitos, El Taste, and Early Culiacán Polychromes. Also found were notched-edge (gear-like in appearance) spindle whorls and copper artifacts. Group C was primarily recovered from late Río Tunal contexts.

The Group A assemblage was derived from the Chametla area. The Group B assemblage contained traits and materials common in the Aztatlán complex at Chametla and Culiacán but only partially represented at Guasave. The Group C assemblage was characterized by traits associated with the Aztatlán complex at Guasave and in part by materials that postdate the Aztatlán complexes at both Chametla and Culiacán. It should also be noted that contexts tentatively identified as Calera phase, ca. A.D. 1150–1350, produced some Dunn ware. Dunn ware is diagnostic of the Middle Culiacán complex that postdates Aztatlán materials. The distribution of these intrusives and Kelley and Winters's ability to place them within meaningful temporal contexts at the Schroeder site confirmed the relative positions of the west coast sequences as originally defined by Kelly and Ekholm.

Kelley and Winters (1960:555–559) went on to carefully evaluate the distribution and relative percentages of Aztatlán-related ceramic types as reported by Ekholm (1942), Kelly (1938, 1945), and Sauer and Brand (1932). They made several observations important for better understanding and defining the Aztatlán phenomenon:

• The Aztatlán phenomenon is not nearly as homogenous as suggested by those initially describing the nature and extent of the Aztatlán phenomenon (a point also made by Kelly [1945]).
• The only ceramic wares common at Chametla, Guasave, and Culiacán were the utility red-brown, polished red, and polished black wares.
• Red-rimmed decorated wares occur at both Chametla and Culiacán but are local variants; Guasave Red-on-buff is related to the red-rim decorated ware.
• "Furthermore, each Aztatlán locality has its own local ceramic types; Cocoyolitos polychrome and Black-on-buff ware at Chametla; Alamitos engraved, Cerro Izábal engraved, Aguaruto polychrome, and 'coarse Aztatlán ware' at Culiacán; while no less than nine well developed polychrome types, two incised types, one engraved ware, and one red-on-buff ware are found only at Guasave. In terms of ceramics, Chametla and Culiacán appear most closely related during the Aztatlán horizon, Guasave most divergent. Chametla appears to have the simplest expression of the Aztatlán horizon; Culiacán next; and Guasave is the richest of all.... [Additionally,] many of the ceramic traits that are so richly represented at Guasave appear to be elaborations of simpler forms present at Chametla and Culiacán" (Kelley and Winters 1960:555).
• Many artifact types and cultural traits are also common to the three local coastal cultures (e.g., extended inhumations, urn burials, bundle burials, ¾ grooved axes, pipes, plain and incised spindle whorls, cylindrical clay stamps, etc.). However, at Guasave many artifact types not represented at the other two sites were found and others are more elaborate and ornate (see Kelley and Winters 1960:555–556). Kelley and Winters argue that the Guasave Aztatlán assemblage is clearly more elaborate and complex than those of Chametla and Culiacán. They suggest that this represents in part an evolution of traits and ceramic styles seen in earlier times at Chametla and Culiacán. They also suggest that the elaborations seen may have been spurred on in part by incorporation of the local Guasave culture into a central Mexican sphere of influence.
• The final point regards the distribution of red-rimmed decorated ware of the west coast. Kelley and Winters (1960:558–559) noted that in Durango, the local red-rimmed decorated ware, Lolandis Red-rimmed, usually occurred lacking association with Aztatlán ware. Again reviewing the data available from the west coast, they determined that west coast sites with red-rimmed decorated ware but lacking Aztatlán ware were earlier than those with mixed red-rimmed decorated and Aztatlán ware. From this Kelley and Winters (1960:559) concluded, "It appears certain that there was an early period in the development of the Aztatlán horizon in which Lolandis Red Rim was the dominant decorated ware, and a later period in which the two occur together." The term *Lolandis* is now commonly applied to all the red-rimmed decorated ware of the lowlands and highlands of northwestern Mexico.

Based on a reassessment of the coastal data and the evaluation of contextual and chronological data from the Schroeder site in Durango, Kelley and Winters (1960:559–561) offered a revision of the coastal sequences. Phase names and temporal boundaries were offered in place of the earlier general chronological designations (Table 11.1).

The Kelley and Winters revision of the Sinaloa sequences is important for many reasons. They independently verified the relative sequences established by Kelly and Ekholm. Additionally, they provided the first critical review of the nature and extent of the Aztatlán phenomenon of the west coast, noting spatial and temporal variation. Also, the presence of Aztatlán-related materials in the highlands of Durango suggested that the Aztatlán phenomenon itself, or its

Table 11.1. Concordance of West Coast Archaeological Sequences.

A.D.	CHAMETLA (Kelly 1938)	CHAMETLA (Kelley & Winters 1960)	CULIACÁN (Kelly 1945)	CULIACÁN (Kelley & Winters 1960)	GUASAVE (Kelly 1945)	GUASAVE (Kelley & Winters 1960)
1530–1400			Late Culiacán	La Quinta		
1400–1250			Middle Culiacán	Yebalito		
1350–1150						Guasave
1250–1100	Late Chametla I (El Taste–Mazatlán)	El Taste	Early Culiacán I	La Divisa		
1050–900	Late Chametla II (Azatlán Complex)	Acaponeta	Early Culiacán II (Azatlán Complex)	Acaponteta	Guasave (Azatlán Complex)	
900–750		Lolandis				
700–500	Middle Chametla	Baluarte				
500–300	Early Chametla	Tierra del Padre				

influence, may have been more complex and more widespread in northwest Mexico than originally thought.

Subsequently, excavations were conducted on the west coast in the Peñitas area (Bordaz 1964) and at Amapa (Meighan 1976), in northern Nayarit. Beginning in 1968 and continuing for seven seasons, excavations were conducted in the Marismas Nacionales along the Sinaloa-Nayarit border (Scott 1974, 1985). Aztatlán-related materials were identified in all these areas.

The Peñitas sequence was divided into the Tamarindo, Chala, and Mitlan phases, dating between ca. A.D. 400 and 1300 (Bordaz 1964). Most of the ceramic material recovered had strong affinities to Amapa. However, Chala phase ceramics included Early Chametla Polychrome, red-rimmed utility ware, and black-banded ware. Mitlan phase material, apparently dating to the early Postclassic period, parallel Lolandis, Acaponeta, and El Taste phase materials at Chametla and exhibit some similarities to Acaponeta and La Divisa phase materials at Culiacán. Importantly, Bordaz also noted many elemental and design pattern similarities between the Peñitas materials and those of central Mexico, especially Cholula.

The 1959 excavations at Amapa (Meighan 1976) represent the most extensive excavations at a single site on Mexico's west coast. Amapa clearly is a primary center. The site is characterized by numerous mound and plaza complexes, a small ceremonial precinct, some use of adobe bricks in construction, a ball court, and a large cemetery. It generally appears that the occupational history of Amapa parallels that of Chametla (Grosscup 1976). Meighan (1976) has offered an alternative temporal sequence for Amapa, but this author (Foster 1995a) favors that proposed by Grosscup. The Tuxpan (a tentative phase proposed by Grosscup but not identified at Amapa itself), Cerritos, and Ixcuintla phases are Aztatlán related, and associated ceramic types include Tuxpan Red-on-orange, Tuxpan Engraved, Cerritos Polychrome, Botadero Incised, Mangos Engraved, Iago Polychrome, Ixcuintla White-on-orange, and Ixcuintla Polychrome.

Although Amapa's Aztatlán materials were more abundant, varied, and elaborate than those identified at sites to the north, Grosscup (1976:254–264) noted many specific resemblances between the Amapa Aztatlán assemblages and those of Chametla, Guasave, and Culiacán. Also of note is the wealth of copper artifacts present at Amapa (Meighan 1976; Pendergast 1962).

North of Amapa, along the Nayarit and Sinaloa border, lies the Marismas Nacionales, a vast estuary-lagoon system (Scott 1974, 1985). Most of the ceramics recovered from a series of excavations here were stylistically either Chametla or Amapa/Peñitas types. Aztatlán-related types identified in the Marismas include Ixcuintla White-on-orange, Ixcuintla Polychrome, Peñitas Engraved, Mazatlán Polychrome, El Taste Polychrome, red-rimmed utility ware, Red-rimmed utility ware–Mano Colorado, Early Culiacán Polychrome, Navalato Polychrome, El Taste Red-bordered, Aguaruto Polychrome, Cocoyolitos Polychrome, Sentispac Buff, and Tuxpan Red-on-orange, to name a few.

Several vessels recovered from the Marismas had head designs similar to those found on Sinaloa Polychrome from Guasave and several Amapa types. A globular tripod jar similar to ones recovered from Guasave and the Schroeder site was recovered from the site of Chalpa. Typologically, the Chalpa vessel falls into the range of Cerritos Polychrome (Sweetman 1974).

Other artifacts of Aztatlán affinity include smoking pipes, spindle whorls, several Mazapan figurine fragments and ceramic whistles, balls, beads, and pendants. Only several amorphous pieces of copper were recovered. There was surprisingly little use of shell as ornaments or personal adornment and virtually nothing in the way of exotica (turquoise, rare resources) except obsidian.

More recently, research in the Tomatlán River valley of coastal Jalisco has resulted in the identification of Aztatlán-related materials (Mountjoy 1982, 1990). Mountjoy (1982:284–289) identified five complexes dating between 1390 B.C. and A.D. 1525. Specifically, Mountjoy identified two complexes that have Aztatlán affinities: the Aztatlán and Nahuapa complexes. In the Tomatlán Valley, the Aztatlán complex appears sometime in the A.D. 700s. Aztatlán ceramic types include Aztatlán Red-on-buff, Aztatlán Red and White on Incised Buff, Cerritos Polychrome, Iguanas Polychrome, Aguaruto Polychrome, and Mangos Engraved. The Nahuapa complex is dated between A.D. 1000 and 1525; thus only the earlier portion of it would fall in Aztatlán times. Nahuapa complex ceramics include Nahuapa Red Incised, Nahuapa Buff Incised, and Santiago White-on-red.

In addition to the ceramics associated with the Aztatlán and Nahuapa complexes, Mountjoy also recovered a variety of other artifacts. Spindle whorls, obsidian projectile points, knives, scrapers, and shell ornaments, to name a few. The impression is that these other materials are not as elaborate as those found either at Amapa or Guasave.

Mountjoy (1990) has also reported Aztatlán materials at Ixtapa in the Banderas Valley of southern Jalisco. Aztatlán-associated ceramics were found in stratigraphic excavations in a platform mound. In association with these he reports finding molcajetes, comales, a spindle whorl, and fragments of Mazapan figurines. The Aztatlán tradition in the Banderas Valley is dated between A.D. 1070 and 1230 (Mountjoy 1989). Mountjoy (1970) also noted the presence of Aztatlán-related materials in his Santa Cruz complex from the San Blas area of Nayarit.

Resemblances between archaeological materials recovered in the highlands of Nayarit, Jalisco, and northwestern Michoacán and Aztatlán-related materials from the west coast were noted very early. Lister (1949) conducted limited excavations at the site of Cojumatlán, Michoacán. The earliest phase, the Chapala phase, was characterized by red-on-brown pottery and Mazapan figurines. This phase was generally described as "Toltecan." The following Cojumatlán phase was characterized by Mixteca-Puebla traits. Two ceramic types in particular typified this phase, Cojumatlán Polychrome and Cojumatlán Polychrome Incised. Lister (1949:29) noted similarities between the two Cojumatlán polychromes and Aguaruto Polychrome and thus Cojumatlán's ties to the Aztatlán phenomenon.

Meighan and Foote (1968) reported the excavations at Tizapan el Alto, Jalisco, on the south shore of Lake Chapala, west of Cojumatlán. An artifact assemblage very similar to Cojumatlán was recovered. Three phases were defined, the Chapala, Cojumatlán, and Tizapan phases. The Tizapan occupation parallels, but is somewhat longer than, that at Cojumatlán. Suggested dates, based in part on radiocarbon dates, for the Chapala phase were ca. A.D. 600–900; the Cojumatlán phase was dated A.D. 900–1100; and the Tizapan complex was dated A.D. 1100–1250 (Meighan and Foote 1968:36). It appears Aztatlán-related traits seen in the Cojumatlán phase carried over to the Tizapan phase.

Cojumatlán and Tizapan el Alto also shared another interesting set of traits. Several human burials were excavated. Many skulls exhibited fronto-occipital deformation, and tooth mutilation in the form of filed incisors was also present. These traits are common in Aztatlán-related sites in the Marismas Nacionales (see Gill 1985).

Meighan and Foote (1968:156–157) suggest that

Cojumatlán and Tizapan el Alto were probably typical of many sites that ringed the shore of Lake Chapala. This inference has since been proven correct (Kelley 1983; Koll 1982). They suggest that the Cojumatlán and Tizapan phases came under strong Mixteca-Puebla influence from central Mexico resulting in the modification of existing pottery styles to accommodate new stylistic elements and probably worldviews.

Sites in the lake basins west of Guadalajara also exhibit evidence of a strong Aztatlán presence. Glassow (1967) excavated at Huistla, noting many strong parallels between the local ceramic assemblage and those of the west coast. However, he could identify only a single example of what he tentatively believed to be an intrusive type, a red-on-buff. The Huistla assemblage included polychromes, red-on-buff, engraved, and incised types.

In the same general area Weigand and Spence (1982) identified many intrusive west coast types at Las Cuevas. These include Iguanas-Roblitos types from the Nayarit coast, as well as polychromes from Chametla and Culiacán. The Ixtlán de Río area of Nayarit also has an Aztatlán related component (Gifford 1950).

The highlands of northern Michoacán, Jalisco, and Nayarit were clearly integrated into the Aztatlán tradition. It is also apparent that these highland sites and cultures were critical links between central Mexican and coastal west Mexican cultures. Although the cultures of highland and lowland west Mexico shared many traits during Aztatlán times, it is again important to remember that local cultures appear to be functioning as independent polities under the Aztatlán veneer.

In northwest Mexico the Aztatlán phenomenon is manifested primarily in the form of trade items: ceramic wares and other items such as spindle whorls, shell, and copper. As previously discussed, the most extensive analysis of west coast material in the Durango uplands remains that of Kelley and Winters (1960) for the Schroeder site. However, it is worth note that since the excavations at Amapa and Peñitas, it has been possible to identify additional types from the Schroeder site that were only tentatively identified as west coast types by Kelley and Winters. These include Tuxpan Engraved, Botadero Incised, and Ixcuintla Polychrome (Ganot and Peschard 1985).

The occurrence of west coast ceramics in highland sites of the Guadiana Chalchihuites of Durango is common. Brand (1939) defined a red-on-buff, Zape Red-on-buff, for the Zape region of northern Durango. It is clearly a variant of the coastal red-rimmed, red-on-buff wares. Brand also noted the presence of Chametla and Culiacán polychromes in the area. A nearly complete vessel of Ixcuintla Polychrome was recovered from within the modern pueblo of El Zape, which is at the foot of the large hilltop site Cerro de la Cruz (Ganot and Peschard 1990; Ganot et al. 1985). Guasave Red-on-buff is also reported from the Zape area.

Ganot, Peschard, and Lazalde also report west coast types at several other sites in Durango including Puerta de la Cantera, La Brena, Cacaria, Topia, Tepheuanes, Hevideros, Canatlán, and Nayacoyan (Ganot and Peschard 1985, 1990; Howard 1957). To date, the two sites producing the most abundant remains in terms of west coast wares are the Schroeder site (Kelley 1971; Kelley and Winters 1960) and Cañon del Molino (Ganot and Peschard 1990, 1995; Ganot and Peschard 1985).

La Brena (Ganot et al. 1985) produced red-on-brown pottery, probably from the Guasave area. Hervideros produced similar red-on-brown types, as well as Culiacán Polychrome. Nayacoyan produced west coast types identified as Tuxpan Incised, Mangos Engraved, and types of the Amapa and Ixcuintla phases. At Canatlán, plates of Lolandis Red-rimmed have also been identified.

Ceramics from the Amapa, Chametla, Guasave, and Culiacán provinces found at Cañon del Molino include Aztatlán Red-on-buff, Guasave Red-on-buff, Lolandis Red-rim, Iguanas Polychrome, Tuxpan Engraved, Mangos Engraved, Santiago Red-on-orange, and Culiacán Polychrome (Ganot and Peschard 1985, 1990, 1995). Also important, these wares were found along with a wide assortment of other items of west coast origin, including shell pendants, copper bells, spindle whorls, and pipes. Several human skulls exhibiting tabular erect cranial deformation and tooth mutilation were recovered at Molino (Ganot and Peschard 1990). All these materials are clearly and unequivocally Aztatlán related.

To the south, in the canyon lands of southwestern Zacatecas and northern Jalisco, some west coast or west coast–like ceramic types have been identified. Cabrero (1989) reports a type of orange-on-white

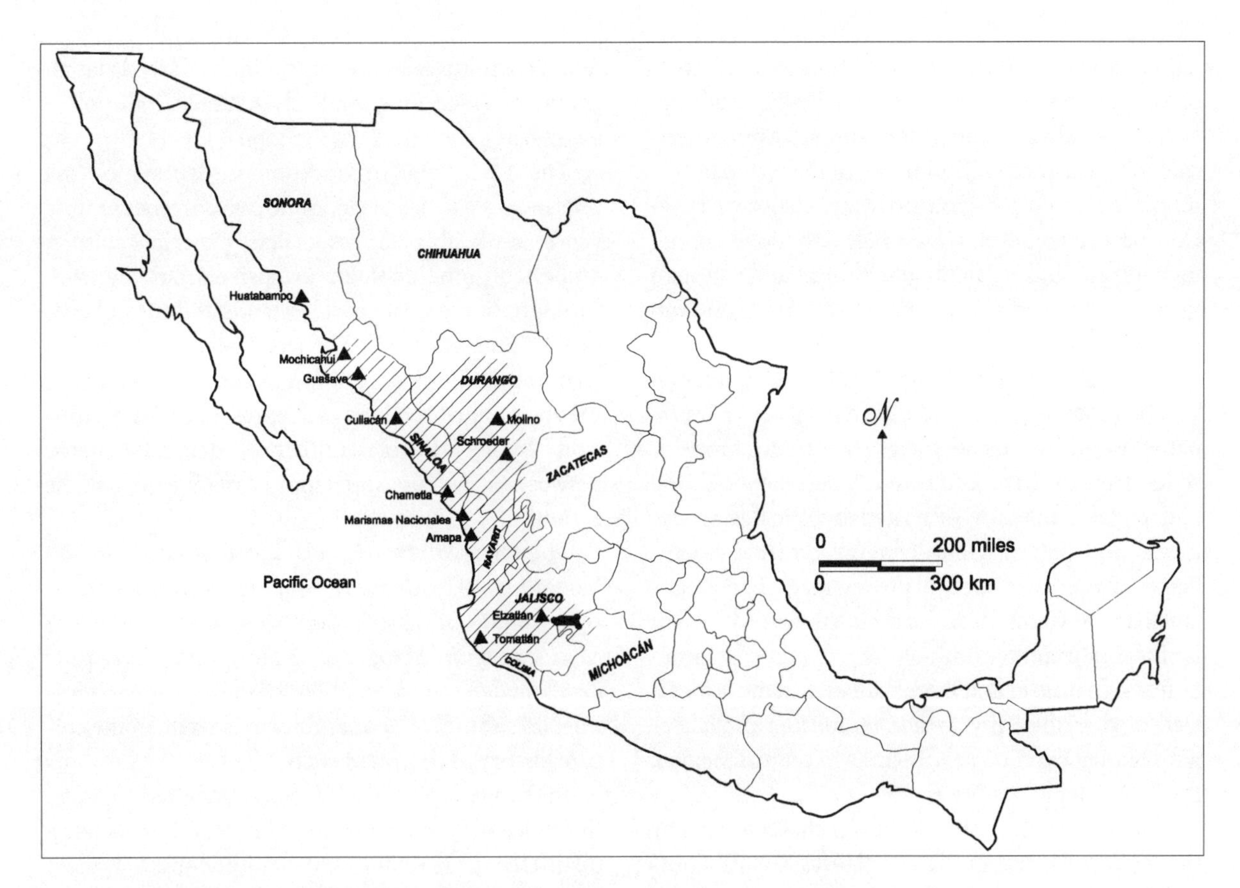

Figure 11.1. The distribution of the Aztatlán tradition in western and northwestern Mexico.

that is apparently a local variant of a west coast type, but she does not report finding any west coast intrusive ceramics as a result of her work in the Bolaños area. However, Kelley (1971:771) reports finding Lolandis and Acaponeta phase types at Totoate in the Río Bolaños area. The lack of west coast– or Aztatlán-related materials in central and southern Zacatecas and northern Jalisco is not fully understood.

In the far northern portions of northwestern Mexico, Chihuahua and Sonora have produced little in the way of west Mexican trade items clearly definable as being from west Mexico and related to the Aztatlán phenomenon. Di Peso (1974:624) believed he had identified some west coast and Chalchihuites sherds at Casas Grandes. However, these were apparently misidentified (Kelley 1993) as to specific types, although they appear to be west and northwest Mexican in origin. Pailes (1972:244–251) reports a number of northern Sinaloa wares in southern Sonora, including Lolandis Red-rim wares, Guasave Red-on-buff, and Navalato Polychrome.

Discussion

Clearly the Aztatlán phenomenon was widespread. The Aztatlán "heartland" included the west coast from northern Sinaloa to southern Jalisco and into the highlands of Jalisco, Nayarit, and northern Michoacán. Its maximum sphere of influence included the highlands of Durango and perhaps the Casas Grandes valley of Chihuahua (Figure 11.1). The Aztatlán tradition may have been the most developed in northern Nayarit and Sinaloa and in the highlands of Jalisco and northern Michoacán. It appears to have evolved out of the red-on-buff ware tradition that preceded it in most areas of west and northwest Mexico. This red-on-buff ware tradition appears to have ties to the similar manifestations in Guanujuato and the Valley of Mexico to the east (Mountjoy 1996). Perhaps as central Mexican influence and contact expanded in west and northwest Mexico and as these areas evolved sociopolitically and economically, central Mexican traits and influences were molded and shared by the local cultures, producing the manifestation known as the Aztatlán tradition. In some areas of west and northwest Mexico, the Aztatlán tradition is the most fully developed and complex Mesoamerican culture achieved. Hallmarks of the Aztatlán tradition include a red-rimmed ware, elaborate polychrome and engraved wares, well-developed copper metallurgy, and a panregional exchange system through which goods and ideas flowed into and out of west Mexico.

It is argued here that the Aztatlán phenomenon best be thought of as a tradition, a persistent cultural pattern identified by characteristic artifact forms or styles. Here the basic and primary persistent cultural pattern takes the form of related stylistic design elements and patterns found in the ceramic assemblages of a series of cultural provenances in the highlands and lowlands of west and northwest Mexico. It is also important to think of the Aztatlán phenomenon as dynamic in that there is an earlier, more localized version, the Early Aztatlán tradition, and a later panregional expression with links to central Mexico, the Late Aztatlán tradition.

The Early Aztatlán tradition was characterized by the appearance and spread of Lolandis Red Rim pottery. As a marker of the Early Aztatlán tradition, this pottery spreads along the northwest coast of Mexico and up into the highlands of Durango. Along the northwest coast its equivalents (see Kelley and Kelley 1971) include Guasave Red-on-buff, Decorated Red Rim Red-on-buff, Red-Rim decorated, and, perhaps, Tuxpan Red-on-orange. Lolandis Red Rim occurs with several polychrome types, engraved types, and a black-on-buff. During the later part of the Early Aztatlán tradition, Lolandis Red Rim is associated with Aztatlán ware. Aztatlán ware is a red-rimmed red-on-buff incised ware sometimes decorated with white paint. Kelley (1992) believes Aztatlán ware marks the initial appearance of stylistic and iconographic elements along the west coast that may be derived from Aztec I ceramics. Sauer and Brand (1932) observed that Lolandis Red Rim occurred at sites without Aztatlán ware. However, Aztatlán ware never occurs without Lolandis Red Rim. Another marker of the Early Aztatlán tradition is a distinctive round, incised spindle whorl decorated with incised circles. These sometimes appear as concentric circles across the face of the whorl or as small circles used to fill geometric patterns on the whorl. In general, the elaborate material culture associated with the Late Aztatlán tradition does not appear in the Early Aztatlán tradition. Dating for the Early Aztatlán tradition is suggested to be ca. A.D. 750 to 1200.

The Late Aztatlán tradition is defined by the presence of a series of elaborate polychrome ceramic types, an elaborate associated material culture, and establishment of an extensive trade network throughout the west coast lowlands and the uplands of west and northwest Mexico. There is a profound elaboration in the decoration of ceramics, including the appearance of codex god representations. Significant Mixteca-Puebla influence, generally dated between A.D. 1200 and 1300, is manifested in the ceramics.

The term *Mixteca-Puebla* was first employed by Vaillant (1938, 1940, 1941), who recognized a distinctive complex of materials both at Cholula and in the Mixteca region of Oaxaca. Although he never fully developed the concept, Vaillant believed the Mixteca-Puebla "culture" to be a significant element of the culture history of central Mexico.

In the 1960s Nicholson (1966) attempted to refine the concept. He suggested that Mixteca-Puebla was a distinctive style rather than a culture and that there were three regionally definable substyles within it: Toltec, the Valley of Mexico Aztec, and the Mixteca proper. Furthermore, because of its distinctive nature and a relatively limited time span, the Mixteca-Puebla phenomenon could be considered a horizon style. Nicholson (1966:260) lists a number of traits (see also Carmack and Larmer 1971) that typify the Mixteca-Puebla style. Nicholson (1982) later revised his initial argument, suggesting that there were actually only two substyles, Cholula and Tula. The interaction between these two centers led to a blending of the substyles that, in turn, provided the basis for the development of an Aztec stylistic tradition.

The Mixteca-Puebla style was executed in a highly precise manner. Many colors, most of which have symbolic significance themselves, are used. Decorative motifs or elements include solar, lunar, calendrical, and various animal (serpents, deer, jaguars) representations. Mixteca-Puebla materials and influence were widely distributed throughout central Mexico and the Maya Lowlands, even crossing into Central America, via an extensive trade and perhaps religious network. The distribution of Mixteca-Puebla materials and influence over such an immense area is clear and powerful evidence of the extent of economic interaction among Mesoamerican cultures during the Late Classic and Postclassic periods. The best dates offered for the Mixteca-Puebla horizon range from between ca. A.D. 650 and 700 to 1300.

As previously discussed, Ekholm (1942:125–132) attributed a number of Aztatlán traits at Guasave to the Mixteca-Puebla "culture" of nuclear Mesoamerica, and the similarities were so strong that he suggested an actual migration of Mixteca-Puebla people must have occurred. The Mixteca-Puebla and Mesoamerican traits identified at Guasave by Ekholm have subsequently been restudied and confirmed by other investigators. Fahmel (1988:148) confirms the Mixteca-Puebla (and Aztec I–II) identification of the ceramics and notes that some ceramic vessel forms in the Guasave material derive from Tohil Plumbate and Fine Orange. These types are widely traded types but are not known to occur north of southern Sinaloa. The Schroeder site produced a cylindrical Guasave Polychrome jar that was decorated on the exterior with three circular medallions. Each contained a codex-style depiction of a god. J. Eric Thompson identified the gods represented (Figure 11.2). One was Xochipilli. Although later used by the Aztecs, the "Xochipilli theme" is thought to be Mixteca in origin (Nicholson 1982). Both the codex-style representations and the depiction of Xochipilli strongly support Ekholm's identification of a Mixteca-Puebla influence at Guasave. Meighan (1971:767) reports a corrected radiocarbon date of A.D. 1220 ± 130 for Guasave, which, based on a stylistic analysis of the Guasave material, seems appropriate. Subsequent archaeological research along the west coast and adjacent highlands suggests the appearance of Mixteca-Puebla influence in west Mexico dates to between A.D. 1200 and 1350. At many of the west Mexican sites the Mixteca-Puebla complex is represented only by Aztec I (Culhuacan Polychrome) ceramic designs and iconography, usually on local ceramic and copper artifacts. "Aztec" I pottery is well represented at Culhuacan and at Cholula. Its iconography is clearly Mixteca-Puebla related, and the presence of that decorative style and iconog-

Figure 11.2. The Guasave jar decorated in codex style from the Schroeder site, Durango. The god Xochipilli is depicted on the left, the god Nanuatzin in the center and right.

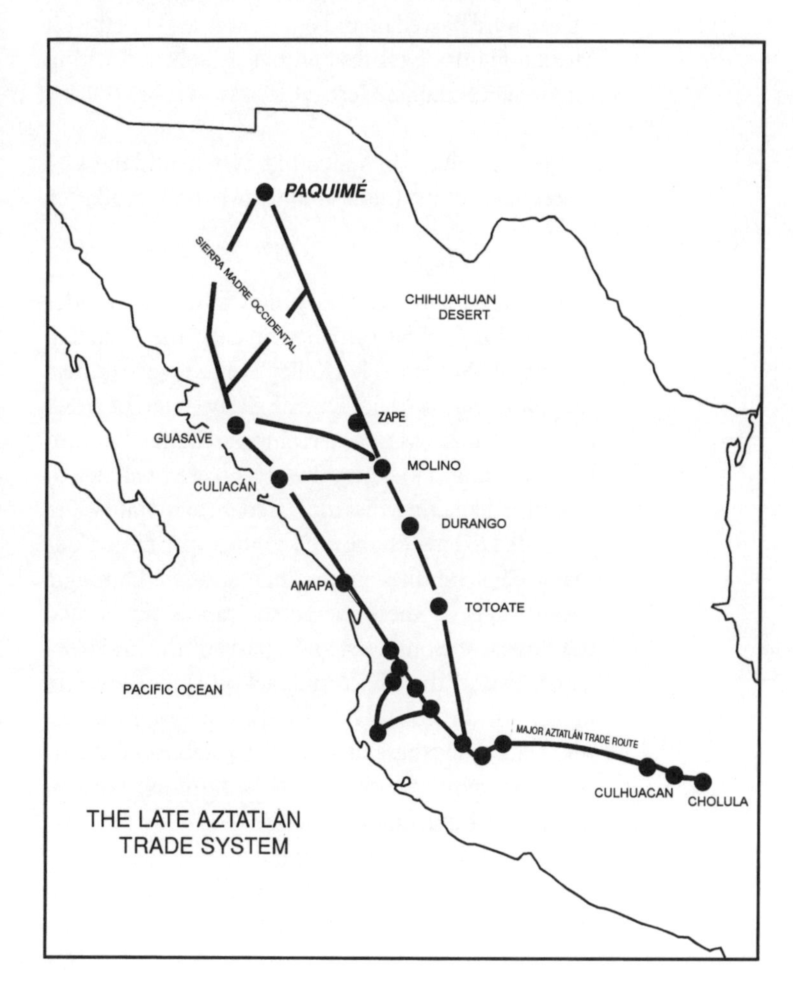

Figure 11.3. The hypothesized route and linkage of the Late Aztatlán mercantile exchange network in west and northwest Mexico.

raphy mark the route (Figure 11.3) of the Aztatlán Mercantile System from central Mexico throughout west Mexico (Kelley 1986, 83–92).

The Greater Aztatlán Mercantile System is a manifestation of the Late Aztatlán tradition, or perhaps vice versa. This Greater Aztatlán Mercantile System acted as a mechanism for the transportation and exchange of a variety of luxury, and probably utilitarian and subsistence, goods over most of west and northwest Mexico. Not only was it a conduit for goods produced and procured in west Mexico, it was a conduit for goods and information flowing out of (and into) central Mexico, and it was clearly and unequivocally linked to the Mixteca-Puebla complex. For example, west Mexican metal artifacts have been recovered in Morelos, Chiapas, the Tehuantepec region, and Belize (Hosler 1994). J. Andrew Darling (personal communication) has identified Pachuca obsidian at Nayacoyan, at the Schroeder site in Durango, and probably at Amapa, Nayarit. Jalisco obsidian (Las Joyas) has also been found at Cañon del Molino. It is quite probable that these goods, the copper and obsidian, were passed in and out of west and northwest Mexico via trade routes and ties established within the Greater Aztatlán Mercantile System.

The Greater Aztatlán Mercantile System and the Florescence of the Casas Grandes Medio Period

The Kelley Model

Kelley's model for the Mesoamerica–Casas Grandes connection focuses on what he calls the "Aztatlán Mercantile System." He (Kelley 1993:249–250) offers the following scenario. During Early Aztatlán times entrepreneurial Mesoamerican merchants, his mobile merchants (Kelley 1986:82) who are pochteca or trocadór-like long-distance trader merchants, are suggested to have established contact with early Guadiana Chalchihuites in the highlands of Durango. Kelley suggests these merchant traders penetrated the American Southwest and "sparked" the initial organization of the Chaco interaction sphere ca. A.D. 900. With the collapse of the Chaco system in the mid–A.D. 1100s these merchants reestablished themselves in a previously established minor base in northern Chihuahua.

Meanwhile, the many cultural provinces along the west Mexican coastal lowlands that were loosely associated economically during Early Aztatlán times became more tightly associated through the development and expansion of the "Greater Aztatlán Mercantile System."

Traders from Aztatlán-related trading outposts established in Durango stimulated the development of the Casas Grandes interaction sphere. The Aztatlán Mercantile System remained a powerful economic force until its links with central Mexico were cut by the expansion of the Tarascan Empire in the late A.D. 1400s. In a subsequent paper Kelley (1992) summarizes: "That Mesoamericans reached Paquime and introduced many traits in architecture, ceramics, copper metallurgy, etc., seems certain. The only probable Mesoamerican source for the conversion of Paquime into a central place (a Mesoamerican Gateway Community) of a major interaction sphere lies in the Mixteca-Puebla Late Aztatlán development east of the Sierra."

Comments

Casas Grandes is clearly unique among sites and cultures of the Southwest, the area north of the Mesoamerican frontier. It is also clear that significant Mesoamerican influence is expressed in the Medio period remains at the site. The idea that Mesoamerican influence and presence at Casas Grandes are simply emulations of Mesoamerican cultures to the south is, to say the least, naive (e.g., McGuire 1980; Minnis 1989). Throughout the history of Mesoamerican culture, starting with the Olmec, large-scale macroeconomic systems existed. The Mixteca-Puebla tradition and its west Mexican expression, the Aztatlán tradition, were Late Classic and Postclassic period expressions of such systems.

Furthermore, the suggestion that Casas Grandes was not a major trading and production center (e.g., Minnis 1988) is fallacious. Substantial quantities and varieties of exotic goods such as macaw remains, turquoise, copper, and marine shell were recovered from the site. Less than half the site was excavated. Such evidence from any other site in the Southwest would be seen as ample proof of specialized production and exchange. In fact, such a site north of the Mexican-U.S. border would be seen by southwestern archaeologists as a major world center of Precolumbian culture.

A variety of Mesoamerican or Mesoamerican-inspired artifacts were recovered from Casas Grandes, including copper bells and other copper items, ceramic drums, spindle whorls, and ceramic sherds. However, these artifacts were not recovered in quantity. Some of the spindle whorls recovered appear to be from the Chalchihuites area of Durango, whereas most of the other items likely derive from the west coast (Sinaloa, Nayarit, and Jalisco). It is further suggested here that the elaborate polychromes of the Mexican west coast and western highlands may have been the inspiration for the Medio period polychromes. Scarlet macaws (*Ara macao*) native to Oaxaca and the tropical lands to the south were imported by the Casas Grandians apparently for macaw aviculture (Di Peso et al. 1974:8:182–185). The remains of some 503 individuals were recovered at Casas Grandes, and other sites have produced nesting boxes as well (Minnis et al. 1993). The birds were probably raised for their feathers, which were traded into other parts of the Southwest, and for ritual purposes. Shell from the Jalisco and Nayarit coasts was also recovered. *Persicula bandera* and *Melongena patula* appear as rare exotic shell at Casas Grandes (Bradley 1993, 1996). Although evidence of metallurgy at Casas Grandes is ambiguous, it is likely that if metallurgical technology was adopted, it came from the copper-producing areas of west Mexico. Similarity between copper bells from Casas Grandes and coastal west Mexico has been noted, but it is premature to discount the possibility that metallurgy was practiced at Casas Grandes, or possibly some outlying site, as has recently been suggested (Vargas 1994, 1995). Again, only half of Casas Grandes has been excavated, and there is a great deal that is not known about the archaeology of the Casas Grandes region.

Another strong indicator of Mesoamerican influence is the ball courts. Casas Grandes has three courts, and other ball courts have been recorded elsewhere in the Casas Grandes valley (Naylor 1995; Whalen and Minnis 1996a). These ball courts, and in particular those with I-shaped configurations, are of considerable importance in documenting the presence of strong Mesoamerican influence at Casas Grandes. The role and significance of the ball game in Mesoamerican culture have been well documented (e.g., Stern 1949; Scarborough and Wilcox 1991). The ball courts found in the northwest Mexican highlands are small open-ended ones (Kelley 1991). An I-shaped court is present at La Quemada and in other sites in the west Mexican highlands and west coast area (Kelley 1991; Clune 1976; Weigand 1991). Ball courts in the Hohokam and Sinagua areas of the American Southwest lack the I-shaped configuration of those in Mesoamerica. The formal I-shaped courts at Casas Grandes suggest a fairly strict adherence to the sociopolitical and ritualistic parameters of the Mesoamerican ball game. Furthermore, it suggests a strong Mesoamerican influence or presence at Casas Grandes.

Thus, it is suggested here that during the Medio period at Casas Grandes, the site was tied to its Mesoamerican neighbors to the south and that the connection was primarily an economic one. However, the tie was sufficiently strong to result in the transmission of ritualistic and ideological knowledge and behavior that greatly influenced the trajectory of sociopolitical and ritualistic development at Casas Grandes, resulting in a unique blend of Mesoamerican and southwestern culture.

Based on the above, the following scenario is proposed. Clearly, Medio period culture and florescence cannot be explained by a single event or a single prime mover. It is suggested here that with the northward expansion of Mesoamerican culture during the Late Classic and Postclassic periods, the Casas Grandes area eventually became integrated into the Mesoamerican interaction sphere. Although this integration reached its maximum between the early A.D. 1200s and the late 1400s, its roots extend back some 1,000 years. As this author (Foster 1986, 1995b) and the Kelleys (Kelley 1966; Kelley and Kelley 1975) have suggested, northwest Mexico was occupied by a series of early agriculturalists participating in a plain- and brownware tradition stretching from Zacatecas and Durango into southern Arizona and New Mexico. The local cultures of this tradition undoubtedly interacted at some level with one another as they exchanged goods, agricultural and collected produce, and technology. It was through this corridor that agriculture and ceramic technology was introduced into the American Southwest. These early agricultural societies eventually gave rise to, or gave way to, more complex developments such as the Canutillo and Chalchihuites cultures of western Zacatecas and Durango, the Casas Grandes culture of Chihuahua, and the Mogollon of New Mexico.

As Mesoamerican culture in the form of the Aztatlán tradition expanded in the western highlands and coastal lowlands, and as these areas became more economically intertwined with central Mexico

(Mixteca-Puebla), new markets opened up and old ones expanded. Especially significant was the demand for exotic and rare resources, as well as the need for more utilitarian goods. It is likely this economic expansion was driven by both a market economy (thus the need for long-distance, entrepreneurial traders) and exchange between the elite of peer polities (e.g., Bradley 1996). As the demand for goods and materials increased, traders working out of west coast centers crossed over the Sierra Madre Occidental and established links with late Chalchihuites peoples in the eastern highlands of Durango (Kelley 1986). This may have stimulated the flow of additional goods and exotica southward out of central and northern Chihuahua and the American Southwest. It is possible that some areas, such as the Casas Grandes valley, became, via either down-the-line exchange or established exchange networks or both, focal points for the collection of materials that were then passed southward. This could have resulted in the formation of a local leadership that gained ever-increasing authority, wealth, and prestige as they organized and administered the acquisition and exchange of goods and resources. By the beginning of Late Aztatlán times, an incipient local or perhaps regional elite may have been established at Casas Grandes. Long-distance traders working primarily out of centers on the west coast are suggested to have penetrated Casas Grandes via a coastal route (see Figure 11.3), establishing ties with the local leadership. Taking advantage of the newly established links with groups to the south, the local Casas Grandes leadership quickly established itself as the dominant force in the Casas Grandes valley and adjacent area. Being able to oversee the production and extraction of a variety of resources locally and acquiring resources, such as New Mexican turquoise, from more distant places enabled the Casas Grandes elite to grow in power.

Simultaneously, not only did the ties to the Late Aztatlán Mercantile System strengthen, but so did the influence of Mesoamerican culture. The coastal route was probably complemented with an inland route coming out of Durango and up the eastern foothills of the Sierra (see chapter four of this volume). It is possible as Casas Grandes grew in importance that it attracted Aztatlán traders, craftsmen, and technicians of one kind or another from west and northwest Mesoamerica. Perhaps the situation was akin to that seen earlier as Teotihuacán's influence expanded into the Maya area at sites like Tikal and Kaminaljuyú or like the Oaxaca barrio at Teotihuacán. Perhaps it was an influx of Mesoamericans into Casas Grandes, there to profit from Casas Grandes's advantageous location and florescence, that resulted in the site's adoption of a Mesoamerican facade. The elite may have been able to maintain their positions through prestige and gift exchange with neighbors to both the south and north. Their connections to the south may have also provided them with esoteric and ritualistic knowledge that also helped them maintain their positions in Casas Grandes society.

It is also believed that Kelley (1993) is correct regarding the decline of the Casas Grandes polity. As he suggests, it is believed that as the Tarascan Empire expanded into central Jalisco, it cut Mixteca-Puebla Aztatlán trade routes. This resulted in the decline of the Aztatlán Mercantile System as demand for goods and exotica dropped. The Casas Grandes elite held on for a while, but as environmental shifts and resulting cultural realignments occurred across the Greater Southwest their position in Casas Grandes society surely weakened, as did the economic and political power of the Casas Grandes polity itself. The culmination of the decline and collapse of the Medio period came when the site was overrun and destroyed.

The above speculation builds on and incorporates several competing explanations in an attempt to better understand the unique character of Casas Grandes. The notion that long-distance Mesoamerican merchant traders were not responsible for the founding, or the direct reorganization, of an earlier Viejo period ranchería into Paquimé is not argued for. It is believed that direct and indirect interaction with Mesoamerican polities along the west coast and in the northwestern highlands contributed to growth of a local Casas Grandes elite and the florescence of the Medio period. It is further argued that without the expansion of the Aztatlán tradition and the development of the Late Aztatlán Mercantile System and its ties to the Mixteca-Puebla tradition of central Mexico, it is unlikely Casas Grandes would have achieved its unique place in the prehistory of the Greater Southwest.

ACKNOWLEDGMENTS. I would like to thank J. Charles Kelley and Ellen Abbott Kelley for the use of Figure 11.1. I would also like to thank J. Charles for his years of friendship, tutelage, and patience. All of us who dabble in Chichimecan and northwest Mesoamerican frontier studies are in debt to the pioneers of the Gran Chichimeca, Charles Di Peso, J. Charles Kelley, Carroll Riley, Isabel Kelly, Campbell Pennington, Gordon Ekholm, Carl Sauer, Donald Brand, Pedro Armillas, Wigberto Jiménez Moreno, and Roman Piña Chan. Their contributions, efforts, sacrifice, insights, and scholarship will likely never be overshadowed.

12

Tlalocs, Kachinas, Sacred Bundles, and Related Symbolism in the Southwest and Mesoamerica

Polly Schaafsma

RECENT YEARS HAVE witnessed a resurgence of interest and attention to the issues of cultural similarities between the Southwest and Mesoamerica. Although Southwest-Mesoamerican connections have been repeatedly postulated and discussed from various angles, there has been no consensus among archaeologists on the nature of these relationships or even on whether perceived parallels were the result of intersocietal interaction or only apparent and due to endogenous development (Pailes and Whitecotton 1995). In this forum the Southwest has been regarded as both an "island" and a "peninsula" in regard to its relationship with Mesoamerica. Mathien and McGuire (1986:1–2) have noted that the debate has tended to be overly polarized. For example, ecological functionalism of the New Archaeology dominated archaeological thinking during the 1970s and most of the 1980s, supporting an isolationist position, which regarded those who advocated a Mesoamerican presence in the Southwest as "diffusionists" (a decidedly negative label), or subscribing to an archaic historical form of explanation. Nevertheless, the recognition that the Southwest was not a "closed system (Foster 1986:65) persists, and Mesoamerican traits in the north cannot be rejected or dismissed easily. Archaeologists continue to address this "problem." Although the case for ideological parallels and connections is extensive and complex, at the moment the development of various models to explain patterns of Southwest-Mesoamerican interaction prevails over substantive research aimed at looking at evidence for Mesoamerican-southwestern parallels that support this interaction.

Since Di Peso's work at Casas Grandes (1974), explanations of interaction have been dominated by mercantile or economic models that include the *pochteca* model of Di Peso and, more recently, a broader concept of economic interaction: the world systems theory, as proposed by Wallerstein (1974) and Whitecotton and Pailes (1986), or dependency theory (Nelson 1993). The *pochteca* model has now fallen into disfavor (McGuire 1980), and alternative explanations for interaction involving more generalized modes of trade and possibly a concomitant ideological spread are being proposed (Foster 1986; McGuire 1980). Phillips (1991) stresses that interaction was not random and that there were multiple possibilities for cultural exchange, proposing that one possible model was provided in local leadership that drew its incentive from the south. This model does not necessitate a Mesoamerican presence in the north per se but posits culture change based on

Mesoamerican inspiration in combination with local processes of change.

Importantly, a continuity in settled village life between the northern outposts of Mesoamerica and the Greater Southwest is now known to have existed (Foster 1986; Pailes and Whitecotton 1995; Phillips 1991) in spite of the purported gap recently declared by Upham (1992). Mesoamerica reached its maximum northern expansion around A.D. 1150 when the Chalchihuites culture extended to Zape in northern Durango (Table 12.1; see also Figure 2 in the introduction to this volume.) Prior to A.D. 1150 between Zape, Durango, and southern Arizona and New Mexico was a Mogollon-like farming people. After A.D. 1150, rock art and ceramic designs in the Casas Grandes region display specific stylistic and iconographic relationships with both the Southwest and cultures on the Mesoamerican periphery in Mexico; nevertheless, with the exception of some "cartouched" designs, possible ideographic "glyphs," no real spatial continuity between the rock art of Casas Grandes and central Mexico has yet been documented (Schaafsma 1997a). Although only spottily represented in the archaeological record, both the iconography itself and ethnohistoric sources indicate that a great many ideas were shared between Mesoamerica and the Southwest. New explanatory models for the spread of ideas may be needed to explain such iconographic "leapfrogging."

It is not the purpose of this chapter to suggest further mechanisms of interaction but rather to examine within specific ideological frameworks the evidence that some kind of cultural interaction did take place. My aim is to focus on two complexes, specifically the Tlaloc configuration in Mexico and the kachina cult in the Southwest. The kachina complex appears in Pueblo IV rock art, ceramic decoration, and kiva murals around A.D. 1300 with precedents in the Mimbres and Jornada Mogollon (Table 12.1). The dating of the kachina phenomenon has been the subject of lengthy discussions elsewhere (Adams 1991, 1994; Carlson 1982a; Schaafsma 1980, 1992, 1994). For some time similarities between the two complexes have been noted (Brew 1943; Ellis and Hammack 1968:41; Kelley 1966:107–109; Parsons 1933:611–613, 1939:1019). These earlier observations, however, have tended to list shared obvious traits without a deeper exploration of conceptual issues.

This chapter deals in part with southwestern iconography, as well as iconography in wall paintings, codices, and sculpture in Mexico. Second, these visual materials are combined with the extensive use of ethnographic data from both Mexico and the Southwest. Examination of this packet of information dealing with Tlaloc and kachinas in Mesoamerica and the Southwest contributes to the view that the two places are undeniably and inextricably linked. The images of the Tlaloc complex and the kachinas of the archaeological record are but the tip of an iceberg, visual forms that incorporate multilayered complexes of metaphors that encompass a wide range of shared ideas. The latter include metaphorical references to landscape features, the Underworld, and the ancestors. The symbolism and landscape metaphors define a "structural armature" or supporting framework that determines a worldview (Hunt 1977) and functions to reduce experience to meaningful patterns (Knab 1986:52). Eva Hunt (1977:259) stresses that such armatures are "quite fixed over long periods of time, across geographic, social, and culture boundaries." Hunt was referring to basic structural elements within Mesoamerican ideology that this study indicates extend into the Southwest.

Shared metaphors and conceptual systems as outlined below indicate that the kachina complex of the protohistoric farmers in the Pueblo Southwest is a northern peripheral manifestation of a Mesoamerican constellation of ideas in the realm of Tlaloc. Because the Tlaloc complex in Mexico, dedicated to bringing rain for crops, was probably more widespread than any other (Nicholson 1971:414), this is not an unreasonable proposition. Furthermore, Tlaloc iconography is ancient and can be traced in time essentially throughout the Mesoamerican sequence. This temporal factor as well has important implications for the spread and development of concepts throughout an interaction sphere that I argue here included the Southwest. Finally, within this general complex, specific ideological sources for the origins of the kachina configuration are suggested.

Mesoamerican Tlaloc Complex and Related Symbolism

Linked with the earth, clouds, and rain, the Tlaloc complex is one of the oldest identifiable in the iconography of ancient Mexico. Covarrubias (1957: Figure 22) traces this earth/rain god to Olmec were-

Table 12.1. Chronology of Selected Cultures and Areas.

	SOUTHWEST UNITED STATES		MEXICO					
1995	Pueblo V							
1900								
1800								
1680								
1598								
1521				Aztec				
1425	Pueblo IV	Jornada Mogollon	Casas Grandes					
1350								
1325								
1250				Proto Aztec				
1200								
1150					Chalchihuites			
1100		Mimbres				El Tajin		
1000				Toltec				
900								
850								
750								
650							Teotihuacán	
550								
450								
350								
250								
150								
50								
50								
150								
200								
300								
400								
500								
600								Chalcatzingo

jaguar origins. As an anthropomorphic embodiment of this complex of ideas, the deity Tlaloc is present in the archaeological record by the late Preclassic (800–300 B.C.) in the Puebla-Tlaxcala region (Weaver 1981:106). As well, the bas-relief at the highland Olmec site of Chalcatzingo, Morelos (600–400 B.C.) (De La Fuente 1992:Figure 14; Gay 1972:Figure 11), is replete with Tlaloc-related symbolism. Portrayed here is a jaguar mask-cave harboring an ancestor/priest and from which mists emerge in the form of scrolls. The seated ancestor/ruler, functioning as an intermediary between the living and the regenerative forces of the landscape (Townsend 1992a:41), faces Popocatepetl, around which clouds are generated daily. Above this scene float stylized clouds with rain that resemble the cave-like mouth characteristic of later rain god representations.

Tlaloc, the Nahuatl name for the male rain/storm/earth god of Mesoamerica, embodies fundamental aspects of Prehispanic cosmovision that include mountains, mists, a watery underworld, and cult of the ancestors, as well as themes of reciprocity and renewal. His complex nature is reflected in the various attempts to specify his identity. From the sixteenth-century Spanish chronicler Sahagún (1953:20) we learn that Tlaloc and the Tlaloque, Tlaloc in his multiple forms or aspects, appear as clouds around mountaintops. In a recent essay Townsend (1992b:179) proposes that as the name signifies "of the earth" or "from the earth," it refers to rising mist or vapor that forms clouds around the mountains. Sullivan (1974:216), in an in-depth etymological analysis of the name, states that "Therefore the name Tlaloc, which correctly should be spelled Tlalloc means, 'he who has the quality of earth,' 'he who is made of earth,'" and "since the names of Nahuatl gods are literally or figuratively a description of their nature, it would appear that Tlaloc was essentially an earth god." She also notes, however, that there was a strong association of this deity with caves, the latter being associated in turn with springs and sources of water. Thus, in conclusion Sullivan (1974:217) speculates that possibly Tlaloc was originally conceived of as a god of earth and water and that his function as a rain god came later; in a subsequent publication she refers to him as the "God of Rain" (Sullivan 1986:10–11).

It follows that mountains, connected to cults of rain, water, and the earth, are central to the ritual landscape of the Tlaloc complex. Streams and springs emerging from mountains are also part of the picture. The pyramids of the urban centers of central Mexico were equal to the sacred mountains with which they were ritually connected by a system of shrines. Orifices in the earth, such as the hole carved deeply into bedrock within the enclosure on Mount Tlaloc outside of Tenochtitlán and in Aztec temple sites elsewhere, symbolized cave entrances to the Underworld (Townsend 1992b:178). Townsend suggests that such earth navels may have served as symbolic places of emergence, or in southwestern terms, as a kind of *sipapu*.

Ceremonies involving Tlaloc were performed on mountaintops, in Aztec urban centers, and in the fields. Child sacrifice, an act of "paying of debts" to Tlaloc, was carried out "everywhere" on mountaintops (Sahagún 1953; Townsend 1992b). The paying of these debts involved an ancient sense of participation in the natural cycle and reciprocity, giving back or negotiating with the life of an individual for life-granting rains for the social whole. Particularly significant in this context was Mount Tlaloc, where Aztec ceremonies of sacrifice and renewal took place each year before the onset of the rainy season. The last sacrifice on Mount Tlaloc is said to have taken place as recently as 1936 (Timothy Knab, personal communication). Ceramics indicate that the use of the site was not peculiar to the Aztecs, however, but that the mountain has been a place of veneration and ritual use for about 1500 years (Townsend 1991:29).

Tlaloc's female counterpart or sister was Chalchihuitlicue, also known as "Lady Precious Green," goddess of groundwaters—of lakes, oceans, and rivers (an important point to which I will return). Illustrations of Chalchihuitlicue and Tlaloc from the *Códice Borbónico* show waters flowing from both the stool and mountain on which they are each seated respectively. Mexican festivals of Tlaloc and Chalchihuitlicue at the onset of the rainy season included a lake cult (Broda 1991:96).

Other aspects of the Tlaloc complex include associations of Tlaloque with the cardinal directions. Tlaloque of the five directions—the intercardinal points and the center—are illustrated in the *Codex Borgia* (Townsend 1992b:Figure 6). The Tlaloque, assistants to Tlaloc, were also often represented by various mountain peaks that were, in turn, associated with color and directional symbolism. In both the Mayan and Mexican areas the cardinal directions have color symbolism and associations with different aspects of a single god, including the rain deities (Nicholson 1971:414; Riley 1963:51).

The Image

Tlaloc is represented in codices, murals, and architectural sculpture as an anthropomorphic deity (Figure 12.1). Carved wooden and turquoise inlay masks were worn by religious impersonators of Tlaloc in festivals dedicated to rain and fertility (Townsend 1992b:171). His iconography varies somewhat according to time and place and is described and illustrated in numerous works (Pasztory 1974, 1983:Plates 32, 137–141; Townsend 1992b). In summary, representations of Tlaloc are characterized by goggle eyes, sometimes shown with brows formed by serpents that intertwine over the nose to create the "cruller" effect. He may also be portrayed with an upturned mouth or with a mustache-like upper lip above a cavernous maw and in either case is equipped with long fangs. Nicholson (1973:87) describes a serrated paper crown surmounted by heron feathers, often combined with quetzal feathers, as symbolizing the male efflorescence of the maize plant and as typifying the headdress of Tlaloc and allied deities in the Aztec period. In several Aztec examples, the corner fangs are represented, but obvious front teeth are lacking, and a band encircles the entire mouth (Figure 12.2; see also Pasztory 1983:Plates 138, 141). Two Classic forms of Tlaloc, a Jaguar-Tlaloc and a Crocodile-Tlaloc, are distinguished by Pasztory (1974) at Teotihuacán. The Crocodile-Tlaloc, both an earth and a water deity (Pasztory 1974:19), frequently has a water lily hanging from the mouth and a year sign in the headdress. The Jaguar-Tlaloc has a knotted headdress and bifurcate lolling tongue but lacks the water lily and year sign. In sum, however, Pasztory notes that the iconography of the two are occasionally blended, and variability even in these features may occur. Most relevant to the current discussion are the Tlalocs that sometimes hold staffs or lightning serpents, as well as effigy vessels of themselves (Figures 12.3 and 12.4). Taube (1986:70) identifies some of these Teotihuacán "effigy vessels" as sacred bundles with Tlaloc masks (a point considered below). In addition, frogs and toads were among the symbolic repertoire of this deity.

In regard to iconographic stability, Nicholson (1973:90) states that "only a few elements among the most striking and diagnostic insignia of particular deities (such as Tlaloc, Ehecatl-Quetzalcoatl . . .) can be traced back into the Classic and in rare cases beyond." The considerable time depth for the Tlaloc complex was noted previously. Changes in Tlaloc iconography through time are inevitable, but the goggle eyes, the volute over the mouth, and the fangs are relatively constant.

Landscape Features and Vessels of Water

For the purposes of this discussion, the iconic aspects of landscape features and other elements with which Tlaloc is associated are even more important than the various characteristics of his appearance. As described previously, central to this discussion are mountains and caves as generators of clouds and sources of springs, lakes, and streams. Throughout most of Mesoamerica, mountaintops were regarded as homes and meeting places of ancestors and deities (Tedlock 1986:128), and ancestors were thought to dwell in watery domains accessed by caves and springs. Mountains themselves were described metaphorically as containers of water, as "vessels" where water was stored in the dry season to be let loose in the upcoming rainy season (Broda 1991:84; Townsend 1992b:181). A graphic description exists for Mount Malinche, which was said to accommodate huge galleries lined with ollas filled with different types of precipitation, seeds, fruit, and so forth (Rands 1955:344–345). The concept of containers from which issue clouds that produce rain was widespread (Rands 1955:344–347). In the oral traditions describing Tlaloc's home, four jars containing beneficent rain, mildew, drought, and destructive rain were said to stand in the four corners of his patio (Peterson 1959:131). These jars, each associated with different types of weather, symbolized his four-sided domain. Similarly the Mixtec and Zapotec of Oaxaca conceived of jars, especially foot-shaped jars or cook pots, containing clouds, hail, and lightning (Marcus 1983b:347; Parsons 1936a:212). The idea of thunder striking vessels to break them as lightning flashes inside is an extension of this metaphor into the landscape (Rands 1955:344). A picture from the *Codex Selden* shows a rain god mask and jar inside a cave (Heyden 1981:14).

Actual caves housing receptacles for water include, among others, the cave beneath the Pyramid of the Sun at Teotihuacán and, in the Maya region, the watery cave of Balankanché, near Chichén Itzá. In the

Figure 12.1. Masked impersonator of Tlaloc, *Codex Magliabechiano,* Aztec (redrawn from Townsend 1992:Figure 3).

Figure 12.2. Aztec Tlaloc effigy vase from the Templo Mayor, Tenochtitlán. The vase is blue with red and orange accents (after Townsend 1992:Figure 1).

Figure 12.3. Tlaloc holding a lightning serpent surrounded by sparks and flames in one hand and a Tlaloc effigy vessel or bundle wearing a Tlaloc mask in the other. Water pours from the "vessel" marked with water symbols, but this object also sports a large feather. These features contribute to the ambiguous nature of the figure. Teotihuacán mural (after Pasztory 1974:Figure 5).

Figure 12.4. Tepantitla mural fragment, Teotihuacán, showing Tlaloc holding Tlaloc effigy vessels of rain, A.D. 300–600 (after Pasztory 1983:Color Plate 2).

Figure 12.5. Bas-relief Panel 6, South Ball Court, El Tajin. A figure holding a vessel (left) stands over a Tlaloc bundle lying within a Teotihuacán water temple, which could also stand for a cave. A second Tlaloc is seated on the roof (Taube 1986:Figure 2b). (Courtesy of Karl Taube)

latter, numerous effigy vessels with Tlaloc and Chac symbolism were left as offerings in the late ninth or early tenth centuries (Andrews and Sabloff 1986: 439). Accompanying these vessels are miniature manos and metates with possible allusions to corn, bones, and the creation of humankind. Offerings to Tlaloc were often made on a miniature scale. The tradition of placing Tlaloc effigy vessels in strategic architectural contexts may be an extension of landscape metaphors and may have roots at least as far back as Teotihuacán (Matos Moctezuma 1992:193; Taube 1986:71).

It is not surprising, therefore, to find vessels pictured as a significant part of the iconography of Tlaloc from at least as early as Teotihuacán (A.D. 300–750) through the Postclassic. As discussed previously, Crocodile-Tlalocs at Teotihuacán are portrayed in murals with vessels in their hands on which Tlaloc symbolism is depicted (Figures 12.3 and 12.4). Symbolic redundancy makes the metaphor even more powerful in the case of an actual vase from Teotihuacán that pictures a Tlaloc carrying an olla that also bears Tlaloc symbolism (Miller 1986:Figure 56). According to the Aztecs, the Tlaloque poured water on the earth from such vessels (Miller 1986:78; Pasztory 1983:222). Pasztory (1983:222) adds that thunder was caused by hitting the vessels with axes. Even at Teotihuacán "The vessels and lightning staffs carried by Crocodile-Tlalocs refer to the way in which the rain gods are supposed to produce rain by pouring water from vessels and lightning and thunder by hitting these vessels with their staffs" (Pasztory 1974:20).

Another elaboration on the symbolic use of water-filled vessels is their widespread identification with springs. At the Aztec Atamalqualiztli Festival, celebrating the birth of maize, vessels of water with frogs and snakes were placed in front of a statue of Tlaloc (Pasztory 1983:62), while the god impersonators danced dressed as birds, butterflies, and bees. Koontz (1994) proposes that the vessel shown in Panel 6 in the South Ball Court sequence at El Tajin (Figure 12.5) contains the *itzompan* waters of fecundity, that is, the sacred waters from the hole in the center of the ball court that are said to flow to the crops. Corner panels also picture this container. Simultaneously water-filled ollas, like springs, also signified access to the Underworld. Among current Aztec descendants, a jar of water placed on an altar can function as a means of divination and communication with Underworld residents. As described by Knab (1995:151): "I told her aunts and uncles to bring new clothes and gifts if they wanted her to return [from the Underworld] and to put them all in front of the jug of water at the altar so that she would see them through the waters." Reflections seen in containers of water were also used for divination (Alarcón 1983: 162; Pasztory 1983:193). Similar uses and symbolic properties of bowls of medicine water on Pueblo altars are described below.

As mentioned throughout the previous discussion, caves in the landscape context have numerous connotations in the Mexican cosmological scheme. In addition to their linkage to Tlaloc they are regarded as points of access to the Underworld and places of origin. Caves are often viewed as entrances and thus as providing access to the watery Underworld as such. The realm of Tlalocan was accessed via caves, especially caves in mountains. This subterranean paradise of Tlaloc and Chalchihuitlicue, enjoyed by certain of the deceased, was a world of perennial summer and lush vegetation from which emerged all waters of the earth (López Austin 1988:2: 296). It follows that mountain caves, often housing springs and shrines, were regarded as especially sacred. The great maw of the jaguar, abstracted as the mouth of the Jaguar-Tlaloc, symbolizes this landscape feature.

The symbolic conflation of water-filled mountains or mountain caves and the Underworld are made explicit in the bas-relief narratives in a ball court at El Tajin (Koontz 1994). The base of the temple pictured in these reliefs, where a blood sacrifice of Tlaloc is taking place, is probably symbolic of a cave filled with water (Taube 1986:70). The blood goes to creating a man wearing a fish mask, iconographic evidence supporting the Mesoamerican concept of the creation of humankind out of earlier (ancestral) fish forms (Léon-Portilla 1992:17), a subject explored extensively by Taube (1986). (For a possible similar concept formerly present among the Pueblo Tewa, see below.) A nearby scene mentioned previously (Figure 12.5) also includes in a cave-like context a representation of Tlaloc as a personified bundle, the latter signified by the knotted cloth (Koontz 1994:74:Figure 4.37a and 4.37c; Taube 1986:55). This particular figure is thought to represent, in full-figure form, the ballcourt sacrifice (Koontz 1994). Bundles will be discussed further below.

Other pertinent landscape features not previously discussed are clusters of natural boulders left in place within the precinct on Mount Tlaloc (Townsend 1992b:178). Townsend feels that these rocks, roughly arranged to correspond to the four corners and center of the compound, repeated the functions of the idols within the temple chamber, some of which represented the neighboring hills and cliffs surrounding the great mountain (Duran 1971:156). Townsend proposes that the boulders had directional symbolism and compares them with the Central Tlaloc surrounded by Tlaloque at the intercardinal points as illustrated in the *Codex Borgia.*

Additional Iconographic Motifs

An additional iconographic motif often symbolizing clouds, and by extension sometimes affiliated with the Tlaloc complex, is the crosshatched net pattern (Figure 12.5). Although the net motif does not play a particularly prominent role in Tlaloc iconography in Mexico, it is worthy of discussion because of its carryover into rain-related motifs in the Southwest after ca. A.D. 1000 or a little later (see below). In Mesoamerica the net pattern symbolizing clouds goes back to the Olmec period, where net patterns, along with spirals or scrolls, are frequently part of rain propitiation themes (Gay 1972:40). This symbolism extends into the historic period as illustrated by a Tlaloc impersonator wearing a garment with a net design and carrying a crosshatched shield (Townsend 1992b:Figure 2). So-called net jaguars in Mesoamerican iconography are simultaneously associated with weapons and war and water and fertility (Pasztory 1974:19), themes that are linked in Mesoamerican thought by the ideology of sacrifice. The Jaguar-Tlaloc is related to this group. Among the Jornada-style petroglyphs (A.D. 1000–1400) in southern New Mexico, a cat covered with a net design and with a rattlesnake tail may have embodied similar concepts (Schaafsma 1980:Figure 184, upper right).

Kachina Ideology and Art in the Southwest

Juxtaposed to this intricate web of landscape and other symbolism surrounding Tlaloc is the Southwest kachina complex, with a parallel set of concepts and metaphors (see Bunzel 1932; P. Schaafsma 1994). It is the general belief that the anonymous ancestors come in the form of clouds to bring rains to the fields of the living, and when they are impersonated in the Pueblo plazas as kachinas, they wear masks. The masks are thought of as originally having belonged to the kachinas themselves. As stated by Bunzel (1932:710, n. 14), "The impersonator dons the mask and becomes the god, and inversely the god assumes human form." The mask is thus the key to the connection between humans and the kachina spirits.

Kachina masks appear around A.D. 1300 in Pueblo rock art and on ceramics (Adams 1991; Hays 1994; Schaafsma 1975a). Along with masks, goggle-eyed figures resembling Tlaloc, often with their torsos covered with cloud symbolism, are prominent in Mogollon Jornada style rock art in the Chihuahuan desert of southern New Mexico between ca. A.D. 1000 and 1400 (Figures 12.6 and 12.7). The presence of a Tlaloc image on a Mimbres Black-on-white bowl (Davis 1995:171) confirms the presence of this figure in southern New Mexico between A.D. 1000 and 1150 (Figure 12.8).

Figure 12.6. Map of the Southwest with various cultural and Pueblo linguistic provinces indicated.

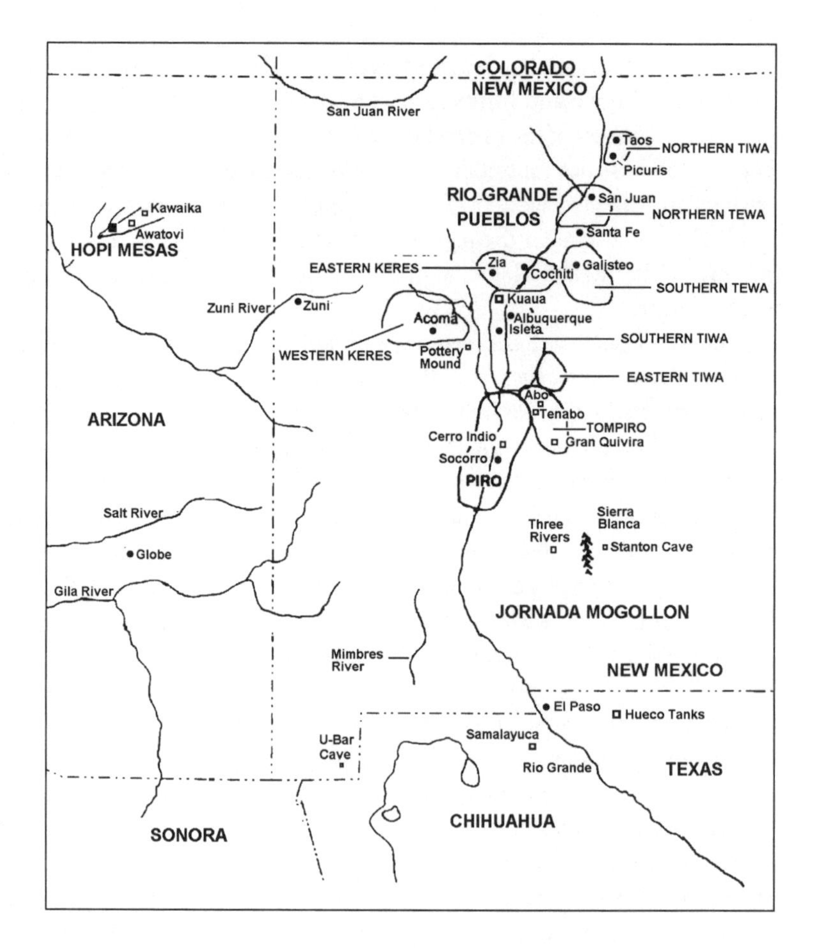

Figure 12.7. Seven Tlaloc figures painted in a single rock shelter, Hueco Tanks State Park, Texas (redrawn from Davis and Toness 1974:Figure 28-A).

Figure 12.8. Design from a Mimbres bowl depicting a female figure carrying a burden basket in the form of a Southwest Tlaloc (redrawn from Davis 1995, p. 171).

Ethnographically and in Pueblo art forms there is no Tlaloc per se. The Hopi god of the earth and death, Masau, overlaps with Tlaloc in certain formal attributes, including the big rings around his eyes and toothed mouth, that in Masau's case are said to resemble a skull. Masau is said to control the earth and the Underworld and the passages in between (Wright 1977:34), and petroglyphs of this god in the Rio Grande valley are found appropriately located in cracks and caves (Schaafsma 1990:149). These Rio Grande examples indicate that Masau was formerly more widespread among the Pueblos and not limited to Hopi as is the case today. Mexica migration and Hopi emergence myths (Pasztory 1983:116; Nequatewa 1947:24–26) also parallel each other, where Tlaloc and Masau, respectively, owners of the earth, grant permission for these people to locate at a chosen spot. Although Masau's association with the dead and the Underworld is very involved (Titiev 1944: 134–135), his association with rain and moisture per se is not particularly significant. If anything, rainmaking powers seem to be limited to his female counterpart, Masau'u Kachin'mana (Wright 1977:56), also known as Tuwapongtumsi, patron deity of all game animals (Titiev 1944:137). Although valuable analogies have also been drawn between Tlaloc of Mexico and Pueblo kachina chiefs such as Pautiwa (Zuni) and Eototo (Hopi) and gods of germination (Parsons 1933:625; Young 1994:117), the parallels between the Tlaloc complex of Mexico and the kachinas of the Southwest rest on much broader common ground (Riley 1995:110–112). Yet unlike Tlaloc, a deity in his own right, kachinas are regarded as anthropomorphic intermediaries between the gods and humankind and as maintaining a general affinity with the ancestors. This important distinction may provide a clue to the ideas that led to the development of the kachina complex as such, a point to which I will return later in this chapter.

Kachinas—the Symbolic Landscape

As with Tlaloc and his assistants, the Tlaloque, of Mexico, Pueblo kachinas are associated both with mountains, around which clouds and mist form, and with the watery underground realm, accessed via springs and lakes, to which the dead return. The latter suggest affiliations with the domain of Chalchihuitlicue, Tlaloc's female counterpart. Certain springs and lakes are simultaneously regarded as the *sipapu,* or place of humankind's emergence to the earth's surface. All of these terrestrial water sources are thought of as being connected under the earth.

Specifically, the San Francisco Peaks, around which the summer cumulus clouds build, are well known for their kachina associations among the Hopi, but there are other "kachina mountains" as well. Kor'kokshi mountain of the Zunis (a name directly referencing the first kachinas at Zuni), or essentially "kachina mountain," is described as having a cave on the summit with a passageway leading to Kolhuwalaaw'a, or Kachina Village in the lake (Stevenson 1904:154). Similarly, Mount Taylor was (is) regarded by the Acoma as "the mother of rain," and a small cave on the summit was used as a "kiva" (Thompson 1879:321) or perhaps a shrine. Thompson reports that the site was visited in mid-June just prior to the beginning of the rainy season, when prayer sticks were left as offerings. Lake Peak, associated with fertility, in the northern Rio Grande valley is likewise regarded as the kachina home and sacred mountain of the East for some northern Tewa, that is,

Nambe Pueblo and probably Tesuque (Lang 1989:19). Nambe Lake, directly beneath the peak itself, is not without significance in this context, possibly the locus of secret ceremonies cited by Harrington (1916:351), as well as a kachina home. For the Tewas of San Juan Pueblo, masked deities associated with winter moiety initiations, however, originate on Truchas Peak to the north (Ortiz 1969:165). Although the kachina cult never took the form of public masked dancing at Taos, conceptual systems surrounding Taos Mountain and Blue Lake partake of kachina ideology elsewhere. The lack of a proliferation of specific kachinas, but instead a more generalized concept of rain deities, is perhaps more akin to the concept of Tlaloc and the Tlaloque in Mexico. In Taos the "cloud boys," or *ła'tsina,* meaning thunder or lightning, are said to live on the mountaintops and in the sky, as well as under the springs. One spring in the communal pasture is called Tsipapapu, and this spring is said to be connected to Blue Lake via an underground passage (Parsons 1936b:109).

Certain caves, as well as small lakes and springs, are regarded by various Pueblos as the Shipap opening, the place of emergence from the Underworld. Zuni ritual poetry metaphorically expresses the idea of rainmakers living inside "the place of our first beginning" and of springs as being the "doorways" of the rainmakers (Bunzel 1932:712). Lakes such as Kachina Lake, or Kolhuwalaaw'a, west of Zuni, Blue Lake at Taos, and other small lakes associated with mountains are regarded as places of access to the watery Underworld of the deceased ancestors, who return as impersonal rain spirits with their cloud masks to ensure the growth of crops in the land of the living. Masked deities brought to the kiva at San Juan to confer blessings on the initiate, or Made Person, welcome him as now "of the lake." Linked to this perhaps is the Tewa word *pa* as signifying both "Made" and "fish" (Ortiz 1969:80). Although Ortiz makes it clear that fish have no ritual or special significance among the Tewa today, conceivably this linkage is far from accidental. The reference to initiated Tewas being "of the Lake," or "Made People," is reminiscent of the Mesoamerican metaphor in which people and fish are related in Underworld contexts. Significantly, in the Popol Vuh the Hero Twins return in the form of channel catfish after surviving their "shamanic initiation," that is, being killed by the Lords of Xibalba and coming back to life imbued with magical powers. That the twins are commonly represented as fish in Mimbres iconography (Thompson 1994:101–103) brings this theme into the Southwest along with the earliest evidence of the kachina cult. At death the initiated Tewas will rejoin the ancestors in the lake (Ortiz 1969:88–89). Similarly at Taos, "Those who believe" and men dying in the mountains become *ła'tsina* under the lake (Parsons 1936b:70). At Blue Lake a ladder is said to be visible, projecting from the underwater kiva that is the home of the Fathers and Mothers (the ancestors). Taos stories refer specifically to the Big House in the lake where the grandfathers live (Parsons 1940:5). Formerly at the first spring near the lake, grinding could be heard below the water. This reference calls to mind the miniature manos and metates inside the cave at Balankanché. People go to the lake following the rain ceremonial in the pueblo in late August, both to have a good time and to worship the *ła'tsina* (Parsons 1936b:98–100).

The conflation of Underworld, emergence, and rain concepts among the Pueblos is well illustrated in kiva murals dating between the fourteenth and seventeenth centuries. In a mural painting from Kawaika-a on the Hopi Mesas, for example, a lower band is filled with images of a fish, corn, and most notably frogs with lightning and clouds attached to them (Smith 1952:Plate D and Figure 60). Fish and corn both carry ancestral connotations in Mesoamerican mythology (Stross 1994; Taube 1986).

Simultaneous with the naming of a kachina home or village, a single place where the kachinas reside when they are not visiting the living, is the concept of linking kachinas to directional symbolism, a characteristic also shared with different manifestations of Tlaloc and the Tlaloque in Mexico. As with the latter, kachinas or different groups of kachinas are also assigned to the six directions with various color associations accordingly (Ortiz 1969:18–19; Parsons 1936b:110). Parsons (1933:613) also proposes that the rain chiefs of the Directions (Uwannami at Zuni, Cloud youths at Hopi, the Shiwanna of the Keres, the Liwane of the Tewa) are more closely equated with the Tlaloque in this respect than are the kachinas. At Acoma, rainmakers of the cardinal points are said to bring different kinds of moisture (White 1932:66), a concept that parallels the previously referenced four jars in the corners of Tlaloc's patio, all filled with diverse offerings. A design on a protohistoric/early historic Tabirá canteen from Gran Quivira graphically illustrates directional symbolism and moisture/cloud associations by four cloud terraces sprouting corn, aligned with the four directions (Hayes et al. 1981:Figure 115j).

Reciprocity and Sacrifice

There are ritual parallels between the Pueblo Southwest and Mexico that emphasize various kinds of sacrificial rites, although in neither place were they confined to rain rituals but were simply part of a larger practice. Sacrifice and offerings are part of a larger and fundamental concept that involves the reciprocal obligations believed to exist between the living and the supernaturals, the earth's surface and the Underworld. Extensive comparisons between Aztec and Pueblo sacrificial rites can be found in Parsons (1939), a subject I touch on only briefly here.

As in the Tlaloc cult, sacrifice in the Southwest did occur in connection with kachina rituals and in the Southwest, at least in the context of the mythology, also involved children. As described by Tedlock (1994:163): "The first step in the development of what will become kachina ideology occurs when the first witch appears among the Zuni and offers yellow corn in exchange for the life of a child." The annual sacrifice of children on Mount Tlaloc in Mexico was mentioned earlier. In the Southwest, offerings exchanged are often based on food or symbols thereof and were (are) accompanied by prayers for rain that include smoke and prayer sticks. It is significant in this context that prayer wands, which were regarded as living beings (Bunzel 1932:710), may have substituted for human sacrifice as such. Prayer offerings made with a good heart require a favorable response from the petitioned deities (Eggan 1994:10).

Sacrifice of the supernaturals themselves, a practice related in Mexican mythology, is actually enacted in conjunction with kachina rituals. Among the Aztecs, accounts of the sacrifice of the gods to the sun in order to nourish this important celestial deity set a precedent for human sacrifice for the sun's continued maintenance. The Earth Monster, as well, claimed her share of food and hearts in order to continue bearing fruit (Nicholson 1971:400–402). In a similar tone, in Zuni ritual poetry the enemy's blood is referenced as "adding to the flesh of our earth mother" (Bunzel 1932:680, 687).

In both Mexico and among the Pueblos there was the institution of sacrificing supernatural impersonators at the end of a ceremony. In the Southwest, rituals resulting in kachina sacrifice include the sacrifice of the Zuni Shalakos (Bunzel 1932:847) and a ritual battle with the kachinas at Acoma. The latter involves the spilling of great quantities of blood (actually blood from a sheep's heart stored in a gut worn around the kachina's neck during the fight) (White 1932:88–94). This rite was held in the spring, and the "blood of the kachinas" was sacrificed in order to fertilize the earth. Bunzel (1932:847) also mentions that in prayers of the scalp dance blood is mentioned as a fertilizing agent. In addition, Acoma whipping rituals at initiations by kachinas were said to have drawn blood: "Tsitsunits [the masked whipper] then strikes the child four times with his soap-weed whip: twice on the back near the shoulder blades, once on the back of the legs between hip and knee, and once on the calves of the legs. The child and his sponsor then exchange places, and Tsitsunits whips the sponsor in the same way. All the while the g'o'maiowic run and jump about the room yelling 'Oh, look at the blood! Look at the blood, how it's running down!' etc." (White 1932:73).

Rock Art, Kiva Murals, and "Tlaloc" in the Southwest

The foregoing discussion consists largely of a review of the conceptual structure pertaining to landscape that underlies kachina ideology in the Southwest, much of which parallels Mexican concepts. In addition, I have touched on some of the acts of reciprocity and sacrifice involving petitions by the living to the ancestors and supernaturals for rain and fertility. Yet to be considered are ideographic parallels suggested by the art, especially rock paintings and petroglyphs situated in landscape contexts. From the fourteenth century on, masks and ceremonial figures are an important part of Pueblo Rio Grande–style rock art and kiva murals that also include clouds, lightning, rain, and other moisture motifs, including pottery vessels.

In Southwest iconography the mask itself, in the context of a specific suite of iconography, is the major criterion for indicating the presence of kachinas in Pueblo prehistory, and this may have been true also for the Jornada Mogollon. This symbolic matrix includes, in addition to the cloud terraces and pottery vessels, horned and sometimes feathered serpents with canine heads, as well as large figures of animals and birds delineated in outline also with clearly

Figure 12.9. Jornada-style petroglyph Tlaloc at Vado, New Mexico. The trapezoidal form of the figure conforms to the shape of the rock. The body is decorated with stepped cloud motifs also found on pottery. (Photo by Karl Kernberger)

Figure 12.10. Jornada-style Tlaloc, Three Rivers, New Mexico. A trapezoidal rock face was selected for this figure. The line at the bottom of the figure was produced by vandals. (Photo by Karl Kernberger)

defined heads. Distinctive in Jornada-style rock art are large geometric patterns made by continuous lines and square "cartouches," or ideographs, containing abstract elements. The latter motifs have a continuous distribution into northern Mesoamerica (Lazalde 1987; Schaafsma 1997a). Southern relationships are suggested by many of these motifs, including the Tlaloc icon discussed below.

The Jornada masks strongly suggest the presence of a conceptually related complex that just precedes the appearance of kachinas among the Pueblos. The Jornada style (ca. A.D. 1000–1400) is immediately antecedent to and in part contemporary with early Pueblo IV Rio Grande–style art (ca. A.D. 1325–1680). Although Rio Grande–style masks in the rock art tend to be simpler than those represented in the Jornada, masks from both styles share stylistic attributes, shapes, and specific decorative symbolic elements that denote historic continuity.

Rock paintings and petroglyphs associated with the Jornada Mogollon culture, in a region embracing much of southern New Mexico, West Texas along the Rio Grande below El Paso, and adjacent parts of northern Chihuahua, feature an earlier mentioned goggle-eyed figure that I have referenced as "Tlaloc" in previous publications (Figures 12.9–12.12; see Schaafsma 1975b; 1980; 1992). Because the Tlaloc complex and ideology surrounding kachinas at the broadest levels share a basic cosmological viewpoint, it is not surprising that evidence for a Tlaloc-like figure is present along with masks in the rock art of the Southwest sometime after A.D. 1000 (Schaafsma 1980:203–211, 1992:64:Figures 85–88). As mentioned previously, a Mimbres bowl pictures such a person-

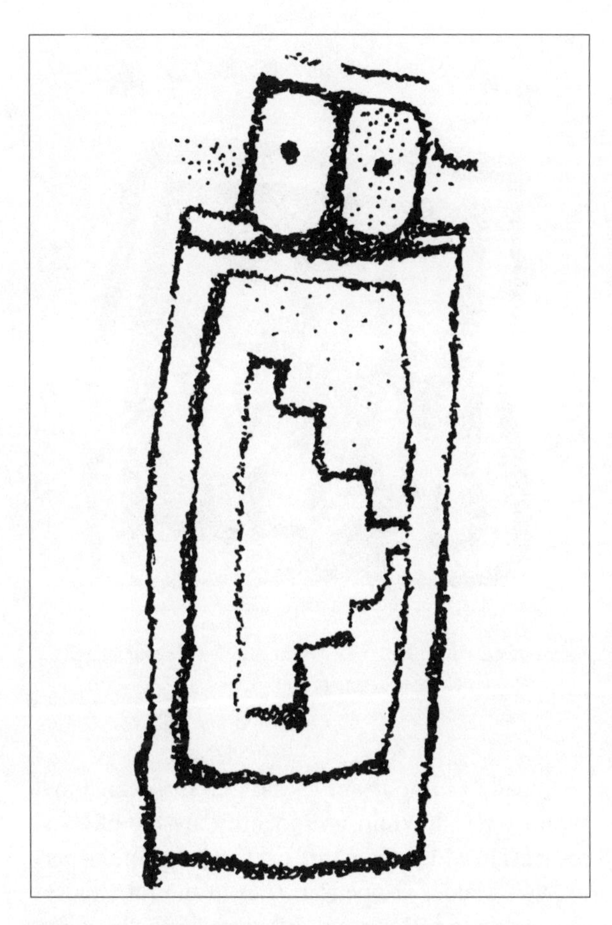

Figure 12.11. Petroglyph Tlaloc with stepped cloud motif, Three Rivers, New Mexico.

Figure 12.12. Goggle eyes attached to a free-form design of scrolls and stepped elements symbolizing clouds. Jornada-style petroglyph, southern New Mexico. (Photo by Curt Schaafsma)

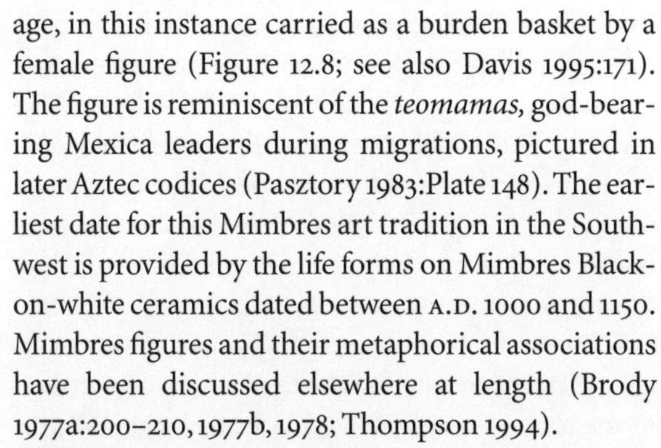

age, in this instance carried as a burden basket by a female figure (Figure 12.8; see also Davis 1995:171). The figure is reminiscent of the *teomamas,* god-bearing Mexica leaders during migrations, pictured in later Aztec codices (Pasztory 1983:Plate 148). The earliest date for this Mimbres art tradition in the Southwest is provided by the life forms on Mimbres Black-on-white ceramics dated between A.D. 1000 and 1150. Mimbres figures and their metaphorical associations have been discussed elsewhere at length (Brody 1977a:200–210, 1977b, 1978; Thompson 1994).

The southwestern "Tlalocs" are represented at most Jornada-style rock art sites in this semiarid region, and there are often several portrayed (Figure 12.7), both factors suggesting a measure of their importance. Of all of the Mesoamerican Tlaloc's distinctive attributes, in almost every case in this peripheral realm, we are left with only the goggle eyes as a distinguishing characteristic, one of his few constant features. Only occasionally is a Tlaloc mask represented with a large square-toothed mouth that might be said to bear some symbolic, if not formal, resemblance to the fanged cavernous mouth of the Jaguar-Tlaloc (Figures 12.13 and 12.14). Typically the southwestern figure consists simply of a pair of large square or round eyes with a central dot, attached to a trapezoidal or rectangular appendageless body. Exceptions to this rule consist of small goggle-eyed figures with arms that variously resemble frogs and owls.

Although the identity of this figure as Tlaloc has been questioned (Crotty 1990:149), further analysis of the design elements and the physical contexts in which these figures occur supports this interpretation.

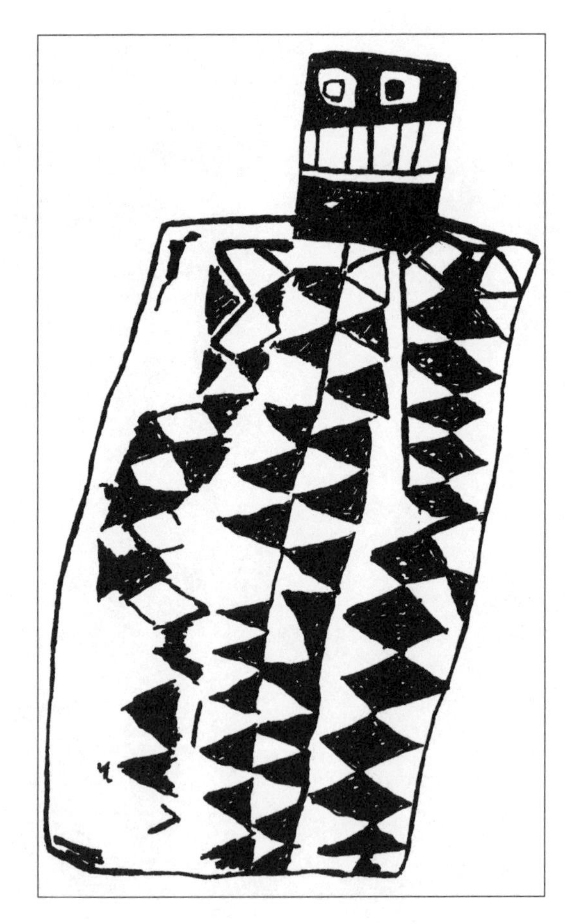

Figure 12.13. Tlaloc painting in red on cave ceiling, Hueco Tanks, Texas.

Figure 12.14. Petroglyph mask with goggle eyes and jagged teeth, Three Rivers, New Mexico.

In Mexico, as in the context of the Southwest kachina complex, the basic identification of a deity depends on the headdress and facial features (Pasztory 1983:84). Thus the goggle eyes as a regular characteristic of the southwestern "Tlaloc" figures can be regarded as diagnostic. In addition to the distinctive eyes, which suggest that we are dealing with a rain god, the identity of this figure is also consistently supported by the stepped fret abstractions for clouds (and in some cases zigzag lightning) that often decorate the torso (Figures 12.9, 12.11, 12.12). One figure at Hueco Tanks, Texas, has stepped cloud elements attached to the head as well (Figure 12.7). Mesoamerican Tlalocs usually lack the cloud symbols on the body, although the above-mentioned historic painting of a Tlaloc impersonator is covered with a net pattern (Townsend 1992b:Figure 2), a design symbolizing clouds, and a Tlaloc bundle (see below) with water signs occurs at Teotihuacán (Taube 1986:Figure 19a).

Equally as important as the graphic details that support a Tlaloc/rain-god identity are the physical contexts in which the figure occurs. Some of the petroglyph Tlalocs at open-air sites in the Jornada region are found, along with other imagery, above dry streambeds that may have standing pools of water. Others encompass a single boulder or rock section delineated by cracks. This integration of image and rock form suggests, following Townsend (1992b:178), a plausible conceptual affinity with the boulders from Mount Tlaloc previously described. The rock selected was often one with a trapezoidal shape that naturally suggests a Jornada-style Tlaloc form (Figures 12.9, 12.10). Tlaloc vases in Mexico also share this configuration. The natural shape of the rock itself was probably regarded as an indication that that particular stone embodied the innate qualities of Tlaloc, a factor that would contribute to the power of the image. On the other hand, the image, once made, would have then contributed to the power already ascribed to the rock (Young 1988:123). A basis for this idea is encountered in contemporary Pueblo thought that confers more power to naturally occurring shapes than human-made effigies (Ellis 1969:161).

The imagery on two such boulders merits further comment. At Samalayuca, Chihuahua, one Tlaloc boulder is inscribed with two full Tlaloc images that utilize all of the available surfaces (two sides and the

Figure 12.15. Tlaloc boulder, Samalayuca, Chihuahua. Visible in the photograph is the head of a Tlaloc figure on the upfacing surface. The vertical face is covered with abstracts such as are normally found on Tlaloc torsos. In addition a second Tlaloc face and a fish with Tlaloc eyes are among the figures depicted. Another full goggle-eyed figure (not visible) is pecked horizontally on the vertical face to the right. (Photo by Curt Schaafsma)

top) (Figure 12.15; see also Schaafsma 1997a). The cloud/pottery design "shirt" area contains, in addition, a fish with Tlaloc eyes attached and a bird. The fish may imply Underworld, ancestral, initiatory, maize, and creation associations all linked with the Tlaloc/kachina themes in both Mesoamerica and the Southwest as previously discussed. Only one Tlaloc impersonator in full anthropomorphic form is known in the rock art, and this petroglyph figure occupies a single boulder near El Paso. This image is shown with a fang, wears a kilt or skirt (suggesting rain), and holds what probably is a lightning staff. The headdress is large but not well defined (Schaafsma 1980:Figure 165).

It is significant that the decorations on the Tlaloc torsos resemble pottery designs as well as clouds, evoking the concept of containers with all their associated metaphors. In the Southwest, as well as in Mesoamerica, bowls and vases were used to contain sacred moisture in various forms. Filled with water they could symbolize springs and access to the Underworld, a subject to which I will return. For the moment, however, it is important to note that such symbolic compounding or redundancy accentuates the meaning of the figure, making its visual message more powerful. The redundancy does not stop here, however. Tlaloc images and cloud symbols in underground caves and deep recesses are locational statements of the Southwest's rain deity's association with the earth, from which all moisture derives. The paintings at Hueco Tanks, Texas, provide good examples. Hueco Tanks itself consists of a tight group of three small intrusive rocky hills that rise above the surrounding desert. These hills are riddled with cracks, dark passages, caves, and overhangs. *Tinajas,* stone basins where water collects, are prevalent in the inner recesses. This special landscape, harboring water in the Chihuahuan desert, where moisture is otherwise scarce, is a perfect embodiment of the Mesoamerican concept of water-filled mountains, or mountains filled with jars (containers) of water. At least seventeen Tlaloc paintings have been located at Hueco Tanks (Davis and Toness 1974; Kirkland and Newcomb 1967), and seven of these are painted within one recess (Figure 12.7). In addition, at least ten more paintings of cloud/ceramic patterns recorded by Kirkland may have been intended as rain-associated imagery. Further, masks are painted in these spaces in even greater numbers than Tlalocs.[1]

Rain-related symbolism within container-like rock-recesses would have functioned to condense the power perceived in the landscape and confirmed the importance of this place as a rain shrine for the Mogollon people of the region. Additional artifacts from this conceptual scheme are the wooden Tlaloc/kachina-like effigies that have been retrieved from dark caves, specifically U-Bar and Stanton Caves, where they had been deposited along with other Jornada Mogollon offerings (Figures 12.16a and 12.16b; see also Laboratory of Anthropology [Museum of New Mexico] 1989:Figure 40; Lambert and Ambler 1965).

The Underworld association of kachinas and

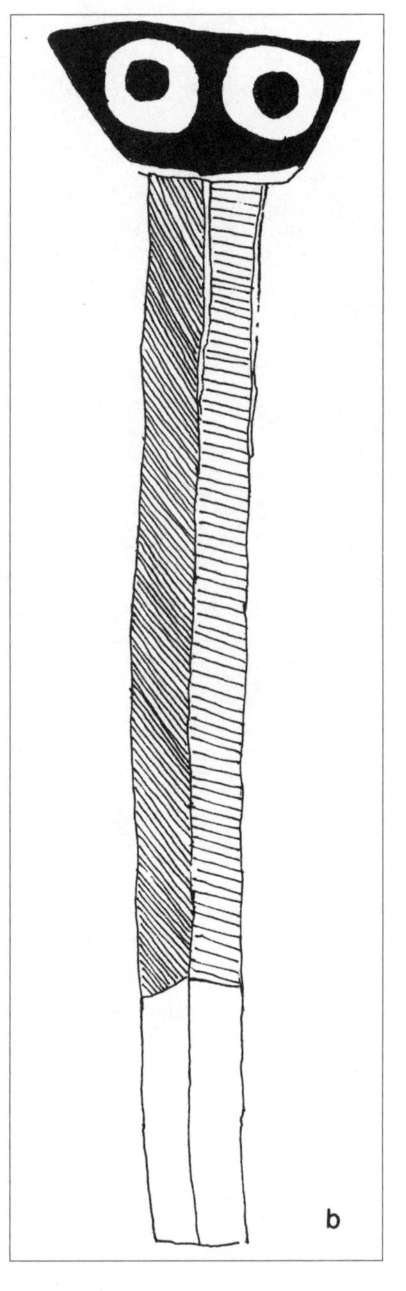

Figure 12.16 (Above and right). Wooden effigies from (a) U-Bar and (b) Stanton Caves in southern New Mexico. Black paint was used on the head. In both cases, the right-hand side of the body is red, the left greenish.

Figure 12.17. Cloud terrace painted in solid black at the bottom of limestone sinkhole near Gran Quivira, New Mexico (drawing from photo). (Courtesy of John Greer)

Figure 12.18. Fifteenth-century kiva mural painting of a stepped cloud terrace with a bird on top, painted in black, red, orange, yellow, and white, Picuris Pueblo, New Mexico.

clouds is reiterated in the southern Pueblo region near Gran Quivira by several masks and a large cloud terrace—an element also seemingly introduced early on by the Mimbres (Brody 1977a:Figures 61, 68, 172, and others)—painted in black inside Surratt Cave (Figure 12.17). This cave is a dark underground chamber in the bottom of a limestone sinkhole accessed by tight passageways. There is some indication that the Tlaloc icon of the Jornada Mogollon was perpetuated in concept among the Pueblos as a conventionalized cloud in the form of a terrace with a face or mask added at the top (P. Schaafsma 1992a: Figure 126). Such figures occur in both the northern Jornada region and in Rio Grande Pueblo rock art. Among the latter there seems to be some overlap with the Heart-of-the Sky deity, who shares affiliations with Quetzalcoatl in Mexico, a subject beyond the scope of this discussion (Schaafsma 1980:295–296; Young 1994:115). Among the paintings from a fifteenth-century kiva in Picuris Pueblo is a terrace with circles that appears to have Tlaloc-like eyes (Figure 12.18). This kiva painting may be graphic evidence of Tlaloc iconography and ideology preserved among the northern Tiwa (note Parsons' accounts about Blue Lake described earlier).

More remains to be said about the metaphorical linkage between pottery vessels and moisture. One should suspect by now that jars and bowls represented in Pueblo art are not simply pots but that they functioned as part of the rain god symbolic complex as derived from Mesoamerica, where, as we have seen, this association is present as early as Teotihuacán. Pueblo IV and Jornada style rock art, as well as kiva murals, also contain examples of vessels bearing clear associations with moisture and rain. Several fourteenth-century kachina masks in the shape of jars and bowls, some bearing explicit cloud symbolism, are represented in the petroglyphs and rock paintings in the Piro and Tompiro Pueblo regions (Figures 12.19 and 12.20; Schaafsma, in press).

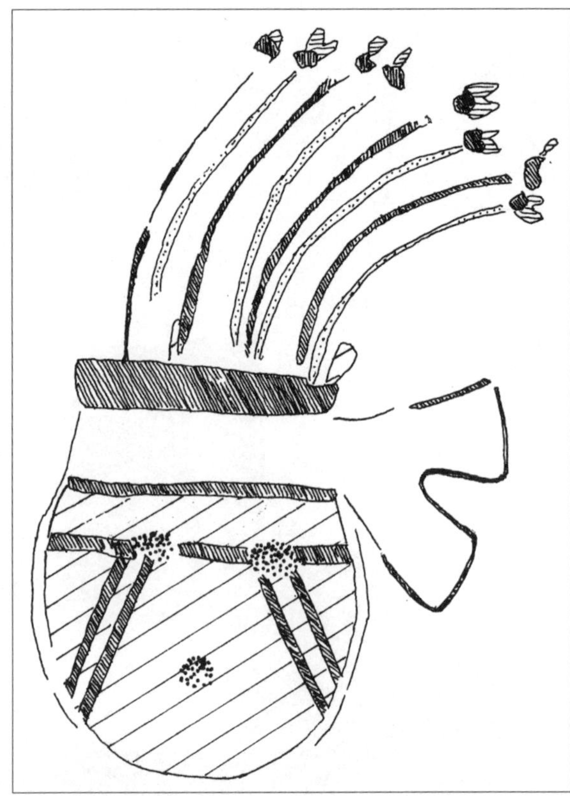

Figure 12.19. (Above and left) Pueblo IV (A.D. 1325–1680) rock paintings of kachina masks in the form of water jars, Tompiro Pueblo province, New Mexico.

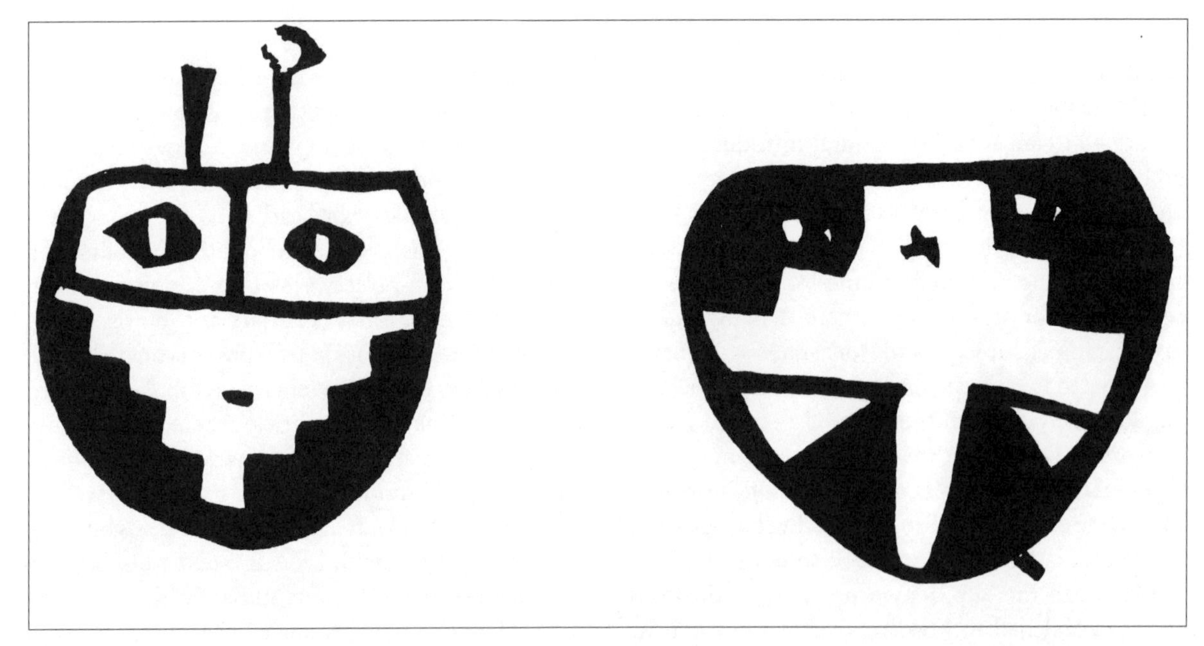

Figure 12.20. Early Pueblo IV petroglyph masks in the form of bowls with cloud symbolism, Piro province, New Mexico.

Additional figures of this type from the same time frame are found in the Pottery Mound kiva murals (Hibben 1975:Figure 16). This synthesis of pottery forms with the rain-bringing supernaturals themselves may have parallels in the Mesoamerican practice of painting Tlaloc images or modeling Tlaloc masks on vessels. In addition, the central Tlaloc effigy on Mount Tlaloc, shattered by the Spanish in 1530 (Wicke and Horcasitas 1957:86), is described by Pasztory (1983:124) as a statue with a vessel on its head. Early chroniclers described offerings of rubber, maize, beans, and chile as being placed in this vessel (Wicke and Horcasitas 1957:84).

From the Southwest, other Pottery Mound paintings show winged figures bearing on their heads water jars out of which emerge clouds and lightning (Hibben 1975:Figures 45 and 61). Pueblo IV kiva murals at Kuaua north of Albuquerque illustrate pots spewing moisture (Figure 12.21; see also Dutton 1963:Plates XVI and XXII). Some vessels containing water pictured in Pueblo murals seem to symbolize earthly water sources. There are several instances where pots and netted gourds are located at the base of kiva mural paintings, either below the level of the ritual participants or below a cloud band, indicating that they are on or beneath the earth's surface or in the Underworld, a concept with strong Mesoamerican parallels (Dutton 1963:Plates XXI and XXIII; Smith 1952:Plate G, or Figure 62a). A meaningful contextual relationship between a curved yellow bowl-like design containing El Paso Polychrome motifs painted at the bottom of a dark crevice above a deep *tinaja* filled with rainwater occurs at Hueco Tanks (Schaafsma 1980:Figure 193).

In contemporary Pueblo ceremonial contexts, water contained in netted gourds and in bowls symbolizes various types of moisture. Water for ritual aspersion is carried in the hands of ritual practitioners in netted gourds, the net itself probably denoting clouds, as described elsewhere. In the Awatovi murals from Hopi a figure holding a netted gourd is dressed in a netted garment (Smith 1952:Figure 65), as if to emphasize his cloud-generating capacity. Bowls on Pueblo altars are routinely filled with yucca suds that simulate clouds (Bunzel 1932:492; Stevenson 1894a: 82; 1904:175). Clay vessels modeled with stepped cloud elements, and sometimes painted with cloud designs, dragonflies, and tadpoles, are used on Pueblo altars or placed with ceremonial caches (see

Figure 12.21. Pueblo IV kiva mural from Kuaua Pueblo on the Rio Grande showing a water jar on top of a raining cloud, the cloud itself decorated with pottery motifs. Water sprays from the vessel, and lightning shoots between the birds and both the vessel and the cloud (redrawn from Dutton 1963: Figure 86).

below). These designs unite concepts of clouds with earthly water sources and are reminiscent of the water-filled vessels containing snakes and frogs described earlier in connection with the Aztec birth-of-maize celebration. Terraced bowls appear in the Pueblo archaeological record during the seventeenth century (Smith 1952:250) and in El Paso Polychrome possibly as early as A.D. 1200 (Peckham 1990:Figure 149).

As suggested by the tadpoles and snakes with the bowls described above, fabricated clay water containers were (are) regarded as analogous to caves and springs, where water is held within the earth in a natural context. A Cochiti story refers to an "inexhaustible bowl of water" in the center of Corn Cob Boy's house, Corn Cob Boy being the son of Heluta, the Father of the Kachinas (Benedict 1931:62). The bowl in the center of the room is also analogous to the sipapu, the passage to the Underworld. Related concepts between kachinas, moisture, and pots are illustrated ethnographically by the Hopi practice of placing vessels of water in cornfields to attract rain (Stephen 1936:483). These vessels containing water, like the one in the Cochiti story, also represent the sipapu, the watery access to the Underworld, and thus emphasize the ultimate chthonic source of water, as does Tlaloc in Mexico. Similarly, a Zia story (Stevenson 1894b:38) describes water brought from springs at the foot of the mountains in gourd jugs and vases to water the earth. Likewise at Zuni "The earth is watered by the deceased Zuni of both sexes, who are controlled and directed by a council composed of ancestral gods. These shadow-people [like the previously described Tlaloque] collect water in vases and gourd jugs from the six great waters of the world, and pass to and fro over the middle plane, protected from view of the people below by cloud masks, the clouds being produced by smoke" (Stevenson 1894a:315).

In a Hopi story, traveling clans were said to have carried "a small perforated vessel containing herbs, different stones, shells, prayer sticks, and a small paaloloqangu," or water serpent, with which they could create springs as needed (Geertz and Lomatuway'ma 1987:178–179). The water serpent was a necessary ingredient and is associated with all springs and contained bodies of water.

Also, as in various Mexican contexts, bowls of medicine water on Pueblo altars may represent springs and, as springs, portals to the Underworld (Parsons 1932:280, n. 48; Stevenson 1904:96). The various contexts in which these medicine bowls function are not confined to kachina related activities, however, but have more general ritual functions. Parsons (1932:316) describes a Medicine Society initiation at Isleta in which the initiate is asked to look into the medicine bowl, where one of the first things he sees are dead persons. A bowl of water described earlier in a contemporary Aztec context as providing a channel between this world and Tlalocan is in line with the Isleta account. In both the Southwest and Mexico, these containers of water also function as mirrors, in themselves doors to the Underworld, and even as mechanisms of divination (Parsons 1932:280, n. 50). Taube (1986:61) discusses Mesoamerican mirrors as supernatural passageways, a concept inherent in the reflective character of water in a bowl. This symbolism is well exemplified in the Caracol at Chichén Itzá, where an olla containing a pyrite mirror was placed over a vertical shaft, which stood for the passage to the Underworld.

As previously discussed, ancestors figure prominently in the rain cults of both central Mexico and the Southwest. Thus it is possible that the Pueblo practice at Acoma, and probably elsewhere as well, of leaving offerings for the dead in pots at designated places in the landscape embraces the symbolic complex of the dead, reciprocity, and rain. In light of the foregoing discussion it is reasonable to suggest that the vessels themselves have a symbolic role in this connection.

Sacred Bundles, Ancestors, and a Proposed Ideological Origin of the Kachina Cult

The various elements and ideological relationships so far described include the goggle-eyed supernatural, masks, and other iconographic elements, as well as landscape metaphors and the multivalent symbolism of water-filled vessels. These involved parallels strengthen the identification of Jornada Mogollon figures as Tlalocs and reinforce the idea of Mexican cosmological origins for the kachina ideology. Central to this discussion, however, is a deeper theme of the linked ideology of ancestors, rain, and sacred bundles that merits further examination.

Although parallels between Mexican rain rituals and kachina rituals in the Southwest and their metaphors in common have been delineated in the previous discussion, the pivotal point on which the kachina system rests has been mentioned only in passing and has not been addressed as such. I am going to propose that kachinas *per se* derived from concepts underlying rituals and funerary practices in Mexico that involved integrating the spirits of the dead with natural forces in order to transform the deceased into rainmakers (Furst 1993). Parallel procedures are carried out among the Pueblos, among whom the connection between the kachinas and the dead is substantiated in oral tradition (Tedlock 1994:165–168). The Mexican process of converting the dead into anonymous masked and bundled spirits that at times wore Tlaloc masks and those of other deities suggests how this came about.

Masks and Funerary Bundles in Mexico

In the United States and Mexico, sacred bundles containing objects of power, or "energy," were associated with emergence or the time of creation and connected with group well-being. These bundles, often wrapped with hides or textiles, contained paraphernalia for rituals and objects that were believed to have the ability to mediate between the living and the supernatural world. Southwestern and Mesoamerican bundles also often embody the concepts of regeneration, as well as fertility and rain symbolism. Mexican rain and lightning bundles representing deities may contain earth renewal/fertility items such as maize, maguey, reeds, water, and blood or the remains of ancestors. In the Southwest, as well, bundles play an important role in the emergence and contain vital elements and the materials for human life, and from Acoma Taube describes a maize bundle wrapped in cloth that is identified with humankind (1986:72). In his discussion on sacred bundles in Mesoamerica, Stenzel (1970) does not particularly address the subject of funerary bundles, except to note that in central Mexico some bundles originated from the death of a deity (Stenzel 1970:348). It would seem that these "deity" bundles, consisting of the gods' mantas and "devices," formed a template for human funerary bundles, some of which bore masks. Crucial to this discussion is that mummy bundles shared symbolism with nature and fertility deities.

Bundles wearing Tlaloc masks are pictured in Mexican art from the Classic period into the Postclassic codices. Tlaloc bundles, supposedly miniature versions of Teotihuacán funerary bundles, were commonly pictured in Teotihuacán, and these objects may have worn life-size stone masks (Taube 1986:70). Mentioned above is a vessel (Pasztory 1974: Figure 5) or bundle (Taube 1986:Figure 19) carried by a Teotihuacán Tlaloc (Figure 12.4). The object in question wears a Tlaloc mask, and water pours from the top of the head. The presence of a feather in addition to the water contributes to Taube's (1986:70) interpretation that this figure is a masked Tlaloc bundle and not a vessel. The figure in question has water signs on the body. Other Classic period masked rain and lightning bundles are pictured on Mayan vessels and stelae and in the ball-court reliefs at El Tajin (Koontz 1994; Taube 1986:Figure 19). The latter, described earlier, is pictured wearing a Tlaloc mask and lies within the context of a cave.

Postclassic narratives of the Highland Maya describe the Headband Twins of the Popol Vuh and, in central Mexico, Quetzalcoatl and Tezcatlipoca descending to the Underworld to retrieve the bones of their fathers. These particular funerary bundles are associated with corn and the creation of humanity, respectively. Bundled remains are a repeated theme and pictured in various contexts in central Mexican codices (Taube 1986:63, 66, 69). Taube (1986:71) suggests that a *nexquimilli,* or funerary bundle, on page 16 of the *Códice Borbónico,* wearing a Tlaloc mask (Figure 12.22), may represent, like the El Tajin sculpture, a Tlaloc bundle in a Teotihuacán cave. A similar figure seated on a gaping cave maw occurs in the *Codex Borgia* (Figure 12.23). These scenes perpetuate the association of bundles with caves and the Underworld.

The connection between masks and ancestors has an ancient history in Mexico. Stone masks found in graves are thought to have been placed over faces of idols and funerary bundles (Peterson 1959:263). In the Basin of Mexico masks are found at ancestral shrines beginning with the Preclassic (Weaver 1981:102). Masks as early as the late Preclassic, lacking holes for seeing but with holes on the peripheries, may have been attached to funerary bundles (Easby and Scott 1970). Easby and Scott (1970:Figure 89) illustrate a mask used as a funerary face dating from 100 B.C. to A.D. 250. The multitude of anonymous masks from Teotihuacán very likely originated with mummy bundles, although a precise archaeological context for these artifacts is usually lacking (Miller 1986:72). Death bundles were often cremated, and many masks show evidence of having been burned. In addition, a unique sculpture from a Teotihuacán tomb represents a probable funerary bundle. Of note is the detachable Teotihuacán mask and the simple bundled torso lacking arms and legs (Berrin and Pasztory 1993:Figure 60).

Later depictions of death customs in Mixtec codices show death masks placed over the faces of deceased notables after their bodies were wrapped (Seler 1963:2:32). Bundles of deceased rulers sometimes wore the mask of one or more gods as a statement of the identity of these personages with several cosmic forces or with the powers of various supernaturals. These masks are shown in polychrome colors and may have been made of wood, although stone masks may have constituted a variant on this theme (Easby and Scott 1970:268).

The manner in which the dead body was clothed indicated the soul's destiny in the afterlife (López Austin 1988:1:331). Specific funerary practices were employed among the Aztecs to turn the appropriate dead into cloud makers, and the living devised rituals to entice these dead to return as rain-bearing clouds

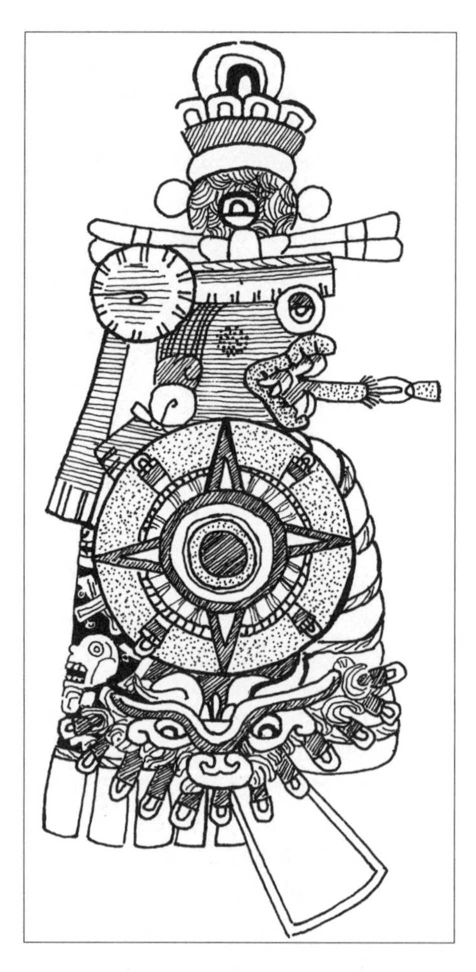

Figure 12.22. Funerary bundle wearing Tlaloc mask and cave, *Codex Borbónicus* (redrawn from *Codex Borbónicus,* p. 16).

Figure 12.23. Masked Tlaloc bundle seated on a cave maw, Borgia Codex (redrawn from Selers 1963:Figure 271).

(Furst 1993). Furst describes Mexica funerary customs that artificially changed people dying from old age and sickness into cloud makers, procedures that linked the dead to specific cosmic elements, for example, earth, water, clouds, and rain. These customs are not unlike burial practices in the Pueblo world (see below). Among the Mexica and other prehistoric Mesoamericans, the dead body was customarily wrapped and bundled. Procedures sometimes included putting a white cloth over the face. Both wrapping and covering the face divest the body of its individuality and place the deceased in the category of the anonymous dead (Furst 1993). Although there is no mention of masks as such, Furst (1993:7) is quick to point out that "covering the corpse, and particularly the face, may give the dead person a form that approximates the white, lumpy shape of a cumulus cloud."

In addition to the masked funerary bundles containing bones of the deceased, the *teixiptla* may be crucial to understanding the origins of the kachina complex. According to Townsend (1979:28), the term *teixiptla* was used in Mexico to define a costumed cult performer or any assemblage or ritual attire on a wooden frame that included a mask (Figure 12.24; Kampen [1972:Figure 34b] provides what is possibly a graphic example of a *teixiptla* from El Tajin). The latter was often associated with a revered ancestral hero. The *teixiptla,* like the dead themselves, might be dressed simultaneously as several gods. Different adornments suggest that the soul, especially the soul of a ruler, could be divided in its relationships (López Austin 1988:1:331), and varied costumes functioned to associate the dead with different aspects of the cosmos. "Placed in urban temples and at many shrines scattered throughout tribal lands, these *teix-*

Figure 12.24. Head resting on a trapezoidal/triangular support, Pyramid of the Niches, Panel 5, El Tajin (redrawn from Kampen 1972:Figure 7a).

iptlas reminded the community that the worship of natural elements was inseparably connected to the memory of the deceased" (Townsend 1979:31). At the same time, the *teixiptla* did not commemorate an individual personality but "the *continuing office of leaders* in preserving a transcendental affinity between cosmic and social orders" (Townsend 1979:31; emphasis in original). As living beings, leaders were responsible for maintaining harmonious relationships with the cosmos as a religious obligation. An effigy, or *teixiptla,* fashioned on the death of such a person, ritually affirmed his or her assimilation into the cosmos (Townsend 1979:31). The deceased did not become gods as such but, sanctified by their association with life forces, acted as mediators between the living and the supernatural realm. In this capacity the deceased were then called upon to perform divine services. At Tlaloc's command, the dead sent beneficial rains, as well as destructive storms with lightning and hail if the situation merited it (López Austin 1988:1: 340).

As well, Furst elaborates on the use of the *teixiptla.* In mourning ceremonies these fake masked bundles (bundles that lacked ancestral remains as such) were constructed that were believed to be efficacious in calling back the ancestors. Within the traditional calendar this occurred in August, after the height of the rainy season had passed (a date now moved to accord with the Christian calendar's Day of the Dead on the first of November [Furst 1995, personal communication]). The August date, however, was in sync with the need for rain as the crops matured, and the ancestors were called back at this critical time specifically for this purpose.

Significantly, in Mexico all deceased were not destined to inhabit the paradise of Tlalocan and return as rainmakers to fructify the earth. Various types of moral behavior and the method of dying (certain types of death were caused by specific deities) determined which souls ended up in Tlaloc's paradise (López Austin 1988:1:337–338). Those claimed by the rain spirits, returning to the earth as clouds, included persons who died by drowning or lightning, those whose birthdays fell on days sacred to the rain spirits, or individuals who contracted illnesses sent by these supernaturals (Furst 1993). Parsons (1939:1018) includes suicide among the various means of reaching Tlalocan. Furst (1993:10) notes that Mendieta's *Historia Eclesiástica Indiana* (1971:97) states that the souls of Tlaxcalan lords and officials return as clouds and mist, as well as birds with beautiful feathers and stones of value. Inferior people, on the other hand, fared poorly. López Austin (1988:1:338) goes on to point out that the marked contrast between a good death and a bad afterlife functioned as "an ideological instrument to lead men along socially established routes."

Southwest Parallels

Mesoamerican concepts regarding sacred bundles, treatment of the dead, and associated beliefs, including ideology concerning rain and clouds, find analogues in the Pueblo world, where they overlap with the ideology of the kachina cult. Descriptions of Pueblo sacred bundles as such by Matilda Coxe Stevenson (1904:163–164), on the basis of her late-nineteenth-century fieldwork in Zuni, constitute some of the most complete information on this subject. These are not funerary bundles, but they embody many of the same properties as funerary bundles from Mesoamerica: themes of creation, emergence, fertility, rain, and regeneration. These paired bundles, heavily wrapped in cotton string, the so-called *et'towe* from the undermost Underworld, are fetishes of the rain priests. The *kia'et'tone,* or water bundle, contains four hollow reeds filled with water and a small live toad or frog. The ends are stopped with cotton and blackish clay, the latter also coming from the Underworld. The second bundle contains eight reeds with all the edible seeds. When not in use these paired bundle sets are kept in sealed jars in sealed cave-like rooms lacking windows within the pueblo. The room where the *et'towe* of the rain priest of the North are kept is supposedly directly over the center of the world. This chamber is referred to in Zuni ritual poetry as a "rain-filled room" (Bunzel 1932:710). A photograph of the room with the *et'towe* of the Corn Clan (Stevenson 1904:Figure 5) shows a stepped cloud vessel along with the jars containing the fetishes.

In essence, these bundles, along with the "rain-filled" rooms in which they reside, retain the symbolic vocabulary of the Tlaloc-like rainmaking system: The rooms and jars in which they are stored and the associated stepped cloud vessels might be compared to the caves of Mount Malinche, with their ollas containing moisture and seeds. The chambers housing the *et'towe* are architectural expressions of the sacred landscape, with caves and springs as portals to the Underworld, and ancestral associations are perpetuated by the emergence symbolism and the mud from the lowest underworld used in sealing the reeds wrapped inside the bundle.

The Pueblo link between kachinas and ancestors has been addressed in the previous discussion and can be elaborated further. Kachinas and masked personages present in abundance in the rock art of the late Pueblo and Jornada Mogollon landscape are reminiscent of the Mexican effigies that merged the deified Aztec ancestors with the topography of the central Mexico plateau as described by Townsend (1979). The rock art in the landscape similarly indicates that one specific function for kachina figures on high points of land, in rock recesses, and in secluded shelters was to tie the deceased into the cosmic forces that inhabit these realms. The Jornada and Rio Grande Pueblo farmers made many more rock art images than did their predecessors, perhaps because of additional motivating ideological forces. Masked figures in the landscape would have functioned to remind the Pueblos of their ancestral connections to place, as well as to activate the rainmaking powers of the dead by uniting them with the forces inherent in certain landscape features. Perhaps simultaneously the power of a location was strengthened by the presence of an image.

As described previously, the Pueblo dead are thought to inhabit springs, lakes, or mountaintops, from which they return as clouds and kachinas to bring the summer rains to the cornfields that provide for the living. As in central Mexico, there are certain procedures followed at death to transform the dead into rainmakers or, in the Southwest, kachinas. The body is wrapped, and at Hopi a cotton cloud mask is placed over the face. This cloud mask makes the body light—a breath body (Titiev 1944:107–108). (Whether the use of this cloud mask is [was] more widespread is not known. Ethnographically there is no record of such a practice elsewhere, although in the Rio Grande valley, funerary practices may have been altered early on by pressure from the Catholic church.) Thus as in Mexico the deceased is relieved of personal identity, along with which was associated a threat of possible danger (Furst 1993). With these attributes gone, the dead become merged in identification with the beneficent ancestors who inhabit Kachina Village and return to the Pueblo in the form of rain clouds.

This connection between the dead and rain-bringing is also activated by the undecorated white cotton wedding garment worn as a bundling garment by deceased married Hopi women (Geertz and Lomatuway'ma 1987:185–189). The relationship between clothing and the fate of the dead among the Aztecs was discussed above, and the use of the wedding garment at Hopi seems to be a related practice. In life this apparel, marked with prayers for fecundity, is worn by new brides with white painted faces on the last day of the Niman ceremony, an act that "establishes her status as a married woman in the eyes of the katsinas" (Geertz and Lomatuway'ma 1987:185). It also confirms her status in the social order, a rank that is equal to that of initiated males. Thus through marriage, she is effectively initiated, and on death these garments assist her in reaching the Underworld, just as the mask assists the Pueblo male in attaining the role of rainmaker. Among the Zuni every adult male kiva member has a mask that is buried with him or "buried at the time you die because when you get to the afterworld, and your spirit comes back to Zuni in the form of rain dances, you have to have your mask to come with" (Ladd 1994:19). Similarly, in regard to the wedding garment, as explained in a Second Mesa myth quoted by Voth (Geertz and Lomatuway'ma 1987:188), "You must wrap up the women when they die in the ówa [the white cotton blanket] and tie the big knotted belt around them, because these ówas are not tightly woven, and when the skeletons move along on them through the sky as clouds, the thin rain drops through these ówas and the big raindrops fall from the fringes of the big belt" (Voth 1905:117). The white cloth signifies the white cloud preceding the rain. Stephen (1936:119) also makes reference to a white cotton blanket that becomes a rain cloud.

This concept also finds a Mexican parallel not previously mentioned, in which rain clouds are also viewed as Divine Women, or Cihuateteo, who are said to wear white vestments and white facial paint and bring rain to make plants grow (Heyden 1986: 38). A complicating factor is that these women are not residents of Tlalocan but are affiliated with deceased warriors and their roles in escorting the sun across the sky each day.

In all cases the dead who are associated with rain clouds have achieved this privilege through status attained in various ways. As in Mexico, not all of the Pueblo dead become rainmakers. Hierarchical affinities between Pueblo dead and kachinas are made explicit. Leaders and society members active in religious organizations are privileged to come back as kachinas. Ortiz (1969:17–18) notes that among the Tewa it is the souls of the officers and religious leaders, or "Made People," who become the rainmakers. This includes the members of the two moiety societies, the medicine men, the Kwirana and Kossa (the Clowns), and members of the Hunt, Scalp, and Women's societies. These rainmakers are associated with the four sacred mountains, and a lake or pond is associated with each as well as a directional color. Similarly at Zuni there is a need for some social status to return as a rainmaker (Ladd 1994:18): "The spirits come to visit in the summer during the rainmaking ceremonies, and in the winter during the winter ceremonies. If you were a person who never attended ceremonies, and didn't participate in any of these activities, you would not come as part of a group; have you ever seen a cloud all by itself, the only little cloud? . . . [T]hat's exactly what spirit you would be. Alone. Because you didn't participate in ceremonies."

Likewise, at Taos the "Cloud Boys"—who live under the springs, in the sky, and in the mountains and who were once human—coming up with the others from under the Lake of Emergence are not the ordinary dead. Returning as clouds are the "good chiefs" who always believe, men who die in the mountains, and the women that grind corn for ceremonies (Parsons 1936b:109).

Going back to the former consideration of Jornada-style rock art and sacred bundles, we can bring a new perspective to the Jornada Tlalocs, covered with pottery designs of stepped frets and scrolls, also interpretable as clouds and moisture symbols. These figures, lacking appendages, masked as rain gods, may in fact represent bundled, anonymous, deified ancestors. Pecked on cliffs above streambeds, on isolated boulders, and painted in grottos near *tinajas* they, like kachina images in Pueblo rock art, embody a many-layered symbolism, merging the rainmakers with the cosmic forces in the landscape, an overlay that contributes to the importance and power of place and vice versa.

Finally, the Shalako kachina of the Pueblo world may merit a further look. The Shalako form in itself manifests some of the specific qualities of an Aztec *teixiptla.* Potential precedents for the conical shape of the Shalako are present in Classic period murals (Bonilla 1992:134) and figurines from Teotihuacán (Berrin and Pasztory 1993:60–61, 95, 97; Taube 1988: Figure IV-11). These figures appear to wear apparel draped over the body. One large clay sculpture, probably representing a funerary bundle found in a mortuary context, wears a detachable mask (Figure 12.25). The El Tajin constructions with heads or masks atop triangular or trapezoidal bases (Figure 12.24 and Kampen 1972:34b) were mentioned previously. There are at least three types of Shalakos extant in contemporary Hopi and Zuni ceremonialism (Hays 1992:73; Wright 1984), and others are pictured in fourteenth- and fifteenth-century rock art. In addition they occur on fifteenth- or early-sixteenth-century Hopi ceramics (Hays 1992). These prehistoric examples indicate that the Shalako complex may have formerly been more diverse and extensive than it is today and that this figure was part of the Pueblo kachina complex from the beginning. The

Figure 12.25. From Teotihuacan tomb, a clay bust with detachable mask thought to represent a funerary bundle, A.D. 400–650 (55 cm tall) (after Berrin and Pasztory 1993: Figure 60).

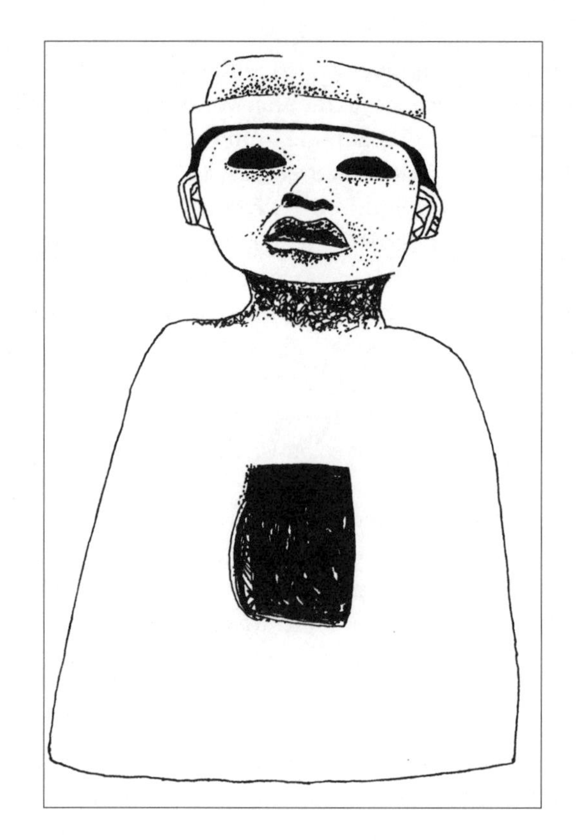

Figure 12.26. Hopi shalako manas. The construction technique of rods and hoops is pictured on the right below the mask (after Fewkes 1903:Plate LVI).

Shalako kachina is unique among kachinas in that it is, like the *teixiptla,* a masked effigy built on a framework (Figure 12.26). The Shalako construct, however, is actually "brought to life" by a dancer who holds and animates the entire armature from within. The effigy is of giant proportions, attaining a height of eight to nine feet. The effigy is armless and wrapped in cotton kilts and mantas or sometimes, as with the Hopi Shalakos, covered with feathers. In addition, the water serpent ceremonies at Hopi are accompanied by the presence of smaller constructed effigies in the form of Shalako marionettes unique to Hopi (Parsons 1939:956).

Although all kachinas in general are associated with clouds and rain, Wright (1984) refers to the Shalakos as the ultimate rain-bringers. Both the winter and summer Shalako forms are said to represent spirits of the dead (Alex Seotewa 1994, personal communication), and there is reference made to their homes in springs (Wright 1982). The bodies of the male and female versions of the Cumulus Cloud kachinas that accompany the Hopi Shalako are painted the blue gray mud from springs. Association with summer thunderstorms and cumulus cloud imagery is particularly prevalent in the Hopi Shalako rituals held during the rainy season in July, a time important for ensuring the maturation of the corn crop. The feather-covered Shalakos wear headdresses replete with cloud iconography (Figure 12.26), and these giant kachinas are accompanied by other sky/storm kachinas. The male Cumulus Cloud kachina, *Turkwinu,* carries a netted gourd filled with water in each hand (Fewkes 1903:Plate XLIII). Fewkes (1903:149) mentions that the Hopi-Tewa call this kachina and the San Francisco Mountains by the same name (*Pompin*).

Shalakos do not appear in the art of the Mimbres or in Jornada-style rock art. The cone-shaped Shalakos are often referred to as being bird-like. There is little formal resemblance between the Shalakos and the square or trapezoidal Tlalocs, or Tlaloc bundles, of the Jornada Mogollon art style, and their masks are quite different as well. Nevertheless, the possibility that the Shalako is analogous to the *teixiptla* of Mesoamerica, just as it is hypothesized that the Tlalocs are representative of sacred funerary bundles, are both possibilities worthy of more research.

Final Remarks and Conclusions

This study, in its search for fundamental metaphors, has made it possible to substantiate earlier claims based on less-extensive evidence that the southwestern kachina cult is related to the ancient Mexican belief system based on earth and water symbolism centered around Tlaloc (Brew 1943; Parsons 1933, 1939). The vast array of associated symbols seems to secure the Mesoamerican origins of this entire complex. This chapter has sought to explore both the iconographic parallels shared between the Southwest and Mexico and, even more important, the underlying structures that unify these ideas. The symbols and metaphors shared between the Southwest and Mexico concerning concepts of a sacred geography involving mountains, caves, lakes, and springs, as well as associated supernaturals and Underworld cosmology, are more involved and redundant than anticipated at the outset of this investigation. The complex ideology of water containers and sacred landscape symbolism—as well as sacred bundles, masked effigies, and funerary practices that integrate the dead with cosmic forces in order that they will become rainmakers—follows a common thread from central Mexico to the peripheries of corn agriculture in the semiarid regions of the Southwest. Acts of reciprocity and sacrifice activate the interaction between the living and the dead to maintain a cosmic balance. Many of the ideas discussed are widespread throughout different cultural contexts in Mesoamerica. The ethnographic data available for both the Aztecs and the Pueblo cultures, however, have facilitated the identification of the patterns and organizing principles that underlie the content of the art, thus amplifying the archaeological record.

This discussion has focused narrowly on Tlaloc and kachinas. Consideration of other deities and their cults would also illustrate common concepts between Mesoamerica and the Southwest. Nicholson (1971) has noted that in Mesoamerica there is a great legion of deities organized around a few fundamental overlapping cults between which clear lines cannot always be drawn. These ambiguities apply to the Tlaloc cult and kachinas of the Southwest. I have said nothing, for example, about the horned and plumed serpent of the Southwest and the Quetzalcoatl-Ehecatl-Xoxotl group with which it shares ideological features. (For parallels see Reyman 1971). The point to be emphasized is that the Tlaloc/kachina complex is part of a wider shared ideological matrix, only a part of which is discussed in this chapter.

This study also makes it evident that iconographic parallels between the Southwest and Mesoamerica are strongest in terms of what is being symbolized, in the content and ideas expressed, rather than in specific visual symbols and forms employed to convey these ideas. In the Southwest the motifs used to express concepts of clouds, water containers, and the portrayal of ceremonial participants, conform for the most part to a Mogollon/Pueblo mode of expression. Specific iconographic similarities that could be cited between the Southwest and Mexico include the Hueco Tanks painted masks and stone masks from Teotihuacán that resemble each other in form and facial details, although the time discrepancy between them was noted previously. Other parallels include the goggle-eyed figures or Tlalocs. Scrolls for water may be shared, but stepped designs as symbols for clouds seem to be distinctive to the Southwest.

One implication of these observations is that, although a spread of Mesoamerican ideology to the frontiers of the agricultural zones in the North seems clear, the lack of strong and detailed iconographic parallels as such indicates a lack of actual Mesoamerican presence in the North.

The mechanisms for the spread and acceptance of Mesoamerican ideas in the Southwest have not been satisfactorily explained, although these problems are being confronted, and models for exploring these issues will be more adequate in the future. Possibly we should be looking for ideological connections that do not imply economic and power dominance but rather regional networks of communication structured along political/religious lines of organization, without the involvement of colonies or outposts as such of Mesoamerican empires. The complexity of the idea systems involved suggests a widely distributed ideographic system that is distinctly Mesoamerican in character but that takes on local or regional character in peripheral areas. Such a system could be regarded as a world-class ideological entity comparable to Judeo-Christian, Hindu, or Buddhist worldviews and religions that have crosscut cultures and linguistic boundaries. Just as these patterns of thought and ways of describing the world are unified by core beliefs, diversity within the system through time and space is also characteristic. Seen from this perspective, the Southwest appears to be a part of a broader ideological program with Mesoamerican relationships.

ACKNOWLEDGMENTS. This essay is a longer version of a paper presented at "Pots, Paintings, and Petroglyphs: Parallels among Mesoamerica, the Southwest, and the Southeastern United States," the Second Conference of the Pre-Columbian Society of Washington, D.C., September 1995. Special thanks go to Lloyd Anderson, who invited me to participate in that symposium. I am indebted to Jill Furst, who introduced me to the mysteries of Mexican codices; to Karl Taube, who provided me with many additional relevant references; and to Laura Holt and Tracy Kimball at the Laboratory of Anthropology library, who patiently dealt with my many requests. John Greer provided a photo of the paintings from the depths of Surratt Cave. The photographs reproduced here are courtesy of Karl Kernberger and Curt Schaafsma. Thanks also to Curt, who critically read various drafts and provided valuable suggestions at several stages of the manuscript.

Note

1. In their general shape, proportions, horizontal banding, and eyes, the highly stylized masks from Hueco Tanks resemble funerary stone masks from Teotihuacán. The latter presumably date from several centuries earlier, but the resemblance described does raise the question of the possibility of a linked stylistic tradition between the two.

13

The Sonoran Statelets and Casas Grandes

Carroll L. Riley

UNTIL RECENTLY THE Serrana area of northeastern Sonora has received comparatively little attention from archaeologists and ethnohistorians. In part this was due to the long involvement by American scholars with the American Southwest, beginning in the late nineteenth century. During this same period Mexican archaeologists and historians understandably concentrated on the rich prehistoric cultures of central, southern, and eastern Mexico and spent little time on the northwestern Mexican frontier. Even Casas Grandes, the most spectacular site in the northwest, was largely left to pothunters for a number of decades. Although Bandelier in 1884 traversed northern and eastern Sonora and reported a number of large sites (Lange and Riley 1970:223–287), these were essentially ignored, and the idea grew of a great cultural sink separating the civilizations of central Mexico from the agricultural and town-building traditions of the American Southwest.

American archaeologists, in a burst of misguided creativity, worked out prehistoric sequences that saw southwestern peoples controlling their own cultural destiny. Most scholars were willing to see early generalized stimuli from Mesoamerica that introduced agriculture and pottery, but they believed that the rich tapestry of culture, growing from those early stimuli, was basically autochthonous. Even such a superb field archaeologist as Earl Morris (1939:22–23) could believe that southwestern pottery might have developed from indigenous, Basketmaker II, sun-dried clay vessels. Any Mesoamerican influence was thought to be the result of vague and indirect diffusion.

The idea of a cultural sink stretching across northern Mexico became firmly entrenched during the first half of the twentieth century. There were, however, some attempts to renew research on the northwestern parts of Mexico beginning around 1930. At that time a group of cultural geographers and anthropologists from the University of California began to study the archaeological sites and the historical records of the west coast of Mexico. These scholars, led by Carl O. Sauer and including Donald Brand and Ralph Beals, published a large new body of data, largely in *Ibero-Americana* but also in the *University of California Publications in Geography.*

Beginning in the 1940s, stimulated in 1943 by the Third Mesa Redonda sponsored by the *Sociedad Mexicana de Antropología,* serious attention began to be given not only to mesoamerican-southwestern contacts but also to filling gaps in the "cultural sink" of northern Mexico. In the years that followed, American archaeologists such as Betty Bell, Gordon F. Ekholm, J. Charles Kelley, Isabel Kelly, Robert H. Lister, Clement Meighan, Joseph B. Mountjoy, and Phil C. Weigand (among others) joined a growing number of Mexican colleagues working on the west coast and in the interior of Mexico, and extending at times to the edges of the Sonoran area. The research on the west coast of Mexico demonstrates that sophisticated groups lived in a series of political entities, stretching from Colima and Nayarit to the Sinaloa River. These included the area devastated by Nuño de Guzmán in the early 1530s. Mendizábal (1928:93–100) called them the *Pequeños Estados* (see also Kroeber 1939: 120–122). Mendizábel listed fifteen of these, including such polities as Xalicso, Centispac, Acaponeta, Chiametla, and Culiacán (Mendizábel 1930:Figure 1). Kroeber pointed out that beyond the line of the Sinaloa River, entering Cáhitan country, there was a simpler culture, extending through "nearly all Sonora except the northeast corner of the state" (Kroeber 1939:123).

Carl Sauer (1935:5) estimated the aboriginal population of this region as approximately 425,000. He included in this number the Pequeños Estados, whose people spoke mostly dialects of Totorame and Tahue, the Cáhitan-speaking region (Mayo and Yaqui and probably the coastal somewhat barbarized Guasave), and the mountain- and barranca-dwelling peoples adjacent to the coast (see also Sauer 1934 and Kroeber 1934). Evidence that these sophisticated contact-period sociopolitical groups also had considerable archaeological depth has been admirably summarized by Publ (1985). All these political units had been largely decimated by European disease by the first decades of the seventeenth century (Reff 1991a:164, 195).

In spite of this renewed interest in the west coast, there was still a strong tendency to see the Sonoran region as a kind of backwater, peopled with low-culture ranchería dwellers of no great sophistication. This was partly a matter of historical accident. Northern Sonora had been contacted quite early in that initial northern thrust of Spaniards up the west coast of Mexico. Diego de Guzmán reached the Yaqui River in 1533, and Cabeza de Vaca and his companions traversed Sonora, north to south, in 1536. The Marcos de Niza and Coronado expeditions (1539–1542) traveled through the region, as did Ibarra in the mid-1560s. After this date, however, the Spaniards shifted their interest to the northern interior of Mexico, following the great silver strikes in Zacatecas, Durango, and Chihuahua. The northwest of New Spain was given over to missionization by the Jesuits, who by about A.D. 1638 had extended their mission stations into the Sonora River valley. Where the Coronado and Ibarra expeditions had reported large towns grouped into confederacies of warlike natives and a vigorous trading culture, the Jesuits found only scattered ranchería settlements of Opata and Lower Pima Indians (Riley 1987:39–96).

Scholars began more and more to doubt the earlier documentary evidence because it seemed to contradict the Jesuit sources. The Jesuits gave firm locations and detailed descriptions, and from the time of their entradas there was historical continuity to the present. There may also have been a tendency to believe that members of a religious community would be less apt to distort their findings than would mere laypeople. In any event, by the 1960s a number of first-rate anthropologists and historians had come to believe that the Jesuits were giving the correct picture and that the sixteenth-century explorers had greatly exaggerated what they found in northeastern Sonora (see, for example, Spicer 1962:86–96; for a more recent example see Hu-DeHart 1981:9–10).

There is, however, reason to believe that *both* the sixteenth-century explorers and the seventeenth-century Jesuits were giving basically correct information and that in the three-quarters of a century between Ibarra and the Jesuits some sort of demographic disaster occurred. Reff (1991a:226) estimates a decline in the Opata from a precontact figure of 70,000 to 40,000 in 1638, a drop-off of nearly 40 percent. He believes this may have been due, at least in large part, to a smallpox epidemic in 1623–1625 (Reff 1991a:164–165, 1997), although earlier epidemics may also have been involved. As with other groups in the Greater Southwest, the Opata continued to decline during the seventeenth and eighteenth centuries. By A.D. 1730 the Opata population was only 10 percent of what it had been in the sixteenth century (Reff 1991a:226, 236).

My own figures for the Opata in Prehispanic times are slightly higher than those of Reff. I calculate perhaps 90,000 people as of the mid-sixteenth century (Riley 1987:57; see also Riley 1985:428–429) in the Serrana country as a whole, including Opata and those town-dwelling Pima Bajo (who together formed the polity that I call the "Sonoran statelets"). This is in line with an estimate of William Doolittle (1984:296).

Even accepting Reff's more conservative maximum, a 40 percent rapid decline in the population must have created a cultural and social crisis of giant proportions. Such catastrophes have been studied in other parts of the world. A very well-documented one is the bubonic plague that struck western Europe from 1348 to 1350. This "black death" caused the death of perhaps 20 percent of the population of England in those years and a decline of 40 percent to 50 percent over the next quarter century (Cartwright 1972:38–41). Although the national government maintained itself, local towns and farming villages were devastated, and the wholesale loss of life produced massive changes that greatly modified the social landscape of the country. What the Jesuits found was an analogous situation, Opata and Southern Pima groups reeling from the demographic blows of introduced European disease. This was probably a factor in the docility of the Opata in the face of missionization, something very different from the warlike and hostile statelets that Ibarra encountered three-quarters of a century before.

That the northeast portion of Sonora originally contained more sophisticated peoples than the scattered ranchería groups described in the seventeenth century was indicated not only by the documents of the sixteenth century but by archaeology done in the latter part of the twentieth. For the modern period, in the Sonora valley this has primarily been work done by Richard A. Pailes (1976, 1980, 1984, 1997), William E. Doolittle (1984, 1988), Daniel T. Reff (1981, 1991a, 1997), and Victoria A. Dirst (1979); see also Pailes and Reff (1985). Pailes and his associates began work in 1975 and continued for a number of years. The major excavation was on the large (25 ha or 60+ acres) site of San José just north of the town of Babiácora in the Sonora valley upstream from the Ures gorge. There have also been studies over a larger section of northeast Sonora by Beatriz Braniff and her associates from the Hermosillo office of the Instituto Nacional de Antropología e Historia (see especially Braniff 1985, 1990, 1993, 1995). Braniff (1986) has also reported on the Ojo de Agua site in the Bavispe drainage east of the Sonora valley.

Pailes and his group excavated extensively at the site of San José and surveyed, tested, and mapped a number of other sites in the Sonora valley, a total of 227 for that region (Pailes 1984:311). This Serrana culture operated for several hundred years, extending to the period of Spanish intrusion. The earliest structures were houses in pits, dating from the latter part of the eleventh century, and Doolittle (1988:37) has postulated an early phase that began sometime around A.D. 1000. As time went on there was a general development of surface structures. These certainly include multiroom buildings of adobe and stone footings and a superstructure of adobe. Pailes (1997) believes that these were one story in height, but Doolittle (1988:26) cites foundations three to five stones wide that suggest to him the multistory structures described in the early Spanish accounts.

The sites are characterized by a brown ware pottery, often with incised or punctated geometric designs, and a decorated red-on-brown pottery. These ceramics fall into a generalized "Mogollon" tradition, mostly of the sort found at Casas Grandes, including pottery similar to Convento Incised, Casas Grandes Incised, and Playas Red Incised from Casas Grandes, as well as Alma-like ceramics from the more northern Mogollon area (Pailes 1997). Locally developed sophisticated polychromes do not occur, but there is a certain amount of trade ware, virtually all of it from the Chihuahuan region. These trade ceramics include Ramos, Carretas, Huérigos, Dublan, Babícora, and Villa Ahumada Polychromes, dating, in other words, from the Medio period at Casas Grandes. There is a small amount of El Paso Polychrome and also Gila Polychrome—although, generally speaking, Jornada Mogollon and Hohokam ceramics are absent or very scantily represented (Pailes 1980:35, 1997; Braniff 1986:77). Many of these ceramic types are also found at the site of Ojo de Agua (Braniff 1986:71–75).

The sites of San José, La Mora (north of San José, near Banámichi), and sites Son K:4:16 and K:4:127 (near Las Delicias and Huepac, respectively) had public architecture, perhaps ball courts and temples, although in such ruined condition that it is hard to make out just what was their original function (Riley 1987:96, 361; Pailes 1997).

One type of structure for which the function is known, because it is described in some detail in the Spanish sources, is that of the pyrosignal system. Doolittle (1988:31–32) documents seven such sites, each with a panoramic view of the valley and each

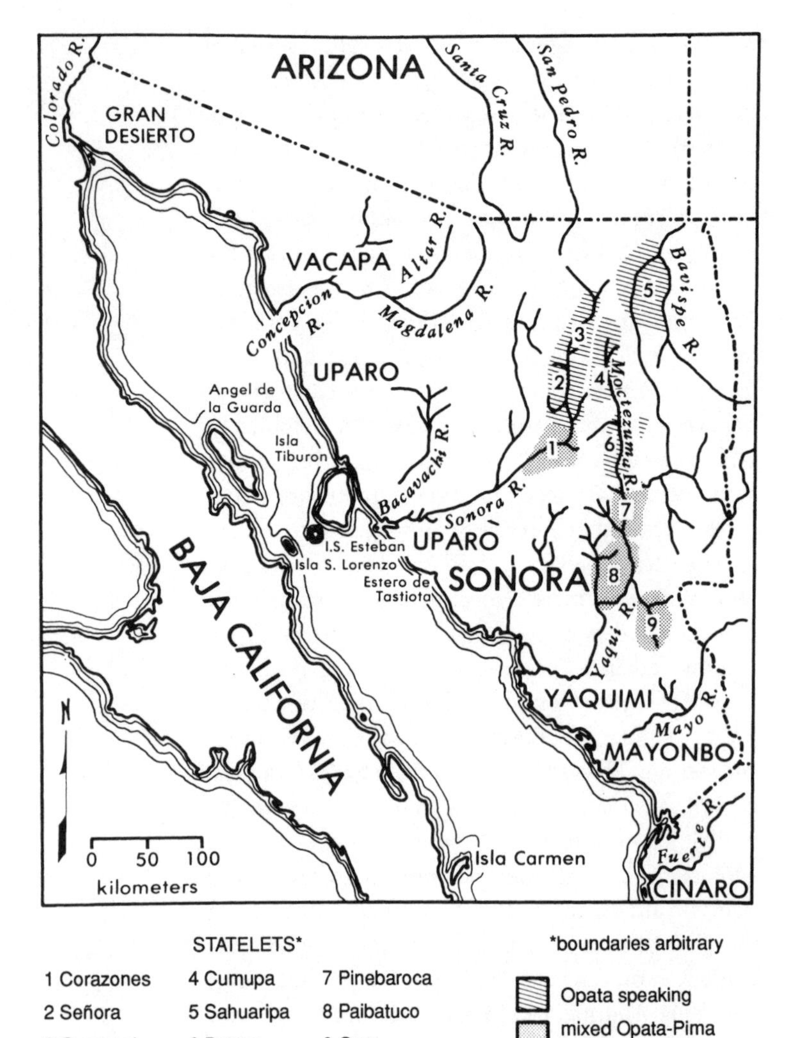

Figure 13.1. Map of Sonoran statelets and related areas in the sixteenth century.

visible from the pyrosignal station on either side. These stations (large boulder-enclosed areas of burned earth) extend from around Banámichi in the north to south of Babiácora, an extent of some 50 km (30 miles). They are roughly in a north-south line except for the ones in the Huepac area, which extend off to the west.

Other finds in the northeast Sonora area include numbers of spindle whorls, often elaborately decorated. There are also female figurines of clay and of turquoise, probably from New Mexico, and copper crotals, the latter traded from Casas Grandes or perhaps directly up the west coast of Mexico (see Vargas 1994:90–94, 1995). The spindle whorls tend to be associated with houses in pits, and Pailes cites a tradition among the historic Opata of weaving in underground structures. The evidence for irrigation agriculture is mostly documentary in nature, but Doolittle (1988:46–47) describes a large elaborately carved boulder discovered near Banámichi in the 1950s that looks very much like a map of irrigation systems in that section of the Sonora valley.

Although the work of Pailes, Doolittle, and Reff clearly discloses a hierarchical settlement with regional centers, smaller villages, and hamlets, Pailes (1997) does not think that the largest excavated sites are the first-tier sites. He points out that the ubiquitous early Jesuit period San Miguel Red and Brown pottery is never found in connection with late prehistoric pottery, suggesting a break in the continuity of those villages actually excavated, tested, or surveyed by the archaeologists. Pailes believes that heavy population loss caused the desertion of many of the late prehistoric settlements. The big modern towns are sited on favorable portions of the Sonora River, and the attractions of these locations would have been the same in pre-Spanish days. The first-tier sites, Pailes believes, are under the plaza areas of such modern towns as Babiácora, Aconchi, and Arizpe.

In the 1970s I became interested in the northeastern Sonoran area because of my work on trade and other contacts between Mesoamerica and the Southwest. Drawing on the various sixteenth-century Spanish documents that relate to the area, on archaeological work in the Sonora and nearby valleys, and on numerous personal visits to archaeological sites, mission stations, and historic towns especially in the Sonora and Moctezuma basins, I suggested a number of small but aggressive polities that controlled the trade routes running from west Mexico to the western Southwest (Riley 1987:39–96).

At some point in the mid-1970s, I coined the term *statelet* to refer to these Sonoran groups, a parallel with the coastal "Pequeños Estados" of Mendizábal and Kroeber (Figure 13.1). This was a period in which archaeologists had borrowed from the social anthropologists a concept of sociopolitical hierarchies, usually in an explicit or at least implied evolutionary context. Terms such as *band, tribe,* and *chiefdom* came with locked-in definitions that some scholars seemed to believe had universal application. It was to avoid this semantic thicket that I used the term *statelet.* I stressed that although the Sonoran statelets had a certain obvious complexity, we knew very little about the specific *forms* of the socioeconomic, political, and religious organization. The same can, of course, be said of the Pequeños Estados.

The Sonoran statelets in my reconstruction were aggressive multitown units, each with a primate center and outlying villages and hamlets. The largest towns had at least several hundred terraced houses, some perhaps multistory, of adobe or jacal construction (Obregón 1924:146–148, 157; Ruiz 1932:55). There were temples, ball courts, other public buildings, and an elaborate irrigation agriculture with double cropping. Trade, both internal and external, was very important. Internally, slaves were traded, as was alum, cotton cloth, and such brightly feathered birds as the military macaw and the thick-billed parrot. There was an external luxury trade in shell and coral, salt, turquoise, and other semiprecious stones, dressed skins, scarlet macaws, polychrome ceramics, copper objects, cotton, and (perhaps) slaves. The turquoise came from the upper Southwest, salt and shells from the Gulf of California region. There is a possibility that scarlet macaw feathers were transshipped from the Mexican southeast (see Riley 1975; 1976a:39–41; 1986:48–50; 1987:39–96, 347–361; 1995a:208–223; 1995b: 201–202).

The religious organization of the region is not securely known. The polemicist and reformer, Bernabé de Las Casas, probably drawing from Marcos de Niza's 1539 journey, indicated that there were very heavy populations in the Sonora valley and described temples of stone and adobe in which animal hearts were offered in sacrifice. These temples also contained mummified bodies of past rulers "leaning against the walls" (Las Casas 1967:2:181–183; see also Riley 1976b:20–21). This may relate to the Casas Grandes area, where seated burials are found in the Medio period (Di Peso et al. 1974:8:327, 328, 355–411). A burial as late as 1624 was reported by the Jesuit missionary Francisco Olindaño for the general Serrana region. It held an "indio principal" seated in his tomb surrounded by a variety of shells, blankets, colored feathers, and other objects (Riley 1987:95).

The statelets were organized into two confederacies. The northernmost was centered on the Opatan-speaking statelet of Señora in the Sonora River valley north of the Ures gorge but also involved the Piman-speaking Corazones to the south of the gorge, as well as other Opata groups, the Guaraspi and Cumapa on the upper Sonora and upper Moctezuma rivers, and Sahuaripa on the Bavispe River. It was east of Sahuaripa, probably along the modern Sonora-Chihuahua frontier, that Ibarra's party in 1564 reached an unnamed town that "marked the limits of the confederation [junta y liga] and the natives lost the opportunity and hope of enjoying plunder from a victory over us (plunder they were already arguing with each other about). Here ended the lands of their friends and we entered the territory of the Querechos, neighbors of the cattle people" (Obregón 1924:173).

The southern confederacy, largely or wholly Pima speaking rather than Opata, was led by Oera and probably included Paibatuco on the Yaqui River and Pinebaroca on the Moctezuma. The statelet of Batuco farther north on the Moctezuma seems to have functioned independently. Warfare was endemic in the region, and both confederacies were characterized by fairly large armies that fought in columns and were armed with spears, bows, macanas, and clubs (Riley 1989:140). The statelets probably fought for control over the trade routes or for material advantages, for example the taking of slaves. Their use of the pyrosignal systems was described graphically by Baltasar de Obregón, chronicler of the Ibarra party, who says that it operated as far south as the Fuerte River (Obregón 1924:172; see also Doolittle 1988:32–33; Riley 1987:93, 1989:140). If this was the case, Doolittle's survey of pyrosignal sites, which was after all limited to the Sonora valley, uncovered only a segment of the system.

A number of specialists have expressed certain reservations about this reconstruction of the Sonoran statelets, usually (and correctly) citing the relative lack of archaeological work in the area (Doelle 1989:165–168; Fontana 1989:8; Naylor 1983:119–121; Sheridan 1996). McGuire and Villalpando (1989; see also Villalpando 1985), however, have a rather different scenario. They concede that the archaeological remains "do suggest larger, more permanent villages than the Jesuits report for the eighteenth-century [seventeenth century?] Opatas" (McGuire and Villalpando 1989:171). They doubt, however, these entities represented "statelets or chiefdom-like polities in the area" (McGuire and Villalpando 1989:171). These authors believe the sixteenth-century documents have been misinterpreted or misread by Reff, myself, and others of the "statelet" school. In their scenario the world that the Spanish invaded in 1540 was "less integrated, less nucleated, less populated, and possibly less militaristic than it had been 100 years before" (McGuire and Villalpando 1989:173). In other words, they see the collapse (or at least serious decline) of these more or less complex Sonoran societies at about the time that the Casas Grandes world ended.

McGuire and Villalpando are productive and perceptive scholars, and I greatly admire their work. I do, however, believe that they have misread the Serrana situation. For one thing, they tend to misinterpret sixteenth-century sources. Witness, for example, the palpably incorrect statement that "many of the documents of the Coronado expedition speak of eastern Sonora as being impoverished and underpopulated" (McGuire and Villalpando 1989:170; but see Hammond and Rey 1940:164, 250, 297, 321). Here, we must assume that the term "eastern Sonora" refers to the statelet area; otherwise the statement is irrelevant. McGuire and Villalpando (1989:130) incorrectly state Marcos de Niza reported gold in Cíbola, a misinterpretation pointed out by Reff (1991b:642–643), who also argues strongly for the basic truth of the Marcos account (1991b:641–647). Much more serious, however, is the fact that McGuire and Villalpando underutilize, or sometimes pretty much ignore, sixteenth-century data, depending instead on the seventeenth-century Jesuit sources (see for example Villalpando 1985:265, 267, 279–285, 288–289).

McGuire and Villalpando do concede the archaeology of the Sonora valley exposes a *somewhat* sophisticated society in the fifteenth century (Kelley and Villalpando 1996:74). But in placing collapse of this culture a century before Coronado, they fly in the face of the archaeological, historical, and epidemiological evidence. For example, the McGuire-Villalpando comment that the sixteenth-century peoples may have been less warlike than the fifteenth-century groups is hard to take seriously. If there was one thing on which the Coronado and Ibarra chroniclers emphatically agreed, it was the militaristic nature of the statelets. Even Cabeza de Vaca mentioned that warring groups broke off their fighting to see the strangers (Riley 1987:90). The pacific Cabeza de Vaca and his companions were handsomely treated; the reason, I (1995b:207) have suggested elsewhere, was that a "traders' protocol" protected small, peaceful groups. This kind of protocol is well known at similar sociopolitical levels around the world. Coronado, with his small advance party in 1540, acted in a totally exemplary way and kept the peace. The powerful main army following a few weeks behind seems to have temporarily overawed the Sonorans. This did not last, and Coronado's relocated way station, San Gerónimo de Corazones in or near Señora, was destroyed with considerable Spanish losses. To Ibarra the powerful statelet of Señora showed implacable hostility.

Had Castañeda and Jaramillo from the Coronado expedition, and especially Obregón and Ruíz with the Ibarra party, found a scattered peaceful ranchería people, it is not credible that they would have described large warlike populations. Ibarra's chroniclers made no bones about the ruinous and uninhabited nature of Paquimé itself. The overriding point to remember here is that *one cannot utilize seventeenth-century documents to reconstruct the sixteenth-century life in northeastern Sonora.* That life disappeared forever sometime between Ibarra's entrada and the first Jesuit settlements.

What was the relationship of this vibrant society of the Sonoran statelets to the greater Casas Grandes world? In an unpublished paper, written sometime around 1977, I suggested that the statelet area might have been somehow closely related to Casas Grandes. I (1979) also brought up the possibility that the Sonora River might have represented the western frontier of this culture, the epicenter lying somewhere in the Yaqui drainage. Although I now think that the center of statelet society was in fact in the Sonora valley, I (1987:48) believe there may well have been Casas Grandes influence in the statelet region. On the other hand, Doolittle (1988:52–56, 59) feels that the Sonoran region had an autochthonous development. He discounts the Casas Grandes presence in the Sonoran area, pointing out that the 700 to 800 Chihuahuan sherds found in the Sonoran sites (0.1 percent of the total sherd count) hardly indicate massive influence.

Phillips, however, sees the possibility of a Casas Grandes base for the statelet area:

> [Pailes and Doolittle] argue that the Río Sonora culture continued into historic times, becoming the Opata. I would like to revive a hypothesis once put forward by Riley (1987, p. 48): that the Opata were descended—at least in part—from Casas Grandes. The Río Sonora hierarchy emerged at a time when the Casas Grandes network was expanding westward. The resulting demographic com-

pression could explain the emergence of small but feisty local hierarchies. This same process may have intensified when the Casas Grandes area was abandoned, after A.D. 1400—its survivors shifting west into Sonora. Such events would explain historic language patterns in northern Sonora, in which Opata displaced Pima and Eudeve. (Phillips 1989:389–390).

The Casas Grandes–Mogollon cast to Sonoran River ceramics, plus similarities in house construction, led Braniff (1995:258–261) to suggest that the northeastern Sonoran peoples were basically Casas Grandes in type and may have represented Casas Grandes control of an Opatan population extending to the Sonora River valley. After the collapse of Casas Grandes, the Sonoran statelets continued their own economic network until it finally crashed sometime before the Jesuits arrived. As Braniff says, "[W]e may argue toward an economic network organized by the Sonoran statelets themselves" (Braniff 1995:261).

Both Di Peso and I believed that certain "provinces" or "kingdoms" mentioned by Marcos de Niza, Melchior Díaz, and Francisco Vazquez de Coronado, but only vaguely or contradictorily located, were really Casas Grandes centers that had collapsed in the fifteenth century. One of those "kingdoms," called Marata, was located by Di Peso (1974:3:808) somewhat to the north and west of Paquimé, extending from the Tres Rios district of Sonora, north into the Playas valley of New Mexico. He (1974:3:807) did not try to map the other two polities, Acus and Totonteac.

For Marata I have postulated an area somewhere in the northern part of the Sonoran-Chihuahuan border region. I (1976a:27) originally suggested that Acus could have been in the Animas drainage of the New Mexico boot heel. If this were the case, however, Acus would have collapsed before A.D. 1400 (see chapter five of this volume). I now prefer to consider Acus, as well as the third polity, Totonteac, unlocated until we have more evidence. Parenthetically, *Marata* may be an Opata word, perhaps an incomplete name in which the Opata preposition *ma* (with) is a part. *Acus* might be Piman (from *aki,* a ravine or arroyo), and *Totonteac* is very likely Piman, meaning something like "Ant Place" (Riley 1995a:216, 218–219). Historians have tended to identify *Acus* with Acoma and *Totonteac* with Hopi, but I (1990a:232; see also Reff 1991b:640–642) have argued against such identifications. In part they are based on misunderstandings by Coronado and his men.

Although the relationship of the northeastern Sonoran region to Casas Grandes still poses many questions, there is a rather plausible scenario, elements of which I have suggested in a recent publication (Riley 1997:18). It seems to me that both the northern Chihuahuan culture and the Sonoran Serrana rose from a Mogollon base sometime in the latter part of the first millennium. Even at that time the Chihuahuan peoples may have been somewhat advanced in terms of population, village size, and sophistication of material culture. This distinction was drastically heightened around A.D. 1150–1200, when the Chihuahuan area went through a dramatic quickening that produced the Medio period of Casas Grandes.

As time went on, the Casas Grandes culture spread its influence in all directions. Northeastern Sonora was at first in a client position, probably, as Braniff (1995:259–261) has suggested, acting as a conduit for shell from the Gulf of California. Some ceramic wares, although not a great deal, were traded from Casas Grandes to the developing statelets. Much of the two-way trade was probably in perishable materials (cotton, salt, brightly colored feathers, slaves, etc.). Some of the materials were probably shipped farther west. At least McGuire, Villalpando, Vargas, and Gallaga (this volume) believe that there was a certain amount of trade into Medio period Casas Grandes from the Trincheras area just west of the Serrana. They do not address the matter of trade routes, but goods from Trincheras to Paquimé must have been funneled through the statelets.

To what extent Casas Grandes religious and sociopolitical ideas penetrated the Serrana is unknown. One problem is the uncertainty of the sociopolitical situation in the Casas Grandes area. Was Paquimé the center of a "kingdom" (Di Peso 1974:2:328)? Alternatively, were there contending primary centers, each with its own stretch of territory (Minnis et al. 1993), or did some other arrangement prevail? Places known only to folk memory by Marcos de Niza's time, for example Marata, suggest a series of more or less autonomous "Casas Grandes" polities at least by the late Medio period.

I very much doubt there was any actual military domination of the Serrana peoples by groups to the east. Still, there may have been hostilities, and this could have been the testing period for the admittedly militaristic statelets of the historic period. With the collapse of the Casas Grandes culture, the statelets were in a position to take over segments of the Casas Grandes hegemony. The fall of Casas Grandes itself may have resulted in part from ethnic shifts deeper in Mexico and the closing of ancient trade routes that ran from north central Mesoamerica into the Casas Grandes region and on into the Jornada and Pueblo regions. Certainly by the late fourteenth and fifteenth centuries, new routes stretching up the west coast of Mexico and into the northern Southwest were beginning to form (Riley 1990b:228–234: Alvarez 1985:256–257). Interestingly, it was at just this time when southwestern Pueblo Indians began to transship large amounts of shell, macaw and parrots and their feathers, and other Mexican materials, along with purely Pueblo products like turquoise and glazed pottery, to the Plains and to the lower Colorado region (Riley 1976a:39–41, 1987:268–272). For the Pueblos at any rate, the new west coast routes may have been richer or more dependable than the older Casas Grandes routes.

In any case, by the sixteenth century Señora, Guaraspi, Corazones, Oera, and the other statelets were fully developed. They were probably not lineal descendants of the Casas Grande polity in the sense that there had been a Casas Grandes political hegemony that extended across northeastern Sonora. But they stood in some relationship to Casas Grandes. Obregón (1924:186) in 1564 picked up information from the Querechos in the Casas Grandes area that the original inhabitants of Paquimé had been driven away by groups from the other side of the sierra (in other words, from the statelet area). In 1884 Adolph F. Bandelier, traveling in northeastern Sonora, recorded a persistent Opata tradition that this group had once been in constant warfare with the Casas Grandes people (Lange and Riley 1970:273). This enmity produced unstable conditions in the Bavispe frontier area until the collapse of Casas Grandes. Indeed, it is probable that there was a "trade and raid" policy between Paquimé and one or more of the statelets, perhaps the Prehispanic precursor of the historic northern or Señora federation. The relationship may have been stressful at times, but it had its value to the statelets, for it seems likely that they partook to one degree or another of the rich cultural sustenance of Casas Grandes.

14

The Postclassic along the Northern Frontiers of Mesoamerica

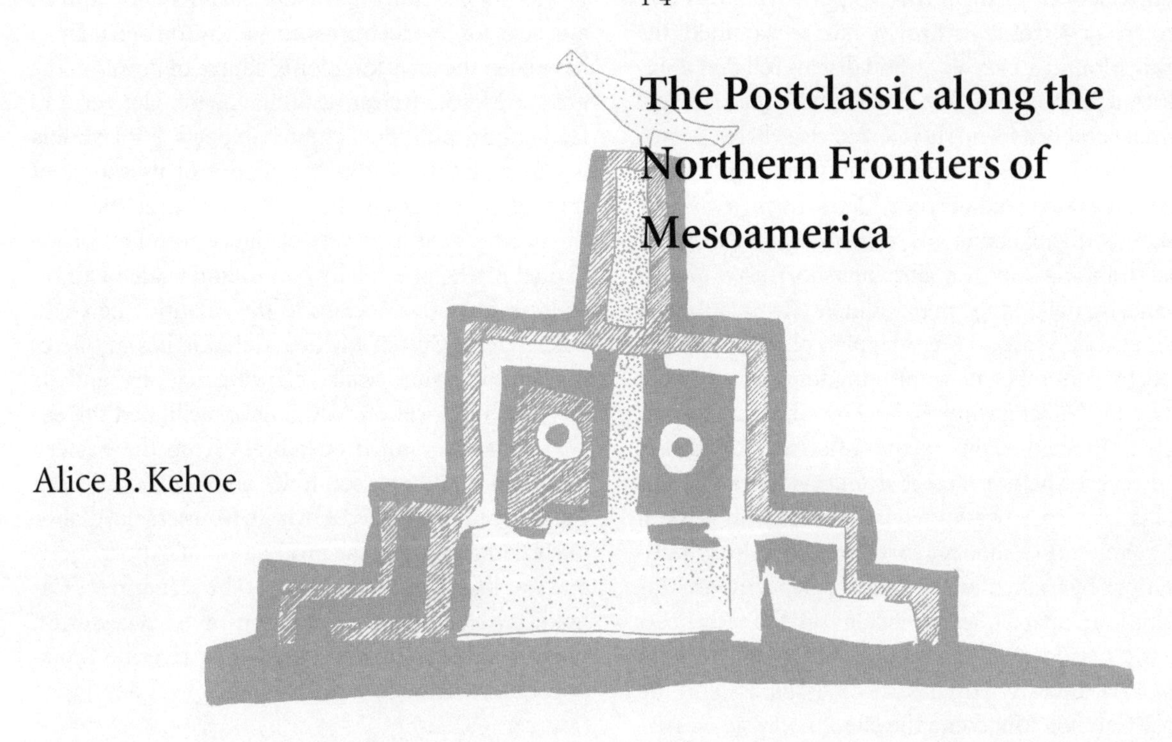

Alice B. Kehoe

IN 1928 KROEBER (1928:389) stated that "practically all American students, seem in agreement... [on] a radiating transmission to and through the Southwest" from Mexico into the United States.[1] That same year, Herbert J. Spinden proposed the source to be a Mesoamerican "cradle" of irrigated maize agriculture accompanied by little female figurines. Spinden (1943:63–64 [1928]) traced these "little fetishes" north into the American Southwest and south into Central America to Panama. As late as 1951 Duncan Strong (1967) reexamined the question of "Nuclear America" and upheld the earlier consensus.

Alfred Kidder summed up the issue in the festschrift for Kroeber:

> Like most archaeologists in this country I am 100 per cent American.... [T]his matter of New World beginnings involves some of the most fundamentally important of all anthropological problems. Were... processes... discovered once and once only?... I am not a polygenist as regards American culture. I believe it had a single point of origin, though this tenet, I grant, is illogical in view of my strong feeling that civilization sprang up independently in the Old and New Worlds. (Kidder 1936:144, 151)

Fifteen years later, Kidder's illogical convictions were challenged by Heine-Geldern and Ekholm's American Museum exhibit on transpacific similarities. Kidder said then, "[D]oubtless because of the obstinacy of increasing age and hardening of mental arteries, I am still one hundred percent American" (Kidder 1951:222).

Philip Phillips attempted to rebut Heine-Geldern and Ekholm's challenge in a chapter in the *Handbook of Middle American Indians* (Phillips 1966). To assist him in the task, Phillips set a 1964 Harvard graduate seminar to come up with a methodology based on stylistic criteria that could refute unacceptable hypotheses of intersocietal contact such as Heine-Geldern's. Data for the seminar were shell engravings from Spiro's Craig Mound: Harvard's best and brightest would demonstrate how to refute claims of transoceanic contact by trashing the preposterous notion of transgulf contact (Williams 1978). Harvard's best failed to produce such a methodology, and Phillips found himself custodian of voluminous stacks of expensive rubbings of shell engravings and in the end produced a beautiful set of volumes on Mississippian shell art (Phillips and Brown 1978).

Phillips accepted contact between Spiro and

Cahokia, both of them Mississippian (Phillips and Brown 1978:170–174). Brown has reexamined the Craig Mound archaeology and discovered that a significant proportion of the artifacts with the principal burial had been formerly interred elsewhere (Brown 1996:195). This discovery, in combination with more, and calibrated, radiocarbon dates (A.D. 1050–1275 [Hall 1991; Pauketat 1995]), provoked the realization that Cahokia was a major but short-lived power (Pauketat 1995) in the midcontinent. Its collapse was followed by a second Mississippian phase characterized by a number of small kingdoms—one could term this *balkanization.* Spiro, Etowah, and Moundville flourished in this second Mississippian phase.

Because I believe there is strong evidence that Cahokia was in a trading relationship with central Mesoamerica (Kehoe 1998:150–171; see series of publications by Griffin for changes in perspective on Cahokia), and that its dates coincide with the early Postclassic period of Mesoamerica, I propose we term Cahokia the early Postclassic Mississippian and the post-Cahokia kingdoms the late Postclassic Mississippian. Southwest dates for Chaco and Classic Mimbres, on the one hand, and for the post-Chaco major population shifts and site developments, including Casas Grandes Medio phase, seem to parallel the Mississippian phenomenon and the Mesoamerican Postclassic well enough that comparisons are facilitated by calling Chaco and Mimbres "early Postclassic" and Pueblo IV and Casas Grandes Medio and Tardio phase, "late Postclassic." Some people will squirm, but "dates" outside the Southwest are after all radiocarbon estimates, and even Southwest tree-ring dates can be debated (Ravesloot et al. 1995a). Radiocarbon estimates and tree-ring dates are ranges within parameters of probability, not to be confused with documented events within Eurasian calendar series.

Given temporal correlations that may be subsumed into the periods early and late Postclassic, the next step is to draw out comparisons. Karen Bruhns and I (1992) found interesting parallels between lower Central America and Cahokia that may indicate frontier states on Mesoamerica's south and northeast margins, respectively. There are some parallels to Hohokam, fewer to Anasazi; the differences appear to necessitate the distinguishing between western and eastern Mesoamerica in the Postclassic.

For the southern frontier (Bruhns 1980, 1989, 1996; Fowler 1989; Schortman 1989; Sharer 1984), climate and soils for producing cacao and cotton are likely to have been the local kingdoms' source of power in the greater Mesoamerican trading sphere. Copper and feathers are additional attested exports. For Cahokia we have almost no direct evidence of its source of trading power other than its position at the confluence of the great rivers of the eastern half of the United States, potentially controlling trade in all resources from the Rockies to the Atlantic, the Great Lakes to the Gulf of Mexico. Cahokia lies in one of the world's prime maize-growing regions, and its riverine hub location would have facilitated the export of finely tanned deer hides from the Eastern Woodlands and of bison hides and pemmican from the Missouri watershed. On both frontiers slave labor likely contributed to the production of export goods and was itself a probable export. The scenario for Cahokia parallels the trade economy of its successor, St. Louis, between 1815 and 1840, when riverine transport dominated and industry had not yet developed (Mercer 1982:80).[2]

Frontier capitals are located in rich agricultural valleys along major interregional trade routes (e.g., Urban 1986; Bruhns 1986). Rulers in frontier capitals, neither puppets of distant emperors nor primitive chiefs, "forge their own solutions" (Schortman and Nakamura 1991:331) to political-economic challenges by expropriating symbols of empire as they simultaneously resist takeover from actual imperial partners. Rich burial offerings often emphasize the ruler's eminence. Mound 72 at Cahokia had 260 bodies, plus copper, shell beads, fine lithics, and undoubtedly perishable luxuries such as feather cloaks, accompanying the central personage.

Cahokia in the north, and the lower Central American kingdoms in the south, adopted the Mesoamerican idea of what a city looks like: public buildings placed on platforms arranged around plazas. This template seems to underlie Hohokam towns, too. Platform mounds on the frontiers show various forms of construction, with earth more common than stone rubble and masonry, especially in the north. On both frontiers many buildings were pole-framed wattle and daub with thatched roofs or, in the south, pole and clay flat roofs. Households show the typical Mesoamerican arrangement of domiciles and their outbuildings around a patio (or along a terrace with connecting patios). In some regions these were separated from other households by their infield gardens, making a kind of garden city; in others the households were tightly contiguous around the ceremonial/administrative center and around the outlying barrio centers but more dispersed on the outskirts. In the early Postclassic the plazas were delineated by walls or terracing, emphasizing the separateness and power of the ruler. Within the terraced/walled area, buildings could be arranged with little apparent relationship to one another or in disparate groups scattered throughout the ceremonial/administrative complex, an idea perhaps earliest seen at Chichén Itzá in the Yucatán but widely adopted from central Mexico (Tula) to El Salvador (Cihuatán) and Honduras (La Sierra)—and Cahokia. Frontier capitals in general lack (or have only quite simple) stone monuments or masonry buildings. They lack vaulted buildings. Inscriptions are lacking and iconographic elements appear more or less out of the full Mesoamerican complex context. Ball courts (in the eastern United States, chunky grounds or ball fields) are a regular part of early Postclassic capitals.

Contacts North and East of the Southwest

That rivers formed the principal transportation system in eastern North America is a well-supported premise, but overland travel was not ignored (Manson 1994). Cahokia occupied the prime location at the junction of the Missouri and Mississippi not far above the Ohio's mouth. To get from the Mississippian domains to the Southwest, traders could go down the Mississippi to the Gulf and then up Texas rivers up the Arkansas past Spiro or up the Missouri to and along the Platte, then south. The Platte route should be considered very seriously because it intersected in Colorado with the Old North Trail running east of the Rockies foothills (approximately Interstate 25) from the Barrens of northern Alberta down through Calgary and Helena to Pecos and on into Mexico (McClintock 1968:434–436 [1910]).[3] It was the Platte route that brought Spanish exploring parties into conflict with Pawnee. Further evidence of overland travel comes from the routes used by Juan Sabeata (Kelley 1955) and the Coronado expedition (Wedel 1994).

Patricia O'Brien (e.g., 1991, 1994) has been investigating the territory of what she (with Gibbon [1974]) is calling the Ramey state, of which Cahokia was the capital. She recognizes territorial markers (bird-man plus cross-in-circle) placed on bluffs controlling the principal riverine approaches to the American Bottom and has found that Mississippian mounds once stood at the confluences of streams with the major rivers radiating from Cahokia. O'Brien has also been overlaying Indian trails and pioneer roads on Mississippian site distribution maps, finding close correlations. These various data—in conjunction with findings of copper, Atlantic shells, and fine cherts from distant sources around the Midwest and Plains—attest to Cahokia's central place in a network of trade and travel from the Rockies to the Appalachians and Gulf of Mexico. Dentalium in Missouri Basin sites demonstrates the prehistoric transmontane trade along the Ac ko mok ki/Lewis and Clark route (Kehoe 1993:94–96). Several of us who work on the Northwestern Plains are convinced pemmican was produced in commercial quantities in the late prehistoric period (as it was in the historic period) for trade downstream to the Mandan entrepôts and on to Cahokia; a pair of Mississippian shell masks found in 1992 in the Sweet Grass Hills (Jaynes 1995) north of the Milk River confirmed Mississippian contacts (see also Hall 1984).

What is the evidence for contacts between the early Postclassic Cahokia network, or the late Postclassic Mississippian, and the Southwest? Practically none. Coronado's route seems to pretty well circumscribe Postclassic Southwest relationships to the north and east; that is, central Kansas was the zone between the outreach of the two culture areas, Southwest and Mississippian. Tangible evidence of movement and contacts between the Pecos and Rio Grande pueblos and Southern Plains nations, principally Caddoan, is common in the Texas-Oklahoma panhandle. Southwest cotton has been found in eastern Oklahoma Caddoan sites, turquoise in Red River Caddoan burials (Vehik and Baugh 1994:259; Brown 1996:199). Jemez Mountains obsidian occurs into western Oklahoma; obsidian from Idaho (Malad) and Utah (Black Rock) also has been found and is more common than Jemez obsidian in western Oklahoma and farther south in Texas (Vehik and Baugh 1994:260).

On the basis of archaeological data, the Southern Plains seem to be the zone of overlap between the two major areas of Postclassic Mesoamerica and to furnish corridors to the north. Mesoamerica's western area runs from Zacatecas west, south, and north through Anasazi/Fremont and tails off around San Francisco Bay. The eastern area includes the Valley of Mexico, the Sierra Oriental and Gulf of Mexico, Yucatán, south to lower Central America and north to include the Gulf Coastal Plain, with its northern boundary at Cahokia. Except for trading turquoise and macaws, the Southwest had little involvement with eastern Mesoamerica. Mississippians' riverine routes favored trade and visiting relations with Gulf of Mexico cities, and cotton cloth may have been the only southwestern product worth the more arduous Santa Fe Trail or Red River procurement routes. Paquimé amply demonstrates the feasibility of imports from West Mexico and the Gulf of California into the interior Southwest, in contrast to the longer, more toilsome routes from the East, so little attested in Chihuahua. What weak resemblances there are between the Southwest and Mississippian in the Postclassic may represent parallel outreaches from Mexico, reflecting differences there between the West and East sectors.

Archaeological data are only a subset of history. "The Indian they called *Turco*," one of Coronado's guides to Quivira in 1541, spoke of a realm on a great river far to the east. Turco was picked up at Pecos. He advocated an east-southeast route to Quivira. "Isopete," another guide picked up at Pecos, insisted Quivira was northeast. Isopete, a Wichita, won out, Coronado ended up in the Wichita villages in central Kansas, and Turco was garroted by his employers. Mildred Wedel (1988:48) believed Turco was probably a Quiviran Wichita, and Riley (1995b:169) suggests he may have been a proto-Pawnee from the nation bordering the Wichita to the north; in either case, Turco was a northern Caddoan.

It was Mildred Wedel's contention that Turco meant to lead Coronado to the Mississippian kingdoms of the lower Mississippi valley, the very kingdoms toward which De Soto was marching. There, Coronado's Spaniards were told, one would meet

> vessels of a great Lord called Aquixo who was lord of many towns and people on the other (west) side of the river, ... 200 vessels [canoes] full of Indians with their bows and arrows, painted with ocher and having great plumes of white and many colored feathers on either side [headdresses?], and holding shields in their hands with which they covered [i.e., protected] the paddlers, while the warriors were standing from prow to stern with their bows and arrows in their hands. The vessel in which the cacique came had an awning spread in the stern and he was seated under the canopy. Also other vessels came bearing other Indian notables. The chief from his position under the canopy controlled and gave orders to the other men. (Quoted by Wedel 1988:41–42)

Garcilaso de la Vega reported that De Soto's men had seen these huge dugout canoes with 14 to 25 oarsmen. "Their crews sang in rhythm of war deeds and victories as the oarsmen propelled the boats forward... [f]illing the broad river, in formation" (quoted by Wedel 1988:42). The Turco is said to have described how "the lord of that land took his siesta beneath a large tree from which hung great quantities of gold jingle bells which in the breeze soothed him. He said further that the ordinary table service of all in general was made of wrought silver and the jugs, plates and bowls of gold. He called the gold Acochis" (quoted by Wedel 1988:43). Wedel (1988:43) suggests *achochis* is probably the Wichita (Caddoan) word *ha:kwicis,* "a generic term for metal in modern Wichita." Turco's *achochis* could have been copper, which was more highly valued than gold by the Mississippians.

I suggest that during the Postclassic, traders—peddlers—such as Isopete, Turco, and Juan Sabeata kept the Southwest and Mississippian kingdoms informed about one another and carried relatively small items to exchange. I think it likely that there was a Postclassic slave trade, also, bringing Numic and Central Plains individuals into the Southwest and Plains individuals into Mississippian kingdoms. Direct trade between the Southwest and Mississippian regions would have been limited by the lack of direct major river routes, discouraging bulk trade. Another limiting factor would have been substantial differences in values, both conceptual and economic, stemming from the differences between West and East Mesoamerica from which the two United States culture areas derived their images of cosmopolitan grandeur.

One small but telling particular, very relevant to the question of trade, is the Mississippian lord's tree jingles. Presumably they were not Mexican-style copper bells because apparently none are reported from Mississippian sites. Sheet copper tinklers were highly popular trade items in eastern North America from the beginnings of European trade. "Arrowhead-shaped pendants" and perhaps some of the "tubular copper beads" recovered from late Postclassic Mississippian sites (Smith 1987:101, 120) may have been tinklers, possibly hung on trees and garment fringes. Substitutive items such as tinklers and bells bedevil our efforts to judge prehistoric contacts.

Conclusion

Surveying archaeological evidence for contacts between Paquimé and regions north of the Gulf of Mexico, we see a clear disjunction with western Oklahoma/central Kansas, the boundary zone. Only in this zone do Southwest and Mississippian materials manifest contact (Schroeder 1994:300), in a context of Caddoan towns culturally similar to the Midwest, not the Southwest. Sheer distance, unmitigated by continuous river routes, militated against significant economic relationships across this disjunction. The few items demonstrating contact are small enough to have been packed on dog or human backs; the plains' low agricultural productivity would not have sustained a class of porters such as carried trade in Mexico.

Knowledge of the great town of Paquimé, and of the Mississippian kingdoms of the Midwest, was carried across the disjunction by individuals such as Turco, Isopete, and Juan Sabeata. Although chiefs of Paquimé and lords of Mississippian kingdoms may have felt curiosity to see the fabled realms, distance prohibited development of any regular and substantial relationships. For each region Mexican powers accessible via the Gulf of California and the Gulf of Mexico were far more feasible trade affiliates and sources of ideas.

Notes

1. I thank Richard B. Woodbury (April 24, 1992, personal communication) for generously collating these references, and the 1951 Kidder paper, in response to my query on inter-war-period opinion.

2. Another parallel is seen in exports from first-century frontier Britain across the Channel into the continental Roman Empire. These exports included grain, hides, slaves, precious and utilitarian metals, and dogs (Elton 1996:83).

3. McClintock was told (1968:436 [1910]) that it took a party of Blackfoot in about 1810 "twelve moons of steady travelling to reach the country of the dark skinned people, and eighteen moons to come north again . . . by a longer route through the . . . Bitter Root country." The party included a married couple, a man, and a twelve-year-old boy. They were remembered because they brought back a medicine pipe and bundle obtained from a "South Man."

Related to the Old North Trail is the Ac Ko Mok Ki map (Moodie and Kaye 1977) depicting 200,000 square miles from the Cypress Hills of southern Alberta to central Wyoming, and from Idaho to North Dakota (not counting the schematic conflation of the Snake and Columbia to indicate a river to the Pacific [shown on the map]). Ac Ko Mok Ki, a Blackfoot leader ("Feathers," a.k.a. Old Swan the Second, died 1814), drew the map in February 1801 for Peter Fidler, who transmitted it to HBC headquarters in London, where the cartographer Arrowsmith published it in 1802. Thomas Jefferson then gave the published map to Lewis and Clark, who used it from Mandan territory to the Columbia. Fidler noted that Ac Ko Mok Ki had personally seen "the greater part" of what he drew.

15

The Mexican West Coast and the Hohokam Region

Clement W. Meighan

It has long been known that the ancient cultures of Mexico had a profound influence on the development of the U.S. Southwest. Delineation of these influences in detail has been quite limited, however, and there is still much to be learned. Because of the increase of archaeological knowledge in both areas, it may be useful to provide further summary and analysis. Comparisons are much helped by the great improvement in chronological placement of archaeological finds in both areas.

Mountjoy (1970:9–10) provides a good summary of the early history of the search for contacts between the west Mexico area and the Southwest. The search for relationships has been one of the central topics of research in west Mexico. One of the earliest scholarly investigations, that of Sauer and Brand (1930), had as a primary purpose the delineation of a cultural corridor between Mexico and the Southwest. Ekholm's (1939, 1942) later work in northern Sinaloa was directed to the same ends. These early investigations were not able to show much in the way of cultural connections, however, let alone a "corridor" of regular influences, and Kelly (1944) was pessimistic about finding evidence of culture contacts. Conclusions were limited, of course, by the scattered excavation evidence of the time, which has since been considerably amplified. In addition, the west Mexican sites were dominated by abundant and distinctive pottery styles (called Aztatlán by Sauer and Brand), not particularly similar to southwestern pottery.

In 1955 the Society for American Archaeology sponsored a number of seminars, one of which was devoted specifically to the question of external relationships of the southwestern culture area (Jennings and Reed 1956). This discussion, which reviewed relationships in all directions from the Southwest, pretty well demolished any remaining notions of autochthonous developments of southwestern culture history and showed the constant interconnections between the Southwest and surrounding areas. Cultural relationships with Mexico were considered in some detail, and this paper of 40 years ago laid the groundwork for contemporary understanding of such relationships. Some comments from this seminar:

> [W]ith the Gila Butte phase of the Colonial period new elements began to appear in great number, of which many, if not all, can be traced to Mesoamerican sources. . . . [T]his process of incorporation reaches its height in the Santa

Cruz and Sacaton phases and dies out in the Classic period. Significantly, these new traits are what give the Hohokam culture its distinctive character and set it off from other Southwestern cultures. In effect, so many Mesoamerican traits are incorporated in the Hohokam culture . . . that it would be quite possible to identify the Hohokam culture as a peripheral manifestation of the Tula-Mazapan horizon, along with other cultures which had by then developed in Northern Mesoamerica. (Jennings and Reed 1956:92)

Subsequent remarks attributed the connections mostly to the Chalchihuites culture of Durango and Zacatecas rather than the west coast cultures represented by such sites as Chametla, Culiacán, and Guasave. Since 1955, however, extensive new excavations along the west Mexican coast, plus much better chronological evidence, make this conclusion less compelling.

With the publication of the large-scale excavations at Casas Grandes (Di Peso 1974), it appeared that most cultural contact problems were resolved. Here was a major site in northern Mexico with abundant evidence of copper artifacts, an extensive trade in marine shells, and even breeding pens for macaws, tropical birds that have been found in both Anasazi and Hohokam cultural contexts far to the north. Important as this site is, however, it does not explain all Mesoamerican influences on the southwestern United States. The major occupation of Casas Grandes is too late in time to be the source of the earlier Mesoamerican influences. It is far too late to be the source of such fundamental elements as corn/beans/squash agriculture and many of the direct trade items found at sites like Snaketown in southern Arizona. For the latter site, Casas Grandes is at a greater distance than Mesoamerican sites along the west coast of Mexico. As always in archaeology, the most obvious interpretation proves to be insufficient to explain everything, and in the case of Mesoamerican/Southwest relationships, the large geographic region and long time span should convince us that multiple lines of connection, spread over many centuries, must have been active. This is no new idea, and it has been recognized by all who have devoted serious thought to the matter. However, making this commonsense observation is not the same thing as providing evidence for relationships, and that is the goal here.

Routes of Connection

Because the southwestern culture area is quite diverse and includes major variants of its own, and because the same is true for Mesoamerica, many kinds of "connections" and "routes" are present. Trading centers in Mexico, such as the site of Casas Grandes, were undoubtedly instrumental in transmitting Mexican objects and ideas to the Southwest (Di Peso 1974).

A trade route through the western mountains (Sierra Madre Occidental) has long been suggested. Kelley argues that Chalchihuites and Canutillo cultures of western Zacatecas and southern Durango "strongly affected the late Pioneer, Colonial, and Sedentary periods of the Southwestern Hohokam" (Kelley 1966:102). In a later paper Kelley stated that "Alta Vista began to influence the Hohokam . . . before A.D. 500" (Kelley 1971:793). He goes on to link some specific Mexican pottery types with the Southwest: "Otinapa Red-on-white ware of the [Chalchihuites] Río Tunal phase is stylistically related to Three-Circle Red-on-White of the Mogollon, corresponding in time to the Sedentary Hohokam, and Nayar White-on-Red ware of the . . . terminal phase of Chalchihuites is clearly related to . . . various White-on-Red wares that are largely Classic Hohokam in age" (Kelley 1971:793). I have not seen the pottery types mentioned, but I think this comparison brings out the difficulties of using sherds as evidence of "relationship," and both Haury and Di Peso were quite cautious in making such linkages. More recent studies have shown a broad distribution in both time and space for White-on-Red pottery in Mexico.

A third possible route of Hohokam-Mexican connection is a west coast connection through the coastal plain. As discussed below, it is an oversimplification to see sites like Guasave as trading outposts on the border of Mesoamerica (Carpenter 1994, 1996a) because the "Gran Chichimeca" was not a cultural vacuum but imposed its own selectivity on elements coming from Mesoamerican centers.

Based on my own field experience in west Mexico (Meighan 1972, 1976; Meighan and Foote 1968), I concentrate here on parallels between the archaeology of west Mexico and the Hohokam region in southern Arizona. Others have summarized well the similarities between Mexico and other areas of the

Southwest (i.e., Reyman 1978; Riley 1978; Lister 1978), and broad relationships over the whole Southwest have been noted. Here, however, I confine the discussion to relationships with the Hohokam region of the Southwest. The definitive studies for Hohokam are Gladwin, Haury, Sayles, and Gladwin 1937; Haury 1976; and Gumerman and Haury 1979.

Geographically, it is not difficult to travel between the Mesoamerican area and the Hohokam sites of Arizona (e.g., the distance from Guasave to Snaketown is less than 800 km). There is a considerable stretch of desert between the Río Fuerte (Sinaloa) and the Gila River in Hohokam territory, sparsely populated in the past and inhabited by potentially hostile hunters and gatherers like the Seri. The residents of desert areas, however, are known for traveling long distances, and at certain seasons the trip through the coastal deserts was not difficult for travelers on foot. For example, the Mojave Indians of the Colorado River regularly traveled far into the Southwest; on one occasion a band appeared at the Santa Barbara Mission, having come, out of curiosity, more than 300 km across one of North America's less-hospitable deserts. Hence, although all of the northern deserts of Mexico were seen by the agricultural settlements of Mesoamerica as the Gran Chichimeca, a region of uncivilized hunters and gatherers, this does not mean that contact and travel did not regularly take place through this zone.

Di Peso (1974:1:263) comments, "One must not scoff at the natives' travelling ability." He goes on to cite visits by Tarahumara Indians to Chihuahua City and Juarez and travels of Tarascan Indians who look for work in the north and enter the United States.

The major large-scale excavations of Di Peso make this long-distance foot travel across the desert abundantly clear, and it would be equally clear for the Mexican west coast except that the latter has seen much smaller excavation samples and more limited excavation evidence. As late as 1966, for example, I (1966) was able to report only four relatively small site excavations for the west coast state of Sinaloa. Of these, only the work at Guasave has been reexamined in detail in recent years (Carpenter 1996a).

The coastal route from west Mexico to the Hohokam is the shortest and easiest way for cultural influences to travel. Haury comments, "The fact that an alternate route of the Inter-American Highway (No. 15) follows a coastal path from Tepic to Guaymas whence it turns directly north to Tucson and Phoenix, the old Hohokam heartland, may represent a modern analog of what happened in antiquity" (Haury 1976:345). Haury (1976) also believes the contacts were direct, by means of traders as long-distance travelers, and he (1976:Figure 17.2) illustrates burden carriers depicted in Hohokam and Mesoamerican art. I agree with Haury, however, that Mesoamerican contacts were probably sporadic and limited rather than the regular *pochteca* trade network developed in Aztec times.

Carpenter (1994, 1996a) has reviewed the nature of aboriginal cultures in northwestern Mexico and suggested that the Sinaloa area, based on reexamination of Ekholm's (1942) excavation reports, was a culturally intermediate area between west Mexico and the American Southwest, sharing elements of both regions but maintaining its own distinctive patterns. Carpenter does not see Guasave as a frontier outpost of Mesoamerica but as representing its own (Cahitan) cultural area. The often-stated idea that the Río Fuerte in Sinaloa marks the northern limit of Mesoamerica is an oversimplified attempt to understand geography and cultural relationships. Actually, the centers of Mesoamerican culture spread quite different and selective influences to the north. Indeed, some well-known west Mexican cultures far to the south of Sinaloa were also not very "Mesoamerican" in their social, political, and material culture manifestations. For example, I (1974) have mentioned that the shaft-tomb assemblages of Mesoamerica, occupying much of Jalisco, Colima, and Nayarit in the early centuries of the Christian era, were not at all typical of what was going on in the Valley of Mexico at that time. The westward and northward spread of Mesoamerican influences was filtered by many locally autonomous groups that did not serve merely as conduits of Mesoamerican ideas and trade objects; hence the differences in routes of transmission and the differences in the receiving culture areas (such as the differences in Mesoamerican diffusion to the Hohokam and the Anasazi).

Evidences of Connection

The evidence for relationships between the Mesoamerican and southwestern culture areas includes cultural patterns of general nature: the use of corn/beans/squash agriculture and the clear priority of

such agriculture in Mesoamerica, objects that could only have been traded from one area to another (southwestern examples include macaws and cast copper objects), and similarities in form and style of artifacts that argue for diffusion from one culture area to another. An example in the Hohokam area is the abundant use of clay figurines, locally produced in their own styles but sharing a deep-seated characteristic of Mesoamerican cultures. These lines of evidence are discussed individually below.

General cultural patterns

Until recently, the ancient connections that must be invoked to explain Hohokam agricultural crops, pottery, and other basic features of sedentary agriculture could not be estimated because the known archaeology of west Mexico was largely confined to later periods; nothing was known that was sufficiently old to have served as a predecessor to Hohokam developments. The picture is still limited, but some early sites are now known for the west coast of Mexico. The late Preclassic (first centuries B.C.) is represented by the Morett site in Colima (Meighan 1972), a site contemporary with earliest Hohokam remains. Interestingly, this site has pottery figurines, sometimes with burials, and also simple shell bracelets, characteristic of Hohokam but not other southwestern cultures.

The other "early" culture of west Mexico is the shaft-tomb assemblage of Nayarit, Jalisco, and Colima, also dating back to the beginning of the Christian era (Meighan and Nicholson 1970, 1989). Known almost exclusively from grave lots, this culture bears little similarity to contemporary Hohokam material, which was far simpler in content and execution.

Still older west Mexican cultures are known but little defined, including the Capacha culture (Greengo and Meighan 1976; Kelly 1980), well back into the Preclassic. Unfortunately, this culture so far is almost entirely known only as a pottery assemblage of small and elaborate vessels, so it contributes no information about possible relationships to the north.

Although we assume that Hohokam culture began with an infusion of cultural elements from the south, and perhaps even with a "colonization" by peoples moving from river valleys in Mexico to the Gila River drainage, compelling evidence for this early contact remains absent from the archaeological record. There is abundant speculation about the size and nature of a "colonization" effort from Mexico; but in the absence of archaeological evidence, the various suggestions are plausible, but none can be confirmed. Although recognizing the reshaping of Mesoamerican elements by the Hohokam, Haury (1976:347) sees the Hohokam of A.D. 500–1100 as an "abridged Mesoamerican society."

On a later time level, after A.D. 500, general similarities with west Mexico are to be seen in the common red and brown pottery and a whole suite of artifact types discussed below (Haury 1976; see also Gumerman and Haury 1979).

Objects that Could Only have been Traded from One Area to Another

A few unquestionable objects must have come to the Hohokam area by way of direct trade from Mexico. Macaws and parrots, not native to the Southwest, have been found in both Hohokam and Anasazi contexts (Haury 1976:115; see also appendix by C. McKusick in this same volume). The most convincing evidence for trade is in the form of metal objects.

Metallurgy

The manufacture of metal objects, one of the key technological advances of human cultures, deserves special attention. In the United States, only in the Southwest are smelted and cast metal objects found in the archaeological record. These objects are compelling evidence for direct contact with Mesoamerica because the forms are identical to those in Mexico and copper bells are clearly to be seen as trade items brought from Mexico. The exact source is unknown, but the bells could have been traded from numerous locations, including Casas Grandes, Amapa, or other places (Vargas 1995).

Preliminary limited efforts to study metal artifacts from west Mexico were made by Meighan (1960) and Mountjoy (1969). Extensive and detailed research by Hosler (1985, 1988a, 1988b, 1988c, 1994) has provided the most complete knowledge of Prehispanic metallurgy in Mexico. Of great significance is her finding that the technology of metallurgy in west Mexico predated metal working in other areas of Mesoamerica by 300 to 400 years. This, in turn, is related to another long-distance connection between west Mexico and northern South America. Those who have studied the subject agree that metallurgy came to west Mexico from South America, probably

by a sea route along the Pacific Coast. Compelling evidence in the form of near identity of artifact types and classes is presented by Mountjoy (1969; see also Hosler 1988c). Although not directly relevant to the present discussion, this evidence of long-distance diffusion of an important technological innovation makes the West Coast/Hohokam contacts appear easy compared to the sea connections with South America.

Haury (1976:Figure 17.3) suggests the arrival of simple copper bells in Hohokam sites in the period from A.D. 500 to 1200, with more elaborate bells in the period after A.D. 1200. Recent studies of the age of copper objects in west Mexico indicate that the earliest date from perhaps A.D. 600, with the great majority of archaeological examples dating from after about A.D. 900. It is unlikely that the Hohokam got metal artifacts immediately after their introduction to Mexico because these items would have been rare and costly and not in regular trade to the hinterland in Arizona. The best guess for introduction of copper items to the Hohokam area would be perhaps A.D. 900, a chronology that agrees not only with that of metallurgy in west Mexico but also with the majority of Hohokam trade elements showing Mexican relationships.

Other Possible Trade Items

Haury (1937) believes the rubber balls found at Snaketown are made of guayule, a rubber-producing plant found in the Southwest and in northern Mexico. It is worth considering, however, that such objects associated with ball courts and ritual behavior might also be trade items. Perhaps trace-element analysis could resolve this question.

Obsidian, a widely traded raw material, was once thought to be obtained by the Hohokam from external areas, possibly California or Mexico. This notion was supported by the perception that there was relatively little obsidian in Hohokam sites. It was mainly, however, a lack of study, and I was surprised at the abundance of obsidian chipping waste on the surface of Snaketown. Shackley (1988) has shown that Hohokam obsidian was derived from local sources in Arizona.

The bracelets of marine shell, common in Hohokam contexts, are known to derive from the northern coast of the Gulf of California, across the present border with Mexico but not far enough south to be related to west Mexican cultures (Woodward 1936). The *idea* of shell bracelets may have originated farther south, however, because such items are found in Colima in the first century B.C. (Meighan 1972).

With the tremendous amounts of pottery found in Hohokam and west Mexican contexts, it would seem that some trade sherds would be present in the archaeological record. These are virtually absent.

Haury (1976:345) discusses 11 sherds from Snaketown believed to be of Mexican origin. The sherds are dated between A.D. 500 and 1100. I examined these sherds and believed they would all fit into the pottery from Amapa, Nayarit. The similarities, however, are generic and not diagnostic; some are plainware, one is a nondescript tripod leg, and some are red-on-brown pottery, which occurs universally in western Mexico. There is nothing conclusive about trade in this material. The reason for this is the widespread local manufacture of pottery, with all areas producing their own wares that were not widely traded. In particular, the exceptional ceramic productions of Mesoamerica, such as plumbate and the many-colored polychromes of later west Mexico, were unlikely to find their way to a comparative cultural backwater in Arizona.

Pyrite mirrors on sandstone backing are generally considered to be trade items from Mesoamerica to the Hohokam region.

The evidence for trade in the north-south direction, from Hohokam to locations in Mexico, is virtually nil. Turquoise, available in the Southwest, may well have gone south and may indeed have been a stimulus for trade relationships. Nothing of recognizable Hohokam origin has so far been identified in west Mexico.

Similarities in Form and Style of Artifacts

Traditional trait lists of similarities between west Mexico and the Hohokam area have been compiled by several scholars. Some of these similarities are in trade items as discussed above. Others provide less-clearcut evidence of connection and may have alternative explanations, including, for example, platform mounds, astronomical observatories such as at Casa Grande (Arizona), and iconographic interpretations of artistic elements. The number and variety of similarities is, however, certainly sufficient to convince any observer that the Hohokam area saw an exten-

sion of basic Mesoamerican cultural ideas, diluted and limited to be sure but enough to show Mesoamerica as a parent culture.

Stylistic similarities in pottery types have been previously mentioned.

Textiles

Cotton is one of the plants introduced from Mexico to the Southwest, being widely distributed by A.D. 500. Anawalt (1992) points out that southwestern cotton garments were similar to Andean-style cotton tunics. She comments on one from Tonto National Monument: "The tunic-like shape of this cotton-fiber shirt appears only in west Mexico and South America."

Anawalt also cites Teague's suggestion that prehistoric southwestern textile traditions do not represent a locally derived development but were introduced from west Mexico.

Pottery Figurines

The unusual abundance of pottery figurines is one of the features that marks off Hohokam from other southwestern cultures. These figurines are merely a stylistic variant of such items in many Mesoamerican areas, dating well back into the Preclassic. They are, however, locally made in the Hohokam area and do not represent trade items. Of note is the number of dog figurines in Hohokam sites, also fairly common in such west Mexico sites as Morret, Colima, beginning in the first century B.C. and extending for centuries thereafter (Meighan 1972).

Stone Sculptures

A comparison that has received little attention involves the presence of small anthropomorphic stone sculptures, often of crude execution. These are not common and not always found in site contexts, but the west Mexico examples are summarized well by Williams (1992), and comparable examples are illustrated from Snaketown (Haury 1976:Frontispiece and Figure 11.24). Williams illustrates several examples from Jalisco of small anthropomorphic sculptures incorporating a bowl (Williams 1992:Figures 12–15, figures ranging from 25 cm to 32 cm in height; there is also a crude seated figure holding a bowl, 51 cm tall). The absence of dating for these figures is related to their known ethnohistoric use as idols and their deposition in shrines, which may be at some distance from residential sites. "Idols" of small and simple human and animal figures of stone extended to historic times and were noted by Lumholtz (1900:24) for the Huichol of west Mexico.

Small zoomorphic stone bowls are also present (Williams 1992:Figures 161–168), all from Jalisco. They are quite shallow, and two are rectangular, suggesting that they may be related to the stone palettes of Hohokam culture.

Finally, Hohokam collections include some stone items that, if found in Mexico, would be referred to as handled "incesarios" of the frying pan type.

Because items of these kinds are associated with religious and ritual behavior, they add to indications of some sort of diffusion of religious ideas from west Mexico northward. This is of particular interest because it does not involve commercial trade in luxury goods but argues for a kind of missionary influence—visitors bringing concepts and ideas to be grafted onto local religious structures. This also supports the consideration that contacts along the west coast route were not merely with traders carrying a sack of goods but probably included many other kinds of visitors as well.

Abstracting from trait lists developed by Haury (1976) and myself (1959), plus a general survey of the literature, artifact similarities are summarized here in Table 15.1.

Problems for the Future

That "more work is needed" is evident. Some of the problems that impede studies of ancient contact along the Mexican west coast include the following:

- The dominance of pottery in the archaeological record, plus the fact that most decorated pottery styles were locally made and used, and very limited amounts of pottery were widely traded. Large excavations such as Snaketown and Casas Grandes have very few evidences of trade in identifiable pottery types, and trade pottery would be largely unrecognizable in the earlier periods when plainwares dominated in both areas.
- The trade in perishable materials (skins, salt, feathers, etc.), which is largely invisible in the archaeological record even though it must have been important.
- The emphasis in the trade record of luxury items (turquoise, copper objects, etc.), which are found

Table 15.1. Parallels between Hohokam Archaeology and that of the West Coast of Mexico.

Architectural	Ball courts with clay walls
	Platform mounds
Burial Practices	Cremations with offerings
Stone Artifacts	Lava metates
	¾ grooved axes
	"Plummets" of lava (may be functional drills or abraders)
	Stone discs, including pyrite-encrusted discs
	Small stone sculptures bearing receptacles on head or in lap
	"Cuchillos" of polished stone
	Turquoise mosaic
	Handled censers ("frying pan incensarios" in Mexico; Hohokam examples are stone, Mexican ones ceramic)
	Stone clubs
Shell Artifacts	Pendants in the form of frogs
	Shell bracelets
	Human effigies in shell
Metal Artifacts	Copper bells
Pottery	Effigy vessels
	Clay figurines, human and dogs
	Tripod vessels
	Spindle whorls
	Ear spools
	Nose plugs
Miscellaneous	Rubber balls
	Macaws and parrots

NOTE: Omitted are stylistic details (such as the intertwined snakes motif) and the generic similarities from early times (such as agriculture, red/brown ceramics, etc.). Where detailed dating is available, most of these parallels date after A.D. 500, and many date after A.D. 900.

only in "high status" contexts, are relatively rare in the everyday archaeological record, and are unlikely to be found in small and limited excavations. It is noteworthy, for example, that the metal artifacts in the Hohokam record are luxury goods and do not include such everyday metal items as awls, needles, and fishhooks, even though the latter are common in west Mexican contexts.

- The transmission of "ideas," which came from contact with other peoples, is only indirectly evident in the archaeological record and can generally be seen only in stylistic elements of architecture, artistic styles, and the like. Because these are generally reinterpreted by the recipients of external ideas, it takes a considerable suite of finds to provide convincing evidence.

Is there any way these problems can be overcome? Perhaps new technological approaches can resolve some of the difficulties. For example, trace element analysis can now pinpoint the origin of many objects. Such trade items as jade, turquoise, and metal objects may well lend themselves to unequivocal identification of their sources. This would be particularly valuable for turquoise because it could establish trade from the Hohokam area to Mesoamerica; at present all evidence is for contacts going the other way.

It is also possible that DNA studies can ascertain the kinfolk of traders and visitors who happened to die far from home. Reyman (1978) looks for Mesoamerican merchants who might be buried in the Southwest; identifications are hard to prove without DNA evidence. Such studies of ancient bones are in their infancy but may prove to be compelling evidence in the future. It would be particularly valuable if DNA studies could establish a "colonization" group entering the Hohokam area from the south. Of course, it is necessary that skeletal material be preserved for such studies to be possible, and the present requirement, issued by the United States government, for returning all bones to Indians for reburial will eliminate the possibility for this kind of study. In addition, the prevalence of cremation in Hohokam sites will also place limits on most kinds of physical anthropological analysis. Nonetheless, it may be the physical anthropologists who will in the future provide some indisputable evidence to clarify the picture seen in the cultural similarities identified by archaeology.

16

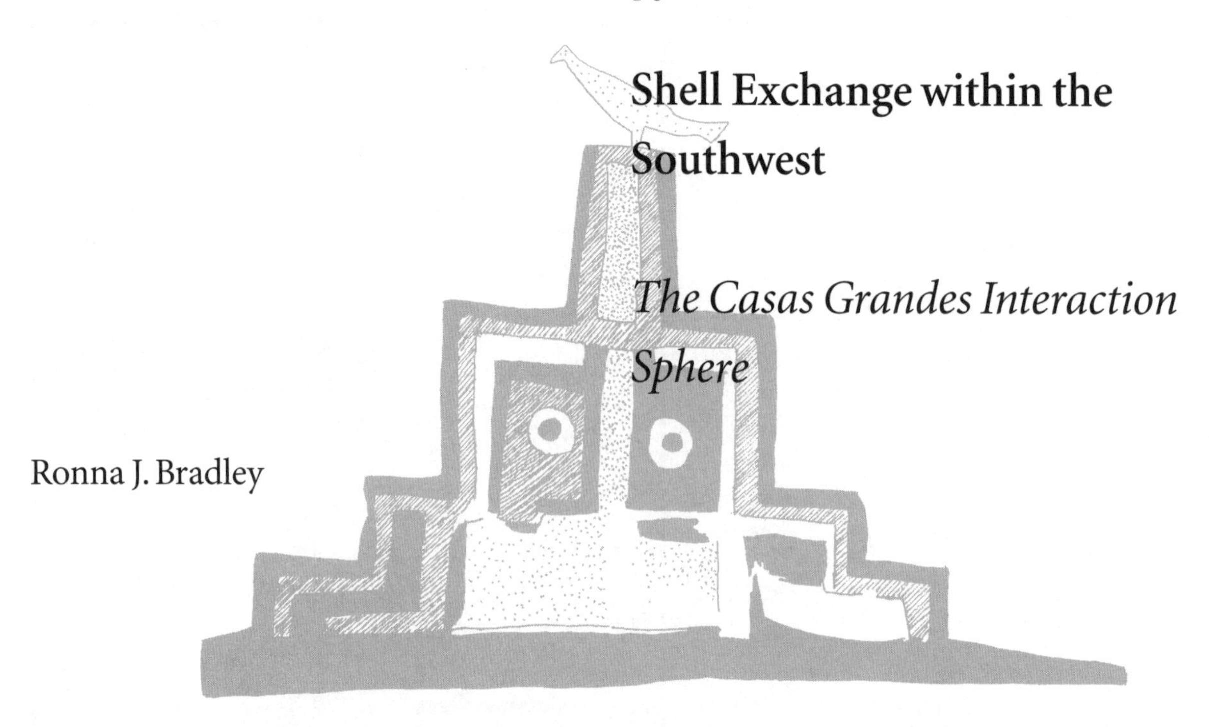

Shell Exchange within the Southwest

The Casas Grandes Interaction Sphere

Ronna J. Bradley

MARINE SHELL ORNAMENTS were widely exchanged across the Southwest during prehistoric times. As early as 1938 Donald Brand traced the sources of southwestern archaeological shell to the Panamic, Californian, and Atlantic faunal provinces. In addition, he defined several routes of trade that followed natural geographical features such as rivers and drainages. Later studies added additional sites and shell species (Kean 1965; Tower 1945).

The north-south and east-west trade routes defined by Brand (1938) converged in the Middle Gila of southern Arizona. Some of the largest quantities of shells occurred in this area, leading Brand to believe that the Hohokam may have been major suppliers of shell ornaments to other parts of the Southwest. Subsequent research has focused on the ritual and economic importance of marine shell in Hohokam society and the Hohokam role as agents in the southwestern shell industry (Haury 1976; Howard 1985; McGuire 1985; McGuire and Howard 1987).

Despite the fact that the Hohokam area and southern periphery of the Papaguería contained quantities of shell ornaments and debris, the largest quantity of shell in the Southwest has been recovered from Paquimé, or Casas Grandes, in Chihuahua, Mexico (Figure 16.1). The most recent revisions in dates place Casas Grandes within an approximate A.D. 1200–1450 time period (Lekson 1984b:59; Ravesloot et al. 1986; Dean and Ravesloot 1993).

Over 3.9 million shell ornaments were excavated from Paquimé during the late 1950s and 1960s (Di Peso 1974). In addition, museums throughout the country contain thousands of nonprovenienced shell ornaments from the Casas Grandes area. It is very clear that shell was an important component of Casas Grandes society. However, in spite of the quantity of marine shell, the vast majority was restricted to storehouses or workshops. Shell does not appear to have been widely available to the general populace. The burial data from Paquimé indicate that very little of the material was interred with the inhabitants during the florescence of the Medio period (Di Peso et al. 1974:8:325–415; Ravesloot 1988), as opposed to the earlier Viejo period at the Convento Site, where 99 percent of the shell was found with burials. Most of the shell at Paquimé was confined to storehouses in Units 8, 14, and 16 (Figure 16.2). Although the shell ornaments are believed to have been used primarily for exchange (Di Peso 1974:2:627–629), there are problems associated with sourcing marine shell, delineat-

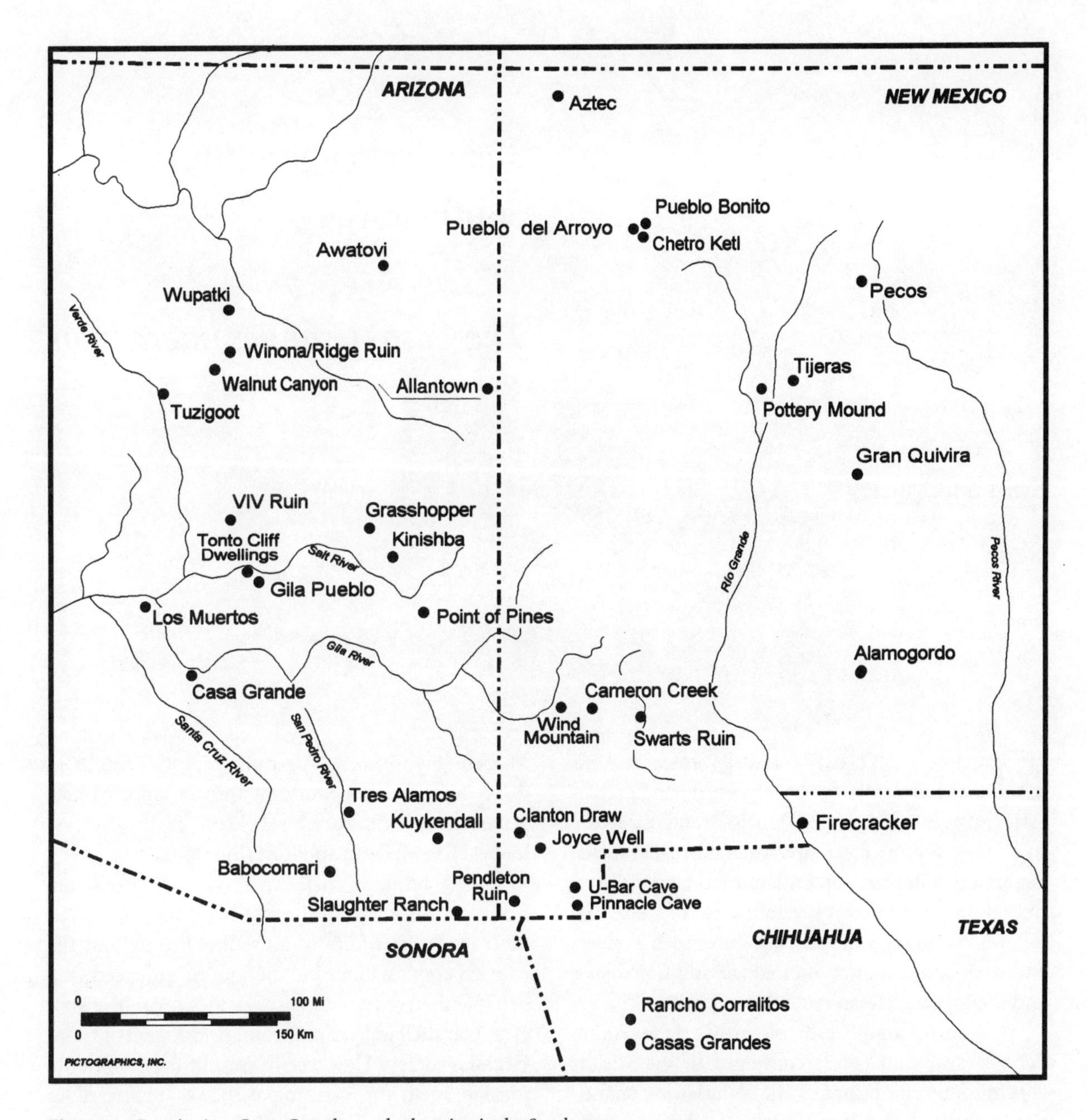

Figure 16.1. Paquimé, or Casas Grandes, and other sites in the Southwest.

ing ornament manufacturing locales, and tracing their distribution across the landscape (Bradley 1986, 1987, 1993).

It has been suggested that a competitive situation developed between the Hohokam area and Casas Grandes over the control of shell ornament production and distribution (Di Peso et al. 1974:8:168), but a more detailed examination of the data is needed. The nature of exchange networks within the Southwest cannot be thoroughly understood until procurement, manufacturing, and distributional data from sites across the region are analyzed and integrated.

The immense quantity of marine shell and other exotica at Casas Grandes raises questions concerning the origins and purpose of the material and the position of Casas Grandes within shell exchange networks in the Southwest and northern Mexico. Were the shells at Casas Grandes used for exchange, or were they stored wealth? Were they dispersed to other sites in the nearby area or used in long distance ex-

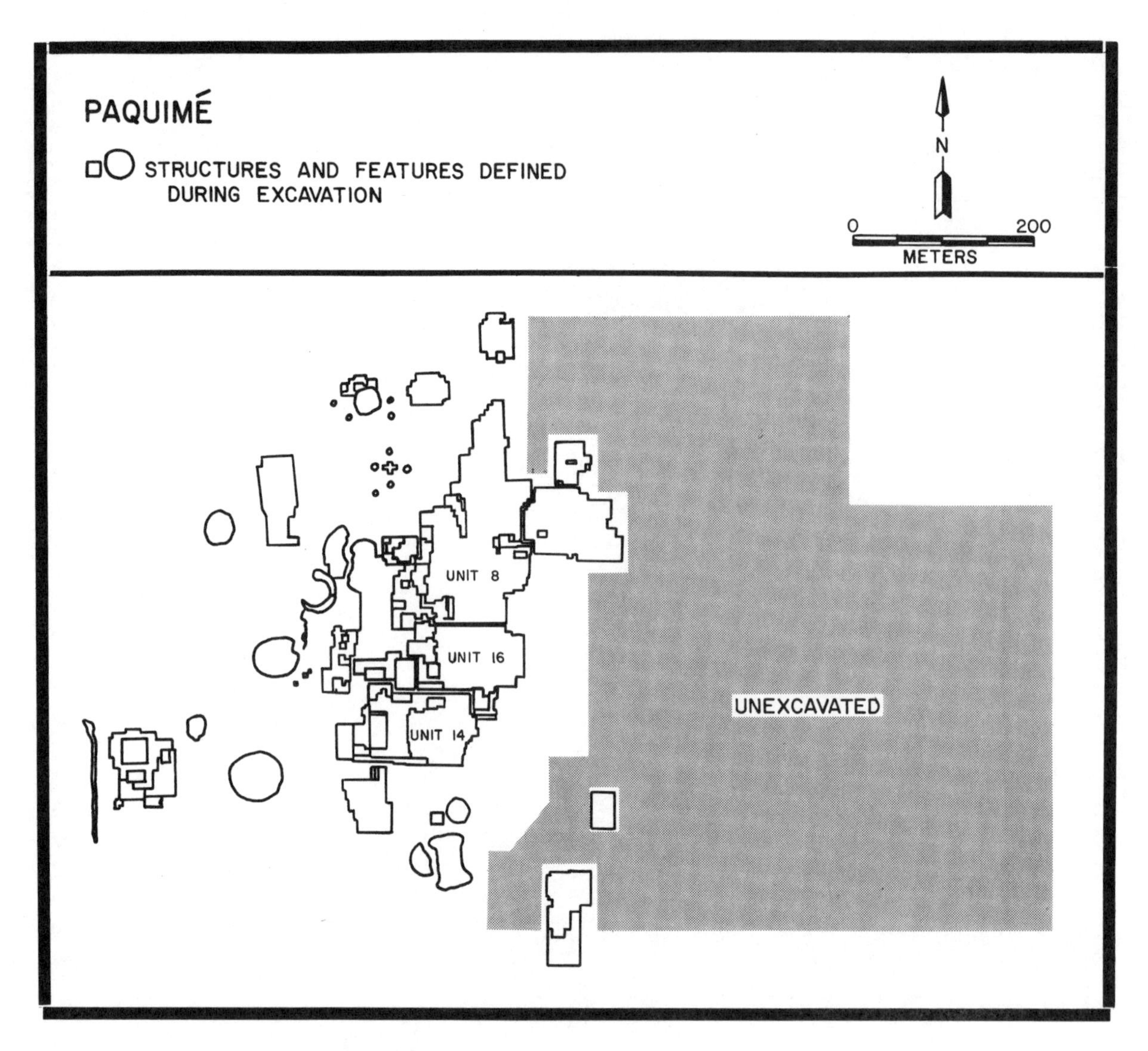

Figure 16.2. Plan map of the site of Paquimé (redrawn from Di Peso 1974).

change? Where were they obtained? How did the rise of Casas Grandes affect the Hohokam shell economy, or did it have any effect at all? These and other questions need to be addressed in order to clarify the role of Casas Grandes and to understand its relationship to other sites in the Southwest and Mesoamerica. This chapter constitutes part of a dissertation project (Bradley 1996) that examined marine shell ornament procurement and distribution in an attempt to define patterns of shell exchange and to address questions concerning the role of Casas Grandes within southwestern exchange networks.

Distributional Patterns in the Southwest: Regional Stylistic Repertoires

In order to define distinct networks using shell ornaments, several expectations were developed. The first proposition asserts that with increased availability of goods through the introduction of new suppliers, there would be a concordant increase in the variation within assemblages. Second, the content of assemblages is expected to be more similar among participants within single exchange systems than between those in different exchange networks. The third expectation suggests that specific stylistic markers follow nodes of interaction. These are discussed in more detail in the following sections.

Table 16.1. Ornament Types by Site.

SITE	BEADS	BEAD PEND	BRACELET	IND. FRAG	TINK-LERS	PEN-DANTS	RINGS	DISK	MISC. OBJECTS	UN-WORKED	WORKED	OTHER	TOTAL
Alamogordo	73	1			5	6			1				86
Allantown	7,884	2,920	4			3		2					10,813
Pueblo del Arroyo	25	14	5	2	1	4							51
Awatovi	64	2	13	19	12	15	2	3		4	5	9	148
Aztec	76	48			1	1					1		127
Babocomari	1,845	2	108	70	4	13					3	1	2,046
Pueblo Bonito	2,342	1,797	97	100		33			5	2	15	19	4,410
Cameron Creek	6,982	26	292		7	17				20			7,344
Casa Grande	385	15	70	112	72	27	12	3	2	140	15	43	896
Casas Grandes	36,324	160	15		334	62				1		2	36,898
Chetro Ketl	4,272												4,272
Chihuahua	6,434	317		1	37	15				3		1	6,808
Clanton Draw	347	22	103	2			1					2	477
Firecracker	67			16									83
Gila Pueblo	11,427	5	21	7	3	38	6	4	2	9	1	1	11,524
Gran Quivira	131	1		13	9	51		1			25	4	235
Grasshopper	14,900	11	121	52	206	100	29	1	3	11	16	8	15,458
Joyce Well	976												976
Kinishba	1,596	6	34	12	18	62	6	1	2	5	5	4	1,751
Kuykendall	2,734		4			1							2,739
Los Muertos	174	4	240	36	11	49	26	22	12	891	68	46	1,579
NA 1785	206	27	172	4		6	3	2	1		5	1	427
NA 2131			17	1							1	4	23
NA 2133	28	5	45	17		1	3		1		1	1	102
NA 2134	196	29	83	4		3	2			5	4	2	328
NA 2135			1			1							2
NA 3474							1						1
NA 3644	10	1	22	1							1		35
NA 3673	85	7	33			3					5	1	134
Pecos	1,043	25	3	260	81	124		3	4	6	63	10	1,622
Pendleton Ruin	6		7	2	2	3			1				21
Pinnacle Cave	56											1	57
Pottery Mound	15	2		1	7	1				3	1		30
Slaughter Ranch	12												12
Swarts Ruin	9,336	48	235		1	21			23		17		9,681
Tijeras	52	11			3	8					1		75
Tonto Ruins	18		10	15	14	4	1	1		3	2		68
Tres Alamos	17	5	418	106	12	44	29	2	6		11	8	658
Tuzigoot	1,903	31	21	15	19	11		1		15	7	2	2,025
U-Bar Cave	546					1							547
VIV	3,885	2				1							3,888
W:10:15	3		3										6
W:10:37	12	1	8	1	8	8	2	1			1		42
W:10:47	4					1					1		6
W:10:50	885	30	42	33	32	40	4	3	11	2	1	6	1,089
W:10:51	1		3		3		1					0	8

Table 16.1 continued

SITE	BEADS	BEAD PEND	BRACELET	IND FRAG	TINK-LERS	PEN-DANTS	RINGS	DISK	MISC. OBJECTS	UN-WORKED	WORKED	OTHER	TOTAL
W:10:52	272		1			1						0	274
W:10:56	2		6	1		1	1					0	11
W:10:57			2			1						0	3
W:10:65	1					1						0	2
W:9:123	1538	122	41	4	1	16	3		11		3	2	1741
W:10:8			1			1						0	2
W:6:5			2									0	2
W:9:10	2	1	3						1			0	7
W:9:39		1	1									0	2
W:9:72	177	25				1						0	203
W:9:83			2	1								0	3
W:10:111			4			1	1					0	6
Walnut Canyon	208	33	8	19	5	3			1	3	2	2	284
Wind Mountain	253	13	64	2		5	1		2		3	3	346
Wupatki	201	38	47	31	45	18	5		3	2	7	10	407
Total	120,031	5808	2432	960	953	827	139	50	92	1125	291	193	132,901

The presence of two or more suppliers or exchange systems within a region would result in an increase in the diversity of assemblages. An increase in diversity would develop through time as more suppliers became involved in the exchange networks or if inhabitants began to participate in more than one exchange network. Richness and diversity measures are useful for addressing these types of issues and are discussed below.

In addition to diversity, other assumptions assert that the general content of assemblages would be similar among participants within an exchange system. The proportions of beads, bracelets, or tinklers would generally be more similar within an individual exchange system than among different systems. In order to evaluate this expectation, principal components and cluster analyses are used to define factors and patterns that account for most of the variability in the assemblages.

Another assumption is that specific stylistic markers may follow the nodes of an exchange system. Because exchange involves social interaction, and ideas and beliefs move within the infrastructure, participants may adopt specific stylistic symbols that represent specific religious or social entities. For instance, in Mesoamerica specific icons representing fertility, fire, death, war, and other concepts are found across great distances and are believed to represent the general spread of religious and social beliefs across a broad area. In the Southwest the spread of the Kachina Cult and Southwestern Cult during late prehistoric times (Adams 1991; Crown 1994) represents a similar phenomenon. Specific artifact styles are used to investigate this expectation.

Diversity and Richness of the Assemblages

Diversity measures of the richness and evenness of artifact assemblages are useful ways of looking at variation on a regional level. It has been suggested that if Casas Grandes became involved in shell exchange late in the prehistoric sequence, that involvement would result in an increase in the diversity of shell ornament types in the Southwest. Rather than a single exchange network stemming from the Hohokam area, the introduction of an additional supplier (Casas Grandes) would be expected to effect an increase in the diversity of artifacts.

With this in mind, analysis of the richness and evenness of the assemblages was conducted using the ornament type counts by site (Table 16.1). Richness describes the number of classes within an assemblage, and evenness refers to the uniformity of distribution or the evenness of the counts across the classes (Kintigh 1984). The diversity program DIVERS, developed by Kintigh (1984, 1989), uses a

Figure 16.3. Diversity plot of type richness.

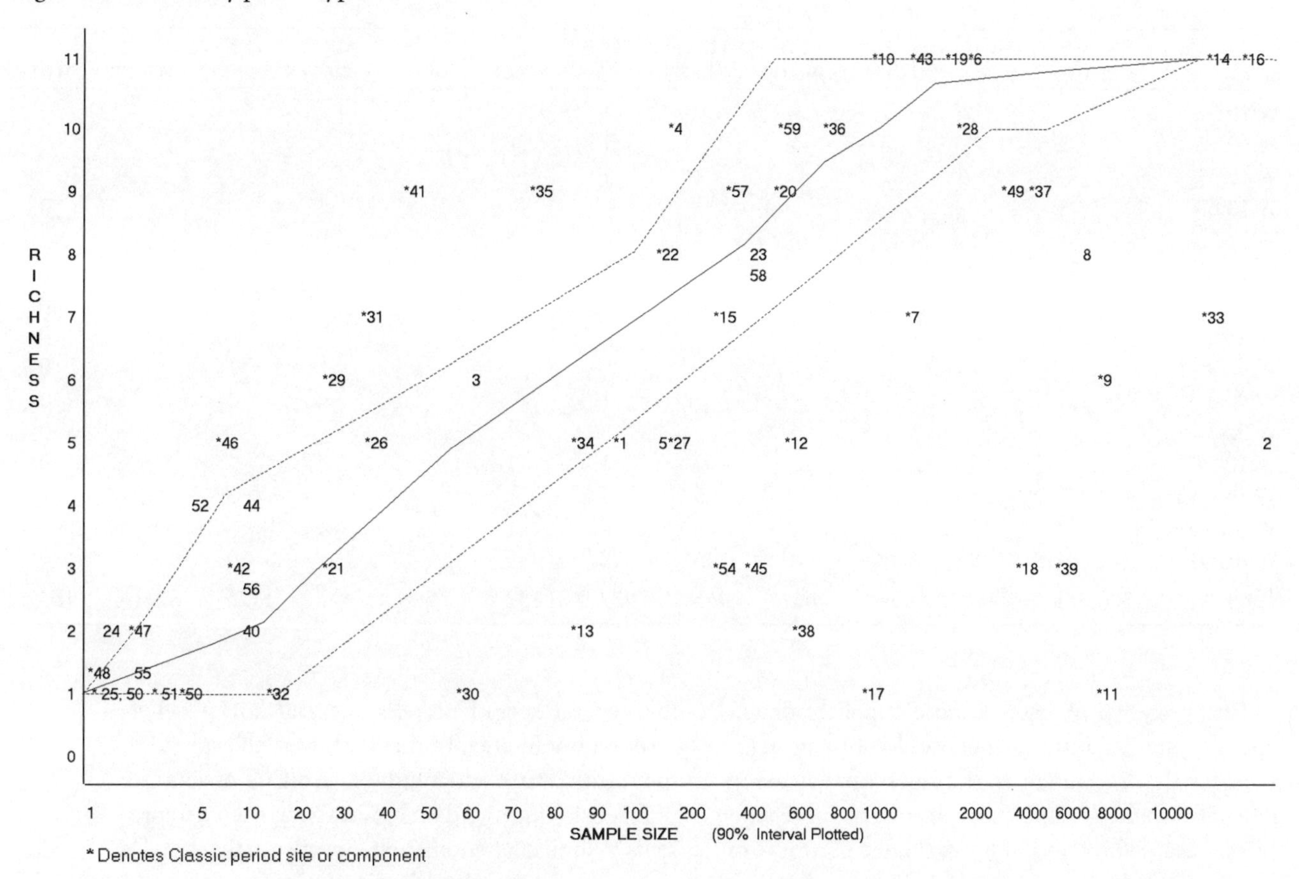

Site Code for Richness and Evenness (Figures 16.3 and 16.4).

Alamogordo	1	Grasshopper	16	Pottery Mound	31	w:10:56	46
Allantown	2	Joyce Well	17	Slaughter Ranch	32	w:10:57	47
Pueblo del Arr	3	Kuykendall	18	Swarts Ruin	33	w:10:65	48
Awatovi	4	Los Muertos	19	Tijeras	34	w:9:123	49
Aztec	5	NA 1785	20	Tonto Ruins	35	w:10:8	50
Kinishba	6	NA 2131	21	Tres Alamos	36	w:6:5	51
Babocomari	7	NA 2133	22	Tuzigoot	37	w:9:10	52
Pueblo Bonito	8	NA 2134	23	U-Bar Cave	38	w:9:39	53
Cameron Creek	9	NA 2135	24	VIV Ruin	39	w:9:72	54
Casa Grande	10	NA 3474	25	w:10:15	40	w:9:83	55
Chetro Ketl	11	NA 3644	26	w: 10:37	41	w:10:111	56
Clanton Draw	12	NA 3673	27	w:10:47	42	Walnut Canyon	57
Firecracker	13	Pecos	28	w:10:50	43	Wind Mountain	58
Gila Pueblo	14	Pendleton Ruin	29	w:10:51	44	Wupatki	59
Gran Quivira	15	Pinnacle Cave	30	w:10:52	45		

Figure 16.4. Diversity plot of type evenness.

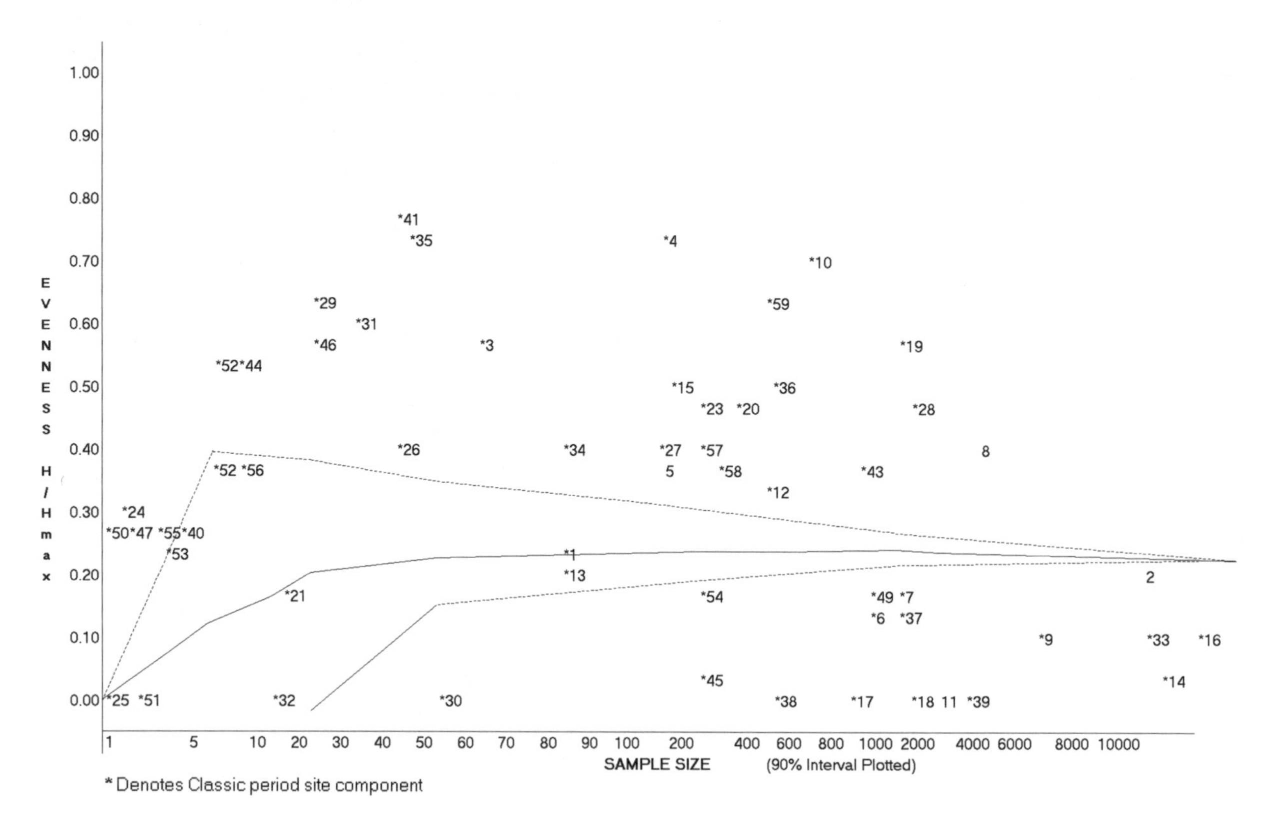

Monte Carlo technique and H/Hmax (also known as a J-score) as a measure of evenness. This particular diversity program is ideal for this project because it controls for differing sample sizes. A companion program, DIVPLT, provides a graphic display of the computations. The program uses a 90 percent confidence interval, with data points displayed around the simulated model distributions.

Figure 16.3 illustrates the distribution of sites by artifact type richness. Note that Classic period sites (post–A.D. 1200) (Bradley 1996:25) tend to exhibit the highest richness overall, and several exceed the 90 percent confidence interval. Interestingly, some of the larger Preclassic sites (pre–A.D. 1200) (Bradley 1996:25) such as Pueblo Bonito, Allantown, Swarts Ruin, and Cameron Creek show lower than expected richness. A group of very low richness sites includes primarily small Salado sites from southern Arizona and New Mexico. Within the expected range is a group comprising Sinagua and Hohokam sites. Exceeding the expected richness are Classic period Hohokam sites, Western Pueblo, and late Anasazi sites.

Figure 16.4 illustrates the evenness of types by site. A large number of sites, such as Casa Grande, Los Muertos, Awatovi, Tonto, and W:10:37, have higher than expected evenness. Others, including Swarts, Cameron Creek, Grasshopper, and Gila Pueblo, exhibit lower than expected evenness. Low evenness generally reflects relatively uneven dispersal of the numbers' different types. In many cases the low scores result from high numbers of beads found within a few contexts, such as at Grasshopper, Gila Pueblo, Cameron Creek, and Swarts.

These data form patterns that appear to be related to general temporal trends of increased diversity through time and suggest a probable increase in the number of exchange networks during the Classic period. With the participation of Casas Grandes in shell exchange during the Classic period, the introduction of new ornament types and species could be expected. The large Western Pueblo and late Anasazi sites exhibit a relatively high diversity or richness of ornament types, whereas early Mogollon and Anasazi sites demonstrate a similar considerably lower richness. Within the trend of ornament richness that increases through time, sites on the fringes of the

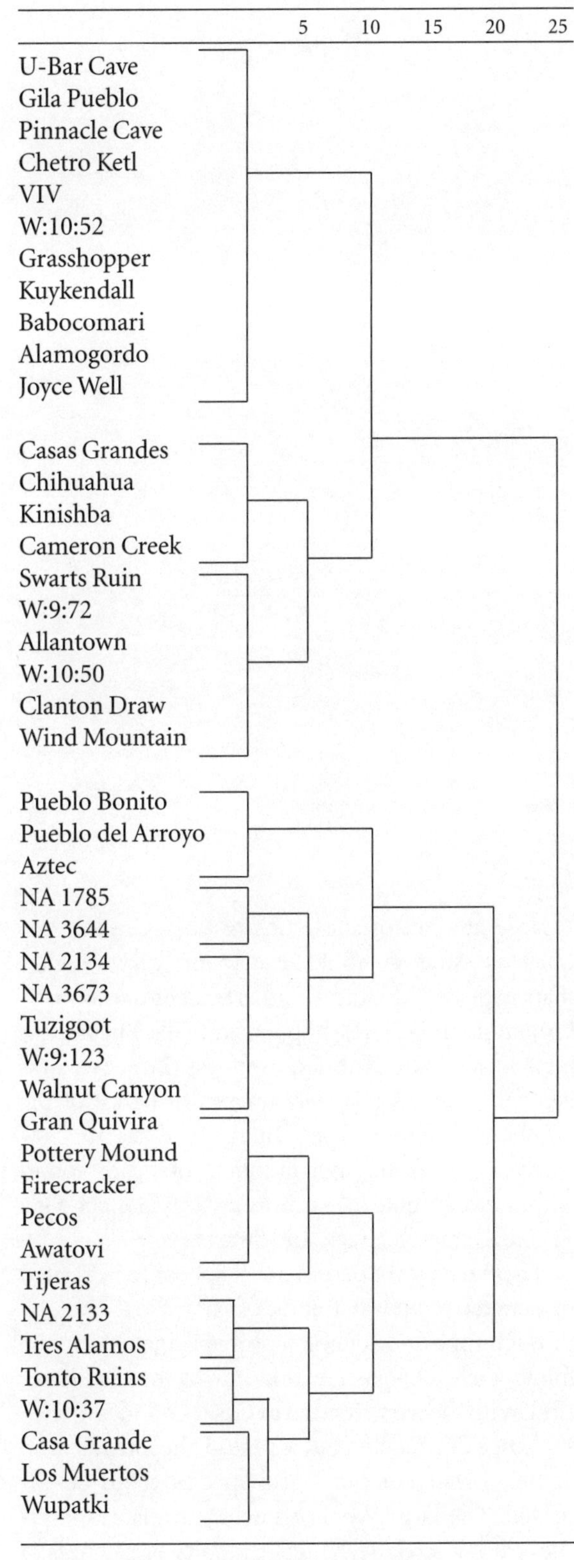

Figure 16.5. Cluster analysis of all shell artifacts.

Southwest, such as Gran Quivira and Pecos, have richness levels that lie within the expected ranges but are not quite as high as some of the Western Pueblo sites. Unlike the Mogollon and Anasazi, Preclassic period sites in the Sinagua area have richness scores that lie within the expected range, showing higher artifact diversity for their sample sizes than larger sites such as Pueblo Bonito. At the same time, contrary to their Western Pueblo contemporaries, notably low richness is demonstrated at some Salado sites in southern New Mexico and Arizona.

This diversity analysis demonstrates an increased richness in shell ornament assemblages through time. Early assemblages do not approach the richness or diversity of many of the late sites in the Hohokam, Western Pueblo, and particularly the Casas Grandes area. Diversity measures are a useful way of observing patterns in the general structure of artifact assemblages over broad regions, but they may mask some of the variability of individual sites (Plog and Hegmon 1993). Two sites with differing sample sizes may have similar richness values, but the two might contain very different assemblages. Therefore, in addition to the diversity measure, other techniques designed to identify more specific patterns are also implemented in an effort to investigate more specific patterns in artifact style.

Defining Regional Stylistic Repertoires

Principal components analysis using the SPSS-PC factor program (Norusis 1988) was initiated on site assemblages with sample totals in excess of 30 artifacts in order to define the major artifact categories in the assemblage. The database was made up of percentages of the following artifact types: disk beads, whole-shell natural beads, modified natural beads, bead pendants, bracelets, unidentified fragments, tinklers, pendants, rings, and other types. The principal components analysis resulted in three factors that account for over 61 percent of the variability.

Factor 1 was negatively loaded for disk beads but had high loadings for indeterminate fragments, tinklers, pendants, and rings. The second factor was loaded for natural beads and bracelets, as well as rings. The third factor loadings included primarily disk and modified natural beads and bead pendants.

A hierarchical cluster analysis (Ward's method) of the factor scores showed regional stylistic repertoires

that form two to three major groupings (Figure 16.5). First, a distinct cluster is formed by sites from the Western Pueblo tradition, Salado, Mogollon, and Casas Grandes areas. A second large grouping is formed by a cluster containing early Anasazi and Sinagua sites and a cluster with late Anasazi sites and Hohokam assemblages. These clusters are in agreement with other data that indicate strong interaction between the Hohokam and Sinagua and the Sinagua and Anasazi (Bradley 1994; Fish et al. 1980), as well as interaction within the traditional Salado/Western Pueblo area (Crown 1994).

The Western Pueblo/Mogollon/Casas Grandes cluster includes Gila Pueblo, Babocomari, other Salado sites, most of the Mogollon assemblages, and the majority of the Western Pueblo sites. Sites in this cluster are contemporaneous with Casas Grandes, although several, such as Swarts and Cameron Creek, have early components as well.

The most compelling patterns are derived when the marine shells alone are considered (excluding the freshwater and land snails). Because some sites, such as Pecos and Gran Quivira, contain quantities of freshwater shell, their groupings may reflect patterns in locally obtainable species rather than marine shell. The results support the patterns derived from the analysis of all shell but provide a clearer picture of the relationship of late Anasazi sites to others in the Southwest.

The principal components analysis defined three factor scores responsible for 62 percent of the variability. Factor 1 has high negative loadings for disk beads and high loadings for fragments, tinklers, pendants, and rings. Factor 2 reveals high negative loadings for natural beads and high loadings for bracelets. Factor 3 features high negative loadings for disk beads and high loadings for modified natural beads and bead pendants.

A hierarchical cluster analysis of the 44 site assemblages resulted in three groupings. Hohokam sites cluster with Wupatki, NA 2133, W:10:37, and Awatovi (Figure 16.6). Another grouping is formed by the early Anasazi sites, other sites in the Winona/Ridge Ruin area, Tuzigoot, Walnut Canyon, and Turkey Creek (W:9:123). Finally, the remaining sites group into two tightly related clusters that contain sites from the Mogollon, Western Pueblo, late Anasazi, and Casas Grandes areas (Figure 16.7). One group contains Grasshopper, Gila Pueblo, W:10:52, Swarts

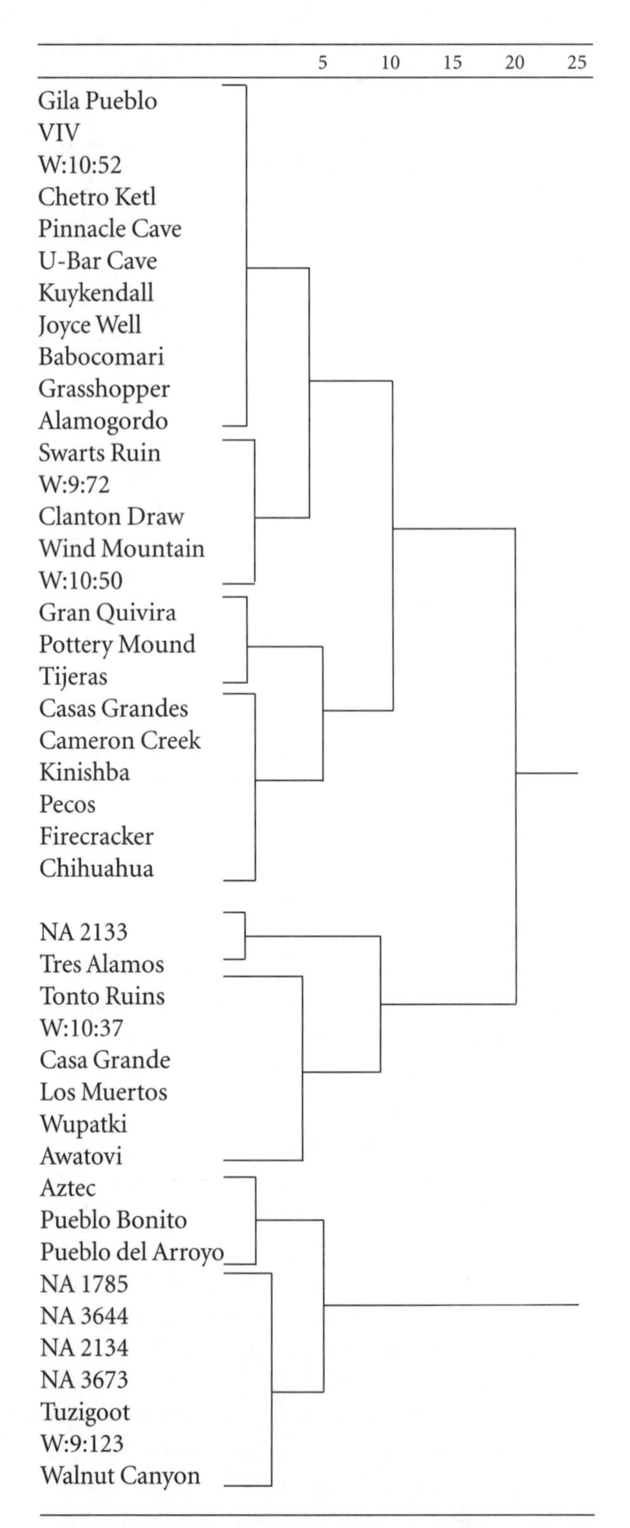

Figure 16.6. Cluster analysis of the marine shell artifacts.

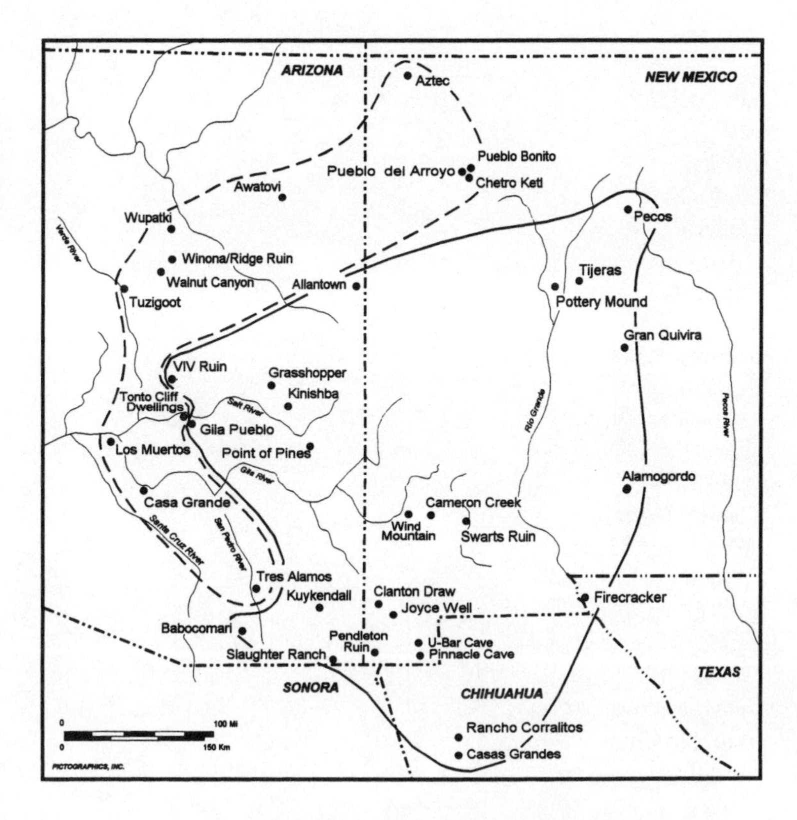

Figure 16.7. Results of the cluster analysis of marine shell, illustrating the Hohokam and Casas Grandes networks.

Ruin, Wind Mountain, and Point of Pines Pueblo (w:10:50), among others. The final grouping consists of Gran Quivira, Pottery Mound, Tijeras, Casas Grandes, Cameron Creek, Kinishba, Pecos, and others.

These clusters represent two to three distinct stylistic repertoires that link different regions. Because marine shell is available primarily through exchange, the repertoires likely represent networks of interaction. One network was centered in the Hohokam, Sinagua, and early Anasazi areas. The distinct cluster formed by the early Anasazi and Sinagua sites is probably related to the Hohokam but represents earlier occupations than the sites in the Hohokam cluster. Another network was associated with the Casas Grandes, Mogollon, late Anasazi, and Western Pueblo traditions. Within the two major networks there is some degree of variability that reflects more complex relationships. In the Hohokam group the Sinagua sites (except for Wupatki and NA 2133) show stronger affinities to the early Anasazi than to late Hohokam assemblages. Similarly, within the Western Pueblo area variability in assemblages results in Kinishba's being more closely related to the Casas Grandes group, whereas nearby Grasshopper is slightly more distant. That is also exhibited in the Mogollon assemblages, with Cameron Creek grouping closely with Casas Grandes and Swarts Ruin showing more affinity to the Wind Mountain and Grasshopper cluster. In addition, several sites are consistently associated with distant areas. In the Point of Pines area, Turkey Creek (w:9:123) and w:10:37 are associated with the Sinagua/Anasazi and Hohokam clusters, respectively, and the remaining Point of Pines sites group with Casas Grandes.

The generalized patterns exhibited by the cluster analyses are mimicked when the Paquimé assemblage is added to the data set. The same groupings of Hohokam, Sinagua, and early Anasazi are defined, along with the Casas Grandes, Mogollon, Western Pueblo, and late Anasazi sites. The patterns indicate regional and panregional stylistic repertoires, but they also display a degree of variability that may reflect more complex relationships. Within specific regions there are sites that consistently align with distant areas, and this variation is supported by data derived from the distribution of specific artifact styles.

Stylistic Markers of Interaction

During the course of this research, several distinctive ornament shapes were noted (Figure 16.8), and their distribution is worthy of discussion. In particular, the distributions of *Glycymeris* rings and perforated pendants show intriguing patterns. *Glycymeris* frogs and *Pecten vogdesi* pendants are among those special forms in the Hohokam area that have been investigated (Nelson 1981, 1991), along with distinctive cut pendant styles and bilobed beads. Within the context of this project, only a small number of these types of ornaments were recorded outside of the Hohokam area.

Glycymeris frogs are found in the Casas Grandes collection, at Gila Pueblo, Grasshopper, Swarts, w:10:37, and Point of Pines Pueblo (w:10:50). Nelson (1991:29, 32, 53) documents other occurrences of frogs (approximately 52 total) at more than 15 sites in the Hohokam area, including Snaketown, Casa Grande, Los Muertos, Las Acequias, Beardsley Canal, Bartley Site, Fortified Hill, Hodges, Rabid Ruin, University Indian Ruin, Whiptail Ruin, Las Fosas, and others, but he indicates that the frogs are primarily

Hohokam Classic period (A.D. 1100–1450) (Haury 1976:338) manifestations. One naturalistic frog was noted in the Paquimé collection, and another stylized zoomorph could represent a frog.

Pecten vogdesi pendants have a much wider distribution than the frogs, with over 900 specimens recorded from over 22 sites in the Hohokam area alone (Nelson 1991:29). Nelson (1991:31) found *Pecten vogdesi* at Snaketown, Grewe, Casa Grande, La Casitas, Los Muertos, Las Acequias, Los Hornos, Pueblo de las Canopas, Valshni Village, Hodges, Cashion, Gu Achi, Frogtown, University Indian Ruin, Gatlin, Citrus, and a number of other sites. Despite his suggestions that these types of pendants have a limited distribution and may be associated with status, they occur in great numbers and appear to be very widespread. During the course of this research, *Pecten vogdesi* pendants were documented at Kinishba, Cameron Creek, Casa Grande, Clanton Draw, Los Muertos, Walnut Canyon, Wind Mountain, NA 1785, NA 2134, Pecos, Tres Alamos, and Point of Pines Pueblo (W:10:50) but not in great quantities. Only two were noted at Paquimé (Di Peso et al. 1974:6:441).

The Hohokam are known for their distinctive cut-shell pendants that are found in a variety of bird, lizard, and other animal forms (Haury 1976). Most are made from thin *Laevicardium elatum* by cutting and grinding. Various cut-shell ornaments were noted at Swarts Ruin, NAN Ranch, and several Hohokam sites. Although sites in the Mogollon area generally fall within the Casas Grandes cluster, early components were associated with Hohokam exchange networks prior to the rise of Casas Grandes. This is particularly apparent at Swarts Ruin and Cameron Creek, where elaborately carved bracelets typical of Hohokam networks were recorded.

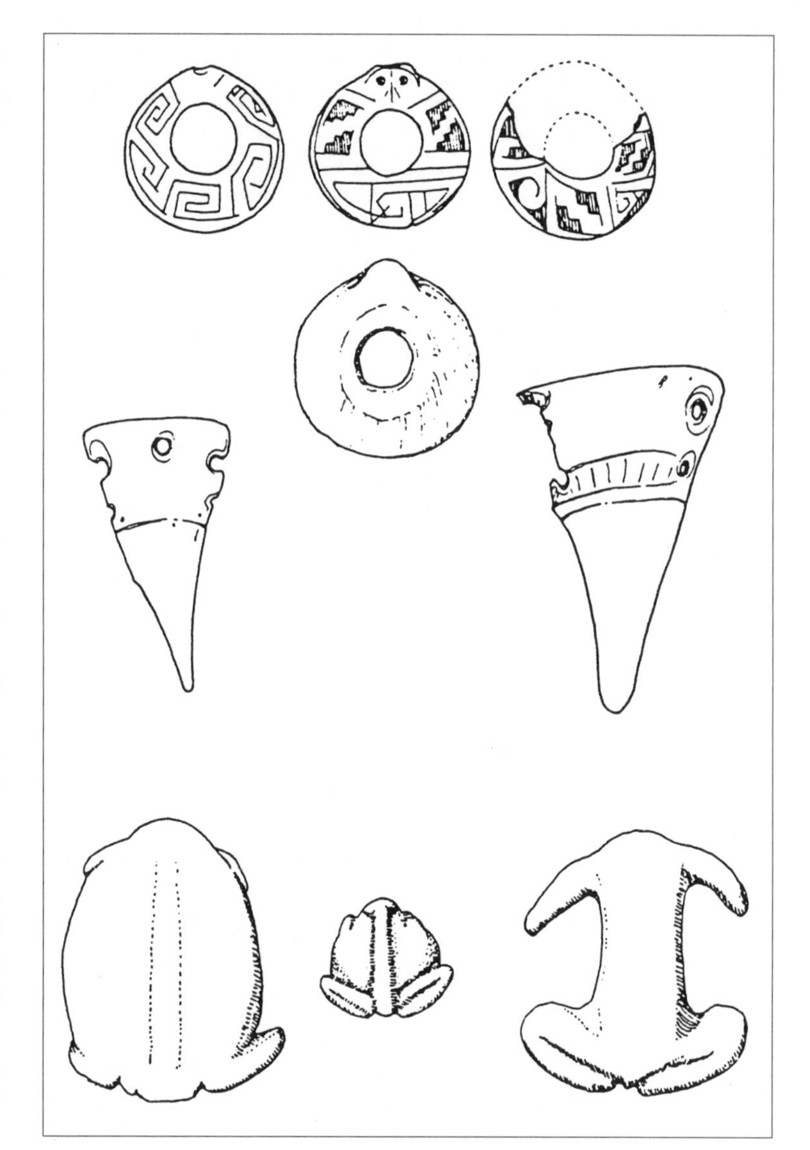

Figure 16.8. Special artifact shapes. Top row: Type III pendants. Middle row: *M. patula* pendants. Bottom row: *Glycymeris* frog pendants. (From Di Peso et al. 1974; Stone and Foster 1994)

Other distinctive styles, such as bilobed bead pendants, occur with much greater frequency but have a distribution that is somewhat unusual. By far, the majority of bilobed bead pendants occur in Anasazi sites (88.6 percent), with others that are confined primarily to Chihuahua (7.3 percent), the Point of Pines area (2.7 percent), and Sinagua contexts (1 percent). In the Anasazi area bilobed beads and disk beads make up the bulk of the bead and bead-pendant assemblages. Unlike the distribution of disk beads, bilobed varieties are found in limited quantities in the Sinagua area but are practically absent in early Mogollon contexts and at many Western Pueblo sites (excluding Point of Pines). Very few bilobed beads occurred in Hohokam sites within the study area, but they were noted at Snaketown (Haury 1976).

Glycymeris rings have an interesting distribution, occurring primarily in Hohokam, Western Pueblo, and Sinagua areas. None were found at Paquimé, indicating that they are probably associated with Hohokam exchange networks. *Glycymeris* rings are produced like bracelets but from smaller, young shell specimens. Because the technology is the same as for

bracelets, it is not surprising that they are associated with the Hohokam network. Substantial quantities of these rings and ring fragments were noted at Los Muertos (n = 24) and Grasshopper (n = 18), with small numbers dispersed throughout a number of other sites.

One unique style of pendant was noticeably common at Paquimé and has a relatively wide distribution at other sites in the Southwest. This pendant of *Glycymeris* has a distinctive, large perforation in the central portion of the bivalve (defined as Type III pendants at Paquimé) (Figure 16.8). The perforation is made by grinding, cutting, and smoothing, forming a finished central hole. Some are decorated with mosaics or incised, but the majority are plain. Approximately 5 percent of the whole-shell pendants at Paquimé were perforated *Glycymeris* pendants known as Type III (n = 25). Sixteen were perforated *Argopecten circularis* and one *Laevicardium elatum.* The distribution of Type III pendants across sites in the Southwest is rather intriguing. A total of 59 Type III pendants have been documented at 18 sites. Most of the pendants are *Glycymeris,* except for a couple of *A. circularis* that occur at Kinishba and Wupatki, *L. elatum* at Grasshopper, and freshwater shell at Swarts. The *A. circularis* pendants are distinctively different from the *Glycymeris* ones and are found on Hohokam sites, such as Snaketown, that predate Casas Grandes. Type III pendants are absent from early Anasazi sites and scarce in other Preclassic contexts. The overwhelming majority of the *Glycymeris* pendants are found on late sites contemporaneous with Paquimé. Substantial numbers of the Type III pendants were found at Kinishba (n = 11), Grasshopper (n = 17), Tres Alamos (n = 6), and Los Muertos (n = 5), as well as a number of other late sites. Interestingly, many Type III pendants at these sites are found with burials. At least six of the items analyzed from Grasshopper accompanied burials, all three of the pendants from Pecos were with burials, and at least one or more from Kinishba and Swarts. In addition, some of the Type III *Glycymeris* pendants at Paquimé were with burials. Information is not available from other sites at this point.

Because of their abundance at Paquimé (n = 25), these *Glycymeris* pendants appear to be associated with the Casas Grandes network. The pendants are primarily a Classic period ornament style that occurs in quantities on several Western Pueblo and some Hohokam sites. They also are found at Pecos, Tijeras, Awatovi, and other sites within the Hohokam cluster. Their abundance at Grasshopper (n = 17) and Kinishba (n = 11) in addition to other associations in other artifact types would suggest interaction between Western Pueblo sites and Casas Grandes.

Discussion and Summary

Analyses of the data using diversity measures and cluster analysis have produced several important patterns. First, diversity measurements indicate that artifact type richness within southwestern assemblages tends to increase through time, with early Preclassic sites containing low to medium richness scores and late Classic sites exhibiting high richness. Not all Classic period assemblages have high richness scores, but all of the richest assemblages are Classic, whereas Preclassic sites lie within the expected 90 percentile or below.

There are clear differences in richness between some regions. For instance, the early Anasazi sites tend to fall well below the expected ranges for artifact type richness, whereas most Sinagua sites fall within the expected 90 percentile range. Both early Mogollon sites and Salado sites such as Kuykendall produced lower than expected richness. Not unexpectedly, the Hohokam sites exhibit higher than expected scores, as do sites in the Western Pueblo area.

In a preceding section I outlined propositions that measure the participation of Casas Grandes within southwestern shell exchange networks. I anticipated that the introduction of new-shell suppliers such as Casas Grandes would result in an increase in the diversity of shell ornament types within the Southwest. Conversely, had Casas Grandes been simply a storehouse or a destination for shell in the Southwest, the diversity measures would be expected to stay the same or drop from previous periods. That is, had Casas Grandes been only a recipient or storehouse for shell, no increase in the diversity of southwestern assemblages would be anticipated. Clearly, there is increased diversity late in the prehistoric period, and associations between the structure of the assemblages in Casas Grandes and some other sites in the Southwest have been demonstrated by the stylistic analyses. This suggests that Casas Grandes was not simply a recipient of shell but an active supplier and participant in the exchange of the material.

The data obtained from the principal components analysis indicate two major networks, one associated with the Hohokam and one with Casas Grandes. The Hohokam grouping includes two Sinagua sites and the late Hohokam assemblages along with Awatovi and w:10:37. The early Sinagua and Anasazi sites form a separate cluster when marine shell only is considered (Figure 16.6) but show affinities to the Hohokam cluster when all shell is considered (Figure 16.5). It is highly likely that the Sinagua and Anasazi group is related to the Hohokam network, although there is a slight possibility that the cluster reflects an east-west exchange network tied to the movement of shell up the Colorado River as has been suggested by Wilcox (1989). Because the Sinagua assemblages exhibit many similarities to the Hohokam, it is more likely that they were involved in the Hohokam network. Two tight clusters form the Casas Grandes grouping, which includes the majority of Western Pueblo, Casas Grandes, late Anasazi, and Mogollon sites.

The early Anasazi sites exhibit a great deal of homogeneity within the assemblages with the exception of Chetro Ketl and Allantown (which fall within the Casas Grandes cluster). Chetro Ketl is an anomalous cache that may not accurately represent the entire assemblage. Despite the fact that the other Anasazi sites cluster with the Sinagua assemblages, they exhibit a distinctiveness that separates them from other areas. All contain a high proportion of bilobed bead pendants and disk beads of shell and other materials.

The Sinagua assemblages from the Winona/Ridge Ruin complex cluster with Tuzigoot and Walnut Canyon. All show affinities with the Anasazi and ultimately the Hohokam. Wupatki is a very diverse assemblage that clusters within the Hohokam group rather than other Sinagua sites. Other evidence suggests that the Sinagua were involved in exchange relationships with both the Anasazi and Hohokam, and the shell data bear this out. The strong affinities between the Sinagua and Anasazi assemblages suggest interaction and exchange, and the fact that the Sinagua assemblages have higher diversity or richness suggests that they were suppliers of shell to the Anasazi, perhaps through their ties with the Hohokam.

There are distinct differences between the late and early Anasazi site assemblages. The early Anasazi sites consistently form a tight cluster that eventually joins with Sinagua and Hohokam sites. The late Anasazi sites (with the exception of Awatovi) also cluster but show affinity to the Casas Grandes and Western Pueblo cluster.

The Casas Grandes/Western Pueblo/Mogollon sites cluster very tightly, with the exception of two Point of Pines sites that are found in other groups. w:10:37 falls in with the Hohokam group, and Turkey Creek (w:9:123) shows more affinities to the Sinagua sites. It is clear that most of the sites in the Mogollon and Western Pueblo areas have assemblages that are very similar to Casas Grandes, suggesting interaction between the two areas.

Consideration of several specific artifact styles provides additional insight into some of the interaction relationships in the Southwest. Very distinctive artifact styles, such as *Glycymeris* frog pendants, *Glycymeris* rings, *Pecten vogdesi* pendants, and Type III pendants, show a distribution slightly different from the clusters of principal component scores, often overlapping the two main exchange networks.

The sample of *Glycymeris* frogs was very small and showed no distinctive patterning in distribution. They are most common in the Hohokam area but appear to be minor or absent in the Anasazi, late Anasazi, and Sinagua areas. The Western Pueblo, Casas Grandes, and Mogollon sites have only small quantities of frogs.

The *Glycymeris* rings have a more widespread distribution, occurring in the Sinagua, Hohokam, Western Pueblo, and some of the Mogollon assemblages. None were found at Paquimé or in the Casas Grandes or Chihuahuan assemblages. They are also absent in Anasazi contexts. Their abundance in the Hohokam area suggests that they were associated with Hohokam networks, particularly because the manufacturing technology of the rings is almost identical to that of the bracelets. In addition, they are most common on late sites, dating to the Classic period.

The *Pecten vogdesi* pendants, believed by some to be associated with status in the Hohokam area (Nelson 1991), are fairly widespread but occur in small quantities with no particular patterning. They tend to be limited to the Hohokam, Sinagua, Western Pueblo, and Mogollon areas.

One pattern is very apparent. The Type III pendants appear most commonly within the sites in the Casas Grandes network, whereas the *Glycymeris* rings occur most commonly within sites in the

Hohokam cluster. In particular, Grasshopper contained the highest number of Type III pendants (n = 17) outside of Paquimé, followed by Kinishba (n = 11), Tres Alamos (n = 6), and Los Muertos (n = 5). The occurrence of Type III pendants crosscuts some of the previously defined clusters and provides intriguing evidence for the movement of particular styles across traditional boundaries. Primarily a Classic period phenomenon, these distinctive pendants were associated with burials, occurring at sites from as far north as Pecos and Tijeras, south to Casas Grandes, and west to Grasshopper and Los Muertos.

In essence, several patterns in the data are distinctive and clear. First, there is evidence for increasing richness in the ornament types in assemblages through time. Casas Grandes, Western Pueblo, and Hohokam sites are among those with the highest richness. This increased richness is attributed to the appearance of Casas Grandes as a supplier of shell ornaments, introducing new variation in ornament types to the Southwest.

Second, there is a significant degree of variability in the proportions of artifact types among assemblages within specific regions, but two to three major groupings are defined. The Hohokam group houses two clusters: Sinagua and early Anasazi sites and late Hohokam assemblages. The Mogollon, Western Pueblo, late Anasazi, and Casas Grandes assemblages form a large cluster representing the Casas Grandes network.

Third, specific artifact styles follow these general patterns but also crosscut some of the major areas, indicating that some of the patterns are more complex than simply the presence of two distinct networks. Particularly, the Western Pueblo area exhibits a mixing of specific styles suggesting influence from both Casas Grandes and the Hohokam areas.

Relationships Within the Southwest: Casas Grandes and the Western Pueblo

Patterns in the archaeological shell reflect important differences in the content of shell assemblages between the Hohokam and Casas Grandes networks. Whereas the Anasazi and Sinagua assemblages show affinities to the Hohokam, others such as the Mogollon and Western Pueblo more closely resemble the Casas Grandes shell. Temporal differences are an important factor in the two networks. The Hohokam repertoire and exchange system appear to have been long-lived, encompassing the early Sinagua and Anasazi regions and surviving into the Classic period relatively intact. The Casas Grandes network appears to have been comparatively short-lived, primarily a Classic period phenomenon. Sites such as Swarts Ruin and Cameron Creek may hold answers to questions concerning the longevity of the Casas Grandes shell-exchange system, but there are problems with sorting out the early and late components. Clearly, some of the early Mogollon shell was from the Hohokam area, but the later manifestations reflect Casas Grandes affinities. The late Anasazi sites fall within the Casas Grandes network, but the paucity of marine shell at these sites and their heavy use and re-use suggest that their connections may not have been direct or very solid. The area that exhibits the strongest ties with the Casas Grandes network is the Western Pueblo region. In addition, these sites also reflect exchange with the Hohokam, resulting in a complexity of relationships centered in the Western Pueblo area.

Concordant with the rise of Casas Grandes in Chihuahua and population migrations and aggregation in the Western Pueblo area came important changes in the social organization of the Hohokam and the introduction and spread of the Salado. The vast changes in southwestern societies late in the prehistoric period resulted in the introduction of new ceramic styles, marked realignments in alliances and exchange networks, and the appearance of the Kachina Cult (Adams 1991; Crown 1994). Salado polychrome ceramics were among the new styles that appeared and spread across the Southwest into Chihuahua, accompanied by what Crown (1994) has defined as the Southwestern Cult. The Salado polychromes reflect local manufacture for the most part, but the iconography and other aspects of the style were transmitted through interaction networks.

The Southwestern Cult is believed to have originated in the Mogollon Rim area of central Arizona in the late 1200s and early 1300s and spread throughout much of the Southwest (Crown 1994:223). First exemplified in the Pinedale style, the Salado polychromes gradually changed through time, with the late styles resembling Chihuahuan Escondida Polychrome and Ramos Polychrome (Crown 1994:190). Although the distribution of Salado polychromes is not believed to be related to exchange (because many

of the ceramics were locally produced), the Southwestern Cult represents an interaction sphere that follows exchange and interaction networks where social and ritual/religious ideas and goods moved across long distances.

Of particular importance to my study is the fact that decorative elements evolve to resemble Chihuahuan polychrome ceramic types late in the developmental sequence (Crown 1994). Escondida Polychrome and Ramos Polychrome were among the most common types recovered from Casas Grandes and have a widespread distribution throughout Chihuahua. In addition, Salado polychromes were recovered from storage rooms at Casas Grandes, where they were stored alongside shell and other exotica. The increasing similarities between ceramic styles in the Salado heartland and Chihuahua and the presence of Salado ceramics at Casas Grandes support the shell data patterns that indicate exchange and interaction among Casas Grandes and Salado groups.

Similarly, Adams (1991:100–101) also indicates that there was significant interaction between the two areas. In discussing the origins of the Kachina Cult, he points out similarities in early Fourmile (Pinedale) style and Ramos and Escondida polychromes. He states that the emphasis on parrots and macaws suggests that northern Mexico, and especially the Casas Grandes area, was a focal point for the initial development of the Fourmile style. The Kachina Cult developments occurred in the Western Pueblo area and spread throughout much of the Southwest during the Late Pueblo period. Ceremony and ritual activities were important, as were costume and ornamentation. Shell was an important part of the various costumes. Pendants and other ornamentation, as well as macaws, have been identified on kiva mural painting at sites such as Pottery Mound (Hibben 1975).

Interestingly, the distribution of macaws closely follows the Casas Grandes shell network. With the exception of Casas Grandes, most of the macaws in the Southwest have been recovered from the Western Pueblo area. Wupatki also contained substantial evidence for macaws, as did Pueblo Bonito. However, they are virtually absent from the Hohokam area, suggesting that the Hohokam were not involved in the movement of macaws, nor were they participants to the same degree within cults that highly valued macaws (such as the Kachina Cult and Southwestern Cult).

Late prehistoric period sites in the Southwest exhibit aggregation of large groups of people and intensified ritual activities. Although there are numerous sites associated with the Casas Grandes network, the most intense relationships appear to be with the Western Pueblo. Not only shell but ceramics, macaws, copper, stone, and other materials moved among large sites. As this study has shown, the larger and most heavily populated sites had access to most of the shell, whereas the small sites received only small quantities.

The need for shell and other items such as macaws in ritual and social realms enhanced and solidified ties to Casas Grandes. Similarly, the transmission of ideas and ritual knowledge perpetuated the exchange of goods by creating a demand for them in ritual and adornment. Crown (1994) has suggested with the Southwestern Cult that information conveyed iconically served as a uniting mechanism resulting in a pansouthwestern religious cult. Shell and macaws traveled along the same paths, serving as components of the ritual and social protocol. As Adams (1991:100) points out, Casas Grandes appears to have been the focal point for the development of the Fourmile (Pinedale) style, an attribute associated with the origin of the Kachina Cult. The similarities in stylistic motifs between Chihuahuan polychromes and Salado polychromes associated with the Southwestern Cult (Crown 1994) demonstrate interaction between the areas.

Despite the fact that many goods and ideas can be traced to Casas Grandes origins, the regularity and degree of participation of Casas Grandes within the Kachina Cult or Southwestern Cult systems is not well understood at this point. Geographically, Paquimé was on the fringes of the major activities that occurred in the Western Pueblo area, where much of the development of both the Southwestern and Kachina cults took place (see chapter 12 of this volume). Although Casas Grandes controlled access to shell, macaws, and possibly ritual knowledge, their degree of participation within the cult systems themselves has not been fully investigated.

Controlled access to ritual goods has important implications. Within the Western Pueblo and Salado heartland, and in the late Anasazi developments, the occupants of many sites had limited access to certain important ritual goods. In many cases emulation was an alternative means of carrying on ritual protocol,

with local manufacture of pottery in the Salado style (Crown 1994) and the adoption of ritual motifs such as macaws and shell in ceramics, mural paintings, and other mediums. Emulation is apparent in the late Anasazi sites with regard to marine shell, where there is obviously a restricted number of marine shell available, and replicas were carved-out stone. In addition, the use of other mediums, such as freshwater shell, may have been a form of emulation as well. The limited quantity of shells and the evidence for heavy use on many late Anasazi sites suggest that they may not have had the well-established ties with Casas Grandes exhibited by the Western Pueblo area.

Finally, although Casas Grandes was an active participant in exchange with the Southwest and West Mexico, the longevity of those trade relationships is not well understood. The bulk of the shell at Casas Grandes was buried under debris when the site was catastrophically abandoned. Questions remain as to whether the exchange network was functioning at its height by the time the site was destroyed. In addition, we lack an understanding of the early occupation of Casas Grandes. Was Casas Grandes a supplier of macaws and marine shell to the Mimbres region early in the sequence, or was it primarily a short-lived, late prehistoric manifestation? These questions and many more have been raised for future research in the Casas Grandes area.

17

The Dentition of Casas Grandes with Suggestions on Epigenetic Relationships among Mexican and Southwestern U.S. Populations

Christy G. Turner II

Teeth are a rich source of information on prehistoric and contemporary intergroup affinities and relationships that can be obtained quickly, easily, inexpensively, and often with large and statistically reliable sample sizes. Because crown morphology results from growth and development regulated largely by polygenic quasi-continuous inheritance, trait frequencies have considerable evolutionary stability and better reflect ancient patterns than do traits with greater susceptibility to genetic and environmental shifts (Scott and Turner 1997). In addition, when environmental stress overrides genetic regulation, the morphological results are usually recognizable, and such teeth can be excluded from analyses of the source population sample. Moreover, not only are there many teeth in an individual, there are also many independent traits. All of this makes for a powerful system for the study of population history. (For illustrations of dental morphology and an extended discussion see Scott and Turner 1997.)

Inasmuch as the analysis reported herein was based only on crown traits, similar sorts of root variation are not considered. Only the crown morphology for 20 largely unrelated traits was used for this chapter because the objective was to see how prehistoric populations compared with certain living Southwest Indian groups, the individuals of which were selected to exclude European and other admixtures as much as possible. Information on living individuals is obtained primarily through dental impressions, the materials of which make contact only with the dental crowns, hence, no root information. Males, females, and children are pooled because these traits exhibit very little sex dimorphism and no age differences. The logic and procedures for scoring and counting these traits are discussed in Turner (1991), Turner and Scott (1977), and Turner et al. (1991).

Because the focus of this brief chapter is on the question of the epigenetic relationship between the people of Casas Grandes, only the frequencies for that sample's crown traits are provided (Table 17.1). Like all other American Indians they exhibit relatively high frequencies of incisor winging, shoveling, double-shoveling, interruption grooves, tuberculum dentale, canine distal accessory ridge, Carabelli's trait, deflecting wrinkles, and the protostylid. They have relatively low frequencies of the other traits listed in Table 17.1. Outside the New World, these frequencies most resemble populations in northeast Asia, where the ancestors of all Native Americans must have originated, a view evidenced as well by

Table 17.1. Casas Grandes Morphological Crown Trait Frequencies (Individual Count, Sexes Pooled, Standard ASUDAS Breakpoints).

	TRAIT	N	FREQUENCY (%)
UI1	Winging	34	47.1
UI1	Shoveling	99	88.9
UI1	Double-shoveling	99	39.4
UI2	Interruption grooves	84	70.2
UI2	Tuberculum Dentale	87	52.9
UC	Mesial ridge (Bushman C)	96	2.1
UC	Distal accessory ridge	64	75.0
UP1	Uto-Aztecan	97	2.1
UM2	Hypocone	84	86.9
UM1	Cusp 5	76	26.3
UM1	Carabelli	79	78.5
UM3	Parastyle	70	12.9
LP2	>1 lingual cusp	85	29.4
LM2	Y groove pattern	82	12.2
LM1	cusp 6	75	33.3
LM2	>4 cusps	85	90.6
LM1	Deflecting wrinkle	49	36.7
LM1	Distal trigonid crest	88	3.4
LM1	Protostylid	92	33.7
LM1	Cusp 7	113	10.6

much other biological data, archaeological findings, and geographic proximity between Siberia and Alaska.

Table 17.2 provides the Mean Measure of Divergence (MMD) matrix of similarity between all possible pairwise comparisons. MMD is a multivariate statistic devised by C. A. B. Smith in which the lower the value, the greater is the similarity between a pair of groups. Hence, inspecting the column for group 1 on the far left of the table, we find that it is very similar to groups 3, 9, and 17 (MMDs = .000), whereas it is least similar to 11 (MMD = .144). The computer algorithm used for the analyses reported here also contains procedures to correct for small sample size and to determine statistical significance (see Turner 1985 for method references).

Table 17.3 extracts and ranks values from the larger matrix for the 23 pairwise MMD values for Casas Grandes. On the one hand, Casas Grandes has no measurable multivariate difference with a series of teeth from Sinaloa (MMD = .000), and on the other, its most marked dissimilarity (MMD = .258) is with a Preclassic Hohokam series from the site of La Ciudad, located in Phoenix, Arizona. The lowest four Casas Grandes MMD values are not statistically significant ($p > .02$), whereas the other 19 are ($p < .02$). Significance herein refers to the probability of getting a specific MMD value by chance alone. Lack of statistical significance can occur when sample sizes are very small or when the trait frequencies in two groups are all very similar. The range in trait sample size for Sinaloa is 4 to 137, and Coahuila is 8 to 54. Sample size does not seem to be the main cause of nonsignificance of MMD values between these groups and Casas Grandes because other series with comparable sample sizes have significant MMD values with Casas Grandes; for example, Sonora ranges from 5 to 29 individuals for its 20 traits and its MMD value (.061) is significant.

Various clustering algorithms have been developed to graphically portray information such as the MMD matrix in Table 17.2. Such graphs are called dendrograms, and they greatly facilitate recognition of the various relationships between groups, in this case 24 groups. All clustering algorithms suffer some loss of information, and all can misclassify one or more groups in a matrix for this reason. This is why it is always advisable to inspect both the matrix and the derived dendrograms. In the case of the Casas Grandes dental morphology, as far as MMD can detect, it is identical to that of Sinaloa, followed very closely by the Mimbres and Pima samples. Figure 17.1 shows the dendrogram based on the Unweighted Pair Group, Arithmetic Averages algorithm.

In the middle of Figure 17.1 Casas Grandes is one of a four-member cluster whose branches include it, Mimbres, Sinaloa, and Coahuila, but not Pima. Pima clusters with the Maricopa and Central Pueblo samples. Even though the Casas Grandes MMD indicates strong similarity with the Pima, there are other samples in the matrix with which the Pima are even more similar. Hence, Casas Grandes is most like Sinaloa and next most like Mimbres, which the dendrogram graphic captures fairly well. The computer program that generates the dendrogram calculates values to very small decimal points, which in the case of the cluster containing Mimbres, Casas Grandes, Sinaloa, and Coahuila caused Casas Grandes to link up first with Mimbres and then Sinaloa because Sinaloa and Coahuila are very slightly more like each other than Sinaloa is like Casas Grandes. However, viewed from

Table 17.2. Mean Measures of Divergence (MMD) Matrix Based on 20 Crown Traits.

	1	2	3	4	5	6	7	8	9	10	11	12	13	14	15	16	17	18	19	20	21	22	23	24
1	0.000																							
2	0.089	0.000																						
3	0.000	0.039	0.000																					
4	0.006	0.036	0.000	0.000																				
5	0.037	0.017	0.029	0.013	0.000																			
6	0.082	0.011	0.037	0.032	0.014	0.000																		
7	0.062	0.019	0.030	0.028	0.010	0.007	0.000																	
8	0.021	0.014	0.011	0.010	0.012	0.039	0.024	0.000																
9	0.000	0.115	0.021	0.027	0.039	0.060	0.041	0.040	0.000															
10	0.024	0.075	0.032	0.018	0.018	0.030	0.040	0.040	0.019	0.000														
11	0.144	0.073	0.153	0.075	0.063	0.093	0.103	0.094	0.149	0.045	0.000													
12	0.045	0.038	0.013	0.019	0.014	0.035	0.010	0.023	0.038	0.036	0.135	0.000												
13	0.072	0.051	0.052	0.075	0.061	0.052	0.049	0.057	0.097	0.101	0.189	0.036	0.000											
14	0.016	0.048	0.000	0.011	0.042	0.051	0.056	0.051	0.062	0.066	0.211	0.011	0.016	0.000										
15	0.076	0.038	0.050	0.054	0.021	0.057	0.049	0.034	0.077	0.091	0.245	0.014	0.000	0.027	0.000									
16	0.038	0.074	0.014	0.037	0.045	0.025	0.042	0.036	0.031	0.031	0.187	0.022	0.083	0.000	0.111	0.000								
17	0.000	0.096	0.021	0.043	0.060	0.077	0.077	0.064	0.049	0.031	0.141	0.060	0.080	0.019	0.126	0.020	0.000							
18	0.073	0.235	0.142	0.164	0.141	0.206	0.189	0.179	0.133	0.138	0.307	0.195	0.165	0.130	0.167	0.147	0.087	0.000						
19	0.021	0.027	0.026	0.009	0.003	0.040	0.012	0.013	0.038	0.040	0.079	0.007	0.019	0.000	0.033	0.043	0.049	0.154	0.000					
20	0.107	0.016	0.058	0.036	0.022	0.020	0.010	0.041	0.072	0.041	0.068	0.051	0.087	0.062	0.079	0.051	0.085	0.164	0.031	0.000				
21	0.027	0.066	0.054	0.028	0.011	0.070	0.044	0.043	0.045	0.034	0.054	0.040	0.073	0.061	0.060	0.110	0.079	0.112	0.001	0.061	0.000			
22	0.077	0.083	0.055	0.045	0.058	0.102	0.082	0.053	0.090	0.080	0.119	0.016	0.061	0.000	0.086	0.045	0.077	0.188	0.022	0.099	0.069	0.000		
23	0.045	0.036	0.033	0.027	0.024	0.014	0.022	0.050	0.050	0.019	0.059	0.026	0.071	0.040	0.061	0.075	0.069	0.223	0.036	0.022	0.033	0.092	0.000	
24	0.105	0.167	0.131	0.112	0.110	0.149	0.145	0.119	0.083	0.096	0.175	0.156	0.269	0.211	0.079	0.225	0.211	0.258	0.189	0.124	0.113	0.258	0.041	0.000

NOTE: *Group numbers are identified in Table 17.3 and Figure 17.1.*

Table 17.3. Ranking of MMD Values of Casas Grandes and Other Dental Samples.

CASAS GRANDES AND:	MMD
14. Sinaloa Region	.000
12. Mimbres Region	.016
19. Pima Live	.022
16. Coahuila Region	.045
4. Kayenta Region	.045
8. Eastern Pueblo Region	.053
3. NE Arizona	.055
5. Central Pueblo Region	.058
13. Sonora Region	.061
21. Maricopa Live	.069
17. Central Mexico Region	.077
1. SE Utah Region	.077
10. Sinagua Region	.080
7. Athabaskans	.081
2. SW Colorad Region	.083
15. Chihuahua Region w/o Casas Grandes	.086
9. Mogollon Region	.090
23. Hohokam w/o La Ciudad	.091
20. Hopi Live	.099
6. Western Pueblo Region	.102
11. Salado Region	.119
18. South Mexico Region	.188
24. La Ciudad Hohokam (Preclassic)	.258

NOTE: Provenience and composition information on these assemblages can be obtained from the author on request.

the point of view of whom the Casas Grandes populations were most like, the MMD values indicate that it was the Sinaloa sample.

There are several clusters containing the live samples that suggest much of this dendrogram is historically acceptable. Hence, the Pima and Maricopa cluster together as would be expected on geographic and culture history grounds. The Hopi cluster with Athabaskans, who today surround the Hopi villages, and with the archaeologically derived Western Pueblo and Southwest Colorado skeletal series. Most of the prehistoric clusters seem reasonable, although there is only archaeological evidence for assessing these, and for the most part such assessments are based mainly on ceramic and architectural considerations (for the most recent extended review of Arizona prehistory see Reid and Whittlesey 1997). Also, all of the more southerly samples, those from Mexico, are in the lower half of the dendrogram, providing another indication that the dendrogram is sound on broad geographic grounds. This is most evident in the outlying South Mexico sample, which originated in Yucatan.

One is tempted to view dendrograms such as Figure 17.1 as if they represent evolutionary relationships, that is, cladistic (genealogical) rather than phenetic (morphological) relationships. If one knows that the characters used to develop the matrix have a genetic basis, then this temptation is not quite so risky. Given that isolation by distance, however, is the primary inhibitor for gene flow in a regional comparison such as Figure 17.1, then a certain amount of misclassification or flaws in the evolutionary tree must be expected. Just how one decides which links are phylogenetically real and which ones are spurious requires evidence of relationships based on some other and independent database. That database is presented in other papers in this compilation.

What is to me most unexpected about this analysis is the relatively great dissimilarity the Casas Grandes dental sample has with the other sample of teeth from Chihuahua, assuming that phenetic similarity should correspond with geographic distance. Whether this unexpected finding is due to some manner of sampling error, actual prehistoric events, or error arising from the statistical methodology can be assessed only with further sampling and analysis using other statistical methods.

In sum, dental crown morphology suggests the population of Casas Grandes had close epigenetic connections with people living in Sinaloa and in the Mimbres area. These relationships are closer than that between Casas Grandes and another sample of Chihuahuan dentition.

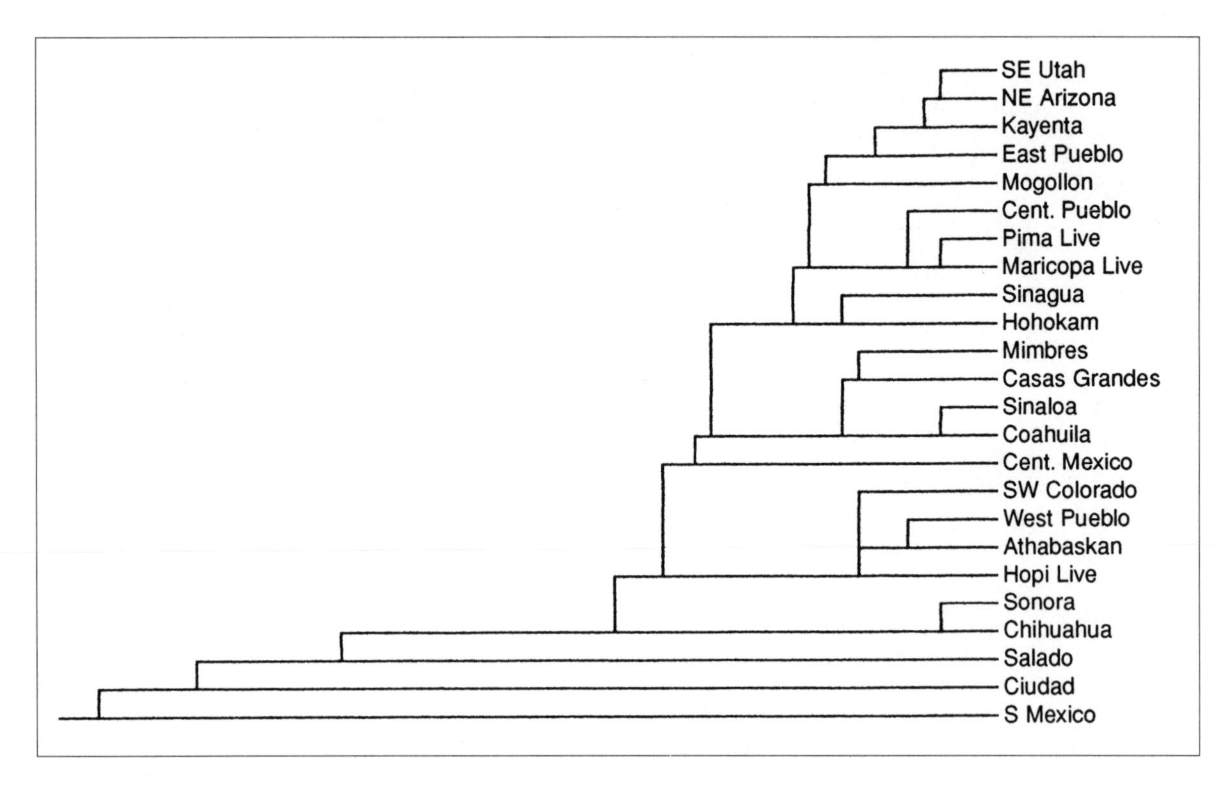

Figure 17.1. Dendrogram of multivariate phenetic relationships based on Mean Measures of Divergence clustered with the Unweighted Pair Group, Arithmetic Averages method. Computer file name: "Regional SW Indian Groups with Casas Grandes Pooled, Pima Live, Hopi Live, Maricopa Live."

V

Toward a New Synthesis

18

The Casas Grandes World

Analysis and Conclusion

Curtis F. Schaafsma

Carroll L. Riley

SINCE AT LEAST 1979 (Schaafsma 1979; LeBlanc 1980) it has been argued that after the passing of the Mimbres culture around 1150 there appeared a widespread regional culture that was remarkably similar in architecture, site layout, settlement pattern, pottery styles, and in the absence of kivas. It was called an "interaction sphere" in 1979 (Ravesloot 1979; Schaafsma 1979), following the meaning of this term as Struever (1972) had defined it by reference to the Hopewell interaction sphere. From the beginning it has been obvious that we have no idea how the region might have been organized politically. It had something to do with the site of Casas Grandes (Di Peso 1974; Di Peso et al. 1974), but in 1979 we did not know (and we still do not know today) the real political situation.

The hundreds and perhaps thousands of sites in the immense region depicted in Figure 1 (see introduction) are still rarely thought of as related to each other. And yet for over 200 years, from about A.D. 1200 to 1425, the people living in these places traded with each other, made coursed-adobe pueblos in the desert country, manufactured magnificent pottery, and produced some of the most extraordinary rock art (P. Schaafsma 1972, 1975b, 1980, 1994, 1997a) to be found anywhere in North America. Bandelier (1892: 541) remarked that this is the region "in which native culture in the Southwest probably attained its highest development."

The Casas Grandes Core Area

The existence of many sites in northwestern Chihuahua related to Casas Grandes has been well known since Bandelier published his Final Report in 1892 (Bandelier 1892). Brand (1935:Figure 1) produced a map showing the extent of the "Chihuahuan complex" based on sites he described in a survey report (Brand 1943). Brand's map is similar to Hewett's 1908 map of the "Region of Chihuahua" (1993:8). Sayles (1936) also worked in northern Mexico, defining essentially the same region. Di Peso et al. (1974: 4:2–6) provided a good summary of this early work, as do Kelley and Villalpando (1996). Wilcox (1996) gives us an excellent summary of current work. This traditionally recognized region is referred to as the Chihuahuan Culture on Figure 1.

Di Peso (1974:1:5–9) described this core area as "The Casas Grandes Archaeological Zone" (Di Peso 1974:1:Figure 5-1). The survey work of the Joint Casas Grandes Expedition in this archaeological zone extended "from Sonora on the west to the desert lands

of the Médanos de Samalayuca on the east, and the international border on the north to the Papagochic River on the south. This is the expanse through which evidence of Casas Grandes material culture is found" (Di Peso 1974:1:5). In the summer of 1959 Mr. M. Harvey Taylor from Brigham Young University conducted a survey in the region (Di Peso 1974:1:38). The sites he recorded and sites visited by other members of the Joint Casas Grandes Expedition between 1959 and 1961 were assigned site numbers and names (Di Peso et al. 1974:4:6) and were mapped (Di Peso et al. 1974:4:Figure 4-4). Their reconnaissance data "were added to the previous excellent work of Sayles and Brand" (Di Peso 1974:1:38). "The reconnaissance, when added to the data obtained by Bandelier, Sayles, and Lister, gave a rather impressive list of sites in northwestern Chihuahua" (Di Peso 1974:1:38). The site data obtained from the above sources were mapped in detail (Di Peso et al. 1974:5:Figure 284-5), showing the overall extent of the "Casas Grandes Archaeological Zone" (Di Peso 1974:1:5, 257).

Whereas Minnis (1989) has called into question the validity of this regional survey database, a careful reading of Brand (1943), Sayles (1936), Carey (1931), and Kidder (1939) will account for most of the sites shown on Di Peso's detailed map (Di Peso et al. 1974:5:Figure 284-5). Were it not for the collection of this site data before the era of intensive agriculture, there would be immense gaps in what we know about the "Casas Grandes Archaeological Zone" inasmuch as many of the sites in the valley bottoms (where the majority were located) have been totally destroyed. We have to rely on the early site data in order to discuss the regional culture. The current effort to locate the sites (Minnis and Whalen 1993 and chapter three of this volume; Kelley et al., this volume) is extremely valuable, but the definition of the basic regional culture must rest on the early data.

On the southwest, Di Peso regarded the Aros (Papagochic) River as the terminus: "Surface surveys indicate that there is little Casas Grandes material culture south of this valley" (Di Peso 1974:1:7). Both Carey (1931) and Kidder (1939) excavated and surveyed sites near Babícora, Chihuahua, that were clearly related to Casas Grandes. More recently this region has received intensive research by Kelley and Stewart (see chapter four of this volume). Di Peso (1974:1:8–9) realized that sites of the "Casas Grandes Archaeological Zone" were restricted to the drainage basins of the Santa María and Carmén rivers, thus defining essentially the same southern boundary as recognized by Brand (1935:Figure 1) (Figure 1). Recent work has confirmed this southern boundary (see chapter four of this volume). Beyond this boundary area, there may well have been Conchos and Tarahumaras that did not "interact" with the people in the "Casas Grandes interaction sphere" (C. Schaafsma 1997).

On the north these sites extend into the southwestern corner of New Mexico (Brand 1935; Sayles 1936; Duran 1992; O'Laughlin et al. 1984), where the Pendleton site, excavated by Kidder and the Cosgroves (Kidder et al. 1949), is located. McCluney (1965a, 1965b) excavated several of them in the early 1960s and concluded they were strongly related to Casas Grandes. De Atley wrote her 1980 dissertation on the sites in southwestern New Mexico and treated them as the northern frontier of the Casas Grandes culture (De Atley 1980). De Atley and Findlow (Findlow 1979; Findlow and De Atley 1976, 1978; De Atley and Findlow 1982) did extensive work on settlement patterns in this area. De Atley (1980:4) presented a very reliable map of the Casas Grandes core area, showing the limits of what she called the Casas Grandes culture. De Atley's (1980:4) work shows clearly that sites of this nature do not extend beyond the town of Animas, New Mexico. Like Brand (1935:Figure 1) De Atley extends the northeastern limits to near Columbus, New Mexico. Fish and Fish (this volume) have recently summarized information on this area.

The northeastern border of Di Peso's Casas Grandes Archaeological Zone extended at least to the dunes of Samalayuca and east of the Laguna de Patos near Villa Ahumada thence southward along the east side of the Carmén River valley (Di Peso 1974:1:6,9, Di Peso 1974:2:Figure 20-2; Di Peso et al. 1974:5:Figure 284-5). Di Peso stated that "this valley marks the eastern border of the archaeological zone" (Di Peso 1974:1:9).

Di Peso stated that "The rough, jagged face of the Sonoran slopes drain into the Bavispe Basin which forms the western margin of the zone" (Di Peso 1974:1:7). This would closely agree with the western limits of the Casas Grandes culture as mapped by De Atley (1980:4). Scholars tend to vacillate about this western boundary, with Brand (1935:Figure 1) having extended it somewhat farther west. It would seem

obvious that more work is needed in this area, especially on the relationship of Casas Grandes to the relatively sophisticated cultures of northeastern Sonora (Phillips 1989; Riley 1985, 1986, 1987, 1990a, 1990b, 1995b, 1997, this volume).

These studies and others define the region that is here treated as the core area of the Casas Grandes interaction sphere (Figure 1). In this primary core area are hundreds of sites that are remarkably similar, particularly in architecture and ceramics. Many of them in the mountains of the Sierra Madre Occidental (Martínez and Pearson 1994; Sayles 1936; Kidder 1939) survive in dry caves, where extraordinary architectural details can still be seen. A number are distributed along the three main river valleys of the Casas Grandes, Santa María, and Carmén rivers (Brand 1943; Di Peso et al. 1974:5:Figure 284-5). When Baltasar de Obregón accompanied Francisco de Ibarra to Paquimé in 1565, he reported houses northward from Paquimé down the Casas Grandes River for about 21 miles:

> This large cluster and congregation of houses is not in one place but scattered over a distance of eight leagues down the river, extending northward from the first tableland in the large mountain range. Rodrigo del Rio and I visited and explored this ridge by order of the governor. Houses continued to be found down the river and we did not lose sight of them.... Most of these houses were in ruins, worn away by the rains and torn down. It seemed that they had been abandoned and given up by their owners many years past. (Hammond and Rey 1928:207)

There seems every reason to believe these river bottom sites depended on extensive irrigation systems (Di Peso 1974:2:336–343; Doolittle 1993). In the intermittent drainages of the eastern margin of the Sierra Madre, such as those in the Carretas Basin (Brand 1943), there are many sites. When the Ibarra party went over the Sierra Madre, probably into the Carretas Basin (Hammond and Rey 1928:General Reference Map; C. Schaafsma 1997), they "began to discover abandoned houses of two and three stories" (Hammond and Rey 1928:197). The current work of Minnis and Whalen (1993) is adding greatly to our knowledge of the sites in the drainages west of Casas Grandes and the region generally. Thus the primary core of the Casas Grandes culture (Figure 1) is well established, albeit in need of a great deal more research (Phillips 1989). The regional context of the sites related to Casas Grandes, or "Paquimé," has become a matter of considerable interest because these sites greatly affect how the major site of Casas Grandes is interpreted (Minnis 1989; Minnis and Whalen 1993).

Di Peso's Mercantile Model

Di Peso's interpretation of the regional culture was closely linked to his mercantile model of the origin of the culture: "It is believed that sometime around the year A.D. 1060 a group of sophisticated Mesoamerican merchants came into the valley of the Casas Grandes and inspired the indigenous Chichimecans to build the city of Paquimé" (Di Peso 1974:2:290). In a later publication Di Peso expanded on this idea: "In the course of time, economic exploitation of the northern region from the south would bring these people together. For the Casas Grandes Valley, this came about in a dramatic way in the eleventh century when a southern merchant family, living somewhere along the Pacific coast of Middle America, inaugurated a well-designed plan of cultural conquest of the Casas Grandes sector of the Chichemecan frontier" (Di Peso 1979b:11). Speaking of the Casas Grandes river drainage, Di Peso said, "Along its banks, literally hundreds of satellite farming villages were built and associated with a large capital city. Together, this population formed an inland entrepôt or Mesoamerican gleaning center that thrived between A.D. 1050 and 1350. In a sense, it functioned somewhat as an elaborate, prehistoric Hudson's Bay trading post" (Di Peso 1979b:12).

In Di Peso's model the "Casas Grandes Sovereignty" (Di Peso 1974:2:Figure 20-2) encompassed essentially the region mapped by Brand (1935:Figure 1) as the "Chihuahuan Culture." In Di Peso's model the hundreds of villages in the region served mainly to supply the needs of the "capital city": "Foodstuffs, for example, were most likely supplied by the many satellite villages that flourished around the business center" (Di Peso 1974:2:333). There is no question that Di Peso regarded this as a hierarchical society: "A bureaucracy arose to control the new farmers and attend to the socio-economic needs of the growing community. It consisted of a group of reigning merchants and priests who lived in exclusive quarters within the big city.... The new lords and masters supplied the people with raw goods and marketed their finished products" (Di Peso 1974:2:18).

According to Di Peso, at its peak the "Casas Grandes Sovereignty" governed the entire region: "In the Paquimé Phase, hundreds of mountain and valley satellite villages located within the Casas Grandes province bowed to the needs of the capital city" (Di Peso 1974:2:314–315).

Di Peso's mercantile model seems to reflect his familiarity with medieval European mercantile practices learned when he earned a Bachelor of Foreign Trade degree from the American Institute of Foreign Trade at Glendale, Arizona, in 1947 (Riley 1993:12). Certainly his basic model more closely resembles the Hanseatic League or the merchants of Venice than anything known in Mesoamerica. Indications that European medieval economic practices were the source of his model can be discerned in this statement:

> Sometimes cities spring up because of some deep underlying economic motive, especially along established transportation routes where they are needed as a protective device for merchants, guildsmen, and goods, or as a result of a religious impulse. These motivational origins, which are familiar to many medieval towns of Europe, may also apply to Casas Grandes. (Di Peso 1974:2:368)

Elsewhere, when discussing the appearance of merchants who established "alien exploitative economic units" (Di Peso 1974:2:331), Di Peso advises the reader to read Fremantle (1965:71–90) and Van Loon (1921: 174–205) to learn more about the merchants of late medieval Europe. These two sources describe social and economic practices that are essentially what Di Peso uses as his mercantile model. In other words, it appears that his mercantile model was derived from his understanding of European medieval political and economic practices, not from practices known for Mesoamerica. According to Riley,

> Throughout the later part of the 1950s, Di Peso developed and refined his motif of the incoming group of overlords or power brokers who shaped and changed the recipient cultures of the Southwest.... This became a consistent theme in Di Peso's later studies at Casas Grandes and was central to his vision of the development of the Greater Southwest (Riley 1993:14–15).

Di Peso called his power brokers *puchteca* or *pochteca*, the term borrowed from the merchant class of the sixteenth-century Aztecs of central Mexico (Riley 1993:17–18). Later, in the 1970s, Di Peso added the concept of the *world systems* as developed by Wallerstein (1974). However, as Riley comments:

> Let me make the point that to Di Peso, the world system ideas fitted comfortably with his earlier pochteca configuration approach. In fact, Di Peso's world systems approach is to a large degree the rewording of his old pochteca configuration model with an added stress on the economic sophistication of Mesoamerica, something largely implicit in the earlier model (Riley 1993: 21).

One of the first studies to question Di Peso's model of regional political control was De Atley's (1980) work on the northwestern corner of the "Casas Grandes Sovereignty" in southwestern New Mexico. Di Peso had included this area in a schematized map of the Medio period extent of Casas Grandes sovereignty (Di Peso 1974:2:Figure 20-2). De Atley (1980:4) regarded this area as firmly within the Casas Grandes culture area. However, she provided good evidence that those sites were largely self-sufficient economically (De Atley 1980:151–159). Her study integrated this frontier area into the Casas Grandes primary culture area but asserted its political independence.

Since then, many studies have grappled with the question of the political nature of the Casas Grandes culture area (Ravesloot 1988; Minnis 1989; Minnis and Whalen 1993; Whalen and Minnis 1996a; Kelley and Villalpando 1996), with none of them endorsing the monolithic "sovereignty" of Di Peso's original model. At this point, the whole topic is a very unstable flux. Whereas some scholars have found that major revisions are needed for Di Peso's (Di Peso 1968, 1974) mercantile model derived from his emphasis on the site of Casas Grandes (Paquimé), others have been extending the general culture even farther in space than Di Peso originally intended. This too has forced new interpretations. He was aware of certain of these efforts. In regard to the extensions into the Jornada Mogollon (Lehmer 1948), Di Peso noted that

> these clues suggest the possibility that the middle valley culture [Jornada Mogollon] was strongly flavored by Casas Grandian culture contacts.... If this is ever verified,

it will have serious implications in matters appertaining to the historical continuum of the upper valley [Rio Grande Pueblos] . . . and it will have serious repercussions in terms of the total human history of the Rio Grande system. (Di Peso 1981:31)

However, Di Peso failed to deal with another serious implication: that the Jornada Mogollon could hardly have been under the political control of Paquimé (Schaafsma 1979; Minnis 1989). Extending the regional culture related to Casas Grandes past the original "Casas Grandes Archaeological Zone" opened major cracks in the Di Peso model that have still not been closed. It is essential to review the history of this effort to extend the Casas Grandes "Phenomenon" (Schaafsma 1979; LeBlanc 1989).

The Black Mountain and El Paso Phases

In 1977 LeBlanc published his work identifying the Black Mountain phase in the Deming/lower Mimbres River area and stated, "It is clear that the Black Mountain sites are closely related to the major site of Casas Grandes, which is situated approximately 94 miles below the border in Chihuahua, Mexico" (LeBlanc 1977:13). LeBlanc pointed out that the Black Mountain phase "appears to have existed between 1175 and 1300" (1977:11). Many of these sites lack Gila Polychrome and related post-1300 Salado polychromes. Nonetheless, at the Black Mountain site itself (LA 49) Gila Polychrome is well represented, indicating this site was occupied after 1300. According to LeBlanc, "We can hypothesize that the Black Mountain phase sites are part of the Casas Grandes cultural system but were on the periphery and the people who occupied these sites participated only to a limited extent in some aspects of the system" (LeBlanc 1977:16). Leblanc added that "The Black Mountain phase material demonstrates that the Casas Grandes phenomenon had a much more marked and direct impact on surrounding areas than had been previously realized" (LeBlanc 1977:21). LeBlanc's initial definition and preliminary impressions of this important phase were followed by Ravesloot's 1979 thesis, in which Ravesloot systematically compared the architecture of the Black Mountain phase sites with Casas Grandes and demonstrated their definite architectural similarity. Speaking in 1980 of these architectural comparisons, LeBlanc stated that "The majority of these traits had no precursors in New Mexico, but bear strong similarity to those at Casas Grandes" (1980:283).

As we said above, Ravesloot (1979) introduced the term *interaction sphere* for discussing the extended regional culture that appears to represent the post-1150 spread of Casas Grandes culture. At about the same time LeBlanc maintained that

By far the most reasonable interpretation of the Animas phase (and the Black Mountain phase) is that it represents a part of the Casas Grandes cultural system. . . . Casas Grandes is one of a large number of very large towns, with room counts in the thousands, that were built in northern Chihuahua at about A.D. 1150. It appears that these towns were not a product of indigenous development; rather, they represent an influx of people from the south who organized local populations into a much more complex organization than had previously existed. (LeBlanc 1980: 284–285)

The revised dating of the site of Casas Grandes by Dean and Ravesloot (1993) to approximately 1200 to 1450 has major implications for regional developments (Table 1). The El Paso phase and the preceding Doña Ana phase were recently regarded by Michael Foster as related to the development of the Casas Grandes regional system: "Another important factor that probably contributed significantly to the development of the El Paso phase was the expansion of Casas Grandes as a regional economic and political power. The time of the increased complexity in the El Paso phase occurred during the Medio period at Casas Grandes, which has now been dated to begin ca. A.D. 1200" (Foster 1993:12). Vernon Scarborough was able to date the pithouse-to-pueblo transition in the El Paso area to the period 1150–1200 (Scarborough 1989, 1992).

LeBlanc recognized in 1980 that it was essential to consider the El Paso phase along with the Animas and Black Mountain phases and particularly noted that "El Paso phase people occupied adobe walled pueblos very similar in architectural form and features to those of the Black Mountain and Animas phases" (LeBlanc 1980:295). Although the El Paso phase sites differ from the others in proportions of pottery types, the same group of types is represented

(LeBlanc 1980:296, 1986:194). "Thus, the El Paso phase is seen to demonstrate a high degree of continuity with both the Black Mountain and Animas phases" (LeBlanc 1980:296).

The regional extent of the El Paso phase villages up the Rio Grande valley was determined by Lekson's survey of Sierra County to be at least the mouth of Alamosa Creek, north of Truth or Consequences (Lekson 1989; Lekson and Wilson 1985). On the northeast the El Paso phase is present to about Carrizozo (Lehmer 1948). The Lincoln phase is distinct (J. H. Kelley 1984) but related in many ways. The Bloom Mound (J. H. Kelley 1984) and the Fox Place Site (P. Schaafsma and Wiseman 1992) near Roswell, New Mexico, define the eastern edge.

Farther afield, the puebloan sites of the La Junta phase near Presidio, Texas, were regarded by J. Charles Kelley as part of the Casas Grandes interaction sphere (1993). The La Junta phase dates from ca. A.D. 1200 to 1400 (Cloud et al. 1994:12). Cloud et al. (1994) provide two new radiocarbon dates for the Polvo site that are in the existing time range. They observed that the construction of the pueblo at the Millington site "is identical to that of El Paso phase pueblos in the Hueco Bolson of El Paso" (Cloud et al. 1994:13).

Thus a wide array of sites over a very large region (Figure 1) would seem to be part of an interacting culture that shared definite architectural and ceramic similarities. As LeBlanc noted:

> It is unfortunate and somewhat confusing that geographically juxtaposed areas containing contemporaneous archaeological remains that demonstrate great similarity and continuity are designated as separate phases. . . . In light of the high degree of similarity and continuity of these phases with the Casas Grandes phenomena, it is suggested that these phases be thought of as regional variants of the Casas Grandes culture. Thus, it may be more reasonable to speak of the Casas Grandes culture in the Animas, Black Mountain, or El Paso regions. (LeBlanc 1980:296)

Schaafsma (1979, 1987, 1988, 1990, 1992a) quite agrees with LeBlanc, having argued several times that these various regional manifestations were all representatives of a once-interacting culture related to Casas Grandes in Chihuahua. The current questions about the nature of this interaction remain a major research domain.

Coursed Adobe Versus Puddled Adobe

Given the fact that the appearance of adobe villages is one of the distinguishing criteria for the Black Mountain and El Paso phases (Leblanc 1989:193), it is essential to define what kind of "adobe" construction is involved. Following Stubbs and Stallings (1953:25–28) there should be a clear distinction between "puddled" adobe, meaning walls that were built by pouring a fluid mix into forms, versus "coursed" adobe, in which "walls were built by taking large handfuls of plastic clay and patting them into place" (Stubbs and Stallings 1953:26). Di Peso confused things by discussing both kinds of walls as "puddled adobe" (Di Peso et al. 1974:4:217–218).

There can be no ambiguity concerning what Di Peso meant by "Cast (Poured) Adobe": "Mud concrete, or poured adobe, walls were made by pouring a fluid mud mix into full-height or movable forms which could be lifted as work progressed. The latter would include the main type of earth wall construction found at Casas Grandes, Chihuahua, and, perhaps, at Casa Grande in Arizona" (Di Peso et al. 1974:4:217). This description was reinforced by very clear drawings (Di Peso et al. 1974:4:Figures 147-4, 148-4, 149-4). Di Peso firmly believed that the newly arrived merchant rulers brought this construction technique with them: "The involved frontiersmen surely must have marveled at the ingenuity of the newcomers, who knew how to cast the thick mud walls" (Di Peso 1974:2:370). The "cast mud concrete load-bearing walls" (Di Peso 1974:2:372), along with other architectural features that marked the Casas Grandes architectural tradition, were "introduced full-blown in the Buena Fé Phase, ca. A.D. 1060" (Di Peso 1974:2:372). Interestingly, "Nowhere in northern Mexico is there evidence which would suggest that this area was the inspiration for the Casas Grandes mode of cast wall construction" (Di Peso et al. 1974:4:216).

Wilcox and Shenk (1977:115) are quite certain that "mud concrete" was not used at Casa Grande in Arizona. On the contrary, "an English Cob [coursed adobe] process was used to build the Casa Grande walls" (Wilcox and Shenk 1977:117). They conclude, therefore, that "Di Peso and his colleagues have not yet published convincing evidence that these most-popular walls at Casas Grandes were built by other than an English Cob technique" (Wilcox and Shenk

1977:127). Future research at Casas Grandes should address this question in much the way Stubbs and Stallings (1953) addressed it at Pindi Pueblo: by taking sample walls apart.

By "English Cob Adobe," Wilcox and Shenk meant essentially the kind of wall construction described by Stubbs and Stallings:

> The walls were built up by taking large handfuls of plastic clay and patting them into place upon the foundation. Each lot added was molded and smoothed with the hands on to the mass below. . . . The top of each course has a general convex surface, still showing the hand-prints of the hand molding process of construction. . . . The courses are usually as long as the wall of which they are a part. . . . The wall was slowly built up, one course on top of another, until the desired height was obtained. . . . Since the term puddling or puddled wall is a misnomer for this type and method of construction, it is suggested a new term be applied to designate this type of wall. The term *coursed adobe* is proposed to describe walls of this type of construction. (Stubbs and Stallings 1953:26)

The coursed-adobe construction technique at Pindi Pueblo is identical to that Kidder described at Las Varas near Babícora (Kidder 1939) and at the Pendleton Ruin in Hidalgo County (Kidder et. al 1949), as well as the walls at the Bradfield and Alamogordo sites (Lehmer 1948). C. Schaafsma, while working on the survey of Chihuahua rock art in 1996 (P. Schaafsma 1997), examined cross-sections of adobe walls in cliff dwellings west of Casas Grandes near Olla Cave that have the characteristic convex surface at the top of each course (Figure 18.1). As nearly as we can determine, in every case where wall construction is carefully addressed (Breternitz and Marshall 1982: 434–437), the technique from Babícora, Chihuahua, to southern Utah is coursed adobe in the sense defined by Stubbs and Stallings (1953). As Wilcox and Shenk noted, "If most of the Casas Grandes was built using an English Cob technique just as the Casa Grande was, in this important respect it looks little different from its neighbors to the north" (Wilcox and Shenk 1977:128).

Dating the appearance of coursed-adobe walls has changed with greater temporal control of sites to the north and the revised dating of Casas Grandes. Creel (this volume) cites evidence that coursed adobe was known to the Mimbres people as early as A.D. 900, although he acknowledges that it was not widely used until the Black Mountain phase, after 1130 or 1150. Coursed-adobe walls have now been well dated to between 1126 and 1133 at Bis sa'ani Pueblo near Chaco Canyon (Breternitz and Marshall 1982: 436; Lekson, this volume). At Bis sa'ani "The adobe architecture of Casa Quemada [a component of Bis sa'ani] and the coincidence of Socorro Black-on-white and Mogollon Brown Ware suggest a unit intrusion from the Cebolleta–Central Rio Grande district" (Breternitz and Marshall 1982:448), which would mean that coursed adobe was being used toward Socorro and the Rio Puerco even earlier,

Figure 18.1. Wall cross section near Olla Cave west of Casas Grandes showing convex upper surface of coursed adobe wall, demonstrating this was not "puddled adobe."

probably at least by 1100. This is comfortably earlier than any contemporary researcher would date the beginning of the Medio period buildings at Casas Grandes. Coursed adobe is an old technique in the north and was not brought in with the hypothesized "newly arrived merchant rulers" from the West Coast of Mexico.

What Is an "Interaction Sphere"?

At this stage the term *interaction sphere* should be used in the sense developed by Struever (1972) to mean a region of shared iconography, architecture, and other indications of cultural commonality whose social and political nature we do not understand:

> The Hopewell Interaction Sphere simply refers to relations of a still undetermined nature, though involving idea and goods exchange, between groups scattered over a broad area of eastern North America. . . . What the mechanisms of interaction were between local groups and between far-distant ones remains to be demonstrated, as do the specific functional contexts within which these items were used in each participating society. And, of course, the degree and form of participation has yet to be explicated for the various local manifestations. (Struever 1972:304)

Most significantly in Struever's definition of an interaction sphere in general as applied specifically to the Hopewell case is a clear understanding that the relations between different groups are of an undetermined nature. We can discuss the apparent relations between groups over a wide region as revealed in shared stylistic and goods exchange without knowing the mechanisms of interaction. There is no indication in Struever's definition of an interaction sphere, implied or explicit, that requires the existence of socioeconomic inequality or any of the specific attributes that Hayden and Schulting (1997:53) believe to be characteristic of "interaction spheres." Indeed, the task of future research is to determine the nature of these attributes. We do not know them beforehand. The definition advanced by Struever (1972) was descriptive but demonstrated a dynamic relationship between groups on a regional level. In Struever's definition there are no presumptions about the nature of the societies involved or the specific mechanisms by which goods were exchanged or ideas shared throughout a wide geographic region.

Dating

Now that there is better temporal understanding of Casas Grandes (Dean and Ravesloot 1993), the regional contemporaneity of these various manifestations is much more apparent (Table 1). Most results indicate the overall culture appeared after 1150–1200 and probably persisted to 1425 or 1450 (Kelley and Villalpando 1996:73).

Some of the most solid evidence for dating the beginning of these sites, before Dean and Ravesloot's work (1993), derives from De Atley's study. She saw the sites in the northern frontier beginning by at least 1200 if not earlier (De Atley 1980). Scarborough (1989) dates the beginning of the El Paso phase to ca. A.D. 1200. The Mimbres–Black Mountain transition remains contentious (LeBlanc 1989:192, 194; Creel, this volume; Shafer, this volume), but there seems little disagreement that the transition was accomplished by 1200. The Medio period sites in the southern area seem to begin somewhat later (see chapter four of this volume). In point of fact, the sites in the peripheral areas have been providing more precise time control in recent years than those in the core region near Casas Grandes.

The termination date remains unstable and in need of careful scrutiny. Dean and Ravesloot ended their careful reevaluation of the Casas Grandes chronology with what we feel is an unwarranted upward revision of the "Medio period termination date to as late as A.D. 1500" (Dean and Ravesloot 1993:98). We are quite dubious about extending Casas Grandes itself past about 1425. In part this is because Dean and Ravesloot have only one projected felling date that confidently extends past 1400 (Dean and Ravesloot 1993:Table 6.2). In addition, all of the pottery types, both at Casas Grandes and at the other sites in the vast region covered by Figure 1, have beginning dates well before 1400. Especially significant are the types from the Show Low-Springerville area of east central Arizona, which we now know was essentially abandoned by 1400 (Kintigh 1996:134).

The once-proposed "Robles phase" is a chimera (Phillips 1990; Phillips and Carpenter, this volume). A working time frame of 1200 to 1425 is thus appropriate for most of the sites, including Casas Grandes, with the recognition that more accurate dating could extend the range (as indicated in Table 1) a few years. We do not believe that any existing reliable data allow extending the Medio period, either at Paquimé or at any of the sites in the general Casas Grandes interaction sphere, past 1450.

Origins

There can be no doubt that major structural reorientation marked the change from the Viejo to the Medio period in Casas Grandes. This was especially true in town planning, house construction, religious architecture, trade, and the intense utilization of shell. For example, the earlier Convento and Pilón phases utilized pithouses scattered around a larger "community house" pit structure with very little perceptible sense of town planning (Di Peso 1974:1:100–101, 107–111, 152–155).

However, starting in the Pilón phase and culminating in the Perros Bravos phase, the terminal period of the Viejo, there was a considerable change in architectural methods. Square contiguous surface rooms replaced pithouses although the community houses continued to be round. A relatively advanced form of jacal construction was used, and the houses were larger than in earlier periods, with both floor and walls plastered with adobe. Although coursed adobe had not yet appeared, the builders were gaining skills in molding substantial adobe walls to the underlying jacal framework (Di Peso 1974:1:Figure 142-1). Town planning becomes evident; as Di Peso said, "The house-clusters, the plazas, and the community house were bound together as an integral unit" (Di Peso 1974:1:190). With the coming of the Medio period, Di Peso (1974:2:372) described a dramatic change in the lifestyles of the Casas Grandes people. Di Peso considered that "T-shaped entries, raised fire hearths, alcove beds, square mud columns, and staircases, associated with cast mud concrete load-bearing walls having drop keys and roughened joints" (Di Peso 1974:2:372) were introduced full-blown in the Buena Fé phase. As discussed above, coursed adobe was already in use in the Rio Grande valley near Socorro, New Mexico, before the beginning of the Medio period.

Although Di Peso stresses the suddenness and depth of the change, one can discern a certain continuity in architecture, with a gradual trend toward greater complexity and an increased use of adobe in surface structures. The town layouts of Perros Bravos phase look in some ways forward rather than backward; that is, they more resemble the early Medio period town planning than the inchoate pithouse villages of the earlier Viejo period.

There are other kinds of continuity between Viejo and Medio periods in the Casas Grandes area. There seems to be an increasing use of Mexican coastal shell, especially as personal ornament, during the Viejo period. A trade in shell appears as early as Convento times, but most of the shell comes from Perros Bravos phase sites (Di Peso et al. 1974:6:390–400). This shell use becomes much more intense and sophisticated in Medio times (see chapter 16 of this volume). In Viejo villages most of the shell was found with burials and tended to be simple pendants, beads, tinklers, or bracelets (Di Peso et al. 1974:6:401–408). During Medio times there developed new ways of handling shell (including techniques of incising, painting, pseudocloisonne, and mosaic).

The earlier pottery traditions in the Casas Grandes area, certainly well represented by Convento times, were the various textured brown- and redwares very similar to other such pottery of a generalized Mogollon tradition (Di Peso et al. 1974:6:21–30, 39–76). There were red and brown bichrome ceramics, popular ones being Victoria red-on-brown textured and its slightly later descendant Mata red-on-brown textured. Mata and Victoria textured pottery seem to have begun in the Pilón phase, although they increased in popularity later in the Viejo period (Di Peso et al. 1974:6:62–65). Developing out of these bichrome wares was Mata Polychrome, made by adding black lines to the red and browns of the Mata textured pottery. This pottery, the only polychrome ware in the Viejo period, was to some degree ancestral to the Medio period Dublan Polychrome (Di Peso et al. 1974:6:75, 220–221). Its origin is not clear, but C. Meighan, in a 1966 communication (Di Peso et al. 1974:6:75), thought that it might be related to early pottery (A.D. 500 or earlier) from the highland Nayarit or Jalisco areas. In Casas Grandes this pottery appears in the Pilón phase but is more common in the Perros Bravos phase (Di Peso et al. 1974:6:75). Like Dublan Polychrome, Mata Polychrome appears as both bowls and jars. The Mata ware shares with Dublan Polychrome tightly composed band layouts with a frequent use of straight-line designs and a predominance of plain corrugated texturing. It differs in that Dublan more commonly has polishing over the designs and in a general difference in vessel shapes (Di Peso et al. 1974:6:221).

Perhaps most significantly, there was a continuity in certain other Medio period Casas Grandes pottery shapes from the Viejo period. Ramos Polychrome and Huérigos Polychrome seem to have their greatest similarity in vessel shape to those of the late Viejo period, especially the Convento wares but also Mata and Pilón ceramics (Di Peso et al. 1974:6:52–74, 249–297).

Although worked copper was primarily a Medio period phenomenon, several metal artifacts (four copper tinklers and a small remnant of sheet copper) found by Di Peso in the Perros Bravos phase indicate that the beginnings of metal use date to the latter part of the Viejo period. In addition, a tubular-shaped piece of turquoise, perhaps part of a necklace, had been found in a Viejo period context (Di Peso 1974:1:210–211, 212; Di Peso et al. 1974:6:499).

It seems likely that at least part of the Medio period population in Casas Grandes descended from Viejo period people. However, there is a troublesome lack of Viejo period sites of any kind (early or late) in the intensive surveys now being conducted by Minnis and Whalen near Casas Grandes (Whalen and Minnis 1996c). From a point of view of cultural connections, ancestral Casas Grandes was part of a larger Mogollon world, that congeries of pithouse-living people who made textured brown and red pottery and whose economies ranged from foraging to simple agriculture. The Mogollon and Mogollon-like cultures extended from the region of southeast and southcentral Arizona and adjacent western New Mexico to Durango and Zacatecas (Foster 1982; Riley 1995b:Map 5). This contains most of the distribution of the Casas Grandes interaction sphere (Figure 2) but extends beyond it especially in the northwest and the south.

What language or languages the people of the interaction sphere spoke is a matter of speculation and considerable disagreement. C. Schaafsma (1997:91) suggests that the Jano and Jocome, who were associated with the historic mission at Janos, north of Casas Grandes, in the seventeenth century, may have spoken a Uto-Aztecan language related to Taracahitan and that they might have been the descendants of the prehistoric inhabitants of at least the northwestern portion of the Casas Grandes interaction sphere (see also Di Peso 1974:1:839–841). By extension people at Paquimè may have spoken a similar language. Alternatively, Riley suggests that Paquimé citizens might have spoken a language closely related to Opata or Tarahumar. Tarahumar forms the modern eastern anchor of the Taracahitan substock, which includes such languages as Opata, Cahita, Yaqui, and Mayo. Beckett and Corbett (1992) suggest that the Manso were Taracahitan-speaking, linguistically related to the Jano and Jocome, and that the Manso ancestors formed at least part of the El Paso phase. This interpretation was recently endorsed by Lockhart (1997).

Another suggestion, made by Bandelier as early as the 1880s (see Bandelier 1892:59; Lange and Riley 1970:276–278; Riley 1987:48, this volume), is that at least the western Casas Grandes interaction sphere may have contained Opata speakers. It would be very surprising if the Casas Grandes populations did not speak some form of Uto-Aztecan, and the Taracahitan subgroup of Uto-Aztecan would make the most sense from a language-distribution point of view.

If Taracahitan was the language of at least the western portion of the Casas Grandes interaction sphere, it suggests a relationship between Casas Grandes and groups westward and southward. The Taracahitan groups from the earliest historical times extended in a northeast-southwest distribution from Chihuahua to Sinaloa. Carpenter (1996:354–357) suggests that influences spreading south to north in Sinaloa involved primarily a flow of ideas rather than people and believes that Taracahitan speakers may have provided the base population in the northern and central Sinaloan region from early A.D. times.

This distribution was broken by a northwest-southeast elongated distribution of another Uto-Aztecan group, the Tepiman (Tepehuan-Pima) speaking peoples. There is a rather shallow time depth of language separation within the Tepiman group, and the four Tepiman languages are closely related (Miller 1983:120). One explanation for that fact would be that they spread down the main cordillera of the Sierra Madre in relatively recent times, overrunning and crosscutting the earlier Taracahitan peoples. Wilcox (1986b:143), however, seems to think that the spread was somewhat earlier, perhaps with a break in the Tepiman chain occurring around A.D. 1000, about the time coastal Sinaloan culture was spreading northward to Guasave (Wilcox 1986b:143).

The final phase of the Viejo period at Casas Grandes, that of Perros Bravos, began around or perhaps a bit before A.D. 1100. If there was a movement of peoples from the Sinaloa area into the general Casas Grandes region at about this time, it might explain the "quickening" that we described above at the beginning of Perros Bravos times.

One interesting bit of research that suggests a tie-up between the people of Casas Grandes and the Sinaloa area comes from the work of the physical anthropologist Christy G. Turner of Arizona State University (1993, this volume). Turner studied the morphology of teeth in approximately 5000 prehistoric and modern southwestern Indians, comparing such features as "the number of molar cusps and roots, the shape of incisors, the occurrence of supernumerary cusps," among other traits (Turner 1993:34). In attempting to link prehistoric populations to historic and modern ones and to get some ideas about ethnic distributions, Turner (1993:44) points us in some interesting directions. The Casas Grandes peoples—at least dentally—are most closely related to populations in Sinaloa and at a slightly greater remove to those of Modern Pima, Coahuila, and the Mimbres region (see chapter 17 of this volume). At the present stage of the research, nothing really definitive can be said about the language situation at Casas Grandes, but Turner's work does strengthen the suggested Uto-Aztecan antecedents of Casas Grandes and probably the more specific Taracahitan tie-up as well.

In spite of a certain continuity with the Viejo period, it must be acknowledged that the Medio period at Casas Grandes presents us with a series of new and dramatically different traits. It does not represent a simple development out of the preceding pithouse world (Foster 1982, 1991) nor the Mimbres culture (see chapters eight and nine of this volume). Something major happened quite abruptly, and the changes were spread throughout the region quickly. The excavator of Paquimé, Charles C. Di Peso, said the main structures were begun and constructed in only a generation or two (Di Peso 1974:2:292), perhaps only 5 to 10 years (Di Peso 1974:2:653, n. 7). As discussed above, Di Peso thought this was due to the arrival of the merchant rulers. It is becoming increasingly apparent that this is an inappropriate model. For one thing it is at variance with both the Pueblo cultures to the north and the nature of Mesoamerican polities to the south. Whatever was going on, the sudden formation of a mercantile empire does not seem the engine that drove these dramatic and rapid changes in the Casas Grandes world. In fact, the evidence for trade, other than shell (Bradley 1993, this volume), is dwindling and being seriously challenged (Vargas 1994, 1995; Young et al. 1994; Mathien and Olinger 1992). For example, it appears that the Casas Grandes people were simply down-the-line consumers of copper items made in western Mexico, and there was a minimal amount of trade in copper to the north (Vargas 1994, 1995).

In the same manner, the turquoise at these sites, including Casas Grandes, was for specialized functions at the villages, and they were the end of the line for turquoise trade (Minnis 1989; Bradley 1993). For example, of the 5,895 pieces of turquoise (constituting 2.6 pounds total) from the entire site (Di Peso et al. 1974:8:187), many of them were in a single Playas Red jar (CG/3485) found at the bottom of a circular pit covered with a stone slab set in adobe (Di Peso et al. 1974:5:Figure 220-5) at the bottom of Reservoir 2, which presumably was filled with water most of the time. The excavators observed that "The distributive association of turquoise indicated that it was primarily used for domestic consumption and then in the realm of the socio-religious, made in the form of ornaments which were placed in subfloor caches as were found in room corners and under Reservoir 2" (Di Peso et al. 1974:8:187). They also note: "Although the turquoise contained in the Reservoir 2 cache was light-colored and would be described as 'poor,' so, too, was most of that from the ruin" (Di Peso et al. 1974:5:837). Not only was the turquoise being used in end-of-the-line contexts, but one really wonders where this "poor" light-colored turquoise was coming from. Mathien and Olinger (1992) have confirmed the observation of Di Peso et al. (1974:8:187) that "it remains for the physical scientists to explore the possibilities of identifying the sources of prehistoric turquoise artifacts. Unfortunately, x-ray diffractograms and chemical analyses alone are not definitive enough to accomplish this chore, as the chemical composition of turquoise from any one mine is often more varied than it is between deposits of differing geographical locales." Maybe new analytic techniques will someday provide reliable answers to this question (Young et al. 1994). The context of use, the difficulties of chemically sourcing, and the quality of the turquoise bring into question the notion that "Turquoise is believed to have been one of the primary materials which originally drew the *puchteca* to the Casas Grandes area" (Di Peso et al. 1974:8:187).

The Cacique Model

Current research on the nature of Mesoamerican polities, based partly on deciphering Maya and Mixtec codices, suggests that mercantile models may be inappropriate for understanding the rise of a place like Paquimé. These entities generally focused on a single person or family as having the ritually sanctioned right to rule. The decipherment of Mixtec codices by Jill Furst (1986) indicates that a ritually sanctioned "cacique," or sacred leader, with his accompanying ritual objects would have to be at the center of any Mesoamerican polity. This is especially true for the widespread, nonstate polities termed "cacicazgos" by Redmond and Spencer (1994). Furst (1986) makes it clear that the ritual objects are what give the cacique his right to rule. These objects in turn are acknowledged for what they are by the people ruled. Such a leader would be very similar to the village chief at the Hopi Pueblo of Old Oraibi (Titiev 1944), who also possesses objects that are recognized and accepted by all as declaring his right to rule. The caciques in the other pueblos appear to be similar to the village chief at Oraibi. In general, they all are in office for life.

Leslie White (1942:183–190) described the mode of government at Santa Ana (one of the eastern Keresan Pueblos) and indicated that this summary would be generally applicable to all the other Pueblos. The head of government at Santa Ana is the cacique, a priest-officer who functions both religiously and politically. The cacique, representing the powerful goddess Iatik, has the mandate to "take care of the people." In theory he owns all the land, and he selects all the pueblo officers, including the powerful war chiefs. Under his rule Santa Ana is a microcosm of the outerworld, with deities, a complete cosmology, and a coherent governing structure. In theory at any rate, the government of Santa Ana operates in terms of divine and absolute powers, one in which only obedience is thinkable or tolerated.

A comparison of White's description with that of Jill Furst regarding the Mixtec caciques will disclose many similarities that we infer are historically related, especially in light of the cosmological similarities that are beginning to become apparent (see chapter 12 of this volume).

Accordingly, it would be concordant with what we are beginning to understand about Mesoamerica, as well as the ethnographic pueblo world to the north, if a "cacique" (Marcus and Zeitlin 1994), with the essential religious objects that declared his right to rule and his accompanying priests and other retainers, moved into the Casas Grandes valley and precipitated the development of Paquimé. Such a leader and his entourage may well have come from the Durango area (Kelley 1993), where the Chalchihuites Culture was flourishing until ca. A.D. 1150–1200 and ball courts similar to those at and near Casas Grandes were found (Kelley 1991; Whalen and Minnis 1996a), or from the sophisticated cultures of the Pacific Coast (Figure 2). This organizational mode, which we call the "Cacique Model," has the advantage of being an "indigenous design" (Redmond and Spencer 1994). Certainly, it is not based on European exploitative practices.

The iconographic depictions of the horned and sometimes plumed serpent and images that relate to Tlaloc throughout the Casas Grandes region (P. Schaafsma 1972, 1975b, 1980, 1992a, 1994, 1997, this volume) imply the former existence of a common religion. Especially significant is the recent finding that rock art depictions of the horned and sometimes plumed serpent are common in the vicinity of Casas Grandes (P. Schaafsma 1997). The presence at Casas Grandes of religious leaders or "caciques," who must have exercised some kind of political control, seems highly likely. However, there is no reason to suggest that the "interaction sphere" was politically controlled by the leaders at Paquimé.

The founders of this culture understood irrigation well (Di Peso 1974:2; Doolittle 1993). Regardless of the ultimate origins of the leaders and the basic ideas, it is becoming increasingly clear that the sudden rise of the culture corresponded with the development of complex irrigation systems along the Casas Grandes, Santa María, and Carmén rivers, as well as along secondary streams like the Piedras Verdes River. Ultimately, the demise of the culture may have related to salinization of the fields and other problems that have confronted other irrigation-dependent cultures elsewhere in the world.

Contacts and Legacy

For over two hundred years the people of the Casas Grandes world occupied the region shown in Figure 1 and were in contact with people in adjacent regions (Wilcox 1991c) (Figure 2). There were strong connections with the Salado people (ca. A.D. 1300–1425) to the northwest (Nelson and LeBlanc 1986) as seen in many shared architectural features and in the common lack of kivas. The Salado polychromes are found in both areas and indicate a strong amount of cultural sharing (Crown 1994). The revised chronology for Casas Grandes (Table 1) is compelling a new look at these similarities. Also to the west, in the river valleys of Sonora, were intriguing connections, as seen in architecture and a limited amount of trade pottery (Braniff 1993:82; Fish and Fish 1994, this volume; McGuire et al., this volume; Riley 1987, 1997, this volume; Kelley and Villalpando 1996). The strongest connections, however, seem to be toward the northeast, where shared iconographic elements in religious art show a major continuity with the emerging Pueblo world in the Rio Grande valley after A.D. 1300 (Schaafsma and Schaafsma 1974; P. Schaafsma 1972, 1975b, 1980, 1994). To the south it is now apparent that Casas Grandes had nothing directly to do with Tula of the Toltecs, nor was it an "outpost" of any other empire. This was an autonomous world that existed in its own terms and was not situated at the northern edge of some major empire. For one thing, the revised chronology for Casas Grandes places it squarely between the Toltec and Aztec empires (Dean and Ravesloot 1993:103). Clarification of the chronology allows the notion of southern domination to dissipate. It should also be noted that to the north the Chaco and Mimbres cultures terminated (ca. 1150) *before* the Casas Grandes culture began.

During the height of Casas Grandes (1300–1400) and the greatest regional extent of the culture, there was considerable contact with the developing Pueblo cultures to the north, most clearly demonstrated by religious art motifs like the horned and sometimes plumed serpent (P. Schaafsma 1980; Stewart et al. 1990; Withers 1976). Other religious motifs are the kachina masks that are remarkably similar from El Paso, Texas, to Santa Fe (Schaafsma and Schaafsma 1974; P. Schaafsma 1980). The kachina cult also is linked to social organization because in the modern pueblos it crosscuts clan affiliations to integrate multiclan communities and may have been the primary means for organizing the post-1300 pueblo towns along the Rio Grande and those to the west at Acoma, Zuni, and Hopi (McGuire et al. 1994; Riley 1995; Schaafsma and Schaafsma 1974; P. Schaafsma 1980). It is important to bring out the fact that the cacique in the modern pueblos is the leader of the kachina cult and that the roots of this theocratic society may have moved northward after 1300 with the kachina cult from the Casas Grandes world (Schaafsma and Schaafsma 1974:543–544; C. Schaafsma 1994:124–125).

The Casas Grandes interaction sphere has come to be one of the most dynamic and significant regions in the area Americans call the Southwest and Mexicans call the Northwest (Braniff 1993; 1994a:15; Phillips 1989:374–375; Kelley and Villalpando 1996; Whalen and Minnis 1996c). For over 250 years these sites formed a nexus with the Pueblos of the American Southwest and the people of Mesoamerica.

REFERENCES

Abbott, P. A.

1966 *A Field Guide to Pacific Coast Shells.* Houghton Mifflin, Boston.

Abonyi, S., and A. Katzenberg

1992 Report on Isotopic Analysis of Materials from the Proyecto Arqueológico Chihuahua. Manuscript on file, Department of Archaeology, University of Calgary, Calgary, Alberta.

Adams, E. C.

1991 *The Origin and Development of the Pueblo Katsina Cult.* University of Arizona Press, Tucson.

1994 The Katsina Cult: A Western Pueblo Perspective. In *Kachinas in the Pueblo World,* edited by P. Schaafsma, pp. 35–46. University of New Mexico Press, Albuquerque.

Adams, K. R.

1988 Carbonized plant remains from the Boss Ranch Site, (AZ FF:7:10), southeastern Arizona. Manuscript on file, Anthropological Resource Center, Cochise College, Douglas, Arizona.

1992 Archaeobotanical and Modern Ecological Perspectives on Ancient Sites in West Central Chihuahua, Mexico: Preliminary Report of 1990 and 1991 Field Seasons. Manuscript on file, Department of Archaeology, University of Calgary, Calgary, Alberta.

Adler, M. A.

1996 The Great Period: The Pueblo World during the Pueblo III Period, A.D. 1150 to 1350. In *The Prehistoric Pueblo World A.D. 1150–1350,* edited by M. Adler, pp. 1–10. University of Arizona Press, Tucson.

Ahlstrom, R. V. N., J. S. Dean, and W. J. Robinson

1991 Evaluating Tree-Ring Interpretations at Walpi Pueblo, Arizona. *American Antiquity* 56:628–644.

Akins, N. J.

1987 Faunal Remains from Pueblo Alto. In *Investigations at the Pueblo Alto Complex, Chaco Canyon, New Mexico, 1975–1979,* edited by F. J. Mathien and T. C. Windes, pp. 445–649. U.S. National Park Service Publications in Archaeology 18F, Santa Fe.

Alarcón, H. R. de

1983 *Treatise on the Heathen Superstitions That Today Live Among the Indians Native to This New Spain, 1629.* Translated and edited by J. R. Andrews and R. Hassig. University of Oklahoma Press, Norman.

Alvarez Palma, A. M.

1985 Sociedades agrícolas. *Historia general de Sonora,* vol. 1, Gobierno del Estado de Sonora, Hermosillo.

Amsden, M.

1928 *Archaeological Reconnaissance in Sonora.* Southwest Museum Papers No. 1. Los Angeles.

Anawalt, P. R.

1992 Ancient Cultural Contacts between Ecuador, West Mexico, and the American Southwest: Clothing Similarities. *Latin American Antiquity* 3:114–129.

Andrews, E. W., and J. A. Sabloff

1986 Classic to Postclassic: A Summary Discussion. In *Late Lowland Maya Civilization: Classic to Postclassic,* edited by J. A. Sabloff and E. W. Andrews V, pp. 433–456. School of American Research, Santa Fe, and University of New Mexico Press, Albuquerque.

Anonymous

1995 An Open Letter to Southwestern Archaeologists. In *Final Program, Durango Conference on Southwest Archaeology,* pp. 14–15. Fort Lewis College, Durango, Colorado.

Anyon, R., and S. A. LeBlanc

1984a The Architectural Evolution of Mogollon-Mimbres Communal Structures. *The Kiva* 45:253–277.

1984b *The Galaz Ruin, A Prehistoric Mimbres Village in Southwestern New Mexico.* Maxwell Museum of Anthropology and University of New Mexico Press, Albuquerque.

Anyon, R., P. A. Gilman, and S. A. LeBlanc

1981 A Reevaluation of the Mogollon-Mimbres Archaeological Sequence. *The Kiva* 46:209–225.

Armstrong, K.

1990 NAN-15 Ceramic Analysis: Sherds from the 1984 Field Season. Manuscript on file, Department of Anthropology, Texas A & M University, College Station.

Bandelier, A. F.

1892 *Final Report of Investigations Among the Indians of the Southwestern United States, Carried on Mainly in the Years from 1880 to 1885.* Papers of the Archaeological Institute of America, American Series 4, vol. 2. Cambridge.

Bartlett, J. R.

1965 [1854] *Personal Narrative of Explorations and Incidents in Texas, New Mexico, California, Sonora, and Chihuahua: Connected with the United States and Mexican Boundary Commission, during the Years 1850, '51, '52, and '53.* 2 vols. G. Routledge, New York. 1965 facsimile ed. Rio Grande Press, Chicago.

Baugh, T. G.

1984 Southern Plains Societies and Eastern Pueblo Frontier Pueblo Exchange during the Protohistoric Period. In *Collected Papers in Honor of Harry L. Hadlock,* edited by N. L. Fox, pp. 157–168. Papers of the Archaeological Society of New Mexico No. 9, Albuquerque.

Baugh, T. G., and J. E. Ericson (editors)
1994 *Prehistoric Exchange Systems in North America.* Plenum Press, New York.

Beckett, P. H., and T. L. Corbett
1992 *The Manso Indians.* COAS Monograph No. 9, COAS Publishing and Research. Las Cruces.

Benedict, R.
1936 *Tales of the Cochiti Indians.* Bureau of American Ethnology Bulletin 98. Washington, D.C.

Berrin, K., and E. Pasztory (editors)
1993 *Teotihuacan: Art from the City of the Gods.* The Fine Arts Museum of San Francisco. Thames and Hudson, New York.

Bertram, J. B., and N. Draper
1982 The Bones from the Bis sa'ani Community: A Sociotechnic Archaeofaunal Analysis. In *Bis sa'ani: A Late Bonito Phase Community on Escavada Wash,* edited by C. D. Breternitz, D. E. Doyel, and M. P. Marshall, pp. 1015–1065. Navajo Nation Papers in Anthropology 14. Navajo Nation Cultural Resource Management Program. Window Rock, Arizona.

Blake, M., S. A. LeBlanc, and P. E. Minnis
1986 Changing Settlement and Population in the Mimbres Valley, SW New Mexico. *Journal of Field Archaeology* 13:439–464.

Bonilla, J. S.
1992 Similitudes entre las pinturas de Las Higueras y las obras plásticas del Tajín. In *Tajín,* edited by J. Brueggemann, S. Ladrón de Guevara, and J. S. Bonilla, pp. 133–159. El Equilibrista, México, D.F., and Turner Libros, Madrid.

Bordaz, J.
1964 *Pre-Columbian Ceramic Kilns at Peñitas, A Post-Classic Site in Coastal Nayarit, Mexico.* Ph.D. dissertation, Columbia University. University Microfilms, Ann Arbor.

Bowen, T.
1976 Esquema de la historia de la cultura Trincheras. In *Sonora: Antropologia del Desierto,* edited by B. Braniff and R. S. Felger, pp. 347–363, Colección Cientifica 27, Instituto Nacional de Antropología e Historia, México, D.F.

Boyd, C.
1996 Shamanic Journeys into the Otherworld of the Archaic Chichimec. *Latin American Antiquity* 7:152–164.

Bradley, R. J.
1986 Shell Species and Exchange: A Brief Review of Shell at Casas Grandes and Its Role in Exchange on the Northwest Frontier of Mesoamerica. Paper presented at the 51st Annual Meeting of the Society for American Archaeology, New Orleans.
1987 Marine Shell Ornament Production at Casas Grandes, Chihuahua: The Role of Shell in Exchange Systems in Northwest Mexico and the Southwest. Paper presented at the 52nd Annual Meeting of the Society for American Archaeology, Toronto.
1993 Marine Shell Exchange in Northwest Mexico and the Southwest. In *The American Southwest and Mesoamerica: Systems of Prehistoric Exchange,* edited by J. E. Ericson and T. G. Baugh, pp. 121–151. Plenum Press, New York.
1994 *Before the Sky Fell: The Pre-Eruptive Sinagua of the Flagstaff Area, across the Colorado Plateau.* Anthropological Studies for the Transwestern Pipeline Expansion Project Vol. XII. Office of Contract Archaeology, The University of New Mexico, Albuquerque.
1995 A Comparison of Shell Ornament Production Strategies in the North American Southwest. Paper presented at the 60th Annual Meeting of the Society for American Archaeology, Minneapolis.
1996 *The Role of Casas Grandes in Prehistoric Shell Exchange Networks within the Southwest.* Unpublished Ph.D. dissertation, Department of Anthropology, Arizona State University, Tempe.

Bradley, R. J., and J. M. Hoffer
1985 Playas Red: A Preliminary Study of Origins and Variability in the Jornada Mogollon. In *Proceedings of the Third Jornada Mogollon Conference,* edited by M. S. Foster and T. C. O'Laughlin. *The Artifact* 23:161–177.

Brand, D. D.
1933 *The Historical Geography of Northwestern Chihuahua.* Unpublished Ph.D. dissertation, Department of Geography, University of California, Berkeley.
1935 The Distribution of Pottery Types in Northwest Mexico. *American Anthropologist,* n.s., 37:287–305.
1938 *Aboriginal Trade Routes for Sea Shells in the Southwest.* Yearbook of the Association of Pacific Coast Geographers 4:3–10.
1939 Notes on the Geography and Archaeology of Zape, Durango. In *So Live the Works of Men. Seventieth Anniversary Volume Honoring Edgar Lee Hewett,* edited by D. D. Brand and F. E. Harvey, pp. 75–105. University of New Mexico Press, Albuquerque, and School of American Research, Santa Fe.
1943 The Chihuahua Culture Area. *New Mexico Anthropologist* 6–7(3):115–158.

Braniff C., B.
1985 La Frontera protohistórica Pima-Opata en Sonora, Mexico. Proposciones Arqueológicas Preliminares. Tésis doctoral, Universidad Autónoma de México, México, D.F.
1986 Ojo de Agua, Sonora and Casas Grandes, Chihuahua: A Suggested Chronology. In *Ripples in the Chichimec Sea: New Considerations of Southwestern-Mesoamerican Interactions,* edited by F. J. Mathien and R. H. McGuire, pp. 70–80. Southern Illinois University Press, Carbondale.
1990 The Identification of Possible Elites in Prehispanic Sonora. In *Perspectives on Southwestern Prehistory,* edited by P. E. Minnis and C. L. Redman, pp. 173–183. Westview Press, Boulder.
1992 *La Frontera Protohistórica Pima-Opata, México.* Instituto Nacional de Antropología e Historia, México, D.F.
1993 The Mesoamerican Northern Frontier and the Gran

Chichimeca. In *Culture and Contact: Charles C. Di Peso's Gran Chichimeca,* edited by A. I. Woosley and J. C. Ravesloot, pp. 65–82. Amerind Foundation Publication, Dragoon, and University of New Mexico Press, Albuquerque.
1994a El Norte de México: La Gran Chichimeca. *Arqueología Mexicana* 1(6):14–19.
1994b *Paquimé.* Instituto Nacional de Antropología e Historia and Salvat Ciencia y Cultura Latinoamérica, México, D.F.
1995 The Opata-Pima Frontier: Preliminary Notes and Comments. In *The Gran Chichimeca: Essays on the Archaeology and Ethnohistory of Northern Mesoamerica,* edited by J. E. Reyman, pp. 252–268. Avebury, Aldershot.

Breternitz, C. D., and M. P. Marshall
1982 Summary of Analytical Results and Review of Miscellaneous Artifacts from Bis sa'ani Pueblo. In *Bis sa'ani: A Late Bonito Phase Community on Escavada Wash, Northwest New Mexico,* vol. 2, pt. 1, edited by C. D. Breternitz, D. E. Doyel, and M. P. Marshall, pp. 433–449. Navajo Nation Papers in Anthropology Number 14. Window Rock, Arizona.

Breternitz, C. D., D. E. Doyel, and M. P. Marshall (editors)
1982 *Bis sa'ani: A Late Bonito Phase Community on Escavada Wash, Northwest New Mexico.* Navajo Nation Papers in Anthropology 14. Window Rock, Arizona.

Breternitz, D. A.
1966 *An Appraisal of Tree-Ring Dated Pottery in the Southwest.* Anthropological Papers of the University of Arizona No. 10. University of Arizona Press, Tucson.

Brew, J. O.
1943 On the Pueblo IV and on the Katchina-Tlaloc Relations. In *El Norte de México y el Sur de los Estados Unidos,* pp. 241–245. Tercera Reunión de Mesa Redonda sobre problemas Antropológicas de México y Centro América. Sociedad Mexicana de Antropología, México, D.F.

Brewington, R. L.
1992 *Mimbres-Mogollon Stylistic and Assemblage Variation: A Comparison of Surface Pueblo Components, West Fork and NAN Ruins, Catron and Grant Counties, New Mexico.* Unpublished thesis for Master's bypass, on file at the Department of Anthropology, Texas A&M University, College Station.
1996 Neutron Activation Analysis of Clays and Ceramics from the Mimbres Area, New Mexico. Paper presented at the 9th Mogollon Conference, Silver City.
1997 *The Production and Distribution of Mimbres Classic Period Ceramics: The Social Implications of Neutron Activation Analysis.* Unpublished Ph.D. dissertation, Texas A & M University, College Station.

Brewington, R. L., H. J. Shafer, and W. D. James
1994 Neutron Activation Studies of Mimbres and El Paso Wares: Social Implications of Trace Element Analysis. Paper presented at the 8th Annual Jornada Conference, El Paso, Texas.

Broda, J.
1991 The Sacred Landscape of Aztec Calendar Festival: Myth, Nature and Society. In *To Change Place: Aztec Ceremonial Landscapes,* edited by D. Carrasco, pp. 74–120. University Press of Colorado, Niwot.

Brody, J. J.
1977a *Mimbres Painted Pottery.* School of American Research, Santa Fe, and University of New Mexico Press, Albuquerque.
1977b Sidetracked on the Trail of a Mexican Connection. *American Indian Art* 2(4):2–31.
1978 Mimbres Painting and the Northern Frontier. In *Across the Chichimec Sea: Papers in Honor of J. Charles Kelley,* edited by C. L. Riley and B. C. Hedrick, pp. 11–21. Southern Illinois University Press, Carbondale.

Brody, J. J., and R. Swentzell
1996 *To Touch the Past: The Painted Pottery of the Mimbres People.* Hudson Hills Press, New York.

Brooks, R. H.
1971 *Lithic Traditions in Northwestern Mexico, Paleo-Indian to Chalchihuites.* Unpublished Ph.D. dissertation, Department of Anthropology, University of Colorado, Boulder.

Brown, J. A.
1990 Spiro Political Economy and the Southern Plains. Paper presented at 48th Plains Conference, Oklahoma City.
1996 *The Spiro Ceremonial Center.* Memoirs of the Museum of Anthropology No. 29. University of Michigan, Ann Arbor.

Bruhns, K. O.
1980 *Cihuatán: An Early Postclassic Town of El Salvador.* Monographs in Anthropology No. 5. University of Missouri, Columbia.
1986 The Role of Commercial Agriculture in Early Postclassic Developments in Central El Salvador: The Rise and Fall of Cihuatán. In *The Southeast Maya Periphery,* edited by P. A. Urban and E. M. Schortman, pp. 296–312. University of Texas Press, Austin.
1989 The Crucible: Sociological and Technological Factors in the Delayed Diffusion of Metallurgy to Mesoamerica. In *New Frontiers in the Archaeology of the Pacific Coast of Southern Mesoamerica,* edited by F. Bove and L. Heller, pp. 221–228. Anthropological Research Papers No. 39. University of Arizona, Tucson.
1996 El Salvador and the Southwestern Frontier of Mesoamerica. In *Paths to Central American Prehistory,* edited by F. Lange, pp. 285–296. University Press of Colorado, Niwot.

Brumfiel, E. M.
1994 Factional Competition and Political Development in the New World: An Introduction. In *Factional Competition and Political Development in the New World,* edited by E. Brumfiel and J. Fox, pp. 3–14. Cambridge University Press, New York.

Bunzel, R. L.
1932a Introduction to Zuni Ceremonialism. In *Forty-*

Seventh Annual Report of the Bureau of American Ethnology, 1929–1930*, pp. 473–544. Government Printing Office, Washington, D.C.

1932b Zuni Katcinas: An Analytical Study. In *Forty-Seventh Annual Report of the Bureau of American Ethnology, 1929–1930*, pp. 843–1086. Government Printing Office, Washington, D.C.

Burrus, E. J. (editor)

1969 *A History of the Southwest* (by A. F. Bandelier), Supplement to Volume I. Reproduction in Color of Thirty Sketches and Ten Maps. Vol. VII. Jesuit Historical Institute, St. Louis University, St. Louis.

Cabrero, G. M. T.

1989 *Civilización en el Norte de México*. Instituto de Investigaciones Antropológicas, Seria Antropología, vol. 103. Universidad Nacional Autónoma de México, México, D.F.

Carey, H. A.

1931 An Analysis of the Chihuahua Culture. *American Anthropologist* 33:325–374.

Carlson, R. L.

1982a The Mimbres Kachina Cult. In *Mogollon Archaeology: Proceedings of the 1980 Mogollon Conference*, edited by P. H. Beckett and K. Silverbird, pp. 147–157. Acoma Books, Ramona, Calif.

1982b The Polychrome Complexes. In *Southwestern Ceramics: A Comparative Review*, edited by A. H. Schroeder, pp. 201–234. The Arizona Archaeologist 15.

Carmack, R. M., and L. Larmer

1971 *Quichean Art: A Mixteca-Puebla Variant*. Museum of Anthropology Miscellaneous Series No. 23. University of Northern Colorado, Greeley.

Carmichael, D. L.

1990 Patterns of Residential Mobility and Sedentism in the Jornada Mogollon Area. In *Perspectives on Southwestern Prehistory*, edited by P. E. Minnis and C. L. Redman, pp. 122–134. Westview Press, Boulder.

Carpenter, J. P.

1992 *The Animas Phase and Paquime (Casas Grandes): A Perspective and Regional Differentiation and Integration from the Joyce Well Site*. Manuscript on file, Department of Anthropology, New Mexico State University, Las Cruces.

1994 The Cahitan Connection: Modeling Mesoamerican-Southwestern Interactions in the Gran Chichimeca. Paper presented at the 59th Annual Meeting of the Society for American Archaeology, Anaheim.

1996a Rethinking Mesoamerican Meddling: External Influences and Indigenous Developments at Guasave, Sinaloa. Paper presented at the 61st Annual Meeting of the Society for American Archaeology, New Orleans.

1996b El Ombligo en la Labor: Differentiation, Interaction and Integration in Prehispanic Sinaloa, Mexico. Unpublished Ph.D. dissertation in Anthropology, University of Arizona, Tucson.

Carr, F. A.

1935 *The Ancient Pueblo Culture of Northern Mexico*. Unpublished Master's thesis, Department of Anthropology, University of Arizona, Tucson.

Cartwright, F. F., in collaboraton with M. D. Biddiss

1972 *Disease and History*. Dorset Press, New York.

Las Casas, B. de

1967 *Apologética Historia Sumaria*. 2 vols, edited by E. O'Gorman. Instituto de Investigaciones Históricas, Universidad Nacional Autónoma de México, México, D.F.

Castetter, E. F., and W. H. Bell

1942 *Pima and Papago Indian Agriculture*. University of New Mexico Press, Albuquerque.

Castro-Leal, M.

1986 *El Juego de Pelota: Una Tradición Prehispánica Viva*. Museo Nacional de Antropología. México, D.F.

Chang, K.

1958 Study of the Neolithic Social Grouping: Examples from the New World. *American Anthropologist* 60:298–334.

Clarke, D. L.

1973 Archaeology: The Loss of Innocence. *American Antiquity* 47:6–18.

Cloud, W. A., R. J. Mallouf, P. A. Mercado-Allinger, C. A. Hoyt, N. A. Kenmotsu, J. M. Sanchez, and E. R. Madrid

1994 *Archeological Testing at the Polvo Site Presidio County, Texas*. Office of the State Archeologist Report 39. Texas Historical Commission and U.S.D.A., Soil Conservation Service, Austin.

Clune, F. J.

1976 The Amapa Ballcourt. In *The Archaeology of Amapa, Nayarit*, edited by C. W. Meighan, pp. 275–298. Monumenta Arqueológica 2, Institute of Archaeology, University of California Los Angeles, Los Angeles.

Códice Borbónico

1981 Comentarios de F. del Paso y Troncoso. Siglo XXI editores, México, D.F., 3rd facsimile ed.

Contreras Sánchez, E.

1986 *Paquimé: Zona Arqueológica de Casas Grandes, Chihuahua*. Ediciones del Gobierno del Estado de Chihuahua. Cd. Chihuahua.

Cordell, L. S.

1994 *Ancient Pueblo Peoples*. St. Remy Press, Montreal.

Cordell, L. S., and G. J. Gumerman

1989 Cultural Interaction in the Prehistoric Southwest. In *Dynamics of Southwest Prehistory*, edited by L. S. Cordell and G. J. Gumerman, pp. 1–17. Smithsonian Institution Press, Washington, D.C.

Cordell, L. S., and G. J. Gumerman (editors)

1989 *Dynamics of Southwest Prehistory*. Smithsonian Institution Press, Washington, D.C.

Cosgrove, C. B.

1947 *Caves in the Upper Gila and Hueco Areas in New Mexico and Texas*. Papers of the Peabody Museum of American Archaeology and Ethnology 24(2). Harvard University, Cambridge.

Cosgrove, C. B., and H. S. Cosgrove

1932 *The Swarts Ruin, A Typical Mimbres Site in Southwestern New Mexico*. Papers of the Peabody Museum of

American Archaeology and Ethnology 15(1). Harvard University, Cambridge.

Covarrubias, M.
1957 *Indian Art of Mexico and Central America.* Alfred A. Knopf, New York.

Craig, D. B.
1982 Shell Exchange along the Middle Santa Cruz River Valley during the Hohokam Pre-Classic. Paper presented at the Tucson Basin Conference, Tucson.

Creel, D.
1989 A Primary Cremation at the NAN Ranch Ruin, with Comparative Data on Other Cremations in the Mimbres Area, New Mexico. *Journal of Field Archaeology* 16:309–329.
1991 *Status Report on Excavations at the Old Town Site (LA 1113), Luna County, New Mexico, Summer 1991.* Report submitted to the U.S. Bureau of Land Management, New Mexico State Office, by the Texas Archeological Research Laboratory, University of Texas at Austin.
1992 *Status Report on Excavations at the Old Town Site (LA 1113), Luna County, New Mexico, Summer 1992.* Report submitted to the U.S. Bureau of Land Management, New Mexico State Office, by the Texas Archeological Research Laboratory, University of Texas at Austin.
1993 *Status Report on Excavations at the Old Town Site (LA 1113), Luna County, New Mexico, Summer 1993.* Report submitted to the U.S. Bureau of Land Management, New Mexico State Office, by the Texas Archeological Research Laboratory, University of Texas at Austin.
1994a Interpreting the End of the Mimbres Classic. Paper presented at the Spring Meeting of the Arizona Archaeological Council, Tucson, Arizona.
1994b Prehistoric Macaws and Parrots in the Mimbres Area, New Mexico. *American Antiquity* 59:510–524.
1995 *Status Report on Excavations at the Old Town Site (LA 1113), Luna County, New Mexico, Summer 1994.* Report submitted to the U.S. Bureau of Land Management, New Mexico State Office, by the Texas Archeological Research Laboratory, University of Texas at Austin.
1996 Environmental Variation and Prehistoric Culture in the Mimbres Area. Paper presented at the 61st Annual Meeting of the Society for American Archaeology, New Orleans.

Creel, D., and B. Adams
1985 Investigation of Water Control Features at NAN-20. In *The NAN Ranch Archaeology Project: 1985 Interim Report,* edited by H. J. Shafer, pp. 50–66. Special Report 7, Anthropology Laboratory, Texas A & M University, College Station.

Creel, D., M. Williams, H. Neff, and M. Glascock
1998 Neutron Activation Analysis of Black Mountain Phase Ceramics and Its Implications for Manufacture and Exchange Patterns, In *Chemical Sourcing in the Southwest,* edited by Donna Glowacki and Hector Neff, UCLA Press, Los Angeles, in press.

Crotty, H. K.
1990 Formal Qualities of the Jornada Style and Pueblo IV Anasazi Rock Art: A Comparison with Implications for the Origins of Pueblo Ceremonialism. In *American Indian Rock Art,* vol. 16, edited by S. Turpin, pp. 147–166. The National Park Service, American Rock Art Research Association, Texas Archeological Research Laboratory, University of Texas at Austin.

Crown, P. L.
1990 Classic Period Hohokam Settlement and Land Use in the Casas Grandes Ruins Area, Arizona. *Journal of Field Archaeology* 14:147–162.
1994 *Ceramics and Ideology: Salado Polychrome Pottery.* University of New Mexico Press, Albuquerque.

Crown P. L., and W. J. Judge (editors)
1991 *Chaco and Hohokam: Prehistoric Regional Systems in the American Southwest.* School of American Research Press, Santa Fe.

Cruz A., R.
1997 Recientes Investigaciones Arqueológicas en Villa Ahumada, Chihuahua. In *Prehistory of the Borderlands—Recent Research in the Archaeology of Northern Mexico and the Southern Southwest,,* edited by J. Carpenter and G. Sanchez, pp. 1–9. Arizona State Museum Archaeological Series 186. Arizona State Museum, University of Arizona, Tucson.

Cushing, F.
1920 *Zuni Breadstuff.* Indian Notes, vol. 8, Museum of the American Indian, Heye Foundation, New York.

Cutler, H. C.
1965a Plant materials from the Joyce Well Site (29 HI SAR 63-16), Hidalgo County, New Mexico. In *The Excavations of the Joyce Well Site, Hidalgo County, New Mexico by E. B. McCluney,* appendix II. Manuscript on file, Laboratory of Anthropology, Santa Fe.
1965b Corn and Cucurbits. In *A Survey and Excavation of Caves in Hidalgo County, New Mexico,* by M. Lambert and J. R. Ambler, pp. 90–93. School of American Research Monograph 25. School of American Research, Santa Fe.

Cutler, H., and M. Eichmeier
1965 Corn and Other Plant Remains from Four Sites in Hidalgo County, New Mexico. In *Clanton Draw and Box Canyon: An Interim Report on Two Prehistoric Sites in Hidalgo County, New Mexico, and Related Surveys,* by E. B. McCluney, pp. 48–54. School of American Research Monograph No. 26. School of American Research, Santa Fe.

Damon, P. E., C. W. Ferguson, A. Long, and E. I. Wallick
1974 Dendrochronologic Calibration of the Radiocarbon Time Scale. *American Antiquity* 39:350–366.

Dart, A.
1986 Sediment Accumulation along Hohokam Canals. *The Kiva* 51:63–84.

Davis, C. O.
1995 *Treasured Earth: Hattie Cosgrove's Mimbres Archaeology in the American Southwest.* SanPete Publications and Old Pueblo Archaeology Center, Tucson.

Davis, J. V., and K. S. Toness
1974 *A Rock Art Inventory at Hueco Tanks State Park,*

Texas. Special Report Number 12, El Paso Archaeological Society, El Paso.

Dean, J. S.

1969 *Chronological Analysis of Tsegi Phase Sites in Northeastern Arizona.* Papers of the Laboratory of Tree-Ring Research No. 3. University of Arizona, Tucson.

1978 Independent Dating in Archaeological Analysis. In *Advances in Archaeological Method and Theory,* vol. 1, edited by M. B. Schiffer, pp. 223–255. Academic Press, New York.

Dean, J. S., J. M. Epstein, R. Axtell, G. J. Gumerman, and S. McCarroll

1995 Creating Alternative Culture Histories in Long House Valley, Arizona: Archaeological Applications of Agent Based Computer Modeling. In *Final Program, Durango Conference on Southwest Archaeology,* p. 9. Fort Lewis College, Durango, Colorado.

Dean, J. S., and J. C. Ravesloot

1988 The Chronology of Cultural Interaction in the Gran Chichimeca. Paper presented at the seminar *Culture and Contact: Charles C. Di Peso's Gran Chichimeca,* Amerind Foundation, Dragoon.

1993 The Chronology of Cultural Interaction in the Gran Chichimeca. In *Culture and Contact: Charles C. Di Peso's Gran Chichimeca,* edited by A. I. Woosley and J. C. Ravesloot, pp. 83–103. Amerind Foundation, Dragoon, and University of New Mexico Press, Albuquerque.

De Atley, S. P.

1980 *Regional Integration on the Northern Casas Grandes Frontier.* Unpublished Ph.D. dissertation, Department of Anthropology, University of California, Los Angeles. University Microfilms, Ann Arbor.

De Atley, S. P., and F. J. Findlow

1982 Regional Integration of the Northern Casas Grandes Frontier. In *Mogollon Archaeology: Proceedings of the 1980 Mogollon Conference,* edited by P. H. Beckett and K. Silverbird, pp. 263–277. Acoma Books, Ramona, Calif.

DeBano, L. F., S. Manzanilla-Naim, R. R. Pollisco, and P. F. Ffolliott

1994 Research and Conservation Literature and Database for the Borderlands Region. In *Biodiversity and Management of the Madrean Archipelago: The Sky Islands of Southwestern United States and Northwestern Mexico,* edited by L. F. DeBano, G. Gottfried, R. Hamre, C. Edminster, P. Ffolliott, and A. Ortega-Rubio, pp. 580–582. Rocky Mountain Forest and Range Experiment Station, U.S. Department of Agriculture, Fort Collins.

De La Fuente, B.

1992 Order and Nature in Olmec Art. In *The Ancient Americas: Art in Sacred Landscapes,* edited by R. F. Townsend, pp. 120–133. The Art Institute of Chicago, Chicago.

Di Peso, C. C.

1953 *The Soibaipuri Indians of the Upper San Pedro River Valley, Southeastern Arizona.* Amerind Foundation Series No. 6. Amerind Foundation, Dragoon.

1956 *The Upper Pima of San Cayentano del Tumacacori: An Archaeohistorical Reconstruction of the Ootam of Pimeria Alta.* Amerind Foundation Series No. 7. Amerind Foundation, Dragoon, and Northland Press, Flagstaff.

1968 Casas Grandes and the Gran Chichimeca. *El Palacio* 75(4):45–61.

ca. 1970–1975 Archaeological Site Survey Forms and Field Records, San Bernardino Valley, Sonora, Mexico (1970–1975). Archives on file, Amerind Foundation, Dragoon.

1974 *Casas Grandes: A Fallen Trading Center of the Gran Chichimeca.* 3 vols. Amerind Foundation Series No. 9. Amerind Foundation, Dragoon, and Northland Press, Flagstaff.

1976 Culture Change in Northern Mexico: The Bureaucratic Conquest of the Gran Chichimeca, A.D. 1540–A.D. 1600. *Actes du XLII Congrès International des Américanistes,* vol. VIII, Paris.

1979a Prehistory: The Southern Periphery. In *Southwest,* edited by A. Ortiz, pp. 152–161. Handbook of North American Indians, vol. 9, W. C. Sturtevant, general editor, Smithsonian Institution, Washington, D.C.

1979b Roots of the New Tradition: Prehistory of the Casas Grandes Valley. In *Juan Quezada and the New Tradition,* edited by D. Frankel, pp. 10–21. California State University Art Gallery, Fullerton.

1981 The Rio Grande as Seen from Casas Grandes. In *Collected Papers in Honor of Erik Kellerman Reed,* edited by A. H. Schroeder, pp. 23–41. Papers of the Archaeological Society of New Mexico No. 6, Albuquerque.

1983 The Northern Sector of the Mesoamerican World System. In *Forgotten Places and Things: Archaeological Perspectives on American History,* edited by A. E. Ward, pp. 11–22. Contributions to Anthropological Studies 3, Center for Anthropological Studies, Albuquerque.

Di Peso, C. C., J. B. Rinaldo, and G. J. Fenner

1974 *Casas Grandes: A Fallen Trading Center of the Gran Chichimeca.* 5 vols. Amerind Foundation Series No. 9. Amerind Foundation, Dragoon, and Northland Press, Flagstaff.

Dirst, V. A.

1979 *The Prehistoric Frontier in Sonora.* Unpublished Ph.D. dissertation, Department of Anthropology, University of Arizona, Tucson.

Dobyns, H. F.

1960 *The Religious Festival.* Department of Anthropology, Cornell University, Ithaca.

Dockall, J.

1991 *Chipped Stone Technology at the NAN Ruin, Grant County, New Mexico.* Master's thesis, Department of Anthropology, Texas A&M University, College Station.

Doelle, W. H.

1989 Review of C. L. Riley's *Frontier People,* University of New Mexico Press. *The Kiva* 54:165–168.

Doolittle, W. E.
1984 Settlements and the Development of "Statelets" in Sonora, Mexico. *Journal of Field Archaeology* 11:13–24.
1988 *Pre-Hispanic Occupance in the Valley of Sonora, Mexico: Archaeological Confirmation of Early Spanish Reports.* Anthropological Papers of the University of Arizona No. 48. The University of Arizona Press, Tucson.
1993 Canal Irrigation at Casas Grandes: A Technological and Developmental Assessment of Its Origins. In *Culture and Contact: Charles C. Di Peso's Gran Chichimeca,* edited by A. I. Woosley and J. C. Ravesloot, pp. 133–151. Amerind Foundation, Dragoon, and University of New Mexico Press, Albuquerque.

Douglas, J. E.
1990 *Regional Interaction in the Northern Sierra: An Analysis Based on the Late Prehistoric Occupation of the San Bernardino Valley, Southeastern Arizona.* Unpublished Ph.D. dissertation, Department of Anthropology, University of Arizona, Tucson.
1992 Distant Sources, Local Contexts: Interpreting Nonlocal Ceramics at Paquimé (Casas Grandes), Chihuahua. *Journal of Anthropological Research* 48(1):1–24.
1995 Autonomy and Regional Systems in the Late Prehistoric Southern Southwest. *American Antiquity* 60:240–257.
1996 Distinguishing Change during the Animas Phase (A.D. 1150–1450) at the Boss Ranch Site, Southeastern Arizona. *North American Archaeologist* 17:183–202.

Downum, C. E.
1993 *Between the Desert and the River.* Anthropological Papers of the University of Arizona No. 57, Tucson.

Downum, C. E., P. R. Fish, and S. K. Fish
1994 Refining the Role of Cerros de Trincheras in Southern Arizona. *The Kiva* 59:271–296.

Doyel, D. E.
1976 Classic Period Hohokam in the Gila River Basin, Arizona. *The Kiva* 42:27–38.

Doyel, D. E., A. Black, and B. Macnider
1995 *Archaeological Excavations at Pueblo Blanco: The MCDOT Alma School Road Project.* Archaeological Consulting Services Cultural Resources Report No. 90. Archaeological Consulting Services, Tempe.

Durán, D.
1971 *Book of the Gods and Rites and the Ancient Calendar.* Translated and edited by F. Horcasitas and D. Heyden. University of Oklahoma Press, Norman.

Duran, M. S.
1992 Animas Phase Sites in Hidalgo County, New Mexico. National Register of Historic Places, Multiple Property Documentation Form. Prepared for the New Mexico Historic Preservation Division, Santa Fe.

Dutton, B. P.
1963 *Sun Father's Way: The Kiva Murals of Kuaua.* University of New Mexico Press, Albuquerque, and Museum of New Mexico Press, Santa Fe.

Easby, E. K., and J. F. Scott
1970 *Before Cortez: Sculpture of Middle America.* Metropolitan Museum of Art, New York.

Eggan, F.
1994 The Hopi Indians, with Special Reference to Their Cosmology or World-View. In *Kachinas in the Pueblo World,* edited by P. Schaafsma, pp. 7–16. University of New Mexico Press, Albuquerque.

Ekholm, G. F.
1939 Recent Archaeological Work in Sonora and Northern Sinaloa. *27th Congreso Internacional de Americanistas, México* 1:69–73.
1942 *Excavations at Guasave, Sinaloa, Mexico.* Anthropological Papers of the American Museum of Natural History 38(2):23–139. American Museum of Natural History, New York.

Ellis, F. H.
1969 Differential Pueblo Specialization in Fetiches and Shrines. *Anales, 1967–1968.* Séptima época, Tomo I, México, D.F.

Ellis, F. H., and L. Hammack
1968 The Inner Sanctum of Feather Cave, a Mogollon Sun and Earth Shrine Linking Mexico and the Southwest. *American Antiquity* 33(1):25–44.

Ellis, L.
1995 An Interpretive Framework for Radiocarbon Dates from Soil Organic Matter from Prehistoric Water Control Features. In *Soil, Water, Biology, and Belief in Prehistoric and Traditional Southwestern Agriculture,* edited by J. Wolcott Toll, pp. 155–186. New Mexico Archaeological Council, Special Publication 2, Albuquerque.

Elson, M. D., and D. Craig
1995 *The Rye Creek Project: Archaeology in the Upper Tonto Basin.* Center for Desert Archaeology Papers No. 11. Center for Desert Archaeology, Tucson.

Elton, H.
1996 *Frontiers of the Roman Empire.* Indiana University Press, Bloomington.

Ericson, J. E., and T. G. Baugh (editors)
1993 *The American Southwest and Mesoamerica: Systems of Prehistoric Exchange.* Plenum, New York.

Fahmel Beyer, B. W. F.
1988 *Mesoamerica Tolteca, sus ceramicas de comercio principales.* Instituto de Investigaciones Antropológicas, Serie Antropológicas Vol. 95. Universidad Autónoma de México, México, D.F.

Feinman, G., S. Upham, and K. G. Lightfoot
1981 The Production Step Measure: An Ordinal Index of Labor Input in Ceramic Manufacture. *American Antiquity* 46:871–884.

Ferguson, T. J., and E. R. Hart
1985 *A Zuni Atlas.* University of Oklahoma Press, Norman.

Ferguson, W. M., and A. H. Rohn
1987 *Anasazi Ruins of the Southwest in Color.* University of New Mexico Press, Albuquerque.

Fewkes, J. W.
1891 A Few Summer Ceremonials at Zuñi Pueblo. In *A Journal of American Ethnology and Archaeology,* vol. 1, edited by J. W. Fewkes, pp.1–62. Riverside Press, Cambridge.
1903 *Hopi Katsinas Drawn by Native Artists.* Annual Report of the Bureau of American Ethnology 21:3–126. Washington, D.C.
Findlow, F. J.
1979 A Catchment Analysis of Certain Prehistoric Settlements in Southwestern New Mexico. *Journal of New World Archaeology* 3(3):1–15.
Findlow, F. J., and L. Confeld
1980 Landsat Imagery and the Analysis of Archaeological Catchment Territories: Test of the Method. *Anthropology UCLA* 10(1–2):31–32.
Findlow, F. J., and S. P. De Atley
1976 Prehistoric Land Use Patterns in the Animas Valley: A First Approximation. *Anthropology UCLA* 6(2):5–18.
1978 An Ecological Analysis of Animas Phase Assemblages in Southwestern New Mexico. *Journal of New World Archaeology* 2(5):6–18.
Fish, P. R., and S. K. Fish
1994 Southwest and Northwest: Recent Research at the Juncture of the United States and Mexico. *Journal of Archaeological Research* 2(1):3–44.
Fish, S. K., and P. R. Fish
1994 Multisite Communities as Measures of Hohokam Aggregation. In *The Ancient Southwestern Community,* edited by W. H. Wills and R. D. Leonard, pp. 119–129. University of New Mexico Press, Albuquerque.
1998 Prehistory and Early History of the Malpais Borderlands. U.S. Forest Service, Rocky Mountain Range and Experiment Station, Fort Collins, Co., in press.
Fish, P. R., P. Pilles, and S. K. Fish
1980 Colonies, Traders and Traits: The Hohokam in the North. In *Current Issues in Hohokam Prehistory,* edited by D. Doyel and F. Plog, pp. 151–175. Anthropological Research Papers No. 23. Arizona State University, Tempe.
Fish, S. K., P. R. Fish, C. Miksicek, and J. Madsen
1985 Prehistoric Agave Cultivation in Southern Arizona. *Desert Plants* 7:102–112.
Fontana, B. L.
1989 Were There Indian Statelets in the Sonora Valley? *Southwestern Mission Research Center Newsletter* 23(79):8.
Foster, M. S.
1982 The Loma San Gabriel–Mogollon Continuum. In *Mogollon Archaeology: Proceedings of the 1980 Mogollon Conference,* edited by P. H. Beckett and K. Silverbird, pp. 251–261. Acoma Books, Ramona, Calif.
1986 The Mesoamerican Connection: A View from the South. In *Ripples in the Chichimec Sea: New Considerations of Southwestern-Mesoamerican Interactions,* edited by F. J. Mathien and R. H. McGuire, pp. 55–69. Southern Illinois University Press, Carbondale.
1991 The Early Ceramic Period in Northwest Mexico: An Overview. In *Mogollon V,* edited by P. H. Beckett, pp. 155–165. COAS Publishing and Research, Las Cruces.
1992 Arqueología del valle de Casas Grandes: Sitio Paquimé. In *Historia General de Chihuahua, Geología, Geografía, y Arqueología,* edited by Arturo Márquez-Alameda, pp. 229–282. Universidad Autónoma de Ciudad Juárez, Juárez, Chihuahua.
1993 *Archaeological Investigations at Pueblo Sin Casas (FB6273), a Multicomponent Site in the Hueco Bolson, Fort Bliss, Texas.* Historic and Natural Resources Report No. 7. Cultural Resources Management Program, Directorate of Environment. U.S. Army Air Defense Artillery Center, Fort Bliss.
1995a The Chalchihuites Chronological Sequence: A View from the West Coast of Mexico. In *Arqueología del Norte y del Occidente de México, Homenaje al Doctor J. Charles Kelley,* edited by B. Dahlgren y Ma. del los Dolores Soto de Arechavaleta, pp. 67–92. Instituto de Investigaciones Antropológicas, Universidad Nacional Autónoma de México, México, D.F.
1995b The Loma San Gabriel Culture and Its Suggested Relationships to Other Early Plainware Cultures of Northwest Mesoamerica. In *The Gran Chichimeca: Essays on the Archaeology and Ethnohistory of Northern Mesoamerica,* edited by J. E. Reyman, pp. 179–207. Avebury, Aldershot.
Foster, M. S., R. J. Bradley, and C. Williams
1981 Prehistoric Diet and Subsistence at La Cabraña Pueblo. *The Artifact* 19(3–4):151–168.
Fowler, W. R., Jr.
1989 The Pipil of Pacific Guatemala and El Salvador. In *New Frontiers in the Archaeology of the Pacific Coast of Southern Mesoamerica,* edited by F. Bove and L. Heller, pp. 229–242. Anthropological Research Papers No. 39. University of Arizona, Tucson.
Fremantle, A.
1965 *Age of Faith.* Time, New York.
Frick, P. S.
1954 *An Archaeological Survey in the Central Santa Cruz Valley, Southern Arizona.* Master's thesis, Department of Anthropology, University of Arizona, Tucson.
Furst, J. L.
1986 "The Lords of Place of the Ascending Serpent": Dynastic Succession on the Nuttal Obverse. In *Symbol and Meaning beyond the Closed Community: Essays in Mesoamerican Ideas,* edited by G. H. Gossen, pp. 57–68. Studies on Culture and Society Vol. 1, Institute for Mesoamerican Studies, State University of New York, Albany.
1993 The Physical Process of Death and the Symbolism of Tlalocan. Paper presented at the International Symposium "La Muerte" sponsored by the Instituto de Investigaciones Históricas, Universidad Nacional Autónoma de México, México, D.F.

Ganot R. J, and A. A. Peschard
1985 La Cultura Aztatlán, Frontera del Occidente y Norte de Mesoamérica en el Post-Clásico. Paper presented at the 19th Mesa Redonda de al Sociedad Mexicana de Antropología, Querétero, México.
1990 El Postclásico Temprano en el Estado de Durango. In *Mesoamerica y Norte de México, Siglo IX–XII,* vol. 2, edited by F. S. Miranda, pp. 401–416. Museo Nacional de Antropología, México, D.F.
1995 The Archaeological Site of Cañon del Molino, Durango, Mexico. In *The Gran Chichimeca: Essays on the Archaeology and Ethnohistory of Northern Mesoamerica,* edited by J. E. Reyman, pp. 146–178. Avebury, Aldershot.

Gay, C. T. E.
1972 *Chalcacingo.* International Scholarly Book Services, Portland.

Geertz, A. W., and M. Lomatuway'ma
1987 *Children of Cottonwood: Piety and Ceremonialism in Hopi Indian Puppetry.* University of Nebraska Press, Lincoln.

Gibbon, G.
1974 A Model of Mississippian Development and Its Implications for the Red Wing Area. In *Aspects of Upper Great Lakes Anthropology,* edited by E. Johnson, pp. 129–137. Minnesota Historical Society, St. Paul.
1989 *Explanation in Archaeology.* Blackwell, Oxford.

Gifford, E. W.
1950 *Surface Archaeology of Ixtalán del Río, Nayarit.* University of California Press, Berkeley.

Gill, G. W.
1985 Cultural Implications of Artificially Modified Human Remains from Northwestern Mexico. In *Archaeology of West and Northwest Mesoamerica,* edited by M. S. Foster and P. C. Weigand, pp. 193–217. Westview Press, Boulder.

Gillespie, W. B.
1989 Faunal Remains from Four Sites along the Tucson Aqueduct: Prehistoric Exploitation of Jackrabbits and Other Vertebrates in the Avra Valley. In *Hohokam Archaeology along Phase B of the Tucson Aqueduct Central Arizona Project, Vol. 1: Synthesis and Interpretations,* edited by J. Czaplicki and J. Ravesloot, pp. 171–237. Arizona State Museum Archaeological Series 178(1). Arizona State Museum, University of Arizona, Tucson.

Gilman, P. A.
1980 The Early Pueblo Period: Mimbres Classic. In *An Archeological Synthesis of Southcentral and Southwestern New Mexico,* edited by S. A. LeBlanc and M. E. Whalen, pp. 256–343. Office of Contract Archaeology, University of New Mexico, Albuquerque.

Gilman, P. A., Veletta C., and R. Bishop
1994 The Production and Distribution of Classic Mimbres Black-on-White Pottery. *American Antiquity* 59:695–709.

Gladwin, H. S.
1957 *A History of the Ancient Southwest.* The Bond Wheelwright Company, Portland, Maine.

Gladwin, H. S., E. W. Haury, E. B. Sayles, and N. Gladwin
1937 *Excavations at Snaketown, Material Culture.* Medallion Papers No. 25. Gila Pueblo, Globe.

Gladwin, W., and H. S. Gladwin
1934 *A Method for Designation of Cultures and Their Variations.* Medallion Papers No. 15. Gila Pueblo, Globe.

Glassow, M. A.
1967 The Ceramics of Huistla, a West Mexican Site in the Municipality of Etzatlán, Jalisco. *American Antiquity* 32:64–83.

Gomolak, A., and D. Ford
1976 *Berrenda Creek, LA 12992, 1976: Field Report and Primary Analysis.* University Museum, New Mexico State University, Las Cruces.

Graybill, D.
1975 *Mimbres-Mogollon Adaptations in the Gila National Forest, Mimbres District, New Mexico.* Archeological Report No. 9, USDA Forest Service, Southwestern Region, Albuquerque.

Greengo, R., and C. W. Meighan
1976 Additional Perspective on the Capacha Complex of western Mexico. *Journal of New World Archaeology* 1:5. University of California Press, Los Angeles.

Griffin, J. B.
1966 Mesoamerica and the Eastern United States in Prehistoric Times. In *Archaeological Frontiers and External Connections,* edited by G. F. Ekholm and G. R. Willey, pp. 111–131. Handbook of Middle American Indians, vol. 4, R. Wauchope, general editor, University of Texas Press, Austin.
1967 Eastern North American Archaeology: A Summary. *Science* 156(3772):175–191.
1985 Changing Concepts of the Prehistoric Mississippian Cultures of the Eastern United States. In *Alabama and the Borderlands,* edited by R. R. Badger and L. A. Clayton, pp. 40–63. University of Alabama Press, Tuscaloosa.
1989 Foreword. In *The Holding Site, a Hopewell Community in the American Bottom (11-Ms-118),* by A. C. Fortier, pp. xvii-xxii. American Bottom Archaeology, FAI-270 Site Reports, vol. 19. University of Illinois Press, Urbana.

Griffith, J.
1992 *Beliefs and Holy Places: A Spiritual Geography of the Pimeria Alta.* University of Arizona Press, Tucson.

Grosscup, G. L.
1976 The Ceramic Sequence at Amapa. In *The Archaeology of Amapa, Nayarit,* edited by C. W. Meighan, pp. 207–272. Monumenta Archaeológica Vol. 2. Institute of Archaeology, University of California, Los Angeles.

Guevara Sánchez, A.
1991 Un Sitio Arqueológico Aldeano de Namiquipa, Chihuahua. In *Tercer Congreso Internacional de Historia*

Regional Comparada, edited by R. L. Garcia, pp. 41–45. Universidad Autónoma de Ciudad Juárez, Juárez, Chihuahua.

Gumerman, G. J.

1994 Patterns and Perturbations in Southwest Prehistory. In *Themes in Southwest Prehistory,* edited by G. J. Gumerman, pp. 3–10. School of American Research Advanced Seminar Series. School of American Research, Santa Fe.

Gumerman, G. J., and E. W. Haury

1979 Prehistory: Hohokam. In *Southwest,* edited by A. Ortiz, pp. 75–90. Handbook of North American Indians, vol. 9, W. C. Sturtevant, general editor, Smithsonian Institution, Washington, D.C.

Gumerman, G. J., and M. Gell-Mann

1994 Cultural Evolution in the Prehistoric Southwest. In *Themes in Southwest Prehistory,* edited by G. J. Gumerman, pp. 11–31. School of American Research Advanced Seminar Series. School of American Research, Santa Fe.

Gumerman, G. J., M. Gell-Mann, and L. Cordell

1994 Introduction. In *Understanding Complexity in the Prehistoric Southwest,* edited by G. J. Gumerman and M. Gell-Mann, pp. 3–14. Addison-Wesley, New York.

Gumerman, G. J. (editor)

1994 *Themes in Southwest Prehistory.* School of American Research Advanced Seminar Series. School of American Research, Santa Fe.

Gumerman, G. J., and M. Gell-Mann (editors)

1994 *Understanding Complexity in the Prehistoric Southwest.* Addison-Wesley, New York.

Hage, P., and F. Harary

1983 *Structural Models in Anthropology.* Cambridge University Press, Cambridge.

Hall, R. L.

1984 A Plains Indians Perspective on Mexican Cosmovision. Paper presented at the 1984 Conference on Archaeoastronomy and Ethnoastronomy in Mesoamerica, Mexico City.

1991 Cahokia Identity and Interaction Models of Cahokia Mississippian. In *Cahokia and the Hinterlands,* edited by T. E. Emerson and R. B. Lewis, pp. 3–34. University of Illinois Press, Urbana.

Hammond, G. P., and A. Rey (editors and translators)

1928 *Obregón's History of 16th-Century Explorations in Western America.* Wetzel Publishing, Los Angeles.

1940 *Narratives of the Coronado Expedition, 1540–1542.* Coronado Cuarto Centennial Publications, 1540–1940, vol. 2, G. P. Hammond, editor. University of New Mexico Press, Albuquerque.

1966 *The Rediscovery of New Mexico, 1580–1594: The Explorations of Chamuscado, Espejo, Castaño de Sosa, Morlette, and Leyva de Bonilla and Humaña.* Coronado Cuarto Centennial Publications No. 3. University of New Mexico Press, Albuquerque.

Hammond, N. D. C.

1972 Locational Models and the Site of Lubaatún: A Classic Maya Centre. In *Models in Archaeology,* edited by D. L. Clarke, pp. 757–800. Methuen, London.

Harary, F.

1969 *Graph Theory.* Addison-Wesley, Reading.

Harrington, J. P.

1916 Ethnogeography of the Tewa Indians. *29th Annual Report of the Bureau of American Ethnology.* Washington, D.C.

Harrington, M. R.

1939 Some Rare Casas Grandes Specimens. *The Masterkey* 13:205–206.

Harris, E. C.

1975 The Stratigraphic Sequence: A Question of Time. *World Archaeology* 7(1):109–121.

1979 *Principles of Archaeological Stratigraphy.* Academic Press, New York.

Haury, E. W.

1936 *The Mogollon Culture of Southwestern New Mexico.* Medallion Papers No. 20. Gila Pueblo, Globe.

1937 A Pre-Spanish Rubber Ball from Arizona. *American Antiquity* 2(4):282–288.

1938 Southwestern Dated Ruins: II. *Tree-Ring Bulletin* 4(3):3–4.

1955 Archaeological Stratigraphy. In *Geochronology,* edited by T. L. Smiley, pp. 126–134. University of Arizona Bulletin Series 26(2). [*Physical Science Bulletin* No. 2]. University of Arizona Press, Tucson.

1976 *The Hohokam, Desert Farmers and Craftsmen. Excavations at Snaketown, 1954–65.* University of Arizona Press, Tucson.

Hayden, B., and R. Schulting

1997 The Plateau Interaction Sphere and Late Prehistoric Cultural Complexity. *American Antiquity* 62:51–85.

Hayes, A. C.

1981 A Survey of Chaco Canyon Archeology. In *Archeological Surveys of Chaco Canyon, New Mexico,* A. C. Hayes, D. M. Brugge, and W. J. Judge, pp. 1–68. U.S. National Park Service Publications in Archeology 18A, Washington, D.C.

Hayes, A. C., J. N. Young, and A. H. Warren

1981 *Excavation of Mound 7.* U.S. National Park Publications in Archeology 16, Washington, D.C.

Hays, K. A.

1992 Shalako Depictions on Prehistoric Hopi Pottery. In *Archaeology, Art, and Anthropology: Papers in Honor of J. J. Brody,* edited by M. S. Duran and D. T. Kirkpatrick, pp. 73–84. Papers of the Archaeological Society of New Mexico No. 18, Albuquerque.

1994 Kachina Depictions on Prehistoric Pueblo Pottery. In *Kachinas in the Pueblo World,* edited by P. Schaafsma, pp. 47–62. University of New Mexico Press, Albuquerque.

Hegmon, M., M. Nelson, and S. Ruth

1998 Abandonment, Reorganization, and Social Change: Analysis of Pottery and Architecture from the Mimbres Region of the American Southwest. *American Anthropologist* 100:148–162.

Heine-Geldern, R.
1966 The Problem of Transpacific Influences in Mesoamerica. In *Archaeological Frontiers and External Connections,* edited by G. F. Ekholm and G. R. Willey, pp. 277–295. Handbook of Middle American Indians, vol. 4, R. Wauchope, general editor, University of Texas Press, Austin.

Heine-Geldern, R., and G. F. Ekholm
1951 Significant Parallels in the Symbolic Arts of Southern Asia and Middle America. In *The Civilizations of Ancient America, Selected Papers of the 29th International Congress of Americanists,* edited by S. Tax, pp. 299–309. Cooper Square, New York.

Hernández, E., and A. F. Glafiro
1970 Estudio Morfológico de 5 Nuevas Razas de Maíz de la Sierra Madre Occidental de México: Implicaciones Filogenéticas y Fitogeográficas. *Agrociencia* 5(1):3–30. Chapingo, México, D. F.

Herold, L. C., and R. F. Miller
1995 Water Availability for Plant Growth in Precolumbian Terrace Soils, Chihuahua, Mexico. In *Soil, Water, Biology, and Belief in Prehistoric and Traditional Southwestern Agriculture,* edited by H. W. Toll, pp. 145–153. New Mexico Archaeological Council Special Publication Number 2, Albuquerque.

Herrington, L.
1979 *Settlement Patterns and Water Control Systems of the Mimbres Classic Phase, Grant County, New Mexico.* Unpublished Ph.D. dissertation, University of Texas at Austin.
1982 Water-Control Systems of the Mimbres Classic Phase. In *Mogollon Archaeology: Proceedings of the 1980 Mogollon Conference,* edited by P. Beckett, pp. 75–90. Acoma Books, Ramona, Calif.

Hewett, E. L.
1993 *Ancient Communities in the American Desert.* Reprinted. Edited by A. H. Schroeder. Monograph Series 1. Archaeological Society of New Mexico, Albuquerque. Originally published 1908, Les Communautés Anciennes dans le Désert Américain, Librairie Kündig, Genéve.

Heyden, D.
1981 Caves, Gods, and Myths: World-View and Planning in Teotihuacan. In *Mesoamerican Sites and World-Views,* edited by E. P. Benson, pp. 1–39. Dumbarton Oaks Research Library and Collections, Washington.
1986 Metaphors, Nahualtocaitl, and Other "Disguised" Terms among the Aztecs. In *Symbol and Meaning beyond the Closed Community: Essays in Mesoamerican Ideas,* edited by G. H. Gossen, pp. 35–43. Studies on Culture and Society Vol. 1, Institute for Mesoamerican Studies, State University of New York, Albany.

Hibben, F. C.
1975 *Kiva Art of the Anasazi at Pottery Mound.* K. C. Publishing, Las Vegas, Nevada.

Hieb, L. A.
1994 The Meaning of Katsina: Toward a Cultural Definition of "Person" in Hopi Religion. In *Kachinas in the Pueblo World,* edited by P. Schaafsma, pp. 23–34. University of New Mexico Press, Albuquerque.

Hill, M.
1997 *Sociocultural Implications of Large Mimbres Sites: Architectural and Mortuary Behavior at the Swarts Ruin, New Mexico.* Unpublished Master's thesis, Texas A&M University, College Station.

Hill, W. D.
1992 *Chronology of the El Zurdo Site, Chihuahua.* Unpublished Master's thesis, Department of Archaeology, University of Calgary, Calgary.

Hillier, B., and J. Hanson
1984 *The Social Logic of Space.* Cambridge University Press, Cambridge.

Hodgetts, L. M.
1996 Faunal Exploitation at the El Zurdo Site (CH-159), A Horticultural Village in North-Central Chihuahua. *The Kiva* 62:149–170.

Hosler, D.
1985 Organización cultural de la Tecnología: Aleaciones de cobre en México precolombino. 45th International Congress of Americanists, pp. 68–86. Universidad de los Andes, Bogotá.
1988a The Metallurgy of Ancient West Mexico. In *The Beginnings of the Use of Metals and Alloys,* edited by R. Maddin, pp. 328–343. Massachusetts Institute of Technology Press, Cambridge.
1988b Ancient West Mexican Metallurgy: A Technological Chronology. *Journal of Field Archaeology* 15:191–217.
1988c Ancient West Mexican Metallurgy: South and Central American Origins and West Mexican Transformation. *American Anthropologist* 90:832–855.
1994 *The Sounds and Colors of Power, the Sacred Metallurgical Techniques of Ancient West Mexico.* Massachusetts Institute of Technology Press, Cambridge.

Howard, A. V.
1985 A Reconstruction of Hohokam Interrregional Shell Production and Exchange within Southwestern Arizona. *Proceedings of the 1983 Hohokam Symposium,* Pt. 2, edited by A. E. Dittert and D. E. Dove, pp. 459–472. Arizona Archaeological Society Occasional Paper No. 2, Phoenix.

Hu-DeHart, E.
1981 *Missionaries, Miners, and Indians.* University of Arizona Press, Tucson.

Hunt, E.
1977 *The Transformation of the Hummingbird: Cultural Roots of a Zinacantecan Mythical Poem.* Cornell University Press, Ithaca.

Huntington, E.
1912 The Fluctuating Climate of North America—The Ruins of the Hohokam. In *Annual Report of the Board of Regents of the Smithsonian Institution,* pp. 383–387, Washington, D.C.

1914 The Climatic Factor as Illustrated in Arid America. *Carnegie Institute of Washington Publication 192,* Washington, D.C.

Ice, R.
1966 LA 6783—The Dinwiddie Site. In *The Cliff Highway Salvage Project,* edited by A. E. Dittert Jr., pp. 12–20. Laboratory of Anthropology Note 40, Museum of New Mexico, Santa Fe.

Jacobs, D.
1995 *Archaeology of the Salado in the Livingston Area of the Tonto Basin, Roosevelt Platform Mound Study.* Arizona State University Anthropological Field Studies 32. Department of Anthropology, Arizona State University, Tempe.

James, D., R. Brewington, and H. Shafer
1995 Compositional Analysis of American Southwestern Ceramics by Neutron Activation Analysis. *Journal of Radioanalytical and Nuclear Chemistry* 192(1):109–116.

Jaynes, S.
1995 Marine Shell Mask Gorgets in Montana. Paper presented at the 53d Plains Conference, Laramie.

Jennings, J. D., and E. Reed (editors)
1956 *The American Southwest: A Problem in Cultural Isolation.* Memoirs of the Society for American Archaeology 11:61–127, Salt Lake City.

Jernigan, E. W.
1978 *Jewelry of the Prehistoric Southwest.* University of New Mexico Press, Albuquerque.

Johnson, A. E.
1960 *The Place of Trincheras Culture of Northern Sonora in Southwestern Archaeology.* Unpublished Master's thesis, Department of Anthropology, University of Arizona, Tucson.

Johnson, A. E., and R. Thompson
1963 The Ringo Site, Southeastern Arizona. *American Antiquity* 28:465–481.

Judd, N. M.
1964 *The Architecture of Pueblo Bonito.* Smithsonian Miscellaneous Collections Vol. 147(1). Washington, D.C.

Judge, W. J.
1981 Chaco: Current Views of Prehistory and the Regional System. In *Chaco and Hohokam: Prehistoric Regional Systems in the American Southwest,* edited by P. L. Crown and W. J. Judge, pp. 11–30. School of American Research Press, Santa Fe.
1984 New Light on Chaco Canyon. In *New Light on Chaco Canyon,* edited by D. G. Noble, pp. 1–12. School of American Research Press, Santa Fe.
1989 Chaco Canyon—San Juan Basin. In *Dynamics of Southwestern Prehistory,* edited by L. Cordell and G. Gumerman, pp. 209–262. Smithsonian Institution Press, Washington, D.C.

Judge, W. J., W. B. Gillespie, S. H. Lekson, and H. W. Toll
1981 Tenth Century Developments in Chaco Canyon. In *Collected Papers in Honor of Eric Kellerman Reed,* edited by A. H. Schroeder, pp. 65–98. Papers of the Archaeological Society of New Mexico No. 6, Albuquerque.

Kampen, M. E.
1972 *The Sculptures of El Tajín Veracruz, Mexico.* University Press of Florida, Gainesville.

Kan, M., C. Meighan, and H. B. Nicholson
1970 *Sculpture of Ancient West Mexico: Nayarit, Jalisco, Colima.* Los Angeles County Museum of Art, Los Angeles.
1989 *Sculpture of Ancient West Mexico: Nayarit, Jalisco, Colima.* Reprinted. Los Angeles County Museum of Art, Los Angeles, and University of New Mexico Press, Albuquerque. Originally published 1970, Los Angeles County Museum of Art, Los Angeles.

Kean, W.
1965 Marine Mollusks and Aboriginal Trade in the Southwest. *Plateau* 38:17–31.

Keen, M. A.
1971 *Sea Shells of Tropical West Mexico: Marine Mollusca from Baja California to Peru.* 2d edition. Stanford University Press, Stanford.

Kehoe, A. B.
1993 How the Ancient Peigans Lived. *Research in Economic Anthropology* 14:87–105.
1998 *The Land of Prehistory.* Routledge, New York.

Kehoe, A. B., and K. O. Bruhns
1992 Cahokia: A Mesoamerican City? Paper presented at the Chacmool Conference, Calgary.

Kelley, J. C.
1955 Juan Sabeata and Diffusion in Aboriginal Texas. *American Anthropologist* 57:981–995.
1966 Mesoamerica and the Southwestern United States. In *Archaeological Frontiers and External Connections,* edited by G. F. Ekholm and G. R. Willey, pp. 95–110. Handbook of Middle American Indians, vol.4, R. Wauchope, general editor, University of Texas Press, Austin.
1971 Archaeology of the Northern Frontier: Zacatecas and Durango. In *Archaeology of Northern Mesoamerica: Part Two,* edited by G. F. Ekholm and I. Bernal, pp. 768–801. Handbook of Middle American Indians, vol. 11, R. Wauchope, general editor, University of Texas Press, Austin.
1983 Hypothetical Functioning of the Major Post-Classic Trade System of West and Northwest Mexico. Paper presented at the 18th Mesa Redonda of the Sociedad Mexicana de Antropologia, Taxco.
1986 The Mobile Merchants of Molino. In *Ripples in the Chichimec Sea: New Considerations of Southwestern-Mesoamerican Interactions,* edited by F. J. Mathien and R. H. McGuire, pp. 81–104. Southern Illinois University Press, Carbondale.
1990 The Early Post-Classic in Northern Zacatecas and Durango: IX to XII Centuries. In *Mesoamérica y Norte de México, Siglo IX–XII,* vol. 2, edited by F. S. Miranda, pp. 487–520. Museo Nacional de Antropología, México, D.F.

1991 The Known Archaeological Ballcourts of Durango and Zacatecas, Mexico. In *The Mesoamerican Ballgame,* edited by V. L. Scarborough and D. R. Wilcox, pp. 87–100. University of Arizona Press, Tucson.

1992 The Aztatlán Mercantile System: Mobile Traders and the Northwestward Expansion of Mesoamerican Civilization. Paper presented at Center for Indigenous Studies in the Americas Roundtable on New World Prehistory, Cultural Dynamics of Precolumbian West and Northwest Mesoamerica. Phoenix.

1993 Zenith Passage: The View from Chalchihuites. In *Culture and Contact: Charles C. Di Pesos's Gran Chichimeca,* edited by A. I. Woosley and J. C. Ravesloot, pp. 227–250. Amerind Foundation, Dragoon, and University of New Mexico Press, Albuquerque.

1997 The Aztatlan Mercantile System: Mobile Merchants and the Northwestward Expansion of Mesoamerican Civilization. In *Greater Mesoamerica: The Archaeology of West and Northwest Mexico,* edited by Michael S. Foster and Shirley Gorenstein, in preparation. Ms. 1997.

Kelley, J. C., and E. A. Kelley

1971 *An Introduction to the Ceramics of the Chalchihuites Culture of Zacatecas and Durango, Mexico. Part I: The Decorated Wares.* Mesoamerican Studies Series No. 5. University Museum, Southern Illinois University, Carbondale.

1975 An Alternative Hypothesis for the Explanation of Anasazi Culture History. In *Collected Papers in Honor of Florence Hawley Ellis,* edited by T. R. Frisbie, pp. 178–223. Papers of the Archaeological Society of New Mexico No. 2, Santa Fe.

Kelley, J. C., and H. D. Winters

1960 Revision of the Archaeological Sequence in Sinaloa, Mexico. *American Antiquity* 25:547–561.

Kelley, J. H.

1984 *The Archaeology of the Sierra Blanca Region of Southeastern New Mexico.* Anthropological Papers No. 74, Museum of Anthropology, University of Michigan, Ann Arbor.

Kelley, J. H., and M. P. Hanen

1988 *Archaeology and the Methodology of Science.* University of New Mexico Press, Albuquerque.

Kelley, J. H., and J. D. Stewart

1991a El Proyecto Arqueológico de Chihuahua: Informe de la Temporada de 1990. In *Tercer Congreso Internacional de Historia Regional Comparada,* edited by R. L. García, pp. 47–50. Universidad Autónoma de Ciudad Juárez, Juárez, Chihuahua.

1991b Proyecto Arqueológico de Chihuahua: Trabajos de Campo 1991. In *Boletín del Consejo de Arqueología,* pp. 157–161. Instituto Nacional de Antropología e Historia, México, D.F.

1992 El Proyecto Arqueológico de Chihuahua: Informe de la Temporada de 1990. In *Actas del Tercer Congreso Internacional de Historia Regional Comparada,* edited by R. L. García, pp. 47–54. Universidad Autónoma de Ciudad Juárez, Juárez, Chihuahua.

Kelley, J. H., and M. E. Villalpando C.

1996 An Overview of the Mexican Northwest. In *Interpreting Southwestern Diversity: Underlying Principles and Overarching Patterns,* edited by P. R. Fish and J. J. Reid, pp. 69–77. Anthropological Research Papers No. 48. Arizona State University, Tempe.

Kelley, R.

1963 *The Socio-Religious Roles of Ball Courts and Great Kivas in the Prehistoric Southwest.* Unpublished Master's thesis, Department of Anthropology, University of Arizona, Tucson.

Kelly, I. T.

1938 *Excavations at Chametla, Sinaloa.* Ibero-Americana 14. University of California Press, Berkeley.

1943 West Mexico and the Hohokam. In *El Norte de México y el sur de Estados Unidos,* pp. 206–222. Tercera Reunión de Mesa Redonda sobre problemas antropológicos de México y Centro America. Sociedad Mexicana de Antropología, México, D.F.

1945 *Excavations at Culiacán, Sinaloa.* Ibero-Americana 25. University of California Press, Berkeley.

1980 *Ceramic Sequence in Colima: Capacha, an Early Phase.* Anthropological Papers of the University of Arizona No. 37. University of Arizona Press, Tucson.

Kidder, A. V.

1924 *An Introduction to Southwestern Archaeology.* Papers of the Southwest Expedition 1. Phillips Academy, Department of Anthropology, Andover.

1936 Speculations on New World Prehistory. In *Essays in Anthropology Presented to A. L. Kroeber,* edited by R. H. Lowie, pp. 143–151. University of California Press, Berkeley.

1939 Notes on the Archaeology of the Babícora District, Chihuahua. In *So Live the Works of Men. Seventieth Anniversary Volume Honoring Edgar Lee Hewett,* edited by D. D. Brand and F. E. Harvey, pp. 221–230. University of New Mexico Press, Albuquerque, and School of American Research, Santa Fe.

1951 Some Key Problems of New World Prehistory. In *Homenaje al Doctor Alfonso Caso,* edited by Juan Comas, pp. 215–223. Imprenta Nuevo Mundo, México, D.F.

1962 *An Introduction to the Study of Southwestern Archaeology with a Preliminary Account of the Excavations at Pecos.* Reprinted. Yale University Press, New Haven. Originally published 1924 for the Phillips Academy by Yale University Press.

Kidder, A. V., H. S. Cosgrove, and C. B. Cosgrove

1949 The Pendleton Ruin, Hidalgo County New Mexico. *Contributions to American Anthropology and History 10, Carnegie Institution of Washington Publication* 585:107–152. Washington, D.C.

Kintigh, K. W.

1984 Measuring Archaeological Diversity by Comparison with Simulated Assemblages. *American Antiquity* 49:44–54.

1989 Sample Size, Significance, and Measures of Diversity. In *Quantifying Diversity in Archaeology,* edited by R. D. Leonard and G. T. Jones, pp. 25–36. Cambridge University Press, Cambridge.

1996 The Cibola Region in the Post-Chacoan Era. In *The Prehistoric Pueblo World,* A.D. *1150–1350,* edited by M. A. Adler, pp. 131–144. University of Arizona Press, Tucson.

Kirkland, F., and W. W. Newcomb Jr.

1967 *The Rock Art of Texas Indians.* University of Texas Press, Austin.

Knab, T. J.

1986 Metaphors, Concepts, and Coherence in Aztec. In *Symbol and Meaning beyond the Closed Community: Essays in Mesoamerican Ideas,* edited by G. H. Gossen, pp. 45–56. Studies on Culture and Society Vol. 1, Institute for Mesoamerican Studies, State University of New York, Albany.

1995 *A War of Witches: A Journey into the Underworld of the Contemporary Aztecs.* HarperCollins, New York.

Koll, R.

1982 Archaeological Reports, Shores of Lake Chapala, Jalisco, Mexico. *PANTOC* 4:19–32.

Koontz, R. A.

1994 *The Iconography of El Tajín, Veracruz, Mexico.* Unpublished Ph.D. dissertation, University of Texas at Austin.

Krickeberg, W.

1966 El Juego de Pelota Mesoamericana y su Simbolismo Religioso. In *Traducciones Mesoamericanistas,* vol. 1, pp. 191–313. Sociedad Mexicana de Antropología, México, D.F.

Kroeber, A. L.

1928 Native Culture of the Southwest. *University of California Publications in American Archaeology and Ethnology* 23(9):375–398.

1934 *Uto-Aztecan Languages of Mexico.* Ibero-Americana 8. University of California Press, Berkeley.

1939 *Cultural and Natural Areas of North America.* Publications in American Archaeology and Ethnology 38. University of California, Berkeley.

Laboratory of Anthropology

1989 *I Am Here: Two Thousand Years of Southwest Indian Arts and Culture.* Museum of New Mexico Press, Santa Fe.

Ladd, E. J.

1994 The Zuni Ceremonial System: The Kiva. In *Kachinas in the Pueblo World,* edited by P. Schaafsma, pp. 17–22. University of New Mexico Press, Albuquerque.

Lambert, M. F., and J. R. Ambler

1965 *A Survey and Excavation of Caves in Hidalgo County, New Mexico.* School of American Research Monograph No. 25. School of American Research, Santa Fe.

Lang, R. W.

1989 *A Cultural Resources Sample Survey of Upper Tesuque Creek, Raven's Ridge, and the Lake Peak Divide of the Santa Fe Range, Sangre de Cristo Mountains, New Mexico.* Prepared for Dames and Moore and Santa Fe Ski Company. Southwest Archaeological Consultants, Santa Fe.

Lange, C. H., and C. L. Riley

1996 *Bandelier: The Life and Adventures of Adolph Bandelier.* University of Utah Press, Salt Lake City.

Lange, C. H., and C. L. Riley (editors)

1970 *The Southwestern Journals of Adolph F. Bandelier, 1883–1884.* University of New Mexico Press, Albuquerque.

Laumbach, K., and D. Kirkpatrick

1985 The Black Range Project: A Regional Perspective. In *Proceedings of the Third Jornada-Mogollon Conference,* edited by M. Foster and T. O'Laughlin, pp. 23–39. *The Artifact* 23:1–2.

Lazalde Montoya, J. F.

1987 *Durango Indígena: Panorama Cultural de un Pueblo Prehispánico en el Noroeste de Mexico.* Impresiones Gráficas México, S. A., Gómez Palacio, Durango.

LeBlanc, S. A.

1977 The 1976 Field Season of the Mimbres Foundation in Southwestern New Mexico. *Journal of New World Archaeology* 2(2).

1980a The Dating of Casas Grandes. *American Antiquity* 45(4):799–806.

1980b The Post Mogollon Periods in Southwestern New Mexico: The Animas/Black Mountain Phase and the Salado Period. In *An Archaeological Synthesis of South-Central and Southwestern New Mexico,* edited by S. A. LeBlanc and M. E. Whalen, pp. 271–316. Office of Contract Archaeology, University of New Mexico, Albuquerque.

1983 *The Mimbres People: Ancient Pueblo Painters of the American Southwest.* Thames and Hudson, London.

1986a Development of Archaeological Thought on the Mimbres Mogollon. In *Emil Haury's Prehistory of the American Southwest,* edited by J. J. Reid and D. E. Doyel, pp. 297–304. University of Arizona Press, Tucson.

1986b Aspects of Southwestern Prehistory: A.D. 900–1400. In *Ripples in the Chichimec Sea: New Considerations of Southwestern-Mesoamerican Interactions,* edited by F. J. Mathien and R. H. McGuire, pp. 105–134. Southern Illinois University Press, Carbondale.

1989 Cultural Dynamics in the Southern Mogollon Area. In *Dynamics of Southwest Prehistory,* edited by L. S. Cordell and G. J. Gumerman, pp. 179–207. Smithsonian Institution Press, Washington, D.C.

Lehmer, D. J.

1948 *The Jornada Branch of the Mogollon.* Social Science Bulletin No. 17. University of Arizona, Tucson.

Lekson, S. H.

1983 Chacoan Architecture in Continental Context. In *Proceedings of the First Anasazi Symposium,* edited by J. E. Smith, pp. 183–194. Mesa Verde Museum Association, Mesa Verde.

1984a Mimbres Settlement Size in Southwestern New Mexico. In *Recent Research in Mogollon Archaeology,* edited by S. Upham, F. Plog, D. Batcho, and B. E.

Kauffman, pp. 68–74. University Museum, New Mexico State University Occasional Papers 10, Las Cruces.
1984b Dating Casas Grandes. *The Kiva* 50:55–60.
1986 The Mimbres Region. In *Mogollon Variability,* edited by C. Benson and S. Upham, pp. 147–154. University Museum, New Mexico State University Occasional Papers 15, Las Cruces.
1989 An Archaeological Reconnaissance of the Rio Grande Valley in Sierra County, New Mexico. *The Artifact* 27(2):1–102.
1990 *Mimbres Archaeology of the Upper Gila, New Mexico.* Anthropological Papers of the University of Arizona No. 53, Tucson.
1991 Settlement Patterns and the Chaco Region. In *Chaco and Hohokam: Prehistoric Regional Systems in the American Southwest,* edited by P. L. Crown and W. J. Judge, pp. 31–56. School of American Research Press, Santa Fe.
1992a *Archaeological Overview of Southwestern New Mexico.* Prepared for New Mexico State Historic Preservation Division, Project No. 35-88-30120.004. Human Systems Research, Las Cruces.
1992b The Surface Archaeology of Southwestern New Mexico. *The Artifact* 30(3):1–36.
1992c Mimbres Art and Archaeology. In *Archaeology, Art, and Anthropology: Papers in Honor of J. J. Brody,* edited by M. Duran and D. T. Kirkpatrick, pp. 111–120. Papers of the Archaeological Society of New Mexico No. 18, Albuquerque.
1993 Chaco, Hohokam, and Mimbres. *Expedition* 35(1): 44–52.
1996a Chaco and Casas Grandes. Poster presented at the 61st Annual Meeting of the Society for American Archaeology, New Orleans.
1996b Scale and Process in the American Southwest. In *Interpreting Southwestern Diversity,* edited by P. R. Fish and J. J. Reid, pp. 81–86. Anthropological Research Paper 48, Arizona State University, Tempe.
1996c Chaco, Casas Grandes, and the Cognitive Structure of the Ancient Southwest. Manuscript on file, University Museum, University of Colorado, Boulder, Colorado.
1997 Rewriting Southwestern Prehistory. *Archaeology* 50(1):52–55.
1998 Salado in Chihuahua. In *Prehistoric Salado Culture of the American Southwest,* edited by J. S. Dean. Amerind Foundation, Dragoon, in press.
1999a *Chaco Meridian: Centers of Political Power in the Ancient Southwest.* Altamira Press, Walnut Creek.
1999b Unit Pueblos and the Mimbres Problem. In *Papers in Honor of Patrick Beckett,* edited by Meliha Duran and David Kirkpatrick. Archaeological Society of New Mexico, Albuquerque.

Lekson, S. H., and C. M. Cameron
1995 The Abandonment of Chaco Canyon, the Mesa Verde Migrations, and the Reorganization of the Pueblo World. *Journal of Anthropological Archaeology* 14:184–202.

Lekson, S. H., L. Cordell, and G. J. Gumerman
1994 Approaches to Understanding Southwestern Prehistory. In *Understanding Complexity in the Prehistoric Southwest,* edited by G. J. Gumerman and M. Gell-Mann, pp. 15–24. Addison-Wesley, New York.

Lekson, S. H., and J. P. Wilson
1985 History and Prehistory of the Rio Grande Valley in Sierra County, New Mexico. Manuscript submitted to the State Historic Preservation Division, Santa Fe.

Léon-Portilla, M.
1992 *The Aztec Image of Self and Society: An Introduction to Nahua Culture.* Edited with an Introduction by J. J. Klor de Alva. University of Utah Press, Salt Lake City.

Leubben, R. A., J. G. Andelson, and L. C. Herold
1986 Elvino Whetten Pueblo and Its Relationship to Terraces and Nearby Small Structures, Chihuahua, Mexico. *The Kiva* 51:165–187.

Levy, J.
1992 *Orayvi Revisited: Social Stratification in an "Egalitarian" Society.* School of American Research Press, Santa Fe.

Lipe, W. D., and M. Hegmon
1989 Historical Perspectives on Architecture and Social Integration in the Prehistoric Pueblos. In *The Architecture of Social Integration in Prehistoric Pueblos,* edited by W. D. Lipe and M. Hegmon, pp. 15–34. Occasional Paper No. 1. Crow Canyon Archaeological Center, Cortez.

Lipe, W. D., and M. Hegmon (editors)
1989 *The Architecture of Social Integration in Prehistoric Pueblos.* Crow Canyon Archaeological Center, Cortez.

Lister, R. H.
1946 Survey of Archaeological Remains in Northwestern Chihuahua. *Southwestern Journal of Anthropology* 2:443–452.
1949 *Excavations at Cojumatlan, Michoacan, Mexico.* University of New Mexico Publications in Anthropology No. 5, Albuquerque.
1978 Mesoamerican Influences at Chaco Canyon. In *Across the Chichimec Sea,* edited by C. L. Riley and B. C. Hedrick, pp. 233–241. Southern Illinois University Press, Carbondale.

Lockhart, B.
1997 Protohistoric Confusion: A Cultural Comparison of the Manso, Suma, and Jumano Indians of the Paso del Norte Region. *Journal of the Southwest* 39(1):113–149.

Longacre, W. A.
1970 *Archaeology as Anthropology: A Case Study.* Anthropological Papers of the University of Arizona No. 17. University of Arizona Press, Tucson.

López Austin, A.
1988 *The Human Body and Ideology: Concepts of the Ancient Nahuas.* 2 Vols. University of Utah Press, Salt Lake City.

Lowdon, J. A.
1969 Isotopic Fractionation in Corn. *Radiocarbon* 11(2): 391–393.

Lucas, J.
1996 *Three Circle Phase Architecture at Old Town, A Prehistoric Mimbres Site in Luna County, Southwestern New Mexico.* Unpublished Master's thesis, University of Texas at Austin.

Lumholtz, C.
1902 *Unknown Mexico: Explorations in the Sierra Madre and Other Regions, 1890–1898.* 2 Vols. Charles Scribner & Sons, New York.

Lyle, R.
1996 *Functional Analysis of Mimbres Ceramics from the NAN Ruin (LA 15049), Grant County, New Mexico.* Unpublished Master's thesis, Department of Anthropology, Texas A & M University, College Station.

McAnany, P. A.
1998 Ancestors and the Classic Maya Built Environment. In *Function and Meaning in Classic Maya Architecture,* edited by S. D. Houston, Dumbarton Oaks, Washington, in press.

McClintock, W.
1968 *The Old North Trail or Life, Legends and Religion of the Blackfeet Indians.* Facsimile reprint. University of Nebraska Press, Lincoln. Originally published 1910, MacMillan, London.

McCluney, E. B.
1965a *Clanton Draw and Box Canyon: An Interim Report on Two Prehistoric Sites in Hidalgo County, New Mexico, and Related Surveys.* School of American Research Monograph No. 26. School of American Research, Santa Fe.
1965b The Excavation of the Joyce Well Site, Hidalgo County, New Mexico. Manuscript on file at the School of American Research and at the Laboratory of Anthropology, Museum of New Mexico, Santa Fe.

McGee, W. J.
1898 The Seri Indians. *Seventeenth Annual Report of the Bureau of American Ethnology,* Smithsonian Institution, Washington, D.C.

McGregor, J. C.
1965 *Southwestern Archaeology.* University of Illinois Press, Urbana.

McGuire, R. H.
1980 The Mesoamerican Connection in the Southwest. *The Kiva* 46:3–38.
1985 The Role of Shell Exchange in the Explanation of Hohokam Prehistory. In *Proceedings of the 1983 Hohokam Symposium,* Pt. 2, edited by A. E. Dittert and D. E. Dove, pp. 473–482. Arizona Archaeological Society Occasional Paper No. 2, Phoenix.

McGuire, R. H., and A. V. Howard
1987 The Structure and Organization of Hohokam Shell Exchange. *The Kiva* 52:113–145.

McGuire, R. H., and D. J. Saitta
1996 Although They Have Petty Captains, They Obey Them Badly: The Dialectics of Prehispanic Western Pueblo Social Organization. *American Antiquity* 61:197– 17.

McGuire, R. H., and M. B. Schiffer
1982 *Hohokam and Patayan: The Archaeology of Southwestern Arizona.* Academic Press, New York.

McGuire, R. H., and M. E. Villalpando
1989 Prehistory and the Making of History in Sonora. In *Columbian Consequences I: Archaeological and Historical Perspectives on the Spanish Borderlands West,* edited by D. H. Thomas, pp. 159–177, Smithsonian Institution Press, Washington, D.C.
1993 *An Archaeological Survey of the Altar Valley, Sonora, Mexico.* Arizona State Museum Archaeological Series 184. Arizona State Museum, University of Arizona, Tucson.

McGuire, R. H., E. C. Adams, B. A. Nelson, and K. A. Spielmann
1994 Drawing the Southwest to Scale: Perspectives on Macroregional Relations. In *Themes in Southwest Prehistory,* edited by G. J. Gumerman, pp. 239–265. School of American Research, Santa Fe.

McGuire, R. H., M. E. Villalpando, J. P. Holmlund, and M. O'Donovan
1993 *Cerro de Trincheras Mapping Project.* Final Technical Report to the National Geographic Society for Grant #4454-91. On file, Department of Anthropology, State University of New York, Binghamton.

Madsen, D. B.
1989 *Exploring the Fremont.* University of Utah Occasional Publication 8. Utah Museum of Natural History, Salt Lake City.

Mallouf, R. J.
1992 La Prehistoria del Noreste de Chihuahua: Complejo Cielo y Distrito La Junta. In *Historia General de Chihuahua I: Geología, Geografía y Arqueología,* edited by A. Márquez-Alameda, pp. 137–162. Universidad Autónoma de Ciudad Juárez y Gobierno del Estado de Chihuahua, Juárez.

Manson, J. L.
1994 Transmississippi Trails: The Buffalo Plains and Beyond. Expanded version of paper read at the 1994 Southeastern and Midwest Archaeological Conference, Lexington.

Marcus, J.
1983a On the Nature of the Mesoamerican City. In *Prehistoric Settlement Patterns,* edited by E. Z. Vogt and R. M. Leventhal, pp. 195–242. Peabody Museum of Archaeology and Ethnology, Cambridge.
1983b Zapotec Religion. In *The Cloud People: Divergent Evolution of the Zapotec and Mixtec Civilizations,* edited by K. V. Flannery and J. Marcus, pp. 345–351. Academic Press, New York.

Marcus, J., and J. F. Zeitlin
1994 *Caciques and Their People: A Volume in Honor of Ronald Spores.* Anthropological Papers No. 89, Museum of Anthropology, University of Michigan, Ann Arbor.

Martin, P., and F. Plog
1973 *The Archaeology of Arizona.* Doubleday/Natural History Press, Garden City, New York.

Martínez, F. S., and D. Pearson
1994 Habitaciones en cuevas en Chihuahua. *Arqueología Mexicana* 1(6):32–35.

Mathien, F. J., and R. H. McGuire
1986 Adrift in the Chichimec Sea. In *Ripples in the Chichimec Sea: New Considerations of Southwestern-Mesoamerican Interactions,* edited by F. J. Mathien and R. H. McGuire, pp. 1–8. Southern Illinois University Press, Carbondale.

Mathien, F. J., and B. Olinger
1992 An Experiment with X-ray Fluorescence to Determine Trace Element Variability in Turquoise Composition. In *Archaeology, Art, and Anthropology: Papers in Honor of J. J. Brody,* edited by M. S. Duran and D. T. Kirkpatrick, pp. 123–134. Papers of the Archaeological Society of New Mexico No. 18, Albuquerque.

Matos Moctezuma, E.
1992 The Aztec Main Pyramid: Ritual Architecture at Tenochtitlán. In *The Ancient Americas: Art from Sacred Landscapes,* edited by R. F. Townsend, pp. 187–196. Art Institute of Chicago, Chicago.

Meighan, C. W.
1959 New Findings in West Mexican Archaeology. *The Kiva* 25:1–7.
1966 Influencias entre culturas de Nayarit, México y de Arizona, E.U.A. Instituto Jalisciense de Antropología e Historia, Eco 24, Guadalajara.
1971 Archaeology of Sinaloa. In *Archaeology of Northern Mesoamerica: Part Two,* edited by G. F. Ekholm and I. Bernal, pp. 754–767. Handbook of Middle American Indians, vol. 11, R. Wauchope, general editor, University of Texas Press, Austin.
1972 *Archaeology of the Morett Site, Colima.* University of California Publications in Anthropology 7. University of California Press, Berkeley.
1974 Prehistory of West Mexico. *Science* 184:1254–1261.
1976 The Archaeology of Amapa, Nayarit. In *The Archaeology of Amapa, Nayarit,* edited by C. W. Meighan, pp. 1–205. Monumenta Archaeologica Vol. 2. Institute of Archaeology, University of California, Los Angeles.

Meighan, C. W., and H. B. Nicholson
1970 The Ceramic Mortuary Offerings of Prehistoric West Mexico: An Archaeological Perspective. In *Sculpture of Ancient West Mexico: Nayarit, Jalisco, Colima,* edited by M. Kan, C. Meighan, and H. B. Nicholson, pp. 17–32. Los Angeles County Museum of Art, Los Angeles.
1989 The Ceramic Mortuary Offerings of Prehistoric West Mexico: An Archaeological Perspective. In *Sculpture of Ancient West Mexico: Nayarit, Jalisco, Colima,* edited by M. Kan, C. Meighan, and H. B. Nicholson, pp. 28–69. Los Angeles County Museum of Art, Los Angeles and University of New Mexico Press, Albuquerque. Originally published 1970, Los Angeles County Museum of Art, Los Angeles.

Meighan, C. W., and L. J. Foote
1968 *Excavations at Tizapán el Alto, Jalisco.* Latin American Studies 11, Latin American Study Center. University of California, Los Angeles.

Mendieta, Fray Gerónimo de
1971 *Historia Eclesiástica Indiana.* Editorial Porrúa, México, D.F.

Mendizábal, M. O. de
1930 Influencia del la Sal en la Distribución Geográfica de los Grupos Indigenas de México. *Proceedings of the 23d International Congress of Americanists* 28:93–100. New York.

Mercer, L. J.
1982 The Antebellum Interregional Trade Hypothesis: A Reexamination of Theory and Evidence. In *Explorations in the New Economic History,* edited by R. L. Ransom, R. Sutch, and G. M. Walton, pp. 71–96. Academic Press, New York.

Merton, R. K.
1993 *On the Shoulders of Giants, The Post-Italianate Edition.* University of Chicago Press, Chicago.

Metcalfe, S. E., A. Bimpson, A. J. Courtice, S. L. O'Hara, and D. M. Taylor
1997 Climate Change at the Monsoon/Westerly Boundary in Northern Mexico. *Journal of Paleoliminology* 17:155–171.

Miller, M.
1992 The Transitional Period in Southern Jornada Mogollon: Archaeological Investigations in the North Hills Subdivision, Northeast El Paso, Texas. Draft report for International City Developers, El Paso.

Miller, M. E.
1986 *The Art of Mesoamerica from Olmec to Aztec.* Thames and Hudson, New York.

Miller, W. R.
1983 Uto-Aztecan Languages. In *Southwest,* edited by Alfonso Ortiz, pp. 329–342. Handbook of North American Indians, vol. 10, W. C. Sturtevant, general editor, Smithsonian Institution, Washington, D.C.

Mills, B. J.
1995 The Organization of Protohistoric Zuni Ceramic Production. In *Ceramic Production in the American Southwest,* edited by B. J. Mills and P. L. Crown, pp. 200–229. University of Arizona Press, Tucson.

Mills, J. P., and V. M. Mills
1969a *The Kuykendall Site.* Special Reports of the El Paso Archaeological Society 6, El Paso.
1969b Burned House: An Additional Excavation at the Kuykendall Site. *The Artifact* 7:21–32.
1971 The Slaughter Ranch Site: A Prehistoric Village Near the Mexican Border in Southeastern Arizona. *The Artifact* 9:23–52.

Minnis, P. E.
1981 *Economic and Organizational Responses to Food Stress by Nonstratified Societies: An Example from Prehistoric New Mexico.* Unpublished Ph.D. dissertation, Department of Anthropology, University of Michigan, Ann Arbor.

1984 Peeking under the Tortilla Curtain: Regional Interaction and Integration on the Northern Periphery of Casas Grandes. *American Archaeology* 4:181–193.

1985 *Social Adaptation to Food Stress: A Prehistoric Southwestern Example.* University of Chicago Press, Chicago.

1988 Four Examples of Specialized Production at Casas Grandes, Northwestern Chihuahua. *The Kiva* 53:181–194.

1989 The Casas Grandes Polity in the International Four Corners. In *The Sociopolitical Structure of Prehistoric Southwestern Societies,* edited by S. Upham, K. G. Lightfoot, and R. A. Jewitt, pp. 269–305. Westview Press, Boulder.

Minnis, P. E., and M. E. Whalen

1990 El sistema regional de Casas Grandes, Chihuahua. *Actas del Sequndo Congreso de Historia Regional Comparada 1990,* pp. 45–55. Universidad Autónoma de Ciudad Juárez, Juárez.

1993 Casas Grandes: Archaeology in Northern Mexico. *Expedition* 35:34–43.

1995 El sistema regional de Casas Grandes, Chihuahua: Informe Pesentado al Instituto Nacional de Antropología e Historia. Manuscript on file, Department of Anthropology, University of Oklahoma, Norman.

Minnis, P. E., M. E. Whalen, J. H. Kelley, and J. D. Stewart

1993 Prehistoric Macaw Breeding in the North American Southwest. *American Antiquity* 58:270–276.

Minnis, P. E., and A. J. Wormser

1984 Late Pithouse Period Occupation in the Deming Region: Preliminary Report of Excavations at the Florida Mountain Site (LA 1839). In *Recent Research in Mogollon Archaeology,* edited by S. Upham, F. Plog, D. G. Batcho, and B. E. Kauffman, pp. 229–249. University Museum, New Mexico State University Occasional Papers No. 10, Las Cruces.

Mitchell, D. R.

1990 *The La Lomita Excavations: 10th Century Hohokam Occupation in South-central Arizona.* Soil Systems Publications in Archaeology 15. Soil Systems, Phoenix.

Moodie, D. W., and B. Kaye

1977 The Ac Ko Mok Ki Map. *The Beaver Outfit* 307(4): 5–15.

Morris, E. H.

1939 *Archaeological Studies in the La Plata District.* Carnegie Institution, Washington, D.C.

Moulard, B.

1981 *Within the Underworld Sky: Mimbres Ceramic Art in Context.* Twelvetrees Press, Pasadena.

Mountjoy, J. B.

1969 On the Origins of West Mexican Metallurgy. In *Precolumbian Contact within Nuclear America,* edited by J. C. Kelley and C. L. Riley, pp. 26–42. Mesoamerican Studies 4. Southern Illinois University, Carbondale.

1970 *Prehispanic Culture History and Cultural Contact on the Southern Coast of Nayarit, Mexico.* Unpublished Ph.D. dissertation, Department of Anthropology, Southern Illinois University, Carbondale.

1982 *El Proyecto Tomatlán de Salvamento Arqueológico: Fondo Ethnohistórico y Arqueológico, Desarrollo del Proyecto, Estudios de La Superficie.* Instituto Nacional de Antropología e Historia Collečión Científica: Arqueológica No. 122. México, D.F.

1989 Proyecto Arqueológico Valle de Banderas: Segunda Temporada (1988). Report on file with the Instituto Nacional de Antropología e Historia, Departamento de Monumentos Prehispánicos, México, D.F.

1990 El desarrollo de la cultura Aztatlán visto desde su frontera suroeste. In *Mesoamerica y Norte de Mexico, Siglo IX–XII,* vol. 2, edited by F. S. Miranda, pp. 541–564. Museo Nacional de Antropología, México, D.F.

1992 Prehispanic Cultural Development along the Southern Coast of West Mexico. Paper presented at the Center for Indigenous Studies in the Americas, Roundtable on New World Prehistory: Cultural Dynamics of Precolumbian West and Northwest Mesoamerica, Phoenix.

Moyer, P.

1980 *The King Collection.* Privately printed.

Myers, R. D.

1985 The Archaeology of Southeastern Arizona: A.D. 1100–1400. Manuscript on file, Anthropological Resource Center, Cochise College, Douglas, Arizona.

Naylor, T. H.

1983 Review of C. L. Riley's *The Frontier People.* Center for Archaeological Investigations edition. *The Kiva* 49:119–121.

1995 Casas Grandes Outlier Ball Courts in Northwest Chihuahua. In *The Gran Chichimeca: Essays on the Archaeology and Ethnohistory of Northern Mesoamerica,* edited by J. E. Reyman, pp. 224–239. Worldwide Archaeology Series 12, Avebury, Aldershot.

Nelson, B. A.

1993 Outposts of Mesoamerican Empire and Architectural Patterning at La Quemada, Zacatecas. In *Culture and Contact: Charles C. Di Peso's Gran Chichimeca,* edited by A. I. Woosley and J. C. Ravesloot, pp. 173–190. Amerind Foundation Publication, Dragoon, and the University of New Mexico Press, Albuquerque.

Nelson, B. A., and R. Anyon

1996 Fallow Valleys: Asynchronous Occupations in the Mimbres Region. *The Kiva* 61:275–294.

Nelson, B. A., and S. A. LeBlanc

1986 *Short-Term Sedentism in the American Southwest: The Mimbres Valley Salado.* Maxwell Museum of Anthropology and the University of New Mexico Press, Albuquerque.

Nelson, M. C.

1993a Abandonment or Reorganization: A Study of Prehistoric Change in the Eastern Mimbres Region. Report to the National Geographic Society, Washington, D.C.

1993b Changing Occupational Pattern among Prehistoric Horticulturalists in SW New Mexico. *Journal of Field Archaeology* 20:43–57.

1993c Classic Mimbres Land Use in the Eastern Mimbres Region, Southwestern New Mexico. *The Kiva* 59:27–47.

Nelson, M. C. (editor)

1984 *Ladder Ranch Research Project: A Report of the First Season.* Technical Series of the Maxwell Museum of Anthropology 1. The Maxwell Museum of Anthropology, Albuquerque.

Nelson, M. C., and M. Hegmon

1996 *Regional Social and Economic Reorganization: The Mimbres.* Unpublished report on file, Department of Anthropology, Arizona State University, Tempe.

Nelson, R. S.

1981 *The Role of a Pochteca System in Hohokam Exchange.* Unpublished Ph.D. dissertation, New York University, New York.

1991 *Hohokam Marine Shell Exchange and Artifacts.* Arizona State Museum Archaeological Series 179. Arizona State Museum, University of Arizona, Tucson.

Nequatewa, E.

1947 *The Truth of a Hopi and Other Clan Stories of Shungopovi,* edited by M. F. Colton. 2d ed. Northern Arizona Society of Science and Art, Museum of Northern Arizona Bulletin No. 8, Flagstaff.

Nicholson, H. B.

1966 The Mixteca Puebla Concept in Mesoamerican Archaeology: A Reexamination. In *Ancient Mesoamerica,* edited by J. A. Graham, pp. 258–263. Peek Publications, Palo Alto.

1971 Religion in Pre-Hispanic Central Mexico. In *Archaeology of Northern Mesoamerica: Part One,* edited by G. F. Ekholm and I. Bernal, pp. 395–446. Handbook of Middle American Indians, vol. 10, R. Wauchope, general editor, University of Texas Press, Austin.

1973 The Late Prehispanic Central Mexican (Aztec) Iconographic System. In *The Iconography of Middle American Sculpture,* pp. 72–97. Metropolitan Museum of Art, New York.

1982 The Mixteca-Puebla Concept Revisited. In *The Art and Iconography of Late Post-Classic Central Mexico,* edited by E. Boone, pp. 227–254. Dumbarton Oaks, Washington, D.C.

Nicholson, H. B., and C. W. Meighan

1974 The UCLA Department of Anthropology Program in West Mexican Archaeology-Ethnohistory, 1956–1970. In *The Archaeology of West Mexico,* edited by B. B. Bell, pp. 6–18. West Mexican Society for Advanced Study, Ajijic, Jalisco, Mexico.

Noguera, E.

1926 *Ruinas Arqueológicas del Norte de México.* Publicaciones de la Sria de Educación Pública. Tomo 11, No. 14. México, D.F.

Norusis, M. J.

1988 *SPSS/PC+ V2.0 Base Manual.* SPSS, Chicago.

Obregón, B. de

1924 *Historia de los descubrimientos Antiguos y Modernos de la Nueva España.* Edited by Fr. M. Cuevas. Departamento Editorial de la Sria. de Educación Pública, México, D.F.

O'Brien, P. J.

1989 Cahokia: The Political Capital of the Ramey State? *North American Archaeologist* 10:275–292.

1990 The Political Economy of Cahokia and Steed-Kisker. Paper presented at the 48th Plains Conference, Oklahoma City.

1991 Early State Economics: Cahokia, Capital of the Ramey State. In *Early State Economics,* edited by H. J. M. Claessen and P. van de Velde, pp. 143–175. Transaction, New Brunswick.

1994 Prehistoric Politics: Petroglyphs and the Political Boundaries of Cahokia. *Gateway Heritage* 15(1):30–47.

O'Donovan, M.

1997 *Confronting Archaeological Enigmas: Cerro de Trincheras, Cerros de Trincheras and Monumentality.* Unpublished Ph.D. dissertation, Department of Anthropology, Binghamton University, Binghamton.

O'Laughlin, T. C.

1985 Jornada Mogollon Occupation of the Rincon Valley, New Mexico. In *Proceedings of the Third Jornada-Mogollon Conference,* edited by M. Foster and T. O'Laughlin, pp. 41–57. *The Artifact* 23:1–2.

O'Laughlin, T. C., M. S. Foster, and J. C. Ravesloot

1984 *Animas Phase Sites of Southern Hidalgo County Thematic Group. Unpublished Site Forms and Draft National Register Form.* On file, New Mexico Historic Preservation Division, Santa Fe.

Ortiz, A.

1969 *The Tewa World: Space, Time, Being, and Becoming in a Pueblo Society.* University of Chicago Press, Chicago.

Pailes, R. A.

1972 *An Archaeological Reconnaissance of Southern Sonora and Reconsideration of the Rio Sonora Culture.* Unpublished Ph.D. dissertation, Southern Illinois University, Carbondale.

1978 The Rio Sonora Culture in Prehistoric Trade Systems. In *Across the Chichimec Sea,* edited by C. L. Riley and B. C. Hedrick, pp. 134–143. Southern Illinois University Press, Carbondale.

1980 The Upper Rio Sonora Valley in Prehistoric Trade. In *New Frontiers in the Archaeology and Ethnohistory of the Greater Southwest,* edited by C. L. Riley and B. C. Hedrick, pp. 20–39. Transactions of the Illinois State Academy of Science Vol. 72, No. 4. Springfield.

1984 Agricultural Development and Trade in the Rio Sonora. In *Prehistoric Agricultural Strategies in the Southwest,* edited by S. K. Fish and P. R. Fish, pp. 309–325. Anthropological Research Papers No. 33. Arizona State University, Tempe.

1997 An Archaeological Perspective on the Sonoran Entrada. In *To Tierra Nueva,* edited by R. Flint and

S. C. Flint, pp. 177–189. University of Colorado Press, Boulder.

Pailes, R. A., and D. T. Reff

1985 Colonial Exchange Systems and the Decline of Paquime. In *The Archaeology of West and Northwest Mesoamerica,* edited by M. S. Foster and P. C. Weigand, pp. 353–363. Westview Press, Boulder.

Pailes, R. A., and J. W. Whitecotton

1995 The Frontiers of Mesoamerica: Northern and Southern. In *The Gran Chichimeca: Essays on the Archaeology and Ethnohistory of Northern Mesoamerica,* edited by J. E. Reyman, pp. 13–45. Avebury, Aldershot.

Parsons, E. C.

1932 Isleta, New Mexico. *Forty-Seventh Annual Report of the Bureau of American Ethnology, 1929–1930,* pp. 193–466. Government Printing Office, Washington, D.C.

1933 Some Aztec and Pueblo Parallels. *American Anthropologist* 35:611–631.

1936a *Mitla, Town of Souls and other Zapotec-Speaking Pueblos of Oaxaca, Mexico.* University of Chicago Press, Chicago.

1936b *Taos Pueblo.* General Series in Anthropology No. 2. Banta Publishing, Menasha. Reprinted, 1970, Johnson Reprints, New York.

1939 *Pueblo Indian Religion.* 2 vols. University of Chicago Press, Chicago.

1969 *Taos Tales.* Memoirs of the American Folklore Society No. 34. Reprinted. Kraus Reprint, New York. Originally published 1940, American Folk-Lore Society, J. J. Augustin, New York.

Pasztory, E.

1974 *The Iconography of the Teotihuacan Tlaloc.* Studies in Pre-Columbian Art and Archaeology 15. Dumbarton Oaks, Washington, D.C.

1983 *Aztec Art.* Harry N. Abrams, New York.

Pauketat, T. R.

1995 Cahokia Political History as Punctuated Disequilibrium. Paper presented at the 60th Annual Meeting of the Society for American Archaeology, Minneapolis.

Peckham, S.

1990 *From This Earth: The Ancient Art of Pueblo Pottery.* Museum of New Mexico Press, Santa Fe.

Pendergast, D. M.

1962 Metal Artifacts in Prehispanic Mesoamerica. *American Antiquity* 27:520–545.

Peterson, F. A.

1959 *Ancient Mexico: An Introduction to the Pre-Hispanic Cultures.* George Allen & Unwin, London.

Phillips, D. A., Jr.

1989 Prehistory of Chihuahua and Sonora, Mexico. *Journal of World Prehistory* 3:373–401.

1990 A Re-Evaluation of the Robles Phase of the Casas Grandes Culture, Northwest Chihuahua. Paper presented at the 55th Annual Meeting of the Society for American Archaeology, Las Vegas.

1991 Mesoamerican–North Mexican Relationships: An Intellectual History. Paper presented at the Symposium Navigating the Chichimec Sea: Internal Developments and External Involvements in the Prehistory of Northern Mexico of the 47th International Congress of Americanists, New Orleans.

Phillips, P.

1966 The Role of Transpacific Contacts in the Development of New World Pre-Columbian Civilizations. In *Archaeological Frontiers and External Connections,* edited by G. F. Ekholm and G. R. Willey, pp. 296–315. Handbook of Middle American Indians, vol. 4, R. Wauchope, general editor, University of Texas Press, Austin.

Phillips, P., and J. A. Brown

1978 *Pre-Columbian Shell Engravings from the Craig Mound at Spiro, Oklahoma,* Pt. 1, vols. 1–3. Peabody Museum of Archaeology and Ethnology, Harvard University, Cambridge.

Plog, S., and M. Hegmon

1993 The Sample Size-Richness Relation: The Relevance of Research Questions, Sampling Strategies, and Behavioral Variation. *American Antiquity* 58:489–496.

Preucel, R. W.

1996 Cooking Status: Hohokam Ideology, Power, and Social Reproduction. In *Interpreting Southwestern Diversity: Underlying Principles and Overarching Patterns,* edited by P. R. Fish and J. J. Reid, pp. 125–131. Anthropological Research Papers No. 48. Arizona State University, Tempe.

Preucel, R. W. (editor)

1991 *Processual and Postprocessual Archaeologies: Multiple Ways of Knowing the Past.* Center for Archaeological Investigations, Occasional Paper No. 10. Southern Illinois University at Carbondale, Carbondale.

Prudden, T. M.

1903 The Prehistoric Ruins of the San Juan Watershed in Utah, Arizona, Colorado, and New Mexico. *American Anthropologist* 5(2):224–288.

Publ, H.

1985 *Prehistoric Exchange Networks and the Development of Social Complexity in México.* Unpublished Ph.D. dissertation, Department of Anthropology, Southern Illinois University, Carbondale.

Rands, R. L.

1955 *Some Manifestations of Water in Mesoamerican Art.* Bureau of American Ethnology Bulletin 157. Washington, D.C.

Rapapport, R. A.

1971 The Sacred in Human Evolution. *Annual Review of Ecology and Systematics* 1:23–44.

Ravesloot, J. C.

1979 *The Animas Phase: The Post Classic Mimbres Occupation of the Mimbres Valley, New Mexico.* Unpublished Master's thesis, Department of Anthropology, Southern Illinois University, Carbondale.

1988 *Mortuary Practices and Social Differentiation at Casas Grandes, Chihuahua, Mexico.* Anthropological Papers of the University of Arizona No. 49. University of Arizona Press, Tucson.

Ravesloot, J. C., J. S. Dean, and M. S. Foster

1986 A New Perspective on Casas Grandes Tree-Ring Dates. Paper presented at the 4th Mogollon Conference, University of Arizona, Tucson.

1995a A New Perspective on the Casas Grandes Tree-ring Dates. In *The Gran Chichimeca: Essays on the Archaeology and Ethnohistory of Northern Mesoamerica,* edited by J. E. Reyman, pp. 240–251. Avebury, Aldershot.

1995b A Reanalysis of the Casas Grandes Tree-Ring Dates: A Preliminary Discussion. In *Arqueología del Norte y del Occidente de México, Homenaje al Doctor J. Charles Kelley,* edited by Barboa Dahlgren y Ma. de los Dolores Soto de Arechavaleta, pp. 325–332. Universidad Nacional Autónoma de México, México, D.F.

Redmond, E. M., and C. S. Spencer

1994 The Cacicazgo: An Indigenous Design. In *Caciques and Their People: A Volume in Honor of Ronald Spores,* edited by J. Marcus and J. F. Zeitlin, pp. 189–225. Anthropological Papers No. 89. Museum of Anthropology, University of Michigan, Ann Arbor.

Reff, D. T.

1981 The Location of Corazones and Señora: Archaeological Evidence from the Rio Sonora Valley, México. In *The Protohistoric Period in the North American Southwest, A.D. 1450–1700,* edited by D. R. Wilcox and W. D. Masse, pp. 94–112. Anthropological Research Papers No. 24. Arizona State University, Tempe.

1991a *Disease, Depopulation, and Culture Change in Northwestern New Spain, 1518–1764.* University of Utah Press, Salt Lake City.

1991b Anthropological Analysis of Exploration Texts: Cultural Discourse and the Ethnological Import of Fray Marcos de Niza's Journey to Cibola. *American Anthropologist* 93:636–655.

1997 The Relevance of Ethnology to the Routing of the Coronado Expedition in Sonora. In *To Tierra Nueva,* edited by R. Flint and S. C. Flint, pp. 177–189. University of Colorado Press, Boulder.

Reid, J., and S. Whittlesey

1997 *The Archaeology of Ancient Arizona.* University of Arizona Press, Tucson.

Reimer, P. J.

1994 Radiocarbon Calibration News. *INQUA Newsletter* 11:21–23.

Renfrew, C.

1986 Introduction: Peer Polity Interaction and Socio-Political Change. In *Peer Polity Interaction and Socio-Political Change,* edited by C. Renfrew and J. F. Cherry, pp. 1–18. Cambridge Press, New York.

Reyman, J. E.

1971 *Mexican Influence on Southwestern Ceremonialism.* Unpublished Ph.D. dissertation, Department of Anthropology, Southern Illinois University, Carbondale.

1978 Pochteca Burials at Anasazi Sites. In *Across the Chichimec Sea,* edited by C. L. Riley and B. C. Hedrick, pp. 242–259. Southern Illinois University Press, Carbondale.

1995 *The Gran Chichimeca: Essays on the Archaeology and Ethnohistory of Northern Mesoamerica.* Worldwide Archaeology Series 12. Avebury, Aldershot.

Riley, C. L.

1963 Color-Direction Symbolism: An Example of Mexican-South-Western Contacts. *América Indígena* 23:49–60.

1975 The Road to Hawikuh: Trade and Trade Routes to Cibola Zuni. *The Kiva* 41:137–159.

1976a *Sixteenth Century Trade in the Greater Southwest.* Research Records of the University Museum, Mesoamerican Studies No. 10. Southern Illinois University, Carbondale.

1976b Las Casas and the Golden Cities. *Ethnohistory* 23:19–30.

1978 Pecos and Trade. In *Across the Chichimec Sea,* edited by C. L. Riley and B. C. Hedrick, pp. 53–64. Southern Illinois University Press, Carbondale.

1979 Casas Grandes and the Sonoran Statelets. Paper presented at the meeting of the Chicago Anthropological Society, Chicago.

1985 Spanish Contact and the Collapse of the Sonoran Statelets. In *The Archaeology of West and Northwest Mesoamerica,* edited by M. S. Foster and P. C. Weigand, pp. 419–430. Westview Press, Boulder.

1986 An Overview of the Greater Southwest in the Protohistoric Period. In *Ripples in the Chichimec Sea: New Considerations of Southwestern-Mesoamerican Interactions,* edited by F. J. Mathien and R. H. McGuire, pp. 45–54. Southern Illinois University Press, Carbondale.

1987 *The Frontier People.* University of New Mexico Press, Albuquerque.

1989 Warfare in the Protohistoric Southwest: An Overview. In *Culture and Conflict: Current Archaeological Perspectives,* edited by D. C. Tkaczuk and B. C. Vivian, pp. 138–146. Proceedings of the 20th Annual Chacmool Conference. The Archaeological Association of the University of Calgary, Calgary.

1990a The Sonoran Statelets Revisited. In *Clues to the Past: Papers in Honor of William M. Sundt,* edited by M. S. Duran and D. T. Kirkpatrick, pp. 229–238. Papers of the Archaeological Society of New Mexico No. 16, Albuquerque.

1990b A View from the Protohistoric. In *Perspectives on Southwestern Prehistory,* edited by P. E. Minnis and C. L. Redman, pp. 228–238. Westview Press, Boulder.

1993 Charles C. Di Peso: an Intellectual Biography. In *Culture and Contact: Charles C. Di Peso's Gran Chichimeca,* edited by A. L. Woosley and J. C. Ravesloot, pp. 11–22. University of New Mexico Press, Albuquerque.

1995a Marata and Its Neighbors. In *The Gran Chichimeca: Essays on the Archaeology and Ethnohistory of Northern Mesoamerica,* edited by J. E. Reyman, pp. 208–223. Avebury, Aldershot.

1995b *Rio del Norte.* University of Utah Press, Salt Lake City.

1997 Introduction. In *The Coronado Expedition to Tierra Nueva,* edited by R. Flint and S. C. Flint, pp. 1–28. University of Colorado Press, Boulder.

Ritchie, W. A.

1969 *The Archaeology of Martha's Vineyard.* Natural History Press, New York.

Robinson, W. J., and C. M. Cameron

1991 *A Directory of Tree-Ring Dated Sites in the American Southwest.* Laboratory of Tree-Ring Research, University of Arizona, Tucson.

Robles, C. A.

1929 *La Región Arqueológica de Casas Grandes.* Imprenta Nuez, México, D.F.

Robles, M.

1973 El Arroyo Bacoachi y El Trafico de Conchas del la Cultural Trincheras. Manuscript on file, Museo de la Universidad de Sonora, Hermosillo.

Rohn, A. H.

1965 Postulation of Socio-economic Groups from Archaeological Evidence. In *Contributions of the Wetherill Mesa Archeological Project,* compiled by D. Osborne, pp. 65–69. Memoirs of the Society for American Archaeology No. 19, Salt Lake City.

Rousseau, D. L.

1992 Case Studies in Pathological Science. *American Scientist* 80:54–63.

Ruiz, A.

1932 From Vol. 316, Historia, AGN, transcribed as an appendix in Carl O. Sauer, *The Road to Cibola,* Ibero-Americana 3:53–58.

Sahagún, Fray Bernardino de

1953 *Florentine Codex: General History of the Things of New Spain. Book 7: The Sun, Moon, and Stars, and the Binding of the Years.* Translated by A. J. O. Anderson and C. E. Dibble. Monographs of the School of American Research No. 14, Pt. VIII. University of Utah Press, Salt Lake City.

Sandor, J. A., and P. L. Gersper

1988 Evaluation of Soil Productivity in Some Prehistoric Agricultural Terracing Sites in New Mexico. *Agronomy Journal* 80:846–850.

Sandor, J. A., P. L. Gersper, and J. W. Hawley

1986 Soils at Prehistoric Terracing Sites in New Mexico. *Soil Science Society of America Journal* 50:166–173.

Santley, R. S., M. J. Berman, and R. T. Alexander

1991 The Politicization of the Mesoamerican Ballgame and Its Implications for the Interpretation of the Distribution of Ball Courts in Central Mexico. In *The Mesoamerican Ballgame,* edited by V. R. Scarborough and D. R. Wilcox, pp. 3–24. University of Arizona Press, Tucson.

Sauer, C. O.

1934 *Distribution of Aboriginal Tribes and Languages in Northwestern Mexico.* Ibero-Americana 5.

1935 *Aboriginal Population of Northwestern Mexico.* Ibero-Americana 10.

Sauer, C., and D. Brand

1930 Pueblo Sites in Southeastern Arizona. *University of California Publications in Geography* 3:415–458.

1931 Prehistoric Settlements of Sonora with Special Reference to Cerros de Trincheras. *University of California Publications in Geography* 5(3):67–148.

1932 *Aztatlán. Prehistoric Mexican Frontier on the Pacific Coast.* Ibero-Americana 1.

Sayles, E. B.

1933 Detail Sheets of the Gila Pueblo Chihuahua Survey. On file at the Arizona State Museum Archives, University of Arizona, Tucson.

1935 Gila Pueblo Field Survey Records from Southwestern New Mexico. On file at the Arizona State Museum Archives, University of Arizona, Tucson.

1936 *An Archaeological Survey of Chihuahua, Mexico.* Medallion Papers No. 22. Gila Pueblo Foundation, Globe, Arizona.

Scarborough, V. L.

1989 Site Structure of a Village of the Late Pithouse–Early Pueblo Period in New Mexico. *Journal of Field Archaeology* 16:405–425.

1992 Ceramics, Sedentism, and Agricultural Dependency at a Late Pithouse/Early Pueblo Period Village. *Research in Economic Anthropology,* Supplement 6:307–333.

Scarborough, V. L., and D. R. Wilcox (editors)

1991 *The Mesoamerican Ballgame.* University of Arizona Press, Tucson.

Schaafsma, C. F.

1979 The "El Paso Phase" and Its Relationship to the "Casas Grandes Phenomenon." In *Jornada Mogollon Archaeology: Proceedings of the First Jornada Conference,* edited by P. H. Beckett and R. N. Wiseman, pp. 383–388. New Mexico State University, Las Cruces, and Historic Preservation Bureau, State Planning division, Santa Fe.

1987 Statement of Curtis F. Schaafsma, New Mexico State Archaeologist and President, American Society for Conservation Archaeology, before the Committee on Interior and Insular Affairs: Oversight Hearing on Phoenix Indian School Property Disposition. *American Society for Conservation Archaeology Report* 14(2):7–11.

1988 Linked to a Larger World: A Review of Anasazi Ruins of the Southwest in Color. *Colorado Heritage* 2:45–47.

1990 The Hatch Site (LA 3135). *The Artifact* 28:1–72.

1992 Statement of Curtis F. Schaafsma, New Mexico State Archaeologist before the Subcommittee on Public Lands, National Parks and Forests; Hearing on S. 2045, Casas Grandes Study Act of 1991. On file, Laboratory of Anthropology Library, Santa Fe.

1994 Pueblo Ceremonialism from the Perspective of Spanish Documents. In *Kachinas in the Pueblo World,* edited by P. Schaafsma, pp. 121–137. University of New Mexico Press, Albuquerque.

1997 Ethnohistoric Groups in the Casas Grandes Region: Circa A.D. 1500–1700. In *Layers of Time: Papers in Honor of Robert H. Weber,* edited by D. Kirkpatrick and M. Duran, pp. 85–98. Papers of the Archaeological Society of New Mexico No. 23, Albuquerque.

Schaafsma, P.
1972 *Rock Art in New Mexico.* State Planning Office, Santa Fe.
1975a *Rock Art in the Cochiti Reservoir District.* Papers in Anthropology 16, Museum of New Mexico Press, Santa Fe.
1975b Rock Art and Ideology of the Mimbres and Jornada Mogollon. *The Artifact* 13(3):1–14.
1975c *Rock Art in New Mexico.* University of New Mexico Press, Albuquerque.
1980 *Indian Rock Art of the Southwest.* School of American Research, Santa Fe, and University of New Mexico Press, Albuquerque.
1990 The Pine Tree Site: A Galisteo Basin Pueblo IV Shrine. In *Clues to the Past: Papers in Honor of William M. Sundt,* edited by M. S. Duran and D. T. Kirkpatrick, pp. 139–258. Papers of the Archaeological Society of New Mexico No. 16, Albuquerque.
1992a *Rock Art in New Mexico.* Museum of New Mexico Press, Santa Fe.
1992b Imagery and Magic: Petroglyphs at Comanche Gap, Galisteo Basin, New Mexico. In *Archaeology, Art, and Anthropology: Papers in Honor of J. J. Brody,* edited by M. S. Duran and D. T. Kirkpatrick, pp. 157–174. Papers of the Archaeological Society of New Mexico No. 18, Albuquerque.
1994 The Prehistoric Kachina Cult and Its Origins as Suggested by Southwestern Rock Art. In *Kachinas in the Pueblo World,* edited by P. Schaafsma pp. 63–79. University of New Mexico Press, Albuquerque.
1997a *Rock Art Sites in Chihuahua, Mexico.* Archaeology Notes 171, Office of Archaeological Studies, Museum of New Mexico, Santa Fe.
1997b Pottery Metaphors in Pueblo and Jornada Mogollon Rock Art. In *Ethnography and Rock Art in Western North America,* edited by D. Whitley. University of New Mexico Press, Albuquerque, in press.

Schaafsma, P. (editor)
1994 *Kachinas in the Pueblo World.* University of New Mexico Press, Albuquerque.

Schaafsma, P., and C. F. Schaafsma
1974 Evidence for the Origins of the Pueblo Katchina Cult as Suggested by Southwestern Rock Art. *American Antiquity* 30:535–545.

Schaafsma, P., and R. N. Wiseman
1992 Serpents in the Prehistoric Pecos Valley of Southeastern New Mexico. In *Archaeology, Art, and Anthropology: Papers in Honor of J. J. Brody,* edited by M. S. Duran and D. T. Kirkpatrick, pp. 175–183. Papers of the Archaeological Society of New Mexico No. 18, Albuquerque.

Schiffer, M. B.
1986 Radiocarbon Dating and the Old Wood Problem: The Case of the Hohokam Chronology. *Journal of Archaeological Science* 13:13–30.

Schackley, M. S.
1988 Sources of Archaeological Obsidian in the Southwest: An Archaeological, Petrological, and Geochemical Study. *American Antiquity,* Vol. 53, No. 4, pp. 752–772, Washington.

Schmidt, R. H.
1973 *A Geographical Survey of Chihuahua.* Texas Western Press, University of Texas at El Paso.
1992 Chihuahua: Tierra de Contrastes Geográficos. In *Historia General de Chihuahua I: Geología, Geografía, y Arqueología,* edited by A. Márquez-Alameda, pp. 45–101. Universidad Autónoma de Ciudad Juárez y Gobierno del Estado de Chihuahua, Juárez.

Schmidt, R. H., and R. E. Gerald
1988 The Distribution of Conservation-Type Water Control Systems in the Northern Sierra Madre Occidental. *The Kiva* 53:165–180.

Schortman, E. M.
1989 Interregional Interaction in Prehistory: The Need for a New Perspective. *American Antiquity* 54(1):52–65.

Schortman, E. M., and S. Nakamura
1991 A Crisis of Identity: Late Classic Competition and Interaction on the Southeast Maya Periphery. *Latin American Antiquity* 2(4):311–336.

Schroeder, A. H.
1994 Development in the Southwest and Relations with the Plains. In *Plains Indians, A.D. 500–1500,* edited by K. H. Schlesier, pp. 290–307. University of Oklahoma Press, Norman.

Scott, G. R., and C. G. Turner II
1997 *The Anthropology of Modern Human Teeth: Dental Morphology and Its Variation in Recent Human Populations.* Cambridge University Press, Cambridge.

Scott, S. D. Jr.
1966 *Dendrochronology in Mexico.* Papers of the Laboratory of Tree-Ring Research 2. University of Arizona Press, Tucson.
1974 Archaeology and the Estuary: Researching Prehistory and Paleoecology in the Marismas Nacionales, Sinaloa and Nayarit, Mexico. In *The Archaeology of West Mexico,* edited by B. B. Bell, pp. 51–56. West Mexican Society for Advanced Study, Ajijic, Jalisco.
1985 Core Versus Marginal Mesoamerica: A Coastal West Mexican Perspective. In *Archaeology of West and Northwest Mesoamerica,* edited by M. S. Foster and P. C. Weigand, pp. 181–192. Westview Press, Boulder.

Seler, E.
1963 *Comentarios al Códice Borgia.* Translated by M. Fenk. 3 vols. Fondo de Cultura Economica, México, D.F.

Shafer, H. J.
1982 Classic Mimbres Phase Households and Room Use Patterns. *The Kiva* 48:17–48.
1985 A Mimbres Potter's Grave: An Example of Mimbres Craft-Specialization? *Bulletin of the Texas Archaeological Society* 56:185–200.
1986 *The NAN Ranch Archaeology Project 1985 Interim Report.* Special Report 7, Anthropology Laboratory, Texas A & M University, College Station.
1991 Archaeology at the NAN Ruin: The 1987 Season. *The Artifact* 29(3):1–43.
1995 Architecture and Symbolism in Transitional Pueblo

Development in the Mimbres Valley, SW New Mexico. *Journal of Field Archaeology* 22:23–47.
1996 The Classic Mimbres Phenomenon and Some New Interpretations. Paper presented at the 9th Mogollon Conference, Silver City.

Shafer, H. J., and A. J. Taylor
1986 Mimbres Pueblo Dynamics and Ceramic Style Change. *Journal of Field Archaeology* 13:43–68.

Shafer, H. J., and C. Judkins
1997 *Archaeology at the NAN Ruin: 1996 Season.* Department of Anthropology, Texas A & M University, College Station.

Shafer, H. J., and R. L. Brewington
1995 Microstylistic Changes in Mimbres Black-on-white Pottery: Examples from the NAN Ruin, Grant County, New Mexico. *The Kiva* 61:5–29.

Shafer, H. J., and R. L. Brewington
1995 Microstylistic Changes in Mimbres Black-on-white Pottery. *The Kiva* 81:5-30.

Shafer, H. J., J. E. Dockall, R. Brewington, and J. P. Dering
1998 *Archaeology at Ojasen and Gobernadora Sites, El Paso County, Texas.* Texas Department of Transportation Investigations. Center for Environmental Archaeology, Texas A & M University, College Station, Texas.

Sharer, R. J.
1984 Lower Central America as Seen from Mesoamerica. In *The Archaeology of Lower Central America,* edited by F. W. Lange and D. Z. Stone, pp. 63–84. University of New Mexico Press, Albuquerque.

Sheridan, T. E.
1996 *Review of C. L. Riley's Rio del Norte.* Southwestern Mission Research Center Newsletter 30(109):13–14.

Smiley, N.
1979 Evidence for Ceramic Trade Specialization in the Southern Jornada Branch. In *Jornada Mogollon Archaeology: Proceedings of the First Jornada Conference,* edited by P. H. Beckett and R. N. Wiseman, pp. 53–60. New Mexico State University, Las Cruces.

Smith, M. T.
1987 *Archaeology of Aboriginal Culture Change in the Interior Southeast.* Ripley P. Bullen Monographs in Anthropology and History No. 6. Florida State Museum, Gainesville.

Smith, W.
1952 *Kiva Mural Decorations at Awatovi and Kawaika-a.* Papers of the Peabody Museum of Archaeology and Ethnology No. 37, Harvard University, Cambridge.

Spicer, E. H.
1962 *Cycles of Conquest.* University of Arizona Press, Tucson.

Spinden, H. J.
1943 *Ancient Civilizations of Mexico and Central America.* 3rd revised ed. Originally published 1928, Handbook Series No. 3, American Museum of Natural History, New York.

Spoerl, P. M., and J. C. Ravesloot
1994 From Casas Grandes to Casa Grande: Prehistoric Human Impacts in the Sky Islands of Southern Arizona and Northwestern Mexico. In *Biodiversity and Management of the Madrean Archipelago,* L. DeBano and P. Ffolliott, pp. 492–501. Rocky Mountain Forest and Range Experiment Station, General Technical Report RM-GTR 264. Fort Collins.

Stein, J. R., and P. J. McKenna
1988 *An Archaeological Reconnaissance of a Late Bonito Phase Occupation near Aztec Ruins National Monument, New Mexico.* National Park Service, Santa Fe.

Stenzel, W.
1970 The Sacred Bundles in Mesoamerican Religion. *Proceedings of the International Congress of Americanists* 38(2):347–352.

Stephen, A. M.
1936 *Hopi Journal of Alexander M. Stephen,* edited by E. C. Parsons. Contributions to Anthropology 23, 2 vols. Columbia University Press, New York.

Stern, T.
1949 *The Rubber-Ball Games of the Americas.* University of Washington Press, Seattle.

Stevenson, C. M., B. E. Scheetz, and J. Carpenter
1989 Obsidian Dating: Recent Advances in the Experimental Determination and Application of Obsidian Hydration Dates. *Archaeometry* 32(2):193–206.

Stevenson, M. C.
1894a A Chapter of Zuñi Mythology. *International Congress of Anthropology, Chicago 1893 Memoirs,* pp. 312–319. Schultz, Chicago.
1894b The Sia. *11th Annual Report of the Bureau of American Ethnology for the Years 1889–1890,* pp. 3–157. Washington, D.C.
1904 The Zuni Indians. *23rd Annual Report of the Bureau of American Ethnology, 1902–1903.* Washington, D.C.

Steward, J. H.
1937 Ecological Aspects of Southwestern Society. *Anthropos* 32:87–104.

Stewart, J. D., J. C. Driver, and J. H. Kelley
1991 The Capitan North Project: Chronology. In *Mogollon V,* edited by P. H. Beckett, pp. 177–190. COAS Publishing and Research, Las Cruces.

Stewart, J. D., P. Matousek, and J. H. Kelley
1990 Rock Art and Ceramic Art in the Jornada Mogollon Region. *The Kiva* 55:301–319.

Stewart, J. D., P. Fralick, R. Hancock, J. H. Kelley, and E. Garrett
1990 Petrographic Analysis and INAA Geochemistry of Prehistoric Ceramics from Robinson Pueblo, New Mexico. *Journal of Archaeological Science* 17:601–625.

Stirling, M. S.
1942 *Origin Myth of Acoma and Other Records.* Smithsonian Institution, Bureau of American Ethnology Bulletin 135. Government Printing Office, Washington, D.C.

Stokes, R.
1996 Mimbres Pottery Micro-Seriation: Determining Where Transitional Rooms May Occur Using Surface Ceramic Collections. Paper presented at the 9th Mogollon Conference, Western New Mexico University Museum, Silver City.

Stone, T., and M. S. Foster
1994 Miscellaneous Artifacts. In *The Pueblo Grande Project: 4. Material Culture,* edited by M. S. Foster, pp. 203–262. Soil Systems Publications in Archaeology No. 20, Tempe.

Strong, W. D.
1967 Cultural Resemblances in Nuclear America: Parallelism or Diffusion? In *The Civilizations of Ancient America: Selected Papers of the 29th International Congress of Americanists,* edited by S. Tax, pp. 271–279. Reprinted. Originally published in 1951, Cooper Square, New York.

Stross, B.
1994 Maize and Fish: The Iconography of Power in Late Formative Mesoamerica. *Res: Anthropology and Aesthetics* 25:10–35.

Struever, S.
1972 The Hopewell Interaction Sphere in Riverine-Western Great Lakes Culture History. In *Contemporary Archaeology,* edited by M. P. Leone, pp. 303–315. Southern Illinois University Press, Carbondale.

Stuart, D. E., and R. P. Gauthier
1981 *Prehistoric New Mexico: Background for Survey.* New Mexico Historic Preservation Bureau, Santa Fe.

Stubbs, S. A., and W. S. Stallings Jr.
1953 *The Excavation of Pindi Pueblo, New Mexico.* Monographs of the School of American Research and the Laboratory of Anthropology No. 18, Santa Fe.

Stuiver, M., and H. A. Polach
1977 Discussion: Reporting of 14C data. *Radiocarbon* 19:355–363.

Stuiver, M., and P. J. Reimer
1993a *CALIB User's Guide Rev 3.0.3 (to be used in conjunction with Stuiver and Reimer, 1993).* Quaternary Research Center, University of Washington, Seattle.
1993b Extended Radiocarbon Data Base and Revised CALIB 3.0 Radiocarbon Age Calibration Program. *Radiocarbon* 35:215–230.

Suess, Hans E.
1970 The three causes of the secular C-14 fluctuations, their amplitudes and time constants. In *Radiocarbon Variations and Absolute Chronology,* ed. by Ingrid U. Olsson, pp. 595–605. Proceedings of the 12th Nobel Symposium. Institute of Physics, Upsala University. Wiley Interscience Division.

Sullivan, T. D.
1974 Tlaloc: A New Etymological Interpretation of the God's Name and What It Reveals of His Essence and Nature. *Proceedings of the 40th International Congress of Americanists* 2:213–219. Rome.
1986 A Scattering of Jades: The Words of Aztec Elders. In *Symbol and Meaning beyond the Closed Community: Essays in Mesoamerican Ideas,* edited by G. H. Gossen, pp. 9–18. Studies on Culture and Society Vol. 1, Institute for Mesoamerican Studies, State University of New York, Albany.

Sweetman, R.
1974 Prehistoric Pottery from Coastal Sinaloa and Nayarit. In *The Archaeology of West Mexico,* edited by B. B. Bell, pp. 68–82. West Mexican Society for Advanced Study, Ajijic, Jalisco.

Szuter, C. R.
1984 Faunal Exploitation and the Reliance on Small Animals among the Hohokam. In *Hohokam Archaeology along the Salt-Gila Aqueduct Central Arizona Project, Vol. 7: Environment and Subsistence,* edited by L. Teague and P. Crown, pp. 139–170. Arizona State Museum Archaeological Series 150. Arizona State Museum, University of Arizona, Tucson.

Szuter, C. R., and W. B. Gillespie
1994 Interpreting Use of Animal Resources at Prehistoric American Southwest Communities. In *The Ancient Southwestern Community: Models and Methods for the Study of Prehistoric Social Organization,* edited by W. H. Wills and R. D. Leonard, pp. 67–76. University of New Mexico Press, Albuquerque.

Talbot, R. K.
1996 Reformulating Fremont Thought: New Perspectives on Old Ideas. Paper presented at the Southwest Symposium, Tempe.

Taube, K. A.
1986 The Teotihuacan Cave of Origin: The Iconography and Architecture of Emergence Mythology in Mesoamerica and the American Southwest. *Res: Anthropology and Aesthetics* 12:51–82.
1988 *The Albers Collection of Pre-Columbian Art.* Hudson Hills Press, New York.

Taylor, R. E., C. V. Haynes Jr., and M. Stuiver
1996 Clovis and Folsom Age Estimates: Stratigraphic Context and Radiocarbon Calibration. *Antiquity* 70:515–525.

Taylor, R. E., M. Stuiver, and P. J. Reimer
1996 Development and Extension of the Calibration of the Radiocarbon Time Scale: Archaeological Applications. *Quaternary Science Reviews* 15:1–14.

Tedlock, B.
1986 On a Mountain Road in the Dark: Encounters with the Quiché Maya Culture Hero. In *Symbol and Meaning beyond the Closed Community: Essays in Mesoamerican Ideas,* edited by G. H. Gossen, pp. 125–138. Studies on Culture and Society Vol. 1, Institute for Mesoamerican Studies, State University of New York, Albany.

Tedlock, D.
1994 Stories of Kachinas and the Dance of Life and Death. In *Kachinas in the Pueblo World,* edited by P. Schaafsma, pp. 161–174. University of New Mexico Press, Albuquerque.

Thompson, G.
1879 Notes on the Pueblos and Their Inhabitants. *Report Upon United States Geographical Surveys West of the One Hundredth Meridian: Archaeology* VII:319–324. Engineer Department, United States Army, Washington, D.C.

Thompson, M.
1990 Codes from the Underworld: Mimbres Iconography

Revealed. Paper presented at the 6th Mogollon Conference, Silver City.

1994 The Evolution and Dissemination of Mimbres Iconography. In *Kachinas in the Pueblo World,* edited by P. Schaafsma, pp. 93–106. University of New Mexico Press, Albuquerque.

Thompson, R. H.

1963 Diagonostic Ceramic Traits of the 14th Century in the Southwest United States and Northwest Mexico. Paper presented at the 9th Mesa Redonda, Sociedad Mexicana de Antropologia, Chihuahua.

Titiev, M.

1944 *Old Oraibi.* Papers of the Peabody Museum of American Archaeology and Ethnology 22:1. Harvard University, Cambridge.

1992 *Old Oraibi: A Study of the Hopi Indians of Third Mesa.* University of New Mexico Press, Albuquerque. Originally published 1944, Papers of the Peabody Museum of American Archaeology and Ethnology 22:1, Harvard University, Cambridge.

Touchon, R.

1988 Growth and Yield of Emory Oak. In *Oak Woodland Management: Proceedings of the Workshop,* edited by P. Ffolliott and J. Hasbrouck, pp. 11–18. School of Renewable Natural Resources, University of Arizona, Tucson.

Tower, D. B.

1945 *The Use of Marine Mollusca and Their Value in Reconstructing Prehistoric Trade Routes in the American Southwest.* Papers of the Excavators Club 2(3). Cambridge.

Townsend, R. F.

1979 *State and Cosmos in the Art of Tenochtitlán.* Studies in Pre-Columbian Art and Archaeology No. 23. Dumbarton Oaks, Trustees for Harvard University, Washington, D.C.

1991 The Mt. Tlaloc Project. In *To Change Place: Aztec Ceremonial Landscapes,* edited by D. Carrasco, pp. 26–30. University of Colorado Press, Boulder.

1992a Landscape and Symbol. In *The Ancient Americas: Art from Sacred Landscapes,* edited by R. F. Townsend, pp. 28–47. Art Institute of Chicago, Chicago.

1992b The Renewal of Nature at the Temple of Tlaloc. In *The Ancient Americas: Art from Sacred Landscapes,* edited by R. F. Townsend, pp. 171–186. Art Institute of Chicago, Chicago.

Turner, C. G. II

1985 The Dental Search for Native American Origins. In *Out of Asia, Peopling the Americas and the Pacific,* edited by R. Kirk and E. Szathmary, pp. 31–78. Reprinted. Originally published in the *Journal of Pacific History,* Australian National University, Canberra, Australia.

1991 *The Dentition of Arctic Peoples.* Garland Publishing, New York.

1993 Southwest Indians: Prehistory through Dentition. National Geographic Society *Research & Exploration* 9(1):32–53.

Turner, C. G. II, and G. R. Scott

1977 Dentition of Easter Islanders. In *Orofacial Growth and Development,* edited by A. A. Dahlberg and T. M. Graber, pp. 229–249. Mouton Publishers, The Hague.

Turner, C. G. II, C. R. Nichol, and G. R. Scott

1991 Scoring Procedures for Key Morphological Traits of the Permanent Dentition: The Arizona State University Dental Anthropology System. In *Advances in Dental Anthropology,* edited by M. A. Kelley and C. S. Larsen, pp. 13–31. Wiley-Liss, New York.

Upham, S.

1992 Interaction and Isolation: The Empty Spaces in Panregional Political Systems. In *Resources, Power, and Interregional Interaction,* edited by E. Schortman and P. Urban, pp. 139–152. Plenum Press, New York.

Urban, P. A.

1986 Precolumbian Settlement in the Naco Valley, Northwestern Honduras. In *The Southeast Maya Periphery,* edited by P. A. Urban and E. M. Schortman, pp. 275–295. University of Texas Press, Austin.

Vaillant, G. C.

1938 A Correlation of Archaeological and Historical Sequences in the Valley of Mexico. *American Anthropologist* 40:535–573.

1940 Pattern in the Middle American Archaeology. In *The Maya and Their Neighbors,* edited by C. L. Hay, R. L. Linton, S. K. Lathrop, H. L. Shapiro, and G. C. Vaillant, pp. 295–305. Dover Publications, New York.

1941 *Aztecs of Mexico: Origin, Rise and Fall of the Aztec Nation.* Doubleday, Doran, New York.

Van Loon, H. W.

1921 *The Story of Mankind.* Boni & Liveright, New York.

Vargas, V. D.

1994 *Copper Bell Trade Patterns in the Prehistoric Greater American Southwest.* Unpublished Master's thesis, Department of Anthropology, University of Oklahoma, Norman.

1995 *Copper Bell Trade Patterns in the Prehistoric U.S. Southwest and Northwest Mexico.* Arizona State Museum Archaeological Series 187. Arizona State Museum, University of Arizona, Tucson.

Vehik, S. C., and T. G. Baugh

1994 Prehistoric Plains Trade. In *Prehistoric Exchange Systems in North America,* edited by T. G. Baugh and J. E. Ericson, pp. 249–274. Plenum, New York.

Villalpando C., M. E.

1985 Cazadores-Recolectores y Agricultores del Contacto. *Historia General de Sonora* 1:263–289. Gobierno del Estado de Sonora, Hermosillo.

1988 Rutas de intercambio y objectos de concha en el noroeste de México. *Cuicuilco* 21:77–82.

Voth, H. R.

1905 *Traditions of the Hopi.* Anthropological Series 8. Field Museum of Natural History Publication 96, Chicago.

Wallace, H. D.

1995 *Archaeological Investigations at Los Morteros: A Pre-*

historic Settlement in the Northern Tucson Basin. Archaeology Anthropological Papers No. 17. Center for Desert Archaeology, Tucson.

Wallerstein, I.

1974 *The Modern World System: Capitalist Agriculture and the Origins of the European World Economy in the Sixteenth Century.* Academic Press, New York.

Ward, G. K., and S. R. Wilson

1978 Procedures for Comparing and Combining Radiocarbon Age Determinations: A Critique. *Archaeometry* 20:19–31.

Warren, A. H.

1981 A Petrographic Study of the Pottery of Gran Quivira. In *Contributions to Gran Quivira Archeology,* edited by A. Hayes, pp. 67–73. U.S. National Park Service Publications in Archeology 17, Washington, D.C.

Weaver, M. P.

1981 *The Aztecs, Maya, and Their Predecessors: Archaeology of Mesoamerica.* 2d ed. Studies in Archaeology. Academic Press, New York.

Webster, C. L.

1912 Archaeological and Ethnological Researches in Southwestern New Mexico. *Archaeological Bulletin* 3(4).

Wedel, M. M.

1988 *The Wichita Indians 1541–1750: Ethnohistorical Essays.* Reprints in Anthropology, vol. 38. J & L Reprint, Lincoln. Originally published 1979, *Nebraska History* 60:193–196.

Wedel, W. R.

1994 Coronado and Quivira. In *Spain and the Plains,* edited by R. H. Vigil, F. W. Kaye, and J. R. Wunder, pp. 45–66. University of Colorado Press, Boulder.

Weigand, P. C.

1982 Mining and Mineral Trade in Prehistoric Zacatecas. In *Mining and Mining Techniques in Ancient Mesoamerica,* edited by P. C. Weigand and G. Gwynne. *Anthropology* 6(1–2):87–134.

1991 The Western Mesoamerican Tlachco: A Two-Thousand Year Perspective. In *The Mesoamerican Ballgame,* edited by V. L. Scarborough and D. R. Wilcox, pp. 73–86. University of Arizona Press, Tucson.

Weigand, P. C., and M. Spence

1982 The Obsidian Mining Complex at La Joya, Jalisco. In *Mining and Mining Techniques in Ancient Mesoamerica,* edited by P. C. Weigand and G. Gwynne. *Anthropology* 6(1–2):175–188.

Whalen, M. E., and P. E. Minnis

1996a Ball Courts and Political Centralization in the Casas Grandes Region. *American Antiquity* 61:732–746.

1996b Studying Complexity in Northern Mexico: The Paquimé Regional System. In *Debating Complexity: Proceedings of the 26th Annual Chacmool Conference,* edited by D. A. Meyer, P. C. Dawson, and D. T. Hanna, pp. 282–289. Archaeological Association of the University of Calgary, Calgary.

1996c The Context of Production in and around Paquimé, Chihuahua, Mexico. In *Interpreting Southwestern Diversity: Underlying Principles and Overarching Patterns,* edited by P. R. Fish and J. J. Reid, pp. 173–182. Anthropological Research Paper 48, Arizona State University, Tempe.

Wheat, J. B.

1955 Mogollon Culture Prior to A.D. 1000. *American Antiquity* 20:4, pt. 2.

Wheeler, M.

1956 *Archaeology from the Earth.* Penguin Books, Baltimore.

White, L.

1932 The Acoma Indians. *Forty-Seventh Annual Report of the Bureau of American Ethnology, 1929–1930* pp. 17–192. Government Printing Office, Washington, D.C.

1942 *The Pueblo of Santa Ana, New Mexico.* American Anthropologist, n.s., Memoir No. 60. American Anthropological Association, Menasha.

Whitecotton, J. W., and R. A. Pailes

1986 New World Pre-Columbian World Systems. In *Ripples in the Chichimec Sea: New Considerations of Southwestern-Mesoamerican Interactions,* edited by F. J. Mathien and R. H. McGuire, pp. 183–204. Southern Illinois University Press, Carbondale.

Whittlesey, S.

1996 Culture History: Prehistoric Narratives for Southern Arizona. In *Cultural Resource Management Plan for the Fairfield Canoa Ranch Property,* edited by C. Van West and S. Whittlesey, pp. 45–78. Statistical Research Technical Series, Tucson.

Wicke, C., and F. Horcasitas

1957 Archeological Investigations on Mount Tlaloc, Mexico. *Mesoamerican Notes* 5:83–95.

Wilshusen, R. H.

1989 Unstuffing the Estufa: Ritual Floor Features in Anasazi Pit Structures and Pueblo Kivas. In *The Architecture of Social Integration in Prehistoric Pueblos,* edited by W. D. Lipe and M. Hegmon, pp. 89–112. Occasional Paper No. 1 of the Crow Canyon Archaeological Center, Cortez.

Wilcox, D. R.

1975 A Strategy for Perceiving Social Groups in Puebloan Sites. *Fieldiana: Anthropology* 65:120–159.

1982 A Set-Theory Approach to Sampling Pueblos: The Implications of Room-set Additions at Grasshopper Pueblo. In *Multidisciplinary Research at Grasshopper Pueblo,* edited by W. A. Longacre, S. J. Holbrook, and M. W. Graves, pp. 19–27. Anthropological Papers of the University of Arizona No. 40. Tucson.

1986a A Historical Analysis of the Problem of Southwestern-Mesoamerican Connections. In *Ripples in the Chichimec Sea: New Considerations of Southwestern-Mesoamerican Interactions,* edited by F. J. Mathien and R. H. McGuire, pp. 9–44. Southern Illinois University Press, Carbondale.

1986b The Tepiman Connection: A Model of Mesoamerican-Southwestern Interaction. In *Ripples in the Chichimec Sea,* edited by F. J. Mathien and

R. H. McGuire, pp. 135–154. Southern Illinois University Press, Carbondale.

1987 New Models of Social Structure at C. C. Di Peso's Paloparado Site. In *The Hohokam Village,* edited by David E. Doyel, pp. 223–248. Southwestern and Rocky Mountain Division of the American Association for the Advancement of Science, Glenwood Springs.

1991a Hohokam Social Complexity. In *Chaco and Hohokam: Prehistoric Regional Systems in the American Southwest,* edited by P. L. Crown and W. J. Judge, pp. 253–276. School of American Research, Santa Fe.

1991b The Mesoamerican Ballgame in the American Southwest. In *The Mesoamerican Ballgame,* edited by V. L. Scarborough and D. R. Wilcox, pp. 101–128. University of Arizona Press, Tucson.

1991c Changing Contexts of Pueblo Adaptation, A.D. 1250–1600. In *Farmers, Hunters, and Colonists: Interaction between the Southwest and the Southern Plains,* edited by K. A. Spielmann, pp. 128–154. University of Arizona Press, Tucson.

1994 Three Macroregional Systems in the North American Southwest, A.D. 750–1450. Paper prepared for the Advanced Seminar on Great Towns and Regional Polities, Amerind Foundation, Dragoon.

1995 A Processual Model of Charles C. Di Peso's Babocomari Site and Related Systems. In *The Gran Chichimeca: Essays on the Archaeology and Ethnohistory of Northern Mesoamerica,* edited by J. E. Reyman, pp. 281–319. Avebury, Aldershot.

1996 Organizational Parameters of Southwest/Mesoamerican Connectivity. Paper presented at the 1996 Southwest Symposium, Arizona State University, Tempe.

Wilcox, D. R., and C. Sternberg

1983 *Hohokam Ballcourts and Their Interpretation.* Arizona State Museum Archaeological Series 160. Arizona State Museum, University of Arizona, Tucson.

Wilcox, D. R., and L. O. Shenk

1977 *The Architecture of the Casa Grande and Its Interpretation.* Arizona State Museum Archaeological Series No. 115. Arizona State Museum, University of Arizona, Tucson.

Wilcox, D. R., T. R. McGuire, and C. Sternberg

1981 *Snaketown Revisited.* Arizona State Museum Archaeological Series No. 155. Arizona State Museum, University of Arizona, Tucson.

Williams, E.

1992 *Las Piedras Sagradas: Escultura prehispánica del Occidente de Mexico.* El Colegio de Michoacán, Zamora.

Williams, M.

1996 A Comparison of Classic Mimbres and Black Mountain Phase Ceramic Manufacture and Exchange Patterns as Determined by NAA. Paper presented at the 9th Mogollon Conference, Silver City.

Williams, S.

1978 Foreword. In *Pre-Columbian Shell Engravings from the Craig Mound at Spiro, Oklahoma,* Pt. 1, vols. 1–3, by P. Phillips and J. A. Brown, unpaged. Peabody Museum of Archaeology and Ethnology, Harvard University, Cambridge.

Wills, W. H.

1994 Evolutionary and Ecological Modeling in Southwestern Archaeology. In *Understanding Complexity in the Prehistoric Southwest,* edited by G. J. Gumerman and M. Gell-Mann, pp. 287–296. Addison-Wesley, New York.

Wilson, C., and E. Blinman

1995 Changing Specialization of White Ware Manufacture in the Northern San Juan Region. In *Ceramic Production in the American Southwest,* edited by B. J. Mills and P. L. Crown, pp. 63–87. University of Arizona Press. Tucson.

Withers, A. M.

1946 *Copper in the Prehistoric Southwest.* Unpublished Master's thesis, Department of Anthropology, University of Arizona, Tucson.

1976 Some Pictographs from Northwestern Chihuahua. In *Collected Papers in Honor of Marjorie Ferguson Lambert,* edited by A. H. Schroeder, pp. 109–112. Papers of the Archaeological Society of New Mexico No. 3, Albuquerque Archaeological Society Press, Albuquerque.

Wobst, H. M.

1977 Stylistic Behavior and Information Exchange. In *For the Director: Research Essays in Honor of James B. Griffin,* edited by C. E. Cleland, pp. 317–342. University of Michigan Museum of Anthropology, Anthropological Papers No. 61. University of Michigan Press, Ann Arbor.

Wolfman, D. W., and C. F. Schaafsma

1989 Recent Archaeomagnetic Dates for the Joyce Well Site in Hidalgo County, New Mexico, and the Implications for Dating the Animas Phase and the Related Casas Grandes Culture. Paper presented at the 1989 annual meeting of the Archaeological Society of New Mexico, Taos.

Woodward, A.

1936 A Shell Bracelet Manufactory. *American Antiquity* 2:117–125.

Woosley, A. I., and B. Olinger

1993 The Casas Grandes Ceramic Tradition: Production and Interregional Exchange of Ramos Polychrome. In *Culture and Contact: Charles Di Peso's Gran Chichimeca,* edited by A. I. Woosley and J. C. Ravesloot, pp. 105–131. Amerind Foundation, Dragoon, and University of New Mexico Press, Albuquerque.

Woosley, A. I., and J. C. Ravesloot

1993 *Culture and Contact: Charles C. Di Peso's Gran Chichimeca.* Amerind Foundation, Dragoon, and University of New Mexico Press, Albuquerque.

Wright, B.

1977 *Hopi Kachinas: The Complete Guide to Collecting Kachina Dolls.* Northland Press, Flagstaff.

1984 The Shalako. Paper presented at the 20th-Century Conference, School of American Research, Santa Fe.

1994 The Changing Kachina. In *Kachinas in the Pueblo World,* edited by P. Schaafsma, pp. 139–146. University of New Mexico Press, Albuquerque.

York, J.

1965 Other Plant Remains. In *A Survey and Excavation of Caves in Hidalgo County, New Mexico,* edited by M. Lambert and J. R. Ambler, pp. 94–95. School of American Research Monograph 25. School of American Research, Santa Fe.

Young, M. J.

1988 *Signs From the Ancestors: Zuni Cultural Symbolism and Perceptions of Rock Art.* University of New Mexico Press, Albuquerque.

1994 The Interconnection Between Western Puebloan and Mesoamerican Ideology/Cosmology. In *Kachinas in the Pueblo World,* edited by P. Schaafsma, pp. 107–120. University of New Mexico Press, Albuquerque.

Young, S. M., D. A. Phillips Jr., and F. J. Mathien

1994 Lead Isotope Analysis of Turquoise Sources in the Southwestern U.S.A. and Mesoamerica. Poster Session, 29th International Symposium on Archaeology, Ankara, Turkey.

CONTRIBUTORS

Ronna Jane Bradley
University of New Mexico
Valencia Campus
Los Lunas

John P. Carpenter
Department of Anthropology
Wichita State University
Wichita, Kansas

Darrell G. Creel
Texas Archaeological Research Laboratory
Pickle Research Campus
The University of Texas at Austin

Rafael Cruz Antillón
Instituto Nacional de Antropología e Historia
Centro Chihuahua
Ciudad Chihuahua

Paul R. Fish
Research Professor and Curator of Archaeology,
Arizona State Museum
The University of Arizona
Tucson

Suzanne K. Fish
Associate Research Professor and Assistant Curator,
Arizona State Museum
The University of Arizona
Tucson

Michael S. Foster
Cultural Resources Management Program
Gila River Indian Community
Phoenix, Arizona

Emiliano Gallaga M.
Instituto Nacional de Antropología e Historia
Centro Sonora
Hermosillo

Alice B. Kehoe
Professor, Department of Social and Cultural Sciences
Marquette University
Milwaukee, Wisconsin

Jane H. Kelley
Professor, Department of Anthropology
University of Calgary
Calgary, Alberta

Stephen H. Lekson
Curator, University Museum, and Assistant Professor,
Department of Anthropology
University of Colorado
Boulder

Randall H. McGuire
Professor, Department of Anthropology
State University of New York
Binghamton

A. C. MacWilliams
Doctoral Candidate, Department of Anthropology
University of Arizona
Tucson

Timothy D. Maxwell
Director, Office of Archaeological Studies
Museum of New Mexico
Santa Fe

Clement W. Meighan
Emeritus Professor, Department of Anthropology
University of California, Los Angeles

Paul E. Minnis
Associate Professor, Department of Anthropology
The University of Oklahoma
Norman

Loy C. Neff
Archeologist, NPS Western Archeological and
Conservation Center
Tucson, Arizona

David A. Phillips Jr.
Principal Investigator, SWCA, Inc.
Adjunct Professor
Department of Anthropology
University of New Mexico
Albuquerque

Carroll L. Riley
Emeritus Distinguished Professor, Department of Anthropology
Southern Illinois University, Carbondale, and
Research Associate, Museum of Indian Arts and Culture/Laboratory of Anthropology
Museum of New Mexico
Santa Fe

Curtis F. Schaafsma
Curator of Anthropology, Museum of Indian Arts and Culture/Laboratory of Anthropology
Museum of New Mexico
Santa Fe

Polly Schaafsma
Research Associate, Museum of Indian Arts and Culture/Laboratory of Anthropology
Museum of New Mexico
Santa Fe

Harry J. Shafer
Professor, Department of Anthropology
Texas A & M University
College Station

Joe D. Stewart
Associate Professor, Department of Anthropology
Lakehead University
Thunder Bay, Ontario

Christy G. Turner II
Regents' Professor, Department of Anthropology
Arizona State University
Tempe

Victoria D. Vargas
Doctoral Candidate, Department of Anthropology
Arizona State University
Tempe

Maria Elisa Villalpando C.
Instituto Nacional de Antropología e Historia
Centro Sonora
Hermosillo

Michael E. Whalen
Professor, Department of Anthropology
University of Tulsa, Oklahoma

David R. Wilcox
Senior Research Archaeologist and Special Assistant to the Deputy Director
Museum of Northern Arizona
Flagstaff

INDEX

Acequia Seca site, 115
Acoma, 90–91, 173, 175, 184, 185, 249
Acus, 199
Adams, E. C., 227
Adobe, coursed, 13, 32–33; at Casa Grande, 242, 243; in cliff dwellings near Casas Grandes, 18; defined, 242; in Mimbres area, 116, 243
Agave, 33, 140
Alamogordo site, 216, 220, 221, 243
Alamo Hueco Caves, 33
Alamo Hueco Mountains, 15
Allantown site, 216, 219, 220, 225
Amapa site, 154, 160, 209, 210
Anasazi: Mimbres and, 89; shell, 219, 220, 222, 223, 224, 225, 226
Anawalt, P. R., 211
Animas phase, 27, 36, 38, 39, 241
Antelope Wells obsidian, 39–40
Anyon, R., 35
Awatovi site, 183; shell, 216, 219, 220, 221, 224
Aztatlán tradition: background of, 150–57; Casas Grandes and, 160–62; definition of, 150–51; distribution of, 157; Early, 158; Late, 158; mercantile system, 159, 160, 162
Aztec, 167, 249; funerary practices, 185–86; sacrifice, 175; Tlaloc of, 168, 170, 175; vessel symbolism, 170, 183
Aztec Ruin, 85, 87, 216, 220, 221
AZ U:9:95, 33
AZ U:9:97, 33
AZ W:6:5, 217
AZ W:9:10, 217
AZ W:9:39, 217
AZ W:9:72, 217, 220, 221
AZ W:9:83, 217
AZ W:9:123 (Turkey Creek), 217, 220, 221, 222, 225
AZ W:10:8, 217
AZ W:10:15, 216
AZ W:10:37: shell, 216, 219, 220, 221, 222, 225
AZ W:10:47, 216
AZ W:10:50 (Point of Pines), 216, 220, 221, 222, 223
AZ W:10:51, 216
AZ W:10:52, 217, 220, 221
AZ W:10:56, 217
AZ W:10:57, 217
AZ W:10:65, 217
AZ W:10:111, 217

Babícora Basin, 63, 67–68, 71, 73–74, 75
Babocomari Village, 143, 216, 220, 221
Balankanché, 168, 170
Ball courts: absence to south of Casas Grandes valley of, 74; integrative role of, 40, 59, 61; I-shaped at Casas Grandes, 51, 161; at Joyce Well site, 16, 36; in Malpais Borderlands area, 36–38, 41–42; near Casas Grandes, 16, 36, 58–59; styles of, 59
Bandelier, A. F., 86, 98
Bartley site, 222
Beardsley Canal, 222
Berrenda Creek site, 117–18
Bis sa'ani site, 243
Black Mountain phase: architecture and community plan, 108, 116–17; Casas Grandes and, 89–90, 241–42; ceramics, 108, 109, 110, 115–16, 132; continuity with Mimbres Classic of, 107, 108–11; dating of, 117–18; discontinuity with Mimbres Classic of, 119, 131–32; mortuary practices, 110, 132; at Old Town, 113–15; settlement pattern, 118–19
Black Mountain site (LA 49), 241
Bloom Mound, 242
Boss Ranch site, 30, 33, 34, 36, 38
Bowen, T., 139
Box Canyon site, 30, 32, 33, 38
Bradford site, 243
Brand, D. D., 34, 44, 63, 150, 213
Braniff, C. B., 199
Buena Fé phase, 99–102, 120

Cabeza de Vaca, Á. N., 198
Caciques, 248
Cahokia, 202–3
Cameron Creek site, 216, 219, 220, 221, 222, 223, 226
Cañon del Molino site, 156, 160
Casa Grande, 210; adobe, 242, 243; shell, 216, 219, 220, 221, 222, 223
Casa Grande Irrigation Community, 35
Casas Grandes: architectural access at, 99–104; Aztatlán tradition and, 160–62; ball courts at and near, 16, 36, 58–59; Black Mountain phase and, 89–90, 241–42; ceramics, 47, 116, 245–46; ceremonial architecture at, 40, 87–88, 101; collared postholes at, 66–67, 75; compared with Cerro de Trincheras, 141–42, 143, 144, 145, 146; connection with Sinaloa, 247; copper at, 76, 161, 209, 246, 247; dating of, 29, 79–80, 244–45; dental morphology, 230; fall of, 200; faunal remains from, 49–50; Fourmile style and, 227; interaction zones around, 60–61; Jornada Mogollon and, 240–41; language of, 246; layout of, 86; Malpais Borderlands and, 29, 38–42; map of, 97, 215; Mesoamerican influence at, 160–61, 162; pilgrimages to, 40–41; as Pueblo, 84–90, 91; in Pueblo tales, 90–91; Salado and, 227, 249; shell at, 143, 144, 145, 161, 213–15, 216, 220, 221, 222, 223, 224, 225, 226, 227, 228, 245; Sonoran statelets and, 197, 198–200; T-shaped doorway at, 19; turkey pens at, 21, 22; turquoise at, 247, 248; uniqueness of, 74; view of, 17; West Mexico ceramics at, 157. *See also* Casas Grandes culture/regional system; Di Peso, C. C.; Medio period
Casas Grandes Archaeological Zone, 237–38, 241
Casas Grandes culture/regional system: ceramics, 38–39; chronology, 7; core area, 237–38, 241; Di Peso on, 50–51, 54; as interaction sphere, 239, 246; Malpais Borderlands and, 27, 38; map of, 8, 9; models of, 50–52; perimeter of, 27
Cashion site, 223
Ceramics: Black Mountain phase, 108, 109, 110, 115–16, 132; Casas Grandes, 38–39, 116, 157, 245–46; Fourmile style, 226; symbolism in Pueblo art of, 181–84; Tlaloc and, 168, 169, 170;

Villa Ahumada, 46–47, 48, 52
Ceramic types: Aguaruto Incised, 151, 152; Aguaruto Polychrome, 152, 153, 155; Alamitos Engraved, 152, 153; Aztatlán Polychrome, 151; Aztatlán Red and White on Incised Buff, 155; Aztatlán Red-on-buff, 155, 156; Babícora Polychrome, 46, 47, 66, 67, 68, 71, 143, 195; Babocomari Polychrome, 143; Botadero Incised, 154, 156; Carretas Polychrome, 38, 46, 56, 67, 75, 195; Casas Grandes Incised, 195; Cerritos Polychrome, 154, 155; Cerro Izábal Engraved, 151, 152, 153; Chametla Black-banded, 152, 154; Chametla Polychrome, 152, 156; Chametla Polychrome Engraved, 152; Chametla Red-rimmed, 152, 154; Chametla Scalloped-rim, 152; Chihuahua indented corrugated, 129; Chupadero Black-on-white, 46, 76, 108, 109, 110, 112, 115, 116, 118, 120, 131, 132; Cloverdale Corrugated, 29, 31, 32; Cocoyolitos Polychrome, 151, 152, 153, 155; Cojumatlán Polychrome, 155; Cojumatlán Polychrome Incised, 155; Convento Incised, 195; Corralitos Polychrome, 67, 75; Culiacán Polychrome, 150, 152, 155, 156; Dublan Polychrome, 195, 245–46; El Paso bichrome, 108, 109, 118; El Paso Polychrome, 44, 47, 52, 71, 109, 110, 112, 115, 116, 118, 120, 131, 132, 183, 195; El Paso Red-on-brown, 129; El Taste Polychrome, 151, 152, 155; El Taste Red-bordered, 151, 155; El Taste Rough, 151; El Taste Satin, 151; Escondida Polychrome, 226, 227; Fernando Red-on-brown, 66; Fine Orange, 159; Gila Polychrome, 47, 139, 142–43, 195, 241; Guasave Polychrome, 151, 152, 159; Guasave Red-on-buff, 151, 153, 156, 157, 158; Huérigos Polychrome, 38, 46, 75, 195, 246; Iago Polychrome, 154; Iguanas Polychrome, 155, 156; Ixcuintla Polychrome, 154, 155, 156; Ixcuintla White-on-orange, 154, 155; Leal Red-on-brown, 66; Lisa Tardia, 142; Lolandis Red Rim, 153, 156, 157, 158; Madera Black-on-red, 67; Madera Red-on-black, 46, 67; Mangos Engraved, 154, 155, 156; Mata Polychrome, 245–46; Mata textured red-on-brown, 66, 245; Mazatlán Polychrome, 151, 155; Médanos Red-on-brown, 46; Mimbres Black-on-white, 46, 76, 171; Mimbres Black-on-white Style II, 109, 116; Mimbres Black-on-white Style III, 108, 109, 110, 115, 116, 118, 126, 128, 129, 130, 131; Mimbres Corrugated, 108, 109, 115, 129; Mimbres Polychrome, 128; Navalato Polychrome, 151, 152, 155, 157; Nayar White-on-red, 207; Nogales Polychrome, 139, 142; Otinapa Red-on-white, 207; Peñitas Engraved, 155; Pilon Red-on-brown, 66; Playas Black, 67; Playas Red, 29, 31, 46, 67, 75, 108, 110, 112, 115–16, 118, 120, 132, 247; Playas Red Incised, 109, 195; Playas Red Obliterated Indented Corrugated, 119; Ramos Black, 46; Ramos Polychrome, 27, 38–39, 46, 47, 67, 75, 90, 143, 144, 195, 226, 227, 246; St. Johns Black-on-red, 109; St. Johns Polychrome, 46, 109, 132; Salado polychromes, 29, 31, 226–27, 249; San Miguel Red and Brown, 196; Santa Cruz Polychrome, 139, 142, 143; Santiago Red-on-orange, 156; Sentispac Buff, 155; Sinaloa Polychrome, 151, 152, 155; Socorro Black-on-white, 243; Three Circle Neck Corrugated, 116; Three Circle Red-on-white, 207; Three Rivers Red-on-terracotta, 109, 112, 115, 132; Three Rivers Terracotta, 46; Tohil Plumbate, 159; Tonto Polychrome, 47; Trincheras Lisa 3, 142; Trincheras Polychrome, 142; Trincheras Purple-on-brown, 142; Trincheras Purple-on-red, 139, 142; Tucson Polychrome, 117, 118; Tularosa Black-on-white, 115; Tularosa Fillet Rim, 110; Tularosa Smudged-Corrugated, 112; Tuxpan Engraved, 154, 156; Tuxpan Incised, 156; Tuxpan Red-on-orange, 154, 155, 158; Victoria red-on-brown textured, 245; Viejo Red-on-brown, 66; Villa Ahumada Polychrome, 46, 47, 52, 71, 75, 115, 118, 195; Zape Red-on-buff, 156
Ceramic wares: Cibola White Ware, 129; Dunn ware, 153; El Paso Brown Ware, 108, 112, 129; Mimbres smoothed/corrugated wares, 46; Mogollon Brown Ware, 243; White Mountain Red Ware, 108, 115
Cerro de la Cruz site, 156
Cerro de Trincheras site: artifacts and features at, 139–41; compared with Casas Grandes, 141–42, 143, 144, 145, 146; culture context of, 141–42; environment, 136; Hohokam and, 136, 142; long-distance trade to, 142–46; map, 138; previous interpretations of, 134, 136; recent work at, 136, 138–39; shell at, 142, 143–46; view of, 137
Cerro Prieto site, 141
Ch-11, 66, 67, 70
Ch-104, 65, 69
Ch-125, 65, 69, 71
Ch-151, 66, 70–71
Ch-152, 66, 69, 70, 71, 73
Ch-156, 66–67, 70, 71, 73, 75
Ch-159 (El Zurdo site), 67–68, 69, 70, 73
Ch-212, 66, 70
Ch-216, 68, 69
Ch-240, 69, 73
Chaco Canyon, 85, 87, 98, 202
Chalcatzingo site, 167
Chalchihuites culture, 67, 165, 248
Chalchihuitlicue, 167, 170, 173
Chalpa site, 155
Chametla site, 151, 152, 153, 154
Chetro Ketl site, 220, 221, 225
Chichén Itzá, 184, 203
CHIH G:2:2, 90
CHIH G:2:3, 79, 81, 83
CHIH H:11:1, 79, 81
Chihuahuan culture, 63–65, 66–68, 69–74, 74–76
Cholula, 158
Cimientos-type architecture, 31, 32
Citrus site, 223
Clanton Draw site, 30, 33, 38; shell, 216, 220, 221, 223
Classic period (Mimbres): continuity with Black Mountain phase of, 107, 108–11; discontinuity with Black Mountain phase of, 119, 131–32; end of, 107, 116–17, 119, 130–31, 132–33; map of, 122, 126; mortuary practices, 110, 126, 131, 132; at Old Town, 111–13; regional variation in, 123
Cliff phase, 132
Cochiti, 183, 184
Cojumatlán site, 155, 156
Colima site, 209
Collared postholes, 66–67, 75
Compounds, 31–32
Convento site, 88, 90, 213

Copper: Aztatlán tradition, 151, 152, 154, 158, 160; at Casas Grandes, 76, 161, 209, 246, 247; Hohokam, 210; in Malpais Borderlands, 39; Mississippian, 204–5
Corn, 33, 50, 140
Coronado, F. V. de, 198, 204
Cotton, 33, 119, 140
Cowboy site, 36–37
Cranial deformation, 155, 156
Cuarenta Casas site, 20
Culberson Ruin, 30, 33, 39
Culiacán site, 150, 151, 152, 153, 154

Dean, J. S., 5–6, 244
De Atley, S. P., 34, 36, 238, 240
Di Peso, C. C., 29; on Casas Grandes and Jornada Mogollon, 240–41; on Casas Grandes Archaeological Zone, 237–38; on Casas Grandes architecture, 98, 99; on Casas Grandes ceremonial rooms, 87–88; on Casas Grandes culture, 50–51, 54; on Casas Grandes faunal remains, 49–50; on Casas Grandes layout, 86; on Casas Grandes turquoise, 247, 248; on Cerro de Trincheras, 134; on Gila Polychrome at Casas Grandes, 47; on Medio period hallmarks, 75; mercantile model of, 84–85, 239–41, 247; on origin of Medio period, 149–50; Robles phase and, 78–82
Doña Ana phase, 13
Double Adobe Cave, 30
Douglas, J. E., 36, 39

Eby site, 119
Ekholm, G. F., 151–52
Elk Ridge Ruin, 117
El Paso phase, 90, 241–42
El Tajin, 170, 171, 185, 187, 189
Escalante Ruin, 143

Ferguson, W. M., 4
Findlow, F. J., 34, 36
Firecracker site, 216, 220, 221
Florida Mountain site, 125
Fortified Hill, 222
Foster, M. S., 241
Fox Place site, 242
Franzoy site, 109
Fremont culture, 89
Frogtown site, 223
Furst, J. L., 186, 248

Galaz site, 109, 111, 117, 131
Galeana site, 43
Gatlin site, 223
Gell-Mann, M., 4
Gila Pueblo site, 216, 219, 220, 221, 222
Gran Quivira, 174, 180, 181; shell, 216, 220, 221, 222
Graph theory, 96, 97, 99–104
Grasshopper site, 216, 219, 220, 221, 222, 224, 226
Grewe site, 223
Gu Achi, 223
Guasave site, 154, 155, 207, 208; Aztatlán tradition at, 151, 152, 153; Mixteca-Puebla "culture" at, 152, 159
Gumerman, G. J., 4–5

Hage, P., 96
Hanson, J., 96, 101, 102
Harary, F., 96
Haury, E. W., 208
Hervideros site, 156
Hidalgo Survey 1, 30
Hidalgo Survey 15, 30
Hidalgo Survey 65, 30
Hillier, B., 96, 101, 102
Hodges site, 222, 223
Hohokam, 27, 28; Casas Grandes looks, 90; Cerro de Trincheras and, 136, 142; copper, 210; Mesoameracan parallels of, 202; shell, 213, 219, 221, 222–23, 224, 225–26; West Mexican influence on, 207–12
Hopi: burial, 188; dental morphology, 232; gods, 173; kachina cult at, 249; Shalako kachina at, 189, 190, 191; village chief, 248; water serpent, 184
Hueco Tanks, 172, 178, 179, 183, 192
Huichol, 211
Huistla site, 156
Ibarra, F. de, 197
Interaction sphere, 244
Irrigation/water control: Casas Grandes, 248; eastern Sierra Madre, 56–57; Mimbres, 125
Isleta, 184
Ixtapa site, 155

Jennings, J. D., 206–7
Joint Casas Grandes Expedition, 54; survey work of, 237–38
Jornada Mogollon: Casas Grandes and, 240–41; Mimbres ceramics in, 128; occupation of Mimbres valley, 131; Tlalocs and kachinas in rock art of, 171, 172, 175–76, 189; Villa Ahumada site and, 44, 46, 50, 52
Joyce Well site: architecture, 21, 31–32, 33, 38; ball courts, 16, 36; Casas Grandes traits at, 21, 38; ceramic production, 39; corn, 33; dates from, 29, 30, 79, 81, 82–83; groundstone, 33; prestige goods, 39; shell, 216, 220, 221

Kachinas: ancestors and, 188; ceremonialism, 132, 226, 227, 249; clouds and, 179–83; masks, 171; Mesoamerican origin of, 191–92; symbolic landscape of, 173–75: Tlaloc complex and, 176
Kawaika-a site, 174
Kelley, J. C., 150, 152–53, 160, 162, 207
Kelley, J. H., 5
Kelly, I. T., 151, 152
Kidder, A. V., 3, 4, 201
Kinishba site: shell, 216, 220, 221, 222, 223, 224, 226
Kivas, 87–88, 123
Kroeber, A. L., 201
Kuaua site, 183
Kuykendall site, 30, 31, 38; shell, 216, 220, 221, 224

LA 3135, 13
LA 18342, 115
La Brena site, 156
La Casitas site, 223
La Ciudad site, 230, 232
Ladd, E. J., 189
Laguna Bustillos Basin, 65–66
La Junta phase, 242
La Lomita site, 33
La Mora site, 195
La Playa site, 134, 136, 139
La Quemada site, 161
Las Acequias site, 222, 223
Las Cuevas site, 156
Las Fosas site, 222
Las Varas site, 243
LeBlanc, S. A., 108, 120, 241–42
Lekson, S. H., 5
Linda Vista site, 141
Livingstone site group, 33
Loma de Montezuma. *See* Villa Ahumada site
Los Hornos site, 223
Los Morteros site, 33
Los Muertos site, 142, 143; shell, 216, 219, 220, 221, 222, 223, 224, 226

McAnany, P. A., 128
Macaws, 161, 227; cages for, 39, 56, 59–60; feathers, 39
McGuire, R. H., 4, 197–98
Maddox Ruin, 30, 36
Malpais Borderlands, 27; architectural variability in, 31–33; ball courts in, 37–38, 41–42; chronology, 29, 30; geographic variability in, 29, 31–33; integration into Casas Grandes polity of, 38–40; population of, 34, 35; role of Casas Grandes in interpreting, 29; settlement organization, 28–29, 36–37; short-term sedentism in, 34–36; subsistence, 33–34
Marata, 199
Maricopa, 230, 232
Marismas Nacionales, 154–55
Masau, 173
Masks, 185, 186, 188–89, 190
Mathien, F. J., 247
Mattocks site, 110
Maya, 128, 130, 185
Medio period: change in lifestyles in, 245, 247; dating of, 80, 99, 149, 244–45;

end of, 80; map of Casas Grandes during, 97; origin of, 149–50; shell in, 213. *See also* Buena Fé phase
Mesilla phase, 13
Millington site, 242
Mimbres, 202; ceremonies and feasting, 129–30, 132; dental morphology, 230, 232; environmental fluctuation and, 124–25; formalized ceramic production, 128; intrusive ceramics, 129; irrigation, 125; kivas, 123; map of, 122; mortuary practices, 126; population model of, 122; as Pueblo, 88, 89–90; Tlaloc on bowl of, 171, 173, 174. *See also* Black Mountain phase; Classic period (Mimbres)
Minnis, P. E., 40, 51
Mixtec, 168, 185
Mixteca-Puebla, 158–60
Mogollon: Casas Grandes as, 88; dental morphology, 232; shell, 219, 220, 221, 226. *See also* Jornada Mogollon; Mimbres
Montoya site, 38, 110, 117
Morrett site, 209, 211
Morris, E. H., 3–4
Moulard, B., 130
Mountjoy, J. B., 155
Mount Tlaloc, 167, 171, 178, 183

NA 1785, 216, 220, 221, 223
NA 2131, 216
NA 2133, 216, 220, 221
NA 2134, 216, 220, 221, 223
NA 2135, 216
NA 3474, 216
NA 3644, 216, 220, 221
NA 3673, 216, 220, 221
Nambe Pueblo, 174
NAN 15, 125
NAN Ranch Ruin, 114, 121, 123; Black Mountain phase at, 131; building episodes, 124–25; dental morphology, 131; household shrines, 126, 128; map of, 124; mortuary practices, 126, 127; occurrence of Classic Mimbres and Black Mountain phase traits together at, 108–9, 110; shell at, 223
Nayacoyan site, 156, 160
Nelson, B. A., 35
Nicholson, H. B., 158, 168
NM EE:5:1 (ASM), 36
North Hills site, 128

Obregón, B. de, 239
O'Brien, P. J., 203
Obsidian, 39–40, 150, 160
Ojo de Agua site, 29, 30, 31, 32, 39, 195
Ojos Calientes de Santo Domingo site, 52
Old Town site, 110; Black Mountain phase at, 113–15, 118, 131; Classic Mimbres at, 111–13; map of, 111, 112; Three Circle phase at, 116
Olinger, B., 247
Olla Cave, 18, 19
Olmec, 165, 167
Opata, 194–95, 197

Paquimé. *See* Casas Grandes
Paquimé phase, 102–4
Paquimé Regional Survey Project, 55–60
Pasztory, E., 168, 170
Pecos site: shell, 216, 220, 221, 222, 223, 224, 226
Pendleton Ruin, 34, 238; coursed adobe at, 243; dates from, 30; groundstone, 33; lack of Casas Grandes architectural traits at, 38; plan, 32; shell, 216
Perros Bravos phase, 120, 245
Phillips, D. A., Jr., 198–99
Phillips, P., 201–2
Picuris Pueblo, 181
Pilón phase, 245
Pima, 230, 232
Pima Bajo, 195
Pindi Pueblo, 243
Pinnacle Cave, 39, 216, 220, 221
Plazas, 31–32, 86, 101–3, 104
Plumed serpent, 22, 248, 249
Polvo site, 242
Pottery Mound, 216, 220, 221, 222, 227
Pottery Pueblo, 183
Proyecto Arqueológico Chihuahua, 64, 65–76
Pueblo Bonito, 216, 219, 220, 221
Pueblo del Arroyo, 216, 220, 221
Pueblo de las Canopas, 223
Pueblo Vinegaroon, 117
Pyrite mirrors, 210
Pyrosignal system, 195–96, 197

Quetzalcoatl, 181, 185

Rabid Ruin, 222
Rancho Baviso, 39
Ravesloot, J. C., 241, 244
Reed, E., 206–7
Reff, D. T., 194, 195
Reyes 2 site, 90
Riley, C. L., 240
Ringo site, 37, 38
Robles phase, 78–80, 81–82
Rohn, A. H., 4
Ronnie Pueblo, 109, 110
Roosevelt Community Development sites, 33
Rubber balls, 210

Sacred bundles, 184–86, 187–89
Sacrifice, 167, 175
Saige-McFarland site, 114
Salado, 27, 28; Casas Grandes and, 227, 249; dental morphology, 232; shell, 219, 221, 224
Samalayuca site, 178–79
San Bernardino site, 36, 39
San José site, 195
San Juan hypothesis, 3–4
San Juan Pueblo, 174
Santa Ana Pueblo, 248
Santa Clara Valley, 68, 71, 75
Santa Cruz site, 37
Santa María Valley, 66–67, 75
Sauer, C. O., 150
Schroeder site, 152–53, 155, 156, 159, 160
Seri, 208
Shalako, 189, 190, 191
Shell: bracelets, 210; at Casas Grandes, 143, 144, 145, 161, 213–15, 216, 222, 223, 224, 225, 226, 227, 228, 245; at Cerro de Trincheras, 142, 143–46; distinctive shapes of, 222–24; diversity and richness of, 217–20, 224; ornament types by site, 216–17; on southern Chihuahuan culture sites, 76; stylistic groups, 220–22; trade networks, 221–22, 225; in Chihuahuan sites, 60, 76
Shenk, L. O., 242, 243
Sierra Madre Occidental, 14, 15, 20
Sinagua: shell, 219, 221, 222, 223, 225, 226
Slaughter Ranch site, 30, 36, 39, 216
Snaketown site, 210, 211, 222, 223, 224
SON K:4:16, 195
SON K:4:127, 195
Sonoran statelets, 194–95, 196–97; relation to Casas Grandes, 197, 198; warfare in, 197, 198
Southwestern Cult, 226–27
Southwest: as closed system, 3–5
Spinden, H. J., 201
Spindle whorls, 66, 67, 150, 151, 152, 153, 196
Spiro site, 201–2
Stallings, W. S., Jr., 242, 243
Stanton Cave, 179, 180
Stevenson, M. C., 184, 187–88
Steward, J. H., 4
Struever, S., 244
Stubbs, S. A., 242, 243
Sullivan, T. D., 167
Surratt Cave, 181
Swartz Ruin, 114, 121, 123, 125; Black Mountain phase at, 131; coursed adobe at, 116; co-occurrence of Classic Mimbres and Black Mountain phase artifacts at, 109–10; shell, 216, 219, 220, 221, 222, 223, 224, 226

Taos Pueblo, 85, 174, 189
Taube, K. A., 185
Tedlock, D., 175
Teixiptla, 186–87, 189, 191
Tenochtitlán, 169
Teotihuacán, 162, 192n1; possible precedents to

Shalako form at, 189, 190; Tlaloc at, 168, 169, 170, 178, 185
Tesuque, 174
Tewa, 189
Thompson, M., 130
Three Circle phase, 121
Three Rivers, 176, 177, 178
Tijeras site: shell, 216, 220, 221, 222, 224, 226
Timberlake Ruin, 36
Tio Benino site, 141
Tizapan el Alto site, 155–56
Tlaloc: bundle, 185; complex, 165, 167; the dead and, 187; image of, 168, 169; landscape features and associations of, 167, 168, 170–71; masks, 185; in Pueblo iconography, 181; sacrifice and, 175; in southwestern rock art, 176, 177–79, 189; vessels of water and, 168, 169, 170
Toltec, 78, 149, 249
Tonto Ruins, 216, 219, 220, 221
Tooth mutilation, 155, 156
Totonteac, 199
Townsend, R. F., 167, 171, 186–87
Tres Alamos site: shell, 216, 220, 221, 223, 224, 226
Tres Rios area, 90
Trincheras villages, 40. *See also* Cerro de Trincheras
Tula, 149, 249
Turco, 204
Turner, C. G., 247
Turquoise, 39, 151, 162, 246, 247–48
Tuzigoot site, 216, 220, 221, 225

U-Bar Cave, 39, 179, 180, 216, 220, 221
University Indian Ruin, 222, 223
Uto-Aztecan language, 246

Valshni Village, 223
Viejo period, 76, 213
Villa Ahumada site, 43; ceramics of, 46–47, 48, 52; dating of, 46; described by Brand, 44; faunal remains, 47–50; INAH excavation of, 44–50; Jornada Mogollon and, 46, 50, 52; map, 45; outside Casas Grandes core area, 50, 52–53; plant remains, 50
Villalpando C., M. E., 5, 197–98
VIV site, 216, 220, 221

Walnut Canyon site, 217, 220, 221
Walsh site, 38, 110, 117
Warfare, 197, 198
Water serpent, 184
Wedel, M. M., 204
Western Pueblo: dental morphology, 232; Kachina Cult, 227; shell, 219, 220, 221, 222, 223, 224, 225, 226
Whalen, M. E., 16, 40, 51
Whiptail Ruin, 222
White, L. A., 175, 248
Wilcox, D. A., 40, 51–52, 86, 242, 243
Wills, W. H., 4
Wind Mountain site, 217, 220, 221, 222, 223
Winters, H. D., 152, 153
Withers, A., 21
Wolfman, D., 21
Wupatki site, 217, 220, 221, 224, 225

Zape site, 165
Zapotec, 168
Zia, 184
Zuni, 91, 174, 249; community-wide ceramic firing, 128–29; sacred bundles, 187–88; sacrifice, 175; mask buried with dead by, 188–89